II KINGS

Volume 11

THE ANCHOR BIBLE is a fresh approach to the world's greatest classic. Its object is to make the Bible accessible to the modern reader; its method is to arrive at the meaning of biblical literature through exact translation and extended exposition, and to reconstruct the ancient setting of the biblical story, as well as the circumstances of its transcription and the characteristics of its transcribers.

THE ANCHOR BIBLE is a project of international and interfaith scope: Protestant, Catholic, and Jewish scholars from many countries contribute individual volumes. The project is not sponsored by any ecclesiastical organization and is not intended to reflect any particular theological doctrine. Prepared under our joint supervision, THE ANCHOR BIBLE is an effort to make available all the significant historical and linguistic knowledge which bears on the interpretation of the biblical record.

THE ANCHOR BIBLE is aimed at the general reader with no special formal training in biblical studies, yet, it is written with the most exacting standards of scholarship, reflecting the highest technical accomplishment.

This project marks the beginning of a new era of co-operation among scholars in biblical research, thus forming a common body of knowledge to be shared by all.

William Foxwell Albright
David Noel Freedman
GENERAL EDITORS

THE ANCHOR BIBLE

II KINGS

A New Translation
with
Introduction and Commentary
by

Mordechai Cogan
and
Hayim Tadmor

DOUBLEDAY & COMPANY, INC.
1988

Library of Congress Cataloging-in-Publication Data
Bible. O.T. Kings, 2nd. English. Anchor Bible. 1988.
II Kings: a new translation.

(The Anchor Bible; v. 11)
Bibliography: p. xxi.
Includes indexes.
1. Bible. O.T. Kings, 2nd—Commentaries.
I. Cogan, Mordechai. II. Tadmor, Hayim. III. Title.
IV. Series: Bible. English. Anchor Bible. 1964; v. 11.
BS192.2.A1 1984 G3 vol. 11 [BS1333] 220.7'7S [222.'54077]
Library of Congress Catalog Card Number: 86-16780
ISBN: 0-385-02388-X

Printed in the United States of America
First Edition

PREFACE TO 2 KINGS

The present commentary is the product of the collaboration of two historians of the ancient Near East, whose specialization in the case of H. Tadmor lies in Assyriology and in the case of M. Cogan in Biblical Studies. H. Tadmor's commitment to Kings goes back almost to the inception of the Anchor Bible series, and in 1978, M. Cogan joined the project as coauthor. A number of preliminary studies preceded the present commentary.

No doubt the customary procedure would have been to start with 1 Kgs 1.1 and to work forward; the finished commentary would have included a detailed introduction, discussing the questions of the place of Kings in the Canon, texts and versions, the literary structure of the book, and the author-editor's identity (though several commentaries on Kings are being issued in fascicles without the introductory material). But as two volumes were planned for Kings at the outset, the commentators chose to follow their major scholarly interest, which is centered in the Assyrian and Babylonian periods, and to give priority to Second Kings, which documents the course of Israelite history during this age. The editor of the Anchor Bible series and the publishers gallantly agreed to this rather unorthodox procedure. The formal introduction to the book of Kings will be given at the head of First Kings, for the present, attention is directed to the special features of the commentary at hand.

The current departmentalization of Bible and Assyriology, as compared with the integration which prevailed at the turn of the century, has not benefited the study of biblical history, or for that matter, biblical studies in general. For in most cases, the student of the Hebrew Bible does not have access to the cuneiform documents from Assyria and Babylonia so vital for understanding the narration in Kings. The present work aims to integrate the pertinent biblical and Assyriological evidence within a single commentary renewed study of this evidence with the aid of the philological tools commonly in use in Assyriology has contributed not only to a better understanding of the political history of the turbulent days at the end of the monarchic period, but quite often has led to an elucidation of knotty textual and literary problems in Kings.

The writing of this volume extended over many years, and the bibliography was periodically updated; but as the first draft was complete by 1982, works that reached us after that date could not be properly considered. The reader will observe that much reference is made to research published in modern

Hebrew, this in an attempt to open this "locked garden" to non-Hebraists. Finally, it is hoped that the appended selection of ancient Near Eastern texts, newly translated, will help the reader follow the historical discussions without finding it necessary to resort to additional textbooks.

The authors owe a special thanks to the editor of the Anchor Bible, Professor David Noel Freedman, who, as colleague and friend, has been a critical correspondent throughout the years. A number of his comments, gleaned from his copious letters, which differ from our own interpretations, are brought in his name (over the signature DNF). Several colleagues in Jerusalem graciously advised us on specialized subjects: Israel Eph'al on maps, Moshe Greenberg on the introduction, and Miriam Tadmor on the selection of the illustrations. Not to be forgotten are the Research Committees at Ben-Gurion University of the Negev and the Hebrew University of Jerusalem; they facilitated our work through generous grants and stipends.

We are also very much indebted to the editorial staff of the Anchor Bible; in Ann Arbor, to Dr. Astrid Beck, and in New York, to Theresa D'Orsogna, administrative editor of the Religion Department at Doubleday and to Eve Roshevsky, formerly of that department, for their various efforts in seeing this volume through its many stages to press.

Beer-sheva,
Jerusalem
December 1985

CONTENTS

History of the Divided Monarchy Resumed

The Kingdom of Judah Until the Exile

PRINCIPAL ABBREVIATIONS

(NOTE Abbreviations for the books of the Bible have not been included, as these are generally known.)

AB	The Anchor Bible
ABL	R F Harper, *Assyrian and Babylonian Letters.* London and Chicago University of Chicago Press, 1892–1914
AcOr	*Acta Orientalia*
AfO	*Archiv für Orientforschung*
AHw	*Akkadisches Handwörterbuch* W von Soden. 3 vols. Wiesbaden Harrassowitz, 1965–81
AION	*Annali dell'istituto orientali di Napoli*
AJBI	*Annual of the Japanese Biblical Institute*
AJSL	*American Journal of Semitic Languages and Literatures*
AKA	E. A. W Budge and L. W King, *The Annals of the Kings of Assyria.* London British Museum, 1902
AnBib	Analecta Biblica
ANEP[2]	*The Ancient Near East in Pictures.* Ed. J B Pritchard. 2nd ed. Princeton, N.J Princeton University Press, 1969
ANET[3]	*Ancient Near Eastern Texts Relating to the Old Testament.* Ed. J B Pritchard. 3rd ed. with supplement. Princeton, N.J Princeton University Press, 1969
AnOr	Analecta Orientalia
AOAT	Alter Orient und Altes Testament
AOATS	Alter Orient und Altes Testament, Supplements
AOS	American Oriental Series
ARAB	D D Luckenbill, *Ancient Records of Assyria and Babylonia.* 2 vols. Chicago· University of Chicago Press, 1926–27
ARI	A K Grayson, *Assyrian Royal Inscriptions.* Wiesbaden Harrassowitz, vol 1, 1972, vol 2, 1976.
ARM	*Archives royales de Mari,* Paris. Geuthner, 1941
ArOr	*Archiv Orientální*
AS	*Assyriological Studies* (Chicago· University of Chicago Press)
ASTI	*Annual of the Swedish Theological Institute*
AThANT	Abhandlungen zur Theologie des Alten und Neuen Testaments (Zürich Zwingli)
BA	*The Biblical Archaeologist*

BAR	*The Biblical Archaeologist Reader*
BASOR	*Bulletin of the American Schools of Oriental Research*
BDB	F. Brown, S. R. Driver, and C. A. Briggs, eds., *A Hebrew and English Lexicon of the Old Testament.* Oxford: Clarendon Press, 1907.
BFCT	Beiträge zur Föderung christlicher Theologie (Gütersloh: Bertelsmann)
BH³	*Biblia Hebraica.* Ed. R. Kittel. 3rd ed. Stuttgart: Privilegierte Württembergische Bibelanstalt, 1937.
Bib	*Biblica*
BibOr	Biblica et Orientalia
BiOr	*Bibliotheca Orientalis*
BWANT	Beiträge zur Wissenschaft vom Alten und Neuen Testament
BZ	*Biblische Zeitschrift*
BZAW	*Beihefte zur Zeitschrift für die alttestamentliche Wissenschaft*
CAD	*The Assyrian Dictionary of the Oriental Institute of the University of Chicago.* Ed. I. J. Gelb et al. Chicago: Oriental Institute, 1964–.
CAH	*The Cambridge Ancient History.* Cambridge: Cambridge University Press, 1925; 3rd ed., 1970–.
CamB	The Cambridge Bible for Schools and Colleges
CBC	The Cambridge Bible Commentary (Cambridge: Cambridge University Press)
CBQ	*Catholic Biblical Quarterly*
ConB	Coniectanea Biblica (Lund: Gleerup)
CRAIBL	*Comptes rendus de l'Académie des inscriptions et belles-lettres*
CT	*Cuneiform Texts from Babylonian Tablets,* London: British Museum.
DB Sup	*Dictionnaire de la Bible, Supplement*
DISO	*Dictionnaire des inscriptions sémitiques de l'ouest.* C.-F. Jean and J. Hoftijzer, Leiden: Brill, 1965.
DOTT	*Documents from Old Testament Times.* Ed. D. Winton Thomas, London: T. Nelson and Sons, 1958.
EA	El-Amarna Tablets according to J. A. Knudtzon, *Die El-Amarna Tafeln.* Leipzig: J. C. Hinrichs, 1908–15.
EAEHL	*Encyclopedia of Archaeological Excavations in the Holy Land.* 4 vols. Jerusalem: Israel Exploration Society, 1975–78.
EI	*Eretz Israel*
EnBib	Encyclopaedia Biblica

EncMiqr	*Encyclopedia Miqra'it* (Encyclopaedia Biblica). 8 vols. Jerusalem: Bialik Institute, 1950–82.
EvTh	*Evangelische Theologie*
ExpTim	*Expository Times*
FRLANT	Forschungen zur Religion und Literatur des Alten und Neuen Testaments (Göttingen: Vandenhoeck & Ruprecht)
GB	W. Gesenius, *Hebräisches und aramäisches Handwörterbuch* . . . bearbeitet F. Buhl, 17th ed.; repr., Berlin: Springer, 1949.
GKC	*Gesenius' Hebrew Grammar.* Ed. E. Kautzsch, rev. A. E. Cowley. 2nd English ed., Oxford: Clarendon Press, 1910. Cited by section.
HAT	Handbuch zum Alten Testament
HTR	*Harvard Theological Review*
HUCA	*Hebrew Union College Annual*
ICC	International Critical Commentary
IDB	*The Interpreter's Dictionary of the Bible.* Ed. G. A. Buttrick et al. 4 vols. New York and Nashville: Abingdon Press, 1962.
IDB Sup	*The Interpreter's Dictionary of the Bible,* Supplementary Volume. Ed. K. Crim et al. Nashville: Abingdon Press, 1976.
IEJ	*Israel Exploration Journal*
IOS	*Israel Oriental Studies*
ITP	H. Tadmor, *The Inscriptions of Tiglath-Pileser III.* Jerusalem: Israel Academy of Sciences and Humanities, in press.
JANES	*Journal of the Ancient Near Eastern Society of Columbia University*
JAOS	*Journal of the American Oriental Society*
JB	*The Jerusalem Bible.* Garden City, N.Y.: Doubleday, 1971.
JBL	*Journal of Biblical Literature*
JCS	*Journal of Cuneiform Studies*
JJS	*Journal of Jewish Studies*
JNES	*Journal of Near Eastern Studies*
JPOS	*Journal of the Palestine Oriental Society*
JPS	The Jewish Publication Society of America translation: *The Holy Scriptures,* Philadelphia, 1917.
JQR	*Jewish Quarterly Review*
JSOT	*Journal for the Study of the Old Testament*
JSOT Sup	*Journal for the Study of the Old Testament,* Supplement Series

JSS	*Journal of Semitic Studies*
JThSt	*Journal of Theological Studies*
JWH	*Journal of World History*
KAI	*Kanaanäische und aramäische Inschriften.* H. Donner and W Röllig, 3 vols. Wiesbaden: Harrassowitz, 1962–64.
KAT[3]	*Die Keilinschriften und das Alte Testament.* E. Schrader, H. Winckler, and H. Zimmern, 3rd ed. Berlin· Reuther and Reichard, 1903
KB	L. Koehler and W Baumgartner, *Hebräisches und aramäisches Lexikon zum Alten Testament,* 3rd ed. Leiden: Brill, 1967–
KJV	*King James Version*
Leš	*Lešonénu*
Luc.	Lucianic recensions of LXX
LXX	Septuagint, according to A. Rahlfs, ed. *Septuaginta.* 5th ed. 2 vols. Stuttgart Privilegierte Württembergische Bibelanstalt, 1952.
MT	Massoretic Text, according to *Biblia Hebraica Stuttgartensia.* eds. K Elliger and W Rudolph, Stuttgart Deutsche Bibelstiftung, 1967/77
MVAG	Mitteilungen der vorderasiatisch-ägyptischen Gesellschaft
NAB	*The New American Bible.* New York Kenedy-Macmillan, 1970.
NEB	*The New English Bible.* Oxford and Cambridge University Presses, 1970.
NJPS	The New Jewish Publication Society of America translations of the Holy Scriptures. *The Torah.* Philadelphia, 1967, *The Prophets.* Philadelphia, 1978, *The Writings.* Philadelphia, 1982.
OIP	Oriental Institute Publications, University of Chicago Press
OLZ	*Orientalistische Literaturzeitung*
Or	*Orientalia*
OTS	*Oudtestamentische Studiën*
PAAJR	*Proceedings of the American Academy of Jewish Research*
PEFQS	*Palestine Exploration Fund. Quarterly Statement*
PEQ	*Palestine Exploration Quarterly*
PJ	*Palästina-Jahrbuch*
PSBA	*Proceedings of the Society of Biblical Archaeology*
RA	*Revue d'assyriologie et d'archéologie orientale*
RB	*Revue Biblique*
RLA	Reallexikon der Assyriologie

RSV	*The Holy Bible, Revised Standard Version.* New York: T. Nelson, 1952.
SBL/SBS	Society of Biblical Literature/Sources for Biblical Study
SBT	Studies in Biblical Theology
SH	*Scripta Hierosolymitana*
SJTh	*Scottish Journal of Theology*
Syr.	Syriac, according to H. Gottlieb and E. Hammershaimb, eds. *The Old Testament in Syriac According to the Peshitta Version.* Part II/fasc. 4. Leiden: Brill, 1976.
TAPS	Transactions of the American Philosophical Society
Targ.	Targum, according to A. Sperber, ed. *The Bible in Aramaic.* Vol. 2. Leiden: Brill, 1959.
TDNT	*Theological Dictionary of the New Testament.* Eds. G. Kittel and G. Friedrich, 10 vols. Grand Rapids, Mich.: Eerdmans, 1964–76.
UF	*Ugarit Forschungen*
UT	*Ugaritic Textbook.* C. H. Gordon, Analecta Orientalia 38, Rome: Pontifical Biblical Institute, 1965.
VDI	*Vestnik Drevnei Istorii*
VT	*Vetus Testamentum*
VT Sup	*Vetus Testamentum,* Supplements
Vulg.	Vulgate, according to R. Weber, ed. *Biblia sacra iuxta vulgatam versionem I.* Stuttgart: Württembergische Bibelanstalt, 1969.
WCJS	*World Congress of Jewish Studies*
WM	*Wörterbuch der Mythologie.* Ed. H. W. Haussig. Stuttgart: E. Klett, 1965.
WHJP	*World History of the Jewish People,* Jerusalem: Masada, 1963–.
WMANT	Wissenschaftliche Monographien zum Alten und Neuen Testament (Neukirchen-Vluyn: Neukirchener Verlag)
WO	*Die Welt des Orients*
WZKM	*Wiener Zeitschrift für die Kunde des Morgenlandes*
ZA	*Zeitschrift für Assyriologie*
ZAW	*Zeitschrift für die alttestamentliche Wissenschaft*
ZDPV	*Zeitschrift des deutschen Palästina-Vereins*
ZThK	*Zeitschrift für Theologie und Kirche*

OTHER ABBREVIATIONS

Akk	Akkadian
ad, ad loc	at, at the place
Aram.	Aramaic
b.	prefixed to a rabbinic tractate; indicates the Babylonian Talmud
B.C.E.	Before the Common Era (= B.C.)
BH	Biblical Hebrew
ca.	circa
cf	compare
col.	column
contra.	contrast
ed., eds.	editor, editors, edition, editions
e.g.	for example
esp.	especially
E.T	English Translation
et al	and others
Heb	Hebrew
ibid	in the same place
idem	the same, previously mentioned
i.e.	that is
LBH	Late Biblical Hebrew
lit	literally
loc cit	in the place cited
ms., mss.	manuscript, manuscripts
n., nn	note, notes
op cit	in the work cited
p., pp	page, pages
pl	plural
PN	personal name
repr	reprint, reprinted
sing.	singular
s.v	under the word
Ug.	Ugaritic
v., vv	verse, verses
vol	volume
(words)	words added for purposes of translation

<words>	words added to MT
« »	words omitted from MT
16*, 24* [etc.]	asterisks denote page numbers of English-language part of *Eretz Israel*

LIST OF ILLUSTRATIONS

Black and white photographs, following pages 108 and 228

City of David, Jerusalem
Fortification Wall, end of eighth century, B.C.E.
The Siloam Tunnel
The Siloam Tunnel Inscription
King Uzziah's Tombstone
Black Obelisk of Shalmaneser, with close-up of second register
Captives and booty from Ashtaroth
Assyrian soldiers attacking Lachish
Residents of Lachish leaving for exile
Reliefs from Sennacherib's palace at Nineveh
fragments of Assyrian stela from Samaria and Ashdod
seal inpressions of royal officials
Group of pottery vessels, seventh century B.C.E.
Fertility figure, seventh century B.C.E.
Crescent-shaped bronze standard and bell, seventh century B.C.E.
Remains of Late Iron Age Citadel and granary

Maps

SELECT BIBLIOGRAPHY

1. COMMENTARIES ON 2 KINGS

All references to commentaries cite the author's name or name and page numbers.

Abarbanel, Don Isaac. *Peruš ʿal neviʾim rišonim.* Jerusalem: Torah va-Da ʿat, 1957.

Barnes, W. E. *The Two Books of the Kings.* Cambridge Bible. Cambridge: At the University Press, 1908.

Benzinger, I. *Die Bücher der Könige.* Kurzer Handkommentar zum Alten Testament. Freiberg: J. C. B. Mohr, 1899.

Burney, C. F. *Notes on the Hebrew Text of the Book of Kings.* Oxford, 1903 (repr., New York: Ktav, 1970).

Ehrlich, A. B. *Mikrâ ki-Pheschutô.* Vol. 2. Berlin: M. Poppelauer, 1900.

______. *Randglossen zur hebräischen Bibel.* Vol. 7. Leipzig: J. C. Hinrichs, 1914.

Eissfeldt, O. *Könige.* Die Heilige Schrift des Alten Testaments. Vol. 1. 4th ed. Tübingen: J. C. B. Mohr, 1922.

Fricke, K. D. *Das zweite Buch von den Königen.* Die Botschaft des alten Testaments. Stuttgart: Calwer Verlag, 1972.

Gersonides (Levi ben Gershon). Commentary in *Mikraʾot Gedolot.*

Graetz, H. *Emendationes in Plerosque Sacrae Scripturae Veteris Testamenti Libros.* Breslau: Schlesische Buchdruckerei, 1894.

Gray, J. *I and II Kings.* Old Testament Library. 3rd ed. Philadelphia: Westminster, 1979.

Grotius, H. in *Critici Sacri.* Ed. J. Pearson. Annotatures ad Libros Historicus, vol. 2, cols. 2569–2654. London, 1660.

Haupt, P. *See* Stade, B.

Joüon, P. "Notes de critique textuelle," *Mélanges-St. Joseph Beyrouth,* 5 (1912), 473–85.

Kittel, R. *Die Bücher der Könige.* Handkommentar zum Alten Testament. Göttingen: Vandenhoeck & Ruprecht, 1900.

Klostermann, A. *Die Bücher Samuels und der Könige, Kurzgefasste Kommentare.* Eds. H. L. Strack and O. Zöckler. Nördlingen and München: C. H. Beck, 1887.

Landersdorfer, S. *Die Bücher der Könige.* Bonn: P. Hanstein, 1927.

Malbim (acronym of Meir Loeb ben Jehiel Michael). *Sefer Mikraʾe Kodesh* on *Prophets and Writings.* Vol. 3. Jerusalem: Pardes, 1957.

Mikraʾot Gedolot (Rabbinic Bible). Repr. New York: Pardes, 1951.

Montgomery, J. A. and Gehman, H. S. *The Books of Kings.* ICC. Edinburgh: T & T Clark, 1951.

Noth, M. *Könige I.* Biblischer Kommentar. Neukirchen-Vluyn: Neukirchener Verlag, 1968.

Perles, Felix. *Analekten zur Textkritik des Alten Testament.* Leipzig: G. Engel: 1922.

Qimḥi, David. Commentary in *Mikraʾot Gedolot.*

Rashi (acronym of Rabbi Solomon ben Isaac). Commentary in *Mikraʾot Gedolot.*

Rehm, M. *Das zweite Buch der Könige.* Würzburg: Echter Verlag, 1982.

Robinson, J. *The Second Book of Kings.* Cambridge: Cambridge University Press, 1976.

Šanda, A. *Die Bücher der Könige.* Exegetisches Handbuch zum Alten Testament. Münster: Aschendorffscher Verlag, 1911–12.

Skinner, J. *I and II Kings.* Century Bible. Edinburgh: T. C. & E. C. Jack, n.d. (ca. 1893).

Snaith, N. H. *The First and Second Books of Kings.* Interpreter's Bible. New York: Abingdon, 1954.

Stade, B. and Schwally F. with notes by P. Haupt. *The Books of Kings.* The Sacred Books of the Old Testament. Leipzig: J. C. Hinrichs, 1904.

Thenius, O. *Die Bücher der Könige.* Kurzgefasstes exegetisches Handbuch. 2nd ed. Leipzig: S. Hirzel, 1873.

2. BOOKS, ARTICLES AND DISSERTATIONS

Most references to books and to articles cite the author's name, a short title, and the page number(s).

Abramsky, S. "The House of Rechab—Genealogy and Social Characteristics," *EI* 8 (1967), 255–64.

Ackroyd, P. "An Interpretation of the Babylonian Exile: A Study of 2 Kings 20, Isaiah 38–39," *SJTh* 27 (1974), 329–52.

Aharoni, Y. *Archaeology of the Land of Israel.* Philadelphia: Westminster, 1982.

———. *The Land of the Bible: A Historical Geography.* 2nd ed., Philadelphia: Westminster, 1979.

Aḥituv, S. *Canaanite Toponyms in Ancient Egyptian Documents.* Jerusalem: Magnes, 1984.

Albright, W. F. *Archaeology and the Religion of Israel.* 5th ed., Garden City, N.Y.: Doubleday, 1969.

———. *Yahweh and the Gods of Canaan.* Garden City, N.Y.: Doubleday, 1969.

Alt, A. *Kleine Schriften zur Geschichte des Volkes Israel.* 3 vols. München: C. H. Beck, 1953–59.

Amiran, R. "The Water Supply of Israelite Jerusalem," in *Jerusalem Revealed.* Jerusalem: Israel Exploration Society, 1975, 75–78.

Amusin, I. D. "The People of the Land," *VDI,* 1955, No. 2, 14–36.

Astour, M. "841 B.C.: The First Assyrian Invasion of Israel," *JAOS* 91 (1971), 383–89.

Avigad, N. "New Light on the *Naʿar* Seals" in *Magnalia Dei. Essays on Bible and Archaeology in Memory of G. Ernest Wright.* Garden City, N.Y.: Doubleday, 1976, 294–300.

———. *The Upper City of Jerusalem.* Jerusalem: Shikmona, 1980 (Hebrew).

Baillet, M. *Les 'Petites Grottes' de Qumran, Discoveries in the Judaean Desert III.* Oxford: Clarendon Press, 1962.

Barrick, W. B. "The Meaning and Usage of RKB in Biblical Hebrew," *JBL* 101 (1982), 481–503.

Barthélemy, D. *Critique textuelle de l'Ancien Testament.* Orbis Biblicus et Orientalis 50/1. Göttingen: Vandenhoeck & Ruprecht, 1982.

Bartlett, J. R. "The Rise and the Fall of the Kingdom of Edom," *PEQ* 104 (1972), 26–37.

———. "The 'United' Campaign Against Moab in 2 Kings 3:4–27," *JSOT* Sup 24 (1983), 135–46.

Bauer, H. and Leander, P. *Historische Grammatik der Hebräischen Sprache des Alten Testaments.* Halle, 1922; repr.: Hildesheim: G. Olms, 1962.

Baumgartner, W. "Ein Kapitel vom hebräischen Erzählungsstil," in *Eucharisterion,* Festschrift H. Gunkel, FRLANT 19 (1923), 145–57.

Beek, M. A. "The Meaning of the Expression 'The Chariots and the Horsemen of Israel' (II Kings ii 12)," *OTS* 17 (1972), 1–10.

Bergstrasser, G. *Hebräische Grammatik.* Leipzig, 1918; repr. Hildesheim: G. Olms, 1962.

Bernhardt, K.-H. "Der Feldzug der drei Könige" in *Schalom,* Festschrift A. Jepsen, ed. K.-H. Bernhardt, Stuttgart: Calmer Verlag, 1971, 11–22.

Bickerman, E. J. "Nebuchadnezzar and Jerusalem," *PAAJR* 46–47 (1979–80), 69–85.

Borger, R. *Die Inschriften Asarhaddons Königs von Assyrien. AfO* Beiheft 9, 1956.

Borger, R. and Tadmor, H. "Zwei Beiträge zur alttestamentlichen Wissenschaft auf Grund der Inschriften Tiglatpilesers III," *ZAW* 94 (1982), 244–49.

Bright, J. *A History of Israel.* 2nd ed., Philadelphia: Westminster, 1972; 3rd ed., 1981.

Brinkman, J. A. "Merodach-baladan II," in *Studies Presented to A. Leo Oppenheim.* Chicago: Oriental Institute, 1964, 6–53.

———. *A Political History of Post-Kassite Babylonia 1158–722 B.C.* AnOr 43 (1968).

Cassuto, U. *Biblical and Oriental Studies,* vol. 2. *Bible and Ancient Oriental Texts.* Jerusalem: Magnes, 1975.

Childs, B. S. "A Study of the Formula 'Until This Day,'" *JBL* 82 (1963), 279–92.

———. *Isaiah and the Assyrian Crisis.* SBT 2nd Series 3 (1967).

Clements, R. E. *Isaiah and the Deliverance of Jerusalem. JSOT* Sup 13 (1980).

———. "The Prophecies of Isaiah and the Fall of Jerusalem in 587 B.C.," *VT* 30 (1980), 421–36.

Clines, D. J. A. "Regnal Year Reckoning in the Last Years of the Kingdom of Judah," *Australian Journal of Biblical Archaeology* 2 (1972), 9–34.

Cogan, M. ". . . From the Peak of Amanah," *IEJ* 34 (1984), 255–59.

———. *Imperialism and Religion: Assyria, Judah and Israel in the Eighth and Seventh Centuries B.C.E.* SBL Monograph Series 19, 1974.

———. "Israel in Exile—The View of a Josianic Historian," *JBL* 97 (1978), 40–44.

———. "'Ripping Open Pregnant Women' in Light of an Assyrian Analogue," *JAOS* 103 (1983), 755–57.

———. "Tendentious Chronology in the Book of Chronicles," *Zion* 45 (1980), 165–72.

Cohen, H. R. *Biblical Hapax Legomena in the Light of Akkadian and Ugaritic.* SBL Dissertation Series 37, 1978.

Cohen, C. (= H. R.) "Neo-Assyrian Elements in the First Speech of the Biblical Rab-šaqê," *IOS* 9 (1979), 32–48.

Cross, F. M. *Canaanite Myth and Hebrew Epic.* Cambridge, Mass.: Harvard University Press, 1973.

Cross, F. M. and Freedman, D. N. *Early Hebrew Orthography.* AOS No. 36 (New Haven, Conn., 1952).

———. "Josiah's Revolt Against Assyria," *JNES* 12 (1953), 56–58.

Dever, W. G. "Asherah, Consort of Yahweh? New Evidence from Kuntillet ʿAjrud," *BASOR* 255 (1984), 21–37.

DeVries, S. J. *Prophet Against Prophet.* Grand Rapids, Mich.: Eerdmans, 1978.

Dietrich, W. *Prophetie und Geschichte.* FRLANT 108 (1972).

Diringer, D. *Le iscrizioni antico-ebraiche palestinesi.* Florence: F. le Monnier, 1934.

Donner, H. "Art und Herkunft des Amtes der Königinmutter im Alten Testament," in *Festschrift Johannes Friedrich.* Heidelberg: C. Winter, 1959, 105–45.

Driver, G. R. "Geographical Problems," *EI* 5 (1958), 16*–20*.

Driver, S. R. *Notes on the Hebrew Text and the Topography of the Books of Samuel.* 2nd edition, Oxford: Clarendon Press, 1913.

———. *A Treatise on the Use of the Tenses in Hebrew.* 3rd ed., Oxford: Clarendon Press, 1892.

Eissfeldt, O. "Die Komposition von I Reg. 16.29–II Reg. 13.25," in *Das ferne und nahe Wort, Festschrift L. Rost. BZAW* 105 (1967), 49–58.

Elat, M. *Economic Relations in the Lands of the Bible c. 1000–539 B.C.* Jerusalem: Mosad Bialik and Israel Exploration Society, 1977 (Hebrew).

______. "The Campaigns of Shalmaneser III Against Aram and Israel," *IEJ* 25 (1975), 25–35.

Ephʿal, I. "On the Identification of the Israelite Exiles in the Assyrian Empire," in *Excavations and Studies, Essays in Honour of S. Yeivin.* Tel Aviv: University of Tel Aviv, 1973, 201–4 (Hebrew).

______. *The Ancient Arabs.* Jerusalem: Magnes, 1982.

Ewald, H. *Ausführliches Lehrbuch der hebräischen Sprache des Alten Bundes.* 5th ed., Leipzig: Hahn, 1844; 8th ed., 1870.

Falk, Z. W. "Forms of Testimony," *VT* 11 (1961), 88–91.

Feigin, S. I. "Sennacherib's Defeat in the Land of Judah," *Missitrei Heavar.* New York: Hebrew Publication Society of Palestine and America, 1943, 88–117 (Hebrew).

Feliks, Y. *Nature and Man in the Bible.* London: Soncino, 1981.

______. *Plant World of the Bible.* Tel Aviv: Masada, 1957 (Hebrew).

Fohrer, G. *Elia.* AThANT 31 (1957).

______. "Prophetie und Magie," *ZAW* 78 (1966), 25–47.

Forrer, E. *Die Provinzeinteiling des assyrischen Reiches.* Leipzig: J. C. Hinrich, 1920.

Frankena, R. "The Vassal-Treaties of Esarhaddon and the Dating of Deuteronomy," *OTS* 14 (1965), 122–54.

Frankfort, H. *Kingship and the Gods.* Chicago: University of Chicago Press, 1948.

Freedman, D. N "The Babylonian Chronicle," *BA* 19 (1956), 50–60.

Freedy, K. S. and Redford, D. B. "The Dates in Ezekiel in Relation to Biblical, Babylonian and Egyptian Sources," *JAOS* 90 (1970), 462–85

Frick, F S. "The Rechabites Reconsidered," *JBL* 90 (1971), 279–87

Friedman, R. E. *The Exile and Biblical Narrative.* Harvard Semitic Monograph 22, 1981

"From Egypt to Egypt. Dtr[1] to Dtr[2]," in *Traditions in Transformation.* Eds. B. Halpern and J D Levenson. Winona Lake, Ind. Eisenbrauns, 1981, 167–92.

Frost, S. B. "The Death of Josiah A Conspiracy of Silence," *JBL* 87 (1968), 369–82.

Galling, K. "Der Ehrenname Elisas und die Entrückung Elias," *ZThK* 53 (1956), 129–48

Garelli, P "Nouveau Coup d'oeil sur Muṣur," in *Hommages à Andre Dupont-Sommer.* Paris. Adrien Maisonneuve, 1971, 37–48

Geller, M. "A New Translation for 2 Kings XV 25," *VT* 26 (1976), 374–77

Gevaryahu, H. M "The Campaign of Sennacherib Against Hezekiah and the Deliverance of Jerusalem," in *Oz Le-David, Studies Presented to D. Ben-Gurion.* Jerusalem Israel Bible Society, 1964, 351–75 (Hebrew).

Ginsberg, H. L. "The Omrid-Davidid Alliance and Its Consequences," Proceedings of Fourth *WCJS* Jerusalem, 1967, 91–93.

Goedicke, H. "The End of 'So, King of Egypt,' " *BASOR* 171 (1963), 64–66.

Graesser, C. F. "Standing Stones in Ancient Palestine," *BA* 35 (1972), 34–63.

Grayson, A. K. *Assyrian and Babylonian Chronicles.* Texts from Cuneiform Sources No. 5. Locust Valley, N.Y.: J. J. Augustin, 1975.

Green, A. R. (W.) "Regnal Formulas in the Hebrew and Greek Texts of the Books of Kings," *JNES* 42 (1983), 167–80.

———. *The Role of Human Sacrifice in the Ancient Near East.* ASOR Dissertation Series 1 (1976).

Greenberg, M. *Biblical Prose Prayer.* Berkeley, Calif.: University of California Press, 1983.

———. "Ezekiel 17 and the Policy of Psammetichus II," *JBL* 76 (1957), 304–9.

Greenfield, J. C. "The Aramaean God Rammōn/Rimmōn," *IEJ* 26 (1976), 195–98.

———. "The Zakir Inscription and the Danklied," Proceedings of Fifth *WCJS* (1969), 174–91.

Gruber, M. I. *Aspects of Nonverbal Communication in the Ancient Near East.* Studia Pohl 12, Rome: Biblical Institute Press, 1980.

Gunkel, H. "Elisha—The Successor of Elijah (2 Kings ii, 1–18)," *ExpTim* 41 (1929), 182–86.

———. *Geschichten von Elisa.* Berlin: K. Curtius [1922].

Hallo, W. W. "From Qarqar to Carchemish: Assyria and Israel in the Light of New Discoveries," *BAR* 2.152–88.

———. "New Moons and Sabbaths: A Case-Study in the Contrastive Approach," *HUCA* 48 (1977), 1–18.

Halpern, B. *The Constitution of the Monarchy in Israel.* Harvard Semitic Monographs 25. Chico, Calif.: Scholars Press, 1981.

Hanson, P. D. "Song of Heshbon and David's *NÎR,*" *HTR* 61 (1968), 297–320.

Haran, M. "Behind the Stage of History—On the Dating of the Pentateuchal Priestly Source," *Zion* 45 (1980), 1–12.

———. "Book-Scrolls in Israel in Pre-Exilic Times," *JJS* 33 (1982), 161–73.

———. "Observations on the Historical Background of Amos 1:2–2:6," *IEJ* 18 (1968), 201–12.

———. "The Rise and Decline of the Empire of Jeroboam ben Joash," *VT* 17 (1967), 266–97.

Hayes, J. H. and Miller, J. M. eds. *Israelite and Judaean History.* London: SCM Press, 1977.

Held, M. "Studies in Comparative Semitic Lexicography," *AS* 16 (1965), 395–406.

Herrmann, S. *A History of Israel in Old Testament Times.* Philadelphia: Fortress, 1975.

Hestrin, R. and M. Dayagi-Mendels. *Seals from the First Temple Period.* Jerusalem: Israel Museum, 1978 (Hebrew).
Hillers, D. R. *Treaty-Curses and the Old Testament Prophets.* BibOr 16, Rome: Pontifical Biblical Institute, 1964.
Hoffman, H. D. *Reform und Reformen.* AThANT 66 (1980).
Hoffner, H. "Second Millennium Antecedents to the Hebrew *ʾôb,*" *JBL* 86 (1967), 385–401.
Honeyman, A. M. "The Evidence for Regnal Names Among the Hebrews," *JBL* 67 (1948), 13–25.
Honor, L. L. *Sennacherib's Invasion of Palestine.* New York: Columbia University, 1926.
Hulse, E. V. "The Nature of Biblical 'Leprosy' and the Use of Alternate Medical Terms in Modern Translations of the Bible," *PEQ* 107 (1975), 87–105.
Hurvitz, A. *A Linguistic Study of the Relationship Between the Priestly Source and the Book of Ezekiel.* Cahiers *RB* 20 (1982).
Inscriptions Reveal. Jerusalem: Israel Museum, Catalogue No. 100, 1973.
Ibn Janah, Jonah. *Sepher Haschoraschim,* Wurzelwörterbuch der hebräischen Sprache von Abulwalîd Merwân Ibn Gānâh, aus dem Arabischen in's Hebräische übersetzt von Jehuda Ibn Tibbon, hrsg. W. Bacher. Berlin: H. Itzkowski, 1896.
Ishida, T. *The Royal Dynasties in Ancient Israel. BZAW* 142 (1977).
"The House of Ahab," *IEJ* 25 (1975), 135–37.
.. " 'The People of the Land' and the Political Crises in Judah," *AJBI* 1 (1975), 23–38.
Iwry, S. "The Qumran Isaiah and the End of the Dial of Ahaz," *BASOR* 147 (1957), 27–33.
Jastrow, M. *A Dictionary of the Targumim, the Talmud Babli and Yerushalmi, and the Midrashic Literature.* Repr. New York: Pardes, 1950.
Jenkins, A. K. "Hezekiah's Fourteenth Year, A New Interpretation of 2 Kings XVIII 13–XIX 37," *VT* 26 (1976), 284–98.
Jepsen, A. "Israel und Damaskus," *AfO* 14 (1942), 153–72.
Joüon, P "Le costume d'Elie et celui de Jean Baptiste," *Bib* 16 (1935), 74–81
Grammaire de l'hébreu biblique. Rome: Pontifical Biblical Institute, 1923
Kallai, Z. "Baal Shalisha and Ephraim," in *Bible and Jewish History* (Studies in Memory of J Liver). Ed. B. Uffenheimer, Tel Aviv· Tel Aviv University, 1971, 191–204 (Hebrew).
The Tribes of Israel. Jerusalem Mosad Bialik, 1967 (Hebrew).
Katzenstein, H J "Some Remarks on the Lists of the Chief Priests of the Temple of Solomon," *JBL* 81 (1961), 377–84
The History of Tyre. Jerusalem Schocken Institute, 1973
"Who Were the Parents of Athaliah?" *IEJ* 5 (1955), 194–97

Kaufman, S. A. "The Enigmatic Adad-Milki," *JNES* 37 (1978), 101–9.

Kaufmann, Y. *Mikivshonah shel hayiṣirah hamiqra'it* (= Collected Papers). Tel Aviv: Dvir, 1966.

———. *The Religion of Israel.* Chicago: University of Chicago Press, 1960.

———. *Toledot ha'emunah hayisra'elit.* 4 vols. Tel Aviv: Dvir, 1960.

Kitchen, K. A. "Late Egyptian Chronology and the Hebrew Monarchy," *JANES* 5 (1973), 225–31.

———. *Third Intermediate Period in Egypt (1100–650 B.C.).* Warminster: Aris & Phillips, 1973.

Kittel, R. *Geschichte des Volkes Israel.* 5th ed., Gotha: F. A. Perthes, 1909.

Koch, K. *The Growth of the Biblical Tradition.* New York: Scribner, 1969.

Kuenen, A. *The Prophets and Prophecy in Israel.* London: Longmans and Green, 1877; repr. Amsterdam: Philo Press, 1969.

Kuhl, C. "Die 'Wiederaufnahme'—ein literarkritisches Prinzip?" *ZAW* 64 (1952), 1–11.

Kutsch, E. "Die Wurzel *ʿṣr* im Hebräischen," *VT* 2 (1952), 57–69.

Kutscher, E. Y. *The Language and Linguistic Background of the Isaiah Scroll* (IQ Isa[a]). Leiden: Brill, 1974.

Labuschange, C. J. "Did Elisha Deliberately Lie? A Note on II Kings 8:10," *ZAW* 77 (1965), 327–28.

Lemaire, A. "Le stèle arameéne de Barhadad," *Or* 53 (1984), 337–49.

———. *Les écoles et la formation de la Bible dans l'ancien Israel.* Orbis Biblicus et Orientalis 39 (1981).

———. "Les inscriptions des Khirbet el-Qom et l'asherah de YHWH," *RB* 84 (1984), 595–608.

Levine, L. D. "Menahem and Tiglath-pileser: A New Synchronism," *BASOR* 206 (1972), 40–42.

Lewy, J. *Die Chronologie der Könige von Israel und Juda.* Giessen: A. Topelmann, 1927.

Licht, J. *Storytelling in the Bible.* Jerusalem: Magnes, 1978.

Lindblom, J. *Prophecy in Ancient Israel.* Philadelphia: Fortress, 1962.

Lipiński, E. *Studies in Aramaic Inscriptions and Onomastics.* Leuven: Leuven University Press, 1975.

Liver, J. *Chapters in the History of the Priests and Levites.* Jerusalem: Magnes, 1968 (Hebrew).

———. "The Wars of Mesha, King of Moab," *PEQ* 99 (1967), 14–31.

Liverani, M. "L'histoire de Joas," *VT* 24 (1974), 438–53.

Long, B. O. "2 Kings III and Genres of Prophetic Narrative," *VT* 23 (1973), 337–48.

Loretz, A. "Kʿt ḥyh." wie jetzt ums Jahr," Gen 18:10," *Bib* 43 (1962), 75–78.

Luckenbill, D. D. *Annals of Sennacherib.* OIP 2. Chicago: University of Chicago Press, 1924.

Lundbom, J. R. "Elijah's Chariot Ride," *JJS* 24 (1973), 39–50.

Macdonald, J "The Status and Role of the Naʿar in Israelite Society," *JNES* 35 (1976), 147–70.

Machinist, P "Assyria and Its Image in the First Isaiah," *JAOS* 103 (1983), 719–37

Malamat, A "A New Record of Nebuchadnezzar's Palestinian Campaigns," *IEJ* 4 (1956), 246–56.

"Josiah's Bid for Armageddon," *JANES* 5 (1973), 267–78

"The Historical Background of the Assassination of Amon, King of Judah," *IEJ* 3 (1953), 26–29

"The Last Kings of Judah and the Fall of Jerusalem," *IEJ* 18 (1968), 137 56.

"The Twilight of Judah In the Egyptian-Babylonian Maelstrom," *VT* Sup 28 (1975), 123–45

Malamat, A and Eph'al I *The Age of the Monarchies. Political History. WHJP* 4/1 Jerusalem, Masada Press, 1979

Masson, O "Les nom des Carians dans quelques langues de l'antiquité," in *Mélanges É. Benveniste.* Louvain, Ed. Peeters, 1975, 407–14

Mastin, B. A "Was the *šālîš* the Third Man in the Chariot?" *VT* Sup 30 (1979), 124–54

"*Waw explicativum* in 2 Kings viii 9," *VT* 34 (1984), 353–55

Mazar, B *Canaan and Israel.* Jerusalem Mosad Bialik, 1974 (Hebrew)

Cities and Districts in Eretz-Israel. Jerusalem Mosad Bialik, 1975 (Hebrew).

"Gath and Gittaim," *IEJ* 4 (1954), 227–35

"The Aramean Empire and Its Relations with Israel," *BAR* 2 127 51

"The Tobiads," *IEJ* 7 (1957), 229–38

McCarter, P K "'Yaw, son of ʿOmri' A Philological Note on Israelite Chronology," *BASOR* 216 (1974), 5–7

McCarthy, D J *Treaty and Covenant.* AnBib 21A (1978)

McKane, W "A Note on 2 Kings 12 10," *ZAW* 71 (1959), 260–65

McKay, J *Religion in Judah under the Assyrians.* SBT 2nd Series 26 (1973)

Mettinger, T D N *King and Messiah.* ConB Old Testament Series 8, 1976.

Solomonic State Officials, ConB Old Testament Series 5, 1971

"YHWH SABAOTH—The Heavenly King on the Cherubim Throne," in *Studies in the Period of David and Solomon.* Ed. T Ishida, Tokyo Yamakowa-Shuppansha, 1982, 109–38

Milgrom, J *Studies in Levitical Terminology.* Vol 1 Berkeley University of California Press, 1970

Millard, A. R. "Adad-nirari III, Aram, and Arpad," *PEQ* 105 (1973), 161 64

"Assyrian Royal Names in Biblical Hebrew," *JSS* 21 (1976), 1 14

"Baladan, the Father of Merodach-baladan," *Tyndale Bulletin* 21 (1971), 125–26.

Miller, J. M. "Another Look at the Chronology of the Early Divided Monarchy," *JBL* 86 (1967), 276–88.

———. "The Elisha Cycle and the Accounts of the Omride Wars," *JBL* 85 (1966), 441–54.

Moffat, James. *The Old Testament, A New Translation.* London: Hodder and Stoughton, n.d.

Montgomery, J. A. "Archival Data in the Books of Kings," *JBL* 53 (1934), 46–52.

Morag, S. "Meša (A Study of Certain Features of Old Hebrew Dialect)," *EI* 5 (1958), 138–44.

Mowinckel, S. "Die Chronologie der israelitischen und jüdischen Könige," *AcOr* 10 (1932), 161–277.

Mulder, M. J. "War war die am Tempel gebaute 'Sabbathalle' in II Kön. 16, 18?" AOAT 211 (1982), 161–72.

Murphy, R. "Israel and Moab in the Ninth Century B.C.," *CBQ* 15 (1953), 409–17.

Na'aman, N. "Sennacherib's 'Letter to God' on His Campaign to Judah," *BASOR* 214 (1974), 25–38.

———. "The Brook of Egypt and Assyrian Policy on the Border of Egypt," *Tel Aviv* 6 (1979), 68–90.

———. "Sennacherib's Campaign to Judah, and the Date of the *Lmlk* Stamps," *VT* 29 (1979), 61–86.

Napier, B. D. "The Omrides of Jezreel," *VT* 9 (1959), 366–78.

Naveh, J. "Khirbat al-Muqannaʿ-Ekron," *IEJ* 8 (1958), 87–100, 165–70.

Nelson, R. D. *The Double Redaction of the Deuteronomistic History. JSOT* Sup 18 (1981).

Nicholson, E. W. *Deuteronomy and Tradition.* Philadelphia: Fortress, 1967.

———. "II Kings xxii.18—A Simple Restoration," *Hermathena* 97 (1963), 96–98.

Nielson, E. "Political Conditions and Cultural Developments in Israel and Judah During the Reign of Manasseh," Fourth *WCJS* (Jerusalem, 1967), 1.103–6.

Noth, M. *The History of Israel.* New York: Harper, 1960.

———. *The Laws in the Pentateuch and Other Studies.* Philadelphia: Fortress, 1966.

———. *Überlieferungsgeschichtliche Studien.* Originally published in 1943. Repr. Tübingen: M. Niemeyer, 1967; English translation as *The Deuteronomistic History JSOT* Sup 15, 1981.

Oded, B. *Mass Deportations and Deportees in the Neo-Assyrian Empire.* Wiesbaden: L. Reichert, 1979.

———. "Observations on Methods of Assyrian Rule in Transjordania After the Palestinian Campaign of Tiglath-pileser III," *JNES* (1970), 177–86.

———. "The Historical Background of the Syro-Ephraimite War Reconsidered," *CBQ* 34 (1972), 153–65.

Oestreicher, T. *Das deuteronomische Grundgesetz.* BFCT 27/4 (1923).
Olmstead, A. T. *History of Assyria.* Chicago: University of Chicago Press, 1923.
Oppenheim, A. L. "A Fiscal Practice of the Ancient Near East," *JNES* 6 (1947), 116–20.
______. *Ancient Mesopotamia.* Chicago: University of Chicago Press, 1964.
Orlinsky, H. "The Kings—Isaiah Recensions of the Hezekiah Story," *JQR* 30 (1939–40), 33–49.
Otzen, B. "Israel Under the Assyrians: Reflections on Imperial Policy in Palestine," *ASTI* 11 (1977–78), 96–110.
Parker, S. B. "Jezebel's Reception of Jehu," *Maarav* 1 (1978), 67–78.
Parpola, S. "The Murderer of Sennacherib," in *Death in Mesopotamia.* ed. B. Alster. *Mesopotamia 8.* Copenhagen: Akademisk Forlag, 1980, 171–82.
Paul, S. "Sargon's Administrative Direction in II Kings 17:27," *JBL* 88 (1969), 73–74.
Puech, É. "Athalie, fils d'Achab et la chronologie des rois d'Israël et de Juda," *Salamanticensis* 28 (1981), 117–36.
Rad, G. von. *Old Testament Theology.* 2 vols. New York, Evanston: Harper & Row, 1962.
______. *Studies in Deuteronomy.* SBT 9 (1953).
Rainey, A. *A Social Structure of Ugarit.* Jerusalem: Mosad Bialik, 1967 (Hebrew).
______. "The Identification of Philistine Gath—A Problem in Source Analysis for Historical Geography," *EI* 12 (1975), 63*–76*.
Reed, W. L. *The Asherah in the Old Testament.* Fort Worth: Texas Christian University Press, 1949.
Reed, W. L. and Winnett, F. V. "A Fragment of an Early Moabite Inscription from Kerak," *BASOR* 172 (1963), 1–9.
Rendsburg, G. "A Reconstruction of Moabite-Israelite History," *JANES* 13 (1981), 67–73.
Reviv, H. *The Elders in Ancient Israel, A Study of A Biblical Institution.* Jerusalem: Magnes, 1983 (Hebrew).
"On the Days of Athaliah and Joash," *Beth-Mikra* 47 (1971), 541–48.
"Types of Leadership in the Period of the Judges," *Beer-sheva* 1 (1973), 204–15 (Hebrew).
Ritter, E. "Magical-Expert (= Āšipu) and Physician (= Asû) in Mesopotamian Texts," *Studies in Honor of Benno Landsberger . . .*, *AS* 16 (1965), 299–321
Robinson, T. H. *A History of Israel.* Vol. 1 Oxford. Clarendon Press, 1932.
Rofé, A. *Israelite Belief in Angels in the Pre-exilic Period as Evidenced by Biblical Traditions.* Unpublished Ph.D dissertation, Hebrew University, 1969 (Hebrew).

———. "The Classification of the Prophetical Stories," *JBL* 89 (1970), 427–40.
———. *The Prophetical Stories.* Jerusalem: Magnes, 1982 (Hebrew).
Rudolph, W. "Die Einheitlichkeit der Erzählung vom Sturz der Atalja (2 Kön 11)," in *Festschrift Bertholet.* Tübingen: J. C. B. Mohr, 1950, 473–78.
Sarna, N. "The Abortive Insurrection in Zedekiah's Day (Jer. 27–29)," *EI* 14 (1979), 89*–96*.
Saydon, P. "The Meaning of the Expression *ʿāṣûr weʿāzûb,*" *VT* 2 (1952), 371–74.
Seeligmann, I. L. "Etiological Elements in Biblical Historiography," *Zion* 26 (1961), 141–69.
———. "On the Problems of Prophecy in Israel, Its History and Nature," *EI* 5 (1958), 125–32.
Segert, S. "Zur Bedeutung des Wortes Nōqēd," *VT* Sup 16 (1967), 279–83.
Shenkel, J. D. *Chronology and Recensional Development in the Greek Text of Kings.* Cambridge, Mass.: Harvard University Press, 1968.
Shiloh, Y. *Excavations at the City of David. Qedem* 19 (1984).
———. "The Population of Iron Age Palestine in the Light of Urban Plans, Areas and Population Density," *EI* 15 (1981), 273–82.
Simon, U. "I Kings 13: A Prophetic Sign—Denial and Persistence," *HUCA* 47 (1976), 81–117.
Simons, J. *The Geographical and Topographical Texts of the Old Testament.* Leiden: Brill, 1959.
Smend, R. "Der biblische und der historische Elia," *VT* Sup 28 (1975), 167–84.
Smirin, S. *Josiah and His Age.* Jerusalem: Mosad Bialik, 1951 (Hebrew).
Smith, M. "A Note on Burning Babies," *JAOS* 95 (1975), 477–79.
Snaith, N. H. "The Meaning of *śĕʿîrîm,*" *VT* 25 (1975), 115–18.
Soggin, A. "Der judäische ʿAm-haʾareṣ und das Königtum in Juda," *VT* 13 (1963), 187–95.
Spalinger, A. "Egypt and Babylonia: A Survey (c. 620 B.C.–550 B.C.)," *Studien zur ägyptischen Kultur* 5 (1977), 221–44.
Speiser, E. A. *Oriental and Biblical Studies.* Philadelphia: University of Pennsylvania Press, 1967.
———. "Unrecognized Dedication," *IEJ* 13 (1963), 69–73.
Stager, L. E. "The Archaeology of the East Slope of Jerusalem and the Terraces of the Kidron," *JNES* 41 (1982), 111–21.
———. "The Rite of Child Sacrifice at Carthage," in *New Light on Ancient Carthage.* Ed. J. G. Pedley. Ann Arbor, Mich.: University of Michigan Press, 1980, 1–11.
Stamm, J. J. "Hebräische Frauennamen," *VT* Sup 16 (1967), 301–39.
Steck, O. H. "Die Erzählung von Jahwes Einschreiten gegen die Orakelbefragung Ahasjas (2 Kön 1, 2–8*, 17)," *EvTh* 27 (1967), 546–56.

Stern, E. "Israel at the Close of the Period of the Monarchy: An Archaeological Survey," *BA* 38 (1975), 26–54.

Streck, M. *Assurbanipal und die letzten assyrischen Könige bis zum Untergange Ninivehs.* Leipzig: J. C. Hinrich, 1916.

Tadmor, H. "Azriyau of Yaudi," *SH* 8 (1961), 232–71.

"Chronology of the Last Kings of Judah," *JNES* 15 (1956), 226–30.

"Philistia Under Assyrian Rule," *BA* 29 (1966), 86–102.

"Que and Muṣri," *IEJ* 11 (1961), 143–50.

"Rab-saris and Rab-shakeh in 2 Kings 18," in *The Word of the Lord Shall Go Forth. Essays in Honor of D. N. Freedman.* Eds. C. L. Meyers and M. O'Connor, Winona Lake, Ind.: Eisenbrauns, 1983, 279–85.

"Some Aspects of the History of Samaria During the Biblical Period," *The Jerusalem Cathedra* 3 (1983), 1–11.

"The Aramaization of Assyria," in *Mesopotamien und seine Nachbarn.* Ed. H. J. Nissen and J. Renger, Berliner Beiträge zum Vorderen Orient 1 (1983), 449–70.

"The Campaigns of Sargon II of Assur: A Chronological-Historical Study," *JCS* 12 (1958), 22–40, 77–100.

"The Conquest of the Galilee by Tiglath-pileser III, King of Assyria," in *All the Land of Naphtali.* Jerusalem: Israel Exploration Society, 1968, 62–67 (Hebrew).

" 'The People' and the Kingship in Israel," *JWH* 11 (1968), 46–68.

"The Southern Border of Aram," *IEJ* 12 (1962), 114–22.

"Treaty and Oath in the Ancient Near East," in *Humanizing America's Iconic Book. Society of Biblical Literature Centennial Addresses, 1980.* Eds. G. M. Tucker and D. A. Knight, Chico, Calif.: Scholars Press, 1982, 127–52.

Tadmor, H. and Cogan, M. "Ahaz and Tiglath-pileser in the Book of Kings: Historiographic Considerations," *Bib* 60 (1979), 491–99.

"Hezekiah's Fourteenth Year: The King's Illness and the Babylonian Embassy," *EI* 16 (1982), 198–201.

Talmon, S. "Double Readings in the Massoretic Text," *Textus* 1 (1960), 144–84.

"Polemics and Apology in Biblical Historiography: 2 Kings 17:24–41," in *The Creation of Sacred Literature.* Ed. R. E. Friedman, Berkeley, Calif.: University of California Press, 1981, 57–75.

"The Judaean ʿAm haʾareṣ in Historical Perspective," Fourth *WCJS* (Jerusalem: 1967), 71–76.

Tawil, H. "The Historicity of 2 Kings 19:24 (= Isaiah 37:25): The Problem of *Yeʾōrê Māṣôr,*" *JNES* 41 (1982), 195–206.

Thiele, E. *Mysterious Numbers of the Hebrew Kings.* 1st ed., Chicago, University of Chicago Press, 1951; 2nd ed., Grand Rapids, Mich.: Eerdmans, 1965.

Timm, S. *Die Dynastie Omri.* FRLANT 124 (1982).

Torrey, C. C. "The Evolution of a Financier in the Ancient Near East," *JNES* 2 (1943), 295–301.

Tov, E. "Some Aspects of the Textual and Literary History of the Book of Jeremiah," in *Le Livre de Jérémie,* ed. P.-M. Bogaert, Leuven: Leuven University Press, 1981, 145–67.

Trebolle, J. "From the 'Old Latin' through the 'Old Greek' to the 'Old Hebrew' (2 Kgs 10:23–25)," *Textus* 11 (1984), 17–36.

Tur-Sinai, N. H. *Peschuto shel Miqra.* Jerusalem: Kiryat Sefer, 1967 (Hebrew).

———. *The Language and the Book.* 2nd ed., Jerusalem: Mosad Bialik, 1954 (Hebrew).

Uffenheimer, B. "The Meaning of the Story of Jehu," in *Oz Le-David, Studies Presented to D. Ben-Gurion.* Jerusalem: Israel Bible Society, 1964, 291–311 (Hebrew).

Unger, M. F. *Israel and the Aramaeans of Damascus.* London: J. Clarke, 1957.

Ussishkin, D. "Excavations at Tel Lachish—1973–1977, Preliminary Report," *Tel Aviv* 5 (1978), 1–97.

———. "The Necropolis from the Time of the Kingdom of Judah at Silwan, Jerusalem," *BA* 33 (1970), 34–46.

Van Zyl, A. H. *The Moabites.* Leiden: Brill, 1960.

Vaugh, P. H. *The Meaning of "Bama" in the Old Testament.* Cambridge, U.K.: Cambridge University, 1974.

de. Vaux, R. *Ancient Israel.* New York: McGraw-Hill, 1961.

———. "Les sens de l'expression 'Peuple du Pays'," *RA* 54 (1964), 167–72.

Vinnikov, I. N. "L'enigme de *ʿāṣûr* et *ʿāzûb,*" in *Hommages à Andre Dupont-Sommer.* Paris: A. Maisonneuve, 1971, 343–45.

Vogelstein, M. *Fertile Soil.* New York: American Press, 1957.

Weinfeld, M. "Burning Babies in Ancient Israel," *UF* 10 (1978), 411–13.

———. "Cult Centralization in Israel in the Light of a Neo-Babylonian Analogy," *JNES* 23 (1964), 202–12.

———. *Deuteronomy and the Deuteronomic School.* Oxford: Oxford University Press, 1972.

———. "The Worship of Molech and of the Queen of Heaven and Its Background," *UF* 4 (1972), 133–54.

Weippert, M. "Jau(a) mār Ḫumrî-Joram oder Jehu von Israel?" *VT* 28 (1978), 113–18.

———. "Menachem von Israel und seine Zeitgenossen," *ZDPV* 89 (1973), 26–53.

Wellhausen, J. *Die Composition des Hexateuchs.* 4th ed., 1899, repr.: Berlin: W. de Gruyter, 1963.

Williams, J. G. "The Prophetic 'Father'," *JBL* 85 (1966), 344–48.

Williamson, H. G. M. "The Death of Josiah and the Continuing Development of the Deuteronomic History," *VT* 32 (1982), 242–48.

Wilson, R R *Prophecy and Society in Ancient Israel.* Philadelphia Fortress, 1980

Winckler, H *Altorientalische Forschungen.* Vol 1 Leipzig Pfeiffer, 1893

Alttestamentliche Untersuchungen. Leipzig Pfeiffer, 1892

Wolff, H W "Das Kerygma des deuteronomistischen Geschichtswerkes," *ZAW* 73 (1961), 171–86; English translation in *The Vitality of Old Testament Traditions.* Eds. H W Wolff and W Brueggemann Atlanta John Knox Press, 1975, 82–100

Würthwein, E. *Der ʿamm haʾarez im Alten Testament.* BWANT 4/17 (1936)

Yadin, Y "Beer-sheba. The High Place Destroyed by King Josiah," *BASOR* 222 (1976), 5–17

The Art of Warfare in Bible Lands. New York McGraw-Hill, 1963

"The Dial of Ahaz," *EI* 5 (1958), 91–96.

"The 'House of Baal' of Ahab and Jezebel in Samaria, and That of Athalia in Judah," in *Archaeology in the Levant, Essays for Kathleen Kenyon.* Eds. R. Moorey and P Parr, Warminster· Aris & Phillips, 1978, 127–35

Yalon, H *Studies in the Hebrew Language.* Jerusalem Mosad Bialik, 1971 (Hebrew)

Yaron, R *"Kaʿeth Ḥayyah* and *Koh Leḥay,"* *VT* 12 (1962), 500–1

Yeivin, S "The Sepulchers of the Kings of the House of David," *JNES* 7 (1948), 30–45

"Families and Parties in the Kingdom of Judah," *Tarbiz* 12 (1941), 241–67

Zadok, R "Geographical and Onomastic Notes," *JANES* 8 (1976), 113–26.

The Jews in Babylonia During the Chaldean and Achaemenian Periods. Haifa. University of Haifa, 1979

Zakovitch, Y "2 Kgs 20·7—Isaiah 38.21–22," *Beth-Mikra* 17 (1972), 302–5

The Pattern of the Numerical Sequence Three-Four in the Bible. Unpublished Ph D dissertation, Hebrew University, 1977 (Hebrew).

Ziegler, J "Die Hilfe Gottes 'am Morgen'," in *Studien Nötscher, Bonner Biblische Studien* 1 (1950), 281–88

Zuckerbram, J "Variants in Editing," *Melilah* III IV (1950), 1 54 (Hebrew).

Introduction

Content

The books of Kings were originally one book, but were subdivided into two by the translators of the Hebrew Bible into Greek. They narrate the history of the Israelite monarchy from the last days of David, through the division of the United Kingdom into the rival kingdoms of Israel and Judah, down to the destruction of Jerusalem and the exile to Babylonia. From the point of view of structure, Kings is a complex composition which employs a synchronic method of narration, not unlike older Mesopotamian models, which coordinate the histories of Assyria and Babylonia.[1] Following a generally chronological order, the narration alternates between the reigns of the kings of Israel and Judah. The narrative framework consists of chronological formulae: a statement about the length of reign of a particular king and its synchronism with that of his counterpart in the rival kingdom—e.g., "Ahaziah son of Ahab became king in Samaria in the seventeenth year of Jehoshaphat king of Judah; he reigned two years over Israel" (1 Kgs 22:52). As analogues suggest, such a framework might have existed independently in annotated king lists or in royal and temple chronicles. But unlike Mesopotamian chronicles, the chronological formulae in Kings are placed at the beginning of each reign, not at its close.

For the author of Kings (henceforth, the historian), the historical approach, the choice of events reported, and the manner of presentation are governed by a single idea: the loyalty of the monarch to the God of Israel as worshipped in Jerusalem determines the course of history. In view of the catastrophic end of the northern kingdom and the pending doom foretold against Judah, the historian leveled severe criticism at the conduct of every monarch of Israel and most of those of Judah. In doing so, the historian chose to relate only those events that were pertinent to his message. For his was a didactic presentation addressed to a contemporary audience, if not also to future readers, its purpose to avert a recurrence of the calamities that befell the nation by avoiding a repetition of the misdeeds of the past. All the while, this predominant ideological component did not disturb the synchronic pattern of narration that was faithfully followed.

The historian, whose ideological premises and *modus operandi* will be treated in the Introduction to 1 Kings, was an adherent of the Deuteronomic school (Dtr., according to the common nomenclature in biblical scholarship).

[1] An Assyrian chronicle, *The Synchronistic History,* which surveys eight hundred years of Assyro-Babylonian relations has been translated and is discussed by A. K. Grayson in *Assyrian and Babylonian Chronicles* (Locust Valley, N.Y.: Augustin, 1975), 51–56, 157–70. For a Synchronic King List recording the names of the kings of Assyria and Babylonia from the early nineteenth century B.C.E. to 627 B.C.E., see *ANET*[3], 272–74, and A. K. Grayson, RLA 6.116–25.

With several scholars, past and contemporary,[2] the present commentators hold that the Book of Kings, in the main, was composed during the reign of Josiah, toward the close of the seventh century B.C E., and that a generation after the destruction of the Temple, the work was updated and partially revised by another Deuteronomistic historian (see Comment at 17 7–23, 22–23). However, the Deuteronomistic historians were not the first to relate the history of Israel, as it is possible to identify parts of an earlier composition of north-Israelite origin embedded in Kings (see Comment at 13 1–9; 14 23–29).[3]

The primary sources used by the authors of Kings are no longer extant, some of them are known only by quotations from the "Annals of the Kings of Israel" and "Annals of the Kings of Judah," or from what seems to have been a Temple Chronicle (see Comment at 16 1–20). At many points, the quotations have been edited and adjusted to the overall conceptual viewpoint of the Deuteronomistic history, although it must be admitted that certain items taken over from the posited north-Israelite composition have not been fully integrated into the larger work (see Comment at 14.23–29).

Extrabiblical Documentation

The use of extrabiblical documentation for elucidating Kings, so prevalent in this commentary, is by no means novel. It started almost from the very onset of archaeological discoveries in the mid-nineteenth century and decisively transformed the study of the Divided Monarchy The decipherment of the Assyrian monuments unearthed at Nimrud (ancient Calah) and Nineveh yielded astonishing revelations, already in 1850, the name of "Jehu, son of Omri" was read on the Black Obelisk of Shalmaneser III, and a detailed account of the Assyrian campaign to Judah and of Hezekiah's tribute was

[2] R D Nelson amply reviews the history of the "dual redaction hypothesis" as regards the composition of the Book of Kings, from its basic formulation by A Kuenen (1887 92) and its adoption by J Wellhausen and S. R Driver to its recent reappraisal by F M Cross (1973). See Nelson, *The Double Redaction of the Deuteronomistic History*, *JSOT* Sup 18 (1981), 13–22

[3] Literary analysis of the regnal summaries and judgment formulae in the book of Kings led H Weippert to posit the existance of an early historical survey of northern provenance from the last days of Samaria, one of three in the book of Kings, see Weippert, "Die 'Deuteronomistischen' Beurteilung der Könige von Israel und Juda und das Problem der Redaktion der Königsbücher," *Bib* 53 (1972), 301 39, and cf S. R Bin-Nun, "Formulas from Royal Records of Israel and of Judah," *VT* 18 (1968), 414–32 The relationship between this northern chronistic stratum within Kings and the pre-Deuteronomistic composition posited here will be evaluated in the Introduction to 1 Kings. See, too, Nelson, *Double Redaction* (above, n.2), 31, and A D H Mayes, *The Story of Israel Between Settlement and Exile* (London SCM Press, 1983), 120–25

found incised on colossal stone bulls from Sennacherib's palace.[4] The spate of materials from the homeland of the empires was not matched by similar discoveries in ancient Israel itself; relatively little that related directly to the history of the monarchy was recovered, though two monuments of note—the Mesha Stone and the Siloam Inscription—did come to light.[5] The relevance of the extrabiblical documents quickly became recognized through the works of George Smith[6] and Eberhard Schrader,[7] and were soon incorporated in biblical commentaries on Kings.[8]

And indeed, the extrabiblical documentation provides a variety of information, some complementary and corroborative, some supplementary and discordant, but in each instance broadening the horizon of 2 Kings. Several examples of the many to be found throughout the present commentary are here adduced.

The inscriptions of the neo-Assyrian monarch Tiglath-pileser III (745–727), though very fragmentary, preserve the names of three kings of Israel: Menahem, Pekah, Hoshea, and one king of Judah: Ahaz. Menahem's tribute to Pul (= Tiglath-pileser) recorded in 2 Kgs 15:19 is matched by the mention of tribute paid by *Miniḫimme Samerināya,* Menahem of Samaria to Tiglath-pileser in 738 B.C.E. So, too, is the deposition of Pekah and the accession of Hoshea (2 Kgs 15:30). In the case of Ahaz, who submitted to Tiglath-pileser in 734 (cf. 2 Kgs 16:7), his name is recorded in a list of tribute-bearing kings; in cuneiform, the name appears in its full form *Iauḫazi Iaudāya,* Jehoahaz of Judah, while in 2 Kings, he is known only by his hypocoristicon, Ahaz. Finally, collation of a recently discovered text of Tiglath-pileser shows that Hoshea of Israel rendered tribute to Assyria in 731, thus providing the modern historian with another fixed chronological date.

The inscriptions of Sargon II (722–705), though of a king not mentioned by name in 2 Kings (cf. Isa 20:1), clarify the sequence of events during the final

[4] See A. H. Layard, *Discoveries in the Ruins of Nineveh and Babylonia* (London: J. Murray, 1853). For a survey of the early history of these discoveries, see H. Tadmor, "Nineveh, Calah and Israel: On Assyriology and the Origins of Biblical Archaeology," in *Biblical Archaeology Today,* Proceedings of the International Congress on Biblical Archaeology, Jerusalem, April 1984 (Jerusalem: Israel Exploration Society, 1985), 260–68.

[5] The strange and tangled history of the Mesha Stone is retraced by S. H. Horn, "The Discovery of the Moabite Stone," in *The Word of the Lord Shall Go Forth.* Essays in Honor of D. N. Freedman, eds. C. L. Meyers and M. O'Connor (Winona Lake, Ind.: Eisenbrauns, 1983), 497–505.

[6] George Smith, *Assyrian Discoveries* (London: S. Low, 1875).

[7] E. Schrader, *Die Keilschriften und das Alte Testament* (Giessen: J. Ricker, 1872); the second edition of this work (1883) was translated and appeared as: *The Cuneiform Inscriptions and the Old Testament* (London and Edinburgh: Williams and Norgate, 1885).

[8] O. Thenius acknowledges the use of Schrader's "valuable work" in the revised edition of his commentary *Die Bücher der Könige* (Leipzig: S. Hirzel, 1873), xi.

years of the northern kingdom. Sargon claims to have conquered Samaria at the beginning of his reign, a statement in open conflict with 2 Kgs 17:5–6 and the Babylonian chronicle entry, which credit Shalmaneser V, his predecessor, with this conquest. But Sargon's annals, an example of retrospective historical narration, preserve evidence of Samaria's reconquest in 720, Sargon's second year, and show that Shalmaneser's sudden death in 722 had left the city to its own devices after the first defeat. The record in 2 Kings 17:1–6 is seen to contain a "telescoping" of events and thus the "king of Assyria" who exiled Israel (17:6) is not Shalmaneser V but Sargon.

The Babylonian Chronicle Series provides documentation of another sort; its yearly entries for 625–595 B.C.E. record, in staccato fashion, the downfall of the Assyrian empire, the military intervention of Egypt on its behalf, and the unsuccessful struggle with Chaldean Babylonia allied with the Medes. It is in conjunction with the events of these turbulent years that the terse report of Josiah's meeting with Necho II in 2 Kgs 23:29 can be interpreted. In addition, the Chronicle Series establishes a solid chronological framework for the last years of the kingdom of Judah. An explicit reference to the capture of Jerusalem and the replacement of its king is recorded for the "seventh year of Nebuchadnezzar," i.e., 597 B.C.E. (cf. 2 Kgs 24:8–17); the city's submission on "2 Adar" is a datum not recorded in 2 Kgs 24 or any other biblical source.

Babylonian administrative documents, whose bearing on biblical issues is usually oblique, if there is any at all, in one instance reveal a detail concerning the conditions of Jehoiachin's imprisonment in Babylon. Recorded in texts dating from the thirteenth year of Nebuchadnezzar is the distribution of fixed allotments of oil (probably for food preparation) to him, his five sons, and Judaean courtiers in the service of the king (see note to 2 Kgs 24:8).

Turning to the land of Israel and its immediate neighbors, there is little in the way of inscriptional material to rival the riches of the cuneiform world. Though it is a fair assumption that monumental inscriptions were composed on behalf of the kings of Israel and Judah (cf. 1 Sam 15:12; 2 Sam 18:18), other than the Siloam Tunnel Inscription, only a few fragments composed in Hebrew survive.[9] The Mesha Stone, a royal commemorative stela of the Mesopotamian type, not only records Moab's rebellion and its wars with Israel (2 Kgs 1 1, 3.1–27), but provides an insight into Moabite historiography. The mode of narration and the view of history in which Chemosh, the national god of Moab, controls the destiny of his subjects, bringing defeat upon them

[9] In the excavations of Samaria, the single word *ʾăšer* ("which") incised in large letters on a piece of limestone, was found. See J W Crowfoot, G M. Crowfoot, K. M. Kenyon, *The Objects from Samaria* (London Palestine Exploration Fund, 1957) 33, Plate IV, I A fragment of four broken lines has recently come to light in Jerusalem, though no continuous text can be made out, see J Naveh, "A Fragment of an Ancient Hebrew Inscription from the Ophel," *IEJ* 32 (1982), 195–98.

at the hands of "Omri, king of Israel" or granting them victory over Israel, are strikingly similar to those prevalent in ancient Israel.[10]

From the small finds recovered, mainly ostraca, seals, and bullae, a corpus of personal names numbering in the hundreds can be gleaned; royalty and notables, as well as private individuals, active during the last two centuries of the kingdom of Judah, are represented. A few can be identified with persons mentioned in 2 Kings (and the parallel chapters of Jeremiah)—e.g., Gedaliah, son of Ahikam (2 Kgs 25:22); Jaazaniah, son of the Maacathite (25:22); King Hezekiah (on the seal of one of his servants, cf. 18:1). In addition, the ostraca attest to the formulae and the "manual of stylistics" which governed Hebrew epistolography (cf. e.g., note to 5:6).

For the convenience of the reader, the most important of the extrabiblical documents have been translated anew and appear in Appendix I.[11]

Philology

The historical focus of this commentary is complemented by philological discussions that give much weight to evidence drawn from Akkadian and Aramaic sources in elucidating words and phrases that have puzzled earlier commentators. The validity and advantage of the investigation into cognate Semitic languages rest upon two premises: (1) During the period covered by 2 Kings, the kingdoms of Israel and Judah were thoroughly integrated into the Syro-Mesopotamian cultural sphere. In the Assyrian provinces established in northern Israel, the official language of imperial administration seems to have been the Assyrian dialect of Akkadian; evidence for this is seen in several cuneiform tablets found at Samaria and Gezer. In addition, it is most probable that Aramaic enjoyed the status of an alternate official language, as was the case in other areas west of the Euphrates. At the same time, Aramaic was the language of converse between native Israelites and the mixed communities from all areas of the Near East resettled in the land. Thus whether the result of political coercion or military conquest, or whether stemming from commercial and trade interests, the everyday contact between speakers of Hebrew and other languages created the setting in which multilingualism developed; lexical borrowings and calques into Hebrew were the result.[12] (2) Akkadian and Aramaic, being contemporary with standard biblical Hebrew,

[10] A discussion of the affinities of the Mesha Stone with biblical and ancient Near Eastern thought can be found in B. Albrektson, *History and the Gods,* ConB, OTS 1 (1967), 100–1.

[11] In this matter, the present commentators have followed the lead of C. F. Burney, who in his *Notes on the Hebrew Text of the Books of Kings* (Oxford: Clarendon Press, 1903), appended a short collection of "the more important contemporary inscriptions which throw light upon the narrative of Kings" (Preface).

[12] Concerning the influence of Aramaic on Hebrew, see the remarks of E. Y. Kutscher, *A History of the Hebrew Language* (Jerusalem: Magnes, 1982), 71–77; and for

have greater relevance for comparative purposes than other Semitic languages which are removed from BH by many hundred of years, as e.g., Ugaritic of the mid-second millennium B.C.E. or Arabic of the first millennium C.E.[13]

Accordingly, an expression like *kāʿēt ḥayyâ* (2 Kgs 4 16) can be explained by reference to the analogous Akkadian *ana balaṭ* "next year" (lit "to life") The ancient crux *kibrat ʾereṣ* (5 19) is etymologically related to Akkadian *bēr qaqqari* and means "a mile of land," a short distance. The term *rōʾê pĕnê hammelek* (25 19, lit "those who see the face of the king") has its semantic equivalent in *dāgil pān šarri* and signifies "subject, royal servant" The obscure *ḥryywnym,* which in the Massoretic tradition was felt to be obscene and so read as *dbywnym,* "excrement" (6:24), on being compared with Akkadian botanical terminology, turns out to be the somewhat picturesque name of the seed of the carob tree, popularly called "dove's dung."

On the other hand, because the state of lexical knowledge of Akkadian has been greatly advanced in the last quarter century with the completion of the *Akkadisches Handwörterbuch* and the continuing publication of the encyclopedic *Assyrian Dictionary of the Oriental Institute of the University of Chicago* (eighteen volumes, to date), cases in which the uncritical use of Akkadian has sometimes led to erroneous etymologies have been corrected. Thus, the Hebrew expression **ʾāsōp miṣṣaraʿat,* lit. "gathered in (after quarantine) because of leprosy" (5 3) is not related to the Akkadian noun *āšipu,* "exorcist," nor does a verb **ašāpu* exist Similarly, the hapax legomenon *wayĕḥappĕʾû* (17·9) can no longer be connected with the Akkadian *ḫapû,* which is now to be read *ḫawû* and means "to growl"

The titles of Assyrian and Babylonian officials, often transliterated into Hebrew and misunderstood during centuries of transmission, are elucidated by the attested usage in cuneiform texts of the period. For this reason, *rab sārîs* (18 17) is "chief eunuch," *rab šāqēh* "chief cupbearer" *Rab ṭabbāḥîm* (25 8) upon closer inspection is "chief cook" and not "chief executioner", in this case, the title is a translation of the native Babylonian *rab nuḫatimmu.*

Above and beyond the use of Comparative Semitics in elucidating individual lexical items in the text of 2 Kings, attention has been directed to inner-biblical semantics, considering that "words can only be intelligibly interpreted by what they meant at the time of their use, within the language system used by the speaker or writer"[14] Thus, e.g., *šōḥad* in 2 Kgs 16:8 is interpreted to mean "bribe" and not "present" as suggested in some recent

Akkadian on Aramaic, see S. A Kaufman, *The Akkadian Influence on Aramaic,* AS 19 (Chicago· University of Chicago, 1974), esp. 5–29

[13] This is not to deny that Ugaritic texts may be of help in the retrieval of certain lexemes which appear in the Hebrew Bible as hapax legomena—e.g., *bṣql,* "ear of grain" in 2 Kgs 4·42, *byt hḥpšt* in 15 5

[14] So J Barr, *The Semantics of Biblical Language* (Oxford Oxford University Press, 1961), 139–40. In general, Barr's common-sense approach is to be preferred to the sometimes obsessive use of etymologies.

discussions. The verbal root **rkb* was found to cover "all aspects of riding, from mounting of an animal to moving forward toward one's destination" (see note to 9:16). Furthermore, evidence for a residue of the north-Israelite dialect of Hebrew embedded in the Elisha cycle, which was earlier collected and commented upon by Burney (208–9), has been confirmed.

Texts and Versions

The goal of the present commentary has been to elucidate the Massoretic Hebrew text of Kings (MT). Unlike other books of the Bible—e.g. Samuel, Isaiah, Psalms—extensive copies of which were discovered at Qumran by the Dead Sea, only scattered fragments of a scroll containing 2 Kings have been identified, and these reflect a text which varies only slightly from MT (cf. e.g. 8:1–6).

Whenever a textual difficulty in MT appeared, the ancient versions, the Septuagint, and its Lucianic recension in particular have been consulted; in some cases this led to a suggested emendation for what seems to be a faulty MT reading.[15] But as a rule, no attempt was made to retrieve the Hebrew *Vorlage* of the book of Kings which likely served the ancient translators. For since the discovery of the biblical texts at Qumran, it has become increasingly recognized that attempts to reconstruct a single *Urtext* from which MT ultimately developed is an impossible, perhaps even an inappropriate task. S. Talmon sums up his masterly study of the transmission of the Bible as follows:

> All we can say is that from the very first stage of manuscript transmission of the Old Testament, the material which is available to us witnesses to a wide variety of textual traditions which seemingly mirror fairly exactly the state of affairs which obtained in the pre-manuscript state of transmission. In other words, the extant evidence imposes upon us the conclusion that from the very first stage of its manuscript transmission,

[15] The Lucianic recension is particularly helpful in text restoration because it is an example of an early, pre-Massoretic text form. For a convenient statement on the characteristics of this recension, see J. D. Shenkel, *Chronology and Recensional Development in the Greek Text of Kings* (Cambridge, MA.: Harvard University Press, 1968), 5–21. Cf., too, E. Tov, "Lucian and Proto-Lucian—Toward a New Solution of The Problem," *RB* 79 (1972), 101–13, K. G. O'Connell, *IDB* Sup 377–81, E. C. Ulrich, *The Qumran Text of Samuel and Jospehus,* Harvard Semitic Monograph 19 (1978), 15–37, and N. Fernandez Marcos, "The Lucianic Text in the Books of Kingdoms: From Lagarde to the Textual Pluralism," in *De Septuaginta,* Studies in Honour of John William Wevers, eds. A. Pietersma and C. Cox (Mississauga: Benben Publications, 1984), 161–74.

the Old Testament was known in a variety of traditions which differed from each other to a greater or less degree.[16]

Moreover, since the application of text-critical rules—e.g. *lectio difficilior,* "the more difficult reading" is to be preferred, or *lectio brevior,* "the shorter reading" is to be preferred—can be subjective and arbitrary, MT has generally not been emended by retroverting into Hebrew from the ancient translations. The strictures recently set out by E. Tov caution against such a procedure:

> The quintessence of textual evaluation is to select from the different transmitted readings the *one* reading which is the most appropriate in the context . . . "context" is taken in a wide sense, referring to language, style, and content of both the immediate context and of the literary unit in which the reading is found. This procedure necessarily allows the scholar much liberty . . .[17]

Therefore MT remained the primary text for interpretation in the present commentary, "not because it is the best or the oldest, but because it is the only complete text of the Hebrew Bible and only through it can sound exegesis, interpreting the Hebrew by the Hebrew, be achieved."[18]

On the Translation and Commentary

Translating 2 Kings for the present Commentary posed a particular challenge, inasmuch our generation has been particularly fortunate to witness the publication of four new renderings of the Bible into modern English: *The New English Bible; The New American Bible; The Torah, the Prophets, the Writings* of the Jewish Publication Society; and *The Jerusalem Bible,* each produced by a representative team of eminent scholars. The warrant for yet another translation, though limited in the present instance to the book of Kings, can be found in the persuasive words of the late E. A. Speiser, in his introduction to *Genesis,* the first volume of the Anchor Bible Series:

> The stepped-up pace of translational effort is but an index of the swelling flow of discovery. Desire to keep up with changing English usage has been a relatively minor factor It is not the language of this or that

[16] S. Talmon, "The Old Testament Text," in *The Cambridge History of the Bible,* vol. 1, *From the Beginnings to Jerome,* eds. P R Ackroyd and C. F Evans (Cambridge Cambridge University Press, 1970), 159–99 (= *Qumran and the History of the Biblical Text,* eds. F M Cross and S. Talmon [Cambridge, Mass. Harvard University Press, 1975], 1–41).

[17] E. Tov, "Criteria for Evaluating Textual Readings: The Limitations of Textual Rules," *HTR* 75 (1982), 429–48, see, in particular, 444–45

[18] So, with M Greenberg, "The Use of the Ancient Versions for Interpreting the Hebrew Text A Sampling from Ezek II,1 III,11," *VT* Sup 29 (1978), 147

> version of the Bible that has needed revising, but the underlying image of the biblical age, as reflected in the text, the grammar, the lexicon, and—above all—in the enormous volume of new material on the ancient Near East as a whole.[19]

Thus the thrust has been to reflect the original Hebrew idiom, without slavishly reproducing familiar, biblical-sounding phrases which originated with the King James Version. In places where the text is unclear or ambiguous, the translation preserves the textual difficulty; suggested interpretations have been relegated to the notes.[20] These notes bear the burden of the philological argument; the Comment is given over to discussion of matters relating to the editorial practice of the Deuteronomistic historian(s) and to literary questions.

The present commentary gives priority to historical matters. When appropriate, the reader is provided with historical surveys drawn from the records of the ancient Near East; the contacts with Assyria and Babylonia, the encounters with Aram-Damascus, and the relations with other neighboring states—all matters with which 2 Kings abounds—have been extensively elucidated. The order of the Hebrew text is followed, even in cases where it appears obvious that some chronological displacement has occurred. To help overcome the disjunctures created by the synchronic method, connective and summarizing comments are offered.

Outline of Historical Events

Finally, for the benefit of the reader of this commentary, a synchronous outline of the historical events in 2 Kings is offered. In this outline, the historical events follow a chronological sequence, not their respective order in 2 Kings. Excluded are the "wonder stories" of the Elijah and Elisha cycles, to which, in any case, no specific dates can be assigned.[21]

[19] Speiser, *Genesis,* AB, lxxvi.

[20] Following T. J. Meek, "Old Testament Translation Principles," *JBL* 81 (1962), 143–54: "All translation is to some degree interpretation, but there should be as little of this as possible. Translation should be definitely objective . . ."

[21] Many of the stories in the Elisha cycle have no clear context; so the Dtr. historian placed the cycle *en bloc* within the account of the reign of Jehoram, i.e., the last decade of the Omri dynasty. Internal analysis, however, has shown that Elisha's career extended down to the days of Joash, grandson of Jehu, some forty years after the beginning of Elisha's ministry. Hence several of the prophetic stories are to be assigned to the reign of Jehu and his successors, especially those stories in which the king of Israel is unnamed. See, e.g., comment at 2 Kgs 6:24–7:20.

TABLE 1: SYNCHRONOUS OUTLINE OF HISTORICAL EVENTS IN 2 KINGS

DATE	KINGDOM OF ISRAEL	KINGDOM OF JUDAH
850	AHAZIAH, SON OF AHAB (852–851)	JEHORAM, SON OF JEHOSHAPHAT (851–843)
	Rebellion of Mesha, King of Moab 1:1	Edom rebels and regains independence 8:20–21
	JORAM, SON OF AHAB (851–842)	Uprising in Libnah 8:22
	Joint campaign of Israel, Judah, and Edom against Moab; unsuccessful siege of Qir; Israel retreats 3:1–27	
	Dynastic changes in Damascus: Hazael succeeds Ben-hadad II 8:7–15	AHAZIAH, SON OF JEHORAM (843–842)
	Renewed battles between Aram-Damascus and Israel at Ramoth-Gilead 8.28f	Supports Joram at Ramoth-Gilead 8.28
	JEHU, SON OF JEHOSHAPHAT (842–814)	Murdered by Jehu 9·15–28
	Downfall of the Omrides. Jehu leads revolt, kills Joram, Ahaziah, and Jezebel; exterminates sons of Ahab and Baal priesthood 8.29–10:29	ATHALIAH (842–836) Bloody seizure of throne 11 1 3
840		
		Jehoiada restores a Davidide to throne: Joash anointed king and Athaliah executed 11·4–20
		JEHOASH, SON OF AHAZIAH (836–798)

DATE	KINGDOM OF ISRAEL	KINGDOM OF JUDAH
830		
	Aram-Damascus seizes areas settled by Israel east of the Jordan in Bashan and Gilead 10:32	
820		Renovation of temple in Jerusalem; new fiscal order for collection and distribution of sacred dues 12:1–17
	JEHOAHAZ, SON OF JEHU (817–800)	
	Aramaean attacks west of Jordan 6:8–23	
	Siege of Samaria by Ben-hadad III 6:27–7:30	
810	Israel humbled by Hazael 13:3–7, 22	Aramaean incursions as far as Gath; threat to Jerusalem averted by tribute payment to Hazael 12:18–19
		King assassinated by courtiers 12:21–22
800	JOASH, SON OF JEHOAHAZ (800–784) Israel relieved from Aramaean pressure 13:5 Recovery of territories lost to Aram; defeat of Ben-hadad III at Aphek 13:24–25	AMAZIAH, SON OF JEHOASH (798–769) Battles in northern Edom 14:7 War with Israel ends in looting of Jerusalem and Amaziah taken hostage 14:8–14 Assassinated at Lachish 14:19–20
790	JEROBOAM, SON OF JOASH (789–748)	AZARIAH, SON OF AMAZIAH (785–733)
780		
770	Israelite hegemony over Damascus and Hamath 14:23–29	Occupies Eilat on Red Sea 14:22

DATE	KINGDOM OF ISRAEL	KINGDOM OF JUDAH
760		JOTHAM, SON OF AZARIAH (758–743) De facto king of Judah due to father's leprosy 15:5
750		
	ZECHARIAH, SON OF JEROBOAM (748–747) Assassinated; end of Jehu dynasty 15:8–12	
	SHALLUM, SON OF JABESH (748/7) Assassinated after one month rule 15:3–15	
	MENAHEM, SON OF GADI (747–737)	
		Attacks by Rezin and Pekah against Judah 15:37
		AHAZ, SON OF JOTHAM (743–727)
740	Recognizes Assyrian hegemony in Syria; pays tribute to Tiglath-pileser III 15:17–22	
	PEKAHIAH, SON OF MENAHEM (737–735) Assassinated by Pekah and Gileadite rebels 15:25	
	PEKAH, SON OF REMALIAH (735–733) Anti-Assyrian alliance with Rezin of Damascus; siege of Jerusalem 16:5	Jerusalem besieged by Israel and Aram; Ahaz appeals to Tiglath-pileser for help
		Judah becomes an Assyrian vassal state 16:5, 7–9
	Assyrian campaign; Tiglath-pileser annexes Galilee and Gilead 15:29	Ahaz introduces cultic reform in Jerusalem 16:10–15

DATE	KINGDOM OF ISRAEL	KINGDOM OF JUDAH
	Capture and exile of Damascus 16:9	
	Assassinated by Hoshea 15:30	Eilat lost to Edom 16:6
	HOSHEA, SON OF ELAH (733–724)	
730		
		HEZEKIAH, SON OF AHAZ (727–698)
	Tribute paid to Shalmaneser V 17:3	
	Rebels against Assyria in alliance with Egypt. Imprisoned by Shalmaneser 17:4	
	Samaria besieged and taken after "three years" 17:5	
720	King of Assyria (i.e., Sargon II) deports Israelites to Assyria; transfers new settlers to Samaria 17:6	Cult reform in Jerusalem and Judah 18:4
		Illness of Hezekiah and his recovery 20:1–11
		Embassy of Merodach-baladan to Jerusalem 20:12–13
710		
		Rebellion against Assyria (after death of Sargon II)
		Attacks against Philistine cities 18:7–8
		Excavation of Siloam conduit 20:20
		Sennacherib campaigns against Judah: major Judaean cities assaulted and captured; Jerusalem threatened. Assyrian-

DATE	KINGDOM OF ISRAEL	KINGDOM OF JUDAH
700		Judaean negotiations over terms of surrender; Hezekiah submits and renders heavy tribute. Siege of Jerusalem lifted; Sennacherib withdraws 18:14–19:36
690		MANASSEH, SON OF HEZEKIAH (698–642)
680		Sennacherib murdered by his sons in Nineveh 19:37
670		Cultic aberrations introduced into Jerusalem Temple 21:1–18
660		
650	Additional resettlement of deportees in Assyrian province of Samaria; cultic developments among settlers 17:24–33	
640		AMON, SON OF MANASSEH (641–640) Assassinated by courtiers 21:19–26
		JOSIAH, SON OF AMON (639–609)
630		
620	Reform activities of Josiah in Bethel and other cities of province of Samaria 23:15–23	Temple repaired; major reform to centralize cult in Jerusalem Temple 22:1–23:14
610		Killed at Megiddo by Necho II 23:29–30
		JEHOAHAZ, SON OF JOSIAH (609) Imprisoned by Necho II; heavy indemnity placed upon Judah 23:31–33
		JEHOIAKIM, SON OF JOSIAH (608–598) Appointed king by Necho II 23:34

DATE	KINGDOM OF ISRAEL	KINGDOM OF JUDAH	
		Recognizes Babylonian suzerainty; revolts after three years	24:1
600		Judah under attack	24:2
		JEHOIACHIN, SON OF JEHOIAKIM (597)	
		Jerusalem besieged; surrenders to Nebuchadnezzar; spoliation of temple and palace treasures; exile of royal family and elite to Babylon	24:10–16
		ZEDEKIAH, SON OF JOSIAH (596–586)	
		Appointed king by Nebuchadnezzar	24:17
590			
		Rebellion against Babylon	24:20
		Jerusalem under long siege; city walls breached; pillage and burning of Temple and royal residences; Zedekiah taken captive and his sons executed	
586		End of Judaean monarchy Babylonian rule in Judah	25:1–21
585		GEDALIAH, SON OF AHIKAM	
		Appointed Babylonian "governor" Murdered by dissident Judaeans	25:22–25
		Voluntary exile to Egypt of Judaean remnant	25:26
561		JEHOIACHIN released from prison	25:27–30

2 KINGS

Translation, Notes, and Commentary

I. THE REIGN OF AHAZIAH (ISRAEL)

(1 Kings 22:52–54; 2 Kings 1:1)

1 Kings 52 52 Ahaziah son of Ahab became king over Israel in Samaria in the seventeenth year of Jehoshaphat king of Judah; he
reigned two years over Israel. 53 He did what was displeasing to
YHWH. He followed the way of his father and the way of his mother
and the way of Jeroboam son of Nebat, who caused Israel to sin. 54 He
worshipped Baal and bowed down to him, so that he angered YHWH,
God of Israel, just as his father had done. **2 Kings 1** 1 Moab rebelled
against Israel after the death of Ahab.

Notes

1 Kgs 22 52. *he reigned two years.* The two years of Ahaziah were of less than a twelve-month duration, according to our calender; he came to the throne in Jehoshaphat's seventeenth year (22:52) and died in his eighteenth year (2 Kgs 3:1). This synchronism shows the use of the antedating system in the counting of regnal years in Israel, according to which the first official year of the king was reckoned from the time he ascended to the throne until the next New Year's festival. A synchronism stemming from an alternate chronological record is given in 2 Kgs 1:17, on which see below.

The order of the words in the verse, with the synchronism following the name of the king, is found earlier in 15:25, 16:29, and 22:41, and again in 2 Kgs 3:1.

53. to *YHWH.* This transcription of the divine name, which represents the consonantal text of MT, was first used in the Anchor Bible series by M. Greenberg in his commentary *Ezekiel 1–20,* AB 22. Among current translations into English, only JB renders the name as "Yahweh"; the others keep to the traditional "the Lord." P. K. McCarter, 1 Samuel, AB, 59, and R. G. Boling and G. E. Wright, *Joshua,* AB, 118–20, summarize scholarly opinion as to the vocalization of the tetragram.

the way of his father and the way of his mother. The sinful ways of Ahab and Jezebel are recalled with reference to their children (cf. 2 Kgs 3:2) and two kings of Judah: Jehoram, a son-in-law of Ahab (8:18) and Manasseh, the arch-apostate (21:3).

2 Kgs 1 **1.** *Moab rebelled against Israel.* Heb. *wayyipšaʿ,* "he transgressed," a frequent term in legal and cultic contexts, is here extended to the political sphere to denote rebellion of a vassal king against his overlord—cf. 8:22 and with similar overtones, 1 Kgs 12:19. Judah's rebellions against Assyria or Babylonia, however, are defined by the "neutral" term *wayyimrōd*—cf. 2 Kgs 18:7; 24:1, 20. In Assyrian historical inscriptions, Akk. *ḫaṭû*, "to make a mistake, to commit an offense," conveys the sense of breaking a vassal relationship, see *CAD* Ḫ, 157.

Verse 1 appears again in 3:5 in conjunction with the prophetic story of Jehoram's campaign against Mesha. It is based on Israelite annals and is not out of place here (so, Benzinger).

Comment

The literary unit describing the reign of Ahaziah begins in the last four verses of 1 Kings 22. The division of the unit as it is presently found in our Bibles is secondary; it was originally introduced into the codices of the Septuagint, which divided the lengthy manuscript of the book of Kings into two smaller "books." In order to indicate the connection between the two, the last line of book one repeated the opening verse of book two as a "catch-line," a common scribal convention in works of multiple parts/tablets in cuneiform literature. This catch-line—"Moab rebelled against Israel after the death of Ahab"—is repeated at the end of the 3rd Kingdoms and the beginning of the 4th Kingdoms in the LXX Vaticanus manuscript; the Hebrew text tradition which considered Kings as a single book omits this repetition.[1] The division into two books of Kings first appears in Massoretic tradition in the Bomberg Rabbinic Bible (Venice, 1516) with the following marginal note: *ka'n mathîlîn hallôʿăzîm sēper mĕlākî(m) rĕbîʿî*, "Here the foreign speakers (i.e., non-Jews) begin the fourth book of Kings."[2]

Ahaziah reigned only one year (852–851) and died unexpectedly: apparently the northern annalists had little to report of historical significance about his reign.[3] What was noted was the outbreak of Moab's rebellion soon after Ahab's death. But because of Ahaziah's fatal accident, the handling of the rebellion was left to his brother Jehoram who succeeded him (see Comment on 2 Kgs 3).

[1] So *b. B.Bat.* 14b. Jerome noted that the Hebrews considered Samuel and Kings as individual books; at the same time, he followed the Greek tradition of referring to them as the "four books of Kings;" more in Kittel, *Könige*, Introduction.

[2] See C. D. Ginsburg, *Introduction to Massoretico-Critical edition of the Hebrew Bible* (London, 1897; repr. New York: Ktav, 1966), 45, 930–31.

[3] On Ahaziah's offer to join Jehoshaphat in a Red Sea trading venture, see note to 22:51.

II. ELIJAH AND AHAZIAH

(1:2–18)

1 2 Now Ahaziah fell through the lattice in his upper chamber at
Samaria and was injured. So he sent messengers, instructing them,
"Go, inquire of Baal-zebub, god of Ekron, whether I shall recover
from this injury."[a] 3 The angel of YHWH then spoke to Elijah the
Tishbite, "Up, go meet the messengers of the king of Samaria and
speak to them, 'Is it for lack of a god in Israel that you are going to
inquire of Baal-zebub, god of Ekron? 4 Therefore, thus says YHWH,
"You shall not leave the bed you are upon,[b] for you shall certainly
die!" ' " And so Elijah set out.

5 When the messengers returned to him (Ahaziah), he said to them,
"Why have you returned?" 6 They said to him, "A man came to meet
us and said to us, 'Go, return to the king who sent you and speak to
him, "Thus says YHWH: Is it for lack of a god in Israel that you send
to inquire of Baal-zebub, god of Ekron? Therefore, you shall not leave
the bed you are upon, for you shall certainly die!" ' " 7 He said to
them, "What was the appearance of the man who came to meet you
and who spoke these things to you?" 8 They said to him, "A hairy
man, girt with a leather belt around his waist." And he said, "It is
Elijah the Tishbite."

9 Then he sent an officer of fifty and his company of fifty to him. He
climbed up to where he was, for he was sitting on a hilltop, and spoke
to him, "O Man of God, the king orders, 'Come down!' " 10 But Elijah
replied and spoke to the officer of fifty, "And if I am a man of God, let
fire descend from heaven and consume you and your company of
fifty." Whereupon fire descended from heaven and consumed him and
his company of fifty. 11 So again he sent another officer of fifty and his
company of fifty. He climbed up[c] and spoke to him, "Man of God,
thus says the king, 'Come down quickly!' " 12 But Elijah replied and

[a] LXX, Syr., Vulg., Targ. read "my injury" (*ḥlyy*).
[b] Lit. "come down from the bed to which you have gone up."
[c] Read *wyʿl* with Luc. for MT *wyʿn*, "he replied."

spoke to him,[d] "If I am a man of God, let fire descend from heaven and consume you and your company of fifty." Whereupon an awesome fire[e] descended from heaven and consumed him and his fifty men. 13 So again he sent a third[f] officer of fifty and his company of fifty. When the third officer of fifty climbed up and drew near, he fell on his knees in front of Elijah, and pleaded with him and said, "O man of God, do value my life and the lives of these fifty men,[g] your servants. 14 Indeed, fire descended from heaven and consumed the first two officers of fifty and their companies of fifty, so now value my life." 15 Then the angel of YHWH spoke to Elijah, "Go down with him. Do not be afraid of him."[h] So he left and went down with him to the king. 16 He spoke to him, "Thus says YHWH, 'Since you sent messengers to inquire of Baal-zebub, the god of Ekron, as if there were no god in Israel to consult his word, therefore, you shall not leave the bed you are upon, for you shall certainly die.' " 17 And so he died in accordance with YHWH's word, which Elijah had pronounced.

Jehoram, <his brother,[i]> succeeded him, in the second year of Jehoram, son of Jehoshaphat king of Judah, because he did not have a son. 18 The rest of the history of Ahaziah (and) what[j] he did are indeed recorded in the annals of the kings of Israel.

[d] Read *ʾlyw* with LXX for MT *ʾlyhm,* "to them."
[e] Lit. "a fire of God." Some versions—LXX, Vulg., Targ.—omit *ʾlhym.*
[f] Read *šlšy* with Luc., Vulg., Targ. for MT *šlšym.*
[g] Read *ḥmšym, he* lost through haplography.
[h] Many mss. read *ʾtw* for *ʾwtw.*
[i] Add <*ʾḥyw*> with Luc., Syr., Vulg. (cf. 2 Kgs 3:1).
[j] Some mss., Luc., and Syr. add *wkl,* "and all."

Notes

1 2. *Ahaziah fell through the lattice.* Heb. *śĕbākâ* from **śbk,* "intertwine, weave," describes the netlike design on the two bronze pillars adorning the entrance of Solomon's Temple (1 Kgs 7:17); in Job 18:8 it appears in parallel to *rešet,* "net." But what particular architectural feature the word connotes in our verse cannot be fixed with certainty. Most commentators think the reference is to a trellis or screenlike structure over a window or the open area of the roof (so Thenius, Kittel, Burney). Qimḥi took it to be a skylight covering.

inquire of Baal-zebub. Heb. *dārôš bĕ-,* "to inquire of, consult," is a technical term for oracular inquiry. In the early literature, the term *šāʾōl bĕ-* is employed when referring to mantic activity of all sorts; whether licit, as *šāʾōl bĕʾûrîm,* "to inquire through the Urim (and Thummim)" (cf. Num 27:21; 1 Sam 28:6) or illicit, as *šāʾōl (bĕ)ʾôb/yiddĕʿōnî,* "to inquire of ghosts/spirits" (Deut 18:11). A similar term is attested for inquiry directed to YHWH, the means, however, not being specified, *šāʾōl ʾet*

YHWH, "to inquire of YHWH" (Gen 25:22; Judg 1:1; 20:18; 1 Sam 14:37; 23:2,4). The term in our verse, *dārôš bě-* contains the *beth* of instrumentality; however the medium through whom the question is placed is not designated, contrary to the case in 1 Sam 28:7. The Chronicler occasionally interchanges *ʾet* and *bě-* (e.g. 2 Chr 18:4, 7; 34:26); but this cannot be taken as evidence for the lateness of the term in our passage (as is suggested by A. Rofé, *The Prophetical Stories* [Jerusalem: Magnes, 1982], 38 [Hebrew]).

Baal-zebub, god of Ekron. Heb. *zěbûb* means "flies"; the rendering in LXX and Josephus (*muian*) supports this reading of the Hebrew text. The compound name with Baal indicates that the reference is to a local manifestation, in a Philistine town, of the prominent Canaanite deity Baal. But "Baal-of-the-flies" is so far unattested in extrabiblical documents, and scholarly interests have been directed to the classical world to find a connection between a "fly-catcher" god (Zeus Apomuios) and the healing aspect of the deity mentioned in 2 Kgs 1. (See T. K. Cheyne, EnBib 1.407–8; Montgomery-Gehman.) A hostile god(?) el-Dhubub does appear in the Ugaritic Baal epic, but nothing further is known of him (See *ANET*³ 137a; cf. T. H. Gaster, *Iraq* 6 [1939], 140, n. 216).

It was noted long ago that Baal-zebub is referred to in the New Testament (Matt 10:25; 12:24; Mark 3:22; Luke 11:15), with many manuscripts reading the name as Beel-zebul. Zebul is an epithet of Baal in Ugaritic literature (*zbl bʿl arṣ,* "The Prince, Baal of the earth," cf. M. Held, *JAOS* 88 [1968], 91–92), and the interchange of names in NT can be explained plausibly as an example of the pejorative rendering of non-Israelite divine names (so e.g. *bōšet* "shame" for Baal). It would have to be admitted then that the original name *Baal-zebul was preserved in popular circles among the Jews, so that he was known to Jesus' audience when he spoke of the god as "prince of devils/demons" (see TDNT 1.605–6). But the connection between the god worshipped at Ekron and the demonic Baal-zebul is yet to be established (cf. M. Pope, WM 1.254).

For a suggestion that *zěbûb* is a corruption of an originally Philistine divine name, see M. Riemschneider, *Acta Antiqua* 4 (1956), 17–29.

Ekron was one of the five Philistine cities on the border of the territory settled by the Israelite tribes (Josh 13:3). It has been identified with the large Iron Age site of Kh. al-Muqannaʿ, on one of the tributaries of wadi Sorek, 3 km east of Revadim. See. J. Naveh, "Khirbat al-Muqannaʿ-Ekron," *IEJ* 8 (1958), 87–100, 165–70; cf. Aharoni, *Land of the Bible*². On the form of the name reflected in Akk. transcription *Amqar(r)una* as compared with the Heb. *ʿeqrôn,* see A. Hurvitz, "*Akkaron* = Amqar(r)una = *ʿeqrôn,*" *Leš* 33 (1969), 18–24.

whether I shall recover from this injury? For a similar oracular query phrased as direct speech, see 8:8: *lēʾmōr haʾeḥyê . . .* (If the reading *ḥolyî,* "my illness," is adopted—cf. above note *a*—the demonstrative *zeh* would remain undetermined, as e.g. Gen 24:8; Exod 10:1; Judg 6:14; 1 Kgs 22:23 [Joüon, 138g].)

3. *angel of YHWH.* For the appearance of the angel of YHWH as intermediary between the prophet and YHWH, see 1 Kgs 19:7 and below in v. 15. Ehrlich suggested that the choice of the word angel *malʾak* was occasioned by the use of *malʾăkê,* "messengers of" the king of Samaria.

Elijah the Tishbite. For the first mention of Tishbe, a town in the Gilead (for MT "the settlers of"), see 1 Kgs 17:7; and cf. 21:17, 2 Kgs 9:36.

king of Samaria. Cf. the same reading in 1 Kgs 21:1, where Luc. reads: "king of

Israel in Samaria." The expression here has its counterpart in Assyrian texts. Both Joash son of Jehoahaz (13:10) and Menahem son of Gadi (15:14) are *Samerināya,* "from Samaria." Therefore, "king of Samaria" is not a sign of late composition, i.e., from the period following the establishment of the Assyrian province of *Samerina* (Šanda, and most recently Rofé, *Prophetical Stories,* 38). Even less does the term "reflect the consciousness that the house of Omri was not truly representative of the people of Israel" (so Gray).

Is it for lack of a god . . . ? For a similar construction with the pleonastic *ʾên,* see Exod 14:11; and cf. GKC 152y.

5. The return of the messengers to the king is somewhat abrupt, for the account of their meeting with Elijah is not related. It comes rather in reply to the king's query as to the quickness of their journey. This is not a lapse of the storyteller, but a case of deferring a key scene to a later sequence in order to heighten the dramatic effect. For examples of this narrative device in other stories, see e.g. Gen 42:21, Exod 14:12.

7. *the appearance of the man.* Heb. *mišpāṭ* expresses both "manner" and "behavior" (cf. Judg 13:12) and here refers to the person's "distinctive characteristics" (Burney).

8. *a hairy man.* Heb. *baʿal śēʿār.* On the analogy of other constructions with *baʿal x* —e.g. *baʿal kānāp,* "winged creature" (Prov 1:17; Eccl 10:20); *baʿal lāšôn,* "charmer" (Eccl 10:11); *baʿal pîpîyôt,* "(thresher of) many teeth" (Isa 41:15)—*baʿal śēʿar* can only be a "hairy man," not a "hairy coat/hair-shirt" (*NEB, NAB*). While Elijah was known to have worn a mantle (see 1 Kgs 19:13, 19; 2 Kgs 2:8, 13, 14), perhaps even a hairy one (cf. Zech 13:4), apparently it was first in intertestamental tradition that the hairy coat became associated exclusively with him. For this reason it was adopted by John the Baptist as part of his costume (Matt 3:4). If all prophets were thus clothed, how did Ahaziah know that the stranger who confronted his messengers was Elijah? (contra. J. A. Montgomery, *JBL* (1932), 201; and P. Joüon, *Bib* 16 [1935], 74–81). M. Buber (*Prophetic Faith* [New York: Harper & Row, 1960], 76) pictured Elijah as a "zealous and inflexible nomad, long-haired, wrapped in a hairy garment with a leather girdle, reminiscent of the Babylonian hero Enkidu of the Gilgamesh epic."

9. *an officer of fifty and his company of fifty.* Fifty men comprise a military unit, headed by an officer (*śar*); cf. 1 Sam 8:12; 2 Kgs 15:25; Isa 3:3. In contemporary Mesopotamian armies, a similar unit was led by a *rab ḫanšê,* "officer/captain of fifty," cf. *CAD* Ḫ 81.

Man of God. Elijah is addressed by the woman of Zarephath as *ʾîš ʾĕlōhîm,* a true prophet of God in 1 Kgs 17:18, 24.

for he was sitting on a hilltop. A late Christian tradition places the site of Elijah's meeting with the messengers at Sheikh Sha'le, in the vicinity of Samaria. See A. Alt, *ZDPV* 48 (1925), 393–97.

11. *He climbed up.* Read *wayyaʿal* with Luc., as in MT vv. 9, 13, for MT *wayyaʿan,* "he replied" (Thenius, Benzinger, Kittel, Šanda). Some commentators have defended MT by suggesting that the second officer did not risk coming into the direct presence of Elijah, and so he shouted up to him from the foot of the hill (so e.g. Malbim; Gray; Fohrer, *Elia*). But to open an address with *wayyaʿan* rather than *wayyōʾmer* would be most unusual in BH. Montgomery-Gehman compared the examples of Deut 21:7; 1 Sam 9:17 and retained MT.

12. *an awesome fire.* Lit. "a fire of God," *ʾēš ʾĕlōhîm.* Certain mss. and versions omit *ʾĕlōhîm,* which is generally accepted as preferable by critics. But the possibility of a

sound play on the preceding *ʾîš ʾĕlōhîm* cannot be dismissed. For *ʾĕlōhîm* used to express the superlative, cf. Gen 30:8, Jonah 3:3, Job 1:16; cf. too the discussion of D. Winton Thomas, "A consideration of Some Unusual Ways of Expressing the Superlative in Hebrew," *VT* 3 (1953), 209–24.

13. *do value my life.* The corresponding Akkadian phrase was first noted by Haupt: *ina pāni / ina īni aqāru,* "to become precious, valuable," cf. *CAD* A2.205–6.

17. *Jehoram <his brother> succeeded him.* The insertion of "his brother" with Luc., Syr., Vulg. is assured by the concluding statement "because he did not have a son." It may have dropped out in MT through haplography which arose from the similarity in spelling of the two adjacent words *ʾḥyw* and *tḥtyw.* (Thenius, Stade, Montgomery-Gehman refer to the error as homoeoteleuton, but it is the first word which has been lost, not the second.)

in the second year of Jehoram, son of Jehoshaphat king of Judah. This clause breaks the syntactic connection between v. 17a ("Jehoram his brother succeeded him") and 17c ("because he did not have a son"); its intrusive nature is marked in MT *pisqāʾ bĕ ʾemṣaʿ pāsûq,* a long spacing. (The function of this massoretic notation is still undetermined, though it surely meant to call the reader's attention to a problem in the text tradition; see S. Talmon, *"Pisqah beʾemṣaʿ pasuq and 11 QPs*[a]*," Textus* 5 (1966), 11–21.)

Moreover, the synchronism of Jehoram's reign here is at variance with that given in 3:1; it is part of an alternate chronological system preserved for the most part in Lucianic manuscripts of LXX, which have four additional verses (1:18[a–d]). For fuller details, see J. D. Shenkel, *Chronology and Recensional Development in the Greek Text of Kings* (Cambridge: Harvard University Press, 1968), 68–82.

18. *(and) what he did.* The present formula appears again in MT in 1 Kgs 16:27; 2 Kgs 14:15; 16:19; 21:25; the addition in Luc. and Syr., "and all that he did," may be due to inadvertent expansion by copyists to the fuller formula.

Comment

The present narrative is the last of the prophetic legends of the Elijah cycle which began in 1 Kgs 17. (In its present form 2 Kgs 2:1–18 is integrated into the Elisha cycle, on which see comment there.) The central theme is Elijah's continuing struggle with the apostate house of Omri: he confronts Ahaziah for turning in his distress to Baal-zebub, god of Ekron, rather than to YHWH, "as if there were no God in Israel" (cf. vv. 3, 6, 16). And, as in the case of Ahab, Elijah utters a curse that the king would die, which, it is editorially noted, came about "in accordance with YHWH's word which Elijah had pronounced" (v. 17a).[1]

An ancillary theme is developed in the scene of the threefold confrontation of Elijah with the king's officers (vv. 9–16). After two unsuccessful attempts

[1] There is little suggestion in the text that Elijah saw himself slighted by the king's act in consulting a non-Israelite medium, even though in other instances of illness and death, prophets of YHWH were sought out. Cf. e.g. 1 Kgs 14:1–18, 2 Kgs 8:7–10.

at ordering the prophet down from his mountain perch, during which two companies met a fiery death, a third officer is shown, on his knees, pleading for his life and the lives of his men. As in other narratives of this cycle, Elijah is portrayed as an uncompromising man of God, zealous in his demand for exclusive loyalty to YHWH and terrifying in his acts of retribution (cf. 1 Kgs 17:40).

For many critics, this second theme is a "later expansion . . . meant to set Elijah in the foreground as a wonder-working 'man of God' to whom respect is due."[2] It is "but a variation" of the scene on Mt. Carmel where Elijah proclaimed 'YHWH is God.'[3] A. Rofé even suggests taking the entire narrative as an epigonic legend of the postexilic period.[4]

But these critical judgments are not warranted, either on the basis of style or of ideology. No special features separate vv. 9–16 from the rest of the narrative;[5] nor are there any sure signs of late linguistic usage. The use of literary repetition, with minor variations (vv. 3, 6, 16, and vv. 9–10, 11–12) is present throughout.[6] Furthermore there is nothing uncharacteristic about Elijah's behavior that does not fit his appearance in other parts of the cycle as a staunch fighter for the exclusive worship of YHWH in Israel.

The Deuteronomistic editor did not comment on the infringement by Ahaziah of the "law of the prophet" in Deut 18:9–22 (contra. R. R. Wilson, *Prophecy and Society in Ancient Israel* [Philadelphia: Fortress, 1980], 200–1).

[2] O. H. Steck, *EvTh* 27 (1967), 547; and so since the remarks of Benzinger, Kittel, Šanda, and Montgomery-Gehman. Cf. also G. Fohrer, *Elia,* AThANT 31 (1957), 42–43; K. Koch, *The Growth of the Biblical Tradition* (New York: Scribner, 1969), 187–88.

[3] R. Smend, *VT* Sup 28 (1975), 178.

[4] Rofé, *Prophetical Stories,* 36–41 (Hebrew).

[5] Rofé correctly observes the essential unity of the narrative, but, wrongly in our opinion, dates the whole to a late period. Fohrer (op. cit. 50) admits that the language suits the era of Elijah and his followers, i.e., mid-ninth- to eighth-century B.C.E.

[6] Cf. Koch, op. cit. 185: "The narrator has therefore gone to particular trouble to vary the repetitions for the sake of his climax . . ." As a sign of the narrative craft, repeated elements ease the task of the storyteller vis-à-vis his audience and are commonly taken to indicate the earliest stages of composition. Cf. H. Gunkel, *Geschichten von Elisa* (Berlin: K. Curtius, [1922]), 8; and the extensive treatment of repetitive situations by J. Licht, *Storytelling in the Bible* (Jerusalem: Magnes, 1978), 51–95.

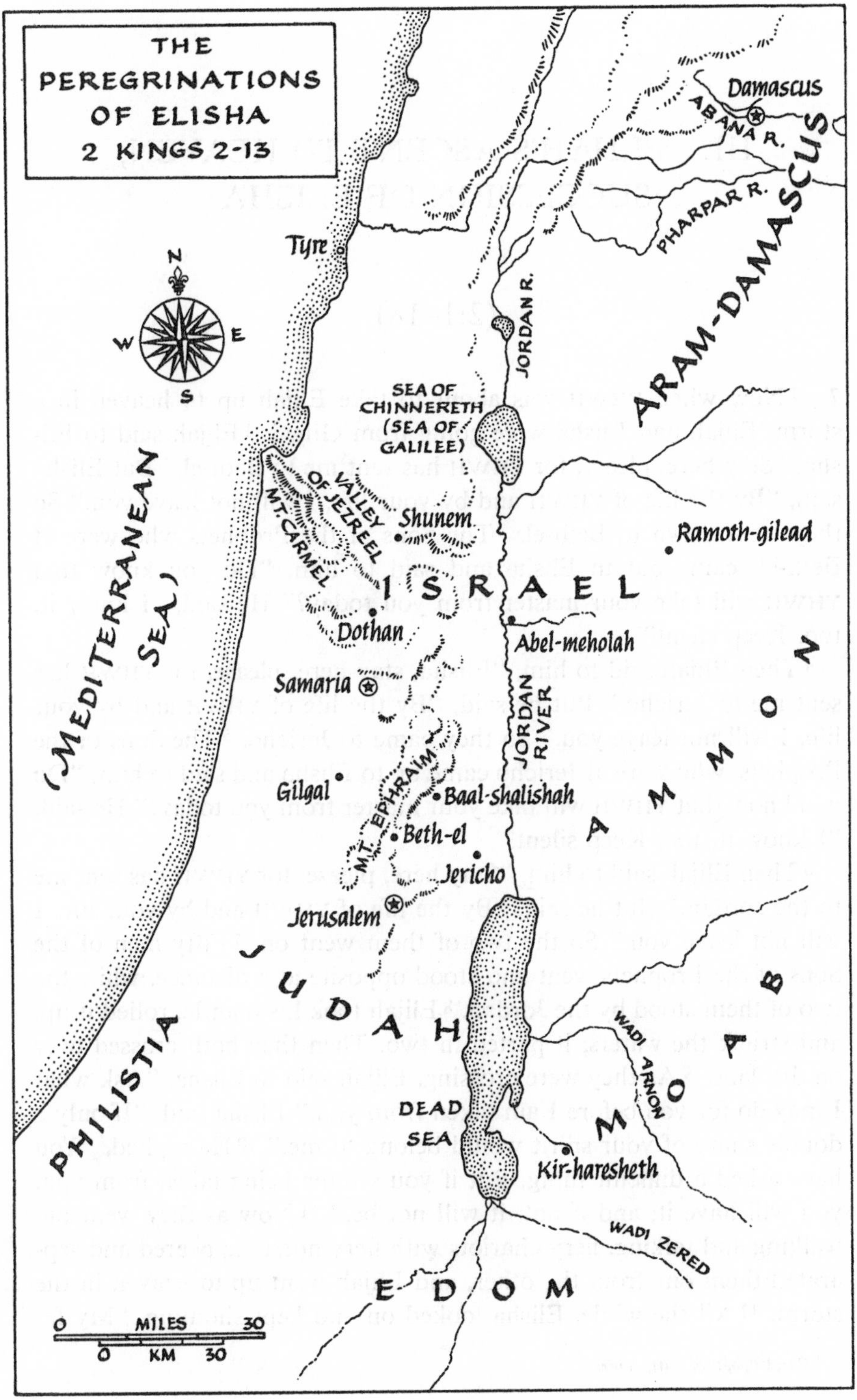
THE PEREGRINATIONS OF ELISHA 2 KINGS 2-13
Damascus
ABANA R.
PHARPAR R.
ARAM-DAMASCUS
Tyre
N
W
E
S
JORDAN R.
SEA OF CHINNERETH (SEA OF GALILEE)
VALLEY OF JEZREEL
MT. CARMEL
Shunem
Ramoth-gilead
ISRAEL
(MEDITERRANEAN SEA)
Dothan
Abel-meholah
Samaria
JORDAN RIVER
AMMON
Gilgal
MT. EPHRAIM
Baal-shalishah
Beth-el
Jericho
Jerusalem
JUDAH
MOAB
PHILISTIA
WADI ARNON
DEAD SEA
Kir-haresheth
WADI ZERED
EDOM
0 MILES 30
0 KM 30

III. ELIJAH'S ASCENT TO HEAVEN; SUCCESSION OF ELISHA

(2:1–18)

2 1 Now when YHWH was about to take Elijah up to heaven in a
storm, Elijah and Elisha were going from Gilgal. 2 Elijah said to Elisha, "Stay here, please, for YHWH has sent me to Beth-el." But Elisha
said, "By the life of YHWH and by your life, I will not leave you." So
they went down to Beth-el. 3 The Sons of the Prophets who were at
Beth-el[a] came out to Elisha and said to him, "Do you know that
YHWH will take your master from you today?" He said, "I know it,
too. Keep silent!"

4 Then Elijah said to him, "Elisha, stay here, please, for YHWH has
sent me to Jericho." But he said, "By the life of YHWH and by your
life, I will not leave you." So they came to Jericho. 5 The Sons of the
Prophets, who were at Jericho came up to Elisha and said to him, "Do
you know that YHWH will take your master from you today?" He said,
"I know it, too. Keep silent!"

6 Then Elijah said to him, "Stay here, please, for YHWH has sent me
to the Jordan." But he said, "By the life of YHWH and by your life, I
will not leave you." So the two of them went on. 7 Fifty men of the
Sons of the Prophets went and stood opposite at a distance, while the
two of them stood by the Jordan. 8 Elijah took his mantle, rolled it up,
and struck the waters; it parted in two. Then they both crossed over
on dry land. 9 As they were crossing, Elijah said to Elisha, "Ask what
I may do for you before I am taken from you." Elisha said, "If only a
double share of your spirit would belong to me." 10 He replied, "You
have asked a difficult thing. But if you see me being taken from you,
you will have it; and if not, it will not be." 11 Now as they went on,
walking and talking, fiery chariots with fiery horses appeared and separated them one from the other, and Elijah went up to heaven in the
storm. 12 All the while, Elisha looked on and kept shouting, "My fa-

[a] Read *bĕbêt ʾēl* with *sebirin.*

ther, my father! The chariots of Israel and its horsemen!" And he saw
him no more. Then he took hold of his garments and rent them in two.
13 He picked up Elijah's mantle, which had fallen from him, and
went back and stood by the bank of the Jordan. 14 He took Elijah's
mantle, which had fallen from him, and as he struck the waters, and
he said, "Where, indeed, is YHWH, God of Elijah?"[b] When he struck
the waters, they parted in two, and Elisha crossed over. 15 The Sons of
the Prophets, who were at Jericho, saw him from the other side, and
they said, "Elijah's spirit has come to rest upon Elisha." So they went
to meet him and bowed down to the ground before him.

16 They said to him, "There are fifty able-bodied men among us,
your servants. Let them go and search for your master. Maybe
YHWH's wind has carried him and thrown him against one of the
mountains or into one of the ravines."[c] But he said, "Don't send
(them)!" 17 They pressed him until he was embarrassed, so that he
said, "Send!" They sent fifty men who searched for three days, but
they did not find him. 18 When they came back to him—he was staying
in Jericho—he said to them, "Didn't I tell you, 'Do not go'?"

[b] Read *ʾēpôʾ* for MT *ʾap hûʾ*; moved up for translation. See note.
[c] Qere reads *haggēʾāyôt* for ketib *haggĕyāʾôt.*

Notes

2 1. *in a storm.* Heb. *śĕʿārâ* is, at times, associated with theophany (Job 38:1, 40:6) and divine punishment (Jer 23:19, Zech 9:14, Ps 83:16); thus it may convey the sense of the numinous. The now familiar translation "whirlwind" stems from *KJV.*

Gilgal. This Gilgal is to be distinguished from the site of the same name (meaning "stone circle") in the Jordan Valley east of Jericho (cf. Josh 4:19). Its location "near the high road between Beth-el and Shechem, the present Jiljilia," was suggested by G. A. Smith, *Historical Geography of the Holy Land* (London, 1894, repr. New York: Harper, 1966), 318, and earlier by Thenius; cf. *IDB* 2.398–99.

2. *By the life of YHWH.* The noun *ḥay,* "life," and its asseverative force when joined to the name of God in oaths, is treated by M. Greenberg, *JBL* 76 (1957), 34–39.

3. *Sons of the Prophets.* Heb. *bĕnê hannĕbîʾîm.* Heb. *bēn* "son" indicates "a member of a guild, order, or class"; see BDB 121 and the examples cited there. The prophetic groups spoken of here appear as loosely organized brotherhoods living together in the towns of northern Israel, and are referred to mostly in the Elisha story cycle. They are not associated with local shrines, as is sometimes claimed, and are probably to be distinguished from the prophets consulted by the Omride kings (e.g. 1 Kgs 22:6). Wilson, in *Prophecy and Society in Ancient Israel,* 141, correctly points out that there is no evidence that they were ecstatics (as the "band of prophets" in 1 Sam 10:5 or 19:20–24).

The honorific title *ʾāb,* "father," was sometimes applied to the group's leader (2 Kgs 2:12, 13:14; cf. earlier 1 Sam 10:12 and possibly 2 Kgs 6:21). On this title, see J. G. Williams, "The Prophetic 'Father'," *JBL* 85 (1966), 344–48; and on this prophetic phenomenon in general, see J. Lindblom, *Prophecy in Ancient Israel* (Philadelphia: Fortress, 1962), 69–70, 183–84.

The same usages are attested in Akk. for *abu,* "father," as a form of address and title (cf. *CAD* A 1.71); and for *māru,* "son," as "a member of a professional or social group"—e.g. *mār bārî,* "diviners" (cf. *CAD* M 1.314–15).

your master from you today. Lit. "from upon your head," which expresses the relationship between Elijah and Elisha as that of master and servant.

Keep silent! The form *heḥĕšû* is imperative, on the analogy of other irregular vocalizations of primae gutturals in Jer 49:8, 30; and cf. 31:31 (so BDB 364 and Burney; contra. Qimḥi and Ehrlich).

8. *rolled it up.* Heb. **gālōm* appears only here and in Ezek 27:24, "wrappings (*gĕlômê*) of blue."

9. *double share.* Elisha's request echoes the legal terminology of Deut 21:17, according to which the first born was to receive *pî šnayim,* "a double share" of his patrimony (so already Gersonides, Grotius, Thenius, and all moderns). In Zech 13:8, the expression means "two thirds." For the equivalent Akkadian term *šinipu,* see A. Goetze, *JNES* 5 (1946), 202, n. 82 (contra. E. A. Speiser, *BASOR* 77 [1940], 19–20); and for the Ug. *šnpt,* see *UT,* 50.

your spirit. The source of Elijah's spirit is YHWH; it is not some inherent personal quality (differently, Z. Weisman, *ZAW* 93 [1981], 225–34). In this regard, Elijah, like Moses, enjoyed a special relationship with YHWH, described in terms of spirit transferable to others (cf. Num 11:16–17, 24–26).

11. *fiery chariots with fiery horses.* Fire is a regular feature of divine manifestation (e.g. Exod 3:2, 13:21, 19:18) and is of the divine essence (cf. Deut 4:24); thus the vehicles beheld by Elisha were those of the Lord (cf. Hab 3:8).

12. *kept shouting.* Heb. *mĕṣaʿēq* in *piel* conveys an iterative sense (Ehrlich).

The Chariots of Israel and its horsemen! The words would seem to be an exclamatory phrase popular during the days of the Aramaean wars of the mid-ninth century. K. Galling (*ZThK* 53 [1956], 129–48) and many commentators seek the original locus of this cliché in the Elisha cycle of stories, especially in 13:14–21; cf. 6:8–23. But even though Elisha is portrayed as more actively involved in military affairs than Elijah (cf. 3:11–19, 6:13–17), this is not reason enough to declare its presence in 2:11 secondary. Elisha beheld YHWH's chariots as Elijah departed this world, and it was this fiery apparition which evoked his excited response.

Other scholars would understand this phrase as an appellation or title of Elijah. Thus the Targum already offered: "You who are better for Israel by his prayers than chariots and horsemen"; and see Ehrlich, who compared Num 10:36; and more recently M. A. Beek, *OTS* 17 (1972), 1–10.

Then he took hold of his garments and rent them in two. As a visible gesture of grief, familiar from Gen 37:34; 2 Sam 1:11, 13:31; Job 1:20.

13. *went back and stood by the bank of the Jordan.* The complementary verb *wayyāšob* usually denotes repeated action (GKC 120d). The narrative is elliptical at this point, not having mentioned that Elijah and Elisha had crossed the Jordan to the farther bank and that the river had returned to its course.

14. *and as he struck the waters . . . When he struck the waters.* Between the re-

peated mention of striking the water, Luc. and manuscripts of Vulg. add: "and they did not part." This remark is exegetical (Montgomery-Gehman), casting doubt on the rank achieved by Elisha vis-à-vis Elijah. (Cf. the repetition of the verb *waybārăkēhû* in Gen 27:23, 27, with temporal aspects similar to those in the present verse, and see the remarks of Speiser, *Genesis,* ad loc.)

Where, indeed, is YHWH, *God of Elijah?* After the question, MT has *ʾap hûʾ,* "even he," connected by the accentuation to the following clause; this is syntactically quite awkward, although defended by Rashi, Qimḥi; cf. Targum. The reading *ʾēpôʾ,* an expletive meaning "then, indeed" (LXX transliterates *aphphō;* cf. 10:10), favored by most moderns, is connected with the first clause. It would be more idiomatic, however, to have the word follow the particle *ʾayyê,* "where" (as in Judg 9:38, Isa 19:12, Job 17:15); but cf. Burney's remarks. The emendation suggested by Graetz and Perles to *ʾēpô hûʾ* ("where is He?"), though repeating the first query, is not to be excluded.

16. *Maybe* YHWH*'s wind has carried him.* The stormy apparition (vv. 1, 11) is here referred to as a mighty wind, through which, at times, the Lord effects his purpose (cf. 1 Kgs 18:12; Exod 10:13; 14:21; Hos 13:15; Ps 148:8).

17. *until he was embarrassed.* Heb. *ʿad bōš.* The phrase seems to have "become equivalent to a long while" when the original significance of the verb may no longer have been felt (so G. F. Moore, *Judges* [ICC, Edinburgh: T. & T. Clark 1895], 101, ad Judg 3:25); cf. 2 Kgs 8:11.

Comment

The present account serves two ends; it is the conclusion of the cycle of tales concerning Elijah and, at the same time, the introduction to the tales of Elisha. It would be artificial to separate this chapter into two traditions, each revolving around one of the prophets, for both men were revered by the same circles of the Sons of the Prophets, who nurtured and preserved these traditions.[1]

As during his life, Elijah is portrayed as an elusive wanderer, appearing and disappearing at a moment's notice (cf. 1 Kgs 18:11–12), so in his death it was told that he vanished from among men for all time. Enoch "was taken by God" (Gen 5:24), but Elijah is the only biblical personality of whom it is said that he "ascended to heaven in a storm" (vv. 1, 11). By utilizing this image, the prophet's followers invested him with the quality of eternal life, surpassing even Moses, the father of all prophets, who died and was buried (albeit by

[1] Critics suggest that the Elisha tradition now dominates the "older" Elijah tradition of the prophet's ascension (so H. Gunkel, *ExpTim* 41, 1929, 486; and similarly Eissfeldt, Gray), neglecting, however, to take account of the chapter's striking unity of style, so ably analyzed by W. Baumgartner in *Eucharisterion,* Festschrift H. Gunkel, FRLANT 19 (1923), 154–55.

God himself: Deut 34:5–6). It was this quality which became the dominant motif in the later Elijah legends.[2]

Thus Malachi proclaimed that the prophet Elijah would be sent "prior to the coming of the great and awesome Day of YHWH," to bring harmony between men, so as to avoid God's destructive wrath (Mal 3:23–24; cf. Sir 48:1–11). In the Hellenistic period, the author of First Maccabees included Elijah among the paradigmatic faithful of Israel, who "for his acts of zeal on behalf of the Torah was taken up as if into heaven" (1 Macc 2:58).[3] Here one observes the reservation entertained in some quarters concerning the actual ascent of a mortal to heaven.[4] But the mystery of Elijah's disappearance and the prophecy of his return continued to engage rabbinic and early Christian circles, among whom Elijah was the acknowledged precursor of the Messiah and of the Messianic Age.[5]

The succession of Elisha to the "fathership" over the Sons of the Prophets is demonstrated by his ability to perform the wondrous splitting of the Jordan; he has indeed inherited his master's qualities. The mantle of Elijah which he now wears is apparently the same one thrown over him when he first met Elijah (see 1 Kgs 19:19–21). The presence of this doublet in Kings does not disturb the reader, for the two stories of Elijah's mantle have been so distributed that 1 Kgs 19:19 reads as Elisha's initiation as personal servant to Elijah; 2 Kgs 2 is the story of his taking office.[6]

Ancient Near Eastern literature does not know of a figure similar to Elijah; individual motifs from that literature, however, may be compared with cer-

[2] Elijah's letter to King Jehoram of Judah reported in 2 Chr 21:12–15 poses chronological problems, since according to MT calculations, Elijah disappeared during Jehoshaphat's reign. This may mean that the Chronicler already knew of the tradition that Elijah did not entirely disappear (so Josephus, *Antiquities* ix. 99). Prophetic communication through a letter is in itself a most unusual act (but cf. Jeremiah's letter to the Exiles in Jer 29); prophets were wont to address their audience directly.

[3] Translation by J. Goldstein, *First Maccabees,* AB (Garden City, N.Y.: Doubleday, 1976), ad loc.

[4] See e.g. Josephus, *Antiquities* ix. 2; LXX and Targum to 2 Kgs 2:1; and cf. *b. Sukk.* 5a, where R. Jose states quite definitely that "Moses and Elijah did not go up to heaven" quoting Ps 115:16.

[5] See the thoroughgoing presentation of the vast Elijah lore by Louis Ginzberg, *The Legends of the Jews* (Philadelphia: Jewish Publication Society, 1913) 4.200–35; 6.322–43; and idem, Jewish Encyclopedia, 5.122–24. For a survey of Elijah as he functions in NT, see at length J. Jeremias in TDNT 2.928–41. The review of the postbiblical sources by M. M. Faierstein, *JBL* 100 (1981), 75–86, suggests that the concept of Elijah as the forerunner of the Messiah is in fact a *novum* in the NT.

[6] Cf. the remarks of O. Eissfeldt, *BZAW* 105 (1967), 50–51, 54–55. Another strand of the tradition, perhaps of later date than its present context in 1 Kgs 19:15–18 suggests, told of Elisha's foreordained nomination as Elijah's successor; but no story of the anointment of Elisha as there intended has been preserved.

tain features in the present narrative. Legendary Etana, king of Kish, for example, ascended to heaven on the back of an eagle in search of the "plant of birth" which would insure him offspring and an heir.[7] Gilgamesh, king of Uruk, however, returned empty-handed from his worldwide quest for eternal life. He learns that only once had a mortal been admitted into the assembly of the gods, a gift granted Utnapishtim, who survived the flood.[8] The ascent of Elijah thus remains unique.[9]

[7] See *ANET³,* 114–18; and cf., too, the entry in the Sumerian King List, *ANET³,* 265.
[8] Cf. *ANET³,* 93–97.
[9] Aggadic and late apocalyptic traditions ascribe supernal life to Enoch as well as to Elijah, at times noting the use of the same verb **lqḥ,* "to take," in describing their disappearances from among men; cf. Gen 5:24 and 2 Kgs 2:3, 5, 9; *Gen. Rab.* 25.1, and see L. Ginsberg, *Legends of the Jews,* 1.125–40; 5.157–64; J. T. Milik, *The Books of Enoch, Aramaic Fragments of Qumran Cave 4,* (Oxford: Clarendon Press, 1976), 4–135. In some circles, Moses, too, was seen as having departed in a cloud, rather than dying (cf. Josephus, *Antiquities* iv.326; and see S. E. Loewenstamm, "The Death of Moses," *Tarbiz* 27 [1958], 142–57).

THE ELISHA CYCLE

IV. SWEETENING THE WATERS

(2:19–22)

2 19 The men of the city said to Elisha, "The city's location is a good
one, as my lord can see, but the water is bad and the land miscarries."
20 He said, "Bring me a new flask, and put salt in it"; and they brought
(it) to him. 21 Then he went out to the water source and threw the salt
into it, and said, "Thus says YHWH, 'I have healed these waters. Death
and miscarriage shall issue from there no longer.' " 22 So the water has
remained healed[a] until this day, in accordance with Elisha's word
which he spoke.

[a] Qere and some mss. read *wayyērāpʾû*.

Notes

2 20. *flask.* Heb. *ṣĕlōḥît,* "jar, flask"; in MH it translates BH *ṣinṣenet* (cf. Targum to Exod 16:33). It is distinct from *ṣallaḥat* "dish" for eating (Prov 19:24) and *ṣĕlēḥâ* a dish for cooking (2 Chr 35:13) (contra. Gray, and J. L. Kelso, *Ceramic Vocabulary of the Old Testament, BASOR* Supplementary Studies 5–6 [1948], 29).

21. *Then he went out to the water source.* The spring ʿAin es-Sultan at Jericho was identified in 1838 by Edward Robinson (*Biblical Researches in Palestine* [London, 1867] 1.554) as the scene of Elisha's miracle.

I have healed. Heb. *rippiʾtî,* taken as tertiae *aleph; wayyērāpû* in v. 22, as tertiae *he* (cf. 1 Kgs 17:14). On this interchange in BH, see GKC, 75oo.

22. *until this day.* This formula is regularly used in etiologies, but in the present case has been secondarily added to the story of Elisha's miraculous sweetening of the waters. Cf. below 8:22, 10:27, 14:7, 16:6, 17:24, and see the study of B. Childs, *JBL* 82 (1963), 279–92, esp. 288–89; and the incisive remarks of I. L. Seeligmann, *Zion* 26 (1961), 149–57.

Comment

The first of the Elisha tales presents the prophet as provider for his followers. When faced with the crisis of the harmful waters at Jericho, Elisha, as YHWH's messenger, effects a cure which makes them potable, thus restoring life to the townspeople. Tales such as this, of miraculous, sustaining acts by holy men of God, are part of the traditional lore—*legenda*—of prophetic circles;[1] thus, it is told of Moses that he sweetened the waters at Marah (Exod 15:23–25),[2] of Elijah that he fed the woman of Sarephath (1 Kgs 17:8–16), and of Elisha farther on, that he brought abundance to the Sons of the Prophets (2 Kgs 4:38–41; 42–44).[3]

[1] A. Rofé, in "The Classification of the Prophetical Stories," (*JBL* 89 [1970], 429–33) offers a cogent treatment of this genre of tale, noting the similarities between the prophetic *legenda* and the "eulogies" of saints and pious rabbis.

[2] An unmistakable literary affinity exists between the tale of Moses and that of Elisha; in both, the prophet acts after hearing a complaint and casts (**hšlk,* cf. Exod 15:25 and 2 Kgs 2:21) a healing agent (**rpʾ,* cf. Exod 15:26; 2 Kgs 2:21, 22) into the bitter source.

[3] Several rationalistic explanations of Elisha's act at Jericho and the efficaciousness of Joshua's curse of the city (Josh 6:26) are discussed in the Comment to 1 Kgs 16:34.

V. YOUNGSTERS AT BETH-EL PUNISHED

(2:23–25)

2 23 He went from there up to Beth-el. As he was on the way, some
young boys came out of the city and mocked him. They said, "Be off,
baldy! Be off, baldy!" 24 He turned around and, looking at them, he
cursed them by the name of YHWH. Whereupon two she-bears came
out of the forest and mauled forty-two of the youngsters. 25 From
there, he went to Mount Carmel and from there he returned to Samaria.

Notes

2 23. *and mocked him.* Luc. has MT *wytqlsw* plus *wysqlw,* "they stoned." Is this addition a true doublet or rather an embellishment which sought to explain the prophet's violent outburst against the children?

Be off, baldy! There is little to support the suggestion that Elisha's baldness was a tonsure of sorts, "one of the distinguishing marks of the prophet's order" (so Montgomery-Gehman; similarly Stade, Šanda, Gray). Lengthy hair, rather than close shaving of the head, was an accepted feature of asceticism as is reflected in the Nazirite law in Num 6:5; cf. Judg 13:5. Moreover the ritual cutting of hair is prohibited in Lev 19:24, 21:5. Perhaps it was Elisha's extreme natural baldness that caught the attention of the rude youngsters of Beth-el.

For *ʿlh (with the preposition *min*) in the sense of "leave, depart," cf. Num 16:27; 1 Kgs 15:19; 2 Kgs 12:19; Jer 21:2, 37:5.

24. *two she-bears.* According to F. S. Bodenheimer, (*Animal and Man in Bible Lands* [Leiden: Brill, 1960], 45), the bears are to be identified as *Ursus arctos syriacus.* The Akkadian lexical evidence distinguishes this animal from the northern brown bear, as shown by B. Landsberger, *Die Fauna des alten Mesopotamien . . .* (Leipzig: S. Hirzel, 1934), 80–83.

forty-two of the youngsters. "Forty-two" occurs again in the number of victims slain by Jehu in 10:14. Was it a figure expressing a large number (cf. Gray), common to the story-telling of that period? In *b. Sota* 47a, the tally of the sacrifices of Balak king of Moab is given as "forty-two."

25. The import of the short itinerary in this verse is not clear; Elisha set out in v. 1 from Gilgal and now returns to Samaria! Perhaps some other ordering of the tales appeared in the Elisha cycle as received by Dtr. before its incorporation into Kings. It should be noted, however, that Samaria, the last stop in v. 25, appears as the starting

point for the campaign in 3:7, in the course of which Elisha does turn up in the army camp (3:11). (This fact led Eissfeldt to suggest that originally the text read "Gilgal," which was editorially altered to "Samaria.") J. R. Lundbom ("Elijah's Chariot Ride," *JJS* 24 [1973], 39–50) argues for a chiastic structural pattern in the ordering of sites in chapters 1 and 2, opening and closing with Samaria.

Comment

Just as the prophetic word heals and gives life (cf. 2:19–22), so, too, it brings death. On his way through Beth-el, Elisha is accosted by a group of jeering urchins—a scene often repeated even today in the streets and markets of the Middle East to the discomfort of the unwary traveler. These he drives off with a curse, potent enough to cut down forty-two of their number.

In a talmudic discussion of the prophet's outburst, the Babylonian *Amora* Samuel treats the story as doubly miraculous: "There was no forest and there were no bears."[1] Early modern critics, like their medieval predecessors, concerned themselves with the seeming immorality of Elisha's act and its justification: "Looking at them, he saw that the young boys were mocking not only him, but his master Elijah as well . . . and this at their parents' command."[2] Others took the verses as didactic in intent, meant to teach children respect for elders.[3] But while the story may have brought smiles to the faces of adult listeners, it is far from being "a puerile tale" or "derogatory to the great public figure and borders on blasphemy."[4] The story of the prophet's effective use of the name of YHWH was set close to the beginning of the Elisha cycle, for it confirmed by a sure sign that he was now "father" to the Sons of the Prophets.

[1] *b. Sota* 46b–47a.

[2] So Abarbanel, cf. Thenius.

[3] E.g. Skinner, Montgomery-Gehman.

[4] So Gray, 479–80.

VI. JEHORAM'S CAMPAIGN AGAINST MESHA OF MOAB

(3:1–27)

3 1 Jehoram son of Ahab became king over Israel in Samaria in the
eighteenth year of Jehoshaphat king of Judah; he reigned twelve years.
2 He did what was displeasing to YHWH, yet not like his father and his
mother; he removed the pillar of Baal which his father had made. 3 Yet
he held fast to the sinful way[a] of Jeroboam son of Nebat who caused
Israel to sin; he did not stray from it.

4 Now Mesha king of Moab was a sheep-breeder and he used to pay
tribute to the king of Israel: one hundred thousand lambs and the wool
of one hundred thousand rams. 5 But when Ahab died, the king of
Moab rebelled against the king of Israel. 6 One day, King Jehoram left
Samaria and enlisted all the Israelites. 7 He went and sent a message to
Jehoshaphat king of Judah: "The king of Moab has rebelled against
me. Will you join me in battle against Moab?" He said, "I will go! I
am (ready) as you are; my forces are as your forces; my horses as your
horses." 8 He said, "Which road shall we take?" and he said, "The
Desert of Edom Road."

9 So the king of Israel, the king of Judah, and the king of Edom set
out, and they circled about for seven days. There was no water for the
camp or for the animals in their train, 10 when the king of Israel said,
"Alas! YHWH must have summoned these three kings in order to hand
them over to the Moabites." 11 Jehoshaphat said, "Isn't there a
prophet of YHWH here through whom we may inquire of YHWH?"
One of the servants of the king of Israel replied, "Elisha son of
Shaphat is here, who poured water on the hands of Elijah."
12 Jehoshaphat said, "He certainly has YHWH's word!" And so the
king of Israel, Jehoshaphat, and the king of Edom went down to him.
13 Elisha said to the king of Israel, "What have I to do with you? Go to
your father's prophets and your mother's prophets!" The king of Israel
said, "No! For YHWH must have summoned these three kings in order

[a] Read *ḥaṭṭa't* in sg.; MT pl. Cf. 13:2.

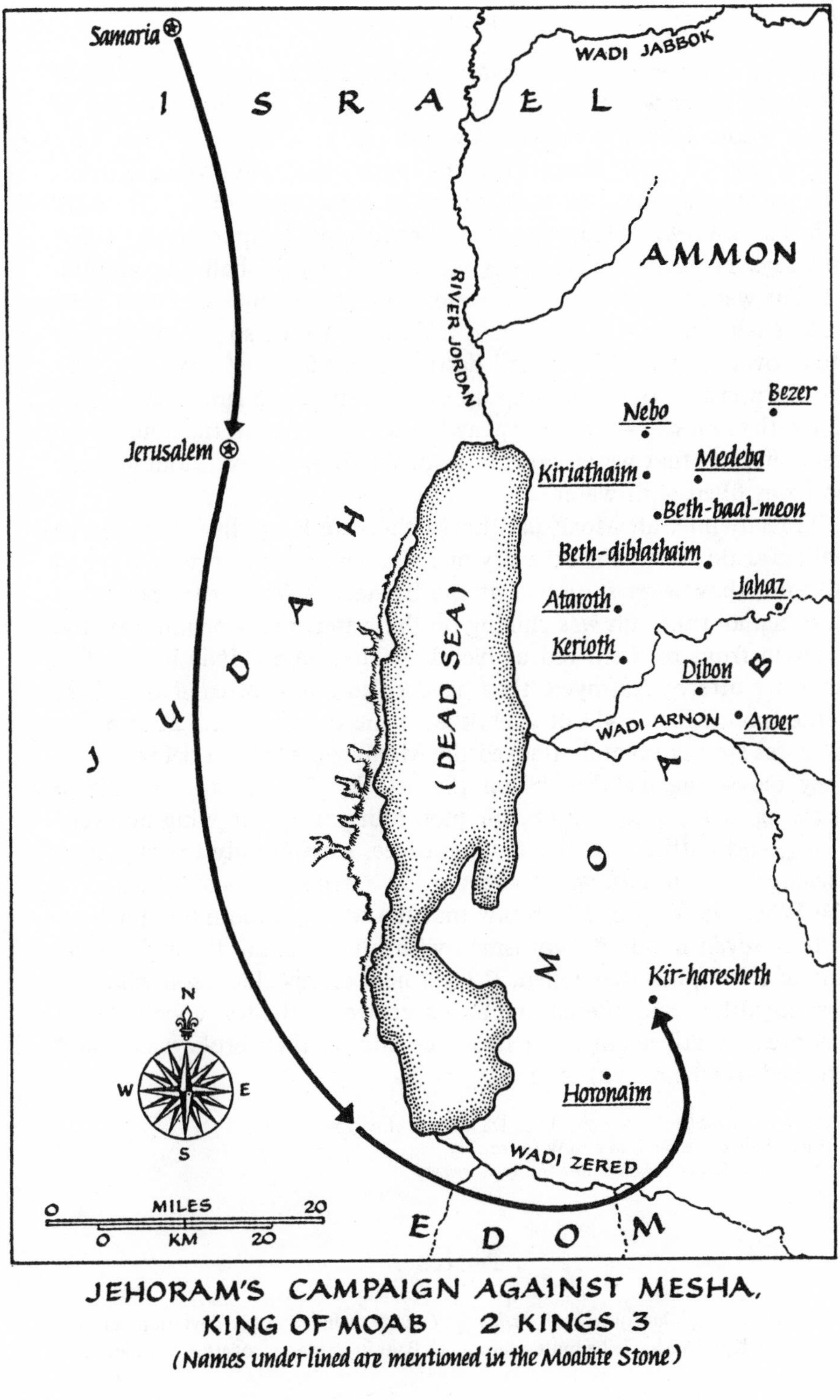

JEHORAM'S CAMPAIGN AGAINST MESHA, KING OF MOAB 2 KINGS 3

(Names underlined are mentioned in the Moabite Stone)

to hand them over to the Moabites." 14 And Elisha said, "By the life of YHWH of hosts whom I serve, were it not for Jehoshaphat king of Judah whom I hold in respect, I would not look at you or even take note of you. 15 Now, then, bring me a musician!"—for when a musician played, the hand of YHWH used to come upon him. 16 He said, "Thus says YHWH, 'This wadi shall produce pools upon pools.' 17 For thus says YHWH, 'You shall not see wind and you shall not see rain, yet that wadi shall fill up with water and you, your flocks, and your herds shall drink. 18 But this is a trifle for YHWH, so he will deliver Moab over to you. 19 You shall destroy every fortified city, « »[b] cut down every good tree, stop up every spring, and ruin every fertile plot with stones.' " 20 So it happened in the morning, at the hour of the meal offering, that water came in from the direction of Edom and the land was filled with water.

21 Meanwhile, all Moab had heard that the kings had marched to make war on them, and so every one who could bear arms was called up[c], and they were stationed at the border. 22 When they rose that morning, and the sun was shining on the water, the Moabites saw the water in front of them red as blood. 23 They said, "It is blood! The kings are utterly destroyed; they have killed one another. Now, then, to the spoil, Moab!" 24 But when they came to the Israelite camp, the Israelites sprang up and attacked the Moabites, who fled before them. They moved against Moab[d] on the attack, 25 destroying the cities, throwing stones into every fertile plot, filling it up, stopping up every spring, and cutting down every good tree, leaving only the stones of Kirharesheth (intact), which the slingers surrounded and attacked.

26 When the king of Moab saw that the war was too much for him, he took seven hundred swordsmen with him to break through to the king of Edom; but they failed. 27 Then he took his eldest son who was to succeed him and offered him as a sacrifice on the (city) wall. There was great wrath against the Israelites and so they broke camp and returned to (their own) land.

[b] Omit *kl ʿyr mbḥwr* with a ms., Luc., LXX^{B}, and cf. v. 25.
[c] Lit. "those old enough to gird (a sword)."
[d] MT *wybw bh* (qere *wayyakkû bāh*); read *wybʾw bʾ*.

Notes

3 2. *the pillar of Baal which his father had made.* Ahab's cultic deviations are recorded in 1 Kgs 16:31–33: he built a temple to Baal in Samaria, together with an altar

and a sacred pole (Asherah). Although it is not mentioned in those verses, there is good reason to accept (contrary to the early critics, e.g. Stade) the reliability of the present reference to a dedication by Ahab of a pillar to Baal. Royal dedications of stela in honor of the gods are too frequent in the ancient Near East to require confirmation. (On this votive function of the *maṣṣēbâ,* among several others, see C. F. Graesser, "Standing Stones in Ancient Palestine," *BA* 35 [1972], 34–63.) For examples from the Phoenician and Aramaean traditions, see *ANEP*² 499, 500, 501. Additional Baal pillars were removed by Jehu; see 10:26–27. This partial rooting out of foreign influence won for Jehoram a tempering of the editorial criticism levelled by Dtr. (On the cult of Baal and its Tyrian character, see above for 1 Kgs 16:31; and W. F. Albright, *Archaeology and the Religion of Israel* [Baltimore: Johns Hopkins University, 1942], 156–58, who identifies this Baal as Melqart.)

4. *Mesha king of Moab.* The name Mesha appears in the opening line of the Moabite stone erected by Mesha himself (for details, see Comment), in which the king's ancestry is given: "I am Mesha, son of Chemosh[yat], king of Moab, the Dibonite." (For the restoration of his father's name, see W. L. Reed and F. V. Winnett, "A Fragment of an Early Moabite Inscription from Kerak," *BASOR* 172 [1963], 1–9.) The interchange between MT *myšʿ* and the LXX transcription *mosa* can be explained by taking the name as derived from **yšʿ,* "to save," which like other primae *yod* verbs shows assimilation in certain dialects to primae *waw* (so e.g. MT *mydd* in Num 11:27 appears in LXX as *modad).* The *hiphil* participle would mean "savior." The Moabite reading of the king's name *mšʿ* shows that the diphthong has been contracted and read either *mêšaʿ* or *môšaʿ* (so with S. Morag, "Meša (A Study of Certain Features of Old Hebrew Dialect)," *EI* 5 [1958], 138–44).

sheep-breeder. Heb. *nōqēd* (Amos 1:1) as well as Akk. *nāqidu* is only "herdsman" (cf. *CAD* N 1.333). The unusual dual designation in an Ugaritic text of a certain *Atrprln* as "head priest" (*rb khnm*) and "head herdsman"(?) (*rb nqdm*) (*UT* 62: 53–57), has misled many into seeking cultic significance for *nōqēd,* such as "hepatoscopist" (e.g. M. Bič, "Der Prophet Amos—ein Haepatoskopas," *VT* 1 [1951], 293–96; followed by Gray). This explanation would attribute a sacral function not only to Mesha, but also to the prophet Amos, who was one of the herders in Tekoa (Amos 1:1, cf. 6:4). But there is no evidence, either linguistic or contextual, for such interpretations, which were correctly rejected by A. Murtonen, *VT* 2 (1952), 170–71; cf. earlier Montgomery-Gehman, and also S. Segert, "Zur Bedeutung des Wortes *Nōqēd,*" *VT* Sup 16 (1967), 279–83. (On *rb nqdm,* see A. Rainey, *A Social Structure of Ugarit* [Jerusalem: Mosad Bialik, 1967], 70–71 [Hebrew].)

he used to pay tribute. Heb. *wĕhēšîb*—cf. 17:3; Ps 72:10—is here frequentative (see Driver, *Tenses,* 120). Targum adds the explanatory *šĕnāʾ bišnāʾ,* "yearly."

one hundred thousand lambs . . . The numbers are extremely high; they may have been used to convey the idea of total submission and were not meant as an accurate head count of animals delivered. Equally large numbers of animals were taken as spoil, cf. e.g. Sennacherib's referring to southern Babylonia: "7,200 horses and mules; 11,703 asses, 5,230 camels, 80,100 cattle; 800,509 sheep—an enormous spoil" *(ARAB* 2.274). Similar large numbers appear in the records of Sarduri, king of Urartu the contemporary of Tiglath-pileser III; cf. F. W. König, *AfO* Beiheft 8 (1955), 115–39, passim.

5. The verse is a repetition of the annalistic notation in 2 Kgs 1:1, which has been prefixed editorially to the story of Jehoram's campaign to explain its circumstances.

6. *One day.* Heb. *bāyyôm hahûʾ,* "on that day," i.e. the day of the story. Cf. the opening in 1 Sam 3:2 (where *NEB*'s "But one night" is more of a commentary than a translation).

7. *He went and sent a message.* The verb *hālak* is used as an auxiliary with the meaning "to be aroused to action" (so Luzzatto ad Ex 2:1) and cf. Gen 35:22; Deut 17:3; 1 Kgs 16:31; Hos 1:3; Jer 3:8.

Jehoshaphat king of Judah. Luc. substitutes Ahaziah (cf. 8:25–26) for Jehoshaphat here, and omits the name altogether in vv. 11, 12, 14. This change suits the alternate chronology in Luc. (cf. above 1:17). But it is unlikely that Ahaziah is original to the prophetic story in 2 Kgs 3; as son of Jehoram and Athaliah daughter of Jezebel, he was a true Ahabite, doing what was displeasing to YHWH (so 8:27), so that Elisha would hardly have spoken of him so highly (see v. 14).

my forces are as your forces; my horses as your horses. Cf. the identical formulation in 1 Kgs 22:4; in both cases, the correspondence between the two kings is signified by the repeated *ka- . . . ka-* (see BDB 454a); cf. too Gen 18:25 and 44:18; Lev 24:22. *NEB* misses the idiomatic Hebrew usage with "What is mine is yours; myself, my people, and my horses." The political overtones of these words, which reflect treaty relations between Israel and Judah (concluded during the reign of Ahab?)—on which see 1 Kgs 22:49–50; 2 Kgs 8:18; 2 Chr 18:3—are illuminated by comparing the statement of King Niqmadu of Ugarit sent to Shuppiluliuma, his Hittite overlord: "I am the servant of the Sun, the great king, my lord. With the enemies of my lord, I am enemy; with his ally, I am ally." (J. Nougayrol, *Le palais royal d'Ugarit* IV [Paris: Impremarie nationale, 1956], No. 17.340, lines 12–13).

8. *The Desert of Edom Road.* Heb. *derek,* "way, road," is taken in most translations as a preposition, "through, by way of." But routes were given names in the Bible by designating their terminal point—e.g. "Shur Road" (Gen 16:7); i.e. the road leading to Shur; "Land of Philistia Road" (Exod 13:17); "Arabah Road" (2 Kgs 25:4), and for further discussion, see Aharoni, *Land of the Bible*², 43–63.

It seems likely that a road east of the Jordan Valley rift, toward the desert, is referred to, and as suggested by N. Glueck (*HUCA* 11 [1936], 150, n. 43) is the road which follows wadi el-Ḥesā (biblical wadi Zered; cf. Num 20:12). Y. Aharoni thought that the text was in error here and identified the road as the one descending from Arad to the northern end of Mt. Sodom and continuing on to the Arabah (*Land of the Bible*², 58). But this goes against the plain sense of the story: the army took a week-long route (v. 9), which would have taken them far from the Judaean desert near Arad.

9. *king of Edom.* The participation of a king of Edom in the campaign disturbs some critics (e.g. Kittel, Benzinger, and lately J. R. Bartlett in *Midian, Moab and Edom* (eds., J. F. A. Sawyer and D. J. A. Clines, *JSOT* Sup 24 [1983], 143–44), because according to 1 Kgs 22:48 "a deputy (of Jehoshaphat) was king" and only during the reign of his son Jehoram was there an independent king of Edom, 2 Kgs 8:20. It would not, however, be unusual for the same official to be referred to as a "deputy" in a chronistic source (so 1 Kgs 22:48) and "king" in a prophetic narrative such as the one before us in 2 Kgs 3. Note a similar alternation in the recently published bilingual inscription from Tel Fekharye. The local ruler Hadad-yisʿi is "king of Gozan" (*mlk gwzn*) in the Aramaic text; at the same time he is called "governor" (*šakin māti*) in Akkadian. See A. Abou-Assaf, P. Bordreuil, A. R. Millard, *La Statue de Tell Fekherye* (Paris: Editions recherche sur les civilisations, 1982), 62, lines 8 and

6. For current discussion of the inscription, apparently to be dated in the third quarter of the ninth century B.C.E., see S. A. Kaufman, *Maarav* 3 (1982), 137–75; R. Zadok, *Tel Aviv* 9 (1982), 117–29; J. C. Greenfield and A. Shaffer, *Iraq* 45 (1983), 109–16; T. Muraoka, *Abr-Naharain* 22 (1983–84), 79–117; and on the archaizing orthography, J. Naveh, *Shnaton* 5–6 (1983), 131–40.

in their train. Heb. *bĕraglêhem,* lit. "at their feet," said of those who follow closely behind a leader; cf. 1 Kgs 20:10; Judg 4:10; 1 Sam 25:27; 2 Sam 15:16, 17.

11. *Isn't there a prophet of* YHWH *here . . . ?* The presence of diviners in army camps is documented in Mesopotamia as early as the Mari Age. Thus e.g. the dispatch to Zimri-lim (*ARM* 2 22:24f.): "The diviner Ilušunaṣir, servant of my lord, will lead the troops of my lord, and a Babylonian diviner will go with the Babylonian troops." Cf. too, *ARM* 1 85: rev 10′; *ARM* 3 80:17. A millennium later, in the days of Ashurnasirpal II, the diviner "who marches in the front of their (the Babylonians') army" was captured (*AKA* 351 iii 20).

who poured water on the hands of Elijah. Targum's *šamēš,* "served," captures the sense of Elisha's role until this time. Cf. 1 Kgs 19:21.

13. *What have I to do with you?* The expression *mal-lî wālak* means "What business can we have together?" (so, 1 Kgs 17:18) or "What have we in common?" (cf. 2 Sam 16:10; 19:23).

14. *whom I serve.* Heb. *ʿāmôd lipnê,* lit. "stand before," is an expression used in court contexts (cf. 1 Kgs 1:2), here distinctively meaning prophetic service of YHWH. Cf. 1 Kgs 17:1; 18:15; 2 Kgs 5:16. For other terms of loyalty, see note to 20:3.

15. *for when a musician played . . .* Syntactically, *wĕhāyâ* is frequentative and describes the recurring ecstasis which took hold of the prophet under the influence of music (Skinner, Šanda, Montgomery-Gehman). Other commentators, however, emend the text to *wayyĕhî,* "When the musician played . . ." (cf. LXX), thus filling in the narrative sequence; but this emendation is superfluous. For another example of a supposed lacuna in a narrative, see the note to 6:33.

The band of prophets met by Saul at Gibeath-elohim, led on by lyre, timbrel, pipe, and harp, was similarly possessed (see 1 Sam 10:5). For a recent anthropological definition of prophetic possession and examples of this from ancient Near Eastern contexts, see Wilson, *Prophecy and Society,* 33–35; 103–6; 129–30.

16. *This wadi shall produce pools upon pools.* Heb. *ʿāśô,* an infinitive absolute, as in 4:43 and 5:10, conveys the basic sense of the verb; cf. *GKC* 113dd. The rendering by an imperative in some versions loses the sense of the miraculous; digging of trenches by the army was not the prophet's intention. See the pointed remarks of Burney.

gēbîm. Traditionally taken as "trenches," they are rather the natural depressions in the wadi bed which fill up when the torrent flows and remain full after the surrounding area dries up. Cf. also Jer 14:3.

18. *But this is a trifle.* Heb. *wnkl zʾt;* for another example of disagreement in gender, see v. 26, *ḥzq . . . hmlḥmh;* and *GKC* 145e.

19. *every fortified city.* The additional *kl ʿyr mbḥwr* in MT grew out of the scribal confusion of *ḥw* for *ṣ* in the preceding phrase *kl ʿyr mbṣr,* the common word for fortification. (The letters are almost identical in the cursive script of the Herodian period.) This erroneous reading was subsequently preserved as a "double reading," on which see further in the note to 10:6.

Elisha's prophecy, worded as a command, of a scorched-earth policy against Moab is at variance with the rules of siege warfare in Deut 20:19; this gave rise to a harmonistic rabbinic exegesis which posited ad hoc legislation by the prophet for a unique military situation (cf. Rashi, Qimḥi, Gersonides, and earlier, *Num. Rab.* 21.6). Yet Elisha's call to devastate Moab may have originated not only in "nationalistic chauvinism, but also . . . tribal pride," he being a Gadite whose territory had previously been destroyed by Mesha (so, G. Rendsburg, "A Reconstruction of Moabite-Israelite History," *JANES* 13 [1981], 67–73).

you shall . . . ruin. Heb. *takʾībû,* lit. "you shall cause pain," in BH usually of bodily harm. Cf. other metaphoric images of "reviving stones" in Neh 3:34 and "healing the destroyed altar of YHWH" in 1 Kgs 18:30 (so Qimḥi).

20. *at the hour of the meal offering.* For a similar reckoning, by the afternoon offering, see 1 Kgs 18:29; and for the components of these daily sacrifices, see Exod 29:38–42.

22. *red as blood.* Commentators labor to find a natural phenomenon which would explain the Moabites' misinterpretation. Explanations offered include: the red color of the sun's reflection on the water (Thenius, Kittel); the reddish color of the water in contact with the red sandstone of the wadi bed (Ewald, Glueck [above n. 8] who quotes A. Musil, *Arabia Petraea* [Wien: A. Hölder, 1907] 1.83; 381, n. 2.).

23. *It is blood!* The image of blood running like water recalls several passages in Assyrian royal inscriptions where the defeat of enemies is described: "I dyed the mountain red with their blood" (*ARAB* 1.500; *ARI* 2.640); "I let their blood run down the surroundings of their city like the water of the stream" (*ARAB* 1.725).

The kings are utterly destroyed. Heb. *hoḥŏrēb neḥerbû;* for another example of *niphal* preceded by an infinitive absolute *hophal,* cf. Lev 19:20. (The emendations listed in Stade are all unnecessary.) Because **ḥrb* generally refers to inanimate objects, *BDB* 352 lists **ḥrb* III; *KB* 355 **ḥrb* II, "smite, attack;" derived from *ḥereb,* "sword"; cf. also Jer 50:21, 27. Here, the modern dictionaries were anticipated by Qimḥi.

24. *They moved against Moab, on the attack.* Reading: *wyb(ʾ)w bʾ whkwt.* MT is faulty; its partial restoration is made possible by the presence of *wĕhakkôt* which determines the preceding verb as infinitive absolute (cf. GKC 75*ff.*); thus for MT *bh* read *bʾ.* MT *wybw,* correctly rendered by LXX *eiselthon,* "they came," is an example of the dropping of *aleph* in forms of the verb *bwʾ* known elsewhere; e.g. 1 Sam 25:8; 1 Kgs 21:21, 29; Ruth 3:5; and see the massoretic note to 1 Kgs 12:12. Thus the ketib of our verse is preferred to the qere (which may have derived from the similarity of *b* and *k,* as well as context).

25. The verbs are all in the imperfect, a tense used to convey a graphic picture of the progress of the battle. Cf. Driver, *Tenses,* 113.4β.

leaving only the stones of Kir-haresheth (intact). Usually taken to be identical with Kir-Moab (Isa 15:1; cf. Isa 16:7; Jer 48:31, 36), this major city in southern Moab is located at el-Kerak (so already in Targum to Prophets). Cf. B. Oded, *EncMiqr* 7.177–81. The steep approaches to the site may have been a factor in Mesha's successful resistance to the rigors of the Israelite siege. For a contemporary example of Assyrian devastations of territories, cf. the punishment of Damascus by Shalmaneser III, *ANET*³, 280; and the monumental reliefs in A. H. Layard, *The Monuments of Nineveh* (London: John Murray, 1849), 1.73, 76.

ʿad hišʾîr, cf. 10:11, best taken as an infinitive construction with *ḥireq* instead of *pataḥ* (with Burney).

which the slingers surrounded. For this attack unit in contemporary armies of the ancient Near East, see Yadin, *Art of Warfare,* 296–97, with illustrations.

to break through to the king of Edom. Heb. *lĕhabqîaʿ ʾel-* in *hiphil* occurs again only in Isa 7:6, but there *ʾel* expresses "to one's benefit, advantage" (the so-called "ethical dative"). In *qal,* the phrase *bāqôaʿ bĕ-* is "breaking through" as in 2 Sam 23:16; with *ʾel* "breaking through (and seizing) for oneself" as 2 Chr 32:1. (Note that the parallel in 2 Kgs 18:13 reads *wayyitpĕśēm,* "he seized them.") Admittedly the present case is the only instance of breaking out of a siege, but the action is described from the Moabite point of view: Mesha sought to break through the Edomite line, the weak link in the chain of forces which encircled his city.

There is scarcely reason to emend the text, following the old suggestion of Winckler (adopted by Eissfeldt, Montgomery-Gehman, Gray), to read *Aram* for *Edom.* There is no indication that Aram-Damascus was allied with Moab at this juncture. An ingenious, though far-fetched, interpretation was put forward by N. H. Tur-Sinai, *The Language and the Book*[2] (Jerusalem: Mosad Bialik, 1954), 1:84–91 (Hebrew). He excised "the king of Edom" entirely from the story and read into our verse *mōlk ʾādām,* a type of human sacrifice (following O. Eissfeldt's study of Moloch rites, on which see 2 Kgs 23:10). The following imaginary vignette emerged from the rewritten verse: Mesha, with the aid of his troops, "cut wood" (**bqʿ*) for a massive sacrifice of propitiation to the angry Moabite god. Tur-Sinai also found reference to this immolation in Amos 2:1, which he read as "who burned bones in a human sacrifice to the demons." See *Peshuto shel Miqra* (Jerusalem: Kiryat Sefer, 1967) 3/2.453.

27. *Then he took his oldest son . . . on the (city) wall.* This is the clearest case of human sacrifice under conditions of stress in biblical literature; the case of Jephthah's daughter belongs to the class of sacrifice offered in fulfillment of vows, cf. Judg 11:30–31; Lev 27:29. Classical sources report the frequent sacrifice of children in cities under siege in Phoenicia and its north African colonies. See, among others, Eusebius, *Praeparatio Evangelica* I, 44; Diodorus, *Bibliotheca Historica* XX, 14:4–6; and the survey of this evidence by M. Weinfeld, "The Worship of Molech and the Queen of Heaven and Its Background," *UF* 4 (1972), 133–40; and below note to 21:6. It is still a question whether or not the depictions on Egyptian reliefs of a child hanging over the wall of a besieged city are ritual in nature and related at all to infant sacrifice; see A. Spalinger, *Journal of the Society for the Study of Egyptian Antiquities* (Toronto) 8 (1978), 47–60. Likewise, the crucial lines in a Ugaritic prayer for a city under siege referring to the consecration of a "first-born" (?) are of disputed interpretation. See A. Herdner, *Ugaritica VII* (Paris: Geuthner, 1978), 31–39, Text RS 24.266; cf. B. Margalit, Seventh *WCJS,* 63–83.

Mesha's sacrifice, performed on the city wall being assaulted by Israelite troops, is best taken as a propitiatory act offered to the angry Moabite deity Chemosh *in extremis,* not as a regular cultic offering. For a suggestion that Ahaz sacrificed his son under similar circumstances, see note to 2 Kgs 16:3.

There was great wrath against the Israelites. This clause is one of the most perplexing items in Scripture. Heb. *qeṣep,* "wrath," describes YHWH's visitation upon wrongdoers—e.g. Num 18:5, Deut 29:27, Josh 9:20, 22:20. The usual idiom is *hāyâ qeṣep ʿal,* as in our verse; but *yāṣāʾ qeṣep,* "the wrath began" (lit. 'issued')—Num 17:11; and *bāʾ qeṣep,* "the wrath came")—2 Chr 32:26, are also attested.

Many commentators assume that originally the subject of the "great wrath" was the Moabite deity Chemosh, who in accepting Mesha's grim sacrifice, struck out at Israel's armies. This reference to an effective display of power by a non-Israelite deity was subsequently edited out of the text (Kittel, Šanda, Gray). Y. Kaufmann, however, has argued that "the wrath of Chemosh is a totally nonbiblical image, but that magical wrath or anger could actually be effective according to biblical thought, as seen in the danger posed by Balaam (cf. Josh 24:10)." Elisha's apparent absence from the camp at the time of Mesha's sacrifice led to the "wrath" which scattered the Israelite forces. See Kaufmann, *Collected Papers,* 205–7 (Hebrew). Rabbinic exegetes transferred the wrath from the divine to the human plane: the king of Edom in his anger turned against Jehoram and Jehoshaphat because of the sacrifice of his son who had been taken captive by Mesha in an earlier attack (a fanciful interpretation which joined v. 26 with the enigmatic Amos 2:1); so Qimḥi, Gersonides. Other commentators interpret *qeṣep* as the "anger" of Israel's own troops over the prolonged siege that brought about such horrors (Thenius), as "panic" and the losing of heart (Keil, Montgomery-Gehman), or even "sorrow and vexation" on the part of the Moabites over Israel's attack (G. R. Driver, *JThSt* 36 [1935], 293). For an analysis of this verse in its compositional setting, see Comment.

Comment

1. *3:1–3.* The eight-year reign of Jehoram (849–842 B.C.E.) is introduced by the standard editorial formula. The closing phrase —"The rest of the history of . . . and what he did"— is lacking, probably overlooked in the final editing of Kings because of the lengthy insertions of prophetic material between the verses here and the description of Jehoram's assassination in 9:1–28.

2. *3:4–27.* A prophetic narrative, vv. 6–25, is set within an editorial framework: vv. 4–5 serve as a prologue, vv. 26–27 an epilogue. This narrative is likely to have been a part of the northern collection of prophetic stories about Elisha, integrated into a pre-Deuteronomistic history of the Israelite kingdom. Recent attempts to narrow down the classification of these stories according to form-critical criteria by introducing terms such as "oracular-fulfullment narrative" (Long) or "instrumental-fulfillment narrative" (DeVries) do not advance our understanding of the societal and historical setting of the narrative and its place in early Israelite historiography.[1]

This is the first instance of Elisha's active involvement in the political affairs of Israel; because of him, victories were granted Israel's armies (cf. 6:24–7:20, 13:14–19). As in the previous accounts of Ahab's wars against Aram-Damascus (1 Kgs 20, 22), the critical role of the prophet as mediator of YHWH's word is the central theme here; the literal fulfillment of Elisha's prophecy as to the devastation of Moab (cf. vv. 19 and 25) serves as the denouement of the story and shows vv. 26–27 to be secondary.

[1] See, among others, K.-H. Bernhardt, "Der Feldzug der drei Könige," in *Schalom,* Festschrift A. Jepsen (ed. K.-H. Bernhardt, Stuttgart: Calmer Verlag, 1971), 11–22; B. O. Long, "2 Kings III and Genres of Prophetic Narrative," *VT* 23 (1973), 337–48; S. J. DeVries, *Prophet Against Prophet* (Grand Rapids, Mich.: Eerdmans, 1973), 65–67; 87–90.

That diviners were consulted prior to going to war or in the course of a battle is not in itself novel. In early Israel, this practice was wholly a priestly function, related to the Urim and Thummim oracle entrusted to their care (cf. Num 27:21; Judg 1:1–2; 1 Sam 30:7–8). Not until the mid-ninth century B.C.E., during the height of the Aramaean wars, do we note the transfer of mantic, divinatory functions from the priesthood to popular prophets.[2] It is nevertheless striking that in no other biblical story is a prophet found among the troops in the army camp.

The role of the king of Judah, both here and in 1 Kgs 22, is pivotal. In addition to being the political ally of Israel, King Jehoshaphat of Judah is portrayed as being the first to request a prophecy by a true prophet of YHWH. Without his participation in these events, there would be no story line; thus reference to him cannot be regarded as a Judaean elaboration of an originally northern prophetic story (so, Skinner). Moreover, the identification of the Judaean king by name and not simply by title appears to be original and cannot be considered a late addition to the text (so e.g. Miller), for it is rather unlikely that Jehoram son of Jehoshaphat and husband of Athaliah would have been treated in a prophetic story with such deference as is Jehoshaphat (see v. 14). The omission of "Jehoshaphat" by name in Lucian is, therefore, a late alteration of the text to accommodate the varying chronological system in the Old Greek.[3]

The similarities between 2 Kgs 3 and 1 Kgs 22 are noted by all commentators. In both chapters, a prophet of YHWH is sought out by Jehoshaphat, who has joined an Israelite king in battle. Validation of the prophet's position and his words come at the time of the prophecy's fulfillment. Identical phraseology lends support to these thematic similarities. Cf. 1 Kgs 22:4 and 2 Kgs 3:7, 1 Kgs 22:7 and 2 Kgs 3:11. These and other prophetic stories (cf. 1 Kgs 20) were preserved by the admirers of the leading prophets and within prophetic circles in general, accounting for literary similarities, which were probably already present at the stage of oral transmission.

Historically, 2 Kgs 3 provides only the barest outline of Jehoram's campaign against Mesha, and this because of the chapter's prophetic focus. The withholding of tribute payment after the death of Ahab signaled Mesha's revolt. Sometime after his succession following the death of his ill-fated brother Ahaziah, Jehoram attacked Moab across its southern border, supported by Jehoshaphat of Judah and an unnamed king of Edom. But his

[2] I. L. Seeligmann (*EI* 5 [1958], 125–32) traces this development through its various stages, finding literary echoes of manticism in late classical prophecy.

[3] For a different opinion, see J. M. Miller, "Another Look at the Chronology of the Early Divided Monarchy" *JBL* 86 (1967), 276–88; J. D. Shenkel, *Chronology and Recensional Development in the Greek Text of Kings,* 87–108; and more recently, A. R. Green, "Regnal Formulas in the Hebrew and Greek Texts of the Books of Kings," *JNES* 42 (1983), 167–80.

initial victories were not enough to subdue Mesha, and the campaign broke off with the retreat of the Israelite forces who had been besieging the Moabite city, Kir-Haresheth.

Complementing the biblical data directly is the report of Moab's wars with Israel as recorded on the Moabite stone, a monumental stele commemorating the heroic deeds of Mesha.[4] Mesha reports: After a long period of oppression beginning under Omri, accounted for by the anger of Chemosh, the chief Moabite deity, toward his land, Moab's fortunes took a turn upward. Mesha drives the Israelite forces out of the major cities north of the Arnon brook in a series of bloody battles, and follows these with public works and cultic dedications, a sign of royal piety in classic ancient Near Eastern tradition.

Most difficult, however, is the historian's task of coordinating the information from this Moabite royal inscription with that from the prophetic narrative in 2 Kgs 3. The crucial stumbling block is the lack of fixed chronological points of contact between the two texts. Jehoram's campaign is undated in 2 Kgs 3, but cannot be later than 846, the last year of Jehoshaphat. Mesha speaks of "forty years" as the period of Israelite rule over Moab, the days of Omri "and half the days of his son" (Moabite stone, line 8), i.e. Ahab. Even if the number "forty" is taken as a typological number meaning "generation," the revolt would have broken out in mid-reign of Ahab, who engaged Mesha in battle at Jahaz (Moabite stone, lines 18–19; contra. 2 Kgs 3:5).[5] Furthermore, Mesha claims to have seen the downfall of Omri and his dynasty (*wʾrʾ bh wbbth,* lit. "I gloated over him and his household": Moabite stone, line 7), which would date the stele sometime after 842, the year of Jehu's rebellion.[6] It follows that the Moabite stone describes events from the perspective of several decades, confining itself to triumphs over the Israelite enemy; neither Jehoram nor the ambiguous encounter with Israel reported in 2 Kgs 3 are mentioned. The reason for this omission lies in the very nature of the Moabite document. It is a royal victory stele recording the triumphs of its author, initiated by the god Chemosh and sanctified by him. But according to 2 Kgs 3:6–25, Moab was ravaged and on the verge of military defeat; the sudden retreat of the allied forces did not change this fact. That being so, Jehoram's

[4] Translated in Appendix, No. 1; cf. *ANET³,* 320; *KAI,* No. 181.

[5] An interpretation of the relationship between 2 Kgs 3 and the Mesha Stone at variance with the one here presented was set forth by F. M. Cross and D. N. Freedman in an extensive note, *Early Hebrew Orthography,* AOS No. 36 (New Haven, 1952), 39, n. 13. They suggest that "his son" (Moabite *bnh*) does not refer to Ahab, but to a "descendant" of Omri, i.e. Jehoram. The reigns of Ahab and Ahaziah are not referred to at all by Mesha. Moreover, "the 40-year datum in line 8 must be regarded as accurate, within definable limits."

[6] For this construing of the text, see W. F. Albright in *ANET³,* 320; and Cross and Freedman, loc. cit. (above, n. 5). More recently, M. Miller ("The Moabite Stone as a Memorial Stela," *PEQ* 106 [1974], 9–18) directed attention to the retrospective character of the inscription, surveying Mesha's reign as a whole.

campaign did not merit recording on the stele. Accordingly, viewed through the perspective of two distinctly different literary genres, 2 Kgs 3 and the Moabite stone depict two different episodes in the history of Israelite-Moabite relations.

Other scholars, however, have found a link between the two documents at the very end of the Moabite stone, in the broken two lines: "And as for Hauronen, there dwelt there [ ] Chemosh said to me, 'Go down, fight against Hauronen.' So I went down [ ], and Chemosh [dwelt] there in my days . . ." (lines 31–31). Hauronen, Heb. Horonaim (cf. Isa 15:5; Jer 48:5, 34), located in southern Moab toward Zoar, may have been in Edomite hands. Did Mesha attack Horonaim after Jehoram's retreat? Or did this attack precede the allied campaign and prompt the attack on Moab from the south? (The northern region, above the Arnon brook, was in Mesha's possession and heavily defended.) Additional epigraphical discoveries from the land of Moab may settle the question of the historical sequence of Mesha's wars, which is now unanswerable.[7]

The epilogue to the prophetic narrative, vv. 26–27, relates the final stages of the campaign: the unsuccessful attempt of the king of Moab to break through the siege; the sacrifice of his firstborn, the crown prince, on the city wall; Israel's retreat. These two verses stand in open contradiction to Elisha's prophecy: "He will deliver Moab over to you" (v. 18), after which the narrative should have told of the taking of Kir-haresheth. The cryptic statement: "There was great wrath against the Israelites" (v. 27) further confounds the reader.

In reality, Elisha's prophecy was fulfilled only in part; Moab remained independent and was never reconquered by Israel. It is this clash between the prophetic tradition (vv. 6–25) and the historical tradition behind vv. 26–27 which the epilogue in its present form attempts to resolve. The editor of the prophetic stories resorted to a theological expedient, a sudden divine wrath, to explain Israel's retreat. The subject of the wrath was left unnamed. The editor could have ascribed it to "the wrath of Chemosh"; but, as Kaufmann pointed out, to do so would have been to admit that a foreign deity was indeed a power source on the level of YHWH and that Mesha's sacrifice was in this sense efficacious, an incredible admission for any biblical writer. Or he could have ascribed the wrath to the god of Israel; but Mesha's sacrifice was obviously not to the god of his enemies. A proper biblical explanation would

[7] For full treatments of the history of Israel-Moab relations, see R. Murphy, "Israel and Moab in the Ninth Century B.C.," *CBQ* 15 (1953), 409–17; B. Mazar, *EncMiqr* 4.921–25, s.v. Mesha; A. H. Van Zyl, *The Moabites* (Leiden: Brill, 1960), 133–48; J. Liver, "The Wars of Mesha, King of Moab," *PEQ* 99 (1967), 14–31 (=*Military History of the Land of Israel in Biblical Times* [Tel Aviv: Maʿarachot, 1964], 221–40 [Hebrew]); J. R. Bartlett, "The Moabites and Edomites," in *Peoples of Old Testament Times* (Oxford: Oxford University Press, 1973), 229–58, and bibliography cited there.

have been to point to some wrongdoing on the part of Israel which then brought on the divine wrath (see the examples in the note to v. 27), but such an act was not part of the prophetic tradition in vv. 6–25. The equivocal "wrath" might have satisfied the ancient editor, but it has been an embarrassment to all his readers.[8]

[8] On this point, D.N.F. comments: "The editor/author has an interest in the House of Omri, and apparently wants to show that God would not permit an Omride to have an undiluted victory . . . Hence the revised account which incorporates a divine judgment against the latest heir to the throne . . . In spite of the prophet and the decision of God against the Moabites, in the end, Jehoram was not allowed to enjoy the fruits of the victory, but had to retreat precipitately."

VII. A HELPER IN TIMES OF DISTRESS

(4:1–44)

4 1 A certain woman, the wife of one of the Sons of the Prophets,
cried out to Elisha, "Your servant, my husband, has died. You know
that your servant feared YHWH; but a creditor has come to take away
my two children as his slaves." 2 Elisha said to her, "What can I do for
you? Tell me, what do you have in the house?" She said, "Your maidservant has nothing at all in the house, except for a container of oil."
3 He said, "Go out and borrow vessels from all your neighbors[a], empty
vessels. Do not skimp! 4 When you come back, close the door behind
you and your sons, and pour (oil) into all these vessels and set aside
the full ones." 5 And so she left him. When she closed the door behind
her and her sons, they kept bringing (vessels) to her and she kept
pouring[b]. 6 When the vessels were full, she said to her son, "Bring me
another vessel." He said to her, "There is not another vessel." Then
the oil stopped. 7 She came and told the man of God, and he said, "Go,
sell the oil and pay off your debt[c], and you and your sons[d] can live on
the remainder."
8 One day, Elisha was passing through[e] Shunem, where there was a
wealthy woman who insisted that he take some food. And whenever
he passed through, he would stop there for some food. 9 She said to her
husband, "Now I know for sure that the man of God who always
passes by our place is holy. 10 Let us make a small roof chamber by the
wall, and put a bed, a table, a chair, and a lamp for him there; and
whenever he visits us, he can stay there." 11 One day, he visited there;
he stopped by the roof chamber and rested there. 12 He said to Gehazi,
his attendant, "Call the Shunammite woman!" He called her and she
presented herself. 13 He said to him, "Please say to her, 'You have
shown all this concern for us. What can we do for you? Can I speak on

[a] Read with qere *šĕkēnāyik,* in pl.
[b] Read with ketib *myṣqt.*
[c] Read with qere *nišyēk.*
[d] Read *wbnyky* with mss., versions, qere.
[e] Read *ʿal* for MT *ʾel;* cf. v. 9.

your behalf to the king or to the commander-in-chief?' " But she said,
"I dwell among my kinsfolk." 14 He said, "Then what can we do for
her?" Gehazi said, "Still, she has no child and her husband is old."
15 He said, "Call her." He called her and she stood in the doorway.
16 He said, "At this season, next year, you shall embrace a son." She
said, "Do not, my lord, man of God, do not deceive your maidservant." 17 The woman did conceive, and she bore a child at the season
next year of which Elisha had spoken to her.

18 The child grew up. One day, he went out to his father among the
reapers. 19 He said to his father, "My head, my head!" He said to his
servant, "Carry him to his mother." 20 He carried him and brought
him to his mother. He sat on her knees until midday and then he died.
21 She went up and laid him on the bed of the man of God, then closed
(the door) on him and went out. 22 She called her husband and said,
"Send me one of the servants and one of the she-asses so that I can
hurry to the man of God and return." 23 He said, "Why are you going
to him today? It is not the new moon or the Sabbath." She said, "All is
well!"

24 She saddled the she-ass and then said to her servant, "Lead on
and proceed! Do not slow the riding for me, unless I tell you." 25 So
she went and came to the man of God on Mount Carmel. The man of
God saw her from a distance; he said to Gehazi his attendant, "Here is
that Shunammite woman. 26 Now[f], run to greet her and say to her, 'Is
all well with you? Is your husband well? Is your child well?' " She
answered, "All is well." 27 When she came to the man of God on the
mountain, she grabbed hold of his feet. Gehazi stepped forward to
push her away; but the man of God said, "Let her alone, for she is
embittered, yet YHWH had hidden it from me and not told me." 28 She
said, "Did I ask for a son of my lord? Did I not say, 'Do not deceive
me'?" 29 Then he said to Gehazi, "Get yourself ready[g] and take my
staff with you and go! If you meet anyone, do not greet him, and if
anyone greets you, do not answer him. Place my staff on the face of
the lad." 30 The mother of the lad said, "By the life of YHWH and by
your life, I will not leave you!" He got up and followed her.

31 Gehazi went on ahead of them, and he placed the staff on the
lad's face, but there was no sound and no response. So he went back to
meet him and told him, "The lad did not wake up." 32 Elisha entered
the house and there was the lad dead, laid out on his bed. 33 He went

[f] Read *wĕʾattā* with mss., Luc.
[g] Lit. "Gird your loins."

in and closed the door on both of them and then prayed to YHWH.
34 He got up (on the bed) and lay down on top of the boy; he put his
mouth to his mouth, his eyes to his eyes, his palms on his palms[h], and
crouched upon him. And the child's body became warm. 35 Then he
walked up and down[i] about the house, and got up (on the bed), and
crouched upon him. The lad sneezed seven times and the lad opened
his eyes. 36 He called Gehazi and said, "Call this Shunammite
woman." He called her and she came to him; he said, "Pick up your
son!" 37 She came in and fell at his feet, prostrating herself on the
ground. Then she picked up her son and went out.

38 Elisha came again to Gilgal, at the time of famine in the land. As
the Sons of the Prophets sat in front of him, he said to his attendant,
"Set the big pot (on the fire) and cook some porridge for the Sons of
the Prophets." 39 One (of them) went out into the field to gather herbs
and found a wild vine; he collected a skirt-full of bitter apples from it.
When he returned, he sliced them into the porridge pot, for he did not
know (what they were).[j] 40 They poured it for the men to eat, and as
they were eating the porridge, they shouted, "There's death in the pot,
man of God!" They couldn't eat (it). 41 He said, "Then bring some
flour." He threw (it) into the pot and said, "Pour out for the men and
let them eat." And now there was nothing harmful in the pot.

42 A man came from Baal-shalisha and brought the man of God
some bread of the first fruits, twenty barley loaves, and some fresh ears
of grain. He said, "Give it to the people that they may eat." 43 But his
attendant said, "How can I set this before a hundred people?" He said,
"Give it to the people that they may eat, for thus says YHWH, 'They
will eat and leave some over.' " 44 So he set it before them, and they ate
and had some left over, in accordance with YHWH's word.

[h] Read *kappāyw* with qere.
[i] Lit. "once this way, once that way."
[j] Read *yādaᶜ* with Luc., Vulg., Syr.; for MT *yādᶜû*.

Notes

4 1. *A certain woman.* Early tradition rescued the woman from biblical anonymity, making her the wife of Obadiah, the steward of Ahab, on the basis of the description in 1 Kgs 18:3, 12, where his "fearing YHWH" is underscored. See Targum ad loc.; Josephus, *Antiquities* ix.47; L. Ginzberg, *The Legends of the Jews* (Philadelphia: Jewish Publication Society, 1913), 4.240–42.

cried out to Elisha. Heb. **ṣāᶜôq ᵓel/lĕ-* conveys "appeal for help," see below note to 6:26; 8:3 and cf. Gen. 41:55; Num 11:2.

your servant feared YHWH. The usual expression of piety is simply "fear God," frequent in Deuteronomic literature (see Weinfeld, *Deuteronomy and the Deuteronomic School,* 332). The emphasis here on loyalty to YHWH may mirror the religious strife of the age of the Ahabites during which exclusive devotion to YHWH was at issue.

a creditor has come . . . Biblical law regulated the seizure of wives and children for nonpayment of debts; see Exod 21:7; cf. Amos 2:6, Isa 50:1. These "salable" persons were to be freed in the jubilee year, according to Lev 25:39–42, or could be released by a special decree, as in Neh 5. According to the Code of Hammurabi §117, the period of service in Babylonia was three years. For discussion of Mesopotamian legal traditions concerning debt slavery, see G. R. Driver and J. C. Miles, *The Babylonian Laws* (Oxford: Oxford University Press, 1952), 1.208–30.

2. *"What can I do for you?"* As in Gen 27:37 and 1 Sam 10:2, Heb. *mâ ʾeʿĕśeh lĕ-* implies being at a loss and unable to help. The prophet could not stop a legal foreclosure, yet it was in his power to produce a miracle (Ehrlich).

a container of oil. Heb. *ʾāsûk,* a hapax, is rendered verbally by LXX *alepsomai;* in the Targum as a noun, *mānāʾ dĕmišḥāʾ* (cf. Qimḥi for comparison to nouns *ʾēzôb, ʾĕgôz*). Thenius, followed by Burney and Montgomery-Gehman, translated "an anointing," a single application; and see Ehrlich. J. L. Kelso's archaeological identification of this "oil jar" (*BASOR,* Supplementary Studies 5–6, 17; *IDB* 3.851b) lacks textual support.

5. *And so she left him.* Luc. adds "and she did so"; but the ellipsis in MT is not unusual and can be maintained (so Stade; otherwise, Klostermann, Benzinger, and recently *NAB*).

she kept pouring. Ketib *myṣqt* is probably to be parsed as a *piel* participle with the sense of intensive action, but this is its only attestion (so Thenius, Stade, Ehrlich). Qere *môṣāqet* is a *hiphil* participle; so *BDB* 472a; cf. Josh 7:23. Note that in v. 4, the *qal* perfect is used.

7. *pay off your debt. Nišyēk,* with qere, from an unattested noun *nĕšî.* Haupt, Montgomery-Gehman, *NAB* prefer the LXX reading *nōšêkî,* "your creditor," which is also behind the Targumic *mārê hôbtîk.*

8. *a wealthy woman.* The adjective *gĕdôlâ,* "great," describes persons of esteem and status—e.g., 5:2; 10:6, 11; Jonah 3:7, Nah 3:10—who may have achieved their positions due to wealth. The legal formulation in Lev 19:15 contrasts *dāl* ("poor") with *gādôl;* but not every "great man" was necessarily wealthy. Nabal (1 Sam 25:2) and Barzillai (2 Sam 19:33) certainly were.

Shunem. A town in the tribe of Issachar (Josh 19:18), identified with the tel near the village of Sulem at the foot of Gibeath-morah in the Jezreel valley. See *EncMiqr* 7.567–68. Cf., too, 1 Kgs 1:3.

9. *the man of God . . . is holy.* It may have been Elisha's comportment that somehow alerted the Shunammite woman to special qualities that set him apart (so, the root meaning of **qdš,* "holy") from the typical man of God of that period (cf. Gersonides). This is the only instance where a prophet is spoken of as "holy"; normally the term is descriptive of cult personnel (e.g. Num 16:5), Nazirites (Num 6:5, 8), and the people of Israel when metaphorically called a "kingdom of priests" (Exod 19:6; cf. Ps 34:10).

10. *a small roof chamber by the wall.* Lacking descriptions of Israelite dwellings, the connotation of *qîr,* "wall," remains in question. The roof area was either "walled

up" to offer a sense of privacy for the holy man (so Qimḥi, Benzinger, Ehrlich, Gray) or was set off "by the wall" (describing its access?). Montgomery-Gehman followed Klostermann's reading *qôr,* "coolness," comparing *mĕqērâ* in Judg 3:20; thus a "cool upper chamber."

13. *"I dwell among my kinsfolk."* The woman's polite refusal of the offer is explained by her being well cared for by her family and clan. She had no need for the prophet's recommendation before the authorities. While the king was the ultimate court of appeal in civil matters (cf. 8:3), the reference to the commander-in-chief may mean that his jurisdiction covered military obligations imposed upon estate owners; cf. Gray, 486.

16. *next year.* Heb. *kāʿēt ḥayyâ,* an ancient crux, has its analogy in the Akkadian expression *ana balaṭ,* "next year," lit. "to life," as was recognized by W. von Soden, cited by W. G. Lambert, *Babylonian Wisdom Literature* (Oxford: Oxford University Press, 1960), 288, note to line 1; and see *AHw* 99a and *CAD* B 51b. Because the idiom is found in only two places in BH (Gen 18:10, 14 and the present passage), most commentators have connected *ḥayyâ,* "life," with the theme of promised births in these two stories. But an inner biblical translation confirms the sense of "next year;" cf. Gen 17:21, *baššānâ hāʾaḥeret.* A useful survey of the various interpretations is given by R. Yaron, *VT* 12 (1962), 500–1, who takes *koh lĕḥāy* in 1 Sam 25:6 as "thus shall it be next year," on the analogy of *ḥayyâ* in the present idiom; cf. *NEB:* "All good wishes for the year ahead!" See, too, A. Loretz, *Bib* 43 (1962), 75–78.

do not deceive your maidservant. **kizzēb bĕ-,* "to lie, to tell a lie"; more frequently *kizzēb lĕ-,* e.g. Ezek 13:19; Ps 78:36; 89:36.

19. *"My head, my head!"* Thenius plausibly suggested that the lad had suffered sun stroke; he was out in the field with his head uncovered. Cf. Ps 121:6; Jdt 8:2, 3.

23. *It is not the new moon or the Sabbath.* The new moon (*ḥōdeš*) was marked by sacrifice (Num 28:11–15) and the sounding of the ram's horn (Num 6:6); it was a day for family feasts (1 Sam 20:5, 26–29) and apparently for paying visits to a prophet. The Sabbath, literally the day of "cessation" from weekday labors, is the central holy day of the biblical calendar, as shown by its inclusion in the Ten Commandments (Exod 20:8–11), the only festival so distinguished, and by its etiology in Gen 2:1–3, as the crowning act of creation.

These popular days of rest and celebration appear together in Hos 2:13; Amos 8:5; Isa 1:14, 66:23.

The Sabbath is an independent Israelite creation based on the cycle of a seven-day week and has no proven relationship to the Babylonian *šapattu,* the day of the full moon, despite its being cognate to the Hebrew term. A full treatment of the nature of the Sabbath and its development is offered by J. Tigay, s.v. *šabbāt, EncMiqr* 7.504–17; and cf. also M. Greenberg, *Encyclopedia Judaica* 14.557–62; M. Tsevat, "The Basic Meaning of the Biblical Sabbath," *ZAW* 84 (1972), 447–59; de Vaux, *Ancient Israel,* 475–83; W. W. Hallo, "New Moons and Sabbaths: A Case-Study in the Contrastive Approach," *HUCA* 48 (1977), 1–18.

25. *that Shunammite woman. hallāz,* m.s.; a feminine sing. form, *hallēzû,* is attested in Ezek 36:35.

27. *yet* YHWH *has hidden it from me . . .* Elisha is taken aback by the woman's outburst, which was so unlike her customary decorum. Seers and prophets were forewarned by YHWH in similar circumstances—e.g., YHWH reveals his plan to Samuel a

day before Saul's arrival, 1 Sam 9:15; Ahijah is told of the impending visit of Jeroboam's wife, 1 Kgs 14:5.

28. *"Do not deceive me."* **šālōh* is more frequent in Aramaic than BH; it translates **šgg* / **šgh*, "to err, go astray" in the Targum to Ps 119:10, Job 12:16. But this does not warrant branding the verb in our passage as a "strong Aramaism" (*BDB* 1017a; Burney, 209); rather it is part of the patois of north Israel which permeates the prophetic literature in Kings.

30. *"By the life of* YHWH *. . ."* So in 2:2, 4, 6. By her oath, the Shunammite forces Elisha to return with her to the side of the lad who was the "prophet's gift." Action by proxy will not do.

Biblical Hebrew formulates oaths by invoking the life of God and/or a person of authority in the second person, in contrast to modern Western usage in the first person. Only God swears, "By My life" (e.g., Num 14:21; Isa 49:18; Ezek 5:11); men use the phrase *ḥālîlâ lî*, lit. *ad profanum!* or "Far be it from me" (e.g. Gen 44:17; Josh 24:16; 1 Sam 12:23, 22:15; note 1 Sam 2:30, in the words of God).

31. *there was no sound and no response.* Cf. 1 Kgs 18:26, 29. Heb. *qešeb* means lit. "attentiveness to spoken words." Should this be taken to mean that the placing of the staff upon the lad's face was accompanied by a verbal command or an incantation of some sort? See below to 5:11 and cf. Mark 5:41.

35. *and crouched upon him.* As in 1 Kgs 18:42, "with his head between his knees." Elisha did not stretch himself out fully over the small frame of the child; and so Burney, noting LXX's rendering as if synonymous with *wayyitmōdēd,* "he stretched himself out," in 1 Kgs 17:21.

the lad sneezed. Heb. **zrr,* a hapax, is used in Aramaic to translate **ʿṭš,* "sneeze," in the Targum to Job 41:10.

38. *Elisha came again to Gilgal.* The reference seems to be to 2:1, but it is a moot question whether this "return" to Gilgal was part of the original Elisha cycle (i.e. "on another occasion") or is a redactional element tying the tales together.

As the Sons of the Prophets sat in front of him. Cf. 6:32. The visit of the man of God was an occasion for a common meal and perhaps a lesson taught by the guest. In the exilic community of Tel-Abib, the elders gathered regularly to hear God's word through Ezekiel; see Ezek 8:1, 14:1, 20:1. Gray's paraphrase "were in session before him" captures the sense.

Set the big pot (on the fire). Heb. *šĕpōt hassīr* is apparently an everyday household expression for preparing a cooked dish and as such is used by Ezekiel in his allegory on rebellious Jerusalem (24:3). For **špt* ("set, place") cf. Isa 26:12, Ps 22:16, and further in the note to 2 Kgs 23:10.

39. *herbs.* Heb. *ʾōrôt,* also Isa 26:19. Rendered "greens" by Targum and "mallow" in Syriac, the exact identification of this wild plant remains uncertain. Y. Feliks, *Plant World of the Bible,* 190, suggests the "rocket" (*Eruca sativa*), an edible herb with medicinal qualities.

bitter apples. Popularly called the "Apple of Sodom." The small yellow melon of the *citrullus colcynthus* is a strong purgative and has been known to be fatal; identified as such already in LXX; see Feliks, *Plant World of the Bible,* 202; idem, *Nature and Man in the Bible,* 67–69; and J. P. Harland, *BA* 6 (1943), 49–52.

for he did not know (what they were). The Luc. reading of the verb in the singular is preferable; the conjunction *kî* introduces the excuse for the preceding action, but cannot explain the following excitement of the group, which would be rendered in BH *wĕhēm lōʾ yādĕʿû*. The additional *waw* results from dittography.

41. *Then bring some flour.* For the demonstrative force of the conjunction *waw*, see Driver, *Tenses,* 122.

42. *A man came from Baal-shalisha.* The identification of Baal-shalisha with Kefr Tilṯ, sixteen miles north of Lydda, in the vicinity of the village of Baithsarisa (given by Eusebius, *Onomasticon*), is adopted by most recent commentators (Šanda, Montgomery-Gehman, Gray); but there is little to recommend it. The land of Shalisha appears together with the lands of Shaalim and Zuph, all of them family districts of the tribe of Benjamin in Mt. Ephraim; see 1 Sam 9:4–5. Kh. el-Marjame, near ʿAin es-Sâmiyah is an important site in this region, which Kallai identified with Baal-shalisha, mentioned here. See Z. Kallai, in *Bible and Jewish History,* Studies in Memory of J. Liver, ed. B. Uffenheimer (Tel Aviv: Tel Aviv University, 1971), 191–204 (Hebrew); *EncMiqr* 2.292; 7.716; B. Mazar, *BASOR* 241 (1981), 81; and the archaeological site report by A. Mazar, *IEJ* 26 (1976), 138–39.

some fresh ears of grain. The variety of translations in the ancient versions for Heb. *bĕṣiqlōnô,* a hapax, indicates that its meaning was lost fairly early. Targum offers *lĕbûš,* "garment"; Vulg. *pera,* "bag"; LXX^{A} transliterates *bakelleth.* A noun *bṣql,* is now known from the Ugaritic Tale of Aqhat (I, 61–66) where it appears in parallel to *šblt,* "ear of grain," as first pointed out by U. Cassuto, *Biblical and Oriental Studies,* 2.197; see H. R. Cohen, *Biblical Hapax Legomena,* 112–13; and the remarks of S. E. Loewenstamm, *Bib* 56 (1975), 118.

43. *"They will eat and leave some over."* For other examples of the infinitive absolute, here used emphatically, cf. 3:16, 1 Kgs 22:30, and see *GKC* 113*ee*.

Comment

Four independent stories of varying lengths appear here; the common theme linking them together is the performance by the prophet of wondrous acts which were witnessed by his admirers. Elisha aids the destitute (vv. 1–7); rewards kindness and revives the stricken (vv. 8–37); and feeds the hungry (vv. 38–41, 42–44).

There are no firm clues as to the date of these events within Elisha's ministry. Drought and the resultant economic hardships were a recurring feature of life in ancient Israel. The historical setting is, moreover, secondary in importance to these stories which heap praise upon the prophetic master.

It is often observed that several deeds told of Elisha—the multiplication of oil (vv. 4–5) and bread (vv. 43–44), and the revival of the woman's son (vv. 33–35)—have their counterpart in the Elijah cycle of stories; cf. 1 Kgs 17:14–16, 17:20–22. Yet the reader is not necessarily faced here with literary borrowing, for the folkloristic motifs which are at the heart of these stories could have developed independently within both the Elijah and Elisha cycles. One cannot deny that within the circles of the Sons of the Prophets among whom these stories circulated, motifs crossed back and forth to the enrichment of each individual story.[1]

Furthermore, beyond the present context of the prophetic cycles, several of the motifs appear in other biblical narratives—for example, the prediction by a divine messenger of the birth of a son to a childless woman (Gen 18:9–15; Judg 13:2–5; cf. 1 Sam 1:17), and the miraculous feeding of the hungry multitudes (Exod 16; Num 11). In one instance the repetition of the unique phrase *kāʿēt ḥayyâ* in 2 Kgs 4:16, 17, and in Gen 18:10, 13, may even serve to suggest that there is a relationship between the two stories in which it appears. A storyteller familiar with the lore of early Israel could unwittingly have transferred expressions or even whole motifs from story to story. Thus a kind of "literary contamination" at the stage of story telling can be posited. To seek an "original setting" or to assign priority in material which had already developed and attained fixity in its oral stage of transmission would seem to serve no useful purpose.[2]

As noted previously with reference to other sections of the Elisha cycle, the present stories, too, are suffused with an air of authenticity; through them the lifestyle of the Sons of the Prophets is discernible. These followers of Elisha assemble at the feet of the master upon his arrival in their town for a communal meal and perhaps to hear some teaching. Elisha is seen to have traveled regularly about the country from his home in the Carmel. At other times, especially on the Sabbath and holy days, he received visitors who came to seek his counsel. A simple lifestyle characterizes the members of these groups; in many instances they appear on the verge of starvation, and these stories recall Elisha's miraculous aid in their time of need.

Traits peculiar to the Hebrew dialect of northern Israel are scattered throughout the chapter, e.g. the second feminine sing. pronoun *ʾattî* (vv. 16, 23); 2nd feminine sing. suffix *-kî* (vv. 2, 3, 7); the unusual noun *ʾāśûk* (v. 2); the root *šlh* (v. 28). (On this dialect, see further in the Introduction.)

[1] See the reasonable statement of Eissfeldt, 547, on the relationship of the two story cycles. Benzinger, 129, credits a redactor, working with written sources, with combining the motifs, a process we assume took place prior to the recording of the individual stories.

[2] On the other hand, it now seems that these stories about Elisha and the distressed women he helps were themselves the object of mimesis; see the suggestive study of T. L. Brodie, "Luke 7:36–50 as an Internalization of 2 Kings 4:1–37: A Study in Luke's Use of Rhetorical Imitation," *Bib* 64 (1983), 457–85.

VIII. THE CONVERSION OF NAAMAN

(5:1–27)

5 1 Now Naaman, commander of the army of the king of Aram, was
greatly esteemed by his master and held in favor, for through him
YHWH had given victory to Aram. But this valorous man was a leper.
2 Once, when the Aramaeans were raiding, they took captive a young
girl from the land of Israel, and she served Naaman's wife. 3 She said
to her mistress, "If only my master would present himself before the
prophet who is in Samaria, he would cure him of his leprosy." 4 [Naa-
man] came and told his master word for word[a] what the girl from the
land of Israel had said. 5 The king of Aram said, "Come, then, let me
send a letter to the king of Israel."

He set out and took with him ten talents of silver, six thousand
(shekels of) gold and ten changes of clothing. 6 He brought the letter
to the king of Israel, (which read) thus: "Now when this letter reaches
you, know that I am sending Naaman my servant to you, that you
may cure him of his leprosy." 7 When the king of Israel read the letter,
he rent his clothes and said, "Am I God, to take life or to give life, that
this fellow sends to me to cure a man of leprosy. Surely you must see
that he is picking a quarrel with me." 8 When Elisha, the man of God,
heard that the king of Israel had rent his clothes, he sent (a message)
to the king: "Why have you rent your clothes? Let him come to me
and he will learn that there is a prophet in Israel."

9 So Naaman came with his horses and chariots and waited at the
entrance of the house for Elisha. 10 Elisha sent a messenger to say to
him, "Go and bathe seven times in the Jordan so that your flesh may
be restored and so that you may be clean." 11 Naaman was angered
and left; he said, "Here I thought that he would surely come out and
stand and invoke YHWH his God by name, and wave his hand over the
spot and cure the leper. 12 Are not the Abana[b] and the Pharpar, the
rivers of Damascus, better than all the waters of Israel? Can I not

[a] Lit. "thus and thus."
[b] Qere: Amanah.

bathe in them and be cleansed!?" He turned and left in a rage. 13 But his servants went up to him and spoke to him; they said, "Sir,[c] if the prophet had told you (to do) a difficult thing, would you not do it? How much more when he said to you, 'Bathe and be clean.' " 14 So he went down and dipped himself in the Jordan seven times in accordance with the word of the man of God, and his flesh was restored as the flesh of a little child and he was clean.

15 He returned to the man of God, he and his entire company, and came and stood before him and said, "Now I know that there is no God in all the world except in Israel. So please accept a gift from your servant." 16 He said, "As YHWH lives, whom I serve, I will not accept anything." He pressed him to accept, but he refused. 17 Then Naaman said, "If not, then let your servant be given two mules' load of earth; for your servant will no longer offer burnt offering or sacrifice to other gods except to YHWH. 18 But may YHWH forgive your servant for this one thing: when my master enters the House of Rimmon to bow down there, and he leans on my arm, and I bow down in the house of Rimmon—when I bow down in the House of Rimmon, may YHWH forgive me for this thing." 19 He said to him, "Go in peace."

He had gone a short distance 20 when Gehazi the attendant of Elisha, the man of God thought, "Here my master has spared this Aramaean Naaman by not receiving from him what he brought. As YHWH lives, I will run after him and get something from him." 21 So Gehazi hurried after Naaman. When Naaman saw someone running after him, he climbed down from his chariot to meet him and said, "Is everything well?" 22 He said, "It is well. My master sent me to say, 'Just now two young men of the Sons of the Prophets from the hill country of Ephraim have come to me. Please give them a talent of silver and two changes of clothes.' " 23 Naaman said, "Kindly take two talents," and he pressed him. Then he tied up two talents of silver in two bags, in addition to two changes of clothing and he gave (them) to two of his servants, and they carried (them) ahead of him. 24 When he reached the citadel, he took (them) from them and deposited (them) in his house. He dismissed the men and they left.

25 As for him, he went in and stood before his master; Elisha said to him, "Where from, Gehazi?" He said, "Your servant has not gone anywhere." 26 He said to him, "Was I not there in spirit[d] when the man got down from his chariot to meet you? Is this a time to accept

[c] Lit. "My father."
[d] Lit. "Did my heart not go."

silver and to accept clothes and olive groves and vineyards and sheep and cattle and male and female slaves? 27 Naaman's leprosy will now cling to you and to your descendants forever." He left his presence, as leprous as snow.

Notes

5 1. *was greatly esteemed by his master.* Lit. "a great man in the view of his master." The preposition *lipnê* ("before, in front") also conveys "the attitude of the party concerned in terms of judgment, will, approval, and the like . . ." Cf. English "countenanced by," as was pointed out by Speiser, *Genesis* AB, lxviii, 51; and see Gen 6:11, 10:9, 17:18, 27:7, 43:32, and Num 32:20. Akk. *pānu,* "face," is sometimes similarly used; cf. *AHw* 819b, 14d.

held in favor. The nuances of *nāśô᾽ pānîm*, "lift up the face," which refer to pleasure and affection as shown by facial expression, are thoroughly studied by M. I. Gruber, "The Many Faces of Hebrew *nś᾽ pnym* >lift up the face<," *ZAW* 95 (1983), 252–60. Cf. Isa 3:3, 9:14; Job 22:8.

valorous man. Gibbôr ḥayīl appears here in its true military significance—cf. 6:15, 7:6; and see the note to 15:20 for its developed sense. Because the term is missing in Luc., most commentators take it as a gloss; Gray, however, retains it.

leper. Heb. *ṣāraʿat,* translated as *lepra* in LXX, refers to a wide variety of skin diseases in man and to molds and fungi on clothes and buildings. In the ritual statute in Lev 13, its distinctive signs include scales and blotches, which suggest the tractable diseases psoriasis and vitiligo. True leprosy (*lepra Arabum* or *elephantiasis Graecorum*), today called Hansen's disease, with its symptomatic swellings, facial distortions, and mutilations, does not appear in the Bible. It has been questioned whether leprosy was even known before the late pre-Christian period, despite the loathsome affliction mentioned in the Ebers medical papyrus (Egypt, sixteenth century B.C.E.). The Akkadian terms *saḫaršubbû, epqu,* and *garābu,* though rendered "leprosy" by the dictionaries (*AHw* 230, 281, 1005; *CAD* E 246; G 46; S 36–37), appear to refer to scaly afflictions and other skin disorders. Naaman's "leprosy" would seem to have been something less severe, considering his access to the court of the King of Aram-Damascus. The ouster of "lepers" from society (cf. below 7:3 and 15:5) may have been prompted more by aesthetics than by concerns for contagion. For discussions of *ṣāraʿat* and bibliographies, see *IDB* 3.111–13; *EncMiqr* 6.774–78; J. Tas, *Actes du 7ien congrès international d'histoire des sciences* (Jerusalem, 1953), 583–87; R. D. Biggs, RLA 6.605.

2. *when the Aramaeans were raiding.* Cf. 6:23. Note the borrowing of this West Semitic idiom, *ṣē᾽t gĕdûdîm,* "to set out in detachments" into the Akkadian of the Assyrian empire: *gudūdānu lūṣûma ṣābēšunu . . . liṣabitūma,* "let the detachments make a sortie and capture their soldiers;" *CAD* G 120a. A. Malamat proposed that a *gĕdûd* numbered six hundred men and finds examples of such brigades in Judg 18:11, 16, 17; 1 Sam 22:2; 1 Kgs 11:24. The "six hundred thousand foot soldiers" who left Egypt (Exod 12:37) would be then a thousand *gĕdûdîm* (*EncMiqr* 2.432–34; and *Bib* 51 [1970], 9–10).

she served. Heb. *hāyô lipnê;* cf. 1 Sam 19:7, 28:8.

3. *If only.* The only other occurrence of *ʾaḥălê* is Ps 119:5. Traditionally parsed as a plural noun in construct from *ḥillô* "to entreat," it is now known from Ugaritic *ʾḥl.* See U. Cassuto, *Biblical and Oriental Studies* 2.197 and M. Dahood, *Psalms III,* AB, *ad loc.*

he would cure him. Heb. *yeʾĕsōp,* "he will gather" describes the readmission of the suspected leper into society after his quarantine; cf. Num 12:14–15 (so Qimḥi, Ehrlich). The suggestion of Montgomery-Gehman, uncritically repeated by Gray, to equate Heb. *ʾāsôp* with Akk. **ašapu,* "to exorcise," is wrong. Such a verb does not exist in Akkadian. The noun *āšipu,* "exorcist," (see *CAD* A 2.431–35) is attested in Dan 1:20, 2:2, along with other practitioners of magic. For a full introductory study of magical-Experts and physicians in Mesopotamian texts, see E. Ritter, *Studies Landsberger, AS* 16 (1965), 299–321.

6. *Now.* Cf 10:2. The transition to the main body of a letter after the salutation is marked in Heb. by *wĕʿattâ;* in Aramaic by *kĕʿenet/kĕʿet,* Ezra 4:10, 17. Extrabiblical examples of this usage are collected by D. Pardee, *Handbook of Ancient Hebrew Letters,* SBL/SBS 15 (1982), 149–50.

7. *"Am I God, to take life or to give life?"* For **ḥyh* in *hiphil* in the sense of to "give life, restore to health, revive," cf. Isa 38:16. The same expression is used in praise of YHWH in Hannah's prayer, 1 Sam 2:6; but there the verb is in *piel*—cf. Deut 32:39, Hos 6:2.

he is picking a quarrel with me. Lit. "seek an occasion." Heb. *mitʾanneh* occurs only here in *hithpael;* cf. Judg 14:4, where the idea of "seeking a pretext" is expressed through the noun *tōʾănâ* of the same root.

9. *waited . . . for Elisha.* For Heb. *ʿāmôd lĕ-,* "to stand waiting," see 1 Kgs 20:38. (The present verse is misconstrued in all modern translations.)

10. *and that you may be clean.* For the use of the imperative, sometimes in place of a jussive, to give added force to the preceding verb, see Driver, *Tenses,* 65; cf. 1 Kgs 1:12 and Gen 12:2 (the revocalization of the verb there by Speiser, *Genesis,* AB, *ad loc.* is unnecessary).

11. *he would surely come out.* The infinitive absolute after the verb (*yṣʾ yṣwʾ*) intensifies the idea of the verb, as it does when placed before the verb; cf. *GKC* 113r and Josh 24:10.

wave his hand over the spot. The expected rite of exorcism included a gesture of some sort over the affected area; for the use of *māqôm* as "place, site" of the boil, see Lev 13:19. *Māqôm* is not "ambiguous" (so, Gray, following Šanda, Kittel); its referent can hardly be the place of the sanctuary or YHWH himself (cf. Gersonides).

12. *the Abana and the Pharpar, the rivers of Damascus.* For ketib *Abana,* qere and Targum have *Amanah,* which is the form of the toponym in Cant 4:8 and all extrabiblical references. Thus it is hard to take Amanah as an example of dissimilation, as e.g. *dybwn* > *dynwn,* Isa 15:2, 9; G. Bergsträsser, *Hebräische Grammatik* 20c, *c* considers the form a "mistake." The mountain height Amanah gave its name to the river which descends from the Anti-Lebanon range and waters the plain of Damascus, today known as the Baradā. The river el-Auwaj, which is south of the city, may be the Pharpar. (The ancient name may still be preserved in wadi Barbar, a stream/canal near the village of Dareiya, south of Damascus. See R. Dussaud, *Topographie historique de la Syrie antique et médiévale* [Paris: Geuthner, 1927], 313, n. 13.) According to cuneiform sources, cedar and alabaster were brought from Mt. Amanah (Akk.

Ammananu) to adorn the royal palaces and temples of Assyria and Babylonia (see M. Cogan, *IEJ* 34 [1984], 255–59).

13. *Sir.* Lit. "my father." This is a most irregular form of address for a servant to his master. One expects *ʾădōnî,* "my lord," as e.g. 6:15; cf. too Gen 44:5, Num 11:28, 2 Sam 9:11. But *ʾābî,* "my father," is attested in Luc. and most versions; LXX adds *ʾim,* "if," which is syntactically required. If MT is retained, the informal address may convey the personal concern of Naaman's attendants for their lord. But an opening with *bî,* "please," would be more in place—cf. Gen 43:20, 1 Sam 1:26, 1 Kgs 3:26; and see Montgomery-Gehman.

14. *So he went down and dipped himself in the Jordan.* A fifth-century Byzantine tradition preserved on a pavement inscription at Hammat Gader in the Yarmuk Valley associates Elijah rather than Elisha with healing the lepers who bathed there at the hot springs. See J. Green and Y. Tsafrir, *IEJ* 32 (1982), 84, 88.

15. *please accept a gift.* For Heb. *bĕrākâ,* "blessing," in the sense of "present," so called for "the feelings of good will of which it is the expression" (with Driver, *Samuel* ad 25:27); cf. Gen 33:11, Josh 15:19, Judg 1:15, 1 Sam 30:26, and see note to 2 Kgs 18:31.

18. Most commentators have noted the repetition of the phrases "in this thing" and "to bow down"; they have excised one or the other, considering them "a misplaced gloss" (Stade) or "clumsy" (Montgomery-Gehman). But the wordiness of Naaman's statement reflects his halting speech, as he apologizes for his continued worship of the god Rimmon, a custom which he perceives to be offensive to Israel's God.

the House of Rimmon. The god Rimmon appears in Akkadian transcriptions as *ᵈRamman* and in the name of the Aramaean dynast Tabrimmon in 1 Kgs 15:18. It is an appellative of Hadad, the god of storm and thunder, and derives from the root **rmm,* "to thunder"; cf. the identification in Zech 12:15. The present verse is the single instance in which the cult of Rimmon is referred to. J. C. Greenfield surveys the material in "The Aramaean God Rammōn/Rimmōn," *IEJ* 26 (1976), 195–98.

19. *"Go in peace."* Note the laconic answer of the prophet—just two words—as compared with the rambling remarks of Naaman (vv. 15–18). Elisha maintains the distance he established at the outset (v. 10) and refrains from commenting, even in victory, upon Naaman's conversion.

a short distance. Heb. *kibrat ʾereṣ* is of uncertain etymology; cf. Gen 35:16, 48:7, where LXX has *hippodromos* perhaps "as far as a horse can gallop." Rabbinic commentators, for the most part, took the *kaph* as prepositional and posited a noun *bā/ĕrâ* meaning "a measure of distance" (cf. Ibn Ezra, Nachmanides). The *kbrt,* which appears in Phoenician and is related to Akk. *kibru/kibrātu* or "regions" (see *CAD* K 331–33), is sometimes cited as a comparable term. Cf. Burney and *KAI* 19, note to line 1. Tur-Sinai's suggestion to derive *kibrat ʾereṣ* from Akk. *bēru,* "mile," a measure of length; "double hour" (*CAD* B 208–11) is enticing, especially in light of the expression *bēr qaqqari,* "a mile of land," the exact equivalent of our term. See N. H. Tur-Sinai, *Tarbiz* 20 (1956), 2–3; idem, *EncMiqr* 4. 11–12.

20. *I will run after him.* For *kî ʾim* expressing certitude, cf. Judg 15:7, Jer 51:4, and see Driver, *Tenses,* 139, n. 1.

21. *he climbed down from his chariot.* Heb. *nāpôl,* "to fall," is properly used for dismounting; cf. Gen 24:64 "from a camel" (so already Ibn Janah). Other verbs used for alighting include *hāpôk* (v. 26) and *ṣānôaḥ* (Judg 1:14; *NEB*'s infelicitous transla-

tion, "she broke wind," is based on a misunderstanding of the Akk. *ṣanāḫu,* "to vomit" [*CAD* Ṣ 96]).

23. *he pressed him.* Heb. *wayyiprōṣ,* usually "he broke/burst forth." But the root **prṣ* often appears when **pṣr* in *hiphil* is expected; it is a case of metathesis of the sibilant and the sonant and need not be emended (as do Burney, Šanda, and Gray); cf. 1 Sam 28:23; 2 Sam 13:25, 27. Nor should the word be omitted altogether because it is lacking in LXX^B (as Stade and *BH³*).

he tied up . . . in two bags. Heb. *wayyāṣar . . . bišnê ḥărīṭîm. Ḥărîṭ* appears again in Isa 3·22 in a list of woman's apparel and seems to signify an item made of a large piece of cloth. In Exod 32:4, the same terms describe Aaron's activity in collecting gold for the calf: "he tied it in a bag" (*ḥereṭ*); so with Luzzatto, *ad loc.;* and *NJPS,* note to the verse; cf. Judg 8:25 (using the parallel *śimlâ*). For "tying" (from **ṣwr* and **ṣrr*) money, cf. Deut 14:25.

24. *the citadel.* Heb. *ʿōpel* is a topographic term describing the elevated part of a city; the verb *haʿăpîl,* "to ascend recklessly" (Num 14:44), may derive from the same root. An *ʿōpel* is attested for Samaria (v. 24), Dibon (Moabite Stone: lines 21, 22) and Jerusalem (Isa 32:14; Mic 4:8; Neh 3:26–27; 2 Chr 27:3, 33:14), where frequent reference is made to the strengthening of its defenses. Josephus referred to the *Ophlas* of Jerusalem, the area south of the Temple mount in the direction of the lower city (*Wars* v. 145, 254), an identification which suits pre-exilic traditions. The most recent archaeological finds concerning the Ophel of Jerusalem are treated by Y. Shiloh, *Qedem* 19 (1984), 27, who defines Ophel as "an urban architectural term denoting the outstanding site of the citadel or acropolis."

25. *Where from?* Qere *mēʾayin* for ketib *mēʾān;* for other examples of the contracted form of the adverb, cf. 1 Sam 10:14, Job 8:2. (1 Sam 27:10 *ʾal* is better read as *ʾel mî* rather than *ʾān* [so BDB 39a]; cf. P. K. McCarter, *1 Samuel,* AB, ad loc.)

26. *Was I not there in spirit . . . ?"* Understood as if *lōʾ* included the interrogative particle; cf. GKC 150a.

Is this a time to accept . . . ?" Cf. Hag 1:4 for a similar construction (*haʿēt* + infinitive). Some commentators have perceived a logical difficulty in the second half of the verse: Gehazi had not taken real property; at most it can be argued that he had plans to purchase such (cf. Targum, *NEB, NJPS*). LXX seems to have read MT: "Now you took . . . and took . . ." (*wĕʿattâ* + perfect); but this is hardly superior to MT (Burney). Luc. has a double reading: in addition to *bgdym,* "clothes," it has *bw gnym,* (to get) "with it gardens" (which Montgomery-Gehman consider original).

27. *as leprous as snow.* This image, which appears again in Exod 4:6 and Num 12:10, may refer to the peeling off of dead skin—desquamation—which resembles the flakiness of snow. See E. V. Hulse, "The Nature of Biblical 'Leprosy' and the Use of Alternate Medical Terms in Modern Translations of the Bible," *PEQ* 107 (1975), 87–105.

Comment

The present chapter contains more than just another miracle story in which Elisha is credited with a saving act, in this case the healing of the Aramaean general Naaman of his leprosy. Indeed, the role of the prophet in the cure is minimized: Elisha suggests through an intermediary that Naaman bathe in the Jordan, and the general's disappointment that Elisha did not behave as a true exorcist (v. 11) underscores this point.

The opening verse sets out the theme: Naaman, whose victories over Israel earn him a high position at the court of Damascus, does not recognize that the author of his good fortune is YHWH, the God of Israel. It is through his cure, then, instigated by the prophet, that he is brought to the awareness: "Now I know that there is no God in all the world except in Israel" (v. 15). By forsaking his master's gods and acknowledging the supremacy of YHWH, Naaman, in effect, becomes a "proselyte." Like other foreigners in this early period (e.g., Ruth), he is admitted into the community of the worshippers of YHWH without the requirements of rite of conversion or polemic which were the hallmarks of the post-exilic period.

But while Israel's God is renowned and rules worldwide, worship of him is restricted to the land of Israel proper. YHWH is inaccessible for fugitives and exiles (cf. 1 Sam 26:19; Ps 137:4), for unlike the land of Israel, foreign lands, polluted as they were by idolatry (cf. Josh 22:19; Hos 9:3–5; Amos 7:17), are not suited for cultic worship of YHWH. Naaman's startling request for a load of earth conforms with this notion of the cultic sanctity of the land; von Rad's implied criticism of his "inability to rise to the level of the spiritual"[1] misinterprets pre-exilic thought. Nor should a historical reality in the late eighth-century B.C.E. among Israelite exiles be sought for this story, as does Rofé. He supposes that the plan of Naaman to erect an altar in Damascus gave legitimacy to those Israelites who sought to continue the cult of YHWH in the "impure lands" of their deportation.[2] But it is hard to believe that Naaman's individual solution could serve as a sanction for the thousands in Assyrian exile who would worship YHWH on soil transported all the way from the holy land. The story of Naaman's conversion is rather an expression of "ancient Israelite universalism,"[3] an idea which surfaces frequently in the Elijah-Elisha cycles of stories. Through His prophets, YHWH works abroad and is recognized as the sole God (cf. e.g. 1 Kgs 17:14; 19:15; 2 Kgs 5:1; 8:13). This faith is still landbound and nonmissionizing, signs of a stage which preceded classical prophecy.

Naaman's commitment to his newly won faith in the story's denouement contrasts with the faithless acts of the Israelite king and Gehazi. The king does not consult Elisha even though it was to him that Naaman was recommended; the king, too, must be taught "that there is a prophet in Israel" (v. 8). Gehazi, in his greed, betrays his master; Elisha had refused the reward offered him by Naaman, thus freeing the true prophetic word from personal gain.

[1] von Rad, *Old Testament Theology* 2.31.

[2] Rofé, *Prophetical Stories,* 111–12.

[3] See the persuasive remarks of Kaufmann, *Toledot,* 2.277–79.

Finally, the suggestion to take vv. 20–27 as a secondary development (so Gray) should be rejected. The artful reversal of roles exhibited in the opening and closing verses points to the primary unity of the chapter: the notable foreigner who trusts in the prophet is healed of his leprosy, while the unfaithful attendant trades places with him, afflicted now by this same terrible disease.[4]

[4] For a detailed analysis of the points of contact between the two parts of 2 Kgs 5, see Rofé, *Prophetical Stories,* 108.

IX. THE FLOATING AXHEAD

(6:1–7)

6 1 The sons of the Prophets said to Elisha, "See now, the place
where we meet with you[a] is too cramped for us. 2 Let us go to the
Jordan, and each person will take a beam from there and we will build
ourselves a place to meet in." He said, "Go!" 3 Then one of them said,
"Will you please come with your servants?" He said, "I will come";
4 and so he went with them. When they came to the Jordan, they cut
down trees. 5 As one of them was felling a beam, the ax head[b] fell into
the water. He cried out, "Alas, my master, it was borrowed!" 6 The
man of God said, "Where did it fall?" He showed him the place. Then
he cut off a stick and threw it in there, and he made the ax head[b] float.
7 He said, "Pick it up!" So he reached out and took it.

[a] Lit. "where we sit in front of you."
[b] Lit. "iron."

Notes

6 1. *where we meet with you.* For Heb. *yōšĕbîm lĕpānêkā,* see note to 4:38. The words refer to the cramped quarters in which the Sons of the Prophets gather ("a conventicle"—Montgomery-Gehman) and not to a population explosion which forced the community "to establish a new settlement" (so Skinner, Gray).

Though not "a school house" in the proper sense of the word, the reference in this verse to a specific place of meeting does suggest that during his circuit to the various prophetic communities, Elisha was in the habit of gathering the Sons of the Prophets for instruction and guidance. See the remarks of A. Lemaire, *Les écoles et la formation de la Bible dans l'ancien Israël,* Orbis Biblicus et Orientalis 39 (1981), 36, 50–51.

3. *"Will you please come . . . I will come."* Speiser pointed out that Biblical Hebrew lacks a term indicating the affirmative reply equivalent to "yes"; the answer is formulated by repeating the verb without the interrogative particle. See Speiser, *Genesis,* AB, lxix; cf. Gen 29:6; Exod 2:7; 1 Sam 23:11–12.

4. *they cut down trees.* Heb. *wayyigzĕrû,* appears only here with reference to trees. More frequent is **kārôt,* "to cut"—cf. 1 Kgs 5:20; 6:36; 7:2, 12; 2 Kgs 19:23. The use of the verb here may reflect northern dialectical usage. Note that for *kārôt bĕrît* "to cut/make a treaty" in BH, Aramaic uses *gĕzar ʿadāyaʾ* (*KAI* 222 A7).

5. *a beam.* Heb. *qôrâ,* properly "beam" (Gen 19:8; cf. Neh 3:3, 6), is here used proleptically (cf. Stade); consequently the clause need not be rewritten (as does Burney).

the ax head fell into the water. If *w'ṭ,* the *nota accusativi,* which is used before the subject, is not an error (so Šanda, Montgomery-Gehman), it may introduce the second subject in an emphatic manner, as, e.g., Jer 36:22; Ezek 17:21; Neh 9:19, 34 (cf. *GKC* 117m, where our verse, however, is considered corrupt).

6. *he cut off a stick.* The sense of the noun *qeṣeb,* "an item cut to shape and size," in 1 Kgs 6:25, 7:37 suits the present context. Otherwise, **qāṣôb* is better attested in Mishnaic Hebrew (see Jastrow, *Dictionary,* 1404).

he made the ax head float. The verb *wyṣp* was read as *qal* in all versions (adopted by Gray); but MT vocalization as *hiphil* is preferable (cf. Stade, Montgomery-Gehman).

Comment

The recovery of a sunken ax head is recorded immediately following the story of Naaman because of the associative link created by their common reference to the Jordan. It is as if the storyteller had said, "Here is another tale about Elisha and the River Jordan." Most commentators either pass over these verses without particular notice or attempt to explain Elisha's actions in rationalizing terms. Gray, for example, speaks of the "prophet's sagacity" in probing the muddy waters with a long pole until he pushed the object to within the man's reach. Qimḥi's comment is recommended for its attention to the operation of the miracle:

> Why didn't he throw the wooden handle of the ax there to begin with? Why did he have to cut a piece of wood to size? It is apparent that miracles are performed by (the use) of new devices; cf. the new flask (2:20). He cut the stick so that it would be like the handle of the ax that had fallen, and so the stick would enter the eye of the ax. When the handle entered it, the ax head floated together with its handle. . . .

X. ELISHA AT DOTHAN: THE SEEING AND THE BLIND

(6:8–23)

6 8 Now the king of Aram was at war with Israel. Once he took counsel with his servants, "Attack[a] at such and such a place." 9 But the man of God sent to the king of Israel, "Be careful not to pass by that place, for the Aramaeans attack there." 10 So the king of Israel sent to the place of which the man of God had told him; he would warn it and would be on guard there, more than once or twice. 11 This matter infuriated the king of Aram, so he called his servants and said to them, "Won't you tell me who among us is supporting the king of Israel?" 12 One of his servants said, "No, my lord king, it is Elisha, the prophet in Israel who tells the king of Israel the words you speak in your bedroom." 13 He said, "Go and find out where[b] he is and I will send to seize him." It was reported to him, "He is in Dothan." 14 So he sent there horses and chariots, a strong force; they came at night and surrounded the city.

15 The servant of the man of God went out early and lo, a force with horses and chariots was all around the city. His attendant said to him, "Alas, master, what shall we do?" 16 He said, "Fear not! There are more on our side than with them." 17 Then Elisha prayed and said, "YHWH, open his eyes and let him see." YHWH opened the eyes of the attendant, and he saw the hill filled with fiery horses and chariots all around Elisha.

18 When (the Aramaeans) came against him, Elisha prayed to YHWH and said, "Please strike this people with a blinding light"; and he struck them with a blinding light in accordance with the word of Elisha. 19 Then Elisha said to them, "This is not the road and this is not the city. Follow me and I will lead you to the man you are looking for." He led them to Samaria. 20 When they entered Samaria, Elisha said, "YHWH, open the eyes of these men and let them see." YHWH

[a] Read *tinḥātû,* conjecture; see note.
[b] MT *ʾēkô;* some mss. *ʾēpô.*

opened their eyes, and they saw that they were inside Samaria. 21 The
king of Israel said to Elisha when he saw them, "Shall I strike (them)
down[c], father?" 22 He said, "Do not strike! Are these ones whom you
have captured with your sword and bow, that you would strike (them)
down? Set food and water before them, and let them eat and drink and
then go back to their master." 23 So he set a lavish feast for them; and
they ate and drank. Then he sent them off and they went back to their
master. And the Aramaean bands no longer raided the land of Israel.

[c] Read: *hhkh ʾkh* for MT *hʾkh ʾkh.*

Notes

6 8. *he took counsel with his servants.* **Yāʿôṣ* in *niphal* is used with the prepositions *ʾet* (1 Kgs 12:6), *ʿim* (1 Chr 13:1) and *ʾel* (2 Chr 20:21), all with the same meaning, "take counsel with, seek advice of." Ehrlich interpreted *yāʿôṣ ʾel* specifically as "let someone know of plans."

Attack. MT *taḥănōtî,* though traditionally associated with the verb **ḥnh* "to camp," thus "encampment" (Qimḥi, Ibn-Janah; GB), remains problematic. From the comment in v. 12 that the prophet overhears the very words the king says in his private quarters, the verbs in vv. 8 and 9 should be parsed from identical roots. Thus *nĕḥittîm* in v. 9 (or perhaps *nōḥătîm* with Joüon, *Mélanges St. Joseph Beyrouth,* 5 [1912], 477–78) suggests reading *tinḥătû* in our verse. **Nḥt* in Jer 2:13, Joel 4:11 appears in the context of military "descent" (and so Montgomery-Gehman and H. Yalon, *Studies,* 7–11). For older emendations, based for the most part on the rendering of LXX, see Stade and *BDB* 334b.

such and such. pĕlōnî ʾalmōnî (also 1 Sam 21:3; Ruth 4:1) is read in Luc. *phelmouni,* the same contraction as in Dan 8:13—*palmōnî.* It is an indefinite pronoun of unknown derivation—Montgomery, *Daniel,* ICC, 344; and *BDB* 811, s.v. **plh.*

By using this pronoun, the narrator avoids naming the place and may be "abstracting, or generalizing, certain specific facts." The hearer/reader does not need to know the name of the ambush site; besides there was more than one such attack. (The poetic device employed here is sensitively described by A. Berlin, *Poetics and Interpretation of Biblical Narrative* [Sheffield: Almond Press, 1983], 99–101).

10. *he would warn it and would be on guard there.* For the use of *waw* with perfect in frequentative sense, see Driver, *Tenses* 114a.

11. *This matter infuriated the king of Aram.* A unique expression describing the king's "storming about." An agitated spirit is also expressed *wattippāʿēm rûaḥ* (Gen 41:8; Dan 2:3).

who among us . . . Mî miššellānû, for the expected *mî mēʾăšer lānû,* (cf v. 16) is a contraction common in Late Biblical Hebrew and in the northern dialect throughout; see *BDB* 979–80; Burney, 208.

The emendations listed in *BH*[3] (so, already Stade) do not recommend themselves (*mglnw,* "reveals us"; *mlšnnw,* "slanders us"), save perhaps *mklnw,* "of all of us" (cf. 9:5; Ewald, *Lehrbuch*[5], 348, n. 1), for the text as given is construable. On the development of the independent relative pronoun *šel,* cf. Cant 1:6, 8:12. See H. Yalon, *Introduction to the Vocalization of the Mishna* (Jerusalem: Dvir, 1964), 26–27; E. Y. Kutscher, *Leš* 26 (1962), 10–11.

13. *where he is.* The reading *ʾēpô* for MT *ʾēkô* is probably a scribal correction, from a dialectical form of standard BH; Haupt suggested vocalizing *ʾēkâ* on the basis of Cant 1:7.

Dothan. The name is transcribed in LXX as Dothaeim, as in Gen 37:17 (MT *dtyn*); cf. Jdt 4:6, 7:3. The *-an/ain* suffix in toponyms, of uncertain meaning, is treated by Tadmor, *JCS* 12 (1958), 40. The identification of the ancient site with Tell Dothan, 22 km north of Nablus, was known to Eusebius and was recorded by Eshtori-hapharhi. Dothan sat astride the western branch of the N–S mountain road, which entered the Jezreel Plain south of Taanach. For a summary of excavation finds from the site, see *EAEHL* 1.337–39; see, too, Aharoni, *Land of the Bible²,* 51–52 and the note to 2 Kgs 9:27. (It is not identical with Dutin in the list of Thutmose III; see Aḥituv, *Canaanite Toponyms,* 90.)

14. *surrounded the city.* Heb. *hāqîp ʿal* is parallel to *sābôb* in Ps 17:9–11, 88:18; note the use of the second verb in v. 15 (translated as "all around"), which creates a poetic touch in a prose text. Cf. too 2 Kgs 11:8.

15. *The servant of the man of God . . . His attendant . . .* This repetition of the subject has caused difficulties for modern commentators; most have followed Klostermann and emended the text to read *mmḥrt* for *mšrt,* thus obtaining "the man of God went out early the next day . . ." This, however, is not supported by any of the ancient versions; the sentence is explicable as it stands. Reintroduction of the subject occurs further on; cf. v. 27, "he said"; and v. 28, "the king said." As for the interchange of the subject "servant," *mĕšārēt,* and "attendant," *naʿar,* this is attested in 4:38 and 43.

naʿar is a traditional title known from pre-Israelite Canaan (*nʿrn* in Egyptian transcription; cf. *ANET³,* 256, n. 12) and has been compared to Akk. *ṣuḫāru* in Mari, Alalakh, and to the form *nʿrm* in Ugaritic. The word *naʿar* refers to a man of rank, serving in various capacities: as armsbearer (Judg 9:54; 1 Sam 14:1), steward and estate manager (e.g. 2 Sam 19:18), and personal attendant in nonmilitary contexts (Exod 33:11; 1 Kgs 18:43; Ruth 2:15. Note 2 Sam 13:17, where *naʿărô mĕšārĕtô* appear together, "his attendant who serves him"). For early discussion, see de Vaux, *Ancient Israel,* 125–26; for later considerations, see J. MacDonald, *JNES* 35 (1976), 147–70; idem, *UF* 8 (1976), 27–35; idem, *JAOS* 96 (1976), 57–68. N. Avigad discusses the seals of high-ranking Israelite *naʿar* in *Magnalia Dei* (Garden City, N.Y.; Doubleday, 1976), 294–300.

went out early. Heb. *wayyaškēm* remains etymologically obscure. The lexicons offer a denominative verb in *hiphil* from *šekem,* "shoulder," meaning the loading up of pack animals, usually an early morning activity, hence "to get up early" (*BDB* 1014b; *KB* 970). But as Ehrlich (*Randglossen,* ad Gen 19:2) and E. A. Speiser (*Genesis,* AB, ad loc.) point out, *hškm* is used adverbally, often in coordination with another verb, and conveys the sense of "persistently, diligently," or the like (cf. 2 Kgs 19:35; Jer 7:13, 15; Zeph 3:7); it has nothing to do with "morning" (Heb. *bōqer*). If connected with "shoulder," then it is best understood as "to shoulder a task" (so Speiser, orally, 1962).

16. *Fear not!* The phrase *ʾal tîrāʾ* is the formulaic opening of "salvation" prophecies, familiar from all strata of biblical literature; cf. Gen 15:1, 26:24; Jer 1:8; Isa 41:10;

Lam 3:57. It is attested in the Aramaic Zakur inscription (*ANET³*, 501b; *KAI* 202, line 13: *ʾl tzḥl*) and in Neo-Assyrian prophecies (*la tapallaḫ*). J. C. Greenfield considers the use of this phrase in the ancient Near East in Proceedings of Fifth *WCJS*, 1969, 174–91; and cf. M. Weippert's recent study of the Assyrian material, in *Assyrian Royal Inscriptions: New Horizons* (ed. F. M. Fales, Rome: Istituto per l'Oriente, 1981), 71–115.

17. *the hill . . . all around Elisha.* The sense requires that the hill be the *tell* upon which the city of Dothan stood; the divine contingent served as a protective cordon. The translations in *NEB, NJPS,* and *NAB,* "hills, mountainside," miss the point.

fiery horses and chariots. For this phenomenon, see the note to 2:11.

18. *when (the Aramaeans) came against him.* For *yārôd ʾel,* lit. "come down," in a hostile sense—cf. 1 Sam 17:8; 2 Sam 23:21.

a blinding light. Heb. *sanwērîm,* again in Gen 19:11. A loan word from Akk. *šunwurum,* "to make radiant, to keep (eye) sharp" (*CAD* N 1.217); here an adjective form with elative force. Speiser, *Genesis,* AB, 139–40, distinguishes between ordinary blindness (*ʿwr) and this numinous flash of light which temporarily disables. For the elative in Hebrew, see below to 7:9.

21. *Shall I strike (them) down?* Best read as the infinitive absolute *hkh* with Targ., Syr., and the requirements of syntax (so Burney, Montgomery-Gehman). The cause of this strange form is a scribal slip rather than the "king's excitement" (so Stade).

father. See note to 2:3 and cf. 5:13; here it is used as a term of respect and regard. Note the use of "father" with reference to king (1 Sam 24:11) and priest (Judg 17:10). For the nuance "counsellor," cf. Gen 45:8.

22. *whom you have captured with your sword and bow.* The analogous expression appears in Assyrian royal inscriptions as *nišē ḫubut qašti* "people, prisoners of the bow" (*CAD* Ḫ 216b).

23. *So he set a lavish feast. Wayyikreh kērâ,* a hapax legomenon in Hebrew, appears to be cognate to Akk. *qerītu,* "festival, banquet" (*CAD* Q 240–41), from *qerû,* "to invite." For the *k/q* interchange within Hebrew dialects and between Heb. and Akk., see M. Moreshet and J. Klein, "The Verb *knn* in Mishnaic Hebrew in the Light of Its Akkadian Cognate," *Leš* 40 (1976), 95–116. (The etymological objections of W. von Soden [see *UF* 13 (1981), 162] to this derivation leave *kērâ* unexplained.) The reading suggested by Graetz is based on a manuscript tradition reported in *b. Sand.* 20a (cf. Qimḥi, Ibn-Janah s.v. *brh*) whereby MT to 2 Sam 3:35 *lĕhabrôt,* "to eat," is read *lĕhakrôt.*

no longer raided. Heb. *bôʾ bĕ-* "to raid, plunder" is found again in 13:20 and Judg 6:5.

Comment

The prophet's unique powers are again at stage center in the present story, as in the other stories of the Elisha cycle. Here Elisha shows himself to be the possessor of "second sight." He has the ability to see hidden things: the ambush of the Aramaeans planned in the private quarters of the king of

Aram (vv. 10–12); the fiery cavalry of YHWH (v. 17). At his command, the eyes of his enemies are closed and opened (vv. 18, 20).

The action is set against the background of the Aramaean wars with Israel, but because the storyteller left the kings of Aram and Israel both nameless, a particular historical setting cannot be recovered. The fact that the Aramaean bands reached as far as Dothan need not mean that Israel was at its nadir, unable to prevent such deep penetrations of its territory because of weakened military position (as assumed by Šanda, relying upon 13:1–7). Raids and ambushes across the border are likely to have characterized relations between Damascus and Samaria all through the ninth century.

In the midst of these general hostilities, Elisha stands out as adviser to the king; through his foresight, Israel's army regularly avoids entrapment.[1] When his own life is threatened, he outsmarts the Aramaeans, who have come to take him, and takes them instead on a trip to Samaria. But once there, he does not permit the king to strike his enemy; since the Aramaeans were not royal prisoners, they were to be treated as invited guests and then sent home.

The paradoxical behavior of the man of God has been described as "generous concern for his prisoners" (Montgomery-Gehman), as an act of "clemency" (Gray), and has been pointed to as a refinement of a later age as compared with the deed related in the story of the she-bears (cf. 2:23–24) (Ehrlich). But another dimension is gained when the release of the soldiers is seen as part of the wider theme: the fame of YHWH's prophet beyond the borders of Israel. The Aramaeans are his prisoners, not the king's; they are spared so that they, like Naaman, may spread the word of his greatness. It is small wonder that a subsequent tradition told of Elisha being so handsomely received in Damascus (8:7–9).[2]

The reader is left wondering whether the end of hostilities noted in the closing "the Aramaean bands no longer raided the land of Israel" (v. 23), resulted from an act of reciprocity to his graciousness or from respect for the powers he displayed: with such a prophet on their side, Israel could not be overcome.

[1] Gray deprives Elisha of his prophetic qualities by reconstructing "his organization of an efficient intelligence service, through general mobility and many local contacts" (Gray, 513); but this kind of historicizing is wide of the mark.

[2] The idea that captives are spared so that they may sing the praises of the victorious monarch is a discernible topos in Neo-Assyrian Sargonid inscriptions—e.g., Ashurbanipal concludes his report of the campaign against the Arab chieftan Uaiteʾ: "I had mercy on him and spared his life so that he would proclaim the fame of Ashur, Ishtar and the great gods, my lords." See *CAD* D 46 for collected citations.

XI. A FAMINE IN SAMARIA

(6:24–7:20)

6 24 Some time later, Ben-hadad king of Aram gathered all his troops
and marched and laid siege to Samaria. 25 There was a great famine in
Samaria, for they were besieging it until a donkey's head was (sold) for
eighty (shekels) of silver and a quarter of a *qab* of "dove's dung"[a] was
five (shekels) of silver.
26 Once when the king of Israel was walking on the city wall, a
woman appealed to him, "Help, my lord king!" 27 He said, "No! Let
YHWH help you! From where can I get help for you, from the threshing floor or from the winepress?" 28 Then the king said to her, "What
is the matter?" She said, "This woman said to me, 'Give up your son
so that we may eat him today; and tomorrow we will eat my son.' 29 So
we cooked my son and we ate him. But when I said to her the next
day, 'Give up your son so that we may eat him,' she had hidden her
son." 30 When the king heard the words of the woman, he rent his
clothes; and as he walked along the wall, the people could see that he
was wearing sackcloth underneath. 31 He said, "Thus and more may
God do to me, if the head of Elisha son of Shaphat remains on his
shoulders[b] this day."
32 Now Elisha was sitting in his house and the elders were sitting
with him, when (the king) sent ahead[c] a man. But[d] before the messenger came, he said to the elders, "Do you see, this son of a murderer
has sent to cut off my head. Look, when the messenger comes, close
the door and press him against the door. No doubt the sound of his
master's feet follows him." 33 While he was still talking with them, the
king[e] came down to him and said, "Indeed this evil is from YHWH.
Why should I still have hope in YHWH?"
7 1 Then Elisha said, "Hear the word of YHWH, thus said YHWH,

[a] Ketib *ḥryywnym;* qere *dbywnym.*
[b] Lit. "on him."
[c] Lit. "from his presence."
[d] Read *ûbĕṭerem* with Luc., Vulg., Syr.; *waw* lost through haplography.
[e] Read *hmlk* for MT *hml'k;* cf. 7:18 and note.

'This time tomorrow, a *seah* of choice flour shall be (sold) for a shekel,
and two *seah*s of barley for a shekel at the market price of Samaria.' "
2 The adjutant, upon whom the king[f] leans, answered the man of God,
"Even if YHWH were to make floodgates in the sky, could this come to
pass?" He said, "You shall see it with your own eyes, but you shall not
eat of it."

3 There were four men, lepers, at the entrance to the gate. They said
to one another, "Why are we sitting here until we die? 4 If we say we
will go into the city, there is famine in the city and we shall die there.
And if we sit here, we shall die. Come, let us desert to the Aramaean
camp. If they let us live, we shall live; if they put us to death, we shall
die." 5 They set out at dusk to go to the Aramaean camp; but when
they came to the edge of the Aramaean camp, there was not a person
there. 6 For YHWH[g] had caused the Aramaean army to hear the sound
of chariots (and) the sound[h] of horses, the sound of a great force, so
that they said to one another, "The king of Israel has hired the kings
of the Hittites and the kings of Egypt against us to attack us." 7 They
started to flee at dusk; they abandoned their tents, their horses, and
their asses, the camp as it was, and they fled for their lives.

8 When those lepers came to the edge of the camp, they went into
one tent, and they ate and drank and then carried off silver and gold
and clothing from it, and went and hid them. They came back and
went into another tent; they carried off (things) from it[i] and went and
hid them. 9 Then they said to one another, "We are not doing right.
This day is a day of good tidings and we are keeping silent. If we wait
until morning light, punishment will overtake us. Come, let us go and
inform the palace." 10 They went and called to the gatekeepers[j] and
informed them, "We came to the Aramaean camp, and there was not a
person there nor the sound of anyone, just the horses tied up, and the
asses tied up, and the tents as they were."

11 The gatekeepers called out[k] and it was reported inside the palace.
12 The king got up in the night and said to his servants, "I will tell you
what the Aramaeans have done to us. They know that we are starving,
so they left their camp to hide[l] in the field, thinking, "When they come
out of the city, we will take them alive and then enter the city." 13 One

[f] Read *hmlk* for MT *lmlk,* with mss., versions.
[g] Read *YHWH;* certain mss. insert qere *ʾdny.*
[h] Some mss. read *wĕqôl.*
[i] For MT *mšm,* 6Q Kgs 10–14 reads *mśwʾm;* cf. Luc.
[j] Read *šôʿărê* for MT *šōʿēr.*
[k] Read *wayyiqrĕʾû* with mss.
[l] Read *lhḥbʾ* for MT *lhḥbh,* with mss.

of his servants answered and said, "Let a few[m] of the remaining horses that are still here be taken; (in any case) they are like the many Israelites « »[n] who have already perished, and let us send and find out."

14 They took two chariot teams, and the king sent them after the Aramaean army, with orders[o]: "Go and find out." 15 They followed them as far as the Jordan; and the entire way was filled with clothing and equipment which the Aramaeans had thrown off in their haste[p]. The messengers returned and told the king. 16 Then the people went out and plundered the Aramaean camp. Thus a *seah* of choice flour was (sold) for a shekel and two *seah*s of barley for a shekel, in accordance with the word of YHWH.

17 Now the king had appointed his adjutant, upon whom he leans, in charge of the gate. The people trampled him to death in the gate, just as the man of God had spoken when the king came down to him. 18 For when the man of God spoke to the king, "Two *seah*s of barley shall be (sold) for a shekel and a *seah* of choice flour for a shekel this time tomorrow at the market price of Samaria," 19 the adjutant answered the man of God and said, "Even if YHWH were to make flood gates in the sky, could this[q] come to pass?" He said, "You shall see it with your own eyes, but you shall not eat of it." 20 This is exactly what happened to him. The people trampled him to death in the gate.

[m] Lit. "five."
[n] Omit the dittography in MT, missing in LXX and in some mss.: *ʾšr nšʾrw bh hnm kkl hhmwn yśrʾl.*
[o] Lit. "saying."
[p] Ketib *bhḥpzm;* qere *bḥpzm.*
[q] MT *kdbr;* mss. *hdbr* (cf. v. 2).

Notes

6 24. *Some time later.* A common editorial phrase connecting independent narratives; it carries no chronological significance for the modern reader.

Ben-hadad, king of Aram. A royal title borne by several kings of Aram-Damascus, meaning "the son of (the god) Hadad." At least two, if not three, persons by this name are known: Ben-hadad, contemporary of Baasha (1 Kgs 15:18); Ben-hadad, foe of Ahab (1 Kgs 20:1; he is identical with *ᵐAdad-idri* of Assyrian inscriptions, cf. E. Michel, *WO* 1 [1947], 59, n. 10); and Ben-hadad, son of Hazael (2 Kgs 13:3). Many follow Albright (*BASOR* 87 [1942], 23–29) in identifying the first two as Ben-hadad I, even though the basis for this suggestion—a disputed reading in the Melqart stele (*ANET³,* 655)—has since been abandoned. For discussions of the Melqart stele, see M. F. Unger, *Israel and the Aramaeans of Damascus* (London: J. Clarke, 1957), 56–

61; E. Lipiński, *Studies in Aramaic Inscriptions and Onomastics* (Leuven: Leuven University Press, 1975), 15–19; and the divergent solutions of F. M. Cross, *BASOR* 205 (1972), 36–42, and of A. Lemaire, *Or* 53 (1984), 337–49.

But it is more likely that the Ben-hadad of 1 Kgs 20 is Ben-hadad II (so B. Mazar, *BAR* 2.134–37), who struggled to defend his realm from the attacks of Shalmaneser III for close to a decade (beginning in 853); Israel, under Ahab, may have been his ally during much of this time. Therefore, the king of Aram referred to in our verse is Ben-hadad III who succeeded Hazael (cf. 2 Kgs 8:15; 13:3); only during his reign, the period of Aramaean supremacy at the close of the ninth century, were the circumstances favorable to Damascus for a siege of Samaria as brutal as the one depicted in 2 Kgs 6:24ff. (The suggestion of A. Jepsen [*AfO* 14 (1942), 153–72] and J. M. Miller [*JBL* 85 (1966), 441–54] to assign 1 Kgs 20 and 22 to the reign of Ben-hadad, son of Hazael at the beginning of the eighth century, thus eliminating the synchronism between Ahab and Ben-hadad, is doubtful. See Comment to 1 Kgs 20.)

25. *they were besieging.* Though some mss. read *whnm,* there is no need to emend MT *whnh* (as does Gray). For *hinnê* without subject, cf. vv. 13, 20, and see Driver, *Tenses,* 135 (6).

a donkey's head was (sold) . . . The effectiveness of the Aramaean siege is described in terms of the extremes to which the population of Samaria was brought: buying repulsive items, which were normally discarded, at exorbitant prices. For similar cases reported in classical sources, see Montgomery-Gehman. During the long siege of Babylon by Ashurbanipal, ca. 650 B.C.E., the Babylonians are depicted as reduced to "gnawing leather straps," not to mention cannibalism (Streck, *Assurbanipal,* 36:45) and see further below, note to v. 28.

a quarter of a qab *of "dove's dung."* A *qab,* only here, equals one sixth of a *seah* in dry measure—i.e. 1.2 liters. See *EncMiqr* 4.853; *IDB* 4.83. MT *ḥryywnym* has been corrected by qere to avoid reciting a word felt to be obscene. Cf. too, MT at 2 Kgs 10:27, 18:27; and see the itemization in R. Gordis, *Biblical Text in the Making* (Philadelphia: Dropsie College, 1937), 30, 86. But qere *dbywnym,* from Aramaic *dîbāʾ,* "flux," seems just as unseemly.

Josephus thought that the dung was used for salt (*Antiquities* ix.62); Qimḥi, for fuel due to the lack of firewood. The translations of *NEB* ("locust beans") and *NJPS* ("carob pods") follow the Akkadian evidence: in a lexical list of plants, *ḫalla/zē summāti,* "dove's dung," is defined as *zēr ašāgi* = *ḫarūbu,* "the seed of the (false) carob." This was first recognized by R. Campbell Thompson, *Dictionary of Assyrian Botany* (London, 1949), 186; and independently by A. L. Oppenheim, *JQR* 37 (1946–47), 175–76. See also the extensive treatment by M. Held, *Studies . . . Landsberger, AS* 16 (1965), 395–98.

"Dove's dung" was, then, the popular name of inedible husks. Oppenheim thought that "donkey's head" was another such name.

26. *a woman appealed to him: "Help, my lord king!"* Heb. **ṣāʿōq ʾel* is the legal term of appeal to the king as chief arbiter; see the remarks of Montgomery-Gehman at 8:3. The proceedings follow formal rules of address: "Help, my lord king!" opens the appeal; "what is the matter?" is the king's invitation to state the case—so, too, in the matter of the woman of Tekoa in 2 Sam 14:4–5.

Evidence from seventh-century Assyria and Babylonia show that a subject might appeal indirectly to the king, by a procedure known as "speaking the word of the king" (*abat šarri qabû/zakāru*), in order to obtain royal intervention in what was perceived to be an unjust act by the administration (J. N. Postgate in *Le Palais et la Royauté,* ed. P. Garelli [Paris: Geuthner, 1974] 421–26; cf. idem, *RA* 74 [1980], 180–82).

27. *No! Let YHWH help you!* The word *ʾal* is taken, against the accentuation, as a deprecation; cf. 3:13 and Gen 19:18; Judg 19:23; Ruth 1:13 (so Burney, Montgomery-Gehman). Josephus, Targum, and others understood it as a curse upon the woman who knew that the king was in no position to help her. For *ʾal* with jussive, in a hypothetical sentence, cf. Driver, *Tenses,* 152(3). In either case, the words are the initial, emotional reaction to the anguished cry of the woman. After calming down, the king begins again in v. 28 with the customary response.

28–29. The gruesome story of the woman belongs to the conventional *topoi* of starvation under siege as depicted in biblical and Mesopotamian literature. See, e.g., Deut 28:52–57; Ezek 5:10; Lam 2:20, 4:10; and *ARAB* 2.794; D. J. Wiseman, *Iraq* 20 (1958), lines 448–50 and 547–50; *ANET*³, 105b, lines 31–37.

30. *as he walked.* For MT *ʿbr,* Luc. reads *ʿmd.* Though this reading is adopted by most moderns, it is not immediately clear why "as he stood" "suits the situation better" (Stade). Either term would serve to explain how the people knew that the king was wearing sackcloth.

32. *and the elders were sitting with him.* The members of the prophetic communities were not the only ones who heard the prophet's teachings (see above to 4:38, 6:1); here city elders seek his counsel and no doubt wait for an oracle of deliverance.

this son of a murderer. This phrase has been recognized, since Winckler, as a piece of invective, without any direct reflection on the father (whether Ahab or Jehu). Cf. 1 Sam 20:30. Like Heb. *ben,* "son," so too Akk. *māru,* "son," signifies a member of a group or profession, as in *mār ḫabbātu,* "robber" (*CAD* Ḫ 13).

33. *While he was still talking with them, the king came down to him.* The corrected reading "king" (*mlk*) for MT "messenger" (*mlʾk*) is confirmed by the repeated description of the scene in Elisha's house in 7:18. The conversation which follows, moreover, shows that the visitor was none other than the king himself. But his appearance is as startling to the reader as it must have been to Elisha who had expected the king's henchman to arrive first (v. 32). Since Wellhausen, it has been customary to eliminate the reference to the messenger altogether and assume that the present state of the text results from scribal misunderstandings and successive additions (Wellhausen, *Composition*³, 285, n. 1; Stade; Skinner). But such radical surgery is unjustified (cf. Šanda). Elisha clearly knew that the king "had placed a price on his head" and that he himself was accompanying the murderer ("No doubt the sound of his master's feet follows him," v. 32). It is hard to imagine that the order to bar the door suggested by Elisha was to prevent the king from entering; such behavior would not have been appropriate toward a royal personage. The abrupt transition from v. 32 to v. 33 is an example of the apocopated style frequent in biblical narratives (Gunkel). Thus when the king arrives before the messenger, the reader is left to figure out just what happened. Josephus offers as reasonable a reconstruction as any:

> "But you," (Elisha) said, "when the man arrives who has been given this order, be on guard as he is about to enter, and press him back against the door and hold him there, for the king will follow him and come to me, having changed his mind." So, when the man came who had been sent by the king to make away with Elisha, they did as he had ordered. But Joram, repenting of his wrath against the

prophet and fearing that the man who had been ordered to kill him might already be doing so, hastened to prevent the murder and even save the prophet.

(*Antiquities* ix. 69–70)

Why should I still have hope in YHWH? For *yḥl l-, expressing hope in divine help, cf. Ps 42:6, 12; 43:5; 130:5; Lam 3:21, 24. The king has resigned himself to the worst, refusing even to pray (cf. Targum) for possible deliverance.

7 **1.** *a* seah *of choice flour shall be (sold) for a shekel . . .* A *seah* in Israel during the age of the monarchy was approximately 7.3 liters; this estimate is based upon the measured volume of the storage jars excavated at several sites; see E. Stern, *EncMiqr* 4.854–55; *IBD* 4.834–35.

the market price of Samaria. The open plaza at the city gate (*šaʿar*) served as the main market place in ancient cities. It was there that most business was transacted (cf. Gen 23:10, 18; 34:20), and legal matters were handled by the elders and judges (e.g. Deut 21:19; 22:15; 25:7; Ruth 4:2, 10). The semantic development attested in MH, in which *šaʿar* means "rate of exchange," is already known in Akk. *bābu / bāb maḫīri*, "gate, market price"; Mesopotamian authorities oversaw the fixing of prices and barter at the city gate and regularly displayed the rates for public use. See B. Landsberger, *VT* Sup 16 (1967), 184, n. 2; and M. Cogan, *EncMiqr* s.v. *šaʿar* 8.231–36. The present verse may be evidence for the meaning "market price" in BH (cf. Ehrlich).

The predicted prices are to be understood as evidence of a break in the famine imposed by the siege. But there are no comparative figures from other biblical texts with which to compare the cost of wheat or barley before and after the siege. In Babylon, in ordinary times, one shekel of silver could buy ten *sûtu* of barley (approximately 100 liters). Under siege conditions, Babylonian documents report that the prices jumped tenfold or even more (orally I. Ephʿal). In the days of Sin-shar-ishkun, a half century later, the cost of food "when the gate of Nippur was closed and the equivalent (of one shekel of silver) was one *sûtu* of barley," parents were forced to sell their children into slavery to keep them alive. (See A. L. Oppenheim, " 'Siege-documents' from Nippur," *Iraq* 17 [1955], 69–89.) Thus if the shekel in Israel was of comparative value, which is still to be proven, Elisha's prediction of abundance was only relative; the cost of choice flour was still many times its normal price. But even that seems to have been taken as a blessing to the siege-weary residents of Samaria.

Finally, for an example of the literary motif of cheap prices resulting from a military victory in Assyrian royal inscriptions, note Ashurbanipal's boasting after his defeat of the Arab tribes: "Camels were bought in my country for less than one shekel of silver on the market price" (*ANET*^{3}, 299b).

2. *the adjutant.* Heb. *šālîš* is of disputed derivation. Besides its obvious connection with *šālōš*, "three," clues have been sought in almost every language of the ancient Near East without consensus. See the comprehensive review of suggestions by B. A. Mastin, *VT* Sup 30 (1979), 125–54; and earlier C. Rabin, *Or* 32 (1963), 133–34. Contextually there is no clear statement as to the function of the *šālîš*. Only Exod 14:7 hints at his possible service in the chariot corps, but Exod 15:4 does not support this interpretation. Nor does the pictorial evidence: Egyptian reliefs of the New Kingdom depict two-man crews on chariots in battle scenes with the Hittites, whose wagons also contain only two men. Only those chariots belonging to Sea Peoples ("Philistines") are manned by a crew of three. By the late eighth century, three-man crews became

standard in Assyria (Yadin, *Art of Warfare,* 104ff.; 298–99). The *šālîš*—in 1 Kgs 9:22; 2 Kgs 7:2, 7, 19; 9:25; 15:25—is an officer, perhaps of "third rank" (so Mastin).

floodgates in the sky. For this image of the damming up of the rain in the heavens, cf. Gen 7:11, 8:2; Mal 3:10.

3. *lepers, at the entrance to the gate.* According to the ritual law in Lev 13, the leper was quarantined outside his settlement (vv. 11, 46; cf. Num 12:14–16). The ouster of the four men here suggests that their affliction was more severe than Naaman's.

4. *Come, let us desert to the Aramaean camp.* Heb. *nāpôl ʾel / ʿal,* well attested in the sense "to desert, defect" (cf. 1 Sam 29:3; 2 Kgs 25:11; Jer 21:9, 37:14, 38:19; 2 Chr 15:9), finds its semantic parallel in Akk. *maqātu,* which also developed the sense "to arrive, fall into some one's hands, flee" (*CAD* M 1.245–46, 255) (Orally, I. Ephʿal).

If they let us live, we shall live; if they put us to death, we shall die. Life and death were in the hands of the victorious king: thus defeated, Aramaean elders came on bended knee and pleaded before Ashurnasirpal, "If it pleases you, kill! If it pleases you, spare! If it pleases you, do what you will!" (Grayson, *ARI* 2.547).

5. *They set out at dusk to go to the Aramaean camp.* Heb. *wayyāqom,* "he arose" when construed with another verb of motion "indicates the start or speed of action" (so Speiser, *Genesis* AB ad 22:3). Cf. v. 7 and 1 Kgs 1:50, 2:40, 11:40, and many times in narrative literature.

6. *For* YHWH *had caused the Aramaean army to hear the sound . . .* Cf. 19:7. Heb. *maḥăneh* like Akk. *karašu* (*CAD* K 210–12), is both the physical "camp" and the "army" which occupies it.

The king of Israel has hired . . . against us . . . The Aramaeans explain their retreat to be the result of Israel's unexpected move in hiring a third party to upset the balance in their favor, a deviation from the accepted rules of war. Cf., similarly, 2 Sam 10:6. Isaiah expresses his objection to the political stance of Ahaz by nicknaming Tiglath-pileser "the hired razor" (Isa 7:20). In the Kilamuwa inscription, the king of Sam'al (Y'DY) boasts of his diplomatic skill in hiring (*śkr*) the Assyrian king against his Danunite enemy at a "bargain" rate (*KAI* 24.7–8; *ANET³,* 500, n. 2; and now, the analysis of "hiring" as an element in royal polemics by F. M. Fales, *WO* 10 [1979], 16–21).

the kings of the Hittites and the kings of the Egyptians. The century-old suggestion of H. Winckler (*Untersuchungen,* 168–74) that *Miṣrayim* here and in 1 Kgs 10:28 refers to Muṣri, a north Syria territory near Que (Cilicia) has gained wide acceptance in biblical scholarship—so e.g. all commentaries as well as *NJPS, NAB* (translating "king of the borderlands"); *NEB* is the only holdout. But this view is untenable. The historical map of the ninth and eighth centuries B.C.E. does not allow positing an independent country by such a name in north Syria or Anatolia. The northern, trans-Tigris Muṣri, adjacent to Assyria, was conquered for the last time and annexed by Ashur-dan II in the late tenth century. After that, all Akkadian references to Muṣri are to Egypt; so, too, *Miṣrayim* in the Hebrew Bible. See H. Tadmor, *IEJ* 11 (1961), 143–50; P. Garelli, *DB* Sup V, 1468–74; idem, *Hommages à Andre Dupont-Sommer* (Paris: Maisonneuve, 1971), 37–48; N. Na'aman, *WO* 9 (1977–78), 225–26. (The identification of *mṣr* in the Sefire treaty remains enigmatic; see Na'aman, loc. cit.) For the plural "kings" of Egypt, as a "rhetorical plural, balancing the two elements, Egypt and the Hittites," see K. A. Kitchen, *Third Intermediate Period,* 326, n. 461. Gunkel's literary approach denies the phrase "any reliable historical recollection"; it is no more than a popular anachronism from past times, when Hittites and Egyptians clashed over rights in Syria and Canaan (mid-second millennium) (Gunkel, *Geschichten von Elisa,* 59).

8. *They carried off (things) from it.* The Qumran manuscript 6Q Kgs 10–14 reads "they carried off their load" (*maśśāʾām;* note the aberrant writings of *ā* with *waw*); so apparently in Luc.

9. *and we are keeping silent.* The verb appears again in 2:3, 5; 1 Kgs 22:3. The *hiphil* of *hāšôh,* "to be silent," is an example of the elative formation in Hebrew, and conveys the sense of "motionless, still," as defined by E. A. Speiser, "The 'Elative' in West-Semitic and Akkadian," *JCS* 6 (1952), 81–92 (repr. in *Oriental and Biblical Studies,* 465–92).

punishment will overtake us. Heb. *ʿāwôn,* both "guilt" and "punishment," is the subject of the verb; for other personifications of evil and hardship with **māṣôʾ* ("to find"), cf. Gen 44:34, Judg 6:13, Ps 116:3, Esth 8:6.

10. *called to the gatekeepers.* For MT *šōʿēr,* LXX reads *šaʿar,* "(into the) gate" (and so also in 2 Sam 18:26). Luc. has a doublet, "into the gate to the princes (*śry*) of the city." But MT "gatekeeper(s)" is required by the subsequent *lāhem,* "to them."

13. The lengthy dittography in MT (see above translation, note *n*) is omitted by modern critics. At the same time, the effect of the major rewriting of the verse by Stade, Burney, and Gray is to produce sentences that are not acceptable as Biblical Hebrew. The least disruptive choice is to recognize the phrase *hnm kkl hmwn* (so with qere) *yśrʾl ʾšr tmw* as parenthetical. It is, nevertheless, somewhat awkward to compare horses to people; the verb **tmm,* "to be finished, consumed, destroyed" (*BDB,* 1070) is used of inanimate objects, but never of animals.

14. *two chariot teams.* So MT. LXX, Josephus, Qimḥi, and many moderns prefer "two riders on horses" (*rōkĕbê*). Burney remarks that it would be more natural for scouts to "be sent on horseback than in chariots." See further in the note to 9:17.

18. Note that in this repetition of the prophet's prediction (cf. v. 1), the elements appear in chiastic order, a feature of narrative literature.

Comment

The siege of Samaria, under historical circumstances left unspecified, serves as the backdrop against which the main theme of this story is acted out: a severe famine in the city is broken in accord with the word of the man of God. As in other stories, Elisha is the possessor of second sight; he knows the course of events prior to their occurrence (cf. vv. 6:32; 7:1). Yet unlike the instances in which he performed some wondrous act in providing food for the hungry (cf. 4:38–44), in Samaria Elisha merely delivers a prophetic announcement in classic fashion: "Thus said YHWH . . ." (7:1).

Famine permeates every scene in this artistically structured story. The teller introduces his theme by reporting the astoundingly high prices being paid for trash items (6:25). In the scene on the city wall, the rigors of famine are shown to have led to cannibalism (6:26–31). At home with the assembled elders as witnesses, Elisha predicts a radical lowering of prices by the morrow (7:1–2). Hunger is also the overriding concern of the lepers who defect to the

Aramaeans (7:4, 8). Before the final scene of rescue, the decimated cavalry comes in for mention (7:13). A stampede for food closes this story of famine and plenty.

All of these many scenes are further united by the narrative device of unity of time; the action takes place within a single day. The walk on the wall by the helpless king (6:27ff.) contrasts with the headlong rush to raid the abandoned enemy camp (7:16–17) just twenty-four hours later. Throughout, the touch of the folk artist is felt in descriptions, often caricatures, that are the stock in trade of the storyteller. So, for example, the outcasts of society bring the good news of rescue; the nonbeliever is punished for his skepticism. This last point is brought home by the reiteration in vv. 18–20.[1] Beyond stressing that the prediction of deliverance by the prophet had been fulfilled, it is the prophet's honor which is defended; punishment awaits the scoffer (cf. Deut 18:19).

The point in history when such a siege could actually have taken place, though thoroughly discussed for over a century, remains an unanswered question. Kuenen was the first to state the obvious: "In the reign of that king [Jehoram], Israel was not in the condition described to us in 2 Kgs 6:24–7:26" [sic! read 20].[2] During Jehoram's short reign (851–842 B.C.E.), Aram-Damascus headed a south Syrian coalition which successfully held off the advance of Shalmaneser III. In 853, Israel, under Ahab, Jehoram's father, sent a large contingent of chariots to fight alongside Adad-idri/Ben-hadad II of Damascus and Irḫuleni of Hamath at Qarqar.[3] It is not out of the question to think that Jehoram, too, was allied with Ben-hadad during the ensuing Assyrian attacks in 849, 848, and 845.[4] Thus a siege of Samaria of the proportions described, in which Israel could hardly muster a few horses for a scouting party, is hard to imagine before the reign of Jehu.

Nor does the reference to the hiring of "the kings of the Hittites and the kings of Egypt" (7:6) aid us in our search for a historical setting. At no point in the first millennium B.C.E. was such an alliance formed against the king of Aram. Egypt never menaced Damascus; nor did the neo-Hittite states. On at least one occasion, Damascus under Ben-hadad III led a group of these north

[1] Because this is the only case of repetition of entire verses in the Elisha cycle, most moderns consider vv. 18–20 secondary expansion, appended by a later editor (so Skinner, Šanda, Eissfeldt, Montgomery-Gehman, Gray, among others). These verses, however, read like the closing of a sermon, a reminder to the audience of the message of the just completed story.

[2] A. Kuenen, *The Prophets and Prophecy in Israel* (London: Longmans and Green, 1877), 396, n. 2. The insertion of the entire block of Elisha stories after the Deuteronomistic notice in 3:1–3 on Jehoram's accession is the immediate cause of the historical misimpression, as Kuenen astutely noted.

[3] See *ANET*[3], 278–79 and the Comment to 1 Kgs 22.

[4] On the breakup of this alliance after the revolt of Hazael in Damascus, a contributing factor to the defeat of Damascus in 841, see the Comment to 2 Kgs 8.

Syrian states against Zakur of Hamath.[5] What is expected in a story of the late ninth century is a reference to Assyria, which raided the West for over sixty years and twice, in 841 and 796, brought Damascus to its knees. It is best, therefore, to understand the reference to Hittites and Egyptians as an old literary image (with Gunkel), of little value for historical purposes.

Finally, the brief biblical chronistic extracts in 10:32–33, 12:18, and 13:7, which record the supremacy of Aram-Damascus in south Syria reaching as far as the Philistian coast, point to the reign of Jehoahaz as the time when a siege of Israel's capital city was most likely.[6]

[5] For a review of the relations between Damascus and the neo-Hittite states, see J. D. Hawkins, *CAH*[3], 3.399–409. For the inscription of Zakur of Hamath, see *ANET*[3], 501–2.

[6] Attempts to pinpoint an exact date for the siege (as advanced by Šanda and accepted by Gray) should be avoided; the evidence is too limited.

XII. THE SHUNAMMITE'S LAND CLAIM

(8:1–6)

8 1 Once Elisha spoke to the woman whose son he had revived, "Up,
go, you and your household, and live wherever you will, for YHWH has
decreed a seven-year famine, and it has already come upon the land."
2 The woman proceeded to act in accordance with the word of the man
of God; she and her household went and lived in the land of the
Philistines for seven years. 3 At the end of the seven years, the woman
returned from the land of the Philistines and she went to appeal to the
king concerning her house and her field. 4 Now the king was talking to
Gehazi, the attendant of the man of God: "Tell me all of the great
deeds that Elisha has performed." 5 And as he was telling the king
how (Elisha) had revived the dead, the woman whose son he had
revived was appealing to the king concerning her house and her field.
Gehazi said, "My lord king, this is the woman and this is her son
whom Elisha revived." 6 The king questioned the woman and she told
him. Then the king assigned a eunuch to her, with orders: "Restore
everything that belongs to her and all the income from her field, from
the day she left the country until now."

Notes

8 1. *"Up, go . . ."* The verb **qûm,* "to arise, get up" is often used in a hendiadys with another verb of motion and indicates the start or speed of action. Cf. e.g., *wayyāqom wayyēlek,* "he started out for . . ." (Gen 22:3); *wayyāqom . . . wayyiśśāʾ* "At once, he lifted . . ." (Gen 31:17).

you and your household. For the dialectal form *ʾty* (ketib) "you," see Comment to 2 Kgs 4.

live wherever you will. Heb. *wĕgûrî baʾ ăšer tāgûrî* is an example of the *idem per idem* idiom, "employed where either the means, or the desire, to be more explicit does not exist." See the discussions by S. R. Driver, *Samuel,* 185–86; idem, *Exodus,* Cam B, 362–63. Other examples: Ex 3:14, 4:13, 16:23, 33:19; Deut 1:46; 1 Sam 23:13; 2 Sam 15:20; Ezek 12:25; Zech 10:8.

YHWH has decreed . . . a famine. Though the use of the preposition *lamed* to introduce the object is a feature of late BH, perhaps under the influence of Aramaic (cf. *GKC* 117n.), in our verse, however, it is dialectal, not "a survival of an earlier substratum of Aramaic" (so Gray; cf. *BDB* 895).

2–3. The Qumran text 6Q Kgs 15, a badly worn fragment upon which the traces of our passage are discernible, has a shorter text than MT:

[2. . . *wtqm h'šh wtlk kdbr*]
[*'yš h'lh*]*y*[*m*] *'l 'rṣ* [*plštym*] *šbʿ šn*[*ym* 3*wtšb h'šh m'rṣ plštym*] [*wtṣ'*]
lṣʿq 'l hmlk 'l byth w'l [*śdh* . . .]

2[. . . and the woman set out and went in accordance with the word] [of the man of God] to the land of the [Philistines] seven yea[rs. 3Then the woman returned from the land of the Philistines] [and she went] to appeal to the king concerning her house and her [field . . .]

At the beginning of v. 3 MT, "at the end of seven years" is missing, probably lost through haplography of the previous words. The reading *lṣʿq* ("to appeal") is almost completely lost. M. Baillet suggested *'*]*l hʿyr,* "to the city" and was followed by Gray; but this makes little sense contextually. See M. Baillet, *Les "Petites Grottes" de Qumran, Discoveries in the Judaean Desert* III (Oxford: Clarendon Press, 1962), 109.

3. *she went to appeal to the king.* See note to 6:26.

4. *the great deeds that Elisha has performed.* The prophet's "great deeds," Heb. *gĕdōlôt,* like those of the Lord, refer to "awesome" and "wonderous" saving acts, cf. Ps 106:21–22.

5. *this is the woman and this is her son.* The presence of the little boy at his mother's side is more than just an artistic touch. He is needed to prove the veracity of Gehazi's story.

6. *eunuch.* On this courtier, see note to 9:32.

income. Heb. *tĕbû'â,* "yield, produce" of the earth, is here secondarily "income"; cf. Isa 23:3.

from the day she left. MT *ʿzbh* is vocalized as *qal* perfect; but it is equally possible to interpret this as *ʿozbāh,* an infinitive with a softening of the *mappiq* marking the pronominal suffix, as observed by Qimḥi; cf. *GKC* 913 (contra. Montgomery-Gehman).

Comment

A sequel to the story of the Shunammite woman in 4:8–37 is presented here; associative literary linking explains its present position after the account of Samaria's rescue (6:24–7:20). In both, Elisha exhibits foreknowledge of future events (cf. 7:1 and 8:1) and the Israelite king acts as chief arbiter of justice in the land (cf. 6:26–30 and 8:5). The man of God continues to aid his patroness from Shunem and warns her of the ensuing famine, and it is his fame which stands her in good stead when she appeals for the return of her lost property.

Of sociological interest is the status of the woman as revealed through her court appeal and the question of land tenure in ancient Israel. There is no way to determine the reason for the loss of the woman's fields. Had they "become crown property" in her absence?[1] Or was the land originally a fief granted by the crown "on the condition that certain services were performed"?[2] On the face of it, however, the story speaks simply of confiscation, "unlawful appropriation,"[3] perhaps even by another family member or a neighbor. The appearance of the woman as plaintiff is in line with her earlier description as being a "wealthy woman" (4:8). The lands were likely hers through inheritance (from a previous marriage?), and it would have been legally proper for her to make claim for their restoration. Conclusions as to her assumed widowhood by all commentators are therefore unjustified.

Beyond the details of the story itself, these few verses offer an unencumbered view of the creative process behind the Elisha cycle. His "great deeds" were retold (v. 4) not only among the Sons of the Prophets, those circles of Elisha's loyal disciples, but also at the court of Samaria (and Damascus, cf. 8:7). The man of God seems to have been a subject of interest to many, and different performers regaled their audiences with stories of his wonders. It was in these settings that the Elisha tradition was first shaped and transmitted.[4]

[1] So Gray; cf. de Vaux, *Ancient Israel,* 124.

[2] See K. H. Henrey, "Land Tenure in the Old Testament," *PEQ* 86 (1954), 10–13; and the examination of scholarly proposals by M. Lahav, "Royal Estates in Israel," in *Sefer Zer-kabod* (Jerusalem: Society for Biblical Research, 1968), 207–45 (Hebrew).

[3] So Skinner; cf. Šanda.

[4] There is no reason to think that 8:1–6 is the "invention" of a later narrator who "spun" his tale on the basis of Elisha's offer in 4:13 (so, Gunkel, 30). On the contrary, the true-to-life atmosphere of these verses speaks for their primacy. Rofé accepts them as "still within the *oral* stage of the *legenda*" but takes 4:8–37 as a "much later phase" in their transmission (*JBL* 89 [1970], 434, n. 27).

XIII. ELISHA AND THE KINGS OF DAMASCUS

(8:7–15)

8 7 Elisha came to Damascus at a time when Ben-hadad the king of
Aram was ill. It was reported to him: "The man of God has arrived
here." 8 The king said to Hazael, "Take a gift with you and go meet
the man of God; inquire of YHWH through him, 'Will I recover from
the illness?' "[a] 9 Hazael went to meet him and took with him a gift of
all the best of Damascus, forty camel loads! He came and stood before
him and said, "Your son Ben-hadad, king of Aram, has sent me to you
to ask,[b] 'Will I recover from this illness?' " 10 Elisha said to him, "Go,
tell him,[c] 'You will surely recover.' But YHWH has shown me that he
will surely die." 11 He kept his face motionless for a long while; then
the man of God wept. 12 Hazael said, "Why does my lord weep?" He
said, "Because I know the harm that you will bring upon the Israelites: you will set their fortresses on fire; you will put their young men
to the sword; you will dash their little ones in pieces and rip open their
pregnant women." 13 Hazael said, "Who is your servant, (but) a dog,
that he should do such a great thing?" Elisha said, "YHWH has shown
me you as king of Aram." 14 He left Elisha and returned to his lord,
who said to him, "What did Elisha say to you?" He said, "He said to
me, 'You will surely recover.' " 15 The next day, he took a cloth and
dipped it in water; he spread it over his face and he died. So Hazael
succeeded him.

[a] LXX, Syr., Targ. read "my illness"; see 1:2.
[b] Lit. "saying."
[c] Read with qere, versions and mss. *lō;* ketib *lōʾ*.

Notes

8 8. *Hazael.* The name of the future king of Damascus (see v. 15 and Comment) is written *plene ḥzhʾl* in vv. 8, 13, 15, 29 (and 2 Chr 22:6). In all other instances in MT it is written *ḥzʾl,* as it is in Aramaic inscriptions (cf. *KAI* 202 A 4, 232). For other cases

of such spellings in personal names, cf. *ʿśhʾl* (2 Sam 2:19), *pdhṣwr* (Num 1:10), *pdhʾl* (Num 34:28). Hazael (*Ḫa-za-ilu*) is first mentioned in inscriptions from 841 B.C.E., the eighteenth year of Shalmaneser III (*ARAB* 1. 672; *ANET*³, 280a). On a large basalt statue of Shalmaneser, Hazael's seizure of power in Damascus is hinted at by the use of the belittling Akkadian epithet, said of usurpers, "Hazael, son of a nobody" (*mār la mammana*); cf. E. Michel, *WO* 2 (1954), 60, n. 15.

" 'Will I recover from this illness?' " The same wording makes up the oracle sought by Ahaziah from Baal-zebub in 1:2. But unlike that case in which the Israelite king bypassed Elijah in favor of an oracle at an idolatrous shrine, in the present instance the foreign monarch sought out the man of God. A striking contrast, which might be more than just fortuitous.

9. *of all the best of Damascus.* Taking *wĕkol* as *waw*-explicative (with B. A. Mastin, "*Waw explicativum* in 2 Kings viii 9," *VT* 34 [1984], 353–55).

forty camel loads! This extravagant gift, worthy of royalty, can only be the product of the storyteller's fancy (cf. Qimḥi). Compare the more modest donation given to Ahijah by Jeroboam's wife in 1 Kgs 14:3.

Your son, Ben-hadad. This address is in line with courtly etiquette. As "son" of the man of God, Ben-hadad put himself in the hands of a superior upon whom he was dependent.

10. *"Go, tell him, 'You will surely recover.' "* The qere *lô* ("him") is attested in all versions. The ketib *lōʾ*, taken together with the following verb, "you will not recover," is a glaring case of late scribal alteration of MT which sought to avoid implicating Elisha in a falsehood. To suggest that Hazael is the subject of the first clause and Ben-hadad that of the second—"you will live, but he will die" (recently C. J. Labuschagne, *ZAW* 77 [1965], 327–28; so too, Rashi)—bears the same apologetic stamp as the ketib. The storyteller had no difficulty with a man of God involved in international political affairs, sometimes dealing underhandedly. In this, Elisha needs no defending; cf. below 9:1–3.

11. *He kept his face motionless for a long while.* Heb. *heʿĕmîd* ("to set, make stand"), together with *pānîm,* can only mean "to make the face stop, keep motionless, expressionless." LXX reads the verb as *qal*—together with the following *wayyāśem:* "he stood by him and presented (the gifts)" (adopted by Stade). But this rendering of the verb as "to serve, be in attendance" (cf. 1 Kgs 12:6) makes little sense in this context, for the gifts would most naturally have been offered at the beginning of the audience. Targum: *wʾsḥr ʾt ʾpwhy,* "he turned aside," suggests a text tradition which read: *wayyāśem ʾet pānāyw,* very likely a double reading of the first clause, *wayyʿămēd ʾet pānāyw.* For *ʿad bōš,* lit. "until embarrassment," see note to 2:17.

Commentators are divided as to the subject of this clause; though most favor Elisha, it is puzzling to have "the man of God" specified at the end of v. 11 as the one who burst into tears if he was the subject of the preceding verbs. Josephus's exposition of the scene recommends itself: "And while the king's servant (i.e., Hazael) was grieving at what he had heard, Elisha began to cry . . ." (*Antiquities* ix. 90). (Note that Vulg. *et conturbatus est,* "he was appalled" [Heb. *wayyiššōm*]—adopted by Klostermann, Benzinger, Kittel, Šanda, Montgomery-Gehman, Gray—may relfect this same tradition.) Hazael was overcome by the implications of the duplicity suggested by Elisha; his stupor was only broken by the prophet's weeping.

12. *Because I know the harm you will bring upon the Israelites.* The syntax of this clause is a bit awkward; the position of *rāʿâ,* "harm," marks it as an "attribute accusative of limitation" (Joüon, 127b), as is *ṭôbâ,* "good," in 1 Sam 24:19. For an older view, cf. Ewald, *Lehrbuch*[8], §333. In either case there is no need to read with Luc. *ʾattâ,* "you," as do Eissfeldt and Gray.

You will set their fortresses on fire . . . The poetic terms used to describe the rampage of the Aramaean armies are similar to those of Amos 1:3, 13; the dry facts of Israel's defeat at the hands of Hazael are recorded in 2 Kgs 10:32; 13:7.

you will dash their little ones in pieces and rip open their pregnant women. A literary phrase used to impress upon the hearer/reader the horrors of war, especially the attack upon defenseless women and children; cf. Amos 1:13, Hos 14:1, and its editorial use in 2 Kgs 15:16. A single extrabiblical reference to this atrocity is known from a hymn to the middle Assyrian monarch Tiglath-pileser I. See M. Cogan, *JAOS* 103 (1983), 755–57.

13. *your servant, (but) a dog.* LXX has "dead dog," a tradition which links this simile with the other instances in OT; cf. 1 Sam 24:14 and 2 Sam 9:8, 16:9. But as a term of self-disparagement, "dog" alone appears three times in Lachish letters: "Who is thy servant (but) a dog . . . ?" (*my ʿabdk klb*) at 2.4, 5.4, 6.3); see *ANET*[3], 322. For the same use in Akkadian epistolary literature of the Amarna and Sargonid periods, see references in *CAD* K 72.

such a great thing. In Deut 4:32 and 1 Sam 12:16, the expression "great thing" conveys the sense of "exceptional, extraordinary," even "awesome," and this may be the connotation here. It is noteworthy that the story captures the Aramaean point of view in these few words; for an Israelite the violence foretold by Elisha would hardly have been considered a "mighty deed" (so *NJPS*).

15. *he took a cloth.* Heb. *makbēr,* a hapax legomenon, is usually related to the nouns *kābîr* (1 Sam 19:13, 16) and *mikbār* (Exod 27:4; 38:4), all with the root meaning "meshed/netted work." The Aramaic Targum to the present verse and to Judg 4:18 (Heb. *śĕmîkâ*) translates *gûnkāʾ* "bed cover, blanket." Are we to understand Hazael's act as premeditated murder? Josephus offers: "he killed him by suffocation" (*Antiquities* ix.92); and cf. Ewald's fanciful reconstruction of murder in the bath (*The History of Israel* [4th ed., London: Longmans, Green, 1883], 4.93). Or is Hazael described here as merely applying cool compresses to his fevered lord, when Ben-hadad died? Medieval commentators favored the latter view; but this interpretation sounds like an attempt to place the man of God above any suspicion of complicity in the death of the Aramaean king.

Comment

Among the stories telling of Elisha's recognition by Damascene officials (cf. 5:1–18, 6:8–23), it is not surprising to find a report of the visit by the man of God to Damascus, the occasion of a divine inquiry through him concerning the health of King Ben-hadad. What is unexpected is that in addition to predicting the death of the king, Elisha announces that Ben-hadad's messenger, Hazael, would himself become king and would greatly harass Israel (v. 12).

This prophetic message asserts that YHWH controls the destiny of all nations, and in particular of Israel and its neighbor Aram. Through his appointment of Hazael, YHWH has set the stage for the decades of war between Aram-Damascus led by Hazael and Israel, under the House of Jehu (cf. 10:32–33, 12:18, 13:22). It is noteworthy that this prophecy, while accounting for the Aramaean oppression as the will of YHWH, lacks a moralizing judgment, which the reader of Kings has come to expect. The passage 8:10–13 is free of Deuteronomistic accretions and is of a piece with the statements of rescue from Aram attributed to YHWH's mercy (cf. 13:4–5, 23; 14:25–27).

A divergent tradition concerning the appointment of Hazael (and Jehu) is preserved in 1 Kgs 19:15–18. There it is Elijah who is commanded to repair to Damascus to anoint the king, and the explanation is offered that the Aramaean wars are wars of divine chastisement: seven thousand of those who did not bow down to Baal will survive (v. 18). This Elijah tradition represents an independent formulation which has not been harmonized with the Elisha cycle in 2 Kgs 8:7–15, 9:1–10.[1] 1 Kgs 19:15–18 looks like the opening of a story whose continuation is missing; the Elisha story, on the other hand, proceeds without any prior divine instruction.

The seizure of power in Damascus by Hazael is alluded to in contemporary Assyrian inscriptions. From the very first, Shalmaneser III faced unexpected opposition in his bid for hegemony over southern Syria. Adad-idri of Damascus (biblical Ben-hadad[II]) and Irḫulenu of Hamath headed a formidable coalition which met him head on at Qarqar in 853. Together with "the twelve kings of the West (*Ḫatti,* i.e., "the Hittite land") and the seashore," they held off the repeated Assyrian attacks in the years 853, 849, 848, and 845. However, in Shalmaneser's eighteenth year, 841, Hazael of Damascus, "son of a nobody," without the allied support enjoyed by his predecessor, suffered a humiliating rout and retreated to the safety of the walls of Damascus. Hazael's coup d'etat, so colorfully sketched in prophetic tradition, can be dated to the four-year interval of 845–841.[2]

It is still an open question as to how long Israel was partner to the anti-Assyrian league. Admittedly Israel is mentioned as fighting at Qarqar, but only for that battle is a detailed list of participants extant. Accounts of the subsequent battles refer to the Syrian opposition in formulaic terms: Damascus and Hamath . . . "and the twelve kings of the West . . . set out to

[1] Cf. the insightful remarks of O. Eissfeldt in *BZAW* 105 (1967), 52–58; and earlier, Wellhausen, *Composition*[4], 280–81.

[2] For the Assyrian texts, see *ANET*[3], 278–81. The discussion of M. F. Unger, *Israel and the Aramaeans of Damascus* (London: J. Clarke, 1957), 64–76, is still useful. See, too, M. Elat, *IEJ* 25 (1975), 29–32; and J. D. Hawkins, *CAH*[3] 3/1, 392–94.

battle." After Ahab's death in 852, Joram may well have honored his father's alliance with Ben-hadad.[3] With the assassination of Ben-hadad, however, Joram was formally released from all treaty commitments; in these new circumstances, he attacked Ramoth-Gilead.

[3] However one understands the circumstances leading to Ahab's attack on Ramoth-Gilead (see Comment to 1 Kgs 22), its outcome was clearly disastrous for Israel: Ahab was killed and Israel's subservient position vis-à-vis Aram-Damascus confirmed.

HISTORY OF THE DIVIDED MONARCHY RESUMED

XIV. THE REIGN OF JEHORAM (ISRAEL)

(8:16–24)

8 16 In the fifth year of Joram son of Ahab, king of Israel,
« »[a] Jehoram son of Jehoshaphat, king of Judah, became king.
17 He was thirty-two years old when he became king, and he reigned
eight years[b] in Jerusalem. 18 He followed the ways of the kings of
Israel, just as the house of Ahab had done, for Ahab's daughter was
his wife; he did what was displeasing to YHWH. 19 But YHWH was
unwilling to destroy Judah for the sake of David his servant, for he
had promised to give him and his offspring[c] a lamp for all time. 20 In
his days, Edom rebelled against the authority of Judah and set up its
own king. 21 Joram crossed over to Zair with all his chariots. He set
out by night and attacked the Edomites, who had surrounded[d] him
and his chariot officers. But the army fled back to their homes.[e] 22 So
Edom has rebelled against the authority of Judah, until this day. Then
Libnah rebelled at that time. 23 The rest of the history of Joram and all
that he did are indeed recorded in the annals of the kings of Judah.
24 So Joram slept with his ancestors and he was buried with his ancestors in the City of David. Ahaziah his son succeeded him.

[a] MT has the additional *wyhwšpṭ mlk yhwdh,* omitted by some mss. and many codices of LXX.
[b] With qere *šnym* for ketib *šnh.*
[c] Read *wlbnyw* for MT *lbnyw* with many mss.
[d] *hassōbēb* written *hsbyb* with additional *yod.*
[e] Lit. "tents."

Notes

8 16. *Jehoram son of Jehoshaphat, king of Judah.* The verse picks up the Judaean monarchic line last treated in 1 Kgs 22:52. The additional phrase in MT *wyhwšpṭ mlk yhwdh* is a dittograph of the concluding phrase.

17. *he reigned eight years in Jerusalem.* According to the synchronism in 2 Kgs 3:1, Joram of Israel came to the throne in the eighteenth year of Jehoshaphat of Judah. If Jehoshaphat reigned twenty-five years (see 1 Kgs 22:42), Jehoram his son ascended the throne in the eighth year of Joram of Israel. But according to the present verse, Jehoram reigned eight years, down to the twelfth year of Joram (v. 25). This four-year discrepancy is usually accounted for by positing a coregency of Jehoram with his father, Jehoshaphat. (Note that 2 Chr 21:3 may hint at Jehoram's special position at court in his father's lifetime.) For these chronological reckonings in detail, see Thiele, *MNHK*[2], 64–72; Tadmor, *EncMiqr* 4.289–94.

Qimḥi's comment is an example of medieval wrestling with these figures; he suggests that the additional words in v. 16 mark the death of Jehoshaphat and the succession of Jehoram as sole king. Cf., too, Thiele, *MNHK*[2], 181–82.

18. *Ahab's daughter was his wife.* On Athaliah, see note to v. 26.

19. *to give him and his offspring a lamp.* Heb. *nîr* is apparently a bi-form of *nēr*, "candle, lamp" (cf. J. Barth, *Die Nominalbildung in den semitischen Sprache* [repr. Hildesheim: Olms, 1967], § 10b); Ugaritic also has two forms of the noun, *nr / nyr*, cf. *UT* 1644, 1702. Though *nîr* appears again in 1 Kgs 11:36, 15:4, and in 2 Chr 21:7, within the same context as our verse, LXX translates it by three different words; here *luchnos*, "lamp." Targum has *malkû*, "rule," a tradition later repeated by Ibn Janah, who connects it with *nîr*, "yoke." *Nîr* as "yoke" is attested in Aramaic (cf. Targum to Jer 27:2) and in Akkadian, where it frequently describes the imposition of a vassal relationship upon the king's subjects; e.g. *kabtu nīr bēlūtiya ēmissunūti*, "I imposed the heavy yoke of my rule on them"; cf. *CAD* N 2.262–63. But this negative connotation of the term in Akkadian cannot serve as support for the suggestion to take BH *nîr* as "dominion" (so P. D. Hanson, "Song of Heshbon and David's *NÎR*," *HTR* 61 [1968], 297–320). Within prophecies of hope to the Davidic kings at times of crises, *nîr* holds out the promise of a remnant. Thus Noth took *nîr* to be a "new break," comparing Jer 4:3, Hos 10:12 ("Break up the untilled ground," *nîrû lākem nîr*, related to a yoked team of oxen?; [*Laws in the Pentateuch*, 137–38, but later withdrawn in *Könige*, ad 11:36]).

The figure of a "lamp" as a sign of life and hope appears in Abishai's oath to David: "You shall not go with us into battle anymore, lest you extinguish the lamp (*nēr*) of Israel!" (2 Sam 21:17). Contrast, too, the simile "They would quench my last remaining ember" (2 Sam 14:7) and its Akkadian counterpart, PN *ša kinūnšu bilû*, "PN whose brazier has gone out"; *CAD* B 73a; K 394b. Finally, the promise of a "lamp" for David finds its late reflection in Ps 132, in which Deuteronomistic echoes are patent: "I have arranged a lamp (*nēr*) for my anointed one" (v. 17).

and his offspring. It is not necessary to emend *wlbnyw* to *lpnyw*, "before him" (as does Klostermann), for the notion of continuity through "offspring" is found in 1 Kgs 15:4.

20. *In his days.* Heb. *bĕyāmāyw* introduces a quotation from a chronistic source like in 1 Kgs 16:34; 2 Kgs 23:29, 24:1. Cf. too the note to 15:19.

21. *Joram crossed over to Zair.* The toponym is otherwise unattested. LXX transcribes *seiōr;* Luc *siōr*—forms which suggest the town named Zoar at the southern tip of the Dead Sea; cf. Gen 13:10, 19:22. The identity of the two names is further supported by the writing *ṣʿwr* for MT *ṣʿr* in IQ Isa[a] 15:5. (On the late Hebrew *qôtôl/ qĕtôl* noun pattern as represented in the Qumran scrolls, see Kutscher, *Isaiah Scroll,* 109–11.) Joram would have used the road through the Jordan Valley from north Israel to reach Zair/Zoar.

He set out by night . . . The translation is, at best, a guess at rendering MT, which is hopelessly faulty; and because significant help is not forthcoming from the versions, MT is retained. As the verse stands, Joram, the only named antecedent, is reported to have made a night attack against Edom. (On the circumstantial construction, cf. Driver, *Tenses,* 165.) But because of the disjointed syntax, it is not clear whether the "chariot officers" are from Judah or Edom. Nor is it specifically stated whose "army fled back to their homes." The repeated statement of Edom's rebellion in v. 22 suggests that Joram failed to resubjugate Edom; therefore, they were his troops that were put to flight for reasons unspecified. Qimḥi relates, in the name of his father Joseph, that the verse might be reporting a rebellion in the Edomite camp. A similar solution is put forth by Stade; he takes Edom to be the subject of v. 21b, but in so doing has to rewrite the verse substantially. In most cases, an emendation like that suggested by Kittel is adopted by commentators: *wykh ʾdwm* or *wyk ʾtw ʾdwm,* "Edom defeated him" (e.g. Šanda, Gray, *NEB*).

the army. Lit. "the people"; cf. note to 13:7. With the definite article, it can only refer to Judah's forces and not to those of Edom. Note that the ending of this campaign is similar to the one in 2 Kgs 3 against Moab; in both cases the victory is not followed up with the total suppression of the rebellion, but the retreat of the Israelite/ Judaean forces.

22. *Edom has rebelled against the authority of Judah.* This sentence repeats the datum recorded in v. 20. While repetition of this sort is not exampled elsewhere in Kings, in the present instance it frames the fragmentary story of the battle at Zair in v. 21.

until this day. A term which marks an editorial notation of non-etiological character (cf. I. L. Seeligmann, *Zion* 26 [1961], 153–55, who defines these "secondary additions"; see, too, B. S. Childs, *JBL* 82 [1963], 288, 292). The term appears again in 14:7 and 16:6; in all three instances, the subject is Judah-Edomite relations. The editor, Dtr_1, gave expression by use of *until this day* to his special interest in the question of territorial claims in the Negev and the Red Sea coast, at the time of renewed Judahite expansion under Josiah.

Then Libnah rebelled at that time. For "then" as an editorial phrase, see note to 16:5.

Libnah was a Levitical city in the Judaean Shephelah (Josh 21:13); its identification is disputed: Noth placed it at Tell Bornaṭ (cf. A. F. Rainey, *Tel Aviv* 7 [1980], 198); Kallai at Tell Judeideh. See Z. Kallai, *EncMiqr* 4.421–23. Libnah came under attack during Sennacherib's campaign against Judah (2 Kgs 19:8) and Josiah's wife Hamutal hailed from this town (cf. 23:31, 24:18).

This short notice is the only reference to a city breaking with the central monarchic administration; but its historical background is irretrievable. Was this a revolt by the city governor of an important border fort, taking advantage of the army's setback in Edom to advance local interests? Far-reaching raids into Judah by Philistines and Arabs at this juncture are recorded in 2 Chr 21:16–17, with which Bright, *History*³, 242, connects the Libnah revolt.

at that time. Heb. *bāʿēt hāhîʾ,* "at that time" is an editorial phrase which introduces quotations from archival records; cf. 16:6; 18:16; 20:12; 24:10. Its appearance together with *ʾāz,* "then," another such phrase, and at the end of a quotation is unattested elsewhere. Was it meant to mark another historical notice no longer preserved in the text?

Comment

Lengthy selections from prophetic material of northern derivation separate the reign of Jehoshaphat in 1 Kgs 22:41–51 from that of Jehoram his son in the present section. The resumption here of the history of Judah is not strictly warranted by the general chronological scheme of Kings. Only after the demise of Joram son of Ahab should a switch to the southern kingdom have been made. (Joram's accession formula is given in 3:1–3.) But inasmuch as the unusual double murder of the kings of Israel and Judah is related in the Jehu narrative in 9:1–10:28, it was necessary for the editor (Dtr_1) to advance his account of the reigns of Jehoram and Ahaziah (8:25–28) to this point.

The negative evaluation of Jehoram's eight-year reign (851–843 B.C.E.), likening the king's ways to those of the house of Ahab, is followed by the editorial statement that Judah was spared because of YHWH's promise to David to maintain a remnant of his dynasty for all times. This promise is invoked in two other instances of severe cultic infidelity; cf. 1 Kgs 11:36, 15:4. On the role of Queen Athaliah in promoting the apostasy of her husband, see the Comment to 8:25–29.

The two chronistic excerpts in vv. 20–22a and 22b, though laconic in the extreme, offer evidence for Judah's continued decline in the mid-ninth century. Edom successfully revolted—encouraged by Moab's example?—and reestablished a monarchy for the first time since David's conquests (2 Sam 8:2, 12–14; cf. 1 Kgs 11:14–22 and the Comment to 2 Kgs 3:7). An insurrection in the town of Libnah on the border facing Philistia even hints at monarchic instability. On this basis, it is not unreasonable to conclude that Judah's appearance on the side of Israel in foreign wars (2 Kgs 3:7, 8:28) was as much due to imposition by the stronger partner as it was to shared economic and political interests.[1]

[1] There is no support for Bartlett's speculative remark that Israel may have had a hand in Edom's revolt; cf. J. R. Bartlett in *Peoples of Old Testament Times* (ed. D. J. Wiseman, Oxford; Clarendon Press, 1973), 236; idem, "The Rise and the Fall of the Kingdom of Edom," *PEQ* 104 (1972), 30–31.

XV. THE REIGN OF AHAZIAH (ISRAEL)

(8:25–29)

8 25 In the twelfth year of Joram son of Ahab, king of Israel,
Ahaziah son of Jehoram, king of Judah, became king. 26 He was
twenty-two years old when he became king and he reigned one year in
Jerusalem; his mother's name was Athaliah daughter of Omri, king of
Israel. 27 He followed the ways of the House of Ahab and did what was
displeasing to YHWH just like the House of Ahab, for he was a son-in-
law of the house of Ahab. 28 He joined Joram son of Ahab in battle
against Hazael king of Aram at Ramoth-Gilead; but the Aramaeans
defeated Joram.

29 But King Joram had gone back to Jezreel to recover from the
wounds which the Aramaeans had inflicted on him at Ramah in his
battle with Hazael king of Aram; and Ahaziah son of Jehoram king of
Judah had come down to see Joram son of Ahab in Jezreel for he was
ill.

Notes

8 25. This verse is repeated in 9:29, where *eleventh* replaces *twelfth.* Luc., Syr. read *eleventh* in our verse; either the number "eleven" is a correction based on 9:29 (so Kittel) or perhaps MT "twelve" developed from a manuscript which represented the number "eleven" in the Aramaic form *ʿaštê ʿāśār,* as in 2 Kgs 25:2, and was subsequently misread.

26. *Athaliah daughter of Omri.* The genealogy of the queen mother given here is contradicted by v. 18, where she is "Ahab's daughter." The term "daughter," however, can be used for "granddaughter," just as "son" can be used for "grandson"—e.g. Jehu son of Jehoshaphat (grand)son of Nimshi in 2 Kgs 9:2, 14, 20; or Laban son of Bethuel (grand)son of Nahor in Gen 22:22–23, 29:5.

Athaliah was the daughter of Jezebel, and her mother's example goes a long way toward explaining the fostering of foreign cults in Jerusalem. A new proposal to fix the main dates in the life of Athaliah—birth, ca. 880 B.C.E.; marriage to Joram, ca. 865 B.C.E.; seizure of throne, ca. 842/41 B.C.E.—is offered by E. Puech, "Athalie, fille d'Achab et la chronologie des rois d'Israël et de Juda," *Salamanticensis* 28 (1981), 117–36. For an alternate chronology of Athaliah, see H. J. Katzenstein, "Who Were the Parents of Athaliah?" *IEJ* 5 (1955), 194–97.

27. *just like the House of Ahab.* Unlike other cases in which the founder's name is commemorated in the dynastic title—e.g. "House of Saul" (2 Sam 3:1, 9:1), "House of David" (1 Kgs 12:19, 13:2), the title "House of Omri" is unknown in the Bible, being replaced by "House of Ahab" (2 Kgs 9:7–9, 10:10–11, 21:13). This designation was preferred as Ahab and his wife Jezebel became symbols of "the most sinful dynasty even when mentioning Omri and Ahab side by side" (T. Ishida *IEJ* 25 [1975], 135–37). In contrast, Assyrian inscriptions consistently refer to Israel as *Bīt-Ḫumri*, "the House of Omri," on which see below, note to 9:2.

28. *Ramoth-Gilead.* A border city between the Israelite Gilead and the Aramaean-held Bashan, identified by Glueck with Tel-Ramith; see *EncMiqr* 7.378–80; Aharoni, *Land of the Bible*², 441. Ramoth-Gilead was the seat of a provincial governor under Solomon (1 Kgs 4:13) and the scene of the debacle in which Ahab fell (1 Kgs 22). The topographical term *(hā)rāmâ,* "(the) height," is associated with sites in Mt. Ephraim/Benjamin (1 Kgs 15:17), the Galilee (Josh 19:29, 36), and the Negev (Josh 19:8; 1 Sam 30:27); thus the additional "Gilead" distinguishes this Trans-Jordanian height from the others. Luc. transliterates *ramath,* influenced by the form in the singular in v. 29. MT is always punctuated plural.

28–29. These verses repeat, in part verbatim, 9:14-15a, 16b, and are considered secondary by many commentators (e.g. Stade, Šanda, Montgomery-Gehman). It has even been thought that the text is in need of correction: the particle *ʾet* is to be excised; thus Ahaziah is removed from the scene of the battle, leaving him the role of visitor of the sick (so Ewald, Benzinger, Kittel). But there is nothing intrinsically unreasonable in MT as given, and it is supported by all versions. Judah had fought at Israel's side in the first battle of Ramoth-Gilead (1 Kgs 22:4) and in the campaign to Moab (2 Kgs 3). The family ties between Samaria and Jerusalem also help account for the joint attack against Hazael at this juncture.

Comment

Ahaziah's single year as king of Judah (843–842 B.C.E.) is presented by the historian in the same critical mode as the reign of his father Jehoram; in both cases the blame for the king's sinful acts are laid at the feet of Athaliah (vv. 18, 26–27). This Israelite princess proved herself to be cut from the same autocratic mold as her mother, Queen Jezebel, as shown in her seizing the throne in Jerusalem after the murder of her son by Jehu's riders (11:1–3). The editorial evaluation of Athaliah, although certainly suggesting the tendency to hold foreign women responsible for the introduction of foreign cults in Israel and Judah (so e.g. 1 Kgs 11:1–10, 16:31–33; cf. Deut 7:3–4, 17:17a), is supported by the tradition of a full-fledged Baal cult operating in Jerusalem during her reign (2 Kgs 11:18).[1]

The standard Dtr. summary concerning Ahaziah of Judah breaks off after

[1] 2 Kgs 11:18 does not specify Athaliah as the cult's sponsor; Josephus made the connection explicit: ". . . the Temple of Baal, which Othlia (i.e. Athaliah) and her husband Joram had built in contempt of the nation's God" (*Antiquities* ix.154).

v. 28 and is not resumed. Instead of the usual concluding formula on the king's death, burial, and successor, the editor let the following narrative about Jehu's rebellion convey this information in its own fashion (cf. 9:27–28). A literary bridge between the framework and this narrative was created by inserting v. 29, a repeat of 9:15a, 16a, foreshadowing the circumstances under which Ahaziah meets his death.

XVI. REVOLT IN ISRAEL: JEHU'S ACCESSION

(9:1–10:36)

9 1 Now Elisha the prophet summoned one of the Sons of the
Prophets and said to him, "Get yourself ready,[a] and take this flask of
oil with you, and go to Ramoth-Gilead. 2 When you arrive, look for
Jehu son of Jehoshaphat son of Nimshi; go and have him get up from
the rest of his companions and take him into an inner room. 3 Then
take the flask of oil and pour (some) on his head and say, 'Thus said
YHWH, "I anoint you king over Israel." ' Then open the door and flee.
Do not delay." 4 So the attendant, the prophet's attendant, went to
Ramoth-Gilead.
5 When he arrived, there were the army officers sitting (together).
He said, "Commander, I have a message for you!" Jehu said, "For
which one of us?" He said, "For you, commander." 6 He got up and
went inside. (The lad) poured the oil on his head and said to him,
"Thus said YHWH, the God of Israel, 'I anoint you king over the
people of YHWH, over Israel. 7 You shall strike down the house of
Ahab your master; thus will I avenge on Jezebel the blood of my
servants, the prophets, the blood of all the servants of YHWH. 8 All the
House of Ahab shall perish[b] and I will cut off every male belonging to
Ahab, even the restricted and the abandoned in Israel. 9 I shall make
the House of Ahab like the House of Jeroboam son of Nebat and the
House of Baasha son of Ahijah. 10 And as for Jezebel, the dogs shall
devour (her) in the plot at Jezreel, with no one to bury (her).' " Then
he opened the door and fled.
11 Jehu went outside to the servants of his master. They said[c] to him,
"Is all well? Why did this madman come to you?" He said to them,
"You know this man and the way he talks." 12 They said, "A lie! Do
tell us!" He said, "Thus and thus he said, 'Thus said YHWH, "I anoint
you king over Israel." ' " 13 Quickly, each one took his garment and
put it under him on the bare steps; they blew the horn and said, "Jehu

[a] Lit. "gird your loins."
[b] Luc., LXX read *wmyd* for MT *wʾbd;* see note.
[c] Read *wyʾmrw* with versions and many mss.

is king!" 14 Thus Jehu son of Jehoshaphat son of Nimshi formed a conspiracy against Joram.

Joram had been on guard at Ramoth-Gilead, he and all Israel, against Hazael king of Aram. 15 But King Joram had gone back to Jezreel to recover from the wounds which the Aramaeans had inflicted on him in his battle with Hazael king of Aram.

Jehu said, "If this is your wish, let no one leave the town to go and report[d] in Jezreel." 16 Then Jehu mounted up and went to Jezreel—that was where Joram was laid up, and Ahaziah king of Judah had come down to see Joram. 17 The lookout standing on the tower in Jezreel saw Jehu's troop as it was coming; he said, "I see a troop!" Joram said, "Take a rider and send out to meet them and have him ask, 'Is all well?' " 18 The horseman went to meet him and said, "Thus said the king, 'Is all well?' " Jehu said, "What concern is it of yours whether all is well? Fall in behind me!" The lookout reported, "The messenger reached them, but is not coming back." 19 Then he sent a second horseman; when he reached them, he said, "Thus said the king, 'Is all well?' "[e] Jehu said, "What concern is it of yours whether all is well? Fall in behind me!" 20 The lookout reported, "He reached them, but is not coming back. And the driving is like the driving of Jehu son of Nimshi, for he drives like a madman." 21 Joram said, "Hitch up!" They hitched up his chariot, and Joram king of Israel and Ahaziah king of Judah went out, each in his own chariot; they went out to meet Jehu. They met him by the plot of Naboth the Jezreelite. 22 When Joram saw Jehu, he said, "Is all well, Jehu?" He said, "What is this 'Is all well?' while the harlotries of your mother Jezebel and her many sorceries (continue)?" 23 Joram turned his hands and fled, and he said to Ahaziah, "Treason, Ahaziah!" 24 But Jehu drew his bow and hit Joram between the shoulders[f]—the arrow went through his heart—and he collapsed in his chariot. 25 Then (Jehu) said to Bidkar his adjutant, "Take and throw him in the plot of land belonging to Naboth the Jezreelite. Remember how you and I were riding side by side behind Ahab, when YHWH made this pronouncement about him, 26 'I swear, as surely as I saw the blood of Naboth and the blood of his sons last night, by YHWH's word, I will requite you in this very plot, by YHWH's word.' So now, take and throw him in the plot in accordance with the word of YHWH."

[d] Ketib *lgyd;* qere *lhgyd.* See note.
[e] Sebirin, some mss. and versions read: *hšlwm.*
[f] Lit. "the arms."

27 When Ahaziah king of Judah saw (this), he fled by the road to
Beth-haggan. Jehu pursued him and said, "Him, too! Shoot him!"
<They shot him>[g] in his chariot at the ascent of Gur near Ibleam.
He fled to Megiddo and died there. 28 His servants drove him to Jeru-
salem, and they buried him in his own tomb with his ancestors in the
City of David.

29 In the eleventh year of Joram son of Ahab, Ahaziah became king
of Judah.

30 Jehu came to Jezreel. When Jezebel heard (of this), she painted
her eyes with kohl and dressed her hair and she looked out of the
window. 31 Jehu was coming through the gate. She said, "Is all well,
Zimri, his master's killer?" 32 He looked up toward the window and
said, "Who is on my side? Who?" Two or three eunuchs looked out
toward him. 33 He said, "Throw her down!"[h] They threw her down,
and some of her blood spattered on the wall and on the horses; he
trampled her. 34 He went in and ate and drank, and said, "Look after
this cursed one; bury her. After all, she is a princess." 35 They went to
bury her, but they found nothing of her save the skull, the feet, and the
palms of the hands. 36 They returned and reported to him. He said, "It
is the word of YHWH which he spoke through his servant Elijah the
Tishbite, 'Dogs shall devour the flesh of Jezebel in the plot of Jezreel,
37 and the carcass of Jezebel shall be like dung on the field in the plot
of Jezreel, so that no one will be able to say "This is Jezebel." ' "

10 1 Ahab had seventy sons in Samaria. Jehu wrote letters and sent
(them) to Samaria, to the officials of the city[i] and to the elders and to
the guardians (of the sons) of Ahab, thus, 2 "Now, when this letter
reaches you, since your master's sons are with you and you have chariots and horses, a fortified city and weapons, 3 choose the best and most
suitable of your master's sons and place him on his father's throne,
and fight for your master's house." 4 But they were very much frightened and said, "Here two kings could not stand up to him, how can we
stand?" 5 The royal steward and the governor of the city and the elders
and the guardians sent to Jehu, "We are your servants, so whatever
you tell us, we will do. We will not make anyone king. Do whatever
pleases you." 6 He wrote them a letter a second time: "If you are on
my side and will obey me, then take the heads of the men, your master's sons, and come to me at this time tomorrow to Jezreel." Now the

[g] Insert *wykhw;* so apparently LXX, though it omits MT *hkhw.* See note.
[h] Read *šmṭwh* with qere for *šmṭwhw* of ketib; final *waw* dittography.
[i] Read *śry hʿyr wʾl* for MT *śry yzrʿʾl,* with Luc., Vulg.

princes, seventy men, were with the nobles of the city who were rearing them. 7 When the letter reached them, they took the princes and
slaughtered (all) seventy men; they put their heads in baskets and sent
them to him in Jezreel. 8 A messenger came and reported to him,
"They have brought the heads of the princes." He said, "Put them in
two heaps at the entrance of the gate until morning." 9 In the morning,
he went out and stood (there); he said to all the people, "You are
innocent! Here I conspired against my master and killed him, but who
has struck down all of these? 10 Take note, then, that nothing of
YHWH's word which YHWH spoke against the house of Ahab shall go
unfulfilled; for YHWH has done what he promised through his servant
Elijah." 11 Then Jehu struck down all who were left of the House of
Ahab in Jezreel, all his nobles, his intimates, his priests, until he had
left no survivor.

12 He then set out to go to Samaria. On the way, when he was at
Beth-eked of the shepherds, 13 he[j] met the kinsmen of Ahaziah king of
Judah. He said, "Who are you?" They said, "We are the kinsmen of
Ahaziah. We have come down (to inquire) after the welfare of the
princes and the sons of the queen-mother." 14 He said, "Take them
alive!" They took them alive and slaughtered them at the pit in Beth-
eked, forty-two men, and did not leave a single one of them.

15 He went on from there and he met Jehonadab son of Rechab
(coming) to meet him. He greeted him and said to him, "Is your heart
true (to mine), as my heart is to your heart?" Jehonadab said, "It is
indeed." (Jehu said,)[k] "Give (me) your hand." He gave him his hand
and (Jehu) lifted him up into the chariot. 16 He said, "Come with me
and see my zeal for YHWH." So he took him along[l] in his chariot.
17 When he came to Samaria, he struck down all who were left of (the
House of) Ahab in Samaria until he had destroyed it, in accordance
with the word of YHWH, which he spoke to Elijah.

18 Then Jehu assembled all the people and said to them, "Ahab
served Baal a little; Jehu will serve him much! 19 Invite all the prophets
of Baal, all his ministrants, and all his priests to me; let no one be
missing, for I am having a great sacrifice for Baal. Whoever is missing
shall not live!" Jehu was acting craftily in order to destroy the ministrants of Baal. 20 Jehu said, "Convoke a solemn assembly for Baal,"
and so it was proclaimed. 21 Jehu sent (word) throughout all Israel and

[j] Read *whwʾ* for MT *wyhwʾ*; see note.
[k] LXX adds the bracketed words, but see note.
[l] Read *wayyarkēb* for MT *wayyarkibû*.

all the ministrants of Baal came; there was no one who did not come.
They came into the House of Baal, and the House of Baal was filled
from end to end. 22 He said to the man in charge of the wardrobe,
"Issue garments to all the ministrants of Baal." He issued the garments to them. 23 Then Jehu and Jehonadab son of Rechab came to
the House of Baal; he said to the ministrants of Baal, "Check carefully
that there are no servants of YHWH here among you, but only ministrants of Baal alone." 24 Then they went in to offer sacrifices and burnt
offerings. Now Jehu had assigned eighty men outside and had said,
"For any one of the men that I hand over to you who escapes, it shall
be a life for a life." 25 When he finished presenting the burnt offering,
Jehu said to the outrunners and the adjutants, "Come in and strike
them down! Let no one get away!" The outrunners and the adjutants[m]
struck them down with the sword; they left (them) lying (there). Then
they went into the interior of the House of Baal. 26 They brought out
the sacred pillar[n] of the House of Baal and burned it. 27 They tore
down the sacred pillar[o] of Baal and then tore down the House of Baal,
turning it into a latrine[p] until today. 28 Thus Jehu rooted out Baal
from Israel.

29 Yet Jehu did not abandon the sins of Jeroboam son of Nebat, who
caused Israel to sin (with regard to) the golden calves at Bethel[q] and at
Dan. 30 YHWH said to Jehu, "Since you have done well by pleasing me,
carrying out all that I had in mind against the House of Ahab, four
generations of your descendants shall sit on the throne of Israel."
31 But Jehu did not follow carefully the teaching of YHWH, the God of
Israel, with all his heart; he did not stray from the sinful way[r] of
Jeroboam, who caused Israel to sin.

32 In those days, YHWH began to reduce Israel. Hazael struck at
them on all the borders of Israel: 33 from the Jordan on the east, all the
land of the Gilead—the Gadites, the Reubenites, the Manassites—
from Aroer by wadi Arnon, including the Gilead and the Bashan.

34 The rest of the history of Jehu and all that he did and all his
exploits are indeed recorded in the annals of the kings of Israel. 35 So
Jehu slept with his ancestors and was buried in Samaria. Jehoahaz his

[m] Brought up for translation from following clause.
[n] Read *maṣṣĕbat* with versions and several mss., for MT *maṣṣĕbôt*.
[o] So MT; perhaps to be read "altar," see note.
[p] Ketib *mḥrʾwt;* qere *mwṣʾwt;* cf. 18:27 and note.
[q] Read *bbyt ʾl* with mss.
[r] Read *ḥṭʾt* with oriental mss. for MT *ḥṭʾwt*.

son succeeded him. 36 Jehu had reigned over Israel for twenty-eight years in Samaria.

Notes

9 1. *Get yourself ready.* Cf. 4:29.

2. *Jehu son of Jehoshaphat son of Nimshi.* It is unusual for the name of the grandfather to be given in a patronymic. Considering that in v. 20 and 1 Kgs 19:16 only Nimshi is mentioned, it may be that Jehu's grandfather was better known in the community than his father (so e.g. Skinner, Gray), unless the additional generation was included in order to avoid confusion with Jehoshaphat of Judah (so Ehrlich). Gray considers Nimshi to be a clan name.

Jehu's name is recorded on the Black Obelisk of Shalmaneser III as: ᵐ*Ia-ú-a mār* ᵐ*Ḫu-um-ri-i* (*WO* 2 [1954-59], 140, line 8; cf. *ANET³*, 281 and *ANEP²*, 355) and once as ᵐ*Ia-a-ú* (*Sumer* 7 [1951], 12, IV:11), lit. "Jehu, son of Omri"—i.e. of Israel. The designation "son" in Assyrian texts refers to the ancestral founder of a dynastic house and not to the name of an individual's father (cf. J. Brinkman, *Post-Kassite Babylonia*, AnOr 43 [1968], 247). It is not possible that the Assyrian scribes were unaware that Jehu had seized the throne in Samaria. Rather they chose to designate Israel by the term *Ḫumrî* or *bīt Ḫumrî*, after Israel's first successful dynast. This usage continued into the eighth century, until the days of Tiglath-pileser III and Sargon II. P. K. McCarter's recent conjecture (*BASOR* 216 [1974], 5–7) identifying *Iaua* with Jehoram was refuted by M. Weippert (*VT* 28 [1978], 113–18) on phonetic grounds. Weippert explains the name Jehu as representing Hebrew **Yaw-hūʾa*, "It is YHWH!" in which the element **yaw* is most naturally represented in Akkadian transcription as *Ia* on the obelisk. In addition, biblical hypocoristica are formed by dropping the theophoric element; thus in the name Jehoram, only *ram* would have been sustained. Cf. Heb. *Ahaz;* Akk. *Iauḫazi*, i.e. *yĕhôʾāḥāz.*

an inner room. Heb. *ḥeder bĕḥāder*, lit. "room within a room," refers to a remote, private chamber; Josephus conceived of this as being underground. Cf. 1 Kgs 20:30; 22:25.

4. *the prophet's attendant.* This phrase looks very much like a gloss (so e.g. Montgomery-Gehman, Gray), added to expressly mark the young man as one of the Sons of the Prophets. But if so, the gloss is early and all ancient versions struggle to translate it.

5. *When he arrived . . .* The young man presents himself, uninvited, to the council of army officers meeting in the open court of a building at Ramoth-Gilead. He immediately recognizes Jehu, though there is no indication that they had met before.

6. *I anoint you king over the people of* YHWH, *over Israel.* Anointing was a regular feature of the coronation ritual in both the kingdoms of Judah and Israel; cf. e.g. 2 Sam 2:4, 5:3; 1 Kgs 1:34, 39; 2 Kgs 11:12, 23:30. But its mention is limited to those instances in which a dynasty is founded or the succession contested. An attempt to reconstruct the development of this rite from its secular roots to its position of signifying the covenant between God and king is persuasively set out by T. N. D. Mettinger, *King and Messiah*, ConB *OTS* 8, 185–232. Whether unction has affinities to the Hittite ceremony of investiture (so M. Noth, "Office and Vocation in the Old Testament," in

Laws in the Pentateuch, 237–40) or, as seems less likely, to an act performed upon Egyptian vassals (so de Vaux, *Ancient Israel,* 103–6), anointing in Israel by a religious personage was the mark of divine approval of the chosen king and his status as "YHWH's anointed" (*mĕšîaḥ* YHWH). A concise discussion of the use of oil in secular and religious ceremonies in the Ancient Near East is given by K. R. Veenhof in *BiOr* 23 (1966), 308–13, in his review of E. Kutsch, *Salbung als Rechtsakt im Alten Testament und im Alten Orient, BZAW* 87 (1963).

8. *All the House of Ahab shall perish.* Heb. *wĕʾābad* was read by Luc. and LXX as *ûmiyyad,* "from the hand of" (the House of Ahab), continuing v. 7; this reading is preferred by Klostermann, Stade, and *NAB.* But since **ʾbd* is attested in the present narrative (10:19) and in Deuteronomistic literature—cf. Deut 11:17; Josh 23:13, 16—MT can be construed as is.

every male. Lit. "who urinates against the wall." This expression is found again in 1 Kgs 14:10, 16:11, 21:21, and 1 Sam 25:22, 34, and though a vulgarism to Western speakers, it may not have been so originally. The Massoretic tradition represented in qere did, however, soften the reading of **šyn,* "urine," in 2 Kgs 18:27 to *mêmê raglayîm,* "water of the legs." Whether the reference is to every male or just to young children (so J. Lewy, *HUCA* 12–13 [1937–38], 100) must be left open, lacking information on sanitary conditions in ancient towns, as well as on public mores. The Talmudic opinion that the reference is to "a dog" (*b. B.Bat.* 19b), though adopted by some medieval commentators, is excluded by the explication of 1 Kgs 14:10 in 15:29: "he did not spare a single soul belonging to Jeroboam."

the restricted and the abandoned. The variety of current translations of *ʿāṣûr wĕʿāzûb* illustrates scholars' inability to get at the meaning of this old proverbial expression: *NAB:* "neither slave nor freeman"; *NEB:* "whether under protection of family or not"; *NJPS:* "bond or free." Besides the three similar cases in which the phrase appears in a prophecy of extirpation (1 Kgs 14:10, 21:21; 2 Kgs 14:26), its use in Deut 32:36 offers a clue: "When YHWH sees that their strength is gone and that there is no one but the *ʿāṣûr wĕʿāzûb.*" Context suggests that incapable or incapacitated persons are being spoken of here (so Luzzatto ad loc. and Driver, *Deuteronomy,* ICC, 376). Thus *ʿāṣûr* is pass. part. of **ʿṣr,* "restrain, shut up," cf. Jer 36:5; Neh 6:10; *ʿāzûb* pass. part. of **ʿzb,* "leave, abandon." Like *hanniš'ār wĕhannāṣûr* in Ezek 6:12, "the survivor and the imprisoned," the present phrase is an expression of the finality of destruction; the House of Omri will be cut off to the very last person, not even the sick and feeble will escape. Among the recent discussions, see E. Kutsch, *VT* 2 (1952), 57–69; P. Saydon, *VT* 2 (1952), 371–74; M. Held, in *A. A. Neuman Festschrift* (Leiden: Brill, 1962), 283, n. 8; I. N. Vinnikov, in *Hommages à Andre Dupont-Sommer* (Paris Adrien Maisonneuve, 1971), 343–45; H. Yalon, *Studies,* 322–25 (Hebrew).

10. *And as for Jezebel, the dogs shall devour (her) . . .* This curse of nonburial appears initially in 1 Kgs 21:23; it is actualized in 2 Kgs 9:35. Cf., too, 1 Kgs 14:11, 16:4, and the notes there. The spectacle of wild dogs dragging off the carcass of a dead person and scattering his bones on the streets and fields brought horror to the ancients; for the spirit of the dead, deprived of proper burial, was destined to roam about endlessly. The analogous conception is preserved in the curse literature of ancient Mesopotamia, e.g., "May dogs and pigs eat your flesh; may your [spiri]t have no one who cares for the libations" (*ANET*[3], 538); cf., too, in the comprehensive study of D. R. Hillers, *Treaty-Curses and the Old Testament Prophets,* BibOr 16 (Rome: Pontifical Biblical Institute, 1964), 68–69. Note, too, Jeremiah's utterance against

Jehoiakim: "He shall be buried like an ass, dragged about and left unburied beyond the gates of Jerusalem" (Jer 22:19); cf. the remarks of M. Cogan, in *Gratz College Anniversary Volume* (Philadelphia: Gratz College, 1971), 29–34.

in the plot at Jezreel. Cf. vv. 36 and 37. The reference is to the vineyard of Naboth the Jezreelite, which Naboth claimed as an ancestral "inheritance" (*nāḥălâ*), 1 Kgs 21:4. *Ḥēleq,* "share, plot," in our verse recalls the legal term *ḥēleq wĕnāḥălâ,* "inherited share," in Deut 12:12; 14:27, 29; 18:1.

11. *Is all well?* The sudden appearance of a prophet in the camp was fraught with significance and prompted the question of Jehu's comrades: Does he bring a good portent?

this madman. Heb. *mĕšūggaʿ* describes wild, uncontrolled behavior; cf. 1 Sam 21:16 and v. 20 below. It is used disparagingly to refer to the ecstatic, dervishlike behavior in some prophetic circles (Hos 9:7; Jer 29:26; cf. 1 Sam 19:23–24). For a sympathetic description of prophetic pathology, see A. Heschel, *The Prophets* (Philadelphia: Jewish Publication Society, 1962), 390–409.

You know this man. Heb. adds the independent pronoun for emphasis—i.e. "I believe you know . . ."

12. *Thus and thus he said.* The idiom *kāzōʾt wĕkāzōʾt* is shorthand, a way of indicating that the repetition of a preceding speech is being avoided; e.g. 5:4, 2 Sam 17:5, and simply *kāzōʾt* in Judg 8:8. The present verse is the only instance in which a direct quotation follows. Some consider the quoted words "Thus said YHWH . . ." as having been added by a later writer (e.g. Stade), but they are represented in all versions. Montgomery-Gehman thought that there is here some indication of Jehu's initial hesitation. Still the stylistic aberration is discordant.

13. *on the bare steps.* Already in ancient times Heb. *gerem hammaʿălôt* was not understood as shown by the LXX transliteration *garem.* Targum, followed by the medieval commentators, translated "stairs of the sundial" with clear reference to 2 Kgs 20:9–11. Graetz's emendation to read *mĕrôm* is adopted by Gray and *NJPS:* "the top step." But *gerem,* "bone," like its synonym *ʿeṣem,* may mean "substance, self"; thus "the steps themselves" (so Ibn-Janah) or the "bare steps" (Gesenius, Ewald).

The spreading of the garments under the feet of Jehu may be compared to a similar act by the crowd who received Jesus when he entered Jerusalem (Matt 21:8).

they blew the horn and said, "Jehu is king!" These acts were regular features of the ritual of accession. After the sounding of the *šôpār,* the ram's horn, the public acclaimed the new king, and thus indicated its formal recognition and submission to him. The cry on such occasions was *yĕḥî hammelek,* "Let the king live!"—i.e. "Long live the king!" Cf. 1 Sam 10:24; 2 Sam 16:16; 1 Kgs 1:25, 34, 39; 2 Kgs 11:12. A second cry, *mālak* PN or PN *mālak,* "PN is king," is attested here and in 2 Sam 15:10, 1 Kgs 1:11, 13, 18 and, as suggested by B. Halpern, represents the formula used for publication of an accession after the elevation ceremony. Note the use of this formula in the "enthronement psalms," Ps 47:9, 93:1, 96:10, 97:1, 99:1 (B. Halpern, *The Constitution of the Monarchy in Israel,* Harvard Semitic Monographs 25 [Chico, Calif.: Scholars Press, 1981], 134–36); cf. the alternate view of Mettinger, *King and Messiah,* 131–37, for whom the present formula "is a summons to arms" by a usurper. See too de Vaux, *Ancient Israel,* 106.

14b–15a. These words, set off in a separate paragraph, relate information needed by the reader in order to understand the sequence of the ensuing drama; they explain the reason for Joram's layover in Jezreel. This consideration argues for their primacy in

1. Aerial view of the City of David, Jerusalem. *Israel Exploration Society.*

2. Fortification Wall, western hill of Jerusalem. Reign of Hezekiah, end of eighth century B.C.E. *Israel Exploration Society.*

3. The Siloam Tunnel (cf. 2 Kings 20:20).

4. The Siloam Tunnel Inscription (cf. Appendix 1, No. 7).

5. King Uzziah's Tombstone, first century B.C.E. (cf. 2 Kings 15:7).

6. Black Obelisk of Shalmaneser III from Nimrud. *Reproduced by courtesy of the Trustees of the British Museum.*

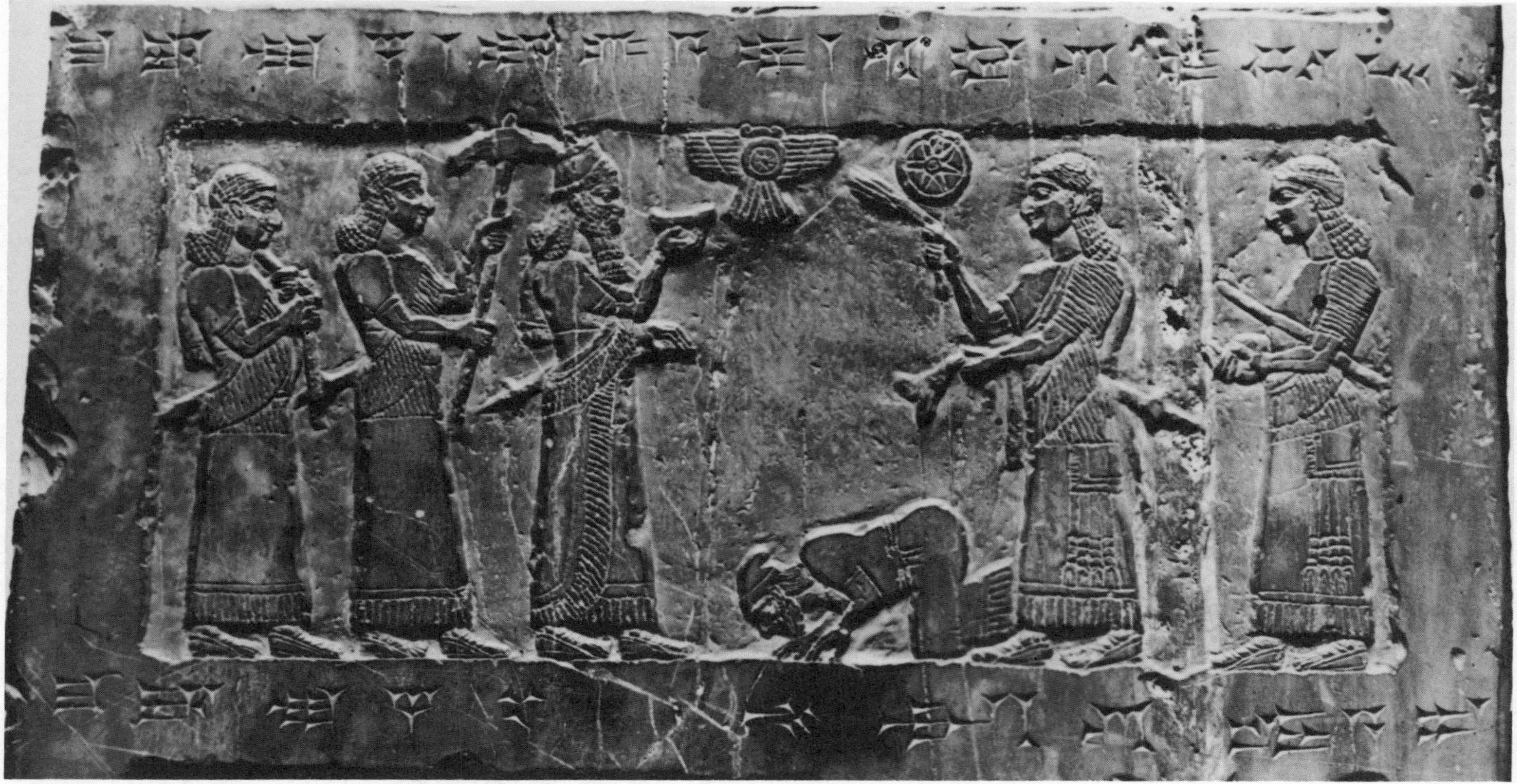

7. Black Obelisk, second register, delivery of tribute of "Jehu, 'son of Omri' " (cf. Appendix 1, No. 2C). *Reproduced by courtesy of the Trustees of the British Museum.*

8. Captives and booty from Ashtaroth on their way to Assyrian exile; Tiglath-pileser III (cf. 2 Kings 15:29). *Reproduced by courtesy of the Trustees of the British Museum.*

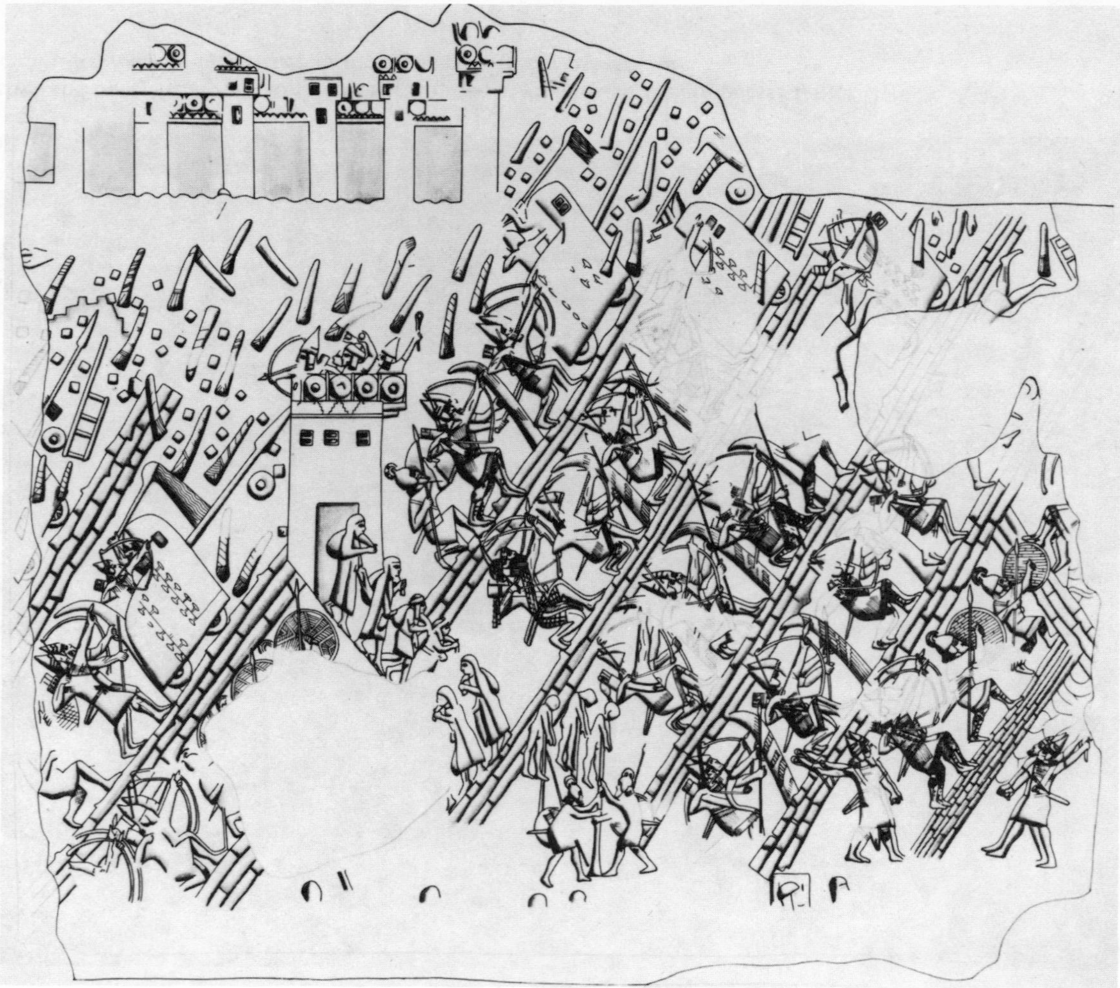

9. Assyrian soldiers attacking Lachish. *Drawing by Judith Dekel. Reproduced from D. Ussishkin,* The Conquest of Lachish by Sennacherib, *Tel Aviv, 1982.*

the present context and that their previous occurrence in 8:28–29 is secondary (see note *ad loc*). MT has *pisqâ* in middle of vv. 14 and 15 as a sign of manuscript bracketing.

15. *King Joram had gone back to Jezreel.* Jezreel was the site of the king's winter residence, chosen previously by Ahab (cf. 1 Kgs 21:1) because of its more clement weather as compared with the hill country of Samaria. Jericho served a similar function for the late Hasmonean monarchs. (See E. Netzer, *BASOR* 228 [1977], 1–14.) The thesis of A. Alt that Jezreel served as a second, "Israelite" capital of the dualistic monarchy, in which Samaria was the "Canaanite" base with a special constitutional status (accepted as a whole by H. Donner, in Hayes and Miller, *Israelite and Judaean History,* 400–3) is "largely inferential" (Bright, *History*^{3}, 244) and now correctly rejected by S. Timm, *Die Dynastie Omri,* FRLANT 124 (1982), 142–56. Nor is B. D. Napier's conclusion that Jezreel was the main royal residence (*VT* 9 [1959], 366–78) better founded; it rests upon the assumption that most references to Samaria prior to Jehu are late glosses.

For MT: *which the Aramaeans had inflicted on him.* (*ʾrmym*), the parallel verse in 2 Chr 22:5 has *hrmym,* with the *aleph* elided after the definite article (cf. Bauer-Leander, 31f.). This reading, however, has spawned the gratuitous emendation suggested by Klostermann *hammōrîm,* "the archers" (and so Burney), and that proposed by Stade *hārōmîm,* "the archers" (so Gray).

The name Joram appears in its unsyncopated form Jehoram in vv. 15, 17, 21, 22, 23, 24; the shorter form Joram in vv. 14, 16. In the translation, the form Joram is used throughout, so as to distinguish this king of Israel from Jehoram of Judah.

15b. *If this is your wish.* The idiom *ʾim yēš (ʾet) napšĕkem* occurs again in Gen 23:8; though many mss. insert the particle *ʾet* in our verse, the present shortened form is preferable, cf. Jer 15:1 and Mishnaic Hebrew *mâ napšāk* (Ehrlich; Montgomery-Gehman; contra. Gray).

and report in Jezreel. For the elision of *he* after the preformative in the *hiphil,* see *GKC* 53q; the qere represents a standardization of a common speech form.

16. *Then Jehu mounted up.* The root **rkb* presents translational difficulties, for its base meaning covers all aspects of riding, from the mounting of an animal or vehicle to the moving forward toward one's destination. Scholarly debate has tried to delimit what is sometimes perceived as an ambiguity, but a consensus has not been reached, as is clear from the recent discussion of W. B. Barrick, "The Meaning and Usage of RKB is Biblical Hebrew," *JBL* 101 (1982), 481–503. Barrick properly stresses the symbolic value of "being mounted" upon the royal mule in 1 Kgs 1:33 (*wĕhirkabtem*). But in that case, as in the present verse, a second verb of motion follows, so that **rkb* can represent the "mounting up." Cf. too Gen 24:61; 1 Sam 25:42; 1 Kgs 13:13, 18:45. In Esth 6:8, 11, and Gen 41:43, **rkb* appears alone and so covers the entire range of "riding." So too *lirkōb* in 2 Kgs 4:24 is "to ride," as the sequence of verbs and context requires. Important examinations of **rkb* include W. L. Moran, *Bib* 43 (1962), 323–27; S. Mowinckel, "Drive and/or Ride in O.T." *VT* 12 (1962), 278–99; and A. Salonen, "Notes on the Stem R-K-B in Akkadian," *ArOr* 17 (1949), 313–22.

17. *"I see a troop!"* Heb. *šipʿat,* lit. "abundance, multitude," is used of droves of camels (Isa 60:6) and horses (Ezek 26:10), and of flood waters (Job 22:11). LXX *koniorton* ("dust cloud") seems to be contextually derived, for in all three instances the verb **ksh* ("cover, hide") appears.

Šipʿat in the absolute form is usually taken to be erroneous; the form simply repeats the preceding construct (so Klostermann, Burney, Montgomery-Gehman). If something has not fallen out of the text, then the form might reflect the excited speech of the lookout.

18. *The messenger reached them.* For the anomalous *ʿad hēm,* cf. Job 32:12 (likely punctuated *ʿădêhem*) and other defectively written prepositions—e.g. *ʾlhm/n;* see *GKC* 32n and the remarks of H. M. Orlinsky, *HUCA* 17 (1942), 283, n. 23.

20. *He reached them.* MT *ʿad ʾălêhem* is a "double reading"; Qimḥi noted that either *ʾălêhem* or *ʿădêhem* (cf. v. 18) alone is necessary.

for he drives like a madman. The rendition of the Targum *bĕnîaḥ mĕdabbār,* "he drives calmly," was also known to Josephus, who relates that Jehu "was going along rather slowly and in good order" (*Antiquities* ix.117); the source of this tradition, which contravenes the plain sense of MT, is unexplained.

22. *the harlotries of your mother Jezebel and her many sorceries.* Harlotry (from the root **znh,* "to follow wantonly") is the standard biblical metaphor for abandoning YHWH to take up the ways of foreign gods (e.g. Exod 34:16; Lev 17:7; Deut 31:16; Judg 2:7). With reference to Jezebel, "harlotry" expresses the contempt in which Israel held pagan practice, seen as suffused with improper sex and magic (cf. Lev 18).

It is of some interest to note that rivalries at the court of the Hittite king Murshili II (mid-fourteenth century B.C.E.) gave rise to charges similar to those brought against Jezebel, against the widow of Shuppiluliuma. The old queen, who had retained a position of influence after her husband's death, was accused of witchcraft and sorcery and importing things from Babylon, the land of her extraction, all of which were excuses for her ultimate deposition. For an exposition of the obscure circumstances of this matter, see S. Bin-Nun, *The Tawananna in the Hittite Kingdom* (Heidelberg: C. Winter Universitätsverlag, 1975), 178–90.

23. *Joram turned his hands.* As in similar circumstances described in 1 Kgs 22:34, the driver signals his team to switch direction by pulling up on one of the reins.

24. *Jehu drew his bow.* Lit. "filled his hand with the bow." I. Ephʿal (orally) notes the use of the verb **millēʾ* for "filling the bow" in Zech 9:13, i.e., setting the arrow to the bowstring and compares the Akk. lexical entry *qaštu malîtu,* "a full bow" (*CAD* Q 147b), from which he would reconstruct an idiom *millēʾ haqqešet bĕyad,* "he filled [i.e. nocked] his bow."

25. *Remember how you and I were riding.* The syntax is a bit unclear. The versions read *zōkēr,* "I remember," for MT *zĕkōr,* on the basis of which Stade thought that a second *kî ʾănî* had fallen out by homoeoteleuton. But MT can be maintained (with Šanda, Montgomery-Gehman). For *ʾēt* as "that, how," see GB 76b and Ehrlich.

side by side. Tentative translation. It is not clear whether *ṣĕmādîm,* lit. "pair, team" (cf. 1 Kgs 19:19), refers to their riding alongside one another on separate horses or together in a single vehicle. Revocalization to the past participle *ṣĕmūdîm* (so Burney, Ehrlich, *BH³*) or *ṣĕmîdîm* (so Gray) does not resolve this ambiguity.

made this pronouncement. Heb. *maśśāʾ,* lit. "something lifted, carried," is also "utterance," in accordance with the idiom *nāśāʾ ʿal śĕpātayîm/pê,* "to utter" (Ps 16:4; 50:16). Thus *nāśā māšāl* is to "utter a parable" (e.g. Num 23:7) and *nāśāʾ qînâ* is "raise a dirge" (e.g. Amos 5:1). Far from the plain sense is Gehman's translation of *maśśāʾ* as "burden," a rendering greatly influenced by the theological considerations expressed by Calvin, who saw the prophet as bearing the Lord's burden until it was laid upon the guilty individual or nation. See H. G. Gehman, *JQR* 31 (1940), 107–21, and Montgomery-Gehman.

26. *last night.* Cf. Gen 19:34; 31:29, 42. H. Yalon, *Studies,* 362 (Hebrew), shows that *ʾemeš* is also "yesterday" in rabbinic Hebrew; and so in Akk., *amšali,* "yesterday," (*CAD* A 2.79).

27. *the road to Beth-haggan.* Modern Jenin in northern Samaria; Gina in EA 250 (Aharoni, *Land of the Bible²,* 175). It is not identical with En-gannim in Josh 19:21; 21:29 in the territory of Issachar (so Gray; Boling, *Joshua,* AB, ad loc.); the tribal holdings of Issachar do not seem to have reached into the hills of Samaria.

They shot him. For MT *hkhw,* Luc. and LXX read *wykhw.* If MT is retained, then a verb describing the fulfillment of the command is required, as felt by Qimḥi; insert with Burney *wykhw.* One of the two verbs was lost in each of the manuscript traditions through haplography.

the ascent of Gur near Ibleam. Ibleam is located in the territory of Manasseh (Josh 17:11; Judg 1:27; 2 Kgs 15:10) and is mentioned after Taanach by Thutmose III (*ANET³,* 242); see Aḥituv, *Canaanite Toponyms,* 120. The ancient name is preserved in wadi Balʿameh leading down to the Jezreel Valley and Khirbet Belʿameh, 2 km south of Jenin.

He fled to Megiddo and died there. A variant tradition which recalled that Ahaziah was in hiding in Samaria, from where he was taken to be executed by Jehu, is found in 2 Chr 22:8–9.

29. A repetition of 8:25, but with a slightly different reckoning of the synchronism between Joram of Israel and Ahaziah of Judah. According to the present verse, since both kings were killed by Jehu in the twelfth year of Joram, Ahaziah, who reigned one year (8:26), must have ascended the throne in the eleventh year of Joram.

The introduction of this item, which is no more than a chronological footnote at this juncture, was determined by the break in the narrative and the change of scene to Samaria.

30. *she painted her eyes with kohl.* Heb. *pûk* is powdered antimony used as paint on the lids, lashes, and brows of the eyes; cf. Jer 4:30; Job 42:14. A synonymous term **kḥl* appears in a verbal form in Ezek 23:40 and is used in the Targum to the present passage; cf. cognates in Akkadian *guḫlu* (*CAD* G 125) and Arabic (noted by Ibn Janah).

The use of the verb **śām,* "to put, place," is unique; as Haupt noted, the usual verb for dressing up is **ʿaśô,* as in "pare her nails" (Deut 21:12) and "pared his toenails and trimmed his mustache" (2 Sam 19:25).

The *beth* of *bĕpûk* can be classed with other *beth instrumenti;* cf. *GKC* 119q.

she looked out of the window. More than just anxiety over developments in the city was behind Jezebel's taking up a position at the window, as is indicated by her dressing up for the occasion; contrast Sisera's mother in Judg 5:28–30. On the basis of late Egyptian practice, Montgomery-Gehman thought that the scene was typical of a royal audience "through the window." Less likely to be pertinent is the frequent motif of the "woman in the window" depicted on carved ivory plaques from many sites in the Near East; cf. *ANEP²,* 131. Barnett interprets this figure as the goddess Astarte, who, bedecked like one of the sacred prostitutes in her service, invitingly leans out of the window (R. D. Barnett, *Iraq* 2 [1935], 182; and idem, *Qedem* 14 [1982], 48). However, a cultic background to Jezebel's meeting with Jehu is nowhere indicated. Nor are references to female demons at the window particularly relevant; cf. H. Zimmern, "Die babylonische Göttin im Fenster," *OLZ* 31 (1928), 1–3; and *CAD* K 357, s.v. *kilili.* See too the remarks of P. K. McCarter, *II Samuel,* AB, 172 ad 6:16. It would appear that Prov 7:6ff. preserves the literary motif in which an alluring woman calls from her window to a foolish passerby hoping to ensnare him. But whether Jezebel thought that her womanly charms would extricate her from certain death is questionable (contra. S. B. Parker, *Maarav* 1 [1978], 67–78). By addressing Jehu as "Zimri" (v. 31)—in every sense an insulting reference—Jezebel continued to display her self-assurance and courage. "The idea is that (as) a queen, (she) meets her destiny in full regalia and made up for the occasion." (D.N.F.)

31. *coming through the gate.* Gray is alone in adopting the LXX *bʿyr,* "into the city," for MT *bšʿr,* "through the gate."

Zimri, his master's killer. The reference is to Zimri, commander of half the chariotry, who slew Baasha king of Israel and declared himself king. He met a fiery death during an attack by Omri after just seven days on the throne; cf. 1 Kgs 16:9–18. For the *casus pendens,* see Driver, *Tenses,* 198, *Obs* 2.

32. *Who is on my side?* For this idiom, cf. 6:16.

Two or three eunuchs. Heb. *sārîs,* loan word from Akk. *ša rēši,* lit. "he who is at the head," i.e. courtier. The millennia-old tradition that *sārîs* means "eunuch" is now conclusively established from the abundant cuneiform evidence. For example, in the middle-Assyrian code, the punishment of castration is termed *ana šarēšen turru* (*AHw* 974b); note too the passage: *kima šūt rēši la ālidi nīlka lībal,* "may your semen dry up like that of a eunuch who cannot beget" (*CT* 23 10:14; cf. *CAD* N 2.234; cf. Isa 56:3). Various Assyrian texts, in describing the personnel of the court, refer to *ša ziqni,* "bearded courtiers," and *ša rēši* (*CAD* Z 126–27), and a similar distinction appears on Neo-Assyrian palace reliefs, on which the beardless figures are identifiable as *ša rēši,* "eunuchs." See the recent survey of J. E. Reade, "The Neo-Assyrian Court and Army: Evidence from the Sculptures," *Iraq* 34 (1972), 91–92. But whether all the many Assyrian state officials titled *ša rēši* were eunuchs is still questioned; certainly the male personnel admitted to the harem had been deprived of their manhood. Reservations as to the inclusiveness of the term were expressed by A. L. Oppenheim, "A Note on *Ša Rēši,*" *JANES* 5 (1973), 325–34; and P. Garelli, "Remarques sur l'administration de l'empire Assyrien," *RA* 68 (1974), 129–40. For further literature and discussions, see J. Kinnier-Wilson, *The Nimrud Wine Lists* (London: British School of Archaeology in Iraq, 1972), 13, 46–48; H. Tadmor, "Rab-saris and Rab-shakeh in 2 Kings 18," in *The Word of the Lord Shall Go Forth: Essays in Honor of D. N. Freedman,* eds. C. L. Meyers and M. O'Connor (Winona Lake, Ind.: Eisenbrauns, 1983), 279–85.

33. *he trampled her.* LXX, Syr. and Targ. vocalized the verb *wyrmsnh* as plural, taking the subject to be the horses. But though this reading is preferred by some (Thenius, Klostermann, Kittel, Burney), MT singular with Jehu as subject is the more striking reading and adds to the characterization of the protagonist.

34. *He went in and ate and drank.* Jehu proceeds as though nothing has happened, his anger still burning hot. Only after he had calmed down did he order Jezebel's burial (Ehrlich).

36. *It is the word of* YHWH . . . The words occur earlier in an abbreviated form in 1 Kgs 21:23; the present rendition is often considered the more original (e.g., Montgomery-Gehman). In any case, Jezebel did not meet her end in the "plot (*ḥlq*) of Jezreel," but in the town Jezreel itself. This discrepancy led O. Eissfeldt (*BZAW* 105 [1967], 57) to favor the reading in 1 Kgs 21:23 "rampart (*ḥl*) of Jezreel" as it reflects better the record in 2 Kgs 9: Jezebel was thrown from the palace window and died on the fortification wall. If Eissfeldt is followed, then the present reading *ḥlq* may be the

result of careless writing, *ḥlqt* having appeared twice earlier in the chapter in vv. 21, 25. (Note that most readers, as far back as Rashi, read *ḥlq* in both instances.)

37. *and the carcass of Jezebel shall be like dung on the field.* For the older form of 3 feminine sing. perfect *lamed he* verbs preserved in the qere of *hayat,* see *GKC* 75m.

The noun *dōmen,* "dung," always appears in the simile of a corpse left lying unburied in an open field; cf. Jer 8:2; 9:21; 16:4; 25:33; Ps 83:11. Targum translates *zebel,* "manure," an Aramaic word of uncertain etymology, thus creating a pun on the name Jezebel. See Montgomery-Gehman and note to 1 Kgs 16:31 on the name Jezebel.

10 1. *Ahab had seventy sons in Samaria.* As in other stories, the writer introduces all possible claimants to the throne by the number "70," a typological number used to express totality, all-inclusiveness. Abimelech "killed all his brothers, the sons of Jerubbaal, seventy men" (Judg 9:5). The descendants of Abdon also totaled "seventy"—forty sons and thirty daughters (Judg 12:14). Bar-rakib king of Sam'al does not hide the fact that his father Panammu took the throne by killing his father and "his seventy brothers" (*KAI* 215.3).

to the officials of the city and to the elders. The Luc. reading is adopted (with Burney, Montgomery-Gehman, Gray) inasmuch as Jehu was writing from Jezreel to Samaria; unless we assume, as did Qimḥi, that the "officials of Jezreel" (so MT) were in Samaria seeking the advice of the royal officials in the capital.

2. *"Now, when this letter reaches you . . ."* As in the letter sent by the king of Aram to the king of Israel in 5:6, the wording of the salutation is dispensed with, as it was seen as nonessential to the story.

5. *royal steward.* For the title *ʾăšer ʿal habbayît,* see note to 1 Kgs 4:6 and 2 Kgs 18:17.

governor of the city. The title *ʾăšer ʿal hāʿîr* appears only here. For its relation to *śar hāʿîr,* see 1 Kgs 22:26.

6. *take the heads of the men.* There is an ambiguity in Jehu's words which Ehrlich and Šanda thought was intentional. Since Jehu did not give an explicit order to murder the king's sons, he could claim his non-involvement in the slaughter; see v. 9.

the men, your master's sons. This translation masks an infelicitous double construction in Hebrew: *ʾnšy bny,* which many mss. resolve by eliminating one of the two elements. MT may be understood as a conflation of two alternate readings, in accord with S. Talmon's suggestion in "Double Readings in the Massoretic Text," *Textus* 1 (1960), 144–84.

the princes. The term *bĕnê hammelek* is taken literally. "The sons of the king" must have been of royal blood; otherwise they would have posed little real threat to Jehu. For a discussion of the accepted view that *ben hammelek* is a title of a royal functionary, not necessarily of the royal line, see note to 1 Kgs 22:26 and provisionally, de Vaux, *Ancient Israel,* 119–20; S. Yeivin, *EncMiqr* 2.160.

7. *in baskets.* Heb. *dûd* is translated in Targum by the more common noun *sal,* "basket"; cf. Jer 24:1. In 1 Sam 2:14 and 2 Chr 35:13, *dûd* is a cooking pot.

8. *Put them in two heaps at the entrance of the gate.* The bloody spectacle of a pile of heads was meant to frighten the citizenry into cooperating with the usurper. It is not unlike the battlefield tactics used by Neo-Assyrian kings. Ashurnasirpal II "cut off the heads" of the troops of Habḫu "and formed a pile" (*ARI* 2.546). Sargon II "heaped up the corpses of its warriors (those of Dūr-Jakīn) in piles in the midst of the marshland" (Lie, *Sargon,* 14:34). Cf. *ANEP*², 236.

until morning. Jehu's insensitivity is underscored by Josephus, who adds the detail that all the while, "he was dining with his friends" (*Antiquities* ix.128).

10. *for* YHWH *has done what he promised through his servant Elijah.* Seeking the approbation of the people, Jehu invokes Elijah's prophecy against the Ahabites (cf. 1 Kgs 21:21–24), a not unreasonable stance for one who was anointed by a prophet sent by Elisha (above 9:6–10a). A discussion of whether this passage and others which refer to Elijah's prophecy stem from a later hand follows in the Comment.

11. *his nobles.* Luc. *gōʾălāyw,* "his kinsmen" (cf. 1 Kgs 16:11), for MT *gĕdōlāyw,* "his nobles," is not a preferable reading (so emended by Stade, Burney). Nobles loyal to Ahab were to be found in Samaria (v. 6) as well as Jezreel.

his intimates. Heb. *mĕyūdāʿ,* "intimate, close friend," from **ydʿ,* "to know," should be distinguished from the court title *rēʿeh hammelek,* "the king's friend"; see 1 Kgs 4:5. In Akkadian texts from Ugarit, the term *mūdē šarri,* "friend of the king," is found (*CAD* M 2.167b); it is interpreted as a designation of high social rank granted by the king. The "friend" paid an annual tax and his status passed on to his heirs. See A. F. Rainey, *Social Structure of Ugarit* (Jerusalem: Mosad Bialik, 1967), 51–53 (Hebrew); and E. A. Speiser, *JAOS* 75 (1955), 163. Cf. too M. Heltzer, *The Internal Organization of the Kingdom of Ugarit* (Weisbaden: Reichert, 1982), 161–63, for a different etymology and view of the *mūdû* as royal functionaries.

his priests. For priests as civil servants, considered together with other royal appointees, see 1 Kgs 4:4.

12. *Beth-eked of the shepherds.* The first part of this toponym was taken as a proper noun by Eusebius and identified by him with Beit Qād, a village some 5 km east of Jenin. A. Alt located it at Kefar Raʿi on the road from Jenin to Samaria (*PJB* 27 [1931], 32–33). See Simons, *Texts,* §919. Beth-eked was translated in Targum as "meeting house"; cf. *NEB* "shepherd's shelter."

13. *he met the kinsmen of Ahaziah.* MT *wyhʾw* is miswritten for *whwʾ* as seen by Driver, *Tenses,* 210 n. 2 (and so Burney, Montgomery-Gehman). *Hûʾ* is required by Hebrew idiom to synchronize the events in vv. 12b and 13a; cf. 1 Sam 9:11, Judg 18:31, Gen 38:25.

the queen-mother. Jezebel is the only queen in the northern kingdom to bear the title *gĕbîrâ.* The influential position of the queen-mother at the court of Jerusalem is exemplified by the case of Maacah, removed by Asa for her cultic offenses in 1 Kgs 15:13; cf. too 11:19. (On this rank in the Bible and ancient Near East, see H. Donner, *Festschrift Johannes Friedrich* [Heidelberg: C. Winter Universitätsverlag, 1959], 105–45.)

14. *"Take them alive!"* The same order is given twice by Ben-hadad in 1 Kgs 20:18.

forty-two men. For another example of this "round" number, cf. 2:24.

15. *Jehonadab son of Rechab.* In early sixth-century Judah, the prophet Jeremiah singled out the House of the Rechabites for their loyalty to the commands of their ancestor Jehonadab son of Rechab (Jer 35). The group's ascetic lifestyle—they did not cultivate the land, nor plant vineyards, did not drink wine nor build houses—represented an extreme rejection of all aspects of the civilization of the land of Canaan. Thus the joining of Jehonadab with Jehu to root out the cult of Baal would seem to have been a natural linking of interests. For the relationship between Rechab and the Kenite clan, cf. 1 Chr 2:55. See S. Abramsky, "The House of Rechab—Genealogy and Social Characteristics," *EI* 8 (1967), 255–64 (Hebrew); idem, *EncMiqr* 7.368–71, F. S. Frick, "The Rechabites Reconsidered," *JBL* 90 (1971), 279–87.

Is your heart true (to mine) . . . ? By no means is *hăyēš ʾet lĕbābĕkā* "non-Hebrew" (so Ehrlich, *Randglossen*), and it need not be rewritten according to Luc., LXX (or most recently, Gray). For *yēš ʾet,* cf. Gen 23:8.

"It is indeed!" Heb. *yēš wāyēš* is taken as emphatic reduplication (with Qimḥi; Gersonides; Ehrlich, *Randglossen; NJPS*). Driver (*Tenses,* 149) understood *wāyēš* as opening a hypothetical statement: "If it be, then, give (me) thine hand"; cf. 5:17; 2 Sam 13:26 (so Burney, Montgomery-Gehman, Gray).

(Jehu said). There is no need to add these words which appear in LXX (so Šanda). The change of speakers is not always noted in Hebrew narratives, cf. e.g. 1 Kgs 20:34.

He gave him his hand. "An act of fidelity" (Montgomery-Gehman): cf. 1 Chr 29:24, 2 Chr 30:8; Ezra 10:19; and see Greenberg, *Ezekiel,* AB, to 17:18. A unique representation of a "handshake" of this sort is depicted on the throne base of Shalmaneser III on which the Assyrian king is shown extending his hand in friendship to Marduk-zakir-shumi, whom he helped reinstate as king of Babylon (D. Oates, "The Excavations of Nimrud (Kalḫu)," *Iraq* 25 [1963], 20–22, plate 7c).

16. *he took him along.* Reading *wayyarkēb* in the singular (so LXX, Syr.) for MT *wayyarkibû* in plural. Others read *wayyirkab ʾitto* "he rode with him" (e.g. *BH*[3]).

17. *until he had destroyed it.* On the vocalization of *hišmîdô,* cf. *ʿad hišʾîr* in 3:25.

19. *the prophets of Baal, all his ministrants, and all his priests.* The noun *ʿōbĕdāyw,* here translated "ministrants," is found in the third position in Luc., and most moderns agree that the order of elements in MT is illogical (so Montgomery-Gehman). This generalizing term appears again in vv. 21, 23, and may be a reading introduced from there. The vocalization of the noun distinguishes, somewhat artificially, these cult personnel (*ʿōbĕdê*) from the "servants" (*ʿabdê*) of YHWH in v. 23.

20. *Convoke a solemn assembly.* The command *qaddĕšû* followed by *wayyiqrāʾû* indicating compliance is an acceptable sequence and should not be emended (as does Stade, cf. too Gray). In Joel 1:14 the two verbs appear in synonymous parallelism; cf. 1 Kgs 21:9. *Qaddēš,* lit. "to sanctify, proclaim holy," signifies a cultic convocation, as does the ritual blessing of the assembled troops prior to battle in Jer 6:4; cf. Mic 3:5.

21. *from end to end.* Cf. 21:16.

22. *the man in charge of the wardrobe.* The translation is based on a contextual guess as there is as yet no satisfactory etymology for Heb. *meltāḥâ,* cf. *BDB* 547. Haupt suggested a derivation from Akk. *maltaktu,* "chamber" (questioned by Šanda; still adopted, *KB* 583); but this may now be dismissed as outdated. *Maltaktu* is a "tested measure" (*CAD* M 1.171). *Maštaku,* "living quarters" (*CAD* M 1.392), is also not related to the Hebrew. More recently a claim for a Ugaritic cognate has been made. Gray, following Eissfeldt, identified Ug. *mʾlḥ* with *meltāḥâ* and translated "cloakroom" (see O. Eissfeldt, *JSS* 6 [1960], 46:271). The strange *ʾel taḥat* in Jer 38:11 is also corrected accordingly to *meltāḥâ.*

For a comparable functionary in the temple of Jerusalem, cf. 22:14.

the garments. Heb. *hammalbûš,* "royal attire," in 1 Kgs 10:5, can be retained, even though earlier in the verse the vestments were referred to as *lĕbûš.* Graphically, the initial *hm* may be a dittography of the preceding *lhm* (so Stade, *BH*[3]), but this is not at all necessary (Montgomery-Gehman).

24. *that I hand over to you.* Cf. the idiom *nātan ʿal yād* in Gen 42:37.

it shall be a life for a life. "The life of the guard for the life of the escapee" (so Qimḥi).

25. *the outrunners and the adjutants.* Heb. *rāṣîm* appear as the royal escort of a

king (1 Sam 22:17), who in addition to their normal guard duties (2 Kgs 11:4, 6), also paraded in state ceremonies (1 Kgs 14:27–28). Pretenders to the throne considered it essential to appear in public accompanied by a squadron of outrunners, cf. 2 Sam 15:1; 1 Kgs 1:5. See the remarks of de Vaux, *Ancient Israel,* 123–24, 221. Runners (*lāsimu*) were often employed in royal service in Mesopotamia; see the lexical evidence collected in *CAD* L 106–7.

For adjutants, see note to 7:2.

they left (them) lying (there). For *hišlîk,* lit. "throw," in the sense of leaving a corpse lying (unburied), cf. 1 Kgs 13:25, Isa 14:19, and the remarks of M. Cogan, "A Technical Term for Exposure," *JNES* 27 (1968), 133–35.

the interior of the House of Baal. This rendering of *ʿîr,* "city," is contextually required, though no other such usage is attested. The troops had already entered the Baal Temple to kill the worshippers there, and the sacred pillar destroyed in v. 26 was without doubt from the same building. Klostermann's conjecture to read *dĕbîr,* "adytum, inner shrine" (cf. 1 Kgs 6:16), was adopted by *NAB. NEB*'s "keep" follows Montgomery-Gehman's "citadel."

Y. Yadin maintained the literal meaning of MT and postulated that the "city of the house of Baal" was located on one of the mountains outside of Samaria (*Archaeology in the Levant, Essays for Kathleen Kenyon,* eds. R. Moorey and P. Parr [Warminster: Aris & Phillips, 1978], 127–35).

27. *latrine.* Thus with LXX and medieval commentaries. But perhaps all that is indicated by *mḥrʾwt* (only here in BH) is a "dung heap"—i.e. public dump.

25–27. Read consecutively, vv. 25–27 offer a confused picture. The words "they left lying" do not have an object; the movement of the troops from the temple to the "city/interior" is enigmatic; the sacred pillar is burned, then smashed to bits. It is possible, in part, to harmonize the account by restoring to emendation. Thus e.g. the "pillar" (*mṣbwt*) in v. 26 is read as "sacred posts" (*ʾašrwt;* cf. 1 Kgs 16:33) (so Stade, Burney, *NEB, NJPS*); or the "pillar" (*mṣbt*) in v. 27 is read as "altar" (*mzbḥ*) (so Stade, Gray, *NJPS*). But a literary tack might do just as well. Josiah's purge of the Temple in Jerusalem included burning of the sacred post and then grinding it to fine dust (cf. 23:6). Otherwise, vv. 26 and 27 may be variants which ultimately derive from two different descriptions of the destruction of the pillar of Baal, set side by side in the present text as complements. A recensional approach to the problem of these verses is presented by J. Trebolle, "From the 'Old Latin' Through the 'Old Greek' to the 'Old Hebrew' (2 Kgs 10:23–25)," *Textus* 11 (1984), 17–36, in which the Old Latin translation emerges as witness to a Hebrew *Vorlage* which arranged the verses as follows: 24b, 23, 24a, 25. In Trebolle's view, this is an "older version of the story with better stylistic qualities."

30. *four generations of your descendants.* The vocalization *bĕnê rĕbīʿîm* (*rĕbîʿîm* in 15:12) is otherwise *ribbēʿîm* (Exod 20:5, 34:7; Num 14:18; Deut 5:9). The blessing of longevity is depicted in terms of living long enough to see great-great-grandchildren. A few ancients of note did attain "length of days"—e.g., Joseph in Gen 50:22; Job in Job 42:16; Si'-gabbari, priest of Nerab (*KAI* 226:5; *ANET³,* 661); and Adad-guppi, mother of Nabonidus, who reached the ripe old age of 104 and saw "great-great-grandchildren, up to the fourth generation in good health" (*ANET³,* 561).

In the Decalogue, the image of "four generations" is turned on its head; the punishment to be visited upon the guilty will reach out to the ultimate extent of his family, even to the fourth generation. See A. Malamat, *AfO* Beiheft 29 (1982), 215–24.

32. *In those days.* An editorial phrase, like "then" and "at that time," which introduces a chronistic entry. See note to 8:22.

YHWH began to reduce Israel. The verb **qṣh,* both in *qal* (Hab 2:10) and in *piel* (Prov 26:6), means "cut off." Ibn-Janah pointed to the related noun *qāṣê,* "edge, extremity," and defined the verb as "to seize border areas." In Mishnaic Hebrew **qṣh* is used for "harvest" of figs (*m. Maʿaś* 2.7). Stade was correct to reject emendations which read here **qṣp,* "be angry" (*BDB* 892), or **qwṣ,* "to loathe" (Klostermann, Burney).

33. *from Aroer by wadi Arnon.* Aroer, modern *ʿArâʿir,* on the Arnon was the southernmost city of Sihon, king of the Amorites (Deut 2:36; Josh 12:2), taken by the Israelites toward the end of their desert sojourn (Num 21:24). Aroer is listed as a Reubenite city in Josh 13:16, but at a later(?) time was apparently settled by Gadites (cf. Num 32:34). See Kallai, *Tribes of Israel,* 266–69; *Land of the Bible*[2], 207–8.

Heb. *naḫal,* sometimes rendered "valley" (RSV), "gorge" (*NEB*), "brook" (JPS), has no adequate equivalent in English. Most modern translations have opted for the Arabic *wadi;* this is the depression which carries off the winter rains, though it is mostly dry during the summer. To signify an ever-flowing wadi, i.e. one fed by a perennial spring, Hebrew seems to resort to the addition of the adjective *ʾêtān,* "firm, mighty" (cf. Deut 21:4, Amos 5:24).

including the Gilead and the Bashan. The repetition of "the Gilead," already mentioned in the opening half of the verse, shows the present clause to be an additional description of Israel's Transjordanian holdings. It is more comprehensive than v. 33a in that the Bashan region, north of the river Yarmuk, is also noted as having been taken by Hazael.

34. *and all his exploits.* Luc. and LXX add, "and the conspiracy which he formed" (cf. 15:15; 1 Kgs 16:20), a superfluous cross-reference after the extensive narrative of Jehu's revolt just completed.

36. *in Samaria.* This word is out of position, cf. 1 Kgs 22:52, and is therefore considered secondary by many (e.g. Stade, Eissfeldt, Montgomery-Gehman). Luc. adds the inaccurate synchronism (see note to 12:2), "in the second year of Athaliah, the Lord made Jehu the son of Nimshi king." It then continues with a lengthy passage concerning Ahaziah, composed of verses culled from the preceding account: vv. 37–38 = 8:26; v. 39 = 8:27; v. 40 = 8:28; v. 41 < 9:14f.; v. 42 = 9:27; v. 43 = 9:28. (On this literary bridge between 2 Kgs 10 and 11, see the remarks of Stade and Burney.)

Comment

1. *The Narrative Source and Its Affinities.* The story of Jehu's overthrow of the dynasty of Omri is related in the longest sustained narrative in 2 Kings; its fifty-nine verses (9:1–6, 10b–28, 30–37; 10:1–27) grip the reader with the same intensity which must have motivated the main protagonist. The drama unfolds in a series of short scenes, and action, not words, carries Jehu from the army camp facing Ramoth-Gilead to the palace at Jezreel and from there to the Temple of Baal in Samaria. By alternating perspectives from time to time, the narrator achieves a fuller characterization of his actors; thus, the

army commanders pass judgment upon the prophetic "madman" (9:11); the lookout on the tower recognizes Jehu by his wild driving (9:20); Jezebel primps herself before meeting her certain fate (9:30); the grisly pile of heads effectively intimidates the crowd at the gate of Jezreel (10:7–10). A single narrator, working under the impact of the dramatic turn of events, was undoubtedly responsible for these vivid descriptions. Only at two points does the reader discern that the narrative has been expanded: 9:7–10a are based upon the stereotypical phraseology of earlier doom prophecies (cf. 1 Kgs 14:10–11; 16:4; 21:23–24); 9:29 is a fragmentary chronological notice concerning Ahaziah.[1]

Gray thinks that the unity of the narrative is "imposed by a compiler . . . that there are indeed two sources reflecting the two aspects of the revolt against the House of Ahab, the religious reaction inspired by the prophets and the political, where a military group took the initiative, using Rechabite fanatics, to the exclusion, apparently, of prophetic elements."[2] But a division such as this into sources underestimates the basic theme which unifies all aspects of the narrative: Jehu's deeds against the House of Ahab fulfill YHWH's word delivered through his prophets. Indeed, Jehu himself is permitted to voice this rationale no less than three times (9:25–26, 36–37; 10:19).

More recently, Rofé found several episodes to be anecdotal in quality; they "were written by a different hand" from that of the main body of the story.[3] For one, 2 Kgs 10:1–10 makes use of folkloristic devices ("seventy sons," v. 1; anonymity of actors) and creates an illogical sequence; how could the Judaean princes innocently proceed to Jezreel (10:12–14) after the mass murder in Samaria? Furthermore, 2 Kgs 10:18–27 is based upon a ruse which would hardly have been believed. Jehu would like to present himself as an enthusiastic Baalist, but "his origin and ideological affiliation certainly could not have been hidden" from public view.[4] But this hypercritical reading of the narrative is excessive. The narrator relates step by step the revenge against the Ahabites; thus associative ordering of episodes demands that the assassination of Joram be followed by the murder of Jezebel and this concluded by the elimination of those remaining in the royal line. Only then, perhaps out of chronological order, does the narrator turn to the incident at Beth-eked. Note that each of these episodes closes with a statement indicating a prophecy fulfilled (9:25–26, 36–37; 10:10). Similarly, Jehu's zeal in Samaria is perfectly in character; modern doubts about the credulousness of the Baal priests is not sufficient reason to posit a second narrator.

[1] Gunkel's essay (*Geschichten von Elisa,* 67–97) is still the most sensitive exposition of the narrative. Of the critics, Kittel, Skinner, Šanda, Eissfeldt, and Montgomery-Gehman are more or less in agreement on the question of unity.

[2] Gray, 537.

[3] Rofé, *The Prophetical Stories,* 72–78.

[4] Rofé, op. cit., 74.

The century-old suggestion of J. Wellhausen to class the present narrative with 1 Kgs 20, 22; 2 Kgs 3; 6:24–7:20, "a group of northern narratives, mainly of political character"[5] is based mostly upon verbal similarities between these chapters (cf. e.g. 2 Kgs 9:2 and 1 Kgs 20:30, 22:25; 2 Kgs 9:23 and 1 Kgs 22:34; 2 Kgs 10:14, 7:12, and 1 Kgs 20:18). But it is the prominent place of the prophetic word and its effect which permits associating 2 Kgs 9–10 with 1 Kgs 22 and perhaps 20.[6] It must be admitted, at the same time, that the connection with the Elisha cycle is peripheral; Elisha's role is limited to instructing the prophet's servant in the procedure of anointing (9:1–3). Moreover, this anointing is at variance with the word of YHWH in 1 Kgs 19:15–18, where Elijah is commanded to anoint Jehu. Quite clearly, the key role in Jehu's divine selection was claimed by the circles loyal to Elijah and to Elisha; Eissfeldt even speculates that the present text preserves the opening drawn from the Elijah cycle, and the conclusion, without its concomitant command of YHWH, from the Elisha traditions.[7]

But our narrator cannot be seen as one of the Sons of the Prophets, a disciple of Elisha; for unlike the stories in the Elisha cycle in which the prophetic "father" stands in relief, 2 Kgs 9–10 is concerned exclusively with Jehu. True, the narrator presents Jehu's acts as fulfilling a prophetic utterance, but this notion is typical of biblical history writing: human action is subject to divine will and proceeds according to an ordained plan announced by the prophet. Thus the latter history of David's reign, in particular the rebellion of Absalom, is understood as divine retribution for the king's sin as foretold by Nathan (cf. 2 Sam 12:7–10). So, too, are Jehu's bloody acts against the House of Ahab. The extermination of a dynasty in Israel called for recording the events, and the present narrative, of outstanding literary quality, preserved the drama and gave meaning to this major turning point in Israel's history. The narrator's objectivity of description leaves the question of his own view of Jehu's violent behavior unsettled. He might well have pitied, or even disapproved of, the murder of the innocent "seventy sons of Ahab"; but it is difficult to find the "implicit protest" against Jehu and his supporters that some scholars have found in these chapters.[8] Jehu's excesses were to come in for criticism in the following century in the prophecies of Hosea son of Beeri (cf. Hos 1:4); 2 Kgs 9–10 relates the events without judgment.

2. *The Revolt and Its Outcome.* Violent dynastic changes in Israel can fre-

[5] So Skinner; cf. Wellhausen, *Composition*[4], 282–87; Kittel, Stade.

[6] So M. Noth, *Überlieferungsgeschichtliche Studien,* 80.

[7] See O. Eissfeldt, *The Old Testament, An Introduction* (New York and Evanston: Harper & Row: 1965), 291–92; idem, "Komposition," *BZAW* 105 (1967), 52–53.

[8] B. Uffenheimer defends the narrator's sense of morality by reading into these chapters a hidden condemnation by one of the disaffected Sons of the Prophets in "The Meaning of the Story of Jehu," *Oz Le-David Studies Presented to D. Ben-Gurion,* (Jerusalem: Israel Bible Society, 1964), 291–311; idem, *EncMiqr* 5.703.

quently be traced to dissatisfaction with foreign military policies, which led army officers to take matters into their own hands (cf. e.g. 1 Kgs 16:8–10, 15–18; 2 Kgs 15:25). Though not explicitly stated, the immediate cause of Jehu's insurrection was the inconclusive outcome of the renewed war with Aram-Damascus by Joram, during which the king himself was wounded (2 Kgs 9:14–15a). On top of this, the combined Israelite-Judaean armies had been forced to retreat from Moab just a few years earlier (2 Kgs 3:27), allowing Mesha to strengthen his position in Trans-Jordan.

The clarion call of the revolt, reechoing throughout the narrative in 2 Kgs 9–10, is: Avenge the blood of Naboth! That this case was taken up by Jehu suggests that the Naboth incident had become a *cause célèbre* and that the outrageous confiscation of one innocent man's property was not an isolated example of royal miscarriage of justice. Resentment over the rule of Ahab and his son Joram was likely widespread.[9] The intermittent wars with Damascus, together with the sometime alliance with Damascus against Assyria, costly public projects, and an extravagant royal lifestyle (1 Kgs 22:39), were all contributing factors to the political and social malaise, of which the lingering presence of Queen Jezebel and her entourage was a constant reminder.

Jehu and his supporters, both in the army and among those who staunchly adhered to the exclusive worship of YHWH, succeeded in extirpating the hated Ahabites, but Israel was left internally weakened, unable to meet the new external challenges which sprang up almost immediately. The assassination of Jezebel abruptly ended the half-century alliance between Samaria and the Phoenician entrepôt, Tyre; Judah, tied by marriage to Israel's royal family, was alienated by the impromptu murder of the family of Ahaziah; and the hostilities between Aram-Damascus and Samaria, already renewed by Joram, continued unabated. Jehu's Israel was isolated on all fronts.

At this juncture, 841 B.C.E., Shalmaneser III reappeared in southern Syria and succeeded in blockading Hazael within Damascus; he claims to have ravaged the countryside, carrying off much booty. The Assyrian marched as far as the mountains of the Hauran—the eastern edge of the Bashan—and then turned west, cutting through the Galilee[10] to reach the Mediterranean at

[9] Because of the paucity of available sources, the class struggle between the "men of means" or *gibbôrê haḥayîl* (the traditional tribal-based aristrocracy in Israel) and the royal establishment (founded upon newly accumulated capital), as reconstructed by A. Wolff, does not leave the realm of the theoretical; see "The Social Background of the Revolt of Jehu," *Hedim* 27 (1961–62), 66–84, 162–75 (Hebrew). For an ample analysis of the early stages of opposition to the Omrides, with considerable "demythologizing" of the legendary Elijah in 1 Kgs 17–21, see M. A. Cohen, "In All Fairness to Ahab," *EI* 12 (1975), 87*–94*.

[10] Shalmaneser may have taken one of two routes, either through the Jezreel Valley or through the lower Galilee; on which see B. Oded, "Darb el-Hawarneh, An Ancient Route," *EI* 10 (1971), 191–97.

Ba'ali-rasi, a promontory facing Tyre.[11] Among the local kings who rendered tribute to Shalmaneser during this campaign was Jehu of Israel.[12] The famous Black Obelisk from Nimrud freezes this moment in time: the Israelite king or his representative is shown on his knees before the Assyrian monarch with the tribute bearers in his train. (For the inscription accompanying this scene and the list of tribute, see Appendix I, No. 2C.)

Under the circumstances prevailing in Israel, Jehu had little choice but to acknowledge Assyrian hegemony. Whereas in the days of Ahab, Israel had been a major partner in the anti-Assyrian alliance of south-Syrian states, a decade later Jehu greeted Shalmaneser III with rich gifts. But this ostensive political realignment was to prove of little worth. Shalmaneser returned in 838 B.C.E. to raid towns belonging to Hazael and to collect dues, and as long as Assyria continued to press its claims in the area, Israel enjoyed a respite from its wars with Damascus. This respite, however, was short-lived.[13]

The attacks upon Israelite districts in the Bashan and the Gilead by Aram-Damascus were renewed once Assyria became embroiled in internal political struggles, and Shalmaneser III, against whom an open rebellion broke out at the end of his reign, could no longer attend to affairs in the West. A temporary decline in the intense military expansion previously known characterizes the reign of his son Shamshi-Adad V (824–811 B.C.E.) and the opening years of his grandson Adad-nirari III (811–783 B.C.E.). It was throughout this

---

An intriguing echo of the destruction and atrocities wrought by Shalmaneser in Trans-Jordan may be heard in the words of the prophet Hosea: "And all your fortresses shall be ravaged, as Beth-arbel was ravaged by Shalman on a day of battle, when mothers and babes were dashed together" (10:14); see M. Astour, "841 B.C.: The First Assyrian Invasion of Israel," *JAOS* 91 (1971), 383–89.

[11] The text translated in *ANET³*, 280 is augmented by another edition of the annals of Shalmaneser; see F. Safar, "A Further Text of Shalmaneser III. From Assur," *Sumer* 7 (1951), 3–21 esp., 11:8–9; see Appendix I, No. 2, A and B. The identification of Ba'ali-rasi, "Baal of the Headland," with Mt. Carmel has long been maintained; see Aharoni, *Land of the Bible²*, 341. But the additional phrase in this inscription, "facing Tyre," favors taking Ba'ali-rasi as referring to Rosh Haniqra (= Rās en-Naqūra); see A. Malamat, "Campaigns to the Mediterranean by Iahdun-lim and Other Early Mesopotamian Rulers," in *Studies . . . Landsberger, AS* 16 (1965), 371–72; and É. Lipiński, "Baʿli-Raši et Raʾšu Qudšu," *RB* 78 (1971), 84–92.

H. J. Katzenstein (*History of Tyre,* 175–77) adopts the older suggestion to identify the mountain with the outcrop at the mouth of Nahr-el-Kalb, where Assyrian reliefs can still be seen.

[12] For Jehu's name, "Jehu, son of Omri" as it appears in the cuneiform text, see note to 9:2.

[13] A suggestive but undemonstrable reading of the events has been broached by Astour (op. cit., above, n. 10): Jehu's extermination of the house of Ahab "was not only a measure to ensure the usurper's unchallenged rule: it was also an act of appeasement of the Assyrian king by wiping out the entire anti-Assyrian party, . . . before the eyes of Shalmaneser when he reached Jezreel."

period that Israel suffered continued losses at the hands of the Aramaeans, reaching its nadir in the decade following Jehu's death (cf. 13:3, 22).

3. *Editorial Evaluation of the Reign of Jehu.* Jehu's act in eliminating Baal worship from Israel (10:28) is noted with some appreciation, but is immediately followed by the editorial remark, standard for all the kings of Israel, that he continued to support the sinful ways of Jeroboam at Beth-el and Dan (v. 29). This critique is further complemented by an excerpt from the royal annals which noted Aramaean successes against Israel in Trans-Jordan and which interpreted them as a sign of divine displeasure (v. 32). Into this unit, a *post eventum* prophecy of unspecified origin has been inserted, which promises Jehu length of dynasty as reward for his loyalty to YHWH (v. 30; cf. 15:12). Not only does this prophecy rationalize Israel's longest surviving dynasty, it is evidence for support of Jehu among prophetic circles despite the military setbacks (Montgomery-Gehman).

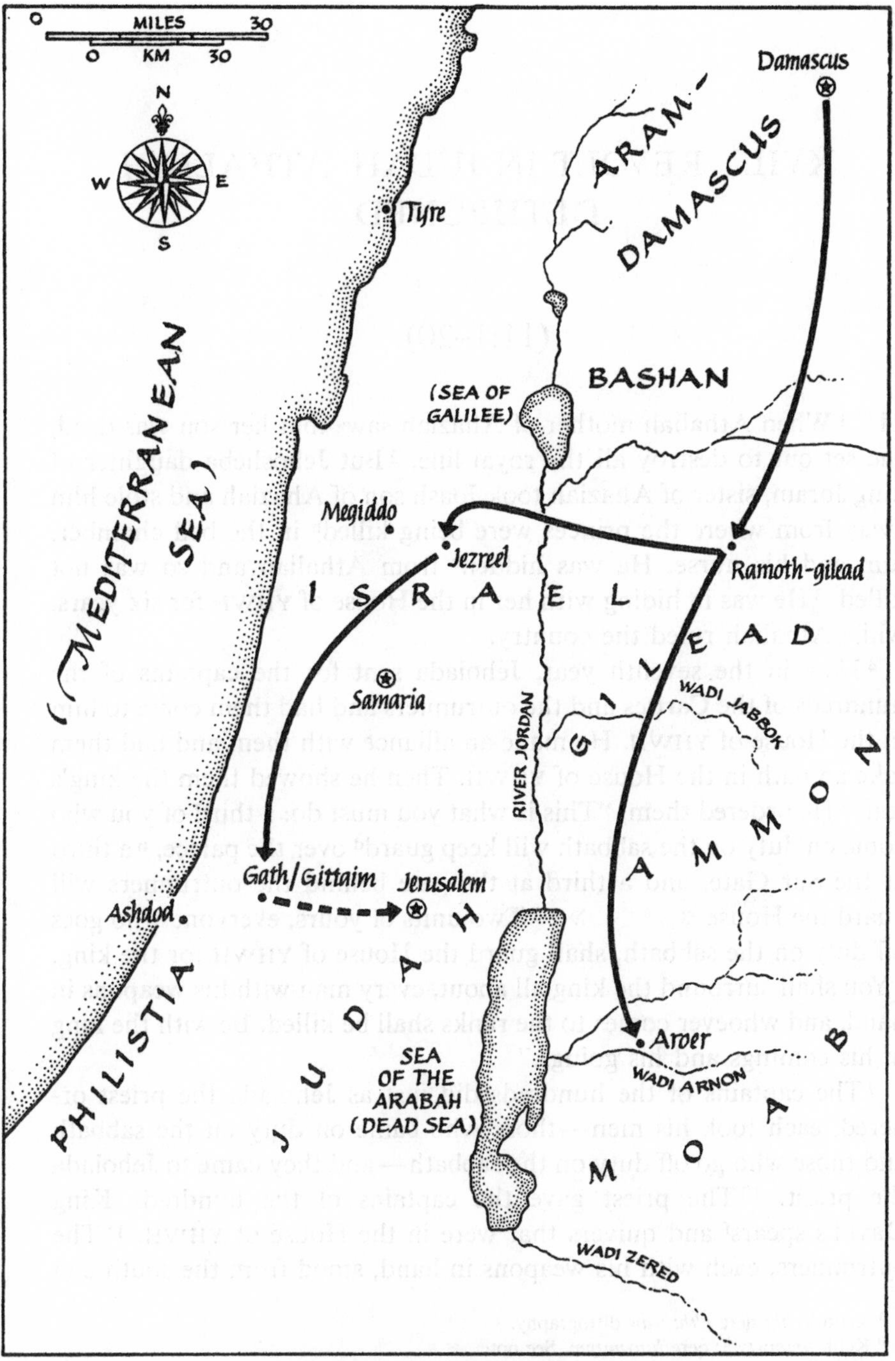

CAMPAIGNS OF HAZAEL,
KING OF ARAM-DAMASCUS
2 KINGS 10:32-33; 12:18-19

XVII. REVOLT IN JUDAH: ATHALIAH DETHRONED

(11:1–20)

11 1 When Athaliah mother of Ahaziah saw[a] that her son was dead,
she set out to destroy all the royal line. 2 But Jehosheba daughter of
king Joram, sister of Ahaziah took Joash son of Ahaziah and stole him
away from where the princes were being killed[b] in the bed chamber,
him and his nurse. He was hidden[c] from Athaliah and so was not
killed. 3 He was in hiding with her in the House of YHWH for six years,
while Athaliah ruled the country.

4 Now in the seventh year, Jehoiada sent for the captains of the
hundreds of the Carites and the outrunners and had them come to him
in the House of YHWH. He made an alliance with them and had them
take an oath in the House of YHWH. Then he showed them the king's
son. 5 He ordered them, "This is what you must do: a third of you who
come on duty on the sabbath will keep guard[d] over the palace, 6 a third
at the Sur Gate, and a third at the gate behind the outrunners will
guard the House « »[e]. 7 Two units of yours, everyone who goes
off duty on the sabbath, shall guard the House of YHWH for the king.
8 You shall surround the king all about, every man with his weapons in
hand, and whoever comes to the ranks shall be killed. Be with the king
in his comings and his goings."

9 The captains of the hundreds did just as Jehoiada the priest ordered; each took his men—those who came on duty on the sabbath
and those who go off duty on the sabbath—and they came to Jehoiada
the priest. 10 The priest gave the captains of the hundreds King
David's spears[f] and quivers that were in the House of YHWH. 11 The
outrunners, each with his weapons in hand, stood from the south end

[a] Ketib *wr'th;* qere *r'th; waw* dittography.
[b] Ketib *hmmwtym;* qere *hmwmtym.* See note.
[c] Lit. "They hid him."
[d] Read *wšmrw* for MT *wšmry;* cf. v. 7.
[e] MT has the additional unintelligible word *msḥ.* See note.
[f] MT *ḥnyt;* 2 Chr 23:9 *ḥnytym.* Read *ḥnytwt,* see note.

of the House to the north end of the House, at the altar and the House,
all about the king. 12 Then (Jehoiada) brought out the king's son and
placed the diadem and the jewels upon him. They made him king and
they anointed him; they clapped their hands and shouted, "Long live
the king!"

13 When Athaliah heard the sound of the outrunners (and) the People, she came to the People in the House of YHWH. 14 She saw the king
standing by the pillar, as was the custom, the officers with the trumpets beside the king, and all the People of the Land rejoicing and
blowing trumpets. Athaliah rent her garments and shouted, "Treason,
treason!" 15 Jehoiada the priest ordered the captains of the hundreds in
charge of the troops and said to them, "Take her out through the
ranks and anyone who follows her, put to the sword"; for the priest
thought, "She should not be put to death in the House of YHWH."
16 They took her away by force, and she entered the palace through the
Horses Entrance; there she was put to death.

17 Then Jehoiada made a covenant between YHWH and the king and
the People that they should be a people belonging to YHWH, and
between the king and the people. 18 Then all the People of the Land
came to the House of Baal; they tore it down, and[g] its altars and
images they smashed to bits. They killed Mattan, the priest of Baal in
front of the altars. (Jehoiada) the priest set guards over the House of
YHWH, 19 and he took the captains of the hundreds, the Carites and
the outrunners and all the People of the Land, and they led the king
down from the House of YHWH. They entered the palace through the
Gate of the Outrunners. And he sat upon the royal throne. 20 All the
People of the Land rejoiced and the city was quiet, whereas Athaliah
they put to death by the sword in the palace.

[g] Read *w't* with mss., 2 Chr 23:17, LXX, and Targ. for MT *'t*.

Notes

11 1. *she set out to destroy.* For the use of **qûm,* "get up," as an auxiliary verb, see note to 8:2.

all the royal line. Heb. *zrʿ hmmlkh.* The regular expression is *zrʿ hmlwkh,* cf. 25:25; Jer 41:1; Ezek 17:13; but the present usage is quite intelligible and need not be emended (so Montgomery-Gehman, contra. Stade). For the term *mmlkh,* both "king" and "kingdom, royal rule," see W. Moran, "A Kingdom of Priests," in *The Bible in Current Catholic Thought* (Herder and Herder: New York, 1962), 7–20 and the note to 1 Kgs 11:11.

2. *Jehosheba, daughter of King Jehoram, sister of Ahaziah.* The unusual mention of Jehosheba's relationship to Ahaziah perhaps means that the brother and sister were children of the same mother; cf. Gen 34:25; Deut 13:7 (with Ehrlich). The narrative carefully notes that the queen's own daughter was her undoing.

stole him away. Heb. **gānôb,* "steal," is used for "kidnapping" in Gen 40:15; Exod 21:16; Deut 24:7.

being killed. Ketib *hmmwtym* is generally regarded as corrupt and read with qere *hmwmtym,* in *hophal;* so mss. and 2 Chr 22:11. Montgomery-Gehman retain the ketib of MT, comparing the *polel* form *mmwtt* in 1 Sam 14:13; but the meaning "dispatch" is inappropriate in the present context.

him and his nurse. In MT, this phrase reads like an awkwardly inserted gloss, whose natural place belongs instead at the end of the clause. The reading in 2 Chr 22:11, "and she put (*wttn*) him and his nurse," is an early attempt at easing the difficulty. Medieval commentators favored the Chronicles' version of the story and took the "bedroom" to be the penthouse where priests retired; cf. Rashi, Qimḥi. But this introduces a Temple bedroom, otherwise undocumented. Stade's sharp eye noted other cases in 2 Kings in which the scene of the murder is specifically recorded (cf. v. 20; 12:21; 15:10, 14).

3. *He was in hiding with her.* I.e. his aunt, who was wife of the priest Jehoiada (see v. 4). What is implied here is that the child was concealed in the lodgings of the high priest within the Temple precinct.

4. *Jehoiada.* In v. 9, he is referred to as "the priest" and in 2 Chr 24:6, as the "high priest"; his wife was Jehosheba daughter of Joram (2 Chr 22:11). Because Jehoiada is introduced abruptly in v. 4 without any accompanying description, the present story may have been part of a longer one in which the priest was previously mentioned.

the Carites. Royal guard of problematic origins. It is often claimed that they are identical with the Carian mercenaries and sailors known from scattered references in Greek sources and inscriptions left in Egypt and Nubia, where they were in the service of Psammetichus I and II. Native to southwest Anatolia, in the territory between Lydia and Lycia, their language is related to the Hittite-Luwian branch of Indo-European. The transcription of the name "Carian" in ancient Near Eastern documents raises problems. Whereas in Greek the form is *kares/karikoi,* in Babylonian the form is *karsā;* in Elamite *kurkā;* in Old Persian *kurkā;* in all instances, three consonants appear as integral components of the name: *krs/k.* Indeed, in newly published texts in Aramaic from Egypt, the Persian form *krky'* is now known. See J. B. Segal, *Aramaic Texts from North Saqqara* (London: Egypt Exploration Society, 1983), 41–42. (Note that other Greeks, *ywnyn,* are mentioned alongside the Carians.) Hence, from the linguistic point of view, the connection between Hebrew *kārî* and sixth-century Carians seems remote. For discussions, see R. Schmitt, RLA 5.423–25; and O. Masson, "Les nom des Cariens dans quelques langues de l'antiquité," in *Mélanges É. Benveniste* (Louvain: Ed. Peeters, 1975), 407–14.

kārî appear again in 2 Sam 20:23 along the *pĕlētî,* Pelethites, commonly taken to be Aegean elements in David's private army. (For the qere *kĕrētî* and the name in 2 Sam 8:18, see P. K. McCarter, *II Samuel,* AB, ad loc.). Perhaps, then, the Carites were the traditional "Swiss guard" of the Davidides, loyal to the family from earliest days (cf. too 2 Sam 15:18).

The parallel account in 2 Chr 23 omits all reference to these foreigners, for according to the priestly law, only Levites were permitted to enter the Temple compound.

He made an alliance with them. Heb. *kārôt bĕrît lĕ-* is distinct from *kārôt bĕrît ʿim,* the latter expressing mutuality between partners of equal status. The preposition *lĕ-* is used to indicate the "granting of a treaty" (Josh 9:6) or "coming to terms" (1 Sam 11:1–2). Ehrlich (*Randglossen*) observed that in Deut 7:2 and 2 Sam 5:3, the idiom is used to note a special grant to former enemies who are rewarded for switching allegiance to a new master. Cf. too 1 Kgs 20:34. Thus Jehoiada, the superior party as well as moving force behind the conspiracy, sets the terms for the queen's guards. Tadmor ("Treaty and Oath" 137, n. 52) points out similar distinctions in Ugaritic and western Akkadian, in which *l* and *ana* are used for "treaty obligations *laid upon* PN."

5–7. Jehoiada's plan of execution is spelled out in these verses; and although v. 6 contains several textual peculiarities, it contains authentic information which makes the judgment that it is an incompatible gloss arbitrary (so, Skinner, Burney, Gray, following Wellhausen, *Composition*⁴, 292 n. 2). But with Joüon ("Notes," 481) and Ehrlich, the passage can be interpreted intact: The royal guard comprises three companies, each one serving one week out of three. (Ehrlich compares the corvée assignment during Solomon's reign, 1 Kgs 5:28.) To insure the success of his scheme, Jehoiada summoned all the guards. Those on duty (*bāʾê haššabbāt*) were subdivided and positioned at three locations: one third at the royal palace; one third at the Sur Gate; one third at the gate behind the outrunners. All the rest, all those off duty (*yōṣĕʾê haššabbāt*), who were two thirds of the total guard, took up positions within the Temple to guard the king. (This elucidation of the passage was also adopted by Montgomery-Gehman.)

6. *the Sur Gate.* An otherwise unknown gate, which appears in 2 Chr 23:5 as the Foundation (*yswd* for *swr*) Gate. Looking ahead to v. 16, some would emend Sur to the Horse (*swsym*) Gate (so Joüon, Galling, Gray). S. Yeiven (*VT* 14 [1964], 334–37) identified the Sur Gate with the New Gate in Jer 26:10.

the gate behind the outrunners. Referred to again in v. 19, where the description allows locating this gate in the southern wall separating the Temple and palace compounds.

msḥ. The additional word *msḥ* in MT is omitted in LXX and transliterated in Luc. and Vulg. The other versions, as well as many of the medieval and modern commentators, etymologize, none very satisfactorily. This unintelligible word is tacked on to the final clause of v. 6, which itself does not follow smoothly as part of the instructions given to the last group of guards. From a comparison with the clauses 5bβ and 7b, 6c looks like a copyist's error. Thus:

v. 5b	:	*wšmry*	*mšmrt byt hmlk*
v. 6c	:	*wšmrtm ʾt*	*mšmrt hbyt msḥ*
v. 7b	:	*wšmrw ʾt*	*mšmrt byt yhwh ʾl hmlk*

8. *whoever comes to the ranks.* Heb. *śĕdērâ,* again in v. 15 (= 2 Chr 23:14). Taken as a feminine noun from **sdr,* meaning "order, arrangement," it appears in 1 Kgs 6:9 in an architectural context describing a row of columns(?) (see note there) and here as a row of troops, thus "ranks." Haupt was the first to point out the Akk. cognate *sidirtu,* "row," which is used in the expression *sidirta šakānu,* "to set troops in battle array" (see *AHw* 1039b). (The interchange of *s* and *ś* is a feature of Hebrew texts written under the influence of Aramaic in which these sibilants merged; see Bauer-Leander, 14d.)

10. *King David's spears and quivers.* MT *ḥnyt,* read in 2 Chr 23:9 as plural *ḥnytym,* is more commonly *ḥnytwt* (Isa 2:4; Mic 4:3). Rather than taking it in a collective sense

(Qimḥi), it is better to emend the text and read the common plural, *-wt* having fallen out through haplography because of the following *wʾt* (so Šanda).

Ancient and modern translations of Heb. *šeleṭ* vary greatly; thus e.g. LXX has "shield"; but in Jer 51:11 "quiver," and in Cant 4:4 "javelin." *NEB* and *NAB* have "shields"; *NJPS:* "quivers." This uncertainty is compounded by the use of the term in the Dead Sea Scrolls, discussed by Y. Yadin (*War of the Sons of Light Against the Sons of Darkness* [London: Oxford University Press, 1962], 133–35), who favors a "javelin-type weapon." With the recent publication of the Aramaic Targum to Job, the tradition behind "quiver" has been elucidated. Heb. *ʾašpâ* in Job 39:23 is there translated by the Aram. *šeleṭ.* See M. Sokoloff, *The Targum to Job from Qumran Cave XI* (Ramat-Gan: Bar-Ilan University, 1974), 156. Meanwhile, R. Borger, "Die Waffenträger des Königs Darius," *VT* 22 (1972), 385–98, adduced textual and pictorial evidence for translating Akk. *šalṭu* as "quiver," or "bowcase," which is now accepted by *AHw* 1151a. (On *šalṭu* as an Aramaic loanword in Akkadian, see W. von Soden, *Or* 46 [1977], 195:144.)

The quivers issued by Jehoiada to the guards were probably the ones taken by David from the servants of Hadadezer and brought to Jerusalem (2 Sam 8:7). They were to serve as symbols of the legitimacy of Joash's succession and the continuity of the Davidic dynasty.

12. *the diadem and the jewels.* A diadem (*nēzer*) of pure gold adorned the priestly turban (Exod 29:6; 39:30; Lev 8:9) and was worn by King Saul (2 Sam 1:10). The present scene and the allusions in Ps 89:40 and 132:18 confirm that it served as a sign of royalty in ancient Israel. Contextually, then, *ʿēdût* ("jewels") should also be some sort of royal "insignia" (so translated by all modern versions). Wellhausen's emendation to read *ʾeṣʿādôt,* "bracelets," based on 2 Sam 1:10, where it appears alongside "diadem," is favored by many critics. Qimḥi had already derived the word from **ʿdh,* "to ornament, bedeck," thus "royal garments." (It is noteworthy that in middle Assyrian ritual texts, the king is crowned by the *šangû*-priest with a "diadem" (*kulūlu*) and decked out with a "golden chain" (*šewer ḫurāṣi*); see K. F. Muller, MVAG 41/3 [1937], 12:25–31. Akk. *kulūlu* [*CAD* K 527] is related to *kilīlu* [*CAD* K 358], "circlet, headband," and passed into Aramaic as *kĕlîlāʾ;* in Targum, it translates Heb. *nēzer.)*

Another possibility, to be found in all ancient translations, is that *ʿēdût* means "testimony." Gersonides explicates: "I believe that he handed over to him the (book of the) Law which is called *ʿēdût* [e.g. Ps 78:5], so that he read it all his days and that it be beside him, as is called for in the Law [Deut 17:18–19]." The same line of reasoning, as well as the evidence for divine legitimation at the king's coronation in Egypt, led von Rad to interpret the term as royal "protocol" (see "Royal Ritual in Judah," in *The Problem of the Hexateuch and Other Essays* [New York: McGraw-Hill, 1966], 222–31; cf. de Vaux, *Ancient Israel,* 103). Weinfeld (*Deuteronomy,* 85–88) takes *ʿēdût* to be a "covenant document" and refers to the ceremony in which Esarhaddon made a binding covenant with the people of Assyria, requiring loyalty to his chosen successor Ashurbanipal (see Streck, *Assurbanipal* 2.4, I:18–23). But in both extrabiblical situations, no charter or covenant is physically handed over to the king, an act required by the Hebrew *wayyittēn ʿālāyw.* In this regard, note the conjecture of Z. W. Falk (*VT* 11 [1961], 88–91) to take *ʿēdût* as an engraved amulet which served as a reminder of the covenant, comparable to the priestly diadem inscribed "Holy to YHWH" (Exod 28:36).

In fine, "the diadem and the jewels" with which the young king was bedecked should be taken together as symbols of royal office.

they clapped their hands and shouted, "Long live the king!" On the acclamation by the onlookers following the ritual of anointing, see the note to 9:13.

13. *the sound of the outrunners (and) the People.* The abrupt introduction of "the People" (*hāʿām*), together with its asyndetic relation to the preceding "outrunners" was partly resolved in 2 Chr 23:12 by reversal of the elements: "the sound of the people running about." Most commentators, however, agree that the Aramaic form of the plural *rāṣîn* indicates that the noun "outrunners" is secondary. S. Talmon (*Textus* 1 [1960], 164–65) suggests that this is but another example of "double reading," though LXX has both elements in a genitival relation similar to 2 Chr 23:12.

The "People" are identical with the "People of the Land" in vv. 14, 18, 20, and so their presence at the coronation seems confirmed. Besides, the People were required to legally confirm the accession. (On the political role of the People of the Land, see note to v. 14.) The guards, with weapons in hand, are not likely to have applauded and shouted (v. 12). The absence of the People from the report up until v. 13 is due to the narrator's concentration on guard duties and protecting the king. On the question of two sources in 2 Kgs 11, based on the presence and/or absence of the People, see Comment.

14. *the king standing by the pillar.* During the covenant ceremony in 2 Kgs 23:3, King Josiah is similarly found standing "by the pillar." The Chronicler, at 2 Chr 23:13, locates the pillar "at the entrance" to the Temple; he may have had one of the two entry pillars, Jachin and Boaz, in mind; see 1 Kgs 7:15–22. Not unlike this custom is the prince's station at the "doorposts of the gate" of the Temple in Ezek 46:2.

the officers with the trumpets. The joyous scene elicited the reading *šārîm,* "singers," in LXX and Vulg. for *śārîm,* "officers," in MT. The parallel text in 2 Chr 23:13 seems to have known both renderings—"the officers with the trumpets . . . blowing trumpets and the singers with musical instruments leading the hymns"—indeed "an alluring correction" (Montgomery-Gehman). Note that Solomon's accession was accompanied by the sound of piping in 1 Kgs 1:40.

the People of the Land. The term *ʿam hāʾāreṣ* refers to a distinct social group in the kingdom of Judah, whose activity at the time of dynastic crisis is recorded several times in 2 Kings. They intervened after the assassination of Amon (21:23–24) and the death of Josiah (23:30) to elevate a proper Davidide to the throne; cf. too 14:21. Jeremiah (1:18, 34:19, 37:2) juxtaposes the People of the Land with other strata of society, and Ezekiel (22:29) berates them for their oppression of the poor, the destitute, and the sojourner; these contexts suggest that they were an elite group of citizens. But it is not a popular "national assembly" (M. Sulzberger, *The Am Ha-aretz, The Ancient Hebrew Parliament* [Philadelphia, 1909]), for the People were never formally convened. Nor are they only the "squirearchy" (M. Weber, *Ancient Judaism* [Glencoe, Ill.: The Free Press, 1952], 26). The term connotes the totality of population—i.e., the people of Judah living on its land. So, too, it can refer to non-Israelite populations in Gen 23:7, 42:6; Exod 5:5. In the single extrabiblical usage of People of the Land, in the Yehawmilk inscription from Byblos, it is an all-inclusive term: "in the eyes of gods (*ʾlnm*) and mankind (*ʿm ʾrṣ*)"; cf. *KAI* 10:10. However, only a small percentage of the People of the Land were active participants in their communities; these were naturally the wealthy who by dint of their influential position could direct public affairs, as they did so often during monarchic upheavals in Judah. Recent studies with bibliographies include: A. Soggin, "Der judäische ʿAm-haʾareṣ und das Königtum in Juda," *VT* 13 (1963), 187–95; R. de Vaux, "Les sens de l'expression "Peuple du Pays . . . ," *RA* 58

(1964), 167–72; S. Talmon, "The Judaean ʿAm-haʾareṣ in Historical Perspective," Proceedings of Fourth *WCJS* (Jerusalem, 1967), 71–76; H. Tadmor, " 'The People' and the Kingship in Israel," *JWH* 11 (1968), 46–68; T. Ishida, " 'The People of the Land' and the Political Crises in Judah," *AJBI* 1 (1975), 23–38.

On the social role of the People of the Land, see E. Wurthwein, *Der ʿamm haʾarez im Alten Testament,* BWANT 4/17 (1936), and I. D. Amusin, "The People of the Land," *VDI* 1955, No. 2, 14–36.

15. *in charge of the troops.* This is the first time in the narrative that the officers are so termed, and the phrase is "intrusive" (Montgomery-Gehman), though it does coordinate the present scene with the earlier one. The vocalization *pĕqūdê* is found again in Num 31:14; correction to *pĕqīdê* (Stade, Burney, Ehrlich) is unnecessary.

Take her out . . . put to the sword. Imperative third person pl. *hôṣîʾû* followed by infinitive absolute *hāmēt* is an attested sequence (*GKC,* 113z) and need not be altered to *yûmat* as in 2 Chr 23:14 (as does Gray).

16. *They took her away by force.* The expression *śîm yādayîm,* lit. "to place the hands", is known only from the present context. Targum and Syr. as well as the medieval commentators, translate *yād* as "space," cf. Josh 8:20, Gen 34:21, Ps 104:25, thus "they cleared a way for her," and so Ehrlich, *Randglossen.* LXX and Vulg. took the words more literally, as if to mean that she was forcibly removed from the Temple; so *BDB* 963a, Burney, Skinner, Montgomery-Gehman. Other expressions in BH for hostile action are *šālaḥ yād bĕ-* (Exod 22:7; 1 Sam 24:10, 26:11; Ps 55:21) and *nātan yād bĕ-* (Exod 7:4).

the Horses Entrance. The Horses Gate of the City of Jerusalem was located east of the Ophel (cf. Jer 31:39, Neh 3:28); through this gate, one reached the Horses Entrance which opened directly into the royal precinct; cf. *EncMiqr* 3.822.

17. *they should be a people belonging to* YHWH. The binding terms of the covenant —to be YHWH's people—is the leitmotif of Deuteronomic literature; cf. Deut 4:20, 7:6, 14:2, 26:18, 27:9; Jer 7:23, 11:4 et al. Its occurrence here, in what is otherwise an early text, is unexpected. See further in Comment.

between the king and the people. The phrase is not represented in 2 Chr 23:16 and Luc. But only a few critics excise it (Stade, Klostermann, Eissfeldt); the others reconstruct a two-covenant ceremony, on which see Comment.

18. *the House of Baal.* There is no reference in the Bible to a Baal Temple in Jerusalem other than the present one; thus its location can only be inferred. Šanda thought that it was located in the vicinity of the palace, it being no more than a private shrine for the apostate Athaliah. Recently Y. Yadin ("The House of Ba'al of Ahab," 130–32) suggested that the monumental structure excavated at Ramat Rahel, 3 km south of Jerusalem, was the Baal Temple of Jerusalem. He noted the building's architectural similarity to the palace at Samaria and compared the location of the Temple outside the acropolis to the "City of the Temple of Baal" (see above, 10:25).

Mattan, the priest of Baal. Mattan is likely a hypocoristicon and admittedly a common name in Phoenician and Punic (see Z. S. Harris, *Grammar of the Phoenician Language,* AOS 8 [1936], 108); but it is also known as a component in Hebrew names, e.g. Mattaniah (2 Kgs 24:17, and seals from Jerusalem and Tell en-Naṣbeh, see R. Hestrin and M. Dayagi-Mendels, *Seals,* No. 66).

set guards over the House of YHWH. Jehoiada took precautions to protect the Temple against acts of revenge by those loyal to Athaliah. J. Liver (*EncMiqr* 3.522) proposed that the priest was also responsible for instituting a permanent system of guard duty still credited to him in the days of Jeremiah, cf. Jer 29:26.

19. *Gate of the Outrunners.* The entrance to the Temple precinct through which the king regularly passed; cf. 1 Kgs 14:28.

20. *whereas Athaliah they put to death by the sword in the palace.* The resumption of the topic of Athaliah's execution is meant to contrast with the jubilation of the People. *NAB* translates the clause: "now that Athaliah . . ." viz., her death was the cause for celebration. In either case, v. 20b is not a second report of Athaliah's death (as taken by some, following Stade). In Josephus' account, she was put to death in the Kidron Valley (*Antiquities* ix.152). (Did he read *šadmôt,* "terraces" [cf. 23:4] for *śĕdērôt* in v. 15?)

Comment

1. The scene of action shifts from the northern kingdom to its southern neighbor, from the tumultuous events surrounding Jehu's overthrow of the dynasty of Omri to the no-less-violent intrigue which replaced Athaliah with a legitimate Davidide on the throne of Judah. This chapter is the first instance in 2 Kings in which the editor of Kings has incorporated a narrative which derives from Judaean sources. Thus even though the chain of events in Jerusalem had its start in the murder of Ahaziah by Jehu (9:27–28), the narrator of 2 Kings 11 concentrates exclusively on the pivotal role played by the priest Jehoiada in restoring the monarchy and renewing the covenant between YHWH and the people. He shows himself to be a close contemporary of Jehoiada, familiar with details of the conspiracy, knowing his way about the Temple and palace compounds. Liverani is certainly correct in viewing this narrative as "political propaganda," in the sense of being an apologia for the unprecedented intervention of a priest in the affairs of state in Judah.[1]

Critics have found reason to suggest that 2 Kings 11 is an amalgamation of two sources, with Stade's analysis still considered the standard treatment:[2]

a. Athaliah's death is reported twice; in v. 16, she was killed on the way to the palace, in v. 20, in the palace itself.

b. The "People" appear suddenly in v. 13; they were not participants in the ceremonies up to this point.

The two sources identified are: (1.) vv. 1–12, 18b–20, a secular, politically oriented narrative; (2.) vv. 13–18a, a fragmentary tradition, emphasizing the religious motivation of the revolt.

The single exception to the critical unanimity on the question of the chapter's unity has been W. Rudolph. He regarded v. 20 as a refrain, not a second

[1] See M. Liverani, "L'histoire de Joas," *VT* 24 (1974), 438–53.

[2] See B. Stade, *ZAW* 5 (1885), 279–88. All commentators follow Stade, the only difference among them being their verdict on the "historicity" of the sources.

murder of Athaliah; but even he was troubled by "the People's" role and excised them as secondary from all verses except v. 20.[3]

Despite the arguments for a separation into sources, 2 Kings 11 is here considered a single source. As Šanda, who followed Stade, admitted, the vividness of description is evident throughout; but it is only because the narrator concentrates on particular aspects of the drama that the illusion of "sudden appearance" is created—e.g., "the People" in v. 13, or "the Carites" in v. 19. Jehoiada acts everywhere in his role as high priest; the crowning of Joash in v. 12, related in the "secular" source 1, is no less a religious act than the conclusion of the covenant in v. 17 in "religious" source 2. As main protagonist, Jehoiada organizes the rebellion, presides over the coronation ceremonies, and orders the death of the queen and the abolition of her cult. At the same time, it must be admitted that the hand of the Deuteronomistic editor can be detected at the crucial stage of covenant making: the language of v. 17 and the placement of v. 18 immediately thereafter raise the suspicion that ideological considerations shaped the present text.

2. The covenant "between YHWH and the king and the people" to be YHWH's people is the first such act reported during the period of the monarchy. Unlike the covenant later undertaken during the reign of King Josiah, at whose center stood the newly recovered Book of Law (2 Kgs 23:1–3), the terms of Jehoiada's covenant are not specified. It is to be expected that the priest would promote the exclusive worship of YHWH in Jerusalem and so the covenant ceremony is quite naturally followed by the eradication of the competing Baal cult (v. 18).

Is there a second covenant referred to in v. 17b in the words "and the king and the people"? These words are missing from 2 Chr 23:16, as well as Luc. and some miniscules of LXX to v. 17. On this evidence, some have concluded that the presence of v. 17b is due to dittography and that only a single covenant was concluded (Stade, Eissfeldt). Yet the Chronicles' account is equivocal; since the Chronicler had already referred to a covenant between king and people in 2 Chr 23:3 (his reworking of 2 Kgs 11:4!), there was no need for him to repeat 2 Kgs 11:17b. Admittedly, special circumstances did prevail and the reinstatement of a true Davidide on the throne could have called for a renewed pledge of loyalty to the dynasty (so Gray).[4] In any event, the case of Joash is not evidence for periodic covenant renewal upon the accession of each Judahite king.[5] Ishida's hesitation concerning v. 17b seems most sound: the covenant with YHWH "in effect implies the Davidic cove-

[3] W. Rudolph, "Die Einheitlichket der Erzählung vom Sturz der Atalja (2 Kön 11)," *Festschrift Bertholet* (Tübingen: J. C. B. Mohr, 1950), 473–78.

[4] See too the remarks of A. Malamat, *BAR* 3.166; H. Tadmor, *JWH* 11 (1968), 61.

[5] As claimed by G. Fohrer, "Der Vertrag zwischen König und Volk in Israel," *ZAW* 71 (1959), 11–13.

nant, in which a Davidic king serves as mediator between Yahweh and the people."[6]

Not surprisingly, even the covenant between YHWH, the king, and the people, has come in for criticism. Thus Noth regarded it as a "later gloss" on the original transaction of "a covenant on a purely human level."[7] And there is almost universal agreement among commentators that v. 18 interrupts the flow of events: the ceremonial climax of the coronation came when the king took his place on the throne, here delayed by the destruction of the Baal cult. The present sequence of verses may be the result of tendentious Deuteronomistic editing, following the pattern "covenant leading to cult reform." But this would not impugn the authenticity of the report in v. 18, which belongs to a later stage. So, too, the presence of Deuteronomistic terms in v. 17a (see note) does not discredit the covenant act altogether.[8] No rigid pattern as to how covenants were concluded is discernible in Kings.[9] Jehoiada stands in isolation from other cult reformers; his act is unlike those of Asa (1 Kgs 15:12–13); Hezekiah (2 Kgs 18:4) or Josiah (2 Kgs 23:1–14), all of whom acted *de novo.* The term *bĕrît,* a key word in the Deuteronomistic presentation of history, is used in 2 Kgs 11 to denote the specific agreement between the priest and the foreign guard (v. 4); in the same way, *bĕrît* in v. 17a refers to a specific agreement to root out all traces of Athaliah's reign.

3. The historical record of the reign of Athaliah (842–836 B.C.E.) is slim; few facts can be recovered from the tendentious narrative in 2 Kings 11. From the point of view of the Deuteronomistic editor of Kings, Athaliah's reign is not granted full legitimacy, for neither an opening nor a closing formula is given for her six years. Yet these years cannot be written off, for example, by including them in the forty years of Joash (12:2), without far-reaching emendations to the chronological data.[10] Mowinckel accepted the historicity of the account that she exterminated all the royal line except for

[6] See T. Ishida, *Royal Dynasties in Ancient Israel, BZAW* 142 (1977), 115. For the suggestion that a single covenant was concluded with two sides, YHWH on one and the king and the people on the other, see G. von Rad, *Studies in Deuteronomy,* SBT 9 (1953), 63–64. See too D. J. McCarthy, *Treaty and Covenant,* AnBib 21A (1978), 215, 260–61.

[7] See M. Noth, *Laws in the Pentateuch,* 115–16.

[8] Montgomery-Gehman expressed indecision: "The term covenant-making . . . if historical, interestingly enough precedes the theme of the so-called Deuteronomic reform (422)."

[9] Recently, H. D. Hoffman, *Reform und Reformen,* AThANT 66 (1980), 104–13, after radical literary analysis, concluded that 2 Kgs 11 is a "unitary narration formed by the hand of Dtr."

[10] See S. Mowinckel, "Die Chronologie der israelitischen und jüdischen Könige," *AcOr* 10 (1932), 235–36; cf. too D. N. Freedman, in *The Bible and the Ancient Near East,* ed. G. E. Wright (Garden City, N.Y.: Doubleday, 1965), 27, n. 40.

young Joash, in whose name, in fact, she ruled.[11] Ginsberg doubts that there were many left to be killed after Jehu's brutal attack on the royal entourage (cf. 10:13–14).[12] Another tradition, in 2 Chr 21:4, recalls an earlier elimination by her husband Jehoram of all his rival brothers. Myers' reconstruction would have Athaliah as queen mother and regent from whose control Joash was kidnapped "not because his life was in danger . . . but because that was the only way to challenge her power."[13] But the narrative acknowledges Athaliah as queen, even though it is highly critical of her usurpation of the throne. Queens were not entirely exceptional in the ancient Near East; in Arabia they were the rule.[14]

Due to the lack of evidence other than 2 Kgs 11, any number of scenarios can be written.[15] In the end, though ousted by a rebellion led by the priest Jehoiada, Athaliah's rule was not discredited by the charge of suppression of the national cult, a sign of the times in Israel when her mother Jezebel was queen. The Temple of YHWH was itself not defiled as later occurred because of Manasseh (2 Kgs 21:4); Athaliah worshiped Baal in a separate shrine. Two major social forces, the priesthood and the People of the Land, joined together to restore the Davidic dynasty. In this, they found support among the foreign mercenaries (v. 4) and the queen's own court ("the city," v. 20).

[11] Mowinckel, loc. cit.

[12] H. L. Ginsberg, "The Omrid-Davidid Alliance and Its Consequences," Proceedings of Fourth *WCJS* (Jerusalem, 1967), 91–93.

[13] J. M. Myers, *II Chronicles*, AB 13, 88.

[14] See I. Ephʿal, *Ancient Arabs*, 82–83.

[15] See H. Reviv, "On the Days of Athaliah and Joash," *Beth Mikra* 47 (1971), 541–48.

XVIII. THE REIGN OF JEHOASH (JUDAH)

(12:1–22)

12 1 Jehoash was seven years old when he became king. 2 In the seventh year of Jehu, Jehoash became king, and he reigned forty years in
Jerusalem; his mother's name was Zibiah from Beer-sheba. 3 Jehoash
did what was pleasing to YHWH all his days, just as Jehoiada the priest
had instructed him. 4 Yet the high places were not removed; the people
continued to sacrifice and make offerings at the high places.

5 Jehoash said to the priests, "All the silver brought as sacred donations to the House of YHWH—silver of the census tax, silver from the
valuation of persons, or[a] any silver that a man may voluntarily bring
to the House of YHWH—6 let the priests take for themselves, each
from his acquaintance, and they shall repair the House wherever damage may be found."

7 But in the twenty-third year of Jehoash, the priests had not (yet)
made repairs on the House. 8 So King Jehoash summoned Jehoiada
the priest and the (other) priests and said to them, "Why are you not
repairing the House? Now, do not keep silver from your acquain-
tances, but donate it for the repair of the House." 9 The priests agreed
not to take silver from the people, nor to make repairs on the Temple.

10 Then Jehoiada the priest took a chest and bored a hole in its side,
and he set it near the altar, on the right[b] as one enters the House of
YHWH; and the priests, keepers of the threshold, would put there all
the silver brought to the House of YHWH. 11 Whenever they saw that
there was much silver in the chest, the king's scribe and the high priest
would come and tie (it) up and count the silver found in the House of
YHWH. 12 They would give the silver that was weighed over to[c] the
workmen in charge[d] of the House of YHWH; they used it to pay the
carpenters and builders working in the House of YHWH, 13 and the
masons and stone cutters, to buy timber and quarry stone to repair

[a] Read *wkl, waw* lost through haplography due to preceding *ʿrkw.*
[b] Ketib: *bymyn;* qere: *mymyn.*
[c] Ketib: *ʿl yd;* qere: *ʿl ydy.*
[d] Ketib: *hpqdym;* qere: *hmpqdym.*

the House of YHWH, and for all other expenditures needed to repair the House. 14 However, no silver basins, snuffers, sprinkling bowls, or trumpets—vessels of gold and silver of any kind—were made for the House of YHWH from the silver brought into the House of YHWH. 15 But they paid it to the workmen who repaired the House of YHWH. 16 Furthermore no accounting was made with the men to whom the silver was given to pay the workmen, for they dealt honestly. 17 Silver from guilt offerings and from sin offerings[e] was not given over to the House of YHWH; it belonged to the priests.

18 Then Hazael king of Aram marched and fought against Gath and captured it; he set out to attack Jerusalem. 19 So Jehoash king of Judah took all the sacred objects dedicated by Jehoshaphat, Jehoram, and Ahaziah, his ancestors, the kings of Judah, and his sacred objects, and all the gold found in the treasuries of the House of YHWH and the palace and he sent (them) to Hazael king of Aram, who then withdrew from Jerusalem.

20 The rest of the history of Joash and all that he did are indeed recorded in the annals of the kings of Judah. 21 His servants rose up and formed a conspiracy; they killed Joash at Beth-millo, which leads down to Silla. 22 The servants who killed him were Jozabad[f] son of Shimeath and Jehozabad son of Shomer. He died and was buried with his ancestors in the City of David. Amaziah his son succeeded him.

[e] Read *ḥṭ't*, sing. with mss. and LXX; MT *ḥṭ'wt*, pl.
[f] So MT and 2 Chr 24:26; many mss. and versions read: Jozacar.

Notes

12 1. *Jehoash was seven years old when he became king.* The standard editorial formula introducing the king's reign is here reversed; his age at accession is followed by the synchronism. Luc. inserts v. 1 after v. 2a and restores the normal sequence. Montgomery-Gehman thought that the reversal links well with the preceding narrative concerning Jehoash's installation and Athaliah's removal, which also begins with a date "in the seventh year" (11:4).

2. *he reigned forty years in Jerusalem.* The forty-year reign does not include the six years of Athaliah, even though Jehoash was, in effect, the sole legitimate heir to the throne. See Comment to 2 Kgs 11.

Calculations based on the synchronisms with the kings of Israel in 12:1, 13:1, 10 during the lifetime of Jehoash and those of his son Amaziah in 14:1, 23 show that in reality Jehoash reigned only thirty-eight full years. The "forty years" credited to him are likely an editorial rounding off to the typological number "forty." Cf., too, Thiele, *MNHK²*, 71–75.

3. *just as Jehoiada the priest had instructed him.* The positive evaluation of Jehoash by Dtr. is recorded again in 14:3, where in reference to Amaziah it is said that he was himself a righteous king, just like his father, although he did not attain to the standard of the founder of the dynasty, David. A dissident (priestly?) tradition, preserved in 2 Chr 24:2, 15–22, qualifies the praise of Jehoash: the king remained loyal to YHWH only during the lifetime of Jehoiada; afterward he came under the influence of the princes of Judah, who led him astray. Burney considered the possibility that v. 3b is "an early marginal note intended to qualify the absolute 'all his days,' " thus bringing Kings into line with the Chronicles narrative. There seems to be no difference in meaning between MT *kl ymyw,* "all his days," and LXX *kl hymym,* "all the days" (contra. Šanda).

5. *silver of the census tax, silver from the valuation of persons.* MT contains a veritable crux, but is construable if it is assumed (with most medieval commentators) that a shorthand is being employed to refer to two priestly levies: *kesep ʿôbēr ʾîš,* lit. "silver for entering, per person"; cf. Exod 30:11–16 for the phrase *ʿôbēr ʿal happĕqūdîm,* "who enters the register" for purposes of the census; *kesep napšôt ʿerkô,* lit. "silver of persons, his valuation"; cf. Lev 27:1–8 for *bĕʿerkĕkā nĕpāšôt,* "the valuation of persons" in payment of vows. Luc. reads only a single levy, "the valuation of persons." In the parallel passage in 2 Chr 24:9, only the "census tax" is referred to: "the tax imposed on Israel in the wilderness by Moses." Thus MT may be suspected of containing a conflated reading of two manuscript traditions, preserved singly in 2 Chronicles and the Greek translation of Kings.

The idiom *ʿōbēr lassōḥēr,* "at the current merchant's price," in Gen 23:16, cited by Ehrlich, *Randglossen,* is extraneous to the present matter (cf. Šanda).

The claim that the Mosaic "census tax" in Exod 30 is a postexilic formulation legitimizing the half-shekel donation of late Hasmonean times was refuted by J. Liver, "The Ransom of Half Shekel," *Y. Kaufmann Jubilee Volume* (ed. M. Haran, Jerusalem: Magnes, 1960), 54–67 (Hebrew).

6. *acquaintance.* A satisfactory solution to the hapax *makkār* has not been found. Current renditions include: "clients" (*NAB*); "from his own funds" (*NEB*); "benefactor" (*NJPS*).

The translation "acquaintance" allows that priests received personal gifts and loans from individuals, a practice discussed in *b. Giṭ.* 30a. Luc. and LXX read the text as *mikrô,* "his sale," apparently understanding priests to have been engaged in private dealings (cf. Deut 18:8). Ugaritic lists of temple personnel include *mkrm* along with priests and attendants, which suggested to some that "temple-tellers" (Montgomery-Gehman) or "business assessors" (Gray) are intended. For *mkrm,* "merchants" at Ugarit, see A. F. Rainey, "Business Agents at Ugarit," *IEJ* 13 (1963), 313–32; and idem, *Social Structure,* 57–62.

they shall repair the House wherever damage may be found. For Heb. *ḥazzēq bedeq,* lit. "to strengthen damage," cf. 22:5; Ezek 27:9, 27. According to *CAD* B 168, the "late substantive *batqu* should be considered an Aramaic loanword (from late Hebrew and Aramaic *bedeq*) and read *badqu.* This seems preferable to assuming a special development in Akkadian (Neo-Assyrian and Neo-Babylonian only)." Cf. earlier, J. C. Greenfield, *HUCA* 29 (1958), 221, n. 24; B. Levine, *Leš* 30 (1965), 10–11; J. N. Postgate, *Taxation and Conscription in the Assyrian Empire* (Rome: Biblical Institute Press, 1974), 40–62; S. Kaufman, *AS* 19, 41.

7. *But in the twenty-third year of Jehoash.* This is one of the few instances in Kings

in which a specific date is noted (cf. e.g. 1 Kgs 14:25); it derives from either a royal or a temple chronicle.

9. *nor to make repairs.* The priests accede to the new regulations arrived at under royal pressure and, at the same time, relieve themselves of all responsibility for repairs to the Temple (Abarbanel).

10. *a chest.* The vocalization of *ʾărôn* in MT gives the appearance of being a noun in construct; with the definite article, the form *hāʾārôn* is attested (e.g. Exod 24:14; Josh 3:15; 1 Kgs 8:3). But the construct form makes little sense here (Qimḥi's "the chest of someone" notwithstanding). Either the punctuators have erred (Burney) or *ʾărôn* is a *qitāl* formation (Bauer-Leander, 61 *eβ),* unrecognized by the dictionaries (cf. Haupt). *Arānu* is a loanword from West Semitic in the late Babylonian dialect of Akkadian (see *CAD* A 2.231).

A "cash box" (*arānu* or *quppu*) located near the temple gates was a regular feature of temple organization in Mesopotamia of the first millennium B.C.E.; cf. A. L. Oppenheim, "A Fiscal Practice of the Ancient Near East," *JNES* 6 (1947), 116–20, who also notes that secular authorities collected funds in a similar fashion.

and he set it near the altar. Stade declared MT "wrong, since the altar stood in the middle of the Temple court, not at the entrance"; and noting the transliteration in LXX *ammazeibe,* he restored *maṣṣēbâ,* "sacred pillar," in place of *mizbēaḥ,* "altar" (adopted by Burney, Montgomery-Gehman). But W. McKane (*ZAW* 71 [1959], 260–65) showed that the Greek cannot be used to support this emendation (cf. now, D. Barthélemy, *Critique textuelle,* ad loc.); *mizbēaḥ* was apparently the reading in all versions. The second half of the verse holds the solution to the commentators' puzzle: the common Judahite did not enter the Temple grounds to approach the collection box positioned on the right side of the altar; he handed over his donation to the Levitical guard at the gate, who deposited the gift in the box.

keepers of the threshold. The title *šōmēr hassāp* appears only in pre-exilic texts (22:4; 25:19; Jer 29:25) and is replaced during the Second Temple by the title *šōʿēr,* "gatekeeper." (Note that the list of returnees from Babylon includes "gatekeepers" in Ezra 2:42 = Neh 7:45.) Their duties remain unspecified and cannot yet be described with any confidence, despite the many references to the families of the gatekeepers in Chronicles (on which see J. Liver, *Chapters in the History of the Priests and Levites* [Jerusalem: Magnes, 1968], 100–26 [Hebrew]).

11. *the king's scribe and the high priest.* In a letter to King Esarhaddon, a reference is made to the fact that the royal delegate must be accompanied by a priest when checking the gold available for repair to the temple of Uruk (*ABL* 476: Obverse 27–Reverse 11; orally V. Hurowitz).

the high priest. The title *kōhēn gādôl* appears in 22:4 and 23:4 with reference to Hilkiah. But in 25:18, Seraiah is *kōhēn hārōʾš,* "head priest;" the sequence of terms in this verse and 23:4 proves the titles identical. The accepted view (e.g. de Vaux, *Ancient Israel,* 377–79; 397–98) is that "high priest" is a Second Temple title; during the pre-exilic era, the head of the Temple bureaucracy was simply "the priest" or "head priest." Accordingly, the titles in 2 Kgs 12 and 22 are seen as accretions from the hand of a later copyist. Yet it cannot be excluded that both titles coexisted in late First Temple times; they were still interchangeble in the days of the Chronicler, when in the opinion of all, the title was *kōhēn gādôl;* cf. e.g. 2 Chr 19:11, 24:11, 26:20.

For a comparable title in Assyrian temples, see note to 25:18.

and tie (it) up. For **ṣwr/*ṣrr,* used for "tying up" silver, see note to 5:23. The often cited suggestion of C. C. Torrey (*JNES* 2 [1943], 300–1) to revocalize MT to read *wayyiṣĕrû,* "they cast" (from **yṣr*), adopted by Montgomery-Gehman, Gray, *NEB,* and *NAB* ("melted down") makes good sense; for as a rule, the miscellaneous objects donated to the Temple were melted down into ingots of standard size and fineness. For cuneiform evidence of this smelting process, see Oppenheim, loc. cit. (above note to v. 10). Yet perhaps only the initial stage of collecting the silver is here described. That is the way the Chronicler (or a later scribe?) understood the verb: *wyʿrw,* "they emptied out" (2 Chr 24:11). (For another example of the interchange of *ṣ* / *ʿ*, cf. *hāṣēr* / *hāʿîr* in 2 Kgs 20:4 and see note there.)

12. *they used it to pay.* For **yṣʾ* in *hiphil,* denoting payment, see note to 15:20.

12–13. The regular maintenance of the Temple buildings was the responsibility of the "workmen in charge of the Temple"; major repairs had to be contracted out to skilled workers, here the carpenters, builders, masons, and stonecutters.

to repair the House. MT *lḥzqh* is vocalized as *qal* infinitive; the versions and many commentators read *lĕḥazzĕqô,* as the *piel,* which is the form of the verb throughout the chapter.

14. All these cultic vessels are referred to in 1 Kgs 7:50 at the time of their fashioning and in 2 Kgs 25:14–15, when they became booty for Nebuchadnezzar.

15. *fought against Gath and captured it.* Several town names are formed from the element *gat,* "press," e.g. Gath (in Philistia), 1 Kgs 2:39; Gath-hepher, 2 Kgs 14:25; Gath-rimmon, Josh 21:24; Gittaim, 2 Sam 4:3. According to B. Mazar ("Gath and Gittaim," *IEJ* 4 [1954], 227–35), the present Gath is identical with Gittaim, located at Ras Abu-Hamid, near modern Ramleh. From this point in the northern Shephelah, Hazael posed a direct threat to Jerusalem. Gath in Philistia is now generally sought farther south at Tell es-Ṣâfi; cf. Aharoni, *Land of the Bible*², 342; Kallai, *Tribes of Israel,* 80. Rainey, however, would identify the Philistine Gath with the Gath in the present verse (A. F. Rainey, *EI* 12 [1975], 63*–76*).

he set out to attack Jerusalem. For Heb. *śîm pānîm,* "to set face (toward)," cf. Gen 31:21; indicating "intention," Jer 42:15, 17; often in a hostile sense, Dan 11:17, and cf. M. Greenberg, *Ezekiel,* AB, ad 6:2.

19. *the sacred objects dedicated by . . . his ancestors.* Royal dedications, a sign of piety and attention to Temple needs, were deposited in the treasury of Temple (1 Kgs 7:51; 15:15); they were often rifled in order to buy off foreign attackers (1 Kgs 15:18; 2 Kgs 18:15).

21. *at Beth-millo, which leads down to Silla.* Assuming that the attack on the king took place in Jerusalem, Beth-millo, "the Millo House," may have been a prominent building in the Millo (cf. 1 Kgs 9:15; 2 Sam 5:9; 1 Chr 11:8), now taken to be the area on the eastern slope of the City of David, filled in and supported by terrace construction. See *EAEHL* 2.595–96. Silla is unidentified. Luc. has the variant reading "on the descent of Alon," which is of little help. Thenius, Stade, Šanda survey the suggested rewritings, while *NAB* and *JB* dismiss the last words altogether.

22. *The servants who killed him . . .* In 2 Chr 24:26, the assassins are reported to have been the sons of foreign women, Shimeath the Ammonitess and Shimrith the Moabitess. This datum appears to be exegetical amplification bringing home the point: "the ungrateful rose up and exacted recompense from Joash the ungrateful, as it is written: 'King Joash disregarded the loyalty which Jehoiada had shown to him' " (*Mek.* 17.8; and so Rashi, Qimḥi). Cf. too, A. Geiger (*Urschrift und Übersetzungen der Bibel* [Breslau: 1857], 49), who notes that the identifications in 2 Chr 24 are an

expression of the antipathy towards these nations during the postexilic period (e.g. Ezra 9:1).

Comment

The reign of Joash (836–798 B.C.E.) is introduced by the usual Deuteronomistic evaluation; the king's commendable behavior is explained as resulting from his following the instruction of Jehoiada the priest (v. 3). Jehoiada's dominant role in the revolution against Athaliah and his crowning the young Joash no doubt earned him a position of considerable influence at court, especially during the king's minority. He may have been guardian of Joash, perhaps even regent in Judah. This priestly rearing would seem to account for the special interest Joash showed in temple affairs.

The report of the repair of the Temple in vv. 5–17 focuses upon the royal initiative, in contrast to the negligence of the priests, as regards the renovations. At first, Joash ordered the use of general priestly revenue for this purpose. But this system proved unsatisfactory; the priests allowed the building to lie in disrepair, inasmuch as the costs were to be covered entirely from their own income. In his twenty-third year, Joash prescribed a new regulation, whereby all private donations (as opposed to obligatory dues, v. 17) were to be earmarked for the repairs; they would be collected separately and paid out directly to those in charge of the work, thus relieving the priests of responsibility and the authority with respect to the work.

Critical opinion is somewhat divided as to the derivation of this report: a few assign it to a Temple History, which included 2 Kgs 11, 22–23 (Wellhausen, Benzinger); many others note the disparaging view taken of the priesthood compared with the approbation of Joash's activity, and thus identify it as the report of the annals of the kings of Judah, if not a temple account edited by a court historian (Skinner, Šanda, Noth, Gray). Should this be the case and a court narrator was responsible for this firsthand look into Temple financing, then the report of 12:5–17 is a further evidence of the prominent role played by Judah's monarchs in the affairs of the country's main sanctuary.

Such a role is consistent with what is known from both Egypt and Mesopotamia, where rulers regularly prided themselves on the construction and endowment of shrines. In Egypt, Pharaoh proceeded "according to the design of his heart," he being god incarnate; in Assyria and Babylonia, the rebuilding of a temple began only after the divinity approved the construction.[1]

[1] A full exposition of the royal service of the gods can be found in H. Frankfort, *Kingship and the Gods* (Chicago: University of Chicago: 1948), 264–74.

From victorious kings the temple expected a share in the booty, especially precious votive gifts to be exhibited to the deity in the cella and the dedication of prisoners of war to increase the labor force of the temple. Under the tutelage of the priests, from the Old Babylonian period onward, kings were made to see that the building of larger and more sumptuously decorated sanctuaries with higher temple towers was an essential part of their duty toward the god, an expression of thanks as well as a guarantee of future successes. The Assyrian kings performed their duties in this respect much more energetically than was the case in Babylonia.[2]

Accordingly, Deuteronomistic notice of royal constructions and dedications in the temple of Jerusalem comes into focus; it goes beyond the routine formula "he did what was pleasing to YHWH," for in Judah, as abroad, kings were expected to concern themselves with the upkeep of the temple.[3] At the same time, the occasional seizure of temple treasures to pay off foreign attackers was not to a king's credit (cf. v. 19).

A supplementary tradition preserved in 2 Chr 24:17–22 tells of a rift between Joash and the priesthood which developed after the death of Jehoiada. It was then that the king came under the influence of the "princes of Judah" and their "idolatries." Chastised publicly by Zechariah the son of his mentor, Joash organized the stoning of his critic. Tensions such as those hinted at here may have had a part in the assassination of Joash by two of his courtiers, whose background is left untreated in the biblical accounts.

The single item of international political interest noted for the reign of Joash is the capture of Gath and the threat posed to Jerusalem (v. 18). No extrabiblical evidence is available to date this campaign, which represents the deepest penetration of Aramaean forces into Israel and the border of Philistia.[4] Hazael had usurped the throne ca. 845, and he continued to rule until close to the end of the ninth century (see Comment to 8:7–15). But it was only during his last decades, when Aram-Damascus was relieved of Assyrian pressures, that he pursued his aggressive policies to the south and the west. The attack on Gath, therefore, should be interpreted in conjunction with those on Israel during the reign of Jehu (cf. 10:32–33) and especially that of Jehoahaz (cf. 13:3, 22).

[2] A. L. Oppenheim, *Ancient Mesopotamia* (Chicago: University of Chicago, 1964), 106.

[3] A view of the Deuteronomistic editing which seems too narrow holds that the present story was included in Kings so that reference to it could be made later in 2 Kgs 22:1–10, the central narrative in the Deuteronomistic history (e.g., Eissfeldt).

[4] The date 814 B.C.E. suggested by B. Mazar (*IEJ* 4 [1954], 230) is apparently based upon a literal reading of v. 18—"Then Hazael king of Aram marched . . . ," i.e., in the twenty-third year, cf. v. 7. But "then" is an editorial term with little chronological significance; see note to 16:5–6.

XIX. THE REIGN OF JEHOAHAZ (ISRAEL)

(13:1–9)

13 1 In the twenty-third year of Joash son of Ahaziah king of Judah,
Jehoahaz son of Jehu became king over Israel in Samaria for seventeen
years. 2 He did what was displeasing to YHWH. He followed the sinful
way[a] of Jeroboam son of Nebat, who caused Israel to sin; he did not
stray from it. 3 YHWH was incensed at Israel, and so he handed them
over to Hazael king of Aram and Ben-hadad son of Hazael for many
years. 4 But Jehoahaz implored YHWH and YHWH heard him, for he
saw the oppression of Israel, how the king of Aram had oppressed
them. 5 So YHWH gave Israel a deliverer and they were freed from the
authority of Aram. The Israelites lived peacefully[b] as in former times.
6 But they did not stray from the sinful way[a] of the house of Jeroboam
who had caused Israel to sin[c]; they followed it. There was even a pole
of Asherah in Samaria. 7 Jehoahaz was left with no force, except fifty
horsemen, ten chariots, and ten thousand foot soldiers; for the king of
Aram had destroyed them and crushed them like dust. 8 The rest of
the history of Jehoahaz and all that he did and his exploits are indeed
recorded in the Annals of the kings of Israel. 9 So Jehoahaz slept with
his ancestors and was buried in Samaria. Joash his son succeeded him.

[a] Read *ḥaṭṭa’t,* in sing.
[b] Lit. "in their tents."
[c] With qere *hḥṭy’.*

Notes

13 1. *Jehoahaz.* The name appears on a stamp seal dated to the end of the seventh century B.C.E.: *lyh’ḥz bn hmlk,* "(belonging) to Jehoahaz, son of the king." See N. Avigad, *EI* 9 (1969), 9. The hypocoristic form of the name, Ahaz, is known from the Davidic dynasty: see below 16:1.

seventeen years. The synchronisms with Joash of Judah in vv. 1 and 10 show that Jehoahaz reigned fourteen years. The number "seventeen years" in MT can be retained either by positing a three-year coregency with his father Jehu (so Tadmor, "Chronology", 280–81) or by suggesting a shift in the reckoning system from post to antedating in both kingdoms (so, Thiele, *MNHK²*, 72–73). The chronology of Josephus resolved the puzzle by reading "the twenty-first year of Joash" (*Antiquities* ix.173).

3. *Hazael king of Aram.* See above note to 8:8, and 10:32, 12:18.

Ben-hadad son of Hazael. Ben-hadad III is mentioned in the Zakur inscription (*ANET³*, 501) and is most likely the Ben-hadad who laid siege to Samaria. See above the note to 6:24. Mariʾ (*Ma-ri-ʾi*) king of Damascus defeated by Adad-nirari III was either Hazael or more probably Ben-hadad III. (*ANET³*, 281–82; and cf. S. Page, *Iraq* 30 [1968], 141–42.) Mari' is either an honorific title of Aramaean kings meaning "the/my lord"; or a hypocoristicon; see W. F. Albright, *BASOR* 87 (1942), 28, n. 16; F. M. Cross, *BASOR* 205 (1972), 41, n. 21.

for many years. Lit. "all the days." Cf. below v. 22, "all the days of Jehoahaz."

5. *a deliverer.* Heb. *môšîaʿ*. The term echoes the phraseology of the book of Judges, in which divinely summoned leaders rescued Israel from their oppressors; cf. e.g. Judg 2:18; 3:9, 15. The identity of the present "deliverer," unnamed in the text, remains disputed. He has been taken to be Joash (Qimḥi, Benzinger, A. Cody *CBQ* 32 [1970], 336–37); Jeroboam II (Thenius, Stade, Skinner, Šanda, Eissfeldt, Montgomery-Gehman, *NAB);* Elisha (Noth, *Überlieferungsgeschichtliche Studien,* 84; Gray); Adad-nirari III (Winckler, *KAT³*, 260; B. Mazar, *BAR* 2.145; Tadmor, *EncMiqr* 3.479); and even Zakur of Hamath (Cooke, *CAH¹* 3.376). To be noted in particular is the use of the verb *hôšîaʿ*, "to deliver" both with reference to Joash (see below v. 17—"an arrow of victory [*tĕšûʿâ*] over Aram") and Jeroboam (see 14:27—"he delivered them" [*wayyôšîʿēm*]). For historical evaluation of these traditions, see further in Comment.

6. Verse 6a is an example of *Wiederaufnahme,* "resumptive repetition," picking up the narrative framework of v. 2 which was broken off by the insertion of vv. 3–5. (On this literary device, see the note to 17:34.)

pole of Asherah. For the term *ʾăšērâ,* both the name of the goddess Asherah and the sacred pole associated with her cult, see the note to 21:7. The venerated object referred to here was erected by Ahab (1 Kgs 16:33) but had not been purged by Jehu (cf. above 10:26–28).

7. *Jehoahaz was left with no force.* Heb. *ʿam,* "kinsman, people," can mean "forces" in military contexts; cf. e.g. Exod 14:6; Num 21:23, 33; 1 Kgs 16:15; 2 Kgs 8:21 and see the comment by Skinner, ad loc. Therefore Gray's proposed emendation (*ʿṣm* for *ʿm*) is gratuitous.

ten thousand foot soldiers. The number seems extraordinarily high. If so, the numeral "ten," *ʿăśeret,* may be an erroneous scribal addition from the preceding "ten" (*ʿăśārâ*) chariots." Perhaps originally the text had *ʾalpayim* "two thousand;" cf. Josh 7:3.

On the other hand, "ten thousand" sets in contrast the depleted chariot and cavalry forces and the relatively larger infantry. In the engagements between Aram-Damascus and Assyria during the preceding decades, it was the number of mobile units mustered which determined the victor (see M. Elat, *IEJ* 25 [1975], 25–35). So, too, here; Israel's small chariot force was no match for Aram, despite the "ten thousand." To take *ʾelep* as "company, contingent" (so R. G. Boling, *Judges,* AB ad 1:4, following G. E. Mendenhall, *JBL* 77 [1958], 52–66), a term which may be applicable to Israel's premonarchic society, does not help in the present context.

and crushed them like dust. For a similar image, see Amos 1:3, where the sharp implement referred to is the threshing sled; cf. Isa 41:15 and 28:27. In analogous fashion, Tiglath-pileser III claimed, "I crushed [the enemy] as if with a threshing sled" (*kīma dayašti adīš*); see *CAD* D 33b.

Comment

The Aramaean oppression of Israel which reached its peak during the days of Jehoahaz is presented in a unit that appears to have been edited in stages. The narrative framework vv. 1–2, 8–9, in formulae used exclusively for Israelite monarchs, is interrupted by vv. 3–5 (note the *Wiederaufnahme* in v. 6a). Verse 7 was appended by a later hand as a footnote; its loose connection with the preceding suggests its marginal origin.

Although the story of the supplication of Jehoahaz and YHWH's favorable response to his prayer is the only one of its kind in the history of the northern kingdom as reported in the book of Kings, it should not be dismissed as a late invention,[1] for it may well derive from genuine Israelite pre-Deuteronomistic traditions, whether oral or written.[2] The beginning of relief is credited to the king's efficacious prayer.[3] If the Israelite king who withstood the siege of Samaria was indeed Jehoahaz as argued earlier (see Comment to 6:24–7:20), then his act of contrition in that city (6:30) complements the tradition in 13:4. Moreover, if a specific event signaling the divine deliverance should be sought, then the sudden lifting of the siege of Samaria would fulfill that requirement.

[1] So e.g. Noth, *Überlieferungsgeschichtliche Studien* 84; and more recently Dietrich, *Prophetie und Geschichte,* 34–35.

[2] The statements in 13:23 and 14:26–27 are similar in tone to the one in 13:3–5 and combine to produce a moderately positive assessment of YHWH's regard for Israel. See further in Comment to 14:23–29.

[3] The contemporary Aramaic inscription of Zakur of Hamath records the deliverance of Zakur from the siege of Hadrach by Bar-hadad (= Ben-hadad III) in terms reminiscent of 2 Kgs 13:4. Zakur says:

> I lifted my hands to Baalshamayn and Baalshamayn answered me . . . through seers and diviners. And Baalshamayn [said] to me: Fear not, for I have made you king and [I shall stand] by you. I shall deliver you from all [the kings] who have besieged you.

For the text and notes see *KAI* No. 202 and cf. *ANET³*, 501–02. For a recent discussion of the historical circumstances of the siege of Hadrach, see A. R. Millard, *PEQ* 105 (1973), 161–64. (The pronunciation of the name Zakur, rather than Zakir, is now known from the unpublished stele of Adad-nirari III in the Antakya Museum, cf. J. D. Hawkins, RLA 5.238.)

XX. THE REIGN OF JOASH (ISRAEL)

(13:10–13)

13 10 In the thirty-seventh year of Joash king of Judah, Jehoash son
of Jehoahaz became king over Israel in Samaria for sixteen years. 11 He
did what was displeasing to YHWH. He did not stray from all the sinful
way[a] of Jeroboam son of Nebat who caused Israel to sin; he followed
it. 12 The rest of the history of Joash and all that he did and his
exploits, that he fought with Amaziah king of Judah, are indeed recorded in the annals of the kings of Israel. 13 So Joash slept with his
ancestors—Jeroboam took the throne—and Joash was buried in Samaria with the kings of Israel.

[a] Read *ḥaṭṭaʾt* in sing.

Notes

13 10. *the thirty-seventh year of Joash king of Judah.* The LXX tradition seems to have corrected the text to "thirty-nine" or "forty," thus coordinating the figure with the seventeen-year reign of Jehoahaz in v. 1 (so, Montgomery-Gehman). But this adds two years to the reign of Joash and complicates the synchronism in 14:1 unnecessarily; see comments there.

Jehoash son of Jehoahaz. In the Tell al-Rimah stele, he is called *Yaʾasu Samerīnāya,* "Joash (of the land) of Samaria"; see S. Page, *Iraq* 30 (1968), 142, line 8. (Alternate readings of the transcription of the name have been suggested: *Yaʾusu* [so W. F. Albright in "Prolegomenon" to Burney, *Notes* (New York: Ktav, 1970) 35], and *Yuʾasu* [so, A. Malamat, *BASOR* 204 (1971), 37–39.])

12–13. These verses are repeated almost entirely in 14:15–16; they are omitted by Luc. here. But if we consider the unit 14:8–14 to be basically a northern story, then the repeated conclusion to the reign of Joash in 14:15–16 was taken over when the whole unit was removed to its present position within the reign of Amaziah (so Burney, Skinner). A later hand added them once again in 13:12–13, so as to conclude Joash's reign. The unique statement, "and Jeroboam took the throne," in v. 13, which departs from the standard formula of succession (cf 14:16), also points to its secondary origin.

Comment

The history of Joash has been curtailed by successive, heavy-handed editing, so that all that remains of the original text is the opening section of the narrative framework, vv. 10–11. Other information relating to the period appears now in separate contexts: Joash's war with Amaziah, in 14:8–14; his victories over the Aramaeans in 13:25. The concluding verses on the king's reign, vv. 12–13, are secondary (see note); the original version of them is preserved in 14:15–16. The reordering of these verses in Luc. which places vv. 12–13 at the end of the chapter after v. 25 is merely an attempt to recreate the concluding part of the narrative framework; but this reordering overlooks the intent of the editorial reprise, vv. 22–25, which follows the prophetic tale (on which, see further below).[1]

[1] Some commentators (e.g. Burney, Gray) thought that Luc. preserved a more original text, prior to displacements, but the evaluation of Montgomery-Gehman is adopted here.

XXI. A PROPHECY OF VICTORY; THE DEATH OF ELISHA

(13:14–25)

13 14 Now Elisha fell ill with a sickness of which he was to die. Joash
king of Israel went down to him; he wept over him and said: "My
father, my father. The chariots of Israel and its horsemen!" 15 Elisha
said to him, "Take a bow and arrows," and he took a bow and arrows.
16 Then he said to the king of Israel, "Put your hand to the bow." He
put his hand (to the bow), and Elisha placed his hands on the king's
hands 17 and said, "Open the window facing east." He opened (it).
Elisha said, "Shoot" and he shot. He said, "An arrow of victory for
YHWH. An arrow of victory over Aram. You will defeat Aram at
Aphek completely." 18 Then he said, "Take the arrows," and he took
(them). He said to the king of Israel, "Strike the ground!" He struck
three times and stopped. 19 But the man of God was angry at him and
said, "Had you struck five or six times, then you would have defeated
Aram completely. Now you will defeat Aram (only) three times."
20 Then Elisha died and was buried.

Moabite bands used to raid the land with the start of the year.[a]
21 Once, they were burying a man and they spotted such a band. They
threw the body[b] into the grave of Elisha and left.[c] When the body[b]
touched the bones of Elisha, it came alive and stood on its feet.

22 Hazael king of Aram oppressed Israel all the days of Jehoahaz.
23 But YHWH was gracious and had mercy upon them. He showed
regard for them because of his covenant with Abraham, Isaac, and
Jacob. He would not destroy them, and so has not rid himself of them
until now. 24 When Hazael king of Aram died, Ben-hadad his son
succeeded him. 25 Jehoash son of Jehoahaz recaptured the cities from
Ben-hadad son of Hazael, which had been taken in war from Jehoahaz

[a] Read *bĕbōʾ haššānâ.* See note.
[b] Lit. "the man."
[c] Read: *wayyēlĕkû* with LXX. Final *waw* lost through haplography.

his father. Joash defeated him three times and thus recovered the cities of Israel.

Notes

13 14. *of which he was to die.* For the concessive force of the imperfect, see Driver, *Tenses,* 39β.

went down to him. Just where the prophet was confined is not stated. Gray (ad loc.) speculates that he died and was buried in Jericho, taking into account the accessibility to Moabite raiders of the lower Jordan valley and the location of Elisha's sepulcher (below v. 20). But also to be considered are Elisha's home town of Abel-meholah (1 Kgs 19:16) in the Jordan Valley or else the eastern plateau in Trans-Jordan as the sites to which he retired and at which he was interred.

The chariots of Israel and its horsemen! For this encomium, formerly proclaimed by Elisha of his master, see the note to 2:12. But unlike Elijah, in the Elisha traditions the prophet is specifically associated with chariots and horses. Cf. 6:8–23.

17. *Aphek.* For the identification of this Aphek on the plateau to the east of the Sea of Galilee, see note to 1 Kgs 20:26. J. M. Miller's recent revival (*ZAW* 80 [1968], 339–40) of the older suggestion of S. Tolkowsky (*JPOS* 2 [1922], 145–48] to locate Aphek on Mt. Gilboa is very problematic, inasmuch as there is neither textual nor archaeological evidence for an Aphek in the region of the Jezreel Valley. See W. F. Albright, *JPOS* 2 (1922), 184–89.

The prophetic specification of the site of the future victories of Joash is unusual and may indeed be an accretion *post eventum* (so, Montgomery-Gehman). In any event, it evokes the earlier victory at Aphek in Trans-Jordan mentioned in 1 Kgs 20:26ff. Ehrlich even suggested reading *kbʾpk,* "as at Aphek," thus explicitly connecting the two traditions.

completely. The infinitive *ʿad kallēh* conveys the sense of "make an end of"; cf. 1 Kgs 22:11.

19. *Had you struck.* Heb. *lĕhakkôt.* All translations beginning with LXX render the infinitive as though it were used paraphrastically; see Driver, *Tenses,* 204. Thus there is no need to emend (with Klostermann, followed by Gray) or repoint the text (with Šanda).

20. *to raid the land.* For the idiom *bôʾ bāʾāreṣ,* see the note to 6:23.

with the start of the year. MT *bāʾ šānâ* is meaningless. The LXX and Targum renditions suggest emending to: *bĕbōʾ haššānâ.* Cf. the expressions for seasonal periods: *ṣēʾt haššānâ,* "end of the year" (Exod 23:16) and *tĕšûbat haššānâ,* "turn of the year" (1 Kgs 20:22, 26) and cf. Exod 34:22. Other proposed readings include: *šānâ bĕšānâ* "yearly" (Kittel, Eissfeldt, *NAB*); *bāh baššānâ* "in that very year" (Vulg., Syr., Qimḥi).

21. *and left.* MT *wylk* is read *wylkw,* the *waw* having been lost through haplography due to the following *wygʿ.* Another explanation, however, can account for the loss of the final consonant. As Luzzatto observed (Commentary to Jer 23:14), in many cases in which the last consonant of a word is identical with the first consonant of the following word, copyists sometimes wrote only one consonant; the second consonant

was later restored (written small), e.g., Gen 27:46; but in other instances, it was left uncorrected, e.g., 1 Sam 19:9, 2 Sam 5:2, 2 Kgs 13:6, Jer 32:35, 39:16. This "shorthand" is also attested in Lachish letter 3.8 where *ky'mr* stands for *ky y'mr,* and in 3.9: *ḥyhwh* stands for *ḥy yhwh.*

22. Luc. has a long addition: *kai elaben Azael ton allophulon ek cheiros autou apo thalasses tes kath esperan eos Aphek,* "and Hazael took Philistia from his hand, from the sea of the West to Aphek." Most critics, beginning with Stade, have accepted this addition as genuine. But as Šanda noted, the geographical terminology is confused. If Aphek east of the Sea of Galilee is meant, then the notice is meaningless, especially since the Philistines never controlled northern Israel as far as Aphek! Hazael must have reached Aphek in Sharon on his way to Gath (12:18), but again Jehoahaz never ruled Philistia. Gray suggested to take *allophulon* as translating an original *haggōy* which was a "corruption of *haggālīl,* 'Galilee' " (601, n. *a*). But this attempt to rescue the verse seems farfetched. Rahlfs (*Septuaginta-Studien,* 3.289) considered the addition a secondary expansion, which was partly based on mistranslation of *yām hāʿărāvâ* (cf. 14:25) as *yām hammaʿărāb,* "western sea" (so Luc. there); and cf. Montgomery-Gehman, 438. Thus, in this case, caution is advisable in using the Lucianic expanded reading as a source of historical information (as adopted by A. Jepsen, *AfO* 14 [1941–44], 168; B. Mazar, *IEJ* 4 [1954], 231, and M. Noth, *History,* 239).

23. *Abraham, Isaac, and Jacob.* The patriarchs of Israel are mentioned only once before in Kings, in the Elijah narrative in 1 Kgs 18:36, and see Comment there.

25. *and thus recovered the cities of Israel.* The cities lost by Jehoahaz to Hazael were apparently all west of the Jordan (cf. 12:18); the Trans-Jordanian territories having fallen to him already in the days of Jehu (cf. 10:32–33). The victories of Joash at Aphek, at the entrance to western Israel from the northeast, curtailed the Aramaean expansion and paved the way for a complete reversal by Jeroboam II (see below on 14:25).

Comment

1. Elisha had made his first appearance toward the end of the reign of Ahab and before the accession of Hazael (see 1 Kgs 19:19–21); the story of his death is set nearly a half century later. Such a lengthy ministry is indeed remarkable, though by no means unreasonable.

From his death bed, Elisha directs the performance of two magical acts, which consist of the following parts: instruction, performance, incantation, and/or interpretation. The shooting of an arrow eastward in the direction of Aram speaks for itself. The very striking incantatory words of the prophet infuse the act with propulsive power. Although this act and many others performed by Elisha resemble non-Israelite magical practices, and are not accompanied by explicit invocation of YHWH, they should not be regarded as a violation of biblical law or a circumvention of the divine will. In the present instance, the arrow is symbolically called YHWH's arrow of victory.[1] In the second act,[2] the hitting of the ground with arrows symbolizes the beating of Aram; the number of foretold victories is linked technically to the number of beats.[3]

The story has still another dimension. It is the testament of a dying man of God, prophesying future victory for Israel. Similar predictive testaments are reported in the early histories of Isaac (Gen 27:27–29); Jacob (Gen 49:1–28); and Moses (Deut 33). Although the story is part of the Elisha cycle, one might speculate upon the unmentioned background of Joash's visit. Prophets were regularly consulted prior to the departure of the army to battle (cf. e.g. 1 Kgs 22); Elisha even accompanied Jehoram on his Moabite campaign (see above 3:11). Might not Joash have sought the advice of the dying Elisha, just as Israel was setting out to attack Aram?

As a footnote to this prophetic tale, a wonder story was added. Not only was Elisha endowed with restorative powers during his life (cf. 4:8–37), but these powers extended beyond his death and into the grave. Thus the Elisha cycle is closed; it opens with a tale about his deadly curse (2:23–25) and ends with one about life-giving contact with his bones.

2. The unit 13:22–25, which is outside the narrative framework, surveys the reigns of Jehoahaz and Joash for a second time, but solely from the point of view of Aram-Israel relations. According to this source, Aramaean pressure upon Israel continued throughout the reign of Jehoahaz (contrary to v. 4); it was not until Ben-hadad succeeded Hazael that Joash was able to push back the Aramaeans and recover Israel's lost cities. The point is made that Joash was victorious over Aram in three battles, but the sites are not specified in the text.

It appears that these verses are not misplaced fragments from the preceding units of the chapter. They have been so constructed and so placed within the chapter as to exemplify the theme "prophecy fulfilled," a theme prominent

[1] See the remarks of J. J. M. Roberts in *Unity and Diversity,* eds. H. Goedicke and J. J. M. Roberts, (Baltimore: Johns Hopkins University Press, 1975), 186; and earlier, G. Fohrer, *ZAW* 78 (1966), 25–47.

[2] Josephus in his recapitulation of the scene (*Antiquities* ix.180–81) combined the second act with the first: Elisha is angered that the king did not shoot three arrows. Y. Kaufmann took this second act as a late expansion, intended to explain away the failure of Elisha's original prediction of complete victory (*Religion of Israel,* 282).

[3] Ezek 21:21 records the unique instance of arrows used in forecasting. This particular ritual is unattested in Mesopotamian sources, but bows and arrows can be found in Mesopotamian prophylactic magic (*namburbi* rituals) and prognostics. See R. Caplice, *Or* 39 (1970), 116, 142f.; and A. L. Oppenheim, *The Interpretation of Dreams in the Ancient Near East,* TAPS 46/3 (1956), 286.

On the evidence for belomancy in Israel and the ancient world, see S. Iwry, *JAOS* 81 (1961), 27–34; and M. Fishbane, *Studies in Biblical Magic* (unpublished dissertation, Brandeis University, 1971), 136–40.

throughout Kings. The unit lays stress upon YHWH's gracious concern for Israel in its adversity, and upon the series of victories granted to Joash, just as had been prophesied by Elisha.

This twice-told history of Israel in 2 Kgs 13 accords well with contemporary regional history. The reign of Jehoahaz (817–800) corresponds with the latter years of Hazael and the first decade of Ben-hadad III, king of Aram. Aramaean ascendance was at its peak. It has already been noted that Assyria, Aram's powerful foe to the north and east, retreated from the area west of the Euphrates during the reign of Shamshi-Adad V (824–811). The latter years of that king were devoted to campaigning in Babylonia, and from the point of view of Damascus, Assyria had entered a period of decline. Another Aramaean state which rose to power during Assyria's absence from the scene was Arpad under the dynasty of Agusi.[4]

It was not until the fifth year of Adad-nirari III (811–783), Shamshi-Adad's successor, that a shift in Assyrian policy was initiated. The Assyrian Eponym Chronicle, the main chronological source at hand, reports what appear to be two thrusts against the West, the first target being Arpad and its vicinity (805–803), the second being Manṣuate, in the Beqaʿ of Lebanon (796). Strangely enough, Damascus is not mentioned, even though in the several extant commemorative inscriptions of Adad-nirari, the defeats of Arpad and Damascus are certainly his main achievements.[5]

Though differing in details, the commemorative inscriptions agree on the main features of the subjugation of Damascus. Here is the account on the Calah slab:

> I set out for Damascus and besieged Mariʾ king of Damascus in Damascus, his royal city. The radiant splendor of (the god) Ashur, my lord overwhelmed him and he took hold of my feet, and became my vassal. 2300 talents of silver, 20 talents of gold, 3000 talents of bronze, 5000 talents of iron . . . I received in Damascus his royal city in his palace.

The Tell al-Rimah stele provides additional information in summary fashion:

[4] The name of the rebellious king of Arpad is now known from the Sheikh Hammad stele of Adad-nirari: Atar-šumki. See A. R. Millard and H. Tadmor, *Iraq* 35 (1973), 58–59. He is the *ʿtrsmk* of the Sefire treaty, father (or grandfather?) of Matiʾel of Arpad (cf. *ANET³*, 659–61).

[5] These inscriptions are all undated: the stone slab from Calah (*ANET³*, 281–82); the Saba'a stele (*ANET³*, 282); the Tell al-Rimah stele (*Iraq* 30 [1968], 141–42). See also H. Tadmor, *Iraq* 35 (1973), 141–50. An unpublished stele of Adad-nirari III from north Syria is mentioned by J. D. Hawkins, RLA 5.239. (Note that in the Saba'a stele, the transcription in *ANET³*, 282 of *Palaštu* should be corrected to read: *māt Ḫatte*, "the land of Hatti;" see H. Tadmor, *IEJ* 19 [1969], 46–48. The translation of *Palaštu* on the Calah slab [*ANET³*, 281] should be *Philistia*, as already in Wiseman, *DOTT*, 51, not "Palestine.") For translation, see Appendix I, No. 3.

> In a single year I made the land of Amurru and Hatti (i.e. the West) in its entirety kneel at my feet; I imposed tribute and tax for future days upon them. . . . He received . . . tribute from Mari' of Damascus, Joash of Samaria, the Tyrians, and the Sidonians.

By all counts, a major victory was rightly claimed by Adad-nirari, one not achieved even by Shalmaneser III; the Assyrian army had entered Damascus and received the submission of Mari' (= Ben-hadad III). This defeat of Aram in a single campaign is probably to be dated 796; the notation "to Manṣuate" in the Eponym Chronicle would then indicate the location of the main Assyrian camp on the road to Damascus at the time the Chronicle entry was made. The tribute payment of Joash, who had come to the throne in Samaria just a few years earlier, obliquely confirms this date.[6]

The extrabiblical data render the deliverance of Jehoahaz and Joash intelligible. Israel was freed from Aramaean hegemony in several stages. At first, Ben-hadad withdrew his blockade of Samaria and its king Jehoahaz in response to the campaigns of Adad-nirari in northern Syria between 805 and 803. Later, in 796, Ben-hadad submitted to Adad-nirari. It was this event which no doubt prompted Joash, who was now on the throne of Israel, to pay tribute to the Assyrian king, the area's ostensible deliverer. (Whether the narrator in 13:5 intended to credit Adad-nirari with the rescue of Israel by the designation *môšîᶜa,* "deliverer," is an open question; see the note at 13:5.) Later, but still suffering from the effects of its earlier reversals, Damascus was dealt a threefold defeat by Joash at Aphek. Though defeated, Damascus did not pass from the scene as a power in southern Syria. It served as the target of a further Assyrian campaign in 773, and again, along with Hadrach, in the years 772, 765, and 755. By then Jeroboam II reigned in Israel, and it was he who was credited with bringing the entire area under Israel's hegemony (see below on 14:23–29).

[6] Numerous studies appeared soon after the publication of the Rimah stele, centering on the questions of the submission of Damascus and the date of Joash's payment of tribute. For the variety of opinions setting the date either in 802 or 796, the following may be usefully consulted: H. Cazelles, *CRAIBL* 1969, 106–18; A. R. Cody, *CBQ* 32 (1970), 325–40; H. Donner in *Archäologie und Altes Testament* Festschrift für K. Galling, eds. A. Kuschke and E. Kutsch (Tübingen: J. C. B. Mohr, 1970), 49–59; A. Jepsen, *VT* 20 (1970), 359–61; J. A. Soggin, *VT* 20 (1970), 366–68; E. Lipiński, Proceedings of Fifth *WCJS,* 157–73; B. Oded, *Studies on the History of the Jewish People and the Land of Israel* (Haifa University, 1972), 2.25–34; A. R. Millard, *PEQ* 105 (1973), 161–64; A. R. Millard and H. Tadmor, *Iraq* 35 (1973), 57–64; H. Tadmor, *Iraq* 35 (1973), 141–50.

XXII. THE REIGN OF AMAZIAH (JUDAH)

(14:1–22)

14 1 In the second year of Joash son of Joahaz king of Israel,
Amaziah son of Joash king of Judah became king. 2 He was twenty-
five years old when he became king, and he reigned twenty-nine years
in Jerusalem. His mother's name was Jehoaddan[a] from Jerusalem.
3 He did what was pleasing to YHWH, yet not like David his ancestor;
he did just as Joash his father had done. 4 Yet the high places were not
removed; the people continued to sacrifice and to make offerings at the
high places. 5 When the kingdom was firmly in his hand, he put to
death those of his servants who had attacked the king his father. 6 But
he did not put to death the sons of the attackers, in accordance with
what is written in the book of the Teaching of Moses which YHWH
commanded: Fathers shall not be put to death for their children; children shall not be put to death for their fathers. Each shall be put to
death[b] only for his own sin.

7 He defeated ten thousand Edomites in the Valley of Salt[c], and he
captured Sela in battle and named it Joktheel, (as it is called) until this
day.

8 Then Amaziah sent messengers to Jehoash son of Jehoahaz son of
Jehu king of Israel: "Come, let us meet face to face!" 9 Jehoash king of
Israel responded to Amaziah king of Judah, "The thistle in Lebanon
sent a message to the cedar in Lebanon, 'Give your daughter in marriage to my son.' But a wild animal in Lebanon passed by and trampled the thistle. 10 You certainly did defeat Edom, but then it has
carried you away. Enjoy your honor, and do stay at home! Now why
provoke trouble in which you and Judah will fall?" 11 But Amaziah
did not take heed. So Jehoash king of Israel set out and they met face
to face, he and Amaziah king of Judah, at Beth-shemesh in Judah.
12 Judah was routed by Israel, and they all fled to their homes.[d] 13 Je-

[a] So with qere and 2 Chr 25:1. Ketib, followed by LXX, read Jehoaddin.
[b] Read *yûmāt* with qere for *yāmût* in ketib.
[c] Read *melaḥ* with qere, without determination *hmlḥ*.
[d] So with ketib *lʾhlw* (lit., "each one to his tent"), rather than qere *lʾhlyw*.

hoash king of Israel captured Amaziah king of Judah son of Jehoash son of Ahaziah at Beth-shemesh. Then he marched[e] to Jerusalem, and breached the walls of Jerusalem from the Ephraim Gate to the Corner Gate, a distance of four hundred cubits. 14 He carried off all the gold and the silver and all the vessels which were found in the House of YHWH and in the royal treasuries and hostages, and then returned to Samaria.

15 The rest of the history of Jehoash (and)[f] what he did and his exploits, and how he fought with Amaziah king of Judah are indeed recorded in the annals of the kings of Israel. 16 So Jehoash slept with his ancestors and he was buried in Samaria with the kings of Israel. Jeroboam his son succeeded him.

17 Amaziah son of Joash king of Judah lived fifteen years after the death of Jehoash son of Jehoahaz king of Israel. 18 The rest of the history of Amaziah is indeed recorded in the annals of the kings of Judah. 19 A conspiracy was formed against him in Jerusalem, and so he fled to Lachish. But they sent after him to Lachish and killed him there. 20 They brought him (back) on horses, and he was buried in Jerusalem with his ancestors in the City of David. 21 Then all the People of Judah took Azariah—he was then sixteen years old—and they made him king to succeed his father Amaziah. 22 It was he who rebuilt Elath and restored it to Judah, after the king slept with his ancestors.

[e] So with qere *wybʾ* for *wybʾw* in ketib.
[f] Some mss. and Syr. add *wĕkōl* "and all."

Notes

14 1. *Amaziah son of Joash.* The verb *ʾmṣ,* "to be strong," appears without the theophoric element in the name Amoz, the father of Isaiah (cf. Isa 1:1) and on the seal of *ʾmṣ hspr,* "Amoz, the scribe" (Diringer, *Iscrizioni,* 235), and see also the inscribed sherd from Tel Dan: *lʾmṣ*[*x*] "to Amoz[x]" (A. Biran, *BA* 37 [1974], 50).

2. *he reigned twenty-nine years.* Amaziah could not have reigned for this length of time. As the synchronisms with the forty-one-year reign of Jeroboam in Israel (14:23; 15:8) indicate, Amaziah's reign is unduly long by fourteen or fifteen years. Therefore, it appears (following J. Lewy, *Chronologie,* 11–14) that after Amaziah's defeat at Beth-shemesh and the raid by Joash on Jerusalem, Azariah his son was placed on the throne as regent, with Amaziah remaining as titular king, but without authority. This would explain the unusual notice in v. 17. A shortened reign of thirteen years, then, may be safely assigned to Amaziah.

Jehoaddan. The name is composed of the theophoric element (YHW) and a form of

*ʿdn, "to have pleasure, delight in." A related name from the same root appears on a seal of the seventh century: *mʿdnh bt hmlk*, "Maʿadanah, the daughter of the king," published by N. Avigad, *IEJ* 28 (1978), 146–51; cf. also J. J. Stamm, *VT* Sup 16 (1967), 313.

4. *Yet the high places were not removed.* For the same formula, see the note to 12:4.

6. *book.* Lit. "a written document, record," here probably in scroll form. Translated as "letter" in 5:5, 10:1, 19:14, 20:12.

written in the book of the Teaching of Moses. The quotation is from Deut 24:16, with the addition of two words *kî ʾim*, here translated as "only." Stade suggested that the passage was a free rendering of text in Deuteronomy. The ketib/qere alteration of *yāmût / yûmāt* may also point to the same phenomenon; but in this case, the qere brought the words into line with the original text.

The practice of blood revenge was common in the ancient Near East and persists in certain traditional societies of the modern Near East. The avenger is duty-bound to slay the murderer or one of his kinsmen, thus righting the imbalance in the community caused by the original loss. Similarly, usurpers insured their throne by exterminating the family of the former king who were potential rivals and avengers. (See M. Greenberg, s.v. "Avenger of Blood," *IBD* 1.321.) Amaziah's act in sparing the sons of his father's assassins was thus a departure from customary practice, and as such is duly stressed by the Deuteronomistic historian. His act was in line with Deuteronomic law (Deut 24:16) quoted in the verse. From the wording of v. 6, it is unclear whether the historian meant that Amaziah actually was guided by the nucleus of the "book of the Teaching of Moses" (which must have existed at that time), or that this is his reflection of Amaziah's act vis-à-vis the norms current at the time the text of Kings was being edited—i.e. after the Josianic reform.

7. *ten thousand Edomites.* Obviously a typological number indicating a vast army, which in poetry would be rendered *rĕbābâ*, e.g. cf. 1 Sam 18:7. The execution of the captured Edomites by hurling them from the top of a cliff (*selʿa*) is described in 2 Chr 25:12. This gruesome detail might be a midrashic expansion of a later date, reflecting the bitter hostility of the Judaean exiles against Edom; cf. Ps 137:9 and Oba 3.

Valley of Salt. Site of earlier battles with the Edomites (so mss., LXX) under David; see 2 Sam 8:13; cf. Ps 60:2. Musil identified it with Wadi el-Milḥ, south of Beer-sheba (*Arabia Petraea*, [Wien: A. Hölder, 190] II, 1.21), but this area was not part of Edom during the days of David or Amaziah. Others identify it with the salt flats south of the Dead Sea, an area unsuitable for military activity. Mazar considers the Valley of Salt identical with Ge-harashim, "Valley of Craftsmen" (cf. 1 Chr 4:13–14), the Kenite center of metal founding in the Arava (B. Mazar, *Tarbiz* 20 [1950], 316, n. 5; and *EncMiqr* 2.479–80).

Sela. Its location is disputed; cf. also Num 24:21 and Judg 1:36. The toponym was taken as a common noun, "rock," in 2 Chr 25:12. Targum offered *kĕrākka*, i.e. Kir-hareseth; cf. Jer 48:31 and the note to 2 Kgs 3:25 above. The LXX identification with Petra, the famous Nabataean capital in southern Edom, followed by many from Eusebius to N. Glueck (*Rivers in the Desert* [Philadelphia: Jewish Publication Society, 1959], 134, 193–94) is highly doubtful (so already Montgomery-Gehman). According to B. Mazar, Sela is to be located in Edomite territory at es-Sela, 8 km southwest of Tapila (*EncMiqr* 5.1050–51; and cf. Aharoni, *Land of the Bible*², 441).

Joktheel. A city of the same name is found in the town list of Judah in Josh 15:38 and is perhaps related to the name Jekuthiel in 1 Chr 4:18. Did the change of name honor the Judaean soldiers who fought at Sela? If the last clause in the verse "until this day" dates from the days of Josiah, then the Hebrew name adhered to the site even after Edom broke loose from Judah's control (cf. 16:6).

8. *Jehoash son of Jehoahaz son of Jehu.* The formal style of presentation, introducing the protagonist by naming his father and grandfather, is known to have been used in Mesopotamian royal inscriptions; for which see R. R. Wilson, *Genealogy and History in the Biblical World,* (New Haven: Yale University Press, 1977), 58–60, and the notes to v. 13 below and to 9:2.

let us meet face to face! Heb. *nitrāʾeh pānîm.* With verb **rāʾô,* "to see," in the *qal,* it is more usual to find *pānîm ʾel pānîm,* cf. Gen 32:31; Judg 6:22. Only here and in v. 11 does the *hithpael* appear and have the hostile sense of confrontation. Likewise the semantic equivalent in Akk. *nanmurru* (N-form of *amāru,* "to see") is used not only for peaceful meetings, but occasionally for confrontations with an enemy as well: e.g. in the Old Babylonian omen (A. Goetze, Yale Oriental Series 10, 36:40) *ṣābaka . . . itti nakrim innammar,* "Your army will meet with (i.e. encounter) the enemy." At this point in the narrative it is not clear whether Amaziah's intentions were warlike from the beginning. In light of the statement in v. 11, however, one can conclude that they were, and the expression *nitrāʾeh pānîm* should be so interpreted.

9. *thistle.* Heb. *ḥôaḥ.* A wild thorny plant which grows in unattended fields (cf. Job 31:40) and abandoned sites (Hos 9:6; Isa 34:13). Identified with *Scolymus maculatus;* see Y. Feliks, *Nature and Man in the Bible* (New York: Soncino, 1981), 70–73.

The use of fables and proverbs in political contexts is well attested. So e.g. Jotham delivers a parable while negotiating with the nobles of Shechem in Judg 7:9–20. Representative examples from Mesopotamia can be cited from eighteenth-century Mari and seventh-century Assyria. For Mari, see the letter of the king Shamshi-Addu to his son Yasmah-Addu in *ARM* 1, 15 (cf. W. Moran, *EI* 14 [1978], 32*–37*); and for Assyria, the letter of Ashurbanipal to the "non-Babylonians" in Babylon in *ABL* 403 (see A. L. Oppenheim, *Letters from Mesopotamia* [Chicago: University of Chicago Press, 1967], 170).

10. *but then it has carried you away.* Heb. *ûnĕśāʾakā libbekā,* lit. "should your heart lift you up." The same idiom is used with reference to the skillful Bezalel "whose heart moved him" to God's service, cf. Exod 36:2; and 35:21, 26. *NEB* renders: "gone to your head"; *NJPS:* "became arrogant," both of which are not applicable in the case of Bezalel. The syntactic construction is explained by Driver, *Tenses,* 119.

Enjoy your honor. Heb. *hikkābēd;* cf. 2 Sam 6:22, 23:23; Isa 43:4, 49:5. The parallel verse in 2 Chr 25:19 reads the verb as a *hiphil* infinitive *lĕhakbîd* and connects it with the preceding, thus: "You are carried away in seeking honor." But it is unnecessary to correct our passage (and so, already Stade).

11. *Beth-shemesh in Judah.* Appears in the district list of Solomon; see the note to 1 Kgs 4:9. Other towns with this name are found in Naphtali (Josh 19:38; Judg 1:33) and Issachar (Josh 19:22). The specification "in Judah" points to the northern provenance of the present account (as observed by Kittel, Benzinger, and Burney). Cf. the similar designation "Beer-sheba in Judah" in 1 Kgs 19:3.

12. *Judah was routed by Israel.* Heb. *wayyinnāgep . . . lipnê.* In the *niphal,* always "to be smitten in battle"—cf. e.g. Judg 20:36; 1 Sam 4:2, 10; 1 Kgs 8:33.

13. In light of the formal style of presentation (see note to v. 8), there is no reaston to consider "son of Jehoash son of Ahaziah" as a scribal expansion (as do Stade,

Gray). At most one might claim that the words "king of Judah" have been transposed from their more usual place after the complete patronymic.

Then he marched to Jerusalem. Heb. *wayyābōʾ* (with qere; pl. in ketib). The text in 2 Chr 25:23 reads *wayĕbîʾēhû,* "he (Jehoash) brought him (Amaziah)." Luc. and Vulg. have this same reading in Kings, which Kittel, Stade and Burney preferred; Montgomery-Gehman, however, rightly considered it secondary.

from the Ephraim Gate to the Corner Gate. For the ablative use of *beth,* recognized in the parallel passage in 2 Chr 25:24 by its replacement with *min,* see N. Sarna, *JBL* 78 (1959), 310–13.

The Ephraim Gate was the main gate in the center of the northern wall of Jerusalem. In Neh 8:16, the city's residents build sukkoth booths in the plaza of the Ephraim Gate. It has been suggested that this gate is the same as the Fish Gate mentioned in Neh 3:3; 12:39, except that there it is referred to by its market name; but this view is uncertain. The Corner Gate may be found 200 cubits distant, in the northwest corner of the city (so B. Mazar, *EncMiqr* 3.818). The Corner Gate is mentioned again in Jer 31:38 and probably in Zech 14:10. It was rebuilt by Uzziah (2 Chr 26:9), who added a watchtower. M. Burrows (*IDB* 2.850) concurs in general with the above picture; the length of 400 cubits (= 200 meters approximately), however, is the full distance from the Ephraim Gate to the Corner Gate, which is located in the vicinity of the present Citadel.

14. *hostages.* Heb. *bĕnê hattaʿ ărūbôt* occurs only here and in the parallel passage in 2 Chr 25:24. For the nominal *taqtūl* form, see Bauer-Leander, *Grammatik,* 61 *yη*. In Assyrian royal inscriptions of the twelfth–eighth centuries, B.C.E., a similar nominal construction is attested with *kî lītūtu,* "in the state / condition of being a hostage." See citations in *CAD* L 224; and note the alliterative boasting of Ashurnasirpal: *ṣābit līṭi šākin līti,* "who takes hostages and establishes victory" (see *CAD* L 223b). The Assyrian records show that often the family of the defeated king was carried off and kept under guard at the Assyrian court as hostages for the good behavior of the king who was allowed to remain on his throne. They might also be held for ransom at a later date. In the present case, the identity of the Judaean hostages is not stated; but one may surmise that they belonged to the nobility.

15–16. These verses are repeated from 13:12–13; for discussion, see the note there.

19–21. These verses come unexpectedly after the closing notice of Amaziah's reign (v. 18). But their placement is explicable, because they report the irregular circumstances surrounding the succession of the next Davidide; and so it is with similar instances elsewhere in the text; cf. 23:29–30 and for Israel, 15:16.

19. *Lachish.* A major city in the Judaean Shephelah (cf. Josh 15:39), located at Tell ed-Duweir. For a survey of 1932–38 excavations, see D. Ussishkin, *EAEHL* 3.735–53; and a report on the renewed investigations at the site, idem, *Tel Aviv* 5 (1978), 1–97; and see below 18:14.

20. *They brought him (back) on horses.* It is hard to decide by what means the body was conveyed to Jerusalem. Was it laid on a litter tied between two horses, or slung over the back of a horse led by another horse and rider? In the case of Josiah, his body was "driven" by his attendants, probably in a wagon (23:30).

21. *all the People of Judah.* Occurs only here and in 2 Sam 19:41. While analogous to the term "People of the Land" (see the note on 2 Kgs 11:14), the "People of Judah," from the limited evidence available, seems to have the wider connotation of the general population of Judah. See T. Ishida, *AJBI* 1 (1975), 32–33.

22. *It was he who rebuilt Elath . . . after the king slept with his ancestors.* A majority of commentators take Azariah to be the unnamed subject of the verse, but it would be most unusual to refer to Azariah's achievements prior to having had the introductory formula to his reign (see 15:1 ff.). Moreover the reference to "the king" is indeed "most obscure" (so Montgomery-Gehman). The expression "slept with his ancestors" does not allow us to consider Amaziah as the subject. It was, then, Azariah who recovered Elath shortly after his accession. Because the relations between Judah and Edom are the leitmotif of 2 Kgs 14, the editor placed this notice concerning Elath here so as to round off his narration.

For other moments in the checkered history of Elath, and Judah's maritime activity from the dual port of Elath-Ezion-geber, see 1 Kgs 9:26; 22:49; 2 Kgs 16:6; and for a thorough historical review, see M. Haran, *IEJ* 18 (1968), 207–12.

Comment

The reign of Amaziah (798–769 B.C.E.) receives the standard Deuteronomistic evaluation of Judaean kings; at the same time, it is augmented here by several novel elements:

1. A notice which credits Amaziah's compliance with the Deuteronomic law of retribution, vv. 5–6.
2. Information deriving from Judaean chronistic sources on the war with Edom, v. 7; and the assassination of Amaziah and the accession of Azariah, vv. 19–22.
3. A narrative, with distinct north Israelite coloration, concerning the war between Israel and Judah and Amaziah's defeat, vv. 8–14.

Amaziah came to the throne at a difficult time for Judah; Hazael of Aram had reached the gates of Jerusalem and forced his father Joash to deliver a heavy payment, shortly after which the latter was assassinated by his courtiers (see 12:18–19, 21–22). But the early part of Amaziah's reign saw a change in the political winds: Aram-Damascus was defeated by Adad-nirari III of Assyria. While his contemporary Joash of Israel fought with the Aramaeans and recovered Israel's lost territories west of the Jordan, Amaziah set out to reassert Judah's control over the Arabah, with its approaches to Eilat and the Red Sea. This control had been lost when Edom rebelled in the days of Jehoram (8:20–22). As retold in 2 Chr 25:5–10, the campaign may originally have been planned as a joint venture by Judah and Israel; but if so the plan collapsed at an early stage.

Spurred on by his victory over Edom at Sela, Amaziah initiated an advance to the west, to the contested border area of the northern Shephelah between Israel, Judah and Philistia. (Note Israel's earlier drive at Gibbethon, 1 Kgs 15:27; 16:15.) Amaziah counted on Israel's weak condition after many years of Aramaean domination to bring him further victories. This miscalculation led to the rout of Judah's armies at Beth-shemesh, the magnitude of which can be appreciated if one considers that it opened the way for the first penetration of Jerusalem by a foreign force and the destruction of its northern defense walls. It is also the only time that a king of Judah is reported to have been taken captive by a king of Israel along with other royal hostages.[1]

The fate of Amaziah after his capture however, remains a riddle. The chronological data in 14:2, 23 and the unusual notation in v. 17—"Amaziah . . . lived fifteen years after the death of Jehoash"—are commonly taken to mean that Azariah was placed on the throne while his father was prisoner in Samaria. There is no way, however, to know just how long he was kept there. Even more obscure are the circumstances surrounding his assassination. The conspiracy originated in Jerusalem; but Amaziah escaped to Lachish, where he found no quarter and was killed. Who were the conspirators and what was their purpose? Had Amaziah attempted to regain the throne and remove Azariah from his regency? From the fact that Azariah is not reported to have avenged the blood of his father (contra. 14:5–6), the conspirators may have been men of rank and of wide following; perhaps Azariah may have himself been implicated in the regicide. Nevertheless, slain Amaziah was returned to the capital and given a royal burial in the sepulcher of the Davidides.

[1] There is nothing to indicate that the tensions between Judah and Israel two generations earlier were a factor in this strange war. Political circumstances had changed sufficiently so that revenge for the murder of Ahaziah and his family (cf. 9:27–28, 10:13–14) and recovery of the throne of Israel for the Omrides (as proposed by H. L. Ginsberg, Proccedings of Fourth *WCJS,* 91–93) played no part.

XXIII. THE REIGN OF JEROBOAM II (ISRAEL)

(14:23–29)

14 23 In the fifteenth year of Amaziah son of Joash king of Judah,
Jeroboam son of Joash became king over Israel[a] in Samaria for forty-
one years. 24 He did what was displeasing to YHWH. He did not stray
from all the sinful ways of Jeroboam son of Nebat who caused Israel
to sin. 25 It was he who restored the boundaries of Israel from Lebo-
hamath to the Sea of the Arabah, in accordance with the word of
YHWH the God of Israel, which he spoke through his servant Jonah
son of Amittai, the prophet from Gath-hahepher. 26 For YHWH saw
Israel's affliction was very bitter indeed;[b] there was no one but the
restricted and the abandoned, and no one to help Israel. 27 YHWH did
not speak of blotting out Israel's name from under the heavens, and so
he rescued them through Jeroboam son of Joash. 28 The rest of the
history of Jeroboam and all that he did, and his exploits, how he
fought and restored Damascus and Hamath for Israel,[c] are indeed
recorded in the annals of the kings of Israel. 29 So Jeroboam slept with
his ancestors <and was buried in Samaria[d]> with the kings of Israel.
Zechariah his son succeeded him.

[a] Read *ʿal yiśrāʾēl* for *melek yiśrāʾēl* with mss., LXX, Targ.
[b] Read *mar hûʾ;* see note.
[c] Omit *lyhwdh;* read *lĕyiśrāʾēl* and see note.
[d] Add with Luc. *wayyiqqābēr bĕšōmĕrôn.*

Notes

14 23. *Jeroboam son of Joash.* The second Israelite monarch to bear this name (cf. 1 Kgs 11:26), Jeroboam II reigned 789–748. A stamp seal of exquisite design of one of the king's courtiers was recovered at Megiddo: *lšmʿ ʿbd yrbʿm* "Belonging to Shema, servant of Jeroboam" (see Diringer, *Iscrizioni,* 224–28; *ANEP*^{2}*,* 276). See Plate 12 (a).

25. *from Lebo-hamath to the Sea of the Arabah.* Jeroboam's victories reestablished the territorial limits of Solomon's realm; cf. 1 Kgs 5:1 and 8:65. For the location of Lebo-hamath (rendered "the Pass of Hamath" by *JB;* cf. Gray), identical with Labʾu

of the ancient sources, in the northern Beqaʿ of Lebanon at modern Lebweh, see B. Mazar, *Cities and Districts in Eretz Israel* (Jerusalem: Mosad Bialik, 1975), 167–81 (Hebrew); Ahiṭuv, *Canaanite Toponyms,* 131; and the note to 1 Kgs 8:65.

The Sea of the Arabah is glossed "the Salt Sea"—i.e., the Dead Sea—in Josh 3:16, 12:3; while in Amos 6:14 the designation of the southern border of Israel is "Wadi Arabah." Corresponding evidence for these successes, with specific reference to Gilead, is found in Amos 6:13. (For the location of Lodebar and Karnaim mentioned by Amos, see Aharoni, *Land of the Bible*², 438–39.)

Jonah son of Amittai. Beyond this reference to the prophet and his message, there is no reliable record of Jonah's life and ministry. The biblical book associated with Jonah is a later product (of the postexilic period), in which the prophet of earlier tradition whose nationalistic prophecies were fulfilled was used as a central figure in a prophetic novella. For a recent survey of the major interpretations of the didactic purpose of the book of Jonah, see B. S. Childs, *Introduction to the Old Testament as Scripture* (Philadelphia: Fortress, 1979), 417–27.

Gath-hahepher. Mentioned again in Josh 19:13 as a town on the Zebulun border. Jerome placed it two miles from Tsippori on the way to Tiberias, near present day Meshed. See F.-M. Abel, *Géographie de la Palestine* (Paris: Gabalda, 1938), 2.326–27; and M. Avi-Yonah, *EncMiqr* 2.572.

26. *very bitter indeed.* MT *mōreh* is inexplicable. It is apparently to be derived from **mrr,* "to be bitter," and read *mar hûʾ mĕʾōd,* as already in LXX, Vulg., Syr. For suggested emendations, see Stade.

there was no one but the restricted and the abandoned. Heb. *ʾepes ʿāṣûr wĕʾepes ʿāzûb. ʾepes* is here "nothing, no one but," as in 2 Sam 9:3 and Isa 45:14. This helps explain the enigmatic *ʿāṣûr wĕ ʿāzûb* as referring to helpless persons, incapable of coming to their own defense. In this meaning, the expression appears in Deut 32:36 in parallel to *ʾāzĕlat yād,* "impotency, inability to act" (cf. the semantic equivalent in Akk. *nīd aḫi, CAD* N 2.209–10). For a fuller discussion of the various scholarly opinions and modern translations, see the note to 2 Kgs 9:8 above.

27. *did not speak of blotting out Israel's name.* Heb. *māḥô šēm* appears only here in Kings and in Deut 9:14; 29:19. The idiom is based on the image of washing a papyrus scroll clean prior to its reuse, as was the practice in ancient Egypt (M. Haran, *JJS* 33 [1982], 168–70), cf. "Erase me from the book," Exod 32:32, 33. In Mesopotamia, "erasing the name" of an ancestor on an inscription and replacing it with one's own called for divine retribution (cf. *AHw* 844, s.v. *šumam pašāṭu*). In the present context, the phrase means that YHWH did not utter a prophecy of doom, but promised salvation; and it evidences awareness of a prophetic word contradicting that of Jonah. See further in Comment.

he rescued them through . . . Heb. *wayyôšîʿēm bĕyad,* as in Judg 6:36, 37; 2 Sam 3:18, means "through the agency of."

28. *restored Damascus and Hamath for Israel.* MT reads: *līyhûdâ bĕyiśrāʾēl,* "for Judah in Israel"; but most agree that this is senseless. The easiest solution is to omit "for Judah" and read "for Israel" (so e.g. Kittel, Montgomery-Gehman). Burney suggested rewriting the phrase as *ʾšr nlḥm ʾt dmśk wʾšr hšyb ʾt ḥmt yhwh myśrʾl,* "how he fought with Damascus and how he turned away the wrath of YHWH from Israel." Although adopted by Šanda and Gray, this suggestion lacks textual warrant and contradicts the tenor of the Jonah prophecy. M. Vogelstein (*Jeroboam II* [Cincinnati, 1945] 10; idem, *Fertile Soil* [New York: American Press, 1957], 27) retained the text

and took "Judah in Israel" to be the official name of the joint state created by Jeroboam II after Amaziah's removal. But such a name and the accompanying historical reconstruction are very dubious.

Most recently *NEB* offered "in Jaudi for Israel," taking *yhwdh* as Iaudi/Sam'al, a north Syrian city. This translation is based upon the century-old suggestion of H. Winckler (*Forschungen* 1.1–23) to identify Y'DY (ancient Sam'al, modern Zinjirli) with *Iaudi* in Assyrian inscriptions. However, this identification can no longer be maintained. All references in Akkadian to *Iaudi* refer to biblical Judah and the kings of Y'DY are always termed the kings of Sam'al. See H. Tadmor, "Azriyau of Yaudi," *SH* 8 (1961), 232–71, and M. Weippert, RLA 5.273. Thus *yhwdh* remains Judah.

Originally, the verse may have read just "for Israel"; the word "for Judah" might be a gloss from the hand of a Judaean scribe for whom the claim to these territories in the far north rested on the achievements of David and Solomon, who were primarily kings of Judah. But this solution, like all the others, is highly speculative. See further in Comment.

29. <*and was buried in Samaria*>. The site of burial is a regular part of the closing formula—cf. 1 Kgs 16:28; 2 Kgs 10:35; 13:9, 13; 14:16—and is probably to be restored on the basis of Luc. (so Stade, Burney).

Comment

Jeroboam II's forty-one year reign, the longest of all kings of Israel, is presented tersely and in no way proportionally to his notable accomplishments in political and military affairs. He pursued the policies of his father Joash; in the north he warred with Aram and pushed beyond Damascus into central Syria, and in Trans-Jordan he extended his control to the Dead Sea. This territorial expansion is described by the narrator as "rescue" of Israel (*wayyôšîʿēm,* v. 27) in response to Israel's sad state and in fulfillment of a prophecy of salvation by one Jonah son of Amittai. The statement that Jeroboam "restored the boundaries of Israel from Lebo-hamath to the Sea of the Arabah" (v. 25), the ideal borders of the Promised Land and the farthest limits of the United Monarchy, reflects an ideology which saw the Israelite king as achieving the glories of David and Solomon.

Such a presentation of YHWH's concern for Israel and the positive appreciation of Jeroboam's role in their rescue, using the terminology of salvation already observed in 2 Kgs 13:5, and most familiar from the framework of the book of Judges (see especially Judg 2:16, 18; 10:12–13),[1] does not accord with the negative Deuteronomistic judgment of Israelite kings. Rather than taking

[1] A. D. H. Mayes (in Hayes and Miller, *Israelite and Judaean History,* 310) argues convincingly that the early traditions in Judges were composed in "northern prophetic circles," where the theme of sin and deliverance was introduced into them. It may be suggested that these same circles were responsible for the pragmatic description of the monarchy in the northern kingdom.

vv. 25–27 as retrospective rationalization of Jeroboam's victories,[2] they should be seen as an affirmation based upon contemporary eighth-century Israelite material. These verses are another example of the existence of a prophetic, pre-Deuteronomistic tradition (see Comment to 13:1–9), which included, as it seems, appraisals of Israel's kings and dynasties.

The international background of Jeroboam's reign is poorly documented. No historical inscriptions of the Assyrian kings Shalmaneser IV (783–773), Ashur-dan III (773–755), and Adad-nirari V (755–745) have survived. The only explicit source dealing with Assyrian military activity during this period is the Eponym Chronicle, in which the name and title of each year's eponym, is listed together with a single major event of this eponymate.[3] Thus we learn that five campaigns were undertaken to the West: in 773, "to Damascus"; 772 "to Hadrach"; 765, "to Hadrach"; 755, "to Hadrach"; and 754, "to Arpad." At least six campaigns are designated as against "Urartu." In the intervening years there were serious troubles inside Assyria: uprisings and revolts in the major cities of the kingdom, plagues, and even the ill omen of a total sun eclipse.[4] Thus it is not surprising that for as many as nine years the chronicle entry reads that the king stayed "in the land"; foreign expeditions could not be undertaken.

How does this picture relate to Jeroboam's Israel? The half century of Assyrian decline saw the emergence of Urartu as a major power in southern Anatolia and northern Syria, competing there with Assyrian interests. As the entries in the Eponym Chronicle clearly point out, it would be wrong to think that Assyria abandoned the West entirely. Jeroboam's involvement as far as Hamath in central Syria could have come about only as a result of an explicit agreement or, at the least, a tacit understanding between Israel and Assyria, their common goal being to contain Damascus.[5]

Since very little is known of the political events during Jeroboam's reign, it is very difficult, if not impossible, to fix chronologically the stages of the expansion of Israel during that half century. M. Haran disagrees with the

[2] Thus e.g. M. Noth (*Überlieferungsgeschichtliche Studien,* 75) credits only v. 25 with being an excerpt from a "diary" source; vv. 26–27 are Deuteronomistic, v. 28 is an even later "erroneous" addition (98, n. 1). For W. Dietrich, (*Prophetie und Geschichte,*) 110–12, v. 25 is a redactional reworking of a historical notice, exemplifying prophetic prediction and fulfillment.

[3] For the standard edition of the Eponym Chronicle, see A. Ungnad, RLA 2.428–35, and esp. 430; cf. *ARAB* 2.435. *ANET*[3], 274 presents an excerpt of the text.

[4] The eclipse in Sivan (= June 15) 763 serves as the basis for the calculation of the absolute chronology of the period.

[5] In 773, during the reign of Shalmaneser IV, a certain Ḫadianu was king in Damascus. Whether he was Ben-hadad III addressed by his personal name (so J. D. Hawkins, *CAH*[3], 3/1.405) or his successor is still unclear. (The Aramaic form of this name appears in 1 Kgs 15:18 as Hezion.)

approach suggested by H. Tadmor[6] that the conquest of Damascus "was conducted with the assent of the Assyrian kings," and suggests narrowing down Jeroboam's moves to 754–748, the last six years of his reign.[7] But this reconstruction is unlikely. The disintegration of "Jeroboam's empire" in the last years of his reign and its rapid decline after his death show that it was the early and middle, not the later, years during which Israel prospered. The internal political and social developments in Israel which grew out of the expansion "beyond Damascus" (cf. Amos 5:27) require positing a much longer period. The picture that emerges from the book of Amos is one of a prosperous Israel, with a rich and powerful elite in Samaria, unaware of the seeds of social breakdown they have sown. Nationalistic prophets such as Jonah son of Amittai supported the military ambitions of the establishment by heralding the "Day of YHWH," as a day of vengeance upon the enemies of Israel (cf. Amos 5:18–20, echoed in Joel 2). Against them appeared Amos of Tekoa, who, breaking with a tradition which traced its roots to the days of Ahab and the early wars with Aram (cf. e.g. 1 Kgs 22:5–6), prophesied the fall of Jeroboam and his dynasty and the exile of Israel—all this prior to the recovery of Assyria under Tiglath-pileser III and his policy of extensive deportations.[8]

[6] See H. Tadmor, *SH* 8, 240. Cf., too, W. W. Hallo, "From Qarqar to Carchemish," *BAR* 2. 166–69.

[7] M. Haran, "The Rise and Decline of the Empire of Jeroboam ben Joash," *VT* 17 (1967), 266–84, esp. 279.

[8] It is remarkable that the historian nowhere refers to Amos or to his social critique. Was this due to the overall tenor of doom in his prophecies, as F. Crüsemann has suggested ("Kritik an Amos im deuteronomistischen Geschichtswerk," in *Probleme biblischer Theologie,* G. von Rad zum 70. Geburtstag, ed. H. W. Wolff [München: Kaiser, 1971], 57–63)?

XXIV. THE REIGN OF AZARIAH (JUDAH)

(15:1–7)

15 1 In the twenty-seventh year of Jeroboam, king of Israel, Azariah
son of Amaziah king of Judah became king. 2 He was sixteen years old
when he became king and he reigned fifty-two years in Jerusalem. His
mother's name was Jecoliah, from Jerusalem. 3 He did what was pleasing to YHWH, just as Amaziah his father had done. 4 Yet the high
places were not removed; the people continued to sacrifice and make
offerings at the high places. 5 YHWH struck the king so that he was a
leper until the day of his death. He resided in *Beth ha-ḥophshith,* while
Jotham, the king's son, was royal steward and judged the People of the
Land. 6 The rest of the history of Azariah and all that he did are
indeed recorded in the annals of the kings of Judah. 7 So Azariah slept
with his ancestors and they buried him with his ancestors in the City
of David. Jotham, his son, succeeded him.

Notes

15 1. *Azariah son of Amaziah.* This king of Judah is known by two names, Azariah and Uzziah, which appear at random in various biblical books. In 2 Kgs 15:1, 6, 7, 8, 17, 23, 27, he is Azariah; in 2 Kgs 13:30, 32, 34 (and throughout 2 Chr 26–27 and Isa 1:1, 6:1) he is Uzziah. This alternation has been taken as evidence for Azariah's having assumed a throne name when he began his single rule in Judah after the death of Amaziah; or it was the name associated with the king during his leprosy. But G. Brin, *Leš* 24 (1960), 8–14, shows convincingly that the roots **ʿzr* and **ʿzz* from which the two names are derived are semantically very close, both conveying the sense of "victory, valor, strength." Following this lead, one notes that the Chronicler punned on the king's two names in 2 Chr 26:15 while referring to his activities: "His (Uzziah's) fame spread wide and far, for he was helped (*lĕhēʿāzēr*) wonderfully." A similar interchange of names can be observed in 1 Chr 25:4, 18, where the pair Azarel/Uzziel appears. Both names occur on Hebrew seals; see R. Hestrin and M. Dayagi-Mendels, *Seals,* Nos. 23, 24, 65, 66.

The name Azariah is also attested in the annals of Tiglath-pileser: *ᵐAz-ri-ia-a-ú* (P. Rost, *Die keilschrifttexte Tiglat-Pilesers III* [Leipzig: E. Pfeiffer, 1893], 22, line 131; Tadmor, *ITP* Ann 19:10; *ARAB* 1.770; cf. *ANET³,* 282), as the name of the rebel who confronted Tiglath-pileser in north Syria in the vicinity of Hamath in 739–738. A cuneiform text fragment (K. 6205) which was considered hitherto as belonging to the annals of Tiglath-pileser contains a reference to a person named [. . . .]*yau* and a land named *Iaudi,* i.e. Judah. On the basis of a restoration of the name as [Azri]yau, he was identified with Azariah/Uzziah of the Bible. For this view, see D. D. Luckenbill, *AJSL* 41 (1925), 217–32; followed by E. Thiele, *JNES* 3 (1944), 155–63; and idem, *MNHK[1],* 75–98; and H. Tadmor, *SH* 8 (1961), 232–71. More recently, however, K. 6205 was joined to another fragment from the reign of a later Assyrian king (Sargon II or Sennacherib), thus leaving Azriyau of the Tiglath-pileser annals without a country. See N. Naaman, "Sennacherib's 'Letter to God' on His Campaign to Judah," *BASOR* 214 (1974), 25–38. Naaman (*WO* 9 [1977–78], 229–39) surmises that Azriyau was king of the north-Syrian city of Hadrach. But it must be borne in mind that the name Azriyau is not Aramaean, but Israelite. (In Akkadian transcriptions, such as Aramaean name would be rendered *Idriau;* cf. Adad-idri for Hadad-ezer; and see R. Zadok, *West Semites in Babylonia* [Tel-Aviv, 1978], 97.) If not the contemporary king of Judah, could Azriyau of the annals, then, have been an Israelite/Judaean of the same name who gained prominence in the region of Hamath, as E. Meyer (*Geschichte des Alterthums[3]* [reprint: Basel: B. Schwabe, 1953] 2/II, 433, n. i) styled him—"an Israelite adventurer"?

2. *he reigned fifty-two years.* Azariah's reign, 785–733, includes the thirteen-year coregency with his father Amaziah (cf. 14:17), the entire reign of his son Jotham (cf. below v. 33), and part of that of his grandson Ahaz (cf. 16:2).

Jecoliah. On the name, which means "YHWH is able/has the power," see J. J. Stamm, *VT* Sup 16 (1967), 311.

5. *he was a leper until the day of his death.* For *ṣāraʿat,* whether leprosy, i.e., Hansen's disease, or some other skin disease, see the note to 2 Kgs 5:1; and cf. 7:3. 2 Chr 26:16–20 relates that this affliction was a punishment from YHWH visited upon Uzziah because of his unorthodox infringement upon priestly prerogatives in the Temple service. Later tradition visualized the famous earthquake of Uzziah's days (Amos 1:1; cf. Zech 14:5) as occurring at the very moment when YHWH's wrath struck the king; see Josephus, *Antiquities* ix.225; cf. Targum to Isa 28:21. For a bizarre attempt to date the earthquake on the basis of the legend, accepted at face value, see J. Morgenstern, *HUCA* 12–13 (1937–38), 1–20.

He resided in Beth ha-ḥophshith. This ancient crux has been resolved in several ways. Targum rendered *wytb br mnyršlm,* "he resided outside of Jerusalem," this in line with the legal provision forbidding lepers to remain in the camp; see Lev 13:46, 2 Kgs 7:3; cf. Num 12:14–15, and so Thenius. However, it is hard to imagine a leper king being sent out of the city gates. It was this consideration that probably led Qimḥi to comment: "When Uzziah became leprous, he lived in a house apart, so that he was free (*ḥopšî*) from the toil (of the monarchy). Therefore that house is called *bêt hāḥopšît* (i.e. 'House of Freedom')." A number of modern scholars have adopted a similar approach. Klostermann (followed by Šanda, Montgomery-Gehman, Gray) read: *bĕbêtōh ḥopšît,* "in his house at freedom," taking *ḥopšît* adverbially. Cf. *NEB:* "relieved of all duties and lived in his own house." New light on *Beth ha-ḥophshith* was shed by the Ugaritic passage in the Baal epic, I*AB v. 15/ /II AB viii 7, in which reference is made to the netherworld as *bt ḫpṯt* (cf. *ANET[3],* 135a, 139a). W. F. Albright (*JPOS* 14 [1934], 131, n. 162) translated "subterranean house, basement"; and so similarly H. L. Ginsberg, *Kitve Ugarit* (Jerusalem: Mosad Bialik, 1936), 142, "pit, underground cave." U. Cassuto offered this observation: "Since the leper is accounted as dead, the house of the lepers was designated by one of the names of Sheol" (*Tarbiz* 12 [1941], 177; English translation *Biblical and Oriental Studies,* 2.160, cf. 2.36). On the Ugaritic evidence, cf. also Montgomery, *HTR* 34 (1941), 321f.; and Montgomery-Gehman, 454. Modern translations apparently followed the Ugaritic lead: *NAB,* "in a house apart; *NJPS,* "in isolated quarters; *JB,* "confined to his room." These interpretations presume that the Ugaritic term *bt ḫpṯt* was preserved in BH, though *ḥopšî* is clearly "free" (cf. 1 Sam 17:25; Job 3:19) and not associated with the netherworld.

It is preferable, then, to leave *bêt hāḥopšît* untranslated, taking it as the name for the separate quarters built for Uzziah, perhaps even outside Jerusalem.

Jotham, the king's son, was royal steward. With King Uzziah incapacitated, Jotham assumed the more important administrative and judicial duties of his father. Heb. *ʿal habbayit* is equivalent to the title *ʾăšer ʿal habbayit,* "royal steward," the highest royal official in Judah at this period. The status achieved by Shebna is a case in point; see Isa 22:15–20 and the note to 2 Kgs 18:18 below.

judged the People of the Land. The People of the Land are the same body mentioned in 11:14, 20; 21:24; 23:30, 35; 25:19. From their appearance in the present verse it emerges that the Davidic king had special obligations to this privileged group of Judaeans in judicial matters. (The issue of the king's accessibility was pivotal in the early stages of the rebellion of Absalom; hence Absalom's promise to personally hear all cases; see 2 Sam 15:2–4.) Jotham was here filling in for his father.

7. *they buried him with his ancestors in the City of David.* According to 2 Chr 26:23, Uzziah was buried in the field, not in the royal cemetery, because of his leprosy. Josephus, *Antiquities* ix.227, reports that "he was buried alone in his own garden"; perhaps this was the garden of Uzza (mentioned in 2 Kgs 21:18, 26). An inscribed plaque, an ancient tombstone of sorts, in Aramaic and dated to the first century B.C.E., was discovered in Jerusalem; its inscription confirms the datum in Chronicles that Uzziah's remains were removed outside the city: "Here were brought the bones of Uzziah, king of Judah. Do not open!" See E. L. Sukenik, *PEFQS* 1931, 217ff.; idem, *Tarbiz* 2 (1931), 288–92. For a photograph of the plaque, see Plate 11.

Comment

Azariah, not unlike his counterpart Jeroboam II in Samaria, enjoyed one of the longest reigns of all the Davidic kings. Yet his fifty-two years were all but left unrecorded by the Deuteronomistic historian. The single detail concerning his reign refers to his malady; Azariah is the only "leper king" attested in antiquity. The brief treatment accorded to him in Kings contrasts sharply with the extensive one in 2 Chr 26. There the Chronicler records how Uzziah/Azariah won victories in Philistia and in the Negev, following a thorough organization of Judah's armies. Also, in keeping with the Chronicler's view of individual retribution, the circumstances which led to the king's leprosy are related: Haughty Azariah sought to offer incense at the altar and was punished in this way by YHWH for his infringement upon priestly prerogatives (see 2 Chr 26:16–20).[1]

The extreme brevity of the account in Kings might be explained in one of two ways: (1.) The historian was acquainted with the priestly story of Azariah's leprosy or at least an early kernel of it, but did not relate it so as not to contradict his positive evaluation of the king's long reign (2 Kgs 15:3). In other instances, however, he did refer to cultic offenses on the part of Judah's king and changed his evaluation accordingly; cf., e.g., Solomon, 1 Kgs 11:1–10; Ahaz, 2 Kgs 16:1–16. (2.) The historian was unable to offer any explanation for the king's leprosy, even though leprosy was commonly seen as a divine affliction (cf. Num 12). Puzzled by this, he also avoided any reference to Azariah's successes.

Taking the account in 2 Chr 26 as the main witness for the period, albeit a late rendition of Judaean sources, Azariah emerges as a militant king who transformed Judah's army and strengthened its defenses. He extended the borders of Judah in the west and in the south, reaching the Mediterranean coast at Ashdod and the Red Sea at Eilat (2 Kgs 14:22). Of particular note is the collaboration of Judah and Israel in the census in Trans-Jordan, in the Gilead and Bashan (1 Chr 5:17), evidence for the joint resettling of the grazing areas formerly controlled by Aram-Damascus.[2] Also in the mountainous and semiarid areas of Judah, Azariah developed agricultural projects and cattle raising. He was, in the words of the Chronicler's unusual accolade, a "lover of the soil" (2 Chr 26:10). During the last third of his reign, he affiliated his son Jotham and his grandson Ahaz as coregents in the rule of Judah, though nominally retaining the title king.[3]

[1] H. L. Ginsberg points out that also at play here was the "more practical motive of discouraging such encroachments," in a history which is pro-priestly (*JBL* 80 [1961], 347, n. 18). On encroachment upon Temple sancta in general, see J. Milgrom, *Studies in Levitical Terminology,* vol. 1 (Berkeley: University of California Press, 1970), part 2.

[2] Note that the census is dated to the reigns of Jotham and Jeroboam. With regard to the tribute paid to Azariah by the Ammonites (2 Chr 26:8), MT *ʿmwnym* should be corrected to *mʿwnym,* Meunites, with LXX. For this nomadic group of the northern Sinai, see J. Liver, *EncMiqr* 5.188–90; I. Ephʿal, *Ancient Arabs* (Jerusalem: Magnes, 1982), s.v. Meunites.

[3] A previous historical reconstruction, according to which Azariah inherited Jeroboam's hegemony over south and central Syria (put forward by H. Tadmor, *SH* 8 [1961], 232–71; and accepted by J. Bright, *History*², 268; and with some hesitation, *History*³, 270; and others) can no longer be maintained, as the main evidence for it was an Assyrian inscription (K. 6205) formerly ascribed to Tiglath-pileser III, but now shown to be of later date. See full discussion of the problematic inscription in the note to v. 1 above.

XXV. FROM ZECHARIAH TO PEKAH: THE DECLINE OF ISRAEL

(15:8–31)

15 8 In the thirty-eighth year of Azariah king of Judah, Zechariah
son of Jeroboam became king over Israel in Samaria for six months.
9 He did what was displeasing to YHWH, just as his ancestors had
done. He did not stray from the sinful ways of Jeroboam son of Nebat,
who caused Israel to sin. 10 Shallum son of Jabesh conspired against
him. He attacked him at Ibleam[a] and killed him; and he succeeded
him as king. 11 The rest of the history of Zechariah is recorded in the
annals of the kings of Israel. 12 This was in accord with the word of
YHWH which promised Jehu, "Four generations of your descendants
shall sit on the throne of Israel." And so it was.

13 Shallum son of Jabesh became king in the thirty-ninth year of
Uzziah king of Judah, and he reigned one month in Samaria.
14 Menahem son of Gadi set out from Tirzah and came to Samaria. He
attacked Shallum son of Jabesh in Samaria and killed him; and he
succeeded him as king. 15 The rest of the history of Shallum and the
conspiracy which he formed are recorded in the annals of the kings of
Israel.

16 Then Menahem attacked Tappuah[b] and all who were in it and its
border areas from Tirzah, because it would not open[c] (its gates). He
defeated it, and even ripped open all its pregnant women.[d]

17 In the thirty-ninth year of Azariah king of Judah, Menahem son
of Gadi became king over Israel for ten years in Samaria. 18 He did
what was displeasing to YHWH; he did not stray from the sinful ways
of Jeroboam son of Nebat, who caused Israel to sin. 19 In his days,[e] Pul
king of Assyria marched against the country. Menahem paid Pul a
thousand talents of silver so that he would support him in holding on

[a] Read with Luc. *byblʿm*. See note.
[b] Read *Tappuah* with Luc. for MT *Tiphsah*. See note.
[c] Read *pātĕḥâ* for MT *pātaḥ*.
[d] Read *wyk ʾth wʾt kl hrwtyh bqʿ* for MT *wyk ʾt kl hhrwtyh bqʿ*.
[e] Read *bymyw* with LXX. At the end of v. 18 MT reads *kl ymyw*.

to the kingdom. 20 Menahem levied the silver from Israel: every man
of means had to pay the king of Assyria fifty shekels of silver per
person. Then the king of Assyria withdrew and did not remain there in
the country. 21 The rest of the history of Menahem and all that he did
are indeed recorded in the annals of the kings of Israel. 22 So Menahem
slept with his ancestors and Pekahiah his son succeeded him.

23 In the fiftieth year of Azariah king of Judah, Pekahiah son of
Menahem became king over Israel in Samaria for two years. 24 He did
what was displeasing to YHWH; he did not stray from the sinful ways
of Jeroboam son of Nebat, who caused Israel to sin. 25 Pekah son of
Remaliah, his adjutant, conspired against him. He attacked him in
Samaria in the citadel of the palace[f] « »[g] with the help of
fifty Gileadites, and killed him; and he succeeded him as king. 26 The
rest of the history of Pekahiah and all that he did are recorded in the
annals of the kings of Israel.

27 In the fifty-second year of Azariah king of Judah, Pekah son of
Remaliah became king over Israel in Samaria for twenty years. 28 He
did what was displeasing to YHWH; he did not stray from the sinful
ways of Jeroboam son of Nebat, who caused Israel to sin. 29 In the
days of Pekah king of Israel, Tiglath-pileser king of Assyria came and
took Ijon, Abel-beth-maachah, Janoah, Kedesh, Hazor—the Gilead
and the Galilee—all the land of Naphtali. He exiled their population[h]
to Assyria. 30 Hoshea son of Elah conspired against Pekah son of
Remaliah. He attacked and killed him; and he succeeded him as king,
in the twentieth year of Jotham son of Uzziah. 31 The rest of the
history of Pekah and all that he did are recorded in the annals of the
kings of Israel.

[f] Read *hammelek* with qere (so 1 Kgs 15:18; 2 Kgs 11:20).
[g] MT has additionally: *ʾt ʾrgb wʾt hʾryh,* "and Argob and the Arieh." See note.
[h] Lit. "them."

Notes

15 10. *Shallum son of Jabesh.* Jabesh (-Gilead) is a town in the northern Gilead (Judg 21:8; 1 Sam 11:1) and so has been taken by some to be an indication of the clan affiliation of Shallum, rather than his lineage, which is not mentioned (so Šanda, Montgomery-Gehman). Gray emends the text without warrant to *Yasib,* following an LXX reading to Josh 17:7. For the history of Jabesh and its identification with Tell Abu-Kharaz, see B. Mazar, *EncMiqr* 3.459–60.

at Ibleam. All modern commentators read *bĕyiblĕʿām* with Luc. MT *qŏbāl ʿām,* "before the people," is most difficult in that it introduces a late Aramaic word into a

Hebrew construction. It also requires correcting the text to *hāʿām* (cf. Qimḥi, *BDB*). As in vv. 14, 25, in which the site of the attacks upon the kings is specified, so, too, in the present instance is a place name to be restored. For the town Ibleam in the hills of Manesseh, see the note to 2 Kgs 9:27.

12. *the word of* YHWH *which promised Jehu.* The fulfillment of the prophetic word to Jehu given in 2 Kgs 10:30; see the note there.

14. *Menahem son of Gadi.* The father's name may be either a hypocoristicon of a name such as Gadiel (cf. Num 13:10) or a clan designation, i.e., the Gadite (cf. 1 Chr 5:18). If indeed a Gadite, then Menahem as well his rival Shallum both hailed from the Trans-Jordanian territories of Israel. In the annals of Tiglath-pileser III, the Assyrian king reports that Menahem of Samaria (*Meniḫimme Samerināya*) rendered tribute along with western vassal kings. See *ANET³*, 283 and Comment.

Tirzah. The royal residence and capital of Israel under Jeroboam I (1 Kgs 14:17) and Ba'asha (1 Kgs 15:33). Tirzah was located in the territory of Manasseh, apparently at Tell el-Far'ah, six miles northeast of Nablus. See the note to 1 Kgs 14:17 and *EncMiqr* 8.937–41.

16. *Menahem attacked Tappuah.* MT reads: Tiphsah. The only Tiphsah known is Thapsacus, the important ford on the bend of the Euphrates, not attested in ancient sources before Xenophon (*Anabasis* I 4, 11, 17). In 1 Kgs 5:4, Tiphsah appears as part of the geographical description of the Solomonic kingdom, which is usually taken as a gloss from the late Persian period (see the note to 1 Kgs 5:4). In any event, even if Tiphsah should one day turn up in an early first millennium document, it would not necessarily imply that Menahem raided as far as the Euphrates (as M. Haran, *VT* 17 [1967], 284–90, would have it), given the external and internal political conditions of the times.

Most commentators and modern translations read *Tappuah,* following the Luc. *taphoe.* For Tappuah on the Ephraim-Manasseh border, cf. Josh 17:7, 8, and Z. Kallai, *EncMiqr* 8.882–83. (Might the source of the erroneous Tiphsah be an early writing of *samekh* for *waw;* note that in some Aramaic cursive hands of the sixth–fifth centuries B.C.E., these letters are sometimes hard to distinguish.)

it would not open (its gates). Read *pātĕḥâ* third-person feminine sing. for MT third-person masculine sing. The law of warfare in Deut 20:11 speaks of the surrender of a city as "opening."

He defeated it . . . MT is clearly faulty. The repetition at the end of 16a of *wyk* is suspect and furthermore lacks an object; most of the versions supply one. The additional *he* in front of *hrwtyh* may be a case of dittography. The proposed emendation is based partly on Luc. and LXX and requires only a minimal adjustment of MT; see, too, Stade, Burney.

ripped open all its pregnant women. This clause hardly stems from the northern chronistic source upon which v. 16a is based. It is rather the critical comment of a later editor (Dtr_1?), who recorded that Menahem in his battle at Tappuah behaved as cruelly as the Aramaeans; see the note to 8:12 and M. Cogan, *JAOS* 103 (1983), 755–57.

19. *In his days.* MT has *kl ymyw,* "all his days," as the last words in v. 18. This alters the well-attested formula describing Jeroboam's sin; cf. e.g. vv. 9, 24, 28. Therefore the LXX reading *bymyw* as the introductory word in v. 19 is preferable. Note that vv. 29, 37 begin with the editorial "in the days . . ." in similar fashion.

Pul king of Assyria. Pul is a hypocoristicon by which Tiglath-pileser III was known in late cuneiform sources and in the hellenistic Ptolemaic Canon. (See F. Schmidtke, *Der Aufbau der Babylonischen Chronologie* [Münster: Aschendorffscher Verlag, 1952], 98–99). There is no evidence to show that this was the throne name of the Assyrian king in any contemporary Babylonian record. *Pūlu* is a well-attested Assyrian name meaning "limestone (block)" and might have been associated in folk etymology with the second element-*pileser* in the full name as a nickname. See discussion in Brinkman, *Post-Kassite Babylonia,* 62, n. 317.

Menahem paid Pul a thousand talents of silver. The very large sum of 1,000 talents of silver paid by Menahem is in line with tribute exacted by Tiglath-pileser from Hulli king of Tabal: 10 talents of gold and 1,000 talents of silver (Tadmor, *ITP* Summary Inscription 7.rev.15′; *ARAB* 1.802) and from Metenna king of Tyre: 50 or 150 talents of gold and [2,000 talents of silver] (*ITP* Summary Inscription 7.rev.16′; *ARAB* 1.803). Both of these vassal kings were usurpers, and their payments bought Assyrian support, thus legitimizing their rule. Menahem's payment seems to have been of the same nature; note in particular the continuation of our verse: "so that he would support him in holding on to the kingdom."

It is usually accepted that Menahem's surrender in v. 19 is the same as the one recorded in the annals of Tiglath-pileser in which Menahem and other kings of the West paid tribute; see *ANET*³, 283. This event should be dated to 738; see H. Tadmor, *SH* 8 (1961), 257–58. But Menahem also appears in the similar list of western tribute bearers on the recently discovered stele from Iran. For a translation of this list, see Appendix I, No. 4A, and for a discussion of whether the tribute dates to 738 or to an earlier year, see L. D. Levine, *BASOR* 206 (1972), 40–42; M. Cogan, *JCS* 25 (1973), 96–99; M. Weippert, "Menachem von Israel und seine Zeitgenossen . . ." *ZDPV* 89 (1973), 26–53.

so that he would support him. Heb. *liheyôt yādāyw ʾittô,* lit. "to have his hands with him," i.e., to make common cause with, to support, to protect; cf. 2 Sam 14:19; Jer 26:24; 1 Chr 4:10. The following clause (omitted by LXX^{B}, Syr.) makes it clear that the subject of "his hands" was Tiglath-pileser, who backed up Menahem's rule, rather than the reverse.

20. *Menahem levied the silver.* Heb. *wayyōṣēʾ,* lit. "he brought out." The use of **yṣʾ* in the *hiphil* with "money" is unique; cf. a similar use in Akkadian of *šūṣû,* "to deliver, make payment" (for examples, see *CAD* A 2.373–79). Stade, Šanda, Montgomery-Gehman were correct in rejecting the emendation suggested by Klostermann (followed by Benzinger, Kittel, Burney) to read *wyṣw,* "he ordered."

every man of means. Heb. *gibbôrê haḥayîl,* lit. "men of valor"; commonly taken as an expression originally denoting bravery in battle, which has undergone transformation and later connotes men of high economic status, i.e., landed gentry or the like. Cf. 1 Kgs 11:28 and 2 Kgs 5:2, and Montgomery-Gehman; de Vaux, *Ancient Israel,* 70, 72.

fifty shekels of silver per person. The Israelite talent contained 3,000 shekels (cf. Exod 38:25–26); accordingly the number of *gibbôrê haḥayîl* would be 60,000. (On the talent, see R. B. Y. Scott, *BAR* 3.353–58; E. Stern, *EncMiqr* 4.861–77.) This datum has considerable bearing upon the question of the size of the population of Israel in the mid-eighth century B.C.E. But as the total number of inhabitants is unknown, the percentage represented by 60,000 cannot be calculated. Furthermore, perhaps a part, if not a considerable part, of the payment came from the royal treasury, with the remainder exacted from the men of means. This consideration would lower proportionately their number in the total population. Or alternately, the payment could have been spread over several years, thus reducing the number of landowners to 20,000 (so Vogelstein, *Fertile Soil,* 123). In any event, the fifty-shekel assessment was high enough to be remembered and recorded by a later narrator. (For a recent attempt to calculate the population of Israel from archaeological evidence, see Y. Shiloh, "The Population of Iron Age Palestine in the Light of Urban Plans, Areas, and Population Density," *EI* 15 [1981], 273–82.)

D. J. Wiseman noted (*Iraq* 15 [1953], 135, n. 1) that the sum of fifty shekels per person was set at the worth of a slave at current Assyrian values as shown in economic documents from Nimrud.

the king of Assyria withdrew and did not remain there in the country. Contemporary Assyrian sources do not confirm the presence of Tiglath-pileser III or of an Assyrian armed force in Israel during the reign of Menahem. Moreover the word "there" would seem to indicate that the notice is phrased from the perspective of a writer not present in the land—i.e., by a narrator residing outside of the north kingdom. Cf. the remarks of Montgomery-Gehman and Comment below.

25. *Pekah son of Remaliah.* Pekah is a shortened form of Pekahiah, the name of the ruling king. Pekah appears as *Paqaḫa* in a text of Tiglath-pileser III (*ANET³,* 284; Tadmor, *ITP* Summary Inscription 4.17′). On a fragment of a jug from the excavations at Hazor, the incised words *lpqḥ smdr* "Belonging to Pekah. Semadar (-wine)" appear (*Inscriptions Reveal,* No. 109). (On this blossom-scented wine, see S. Aḥituv, *Leš* 39 [1975], 37–40.)

his adjutant. Heb. *šālîš.* See note to 2 Kgs 7:2.

the citadel of the palace. Heb. *ʾarmôn bêt hammelek;* as in 1 Kgs 16:18. In Isa 13:22 *ʾarmĕnôtāyw* (for MT *ʾalmĕnôtāyw*) is parallel to "palaces of pleasure." The context suggests that the term refers to a specific structure within the royal palace complex. E. A. Speiser (*JQR* 14 [1924], 329) compared the Akkadian *rimītu,* "foundation"; H. L. Ginsberg (*JBL* 62 [1943], 113f.) translated "fortification."

with the help of fifty Gileadites. Though it is not specifically stated, Pekah, like the usurpers before him (cf. vv. 10, 14), may have been a Gileadite himself. For the military unit "fifty" and its officer, see the note to 1:9 above.

MT has the additional *ʾt ʾrgb wʾt hʾryh,* "and Argob and the Arieh," (lit. "the lion"), two proper nouns in the accusative which offer little sense in this context. Precritical commentators took them to be the names of two outstanding Gileadite warriors, noting the similarity of the name Argob with the district of the same name in the Gilead (cf. Deut 3:4), so e.g. LXX, Targum, Qimḥi, Gersonides; cf. *NJPS.* Stade considered the names "a misplaced gloss" to "the Gilead" in v. 29 and read "Argob and Havvoth-jair" (cf. Num 32:41; 1 Kgs 4:13); and so Burney, Montgomery-Gehman. *NEB* and *NAB* omit the words altogether. Most recently M. Geller (*VT* 26 [1976], 374–77) rendered *ʾrgb* and *ʾryh* as "by the eagle and the lion," (*ʾrgb* is explained by what looks to be a cognate word in Ugaritic), i.e. portal figures at the gates of Samaria's palace; curiously, Rashi had also suggested that "a golden lion stood in that palace."

27. *Pekah . . . became king . . . for twenty years.* A twenty-year reign for Pekah is a datum which cannot easily be coordinated with the chronologically fixed dates for the northern kingdom. According to the present verse, Pekah came to the throne in Azariah's fifty-second year—i.e. 734/3. Hoshea replaced Pekah as king of Israel in 732/1 (see the note to 2 Kgs 17:1), and was confirmed in that position by Tiglath-

pileser in the same year. Therefore Pekah could have reigned for two years at the most. The "twenty years" assigned to him, however, is used in the Israelite synchronisms in vv. 32 and 16:1, and thus the number "twenty" cannot be simply a scribal error for "two" or an incorrect gloss. Vogelstein (*Fertile Soil,* 30–31) and Thiele (*MNHK*[3], 124; *JBL* 93 [1974], 194–98) maintain that Pekah had set up a rival rule in the Gilead even before the death of Jeroboam, and after coming to the throne in Samaria counted those years in the total years of his reign. In a somewhat similar approach, B. Oded (*CBQ* 34 [1972], 162) suggests that Pekah "ruled over northern Transjordania on behalf of the king of Israel" before seizing power.

29. *Tiglath-pileser . . . came and took Ijon, Abel-beth-maachah, Janoah, Kedesh, Hazor . . . —all the land of Naphtali.* It is of interest to note that part of this list appears in the description of Ben-hadad I's attack on northern Israel during the reign of Baasha (1 Kgs 15:20).

On the king's name, see note to 16:7.

Ijon, at Tell ed-Dibin in the fertile valley at the foot of Mt. Hermon, survives in the name of the present-day town of Marj-ʿAyun. See Aharoni, *Land of the Bible*[2], s.v.

Abel-beth-maachah, south of Ijon in the upper Galilee at Abil el-Qamḥ (*EncMiqr* 1.37). The *Abilakka* in a text of Tiglath-pileser (*ANET*[3], 283), taken by all commentators as the Assyrian form of the name Abel-beth-maacah, is not at all certain. The text has *A-bi-il-xx.* Besides, the reference there is to the border between Aram and Israel in Trans-Jordan. For an Abil in the Gilead, see Aharoni, *Land of the Bible*[2], s.v., and the remarks of H. Tadmor, *IEJ* 12 (1963), 114–15; idem, in *All the Land of Naphtali* (Jerusalem: Israel Exploration Society, 1968), 65–66 (Hebrew).

Janoaḥ is of disputed identification. At least three modern sites preserve the name *Yanuḥ.* Aharoni, *EncMiqr* 3.704, prefers a location in the western Galilee on the road leading to the plain of Acre. J. Kaplan, *IEJ* 28 (1978), 159–60, suggests Giv'at hashoqet, a site in the upper Huleh Valley, the area favored by early investigators.

Kedesh is one of several cities with this name, and according to Aharoni, *EncMiqr* 7.37–39, is at Tell Qadis, 10 km northwest of Hazor in the upper Galilee. It is also referred to in Josh 12:22, 20:7, 21:32. Cf. Kallai, *Tribes of Israel,* 194–99 (Hebrew).

Hazor is the largest site in the upper Galilee, situated at Tell el-Qedaḥ. See the summary of excavations in *EAEHL* 2.474–95; and Y. Yadin, *Hazor* (Schweich Lectures, London: The British Academy, 1972); and the note to 1 Kgs 9:15.

the Gilead and the Galilee. Conquest of the Gilead is reported in 1 Chr 5:6, 26. The term Galilee appears here in its late Hebrew, Aramaized form, *haggālîlâ.* Consequently, both of these geographical designations are likely to be glosses, summarizing Tiglath-pileser's conquests east and west of the Jordan; and they correspond in part to the following phrase, "all the land of Naphtali."

all the land of Naphtali. Also in 1 Kgs 15:20. F. Hommel's cautious suggestion on a broken line in Tiglath-pileser's annals—"the wide land of [ ]li, in its entire extent"—"perhaps to be restored as *Naptali*" (see *Geschichte Babyloniens und Assyriens* [Berlin, 1884–88], 665) became scholarly fact in all subsequent editions and translations. See e.g. P. Rost, *Keilschrifttexte Tiglat-Pilesers III,* 78, line 7; *ARAB* 1.815; *ANET*[3], 283. However, H. Tadmor (*IEJ* 12 [1962], 115–16) restored the line: "the wide land of [Bīt-Ḫazai]li, in its entire extent." Accordingly it refers to the southern border of Aram-Damascus, not to Israel. Finally Tiglath-pileser's annals, on a very fragmentary slab, provide the names of additional sites in the Galilee overrun by his forces.

> . . . x captives from the city of [. . .]-bara, 625 captives from the city of [. . .] [. . . captives from the city of] Hannathon, 650 captives from Ku[. . . captives from the city of Jo]tbah, 656 captives from the city of Sa[. . . . . .] the cities of Aruma and Merum[. . .]
>
> (Tadmor, *ITP*, Annals 18:4′–7′; cf. Appendix I, No. 4B; *ARAB* 1.777; *ANET*[3], 283)

Inasmuch as Tiglath-pileser campaigned for two years, 733–732, in the area of northern Israel, one cannot be sure that the biblical and Assyrian lists refer to the same campaign. (For the identification of these towns, see Aharoni, *Land of the Bible*[2], 372–74. Note that some of Aharoni's readings are corrected in the quotation above.)

he exiled their population to Assyria. This is the first recorded exile of Israelites from their land. Earlier references to the Assyrian practice of population transfer appear throughout the prophecies of Amos; see, e.g., Amos 5:5, 27; 6:7; 7:11, 17. In an annal fragment of Tiglath-pileser (edited for the first time in Tadmor, *ITP*, Annals 24:1′–9′), the figure 13,520 is given as the sum total of captives taken during the campaign in the Galilee. Cf. Tadmor, in *All the Land of Naphtali*, 66–67.

30. *Hoshea son of Elah . . . succeeded him as king.* The name Hoshea, a shortened form of *Hôšaʿăyā(hû)*, appears on several Hebrew seals; see Hestrin and Dayagi-Mendels, *Seals*, nos. 22, 53. For a thorough discussion of the derivation of the name from **w/yšʿ* in the *hiphil* and its possible cognates, see I.Ephʿal, in *Excavations and Studies, Essays in Honour of S. Yeivin* (Tel Aviv: University of Tel-Aviv, 1973), 201–3.

The annals of Tiglath-pileser record the deposition of Pekah and Hoshea's accession:

> Pekah, their king [. . .]
> and I installed Hoshea (ᵐ*A-ú-si-ʾ*) as king
> over them. 10 talents of gold, x talents
> of silver, their [. . .] I received from them.
>
> (Tadmor, *ITP*, Summary Inscription 4.17′–18′; cf. Appendix I, No. 4C; *ANET*[3], 284)

(*The manuscripts prepared by G. Smith of this fragment vary as to the amount of silver: 200/1,000/2,000 talents.)

Another text (ND4301+ from Calah; D. J. Wiseman, *Iraq* 18 [1956], 126, reedited in *ITP* as Summary Inscription 9.10–11) provides information on the data of Hoshea's confirmation by Tiglath-pileser.

> [Hosea] over them as king [I placed.]
> [He/his messenger came] before me to the city
> of Sarrabani [and kissed my feet.]

As the siege of Sarrabani in southern Babylonia took place in 731, Hoshea must have come to the throne either at the beginning of that year or at the end of 732. On this date, see R. Borger and H. Tadmor, *ZAW* 94 (1982), 244–49.

Comment

1. *Assyria under Tiglath-pileser III: The Setting for Israel's Decline.* The coming of Tiglath-pileser III to the throne (745–727) inaugurated a new stage in the history of Assyria and the ancient Near East as a whole. His rule apparently began in rebellion; the Eponym Chronicle for 746 B.C.E. records a "revolt in Kalḫu." Unlike other Assyrian kings, Tiglath-pileser does not list his parentage in the opening lines of his inscriptions, though in the Assyrian King List he appears as the son of his predecessor Ashur-nirari V.[1] In the mid-eighth century, the western border of the Assyrian empire stood at the Euphrates, at Bit-Adini, annexed by Shalmaneser III a century earlier. The key to Assyrian political and economic domination of north Syria and the Phoenician coast was control over Arpad (Bit-Agusi). Mati-ilu, king of Arpad, had been forced to swear a vassal oath to Ashur-nirari V, at the same time remaining a power in the area in his own right.[2] However, the major rival of Assyria in north Syria was Urartu (modern Armenia), whose kings Argishti I (early eighth century) and Sarduri II (mid-eighth century) pushed westward through Anatolia during the period of Assyria's internal weakness which preceded Tiglath-pileser.

This weakness found expression in the ascendance of powerful provincial governors and army commanders. Among the better known are Nergal-eresh, governor of Raṣappa[3] and Shamshi-ilu, the *turtānu,* one of whose centers was Til-Barsip. The latter's independence of action is demonstrated by an inscription in which his offices and achievements are enumerated: "viceroy, chief herald, overseer of temples, chief of a vast army, ruler of the land of Hatti, the highlands and all the land of Namri"[4]—all these titles without mentioning the reigning monarch.[5]

[1] For the Assyrian King List, see the edition of I. J. Gelb, *JNES* 13 (1954), 229, line 24. Only in one text, in a brick inscription from Ashur, does Tiglath-pileser mention his parentage. There he is "son of Adad-nirari," evidently Adad-nirari III, (811–783); see *ARAB* 1.822, No. 1. Was he then one of that king's youngest sons?

[2] For the text of the oath sworn by Mati-ilu to Assyria, see *ANET*³, 532–33. Mati-ilu himself defined his own position as overlord of Bar Ga'ya, king of (the land of) KTK by a similar loyalty oath preserved in the texts of the Sefire treaties. See J. A. Fitzmyer, *The Aramaic Inscriptions of Sefire* (BibOr 19: Rome, 1967) and *ANET*³, 659–61.

[3] A stele of Nergal-eresh erected at Tell al-Rimah for Adad-nirari III (the second half of which contained a description of the governor's achievements and which was subsequently defaced), has been published by S. Page *Iraq* 30 (1968), 139–53, and cf. above Comment to 13:14–25.

[4] F. Thureau-Dangin, *Til-Barsib* (Paris: Geuthner, 1936), 145–46.

[5] The reference to "him that holds the scepter in Beth-eden" in Amos 1:5 has plausibly been identified with Shamshi-ilu by A. Malamat in *BASOR* 129 (1953), 25–26.

This state of affairs changed in 745. Tiglath-pileser III set out to reassert the prerogatives of the Assyrian monarch: he circumscribed the role of the provincial governors by subdividing their large domains. In the political and military spheres, he conducted an aggressive imperial policy. In his first regnal year, Tiglath-pileser intervened in Babylonia, thus extending Assyrian supervision as far as southern Chaldea. For the next five years, he campaigned in the north and the west. In 743 he defeated Sarduri king of Urartu and cleared the way for an attack on Arpad. Arpad fell after a three year siege. The other states of north and central Syria yielded and paid tribute. In 738, the neo-Hittite state of Unqi and its capital Kunulua/Kullani (biblical Calneh) also fell to the Assyrian conqueror. It is in connection with these affairs that the fragmentary annals record the defeat of nineteen districts in Hamath and Hatarikka led in rebellion by Azriyau (see the note to 15:1). The Assyrian empire now extended to the Mediterranean coast; Arpad, Kullani, Hatarikka and Ṣimirra were annexed as provinces for the first time.[6]

These new annexations were accompanied by deportations on an unprecedented scale. Deportation of captive peoples, Aramaeans and north Syrians, into Assyria is well documented in the ninth century; Ashurnasirpal II, for example, settled "captured peoples from the land of my conquest" in Kalḫu after its restoration.[7] The novelty of Tiglath-pileser's action was not only its size, but its character. Deportation became a two-way exchange: from newly organized provinces in the West, he transferred populations to Assyria proper, and resettled those areas with people brought from the East and South. This radical procedure of population exchange sought to make the uprooted totally dependent on the central government,[8] forcefully amalgamating them so that "they became Assyrian."[9] This procedure, more than any other, created the new Assyrian empire.

The years 734–732 mark the second stage of Tiglath-pileser's conquest of the West. The Eponym Chronicle records: 734, "to Philistia"; 733, "to Damascus"; 732, "to Damascus." It is not clear whether the initiative for these campaigns was the desire to extend Assyrian hegemony over the profitable

[6] On the north-Syrian provinces in 738, see the discussions of K. Kessler, *WO* 8 (1976), 49–63; and N. Na'aman, *WO* 9 (1977), 228–39. The reference in Amos 6:2 to Calneh and Greater Hamath suggested to N. Na'aman that the prophet was referring to the campaign of 738 in north Syria (*BASOR* 214 [1974], 37). For the location of Calneh/Kullani, see J. D. Hawkins, RLA 6.305–6 and literature cited there.

[7] See the stele inscriptions from Calah published by D. J. Wiseman, *Iraq* 14 (1952), 29–32, lines 33–36.

[8] Transporting captive Aramaeans and dealing with their personal needs are the subjects of two Nimrud letters, part of the royal correspondence from field officers; see H. W. F. Saggs *Iraq* 18 (1956), 41–32, letters nos. 25, 26.

[9] The phrase *itti nišê māt Aššur amnušunuti,* "I considered them (i.e. the captives) as Assyrians," was reintroduced by Tiglath-pileser III (cf. CAD M 1.224). On the lot of the deportees in Assyria and their social position, see B. Oded, *Mass Deportations,* 75–115.

trade centers of Philistia or was undertaken in response to hostile moves on the part of a coalition of area states, among them Damascus, Tyre, Israel, Gaza.[10] (On the place of the appeal of Ahaz of Judah to Tiglath-pileser in this turbulent period, see the Comment on 16:5–9.) Initially Gaza was subjugated and a new vassal oath imposed upon its king. Commercial activity in Philistia was put under Assyrian supervision, with the cooperation of native elements in northern Sinai. A royal stele set up on the banks of *naḫal Muṣri,* "the Wadi of Egypt," i.e. Wadi el-Arish, marked the limit of Tiglath-pileser's rule in the south.[11] But the major achievement of these years was the conquest and destruction of Aram-Damascus after a two-year siege. Aramaean territory as far as the Gilead was annexed and reorganized as Assyrian provinces. Israel, too, felt the impact of the Assyrian onslaught. The entire Galilee as far as Megiddo in the Esdraelon Valley and northern Transjordan up to (Ramoth-) Gilead became provinces of the empire.[12] The states of the west not formally incorporated by Assyria—Israel (restricted to the hills of Ephraim), Judah, Ammon, Moab, and Edom—were brought under imperial control as vassals.

In the final stages of his reign, Tiglath-pileser conquered Chaldea, and for the first time in the history of the neo-Assyrian empire, ascended the throne of Babylonia, assuming the title "king of Assyria and Babylonia." The claim of the Assyrian monarch to being master of all the lands and peoples "from the horizon to the zenith" was indeed no empty boast.

2. *Israel's Decline.* As fate would have it, Assyria's renewed ascendancy under Tiglath-pileser III coincided with the internal strife which racked Israel following the death of Jeroboam II. The social and moral decay already experienced during Jeroboam's reign and so vividly described in the prophecies of Amos helps account for the political disarray chronicled in these verses. Successive rivals contested for the throne of Israel; Shallum "son of Jabesh" (v. 10), Pekah "son of Ramaliah" (v. 25), and perhaps Menahem "son of Gadi" as well (v. 14) all hailed from the Gilead. This agriculturally rich and strategically vital territory, recovered by Jeroboam II after decades of Aramaean domination (14:25), became the base for a new Israelite elite which fought to seize power in Samaria. The only stable reign during this period was that of Menahem (747–737), and this was made possible, in part,

[10] For differing views on this question, see Alt, *Kleine Schriften,* 2.150–62; H. Tadmor, *BA* 29 (1966), 87–90; B. Oded, *ZDPV* 90 (1974), 38–49; B. Otzen, *ASTI* 11 (1977–78), 99–105.

[11] The integration of nomadic elements in imperial affairs at this juncture is set out by I. Ephᶜal, *The Ancient Arabs,* 93–100.

[12] E. Forrer, in his seminal study, *Die Provinzeinteilung des assyrischen Reiches* (Leipzig: J. C. Hinrichs, 1920) argued that at this juncture several additional provinces were created: the province of Dor on the Mediterranean coast, as well as the provinces Qarnaim and Hauran in the territory of Aram-Damascus. Concerning the organization of Trans-Jordan, see too B. Oded, *JNES* 29 (1970), 177–86. For a critical investigation of Forrer's thesis, see I. Ephᶜal in *WHJP* 4/1, 282–86.

by the political (and military?) backing of Assyria. Menahem submitted to Tiglath-pileser "so that he would support him in holding on to the kingdom" (v. 19).[13] At the same time, Pekah with his band of Gileadites may have proclaimed himself king in Trans-Jordan; some scholars suspect that Rezin of Damascus was behind this move (see the note to v. 27).

By 734 a major new coalition headed by Rezin confronted Tiglath-pileser in south Syria, Israel, and on the sea coast. But it could not meet the threat; after a wide-ranging military campaign over three years, 734–732, the area was brought under direct Assyrian control. Israel was stripped of the Galilee and the Gilead (v. 29) and left a rump state in the hill country of Ephraim, with Hoshea son of Elah installed as king and vassal of Assyria (v. 30). Damascus, the major power in southern Syria, which had withstood Assyrian military prowess for over a century, was conquered and severely punished (16:9).

These events, in what proved to be the last decades of Israel's monarchy, are narrated in 2 Kgs 15 within the regular Deuteronomistic framework. An unusually large number of quotations, some of them in a poor state of preservation, drawn from contemporary Israelite chronicles (vv. 8, 10, 13, 14, 16, 23, 25, 27, 29, 30) fills out that framework with details of persons, places, and dates in the ever-changing political picture in Samaria.[14] In addition to these written sources, other northern traditions incorporated by Dtr. seem to have been transmitted in oral form, like the story of Pul's (Tiglath-pileser) campaign "to the land" and Menahem's onerous assessment (vv. 19–20). After the report of the assassination of Zechariah son of Jeroboam, an editorial remark in v. 12 links his death with an earlier prophecy in 10:30. Both verses are a postfactum judgment on Jehu's dynasty in the pattern of "prophecy and fulfillment" favored by the editor of Kings; it is the last statement of this kind in the narration of the history of the north. Also noteworthy is the lack of any reference to prophetic admonitions in this section, although literary prophets such as Amos and Hosea are known to have actively criticized Israel's rulers during this period (note esp. Amos 7:10–11; Hos 5:8–15, 10:7). This omission is in seeming contradiction to Dtr.'s own statement: "YHWH even warned Israel and Judah through all his prophets . . . But they did not listen" (2 Kgs 17:13–14). It may be suggested, therefore, that the editing of the Israelite material in 2 Kgs 15 goes back to an earlier, pre-Dtr. framework from north Israel itself.

[13] The proposal to credit Menahem with leading a raid against Tiphsah on the Euphrates is historically untenable. See the discussion in the note to v. 16.

[14] Might the bad state of the text of vv. 16 and 25 have resulted from these notices being written in the concluding section of an Israelite chronicle on the end of a scroll, which was later damaged in the course of transmission?

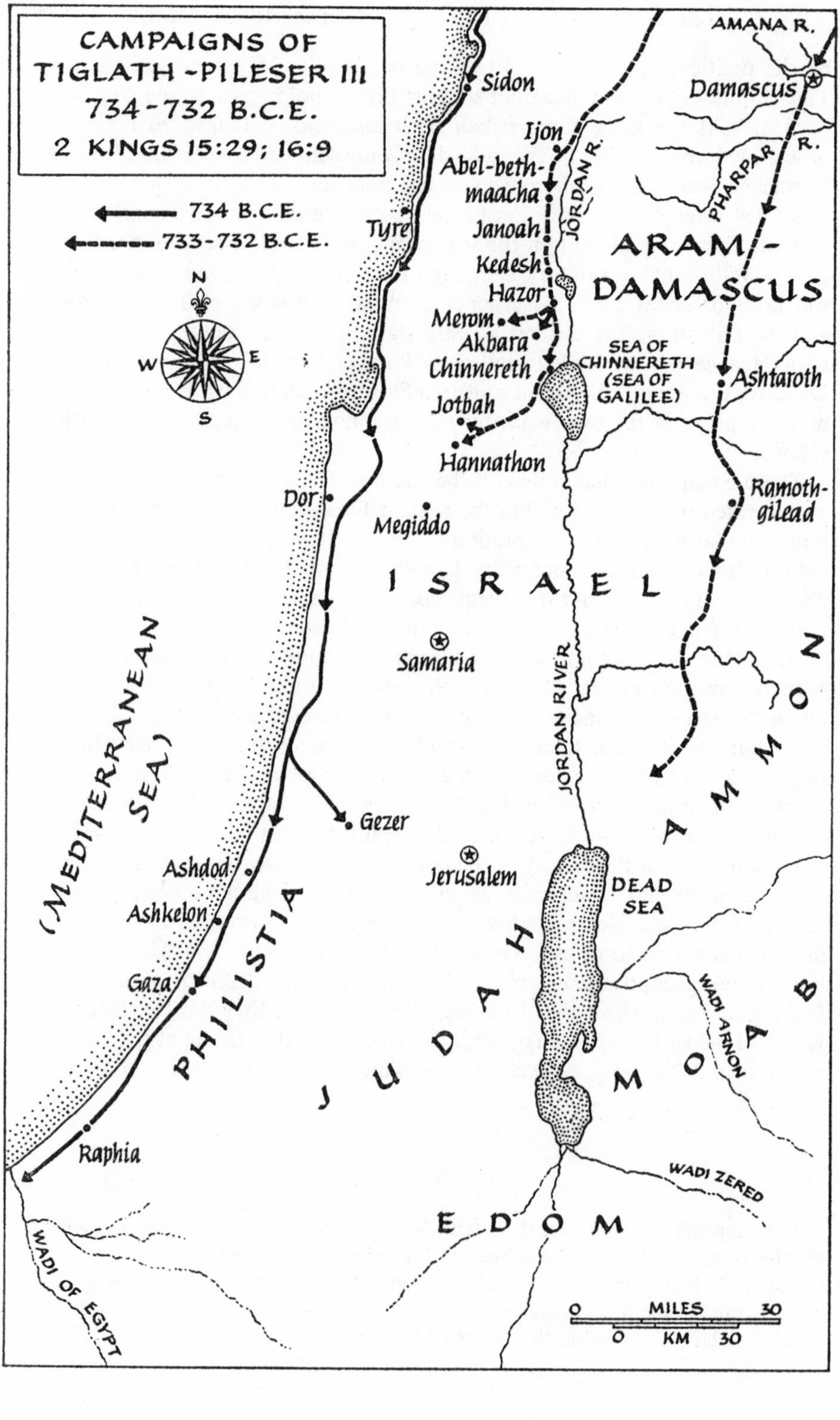
CAMPAIGNS OF TIGLATH-PILESER III 734-732 B.C.E. 2 KINGS 15:29; 16:9
734 B.C.E.
733-732 B.C.E.
N
W
E
S
Sidon
Tyre
Ijon
Abel-beth-maacha
Janoah
Kedesh
Hazor
Merom
Akbara
Chinnereth
Jotbah
Hannathon
JORDAN R.
AMANA R.
Damascus
PHARPAR R.
ARAM-DAMASCUS
SEA OF CHINNERETH (SEA OF GALILEE)
Ashtaroth
Ramoth-gilead
Dor
Megiddo
ISRAEL
Samaria
JORDAN RIVER
AMMON
(MEDITERRANEAN SEA)
Gezer
Ashdod
Jerusalem
Ashkelon
DEAD SEA
Gaza
PHILISTIA
JUDAH
WADI ARNON
MOAB
Raphia
WADI ZERED
EDOM
WADI OF EGYPT
0 MILES 30
0 KM 30

e (*MNHK*², 118–
haz and survived
en."
rûšâ) means "the
at she was "from

is known of the
ind Jotham's en-
nple complex is
ur; Ezek 9:2 (cf.

against Judah.
ence to YHWH's
ne, Lev 26:22 of

ompared with 2
ition and shows
o the attack on
"The Historical
2), 153–65; and
Dtr_2.
Isaᵃ 9:10 reads
u. On the basis
ṣyan, meaning
berger, *Samʾal*
n. 83.
-pileser in 738;
us in 733–732,
orted (*ANET*³,
34).

e Deuteron-
the lifetime
duties from
he Temple's
ed writer.
e traditions
her's policy
n claims in

THAM (JUDAH)

f Remaliah king of Israel,
ne king. 33 He was twenty-
he reigned sixteen years in
a daughter of Zadok. 34 He
st as Uzziah his father had
ved; the people continued to
places. He built the Upper
f the history of Jotham and
nnals of the kings of Judah.
king of Aram and Pekah son
slept with his ancestors, and
City of David his ancestor.

has been taken to mean "YHWH is
men . . . [Stuttgart: W. Kohlham-
eleifeh near Elath reading *lytm* was
-14, and by W. F. Albright, op. cit.
e at the port city (so Montgomery-
3 [1961], 18–22). But the seal is of
e read "Belonging to Yatom," i.e. the
], 381, n. 3).
ixteen-year reign for Jotham contra-
in v. 30, whereby Jotham reigned at
seems to be based on the assumption
nd year of Azariah (v. 27) which was
began his reign in Pekah's first year
(v. 27). But this calculation (by a late
e into consideration Jotham's coreign
Pekah's twenty years may have been

spent as a self-proclaimed king in the Gilead. Other solutions: Th
31) posits that Jotham was deposed in his sixteenth year by his so
another four years. Gray corrected the text to read "six" for "si

Jerusha daughter of Zadok. The name *Yĕrûšā'* (in 2 Chr 27:1
inherited one"; see J. J. Stamm, *VT* Sup 16 (1967), 327. Luc. adds
Jerusalem."

35. *He built the Upper Gate of the House of* YHWH. As so lit
Temple's architectural history after Solomon, the circumstances
dowment must be left open. An Upper Benjamin Gate in the
mentioned in Jer 20:2 as the place of Jeremiah's confinement by Pa
8:3) confirms that this gate opened northward (and cf. Skinner).

37. *In those days,* YHWH *first loosed Rezin . . . and Pekah* .
Heb. *lĕhašlîaḥ bĕ* . . . , "to send against," always said with re
punishments; e.g. Exod 8:17 of plague, Amos 8:11, Ezek 14:13 of
wild beasts.

From the point of view of style and ideology, this verse should
Kgs 10:32. Like the latter, this one derives from sound historical
that the pressure of Aram and Israel upon Judah had started pri
Ahaz described in 16:5. For a defense of this tradition, see B. Od
Background of the Syro-Ephraimite War Reconsidered," *CBQ* 34
the Comment below. Note the similar observation in 24:2 by the

Rezin king of Aram. LXX transcribes the name as *Raasson.*
rṣy'n. In Akk. transcription it appears as *^{m}Ra-ḫi-a-nu* and *^{m}Ra-q*
of these forms the Aramaean original can be reconstructed as
"pleasant, desirable." The Akkadian form has been treated by B. I
(Ankara, 1948) 66, n. 169; cf. M. Weippert, *ZDPV* 89 (1973), 46

Rezin was one of the western kings who rendered tribute to Ti
see the note to 15:14 above and Comment. During the siege of Da
[. . .] Hadara, Rezin's hometown, was taken and its population
283; Tadmor, *ITP,* Annals 22, 13′–15′; and B. Oded, *EncMiqr* 7.

Comment

The presentation of Jotham's sixteen years as king of Judah
omist is quite unremarkable; his entire reign (758–743) fell
of his father. Having recorded that Jotham assumed certain
Azariah in 15:5, the editor credits him with renovating on
gateways (v. 35), an item of special interest to this temple-

A more substantive picture of Jotham's reign emerges fr
behind 2 Chr 27. There Jotham is shown to have continued
of military preparedness; he also took up arms to defend J

Trans-Jordan (27:5). It is suggestive to see the later banding together of Israel and Aram-Damascus against Jotham (2 Kgs 15:37) as an outgrowth of such moves.[1] Chronologically, Dtr. dated these attacks on Judah prior to Tiglath-pileser's campaign.

[1] These affairs are taken as the opening stage of the "Syro-Ephraimite war" by B. Oded (above, note to v. 37). See further in Comment to 16:5–9 below. On the long-standing interests of Judaean families in the Gilead, see B. Mazar, "The Tobiads," *IEJ* 7 (1957), 233–38.

XXVII. THE REIGN OF AHAZ (JUDAH)

(16:1–20)

16 1 In the seventeenth year of Pekah son of Remaliah, Ahaz son of
Jotham king of Judah became king. 2 Ahaz was twenty years old when
he became king, and he reigned sixteen years in Jerusalem. He did not
do what was pleasing to YHWH, his God, like David, his ancestor,
3 but he followed the ways of the kings of Israel; he even passed his
son[a] through fire, imitating the abominations of the nations whom
YHWH dispossessed before the Israelites. 4 He sacrificed and made offerings at the high places, on the hills, and under every leafy tree.

5 Then Rezin king of Aram and Pekah son of Remaliah king of
Israel came to do battle against Jerusalem. They besieged Ahaz, but
they were not able to attack.

6 At that time, the king of Edom[b] restored Elath to Edom[c]; he drove
out the Judahites from Elath[d]. Edomites[e] came to Elath and settled
there until this day.

7 Ahaz sent messengers to Tiglath-pileser king of Assyria: "I am
your servant and your son. Come, rescue me from the hand of the king
of Aram and from the hand of the king of Israel who are attacking
me." 8 Ahaz took the silver and the gold stored in the House of YHWH
and in the palace treasury, and sent a bribe to the king of Assyria.
9 The king of Assyria responded to his plea; the king of Assyria proceeded against Damascus. He captured it and exiled its population[f] to
Kir[g], and put Rezin to death.

10 Now when King Ahaz went to Damascus[h] to greet Tiglath-
pileser, king of Assyria, he saw the altar in Damascus; whereupon
King Ahaz sent a model of the altar and a plan with all details for its

[a] Luc. reads "sons"; so, too, 2 Chr 28:3.
[b] Read *mlk ʾdm* for MT *rṣyn mlk ʾrm;* see note.
[c] Read *lʾdm* for MT lʾ *rm.*
[d] MT reads "Eloth" (*ʾylwt*); versions and a few mss. read "Elath (ʾylt)."
[e] Read *ʾdmym* with qere; *ʾrmym* in ketib. Some mss. *ʾdwmym* qere; *ʾrwmym* ketib.
[f] Lit. "it."
[g] Omitted by LXX[B].
[h] MT *dwmśq.* Mss. correctly read *dmśq.*

construction to Uriah the priest. 11 Uriah the priest built the altar,
according to all that King Ahaz had sent him from Damascus; Uriah
the priest completed it by the time King Ahaz returned from Damascus. 12 When the king returned from Damascus and inspected the altar, he approached the altar and ascended it; 13 he offered his burnt
offering and his meal offering; he poured out his libation, and he
dashed the blood of his offering of well-being against the altar. 14 As
for the bronze altar which (had stood) before YHWH, he moved (it)
from the front of the House, from between the altar and House of
YHWH, and placed it on the north side of the (new) altar. 15 King Ahaz
then ordered Uriah the priest[i]: "On the great altar, offer the morning
burnt offering and the evening meal offering and the king's burnt offering and his meal offering and the burnt offering of all the People of the
Land, and their meal offerings and their libations. All the blood of the
burnt offerings and all the blood of the sacrifices you shall dash against
it. The bronze altar will be for me to frequent." 16 Uriah the priest did
just as King Ahaz ordered.

17 King Ahaz stripped off the frames of the wheeled stands and
removed the basin from them[j]; he took down the (bronze) Sea from
the bronze oxen that supported it and placed it on the stone pavement.
18 He also removed from the House of YHWH the sabbath covering[k]
built in the House and the king's outer entrance, (all) on account of
the king of Assyria.

19 The rest of the history of Ahaz and[l] what he did are indeed recorded in the annals of the kings of Judah. 20 So Ahaz slept with his
ancestors and he was buried with his ancestors in the city of David.
Hezekiah, his son, succeeded him.

[i] Read with qere *wayĕṣawweh* in place of ketib *wayêṣawwēhû.*
[j] MT has *hmsgrwt* and *wʾt-hkyr.* See note.
[k] Ketib *mysk;* qere *mwsk;* see note.
[l] Many mss., Luc., including some Targ. mss., add: "and all."

Notes

16 1. *Ahaz.* The name Ahaz is a hypocoristicon which appears in its full form only in Assyrian inscriptions as *Iauḫazi* (see *ANET*^{3}, 282). The name was borne by another king of Judah, Jehoahaz son of Josiah (23:30), and an earlier king of Israel, Jehoahaz son of Jehu (13:1). The same components, in reverse order, comprise the name Ahaziah (1 Kgs 22:52, 2 Kgs 8:25). The shortened name Ahaz is known from the seal of one of his courtiers: *lʾšnʾ ʿbd ʾḥz,* "(Belonging) to Ashna, servant of Ahaz." See Diringer, *Iscrizioni,* 212.

2. *Ahaz was twenty years old when he became king . . .* Comparing the statement in this verse with 18:2, in which it is reported that Hezekiah his son succeeded his father at the age of twenty-five years, Ahaz had become a father at the age of eleven! Though not entirely impossible, the figure "eleven" seems too low. One may adopt the reading of manuscripts of LXX to 2 Chr 28:1, "Ahaz was twenty-five years old when he became king" and arrive at a more suitable age for the king when his son was born: sixteen years old.

3. *passed his son through fire.* The most serious of the cultic offenses of the king is set at the head of the list. The oft-repeated speculation that Ahaz sacrificed his first-born during the pressing hours of the siege of Jerusalem by the Syro-Ephraimite armies, as Mesha, king of Moab, had once done under similar circumstances (cf. 3:27, so, e.g., Montgomery-Gehman, Gray) has no direct textual support. It depends upon the interpretation of the nature of this offense, on which see the note to 21:6.

4. *He sacrificed and made offerings at the high places.* The worship at the shrines is not ascribed elsewhere to Judahite kings. It is always the people of Judah who are said to have committed this offense; cf., e.g., 1 Kgs 22:44; 2 Kgs 12:4; 14:4, 15:4, 35.

sacrificed and made offerings. Heb. *zibbēaḥ, qiṭṭēr.* On the use of the *piel* to indicate illicit worship at the shrines, as against the *qal* form *zābaḥ,* and *hiphil hiqṭîr* in the legal cult, see 1 Kgs 22:44.

5–6. *Then . . . At that time.* These words are opening formulae which introduce quotations from earlier, perhaps archival, sources. Assyrian and Babylonian historical literature display a similar phenomenon, in which the phrases *ina tarṣi* PN, "in the days of PN" and *ina ūmīšuma,* "at that time" (lit. "in his days") signal verbatim quotations from chronicles. In many cases, the alteration between the use of the first-person and third-person address and the royal titulary complement the formulaic indications. Cf. the early study of J. A. Montgomery, *JBL* 53 (1934), 46–52, and see the remarks on the comparative material by H. Tadmor and M. Cogan, *Bib* 60 (1979), 493–99.

5. On the name Rezin, see note to 15:37.

They besieged Ahaz. In the parallel passage in Isa 7:1, the words *wayyāṣūrû ʿal-ʾāḥāz,* "they besieged Ahaz," are missing. Thus the phrase is usually taken to be an error by an editor or copyist for an original *wayyāṣūrû ʿālehā,* "they besieged it (i.e. Jerusalem)," which is reconstructed from *lammilḥāmâ ʿāleyhā* and *lĕhillāḥem ʿāleyhā* in Isaiah. But lexicographically there is no warrant to cancel *wayyāṣūrû ʿal- ʾāḥāz;* the expression "to besiege someone" appears in 2 Sam 20:15. Both the Kings and the Isaiah texts are independent formulations, based upon the same archival source and should not be used to correct one another.

but they were not able to attack. From this laconic statement, it is difficult to decide whether they tried to engage the defenders in open battle and failed to do so, or were unable to launch an attack against the city and storm it.

6. *restored.* The expression *hēšîb lĕ-,* "to regain control," indicates a battle fought over territory to which there is a claim of ownership made for one's own purposes, not on behalf of a third party, cf. 2 Kgs 14:25. Hence if it was the Edomites (with qere) who reoccupied Elath, it was not the Aramaeans who conquered it.

Edom, Edomites. This is the preferred reading, rather than that of the consonantal text: *Aram, Aramaeans.* The textual corruption, as well as the introduction of the name *Rezin,* entered into v. 6 from v. 5, when the two verses were joined in the present text. Originally, vv. 5 and 6 were separate chronistic entries. This observation is supported by the text of 2 Chr 28:17 in which only Edom is the attacker. Current opinion makes this verse the ground for Aramaean intervention on behalf of Edom—see, e.g., Aharoni, *Land of the Bible*², 371; A. Malamat in *Peoples of Old Testament Times*, ed. D. J. Wiseman (Oxford: Oxford University Press, 1973), 146; M. Ottosson, *Gilead* (ConB; Lund: Gleerup, 1969), 235; and W. Rudolph, *Chronikbücher*, HAT, 292, among others.

Judahites. Heb. *yĕhûdîm* does not appear as the name for the residents of the southern kingdom until Jeremiah's time (e.g., Jer 32:12, 38:19, and others), which may be an indication that this notice was written at the end of the seventh century. See Comment.

Elath, Eloth. The two variant spellings of the city's name in a single verse is surprising. But the interchange of the suffix *at* and *ôt* is not unusual. See W. Borée, *Die alten Ortsnamen Palästinas*² (Leipzig: E. Pfeiffer, 1930), 43–47. The name of Gaza appears in an Assyrian text of Tiglath-pileser as *Ḫazzutu*, i.e., *ʿazôt*, alongside *Ḫazziti*, i.e., *ʿazâ*, *ʿazât*. (Cf. Borée for additional examples of this interchange in the LXX.) This linguistic phenomenon, *a* or *ā* > *ô*, is not necessarily late, and may be documented as far back as the beginning of the second millennium B.C.E. among the speakers of Amorite in Canaan as compared with those in Syria. See I. J. Gelb, "The Early History of the West Semitic Peoples," *JCS* 15 (1961), 42–44, and now, W. W. Hallo and H. Tadmor, "A Lawsuit from Hazor," *IEJ* 27 (1977), 4–5. The more frequent form *ʾylt* appears now in an ostracon from Heshbon, F. M. Cross, "Ammonite Ostraca from Heshbon," *Andrews University Seminary Studies* 13 (1975), 2, 5.

7. *Ahaz sent messengers to Tiglath-pileser.* Tiglath-pileser Heb. *tglt plʾsr;* Akk. *Tukultī-apil-Ešarra*, "My help is the son of Esharra (the temple of the god Ashur in the city of Ashur)." The Assyrian consonant *k* regularly shifts to Hebrew *g* between vowels or in the vicinity of the sonorous *r, l, n;* cf. Akk. *šaknu*, Heb. *sĕgan*, "prefect" (Jer 51:23, 57); Akk. *Šarru-kēn*, Heb. *Sargon*, (the king) Sargon (Isa 20:1). The transcription in Chronicles (1 Chr 5:26) *tlgt plnʾsr* represents a late, dissimilated form. Aramaic inscriptions from the West reproduce the king's name in the same form as the Hebrew; in linguistic areas under the influence of the Babylonian dialect of Akkadian, the transcription was *tkltplsr*. Cf. A. R. Millard, *JSS* 21 (1976), 7.

your servant and your son. The combination of these terms is unique in the Bible, though each is frequently attested separately. "Servant" indicates a relationship of subservience and dependence, with "son" used to moderate the inferior status by arousing fatherly feelings toward the "servant."

In extrabiblical documents, the combined phrase *aradka u marūka anāku*, "I am your servant and your son," is rarely attested; cf. Amarna letter 158.1–2 (in which the addressee is an Egyptian high official) and 288.66 (directed to the Egyptian royal scribe). In the Assyrian royal correspondence, the writer always refers to himself as "servant" when writing to the king, even if the writer is the crown prince himself, e.g., Shalmaneser V, son of Tiglath-pileser, or Sennacherib, son of Sargon. See H. W. F. Saggs, "The Nimrud Letters, 1952-Part V: Administration," *Iraq* 21 (1959), 159; H. Tadmor, *EncMiqr* 7.713–714, and L. Waterman, *Royal Correspondence of the Assyrian Empire* 1 (Ann Arbor: University of Michigan Press, 1930), nos. 196–199. A vassal would not have dared to use the term "son," which expressed familial dependency. Therefore one doubts the originality of the formula as used here by Ahaz; it just may be a combination coined by our storyteller.

who are attacking me. For Heb. *haqqômîm ʿālāy* cf. Ps 92:12 and *qāmîm ʿālāy lĕmilḥāmâ* (cf. Obad 1). On the participle form *qômîm,* see GCK 72p.

8. *bribe.* Heb. *šōḥad,* not "present" as taken by most commentators. This term is rooted in legal parlance and bears negative connotations. The laws of the Pentateuch forbid it (Exod 23:8, Deut 16:19); prophets speak out against it (e.g., Isa 5:23, Ezek 22:12); and in Wisdom literature, the giving of *šōḥad* is considered a corrupt act, a perversion of justice (Prov 17:23; cf. Ps 15:5). In historical literature, *šōḥad* appears but twice; in the account of the war between Asa and Ba'asha (1 Kgs 15) and in the present story.

The use of *šōḥad* within the context of international relations is unusual. But the same usage can be documented from the royal historical literature of the Neo-Assyrian period. A request for aid from a neighboring monarch is defined by the Akk. term *ṭātu,* the semantic parallel of *šōḥad,* which likewise, carries a negative connotation. Thus, for example, on the eve of his conquest of Babylon (710 B.C.E.), Sargon II of Assyria, accused Merodach-baladan II, the Chaldean king of Babylon, of bribing Shutruk-Naḫḫunte, king of Elam: "He sent his gift to Shutruk-Naḫḫunte, the Elamite, that he might avenge him. The wicked Elamite accepted his bribe (*ṭātuš*)" (A. G. Lie, *Inscriptions of Sargon II* [Paris: Geuthner, 1929] 54:367–68).

A term closely related to *ṭātu* is *šulmānu,* frequently employed in Akkadian documents of the second half of the second millennium B.C.E. to convey "gift, present," tendered in expectation of return and reward. Cf. P. Artzi, "The First Stage in the Rise of the Middle-Assyrian Empire: EA 15," *EI* 9 (1969), 26–27. Its use in the texts of the first millennium B.C.E. is rare and archaic and is limited to elevated literary prose. Thus, e.g., Sargon II describes the request sent from Ashdod to Egypt: "They sent their gifts (*šulmānišūnu*) to Pharaoh, king of Egypt, a prince who cannot save them, and sought his aid" (H. Winckler, *Die Keilschrifttexte Sargons,* [Leipzig: E. Pfeiffer, 1889] 188:33–36). But in contrast to the use of *ṭātu,* there is no negative evaluation in describing a gift as *šulmānu,* i.e., the record of Sargon himself receiving *šulmānu* from his vassals; it is hardly likely that the Assyrian king would boast of having taken bribes. Cf. F. Thureau-Dangin, *Huitième campagne de Sargon* (Paris: Geuthner, 1912) line 54; the use of *šulmānu* in the letter, ABL 2, Rev. 17; and now, S. Parpola, *Letters from Assyrian Scholars* (AOAT 5/1, 1970) No. 121. Etymologically, *šulmānu* in Akk. and *šalmōnîm* in BH (cf. Isa 1:22) are identical; but semantically, they are distinct: *šalmōnîm* is a hapax legomenon parallel to *šōḥad.* But from parallelism in biblical poetry one may not deduce that *šulmānu* in Akkadian had a negative sense (as might be inferred from the discussion of *ṭātu* and *šulmānu* in Middle Assyrian texts by J. J. Finkelstein, "The Middle Assyrian *šulmānu*—Texts," *JAOS* 72 [1952], 77–80). In a lexical list from Assur, *šulmānu* is parallel to all three terms: *ṭātu* "bribe"; *igisû* "gift"; *tāmartu* "present" (cf. *AHw* 1268).

In the present verse, the biblical writer expressed criticism by his use of the term *šōḥad.* By describing the gift sent to Tiglath-pileser as "bribe"—"He sent *šōḥad* to the king of Assyria" (2 Kgs 16:8)—the writer took exception to this appropriation of temple property. A similar criticism is implied in the description of the deed of Asa (1 Kgs 15:18–19).

9. *exiled its population.* MT "to Kir" is omitted by LXX. The location of this place is still an enigma, in spite of the vast toponymic material available nowadays from Assyro-Babylonian sources. According to Amos 9:7, Kir was the original home of the Aramaeans, and to Kir they would be forcibly returned (1:5). For a review of current

opinion on the origins of the Aramaeans in the upper Euphrates valley, see A. Malamat, 134–55 (above n. 6).

put Rezin to death. Regrettably, none of the extant documents from the reign of Tiglath-pileser records this execution. G. Smith reported (*Zeitschrift für ägyptische Sprache und Altertumskunde* 7 [1869], 14) that "one valuable fragment discovered by Sir H. Rawlinson which contained a notice of the death of Rezin has been left in Assyria and lost."

10–16. *King Ahaz.* Note the peculiar repetition of *hammelek ʾāḥāz* in these verses, as against *ʾāḥāz* in vv. 5, 7, 8, 19–20. This construction is typical of narrative style. Cf. similarly "King Hezekiah," 18:17; 19:1.

10. *to Damascus.* The spelling of the name of the city in MT as *dwmśq* is unique and some manuscripts read the regular form *dmśq* or indicate this in the qere. *dwmśq* is likely an erroneous copying of the postexilic, dissimilated form of the name: *drmśq* (e.g., 2 Chr 28:33); cf. Kutscher, *Isaiah Scroll,* 3–4.

model. Heb. *dĕmût.* Lit. "likeness, figure"—cf. Gen 1:26, 5:13.

Uriah the priest. Known to be a supporter of the prophet Isaiah (Isa 8:2) and therefore a faithful officiant of the cult of YHWH, Uriah complies with the king's order without hesitation. Though Uriah seems to have been the high priest, his name is missing from the list of Zadokite priests in 1 Chr 5:27–41. Was he a member of a rival priestly family (see the note to 22:4) or are the lists in Chronicles faulty? (So Cross, *Canaanite Myth,* 211–15.) The name Uriah does appear in the list of Josephus, *Antiquities* x.152.

11. *Uriah the priest completed it.* For *ʿāśâ kēn* in the sense "agree, comply," cf. Gen 29:28 and the remarks by Speiser, *Genesis,* AB, ad loc. who compares the use of the cognate Akk. *kēnu* with the verbs *nadānu,* "to give," and *šakānu,* "to place."

12. *he approached the altar and ascended it.* Ahaz's officiating in the inaugural ceremony upon the new altar accords with the practice of the kings of Judah and Israel—cf. David, 2 Sam 6:17–18; Solomon, 1 Kgs 8:63; Jeroboam, 1 Kgs 12:32. All these were inaugural, not everyday, sacrifices—hence the king assumed what appear to be priestly functions.

14. *the bronze altar.* The definite article before *mizbaḥ* is not superfluous; "bronze" (with article) is construed as in apposition, not as a genitive, and see below in v. 17; cf. *GKC* 131d, with examples.

15. *People of the Land.* MT is to be retained, despite the fact that some LXX manuscripts have the shortened form "the People." For the meaning of the political term *ʿam hāʾāreṣ,* see the notes to 11:17ff. and 21:24.

will be for me to frequent. I.e. "for my private use." The meaning of the verb *lĕbaqqēr* in this verse is almost beyond explanation (cf. Stade). The context, however, does not suggest that we are dealing with a ritual innovation ("consulting entrails" [Gray], or the like). The tentative translation "frequent" is based on Ps 27:4. A semantic relationship between *baqqēr* and *dārôš* "to seek, search, inspect," is attested in Ezek 34:11, 12; in this meaning *baqqēr* is similar to *dārôš* in Deut 12:5 ("resort to").

17. *the frames of the wheeled stands.* For this Hebrew construction, see the note above on v. 14. The construction of these stands was detailed in 1 Kgs 7:27–37. It may be that only the bronze frames were removed and sent to Assyria. The stands themselves were to become spoil for Nebuchadnezzar; cf. 2 Kgs 25:13.

18. *the sabbath covering.* The translation is tentative. From the context, it seems that this may have been a metal awning, taking *mûśak* from **śkk,* "to cover, screen."

The translation "seat of the dais" in *JB* and in some commentaries (see Montgomery-Gehman) is based on the LXX *ton themelion tēs kathedras,* i.e., retroverted as an otherwise unattested Heb. *mûsad haššebet* (cf. 1 Kgs 10:19). For *šabbāt* in inner temple terminology, cf. 2 Kgs 11:7. Both renderings of *šbt,* as "seat" and "sabbath," are found in Luc. as a doublet. A full review of the history of interpretation of this crux, with a suggestion to translate as "cast-metal seat" (derived from **nsk,* "to pour out, cast") is now given by M. J. Mulder, "Was war die am Tempel Gebaute 'Sabbathalle' in II Kön. 16, 18?", AOAT 211 (1982), 161–72.

on account of the king of Assyria. That these alterations were made "by order of" (Gray), "in deference to" (*JB*), or "to satisfy" (*NEB*) Tiglath-pileser, does not conform to the known practice of Assyrian kings, who did not interfere with the native cultic practices of their vassals. See the full discussion by M. Cogan, *Imperialism and Religion,* 42–64. The alterations in the Jerusalem Temple were necessitated by the heavy tribute in metal which Ahaz had to pay Tiglath-pileser.

the king's outer entrance. Heb. *mābôʾ* is an architectural term used for the entryway into a city (Judg 1:24–25) or a private building (2 Kgs 11:16, Jer 38:14). It appears in Ammonite as well, in the ʿAmman Citadel Inscription, line 1, where it is recorded that the god Milkom "built entrances" (*mbʾt*). For a recent discussion of the inscription, see W. J. Fulco, *BASOR* 230 (1978), 39–43. The final *he* of the adjective *hḥyṣwnh* is due to dittography.

Comment

The introduction to the reign of Ahaz (743–727) departs, for the first time, from the formulaic language which characterizes the evaluation of the other kings of Judah. The stereotypical expression "He did what was pleasing to YHWH . . . however the high places were not removed" is couched in negative terms. Not only did Ahaz do what was displeasing to YHWH, by himself worshipping at the shrines, but he even "passed his son through fire" (v. 3).

Ahaz faced a major crisis shortly after 735 B.C.E.—the attack upon Jerusalem by the armies of Rezin of Damascus and Pekah of Samaria. A fuller account of these events is related in Isa 7:1ff., where it is related that the two allied kings sought to dethrone Ahaz, replacing him with the "son of Tabeel" (Isa 7:6).[1] The motives behind this campaign are not stated in the biblical sources. Most biblical historians follow the suggestion of J. Begrich[2] that Aram and Israel formed an alliance—"Syro-Ephraimite" in his terminology —against Assyria, and attempted to enlist Judah on their side. To overcome

[1] On the identity of "son of Tabeel," see the suggestions of W. F. Albright, *BASOR* 140 (1955), 34–35; and B. Mazar, *IEJ* 7 (1957), 236–37.

[2] *Zeitschrift der deutschen morgenländischen Gesellschaft* 83 (1929), 213–37.

Ahaz's resistance, they moved against Jerusalem in force, and planned to place a king more agreeable to their political goals on David's throne.[3]

From Assyrian records, it appears that the alliance against Tiglath-pileser was more broadly based than reported in 2 Kgs 16:5. Tyre, under its king Hiram, was in league with Damascus; and perhaps some of Philistia's major cities (Ashkelon and Gaza) sided with Pekah and Rezin.[4] Any historical reconstruction of the events of these turbulent years must take into consideration the long-standing rivalry between Israel, Judah, and Aram, especially considering Judah's expansion into the Gilead during the days of Uzziah and Jotham.[5] Perhaps these last moves prompted Pekah the Gileadite to join forces with Rezin to challenge Judah's weakening supremacy.[6]

Attacks upon Judah by her northern neighbors had already taken place in the days of Jotham, Ahaz's father (cf. above 15:37). An echo of these battles can be detected in a late tradition preserved in 2 Chr 28:7–15, which ultimately derives from a north Israelite source.

The records of Tiglath-pileser III pertaining to these years are badly mutilated, and very little has survived. One relatively firm datum is the reference recorded in a list of tributary kings of Syria-Palestine to the tribute of Iauḫazi, king of Judah, paid to Tiglath-pileser in 734.[7] The Assyrian Eponym Chronicle, our main chronological source for fixed dates, reports an Assyrian campaign to Philistia in 734 and to Damascus in 733 and 732.[8]

The problem, then, is when exactly did Ahaz appeal to Assyria for help? Was it prior to Tiglath-pileser's campaign to Philistia in 734? In that case, this appeal would be the initial act of submission by Judah to Assyria. Or did it follow the Assyrian campaign? If so, then it came after Ahaz had submitted to Tiglath-pileser, and as a vassal petitioned his overlord to come to his aid in a time of stress. The historical problem has no ready solution and the formula "I am your servant and your son" (above v. 7) is of little help in weighing the options. For the Deuteronomist, Ahaz's appeal brought Assyria to the area, and it is for this reason that he is censured by use of the term "bribe" (v. 8).

The rescue of Judah is narrated succinctly. During 732 Damascus was taken, its population was led into exile, and Rezin was put to death. While Damascus was under siege, Trans-Jordan and the Galilee came under attack,

[3] This suggestion has been adopted by J. Bright, *History*², 271–72; M. Noth, *History*, 259–60; H. Donner in J. H. Hayes and J. M. Miller, *Israelite and Judaean History*, 421–41, among others.

[4] See D. J. Wiseman, *Iraq* 18 (1956), 125, rev. 5.

[5] This may be deduced from the reference in 1 Chr 5:17 to a census that took place in Trans-Jordan "in the days of Jotham king of Judah and in the days of Jeroboam king of Israel." See H. Tadmor in *A History of the Jewish People* (ed. H. H. Ben-Sasson, Cambridge: Harvard University Press, 1976), 132.

[6] This point was developed in full by B. Oded, *CBQ* 34 (1972), 153–65.

[7] See Appendix I, No. 4D; cf. *ARAB* 1.801 and *ANET*³, 282.

[8] *ARAB* 2.436.

and were subsequently annexed as Assyrian provinces. (For details, see Comment on 2 Kgs 15:29.) Verses 5–9 consist of two units—vv. 5–6; vv. 7–9—both based upon court and temple archives. These excerpts, though of high historical value, are not verbatim quotations from the archival material (see the note to v. 5). Careful rewriting by the historian colored the story with a negative evaluation of Ahaz.

During his visit to Damascus to greet the victorious Tiglath-pileser III after the Assyrian conquest of that city of 732 B.C.E., King Ahaz of Judah saw an altar, whose design he sent to Jerusalem. The priest Uriah had an altar built according to the specifications of the foreign model, completed for use by the time the king returned. This new altar replaced the old Solomonic bronze altar, henceforth set aside for use by the king in his private worship.

Critical opinion is divided as to the reasons for this innovation and the definition of its model; the altar has been called Assyrian,[9] Phoenician,[10] and Aramaean.[11] The argument for Assyrian cultic imposition and the alleged imperial worship of Assyrian's chief god Ashur was investigated by M. Cogan[12] and J. McKay,[13] who have shown that Assyrian imperial policy did not require the worship of Assyrian gods by vassal states. Only in territories annexed to Assyria as provinces, thus becoming integral parts of the empire (*ana māt Aššur utīr,* "I annexed to Assyria"), was the cult of the god Ashur occasionally established. It then took the form of placing "Ashur's weapon" in the provincial center. Assyrian sources do not report the installation of altars. Moreover, it stands to reason that the temple visited by Ahaz was the main Aramaean shrine in Damascus, the temple of Adad-Rimmon (cf. 2 Kgs 5:18). The rites described here as practiced upon the new altar are typically Israelite (see on v. 13) and do not contradict what is known of the accepted practice of the Jerusalem temple.[14] Mesopotamian ritual, including that of Assyria, did not admit whole burnt offerings and blood sprinkling.[15] It is, therefore, unlikely that the altar in Damascus was of Assyrian origin. The view that the altar was Phoenician is based upon an alleged political alliance between Jerusalem and Tyre in 734; it is hardly more defendable. (For the coalition of Tyre, Damascus, and Samaria against Jerusalem, see above.)

What, then, was the nature of the altar of Ahaz, to which even the priest

[9] A. T. Olmstead, *History of Assyria,* 198.

[10] H. W. F. Saggs, *Assyriology and the Study of the Old Testament* (Cardiff, University of Wales Press, 1969), 19–22.

[11] Snaith, *Kings,* 275.

[12] M. Cogan, *Imperialism and Religion: Assyria, Judah and Israel in the Eighth and Seventh Centuries B.C.E.,* SBL Monograph Series 19 (1974), 42–64.

[13] J. McKay, *Religion in Judah under the Assyrians,* 60–66.

[14] On these sacrifices, see R. Rendtorff, *Studien zur Geschichte des Opfers im Alten Israel,* WMANT 24 (1967), 45–50.

[15] Cf. A. L. Oppenheim, *Ancient Mesopotamia* (Chicago: University of Chicago Press, 1964), 192.

Uriah, closely associated with Isaiah, did not object? The construction of this new altar of striking dimensions (the "great altar," v. 15) should be viewed as motivated rather by a spirit of assimilation to the current international fashions. Syrian art and architectural styles are reported even within Assyria proper, e.g. "the *bīt-ḫilāni* palace in the manner of the land of Hatti" constructed by Tiglath-pileser III and his successors.[16] The voluntary innovation of Ahaz was thus the first wave in the larger movement of acculturation to the practices of the Assyrian empire, which in themselves were heavily Aramaized—a wave which was to reach new heights in the mid-seventh century in the days of King Manasseh. (See in detail below, Comment on 2 Kgs 21.)

The detailed story of the altar of Ahaz, which exhibits a specific interest in the Temple, cultic reforms, and the like, originated in a priestly source, not a royal chronicle. The affinity of this passage to the terminology of the Pentateuchal source "P" (Priestly document) is made evident by such phrases as "blood of the offering of well-being" (cf., e.g., Lev 7:14); "their meal offering and their libations" (cf., e.g., Lev 23:18 and Num 6:15); "plan with all details" (cf. Exod 25:9, 40). The Deuteronomistic historian recorded this narration in full to bolster his indictment of King Ahaz, whose apostasy he set out in the introduction to the king's reign, vv. 1–4. Ahaz's innovations, by no means idolatrous or syncretistic, are criticized, it would seem, because they upset the order of things in the Temple as established by Solomon. Other kings' restorations of the Temple, on the other hand, are highly praised (cf. those of Joash—2 Kgs 12:3; Hezekiah—18:3, 5–7; Josiah—23:25).

As an appendix, vv. 17–18 report that Ahaz stripped the bronze from certain temple vessels in order to pay the "bribe" to the king of Assyria, Tiglath-pileser III. The bronze Sea, set up by Solomon (cf. 1 Kgs 7:23–26) was dismantled, and the bronze oxen were apparently sent to Tiglath-pileser as part of Judah's vassal dues.[17] The verses, which no doubt derive from a temple chronicle, are Dtr.'s last example of the misdeeds of Ahaz.

Finally, the chronological significance of the phrase *ʿad hayyôm hazzeh,* "until this day," should not be overlooked. It occurs three times in Kings in territorial contexts:

2 Kgs 8:22—"So Edom has rebelled against the authority of Judah *until this day.*"
2 Kgs 14:7—"He defeated ten thousand Edomites in the Valley of Salt and he captured Sela in battle, and named it Joktheel (as it is called) *until this day.*"
2 Kgs 16:6—"Edomites came to Elath and settled there *until this day.*"

[16] *ARAB* 2.73, 366.
[17] Cf. the copper bull figures received as tribute by the Assyrian king Ashurnasirpal II, *ARAB* 1.476.

The common denominator in these three verses is their topic: Judahite-Edomite relations. All three verses appear to have been composed by a single writer expressing his special interest in the question of the proprietorship of Elath and the Red Sea Coast. It was as if he said, "Until this day, Edomites dwell here, even though Judah has claims in that region dating back to the days of Solomon and Jehoshaphat" (cf. 1 Kgs 9:26; 22:48–49). Moreover it is becoming increasingly evident that at the end of the seventh century B.C.E. Edom reasserted itself and took up a position hostile to Judah. Therefore, it was probably during the reign of Josiah, with renewed Judahite territorial expansion, that the question of Elath in all its ramifications arose. The three citations may therefore reasonably be assigned to the times of Josiah and not to the Exilic Age or to "Nabatean times" (so Montgomery-Gehman).

XXVIII. THE REIGN OF HOSHEA (ISRAEL): THE FALL OF SAMARIA

(17:1–6)

17 1 In the twelfth year of Ahaz, king of Judah, Hoshea son of Elah became king over Israel in Samaria for nine years. 2 He did what was displeasing to YHWH, yet not as the kings of Israel who had preceded him. 3 Shalmaneser king of Assyria marched against him, and Hoshea became his vassal and rendered him tribute. 4 But when the king of Assyria discovered that Hoshea was part of a conspiracy, for he had sent envoys to Sais <to> the king of Egypt[a] and withheld the yearly tribute to the king of Assyria, the king of Assyria arrested him and put him in prison. 5 The king of Assyria invaded the whole country; he marched against Samaria and laid siege to it for three years. 6 In the ninth year[b] of Hoshea, the king of Assyria captured Samaria. He exiled Israel to Assyria and resettled them in Halah and on the Habor, the river of Gozan, and in the cities[c] of Media.

[a] Read perhaps *ʾl sw <ʾl> mlk mṣrym* for MT *ʾl sw mlk mṣrym;* see note.
[b] Some mss. read *bšnh* for *bšnt.*
[c] LXX *kài ore* translates Heb. *hry,* "mountains;" MT *ʿry* "cities."

Notes

17 1. *In the twelfth year of Ahaz.* The accession of Hoshea to the throne is here synchronized with the reign of Ahaz in Judah, while in 15:30 it was with that of his father Jotham. This double synchronism may be evidence for a coregency. Having completed his treatment of both the reigns of Jotham (in 15:36) and of Ahaz (in 16:19), Dtr. chose to relate Hoshea to the latter, probably to avoid further confusion, in an already confused decade.

nine years. Hoshea reigned nine years, 732/31–724/23; his captivity and the siege of Samaria are not included in this figure. The date in v. 6, which synchronizes the fall of Samaria with Hoshea's ninth year is the artificial calculation of the chronographer (like those in 18:1, 9), who did not know that Samaria held out for over two calendar years without a king. See further in the note to 18:1.

2. *yet not as the kings of Israel who had preceded him.* Dtr. tempers the criticism

leveled at Hoshea. In this case, the usual formula of condemnation, "he did not stray from the sinful ways of Jeroboam son of Nebat," is lacking, though the reader is not told why. Rabbinic interpretation, sensitive to this stylistic change, saw Hoshea as permitting cultic reconciliation with Jerusalem, by removing the roadblocks to the southern capital (*b. Git.* 68a). Cf. M. Greenberg, *WHJP* 4/2, 113; A. Rofé, *Prophetical Stories,* 86, n. 50. Assuming that "the king under whom Israel perished must have been an atrocious sinner" (Stade), the Luc. reading made Hoshea the last and the worst of the northern monarchs (utilizing the formula of 1 Kgs 14:9; 16:25, 30, 33). It was correctly seen as secondary by Burney and Montgomery-Gehman.

3. The information in this verse is drawn from an independent and apparently authentic source, which is not utilized in the capsule history in 18:9–12.

Shalmaneser. On the Hebrew form of the Assyrian name *Šulmānu-ašarēdu,* "(the god) Shulman is preeminent," A. R. Millard (*JSS* 21 [1976], 7–8) remarks, "Loss of the final letter in the Hebrew may result from haplography in the biblical text, or from assimilation to the final element of Tiglath-pileser in the previous chapters."

became his vassal. Heb. *ʿebed,* lit. "servant," as is usual in the political parlance of the period. Cf. 2 Sam 8:6, 2 Kgs 16:7.

rendered him tribute. Heb. *hēšîb minḥâ.* The use of *hēšîb,* lit. "returned," suggests payment of a fixed amount agreed upon under the terms of submission. Such sums were, as a rule, rendered yearly (cf. v. 4), and their interruption signaled rebellion. Cf. 2 Kgs 3:4, Ps 72:10. Other verbs used with *minḥâ,* e.g. *nāśāʾ* (2 Sam 8:2, 6); *hēgîš* (1 Kgs 5:1); *hēbîʾ* (2 Chr 17:11); *nātan* (2 Chr 26:8), describe the ceremonial act of delivering payment and not its legal status.

4. *to Sais* <to> the king of Egypt. According to MT *ʾl swʾ mlk mṣrym,* "to So, king of Egypt," So is a proper name, but Egyptian sources provide no candidate with this name who can be identified as the collaborator of Hoshea. The old identification of So with Sibe, an Egyptian commander who fought against Sargon—cf. *ANET*³, 285a—is ruled out by the new reading of the name as Re'e. See R. Borger, *JNES* 19 (1960), 49–53. A full review of the problems of this and other Egyptological suggestions is given by K. A. Kitchen, *Third Intermediate Period,* 372–75. The emended text adopted here follows the suggestions of H. Goedicke, *BASOR* 171 (1963), 64–66, and W. F. Albright, *BASOR* 171 (1963), 66, to identify So as the Hebrew transcription of the city Sais (transcribed in Akk. texts as *Sâ*), which would make its ruler, Tefnakht, Hoshea's ostensive ally. The same form of the name as the biblical *Swʾ* seems to be found in an epithet "the Saite," derived from Egyptian *p*ꜣ*S*ꜣ*w(w),* which is attached to Manetho's entry for Necho in his list of the 26th dynasty (D. B. Redford, *Journal of the Society for the Study of Egyptian Antiquities [Toronto]* 11 [1981], 75–76). Kitchen, loc. cit., takes So as the abbreviated name of Osorkon IV, king of Tanis and Bubastis in the eastern delta. It should be noted, however, that the use of such an abbreviated form of the name is otherwise unattested.

the yearly tribute. Cf. 1 Kgs 10:35. In Assyrian royal inscriptions, the usual expression is *šattišam la naparkâ,* "yearly without interruption."

arrested him. It is unlikely that Hoshea was arrested "during the later stages of the siege of Samaria" (so Gray). The plain sense of the passage suggests that Hoshea's arrest preceded the Assyrian campaign against Israel (see the note to v. 1). Once the secret embassy to Egypt was uncovered, he was called before his overlord, probably to Assyria, to explain his treasonous behavior, and there detained and jailed.

5. *three years.* Shalmaneser's campaign followed the arrest of Hoshea in 724 or early 723.

6. *in the ninth year.* The interchange in some mss. between *bšnh/bšnt* may be explained as a "formal genitive," which is actually an apposition; cf. *GKC* 128k and 134p.

the king of Assyria captured Samaria. He exiled Israel . . . MT reads as if the same king of Assyria besieged Samaria (v. 5), took it (6aα), and exiled Israel to Assyria (6aβ–6b). Historically, however, this construing of the text cannot stand. Two kings of Assyria oversaw the events referred to in v. 6; Shalmaneser V captured Samaria; Sargon II exiled Israel. The siege of Samaria ended in the winter of 722/21 B.C.E. with the city's surrender to Shalmaneser, but because of the king's death, final determination of the status of Samaria was put off for two years. Sargon II recaptured the city in 720 B.C.E. in his first campaign to the west; the deportations described followed sometime later. See further discussion in Comment. The present telescoping of events might be as early as the Deuteronomic editing of Kings.

The apocryphal Tobit claims to have been exiled by Shalmaneser from his hometown in the Galilee (Tob 1:1–2). But as is clear from the continuation of his story, in which he skips over the reign of Sargon (Tob 1:15), the Tobit tradition is based on MT 2 Kgs 17:6 and therefore has no independent historical value.

Halah and on the Habor, the river of Gozan, and in the cities of Media. The list is repeated in 18:12 and in a garbled form in 1 Chr 5:26, where the reference to the transfer of Trans-Jordanian exiles to these same locations during the days of Tiglath-pileser III seems anachronistic. The LXX reading *Orē Mēdōn* is likely a phonically derived variant retroverted as *hārê māday,* "mountains of Media," for MT *ʿārê māday,* "cities of Media," also reflected in the anomalous *hārāʾ* in 1 Chr 5:26.

Halah. A city and province, northeast of Nineveh on the road to Khorsabad (Dur-Sharruken); cf. RLA 4.58.

Habor. Akk. *Ḫābūr,* a tributary of the Euphrates and district of the same name, northwest of Assyria, which was mostly settled by Aramaeans; cf. J. N. Postgate, RLA 4.28–29.

the river of Gozan. Gozan (Akk. *Guzāna,* modern *Tell Halaf*), on the upper Habor, was the capital of the Assyrian province Bīt Baḫian from the second half of the ninth century. The designation of the Habor as the river of Gozan is so far unique and is apparently an Israelite designation. Israelite personal names, undoubtedly of exiles from Samaria, are attested in Assyrian documents recovered at Gozan, e.g., *Neriyau, Palṭiyau.* See I. Ephʿal, "On the Identification of the Israelite Exiles in the Assyrian Empire," in *Studies Yeivin,* 201–4; R. Zadok, *The Jews in Babylonia,* 7–22, 97ff.; idem., *Or* 51 (1982), 391–93.

A late tradition in 2 Esdr 13:45 has some of the exiles take up a "long journey of a year and a half" to Arzareth, apparently Heb. *ʾereṣ ʾăḥeret,* "a strange land" (cf. Deut 29:27).

Comment

The last years of the kingdom of Israel are chronicled in very terse fashion and though the extant extrabiblical sources are scant indeed, a historical reconstruction is recoverable.[1]

Hoshea came to the throne in 732/31 (see above 15:30), in the twelfth year of Tiglath-pileser III and remained a loyal vassal of Assyria for the remaining part of the latter's reign. Tiglath-pileser's death in 727 seems to have sparked unrest in Phoenicia and Israel.[2] Evidence for events in the West comes from Josephus (*Antiquities* ix.283–87), who quotes an account from Menander, which is ultimately derived from Tyrian annals:

> The Assyrian king Selampsas (Latin version: Salamanasses) invaded Phoenicia during the reign of Elulaios king of Tyre. "After making a treaty of peace with all (its cities), he withdrew from the land." Somewhat later, several Phoenician cities subservient to Tyre revolted and turned to Assyria for protection. This brought the Assyrian army once again to the area. Unable to subdue Tyre, the king of Assyria cut off the mainland water supply to the island city, but Tyre held out for five more years.

The Assyrian Selampsas should be identified with Shalmaneser V,[3] who succeeded Tiglath-pileser; but coordination of the report in Josephus with Assyrian history is somewhat problematic. No Assyrian historical record from Shalmaneser's reign has survived, and the Assyrian Eponym Chronicle is badly mutilated at this point. From the few words preserved there, one learns that of his short five-year reign, Shalmaneser spent at least three years in the field.[4] The two-staged Tyrian affair described by Josephus may, there-

[1] Most of the available presentations of this period are incomplete in that they misrepresent one or more of the extrabiblical pieces of evidence; e.g., Noth, *History*, 261–62; Herrmann, *History*, 250; B. Oded in J. H. Hayes and J. M. Miller, *Israelite and Judaean History*, 432–43; Bright, *History*[3], 275–76.

[2] For reactions in Philistia to the news of the death of the Assyrian conqueror, "the rod which smote you," cf. Isa 14:28–32.

[3] This was suggested already by Šanda, and more recently Katzenstein, *History of Tyre*, 220–29, with full literature.

[4] The Eponym Chronicle lists two events for 727: a campaign, the destination of which is no longer preserved; and the accession of Shalmaneser V. In 726 the king stayed in Assyria. The statement of A. T. Olmstead that in 727 "the last embers of revolt were stamped out in Damascus" (*History of Assyria*, 202) is based on a wrong reading of the text. Collation of K. 3202 shows that the line in question reads: *ana* x[ ]—"to x[ ]." The broken sign was read by George Smith as *di;* and completed by Olmstead (*JAOS* 34 [1915], 357) to read *Di*[*mašqa*]—"Damascus." He was

fore, be dated to 727 and 725 respectively. Hoshea's first submission to Shalmaneser (v. 3) can be coordinated with the first encounter with Tyre in 727, Hoshea's embassy to Egypt, and his subsequent deposition (v. 4) with the siege of Tyre.

Not only the Assyrian records but also Egyptian historical sources are very meager for these years, especially those relating to Egyptian involvement in Syro-Palestinian affairs. During the rebellion, which followed upon the death of Shalmaneser, an Egyptian auxiliary force is known to have been defeated along with the rebels of the Philistine states in the battle of Raphiah in 720 (*ARAB* 2.5). And judging from the overall record of active Egyptian intervention in the area (cf. e.g. the battles of Qarqar in 853 and Eltekeh in 701), it stands to reason that Egypt might have secretly lent its support to Tyre and Israel in an anti-Assyrian league.[5]

Shalmaneser besieged Samaria for at least two calendar years and captured it, before his death, in the winter of 722/21. The fall of the city is reported in the Babylonian Chronicle:

> On the twenty-fifth day of Tebet, Shalmaneser ascended the throne in Assyria. He demolished Samaria (Akk. *Šamara'in*).[6]

It is remarkable that during this whole period, Samaria withstood the attacks, despite the absence of its king, who had been arrested before the siege was imposed (see the note to v. 4). When the throne in Assyria was taken by Sargon, a royal prince but not the direct heir, the Assyrian army apparently withdrew (December 722–January 721). Samaria was left to herself; and when rebellions erupted throughout the West (721), its leaders joined the

---

followed by Luckenbill, *ARAB* 2.437; Thiele, *MNHK*², 213; Unger, *Israel and the Aramaeans of Damascus,* 103; Katzenstein, *History of Tyre,* 225. The name of the place referred to cannot presently be known. Moreover, the campaign is the last item in the reign of Tiglath-pileser and has nothing to do with Shalmaneser V or Israel's Hoshea (as presented by Katzenstein, loc. cit.).

[5] Egypt, at this time, was governed by the weak kings of the twenty-third dynasty from Tanis in the Eastern Delta. At Sais, a rival and powerful line of princes, Tefnakht and Bochchoris (later the twenty-fourth dynasty), ruled independently. To add to this picture of division, a Nubian line of kings had developed (twenty-fifth dynasty) in the South, but was not involved, as yet, in Western Asia. For details, see Kitchen, *Third Intermediate Period,* 362–77.

[6] Grayson, *Chronicles,* 73; cf. Appendix I, No. 5. The Akkadian reading of the city's name *Šamara'in* is the Babylonian rendering of the Aramaic form of the name *Šāmĕrāyin* (cf. Ezra 4:10). The provincial name of Samaria, *Samerina,* is also based on this pronunciation. The Hebrew *Šômĕrôn* shows that there were two contemporaneous forms of the name, one with the ending *-ayin,* and other *-â/ôn.* Other examples of this variation are known—e.g. Dothan/Dothain; cf. note to 2 Kgs 6:13, and H. Tadmor, *JCS* 12 (1958), 39–40.

revived league, together with Hamath and Gaza and the breakaway provinces of Dimašqa (= Damascus) and Hatarikka (= Hadrach).

Despite Sargon's claim in the final edition of the Khorsabad annals, it was in his second year, 720, and not during his accession and first year, that he set out to reconquer the West.[7] Samaria was retaken by Sargon, and subsequently its population was deported to Assyria. The Assyrian account of these events, as restored from two separate inscriptions, reads:

> With the strength of my gods, I fought with and defeated the Samarians, who had come to an agreement with a hostile king not to be my vassals and not to pay tribute, and who opened hostilities (against me). I took captive 27,290 of its inhabitants. From among them, I organized fifty chariots as a royal unit, and the rest of them I resettled within Assyria. The city of Samaria I rebuilt and repopulated more than before; I brought people there from the lands which I had conquered. I placed my courtier over them as governor, and imposed tax and tribute upon them, just as if they were Assyrian. I also had them trained in proper conduct.[8]

This historical record makes it clear that the biblical account in vv. 5 and 6a has telescoped two events: the fall of Samaria to Shalmaneser in 722, after the three-year siege; and the captivity of Samaria two years later in 720 by Sargon.

Sargon's inscriptions record the exile of 27,290 Israelites from Samaria and the induction of chariot units into royal service. Whether these numbers refer to city dwellers alone is not stated. But from the report concerning the transfer of Arab tribesmen to the province of Samaria in 715 (see the note to v. 24), one should consider that areas outside of the capital were also depopulated, during and after the protracted conflict which took place in 725–720.

The main source of information about the centers of the Israelite dispersion is 2 Kgs 17:6; Assyrian sources do not report the destination of the deportees. Reasons for their resettlement in the Habor district and Media can only be surmised, and this from the patterns discernible from the total corpus of Assyrian documents.[9] Two factors seem relevant in the case of the Israelites: (1.) The military units forcibly impressed into the Assyrian army were sent to guard border areas, such as the "cities of Media." Sargon's campaigns to

[7] The critical attitude toward Sargon's claims can be found in A. T. Olmstead, *AJSL* 21 (1904–5), 179–82; idem, *Western Asia in the Days of Sargon of Assyria* (New York: Holt, 1908), 45ff., n. 9; E. R. Thiele, *MNHK*[1], 122–27; and for an evaluation of the Assyrian sources, H. Tadmor, *JCS* 12 (1958), 33–40. The royal scribes, as argued there, covered up the lack of military activity in Sargon's first year by transferring to that year the account of the conquest of Samaria and its exile.

[8] The composite text presented here was treated by H. Tadmor, *JCS* 12 (1958), 34, and Cogan, *Imperialism and Religion*, 49–51; cf. Appendix I, No. 6A.

[9] See the thorough examination of this problem in Oded, *Mass Deportations*, 41–74.

Media are well attested (cf. *ARAB* 2.11, 15, 19, 23, 24). (2.) The bulk of the exiles were brought to the thinly populated areas on the middle Euphrates (traditionally Aram-Naharaim), which had been devastated during the Assyrian expansion during the tenth and early ninth centuries B.C.E.

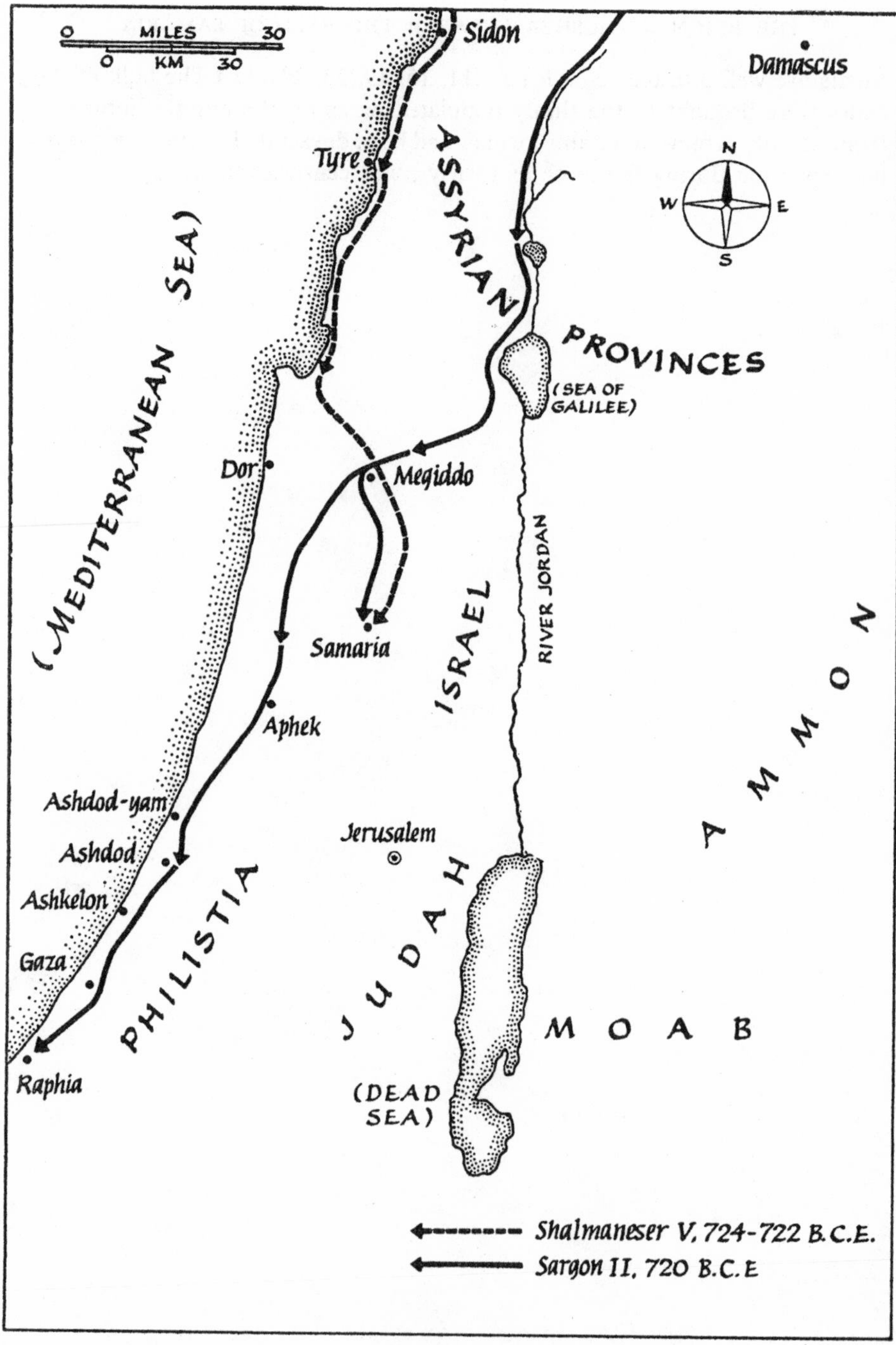

ASSYRIAN CAMPAIGNS TO ISRAEL
724-720 B.C.E.
2 KINGS 17:3-6

XXIX. A HOMILY ON THE FALL OF THE NORTHERN KINGDOM

(17:7–23)

17 7 Now, because the Israelites sinned against YHWH, their God, who brought them up from the land of Egypt, from under the control of Pharaoh, king of Egypt, by revering other gods; 8 and followed the statutes of the nations, whom YHWH dispossessed before the Israelites,[a] and of the kings of Israel which they practiced,[a] 9 the Israelites ascribed untruths to YHWH, their God; and built themselves high places in all their cities, from watchtower to fortified city; 10 and set up pillars and sacred poles for themselves on every lofty hill and under every leafy tree; 11 and made offerings there, at all the high places, as the nations whom YHWH exiled before them; and did evil things, angering YHWH; 12 and worshipped idols, about which YHWH had said to them, "Do not do this thing!" 13 YHWH even warned Israel and Judah by every prophet and every seer,[b] "Turn back from your evil ways and keep my commands and[c] my statutes, in accord with all the Law which I commanded your ancestors, and which I sent to you through my servants, the prophets."

14 But they did not listen. They were as stiff-necked as their ancestors had been, who did not trust YHWH, their God. 15 Moreover they spurned his statutes, and his covenant which he made with their ancestors, and the warnings which he had given to them; and they went after emptiness and became empty themselves, and after the fashion of the neighboring nations which YHWH commanded them not to imitate. 16 They abandoned all the commands of YHWH, their God; they made themselves molten images—two calves; they made a pole of Asherah; they bowed down to all the heavenly host; they worshipped Baal; 17 they passed their sons and their daughters through fire; they practiced divination and sorcery; they gave themselves up to doing

[a–a] Omitted in whole or in part by mss. and some versions.
[b] Read *kl nbyʾ wkl ḥzh* with a few mss. and Targ., Vulg.
[c] Read *wḥqwty* with mss. and versions.

what was displeasing to YHWH, making him angry. 18 (Because of all this,) YHWH was very angry with Israel, and he removed them from his sight; only the tribe of Judah was left.

19 But[d] even Judah did not keep the commands of YHWH, their God; they followed the statutes practiced by the Israelites. 20 Thus YHWH spurned all the seed of Israel; he afflicted them by handing them over to plunderers, until he rid himself of them.

21 When he tore Israel away from the House of David, they made Jeroboam son of Nebat king; Jeroboam led Israel away[e] from following YHWH and caused them to sin greatly. 22 The Israelites followed all the sinful ways[f] practiced by Jeroboam; they did not stray from it; 23 until YHWH removed Israel from his sight, as he had foretold through all his servants, the prophets. So Israel was exiled from its land to Assyria, until this day.

[d] Read *wgm,* with versions; MT *gm, waw* lost through haplography.
[e] Read *wydḥ* with qere and mss.; ketib: *wyd'*
[f] Read *ḥṭ't,* with mss., in agreement with *mmnh.*

Notes

17 7–23. This extensive sermon on the fall of the kingdom of Israel draws upon the entire stock of homiletic phraseology which characterizes the Deuteronomistic critique throughout Kings. (See Burney and esp. Weinfeld, *Deuteronomy,* Appendix A, for the cross-references.) Except for some glosses with reference to Judah (v. 13, "and Judah"; vv. 19–20), the sermon is devoted exclusively to Israel.

7. *Now, because the Israelites sinned . . .* The lengthy protasis which piles up the sins of the Israelites in one sentence and which extends over the next eleven verses finds its apodosis in v. 18—("Because of all this . . .). This peculiarity of Deuteronomistic rhetoric has given rise to a variety of translations. The Luc. addition *kai egeneto orgē kuriou ton Israel,* "and the Lord's anger was against Israel," is not a preferable reading (adopted by Gray), but represents an attempt by the Greek translator to improve the verse by bringing up part of v. 18 into v. 7 (Montgomery-Gehman).

8. *and of the kings of Israel which they practiced.* Israel's kings are linked with the presettlement inhabitants of the land as setting the norms for the illicit cultic practices of Israel. The peculiar syntax of this clause, which interrupts the sequence in which the Israelites are the subject, suggests that it is a gloss. Burney suspects that a corrupt text may have given rise to this addition.

NAB renders: "[and the kings of Israel whom they set up]." The brackets indicate the problematic syntax; the verb *'āśû* is taken in the sense "made for themselves, set up" as in v. 32. This translation introduces a critique similar to the one in Hos 8:4 in which Israel is berated for appointing kings without divine sanction.

JB moves the problematic clause to the next verse: "The Israelites and the kings that they had made for themselves . . ."

9. *the Israelites ascribed untruths to* YHWH, *their God.* The translation is suggested by context: Heb. *wayĕḥappĕʾû* is a hapax legomenon. Early commentators connected the verb with *ḥippâ*, "to hide, to cover" (e.g., Qimḥi; cf. *BDB* 341b). Many moderns have followed V. Scheil (*Nouveaux vocabulaires babyloniens* [Paris, 1919], 12f.), who related the Hebrew root to the supposed Akk. *ḫapû*, "to utter" (quoted in Montgomery-Gehman; cf. Gray, and *CBC*, 157). But that Akk. word is to be read *ḫawû*, meaning "to growl," said of ghosts and dogs (cf. *CAD* Ḫ 163), thus eliminating any etymological similarity and semantic connection. The context suggests that the Israelites followed practices unauthorized by YHWH, yet attributed by them to divine command (cf. the use of the verb *ḥippâ* in *Gen.Rab.* 94.8; and see Rashi, as well as Ehrlich, *Randglossen*). Note the vehement denials by Jeremiah that YHWH ever thought of requiring the sacrifice of children (e.g. Jer 19:5; cf. Mic 6:7).

9b–11. The improper acts listed here are not idolatrous worship *in stricto sensu* but are adaptations of foreign practices introduced into the cult of YHWH after the fashion of the nations. The warning in Deut 12:2–4 went unheeded. In this sense, the verb *ḥippâ* in v. 9a might imply cultic "embellishments" (cf. Ps 68:14; 2 Chr 3:5, 7–9).

12. *idols.* Heb. *gillūlîm.* Cf. 1 Kgs 15:12.

13. *by every prophet and every seer.* "Seer" is the term for divine messenger favored by the Chronicler, in whose work it often appears, sometimes replacing the "prophet" of Kings (cf. e.g. 2 Kgs 21:10 and 2 Chr 33:18).

14. Stade's reading, following LXX and Syr., *mēʿōrep* (for MT *kĕʿōrep*) is preferred by Gray and *JB*. But this introduces the idea that the generations of Israel were successively more disobedient, a thought expressed only in Jer 7:26.

15. *they spurned his statutes.* Heb. **māʾôs*, "despise, reject." The Akk. cognate *mêšu* (*mēsu*) is used in describing contempt for divine ordinances as well as breach of oaths of fealty (*adê*). See citations in *CAD* M 2.41–42. The Qumran reading 1Q Isa[a] 33:8 *mʾs ʿdym* (for MT *mʾs ʿrym*) restores a lost Hebrew idiom, attested in Akk. as *adê mêšu*, "to despise oaths"; note the parallel expression *ḥpr bryt*, "he rejected a treaty," in the same verse (D. R. Hillers, *HTR* 64 [1971], 257, and H. L. Ginsberg, *H. Yalon Jubilee Volume* [Jerusalem: Kiryat Sefer, 1963], 171 [Hebrew]).

16. The words "two calves" may be a gloss on *massēkâ*, "molten image," as suggested by some commentators (Benzinger, Šanda, Montgomery-Gehman); but it is most appropriate nevertheless. The Pentateuchal traditions in Exod 32:4, 8 (cf. Deut 9:12, 16) and the rebuke of the northern prophet Hosea (13:2) describe the calf images by this same term, *massēkâ*. (Note that the identical wording appears in Hosea *wayyaʿaśû lāhem massēkâ*, "they made themselves a molten image.")

a pole of Asherah. Though sacred poles are mentioned in the general indictment in v. 10, this pole may be the one worshipped by Ahab; so, too, the reference to the worship of Baal—see 1 Kgs 16:32–33 and the note to 2 Kgs 21:7.

heavenly host. Astral worship is first mentioned in conjunction with King Manasseh of Judah (see further below on 21:3) and never in relation to the kings of Israel.

17. The offenses listed in this verse are introduced here for the first time, not having been related previously about the Israelites in Kings. Dtr. drew upon the phraseology of Deut 18:9–11 in filling out his indictment.

they gave themselves up. Heb. *wayyitmakkĕrû.* Cf. 1 Kgs 21:20. The Luc. translation adds, "they made an ephod and teraphim." The addition of this phrase illustrates the tendency of translators and copyists to add elements in cataloguelike listings. *Tera-*

phim images are mentioned in conjunction with sorcery in 1 Sam 15:23 and Ezek 21:27, and point to the kind of collocation which may have inspired this tag in Luc.

18. For the syntactic structure of the main sentence, see the note on v. 7.

20. *by handing them over to plunderers.* Heb. *šōsîm;* again only in Judg 2:14, 16. The idea that YHWH punished Israel in stages, through the successive attacks of enemies, is here unique to the Deuteronomistic historiography in Kings. It appears in the pragmatic framework of Judges and may have been introduced from there, since it is not integrated into the theme of unrequited sin which can only be erased by exile, the main contention of Dtr.

21. *When he tore Israel away.* The subject of the clause is YHWH, referring to the divine action directly undertaken against the Davidic dynasty. Cf. 1 Kgs 11:11f.; 14:8.

led Israel away. Jeroboam's act is described by **ḥiddîaḥ,* which harks back to the Deuteronomic law against incitement to idolatry. Cf. Deut 13, especially vv. 11, 14.

and caused them to sin greatly. Heb. *wĕheḥĕtîʾām ḥăṭāʾâ gĕdôlâ;* lit. "and caused them to sin a great sin." It is not accidental that the formulation "great sin" is used here. It appears three times in Exod 32 (vv. 21, 30, 31) in the story of the Golden Calf. On the relationship between Exod 32 and the acts of Jeroboam, see the Comment on 1 Kgs 12.

23. *until this day.* See discussion above, note to 2 Kgs 2:21.

Comment

The indictment against Israel falls into two distinct units: (1.) vv. 7–18; (2.) vv. 21–23a (on the intrusive vv. 19–20, see below). In the first unit, the Israelites are depicted as having come under the influence of the dispossessed Canaanites, and despite repeated attempts by prophets and seers to lead them back to the proper path, they stubbornly forsake YHWH's Law and His covenant. The general accusation at the outset of this unit is specified in v. 16, by reference to particular acts from the historical record. What is singular about the point of view expressed here is that the nation and not its kings is held accountable for the long list of wrongdoings. Monarchic misconduct, the measure of Deuteronomistic judgment elsewhere in Kings, is not considered. Even in v. 16, the royal perpetrators are passed over in silence. In the second unit, the cause of Israel's sin is traced back to Jeroboam, son of Nebat. His erring ways led the nation astray, finally into exile. The warning role of the prophets and the fulfillment of their predictions are particularly noted.

These two units cannot be the product of the same historiographic outlook. Prior to this chapter, the kings of the northern kingdom alone were depicted as straying from YHWH, holding fast to the path first marked out by Jeroboam I (cf. 1 Kgs 13:34; 14:16; 15:26, 30; 16:2, 19; 2 Kgs 10:31; 13:2, 6, 11; 14:22; 15:9, 18, 24, 28). Popular cultic behavior in Israel was not the historiographer's concern. Yet cultic behavior does come under scrutiny in so far as Judah's population is concerned. As for Judah, a distinction is made between the righteous kings of the house of David and the people who continue to practice their illicit cults (cf. 1 Kgs 22:42–43; 2 Kgs 12:3–4; 14:3–4; 15:3–4, 34–35). The homily on Israel's Fall departs from this pattern and applies to Israel the critique that has so far been limited to Judah, giving it precedence over the "sins of Jeroboam."

Because in unit 2 Israel's Fall "is traced to the one sin on which that writer most insisted—the calf worship of Jeroboam I" (Skinner), it is likely that it is part of the first Deuteronomistic edition of Kings (= Dtr_1). Unit 1 is a second strand which, because of its affinity with the description and evaluation of Judah and Manasseh's reign, in particular (cf. 2 Kgs 21), may be assigned to the post-Josianic Deuteronomist (= Dtr_2).

Intrusive in a homily on Israel are vv. 19–20; their subject is Judah and their vantage point is exilic: "all the seed of Israel" (v. 20), i.e. Israel *and* Judah, have been cast out of YHWH's sight. If these verses are not the continuation of unit 1 (i.e. Dtr_2), then they are from a later, third writer, who saw the fate of all Israel as inextricably exile bound.[1]

Verse 23b recapitulates part of v. 6 and brings the focus back to Israel in exile, a subject elaborated upon in 17:34–40.

[1] The division of 2 Kgs 17:7–23 into two discrete units is recognized by a majority of modern scholars, the points of difference between them being the assignment of one or the other unit to the basic edition of the book of Kings. Even Noth, who believed Kings was the work of a single exilic editor, could not link unit 2 with the preceding material and so took it as a "subsequent accretion" (Noth, *Überlieferungsgeschichtliche Studien,* 85, n. 4 [= E.T., 136, n. 60]). The position adopted here is fundamentally that of Stade, Kittel, Skinner, Šanda, and Gray (each with his own reservations as to the question of v. 18 and its relation to vv. 19–20). The most recent work on these questions, with a detailed study of stylistics and the theological issues involved, with whose conclusions the present ones tally, is by R. D. Nelson, *The Double Redaction of the Deuteronomistic History, JSOT* Sup 18 (1981), 55–63.

XXX. SAMARIA RESETTLED

(17:24–41)

17 24 The king of Assyria then brought (people) from Babylon,
Cutha, Avva, Hamath, Sepharvaim[a], and settled them in the cities of
Samaria in place of the Israelites. They took possession of Samaria and
settled in its cities. 25 Now at the beginning of their settlement there,
they did not revere YHWH, so YHWH let lions loose against them, and
they were killing some of them. 26 It was reported to the king of Assyria, "The nations whom you exiled and settled in the cities of Samaria did not know the rites of the god of the land, and so he let lions
loose against them. They are preying upon them, because they do not
know the rites of the local god!" 27 The king of Assyria ordered, "Have
one of the priests whom I exiled[b] from there sent back there. Let him
go and settle[c] there and teach them the rites of the god of the land."
28 Thus one of the priests exiled from Samaria came and settled in
Bethel; he taught them how to revere YHWH. 29 But each nation made
its own gods and set (them) up in the shrines of the high places which
the Samarians had made, each nation in the city in which it was living.
30 The people of Babylon made Succoth-benoth; the people of Cutha
made Nergal; the people of Hamath made Ashima; 31 the Avvites
made Nibhaz and Tartak; and the Sepharvites were burning their sons
in fire to Adrammelech and Anammelech, gods of Sepharvaim.[d]
32 And they revered YHWH; they appointed some of their own number
priests at the high places and they officiated for them at the shrines of
the high places. 33 They revered YHWH and (at the same time) they
served their own gods, after the rites of the nations from among whom
they had been exiled.

34 Until this day, they follow the(ir) earlier practices[e]: they do not
revere YHWH, and they do not do as required by their statutes and

[a] Read with qere and versions: *msprwym.*

[b] Read with Luc., Targ.: *hglytym;* MT: *hglytm.*

[c] Read the verbs as sing., with Luc., Syr., Vulg.; MT pl.

[d] Read *ʾlhy* as pl., with qere and versions.

[e] Luc. reads: *kmšpṭm hrʾšwn* as in v. 40.

their practice—the Teaching and the command which YHWH commanded the sons of Jacob, whose name he changed to Israel. 35 YHWH
had made a covenant with them, and he commanded them, "Do not
revere other gods. Do not bow down to them; do not serve them; do
not sacrifice to them. 36 For it is only YHWH, who brought you up
from the land of Egypt, with great power and outstretched arm whom
you shall revere; to him you shall bow down; to him you shall sacrifice. 37 Carefully observe the statutes and the rules—the Teaching and
the command which he wrote down for you—forever. Do not revere
other gods. 38 Do not forget the covenant which he made[f] with you; do
not revere other gods. 39 For it is only YHWH your God that you shall
revere, and he shall deliver you from all your enemies." 40 But they did
not listen; rather they follow their earlier practices.

41 Now these nations revered YHWH and they served their idols (at
the same time); even their sons and grandsons behave as did their
ancestors, until this day.

[f] MT reads "I"; all versions (except Targ.) read "he."

Notes

17 24. *The king of Assyria.* The king responsible for the transfer of foreigners to Samaria is unnamed. Dtr. simply associates all operations in Samaria with one king. Cf. above vv. 3, 5. Assyrian texts report that Sargon II reorganized the territory in 720, bringing settlers from unspecified lands (*ARAB* 2.4); in 715 he transferred members of several Arab tribes to Samaria (Appendix I, No. 6B; cf. *ARAB* 2.17). But inasmuch as Sargon pursued a policy of conciliation toward Babylon, serving as king of Assyria and Babylon at one and the same time, he can hardly be the one who exiled Babylonians to distant Israel. In this case, one might consider the king to have been Sennacherib (cf. *ARAB* 2.234, 339–41) or even Ashurbanipal (*ARAB* 2.791–98), both of whom warred at length in southern Mesopotamia. Cf. too the biblical references to deportations by Esarhaddon and Ashurbanipal in Ezra 4:2, 9–10.

It follows that in the unit vv. 24–35, several waves of settlement are referred to, without chronological distinction. See the early discussions of Winckler, *Untersuchungen,* 97–100; Šanda; and more recently Tadmor, *The Jerusalem Cathedra* 3 (1983), 4–8.

Babylon, Cutha, Avva, Hamath, Sepharvaim. Settlers were brought to Samaria over the course of many decades, from scattered areas of the Assyrian Empire; identification of their original homelands and the gods they worshipped (vv. 30, 31) is often problematic. This is so because of many homonyms in the geographic lexicon of the Near East and uncommon divine names, which were transmitted orally and only later transcribed into Hebrew. For identifications, see below on vv. 30, 31.

the cities of Samaria. The name of the Assyrian province founded in the hill country of Ephraim was *Samerīna,* with the city Samaria as its capital. The expression "the cities of Samaria" is taken by all commentators to be a reference to this new, Assyrian administrative unit. But as early as the start of the eighth century, the Assyrian king Adad-nirari III referred to King Joash as "the Samarian" (*Iraq* 30 [1968], 142, line 8), and in Tiglath-pileser III's inscriptions Menahem is also "the Samarian" (cf. *ARAB* 1.772). This suggests that the kingdom of Israel was sometimes styled Samaria and, while not frequent, the term "king of Samaria" is to be found in Kings, in two prophetic stories of northern origin (cf. 1 Kgs 21:1, 2 Kgs 1:3). See further below, note to v. 29.

25. *YHWH let lions loose against them.* The ravage of lions among the newly settled residents of Samaria is generally seen as following in the wake of the "devastation" (Montgomery-Gehman) and "depopulation" (Gray) of the Assyrian wars. But this episode seems to be more a literary than just a natural phenomenon; the lions are an instrument of divine punishment sent against the disobedient, as exampled already in 1 Kgs 13:24 and 20:36. All the incidents involving lions in Kings are staged in northern Israel, and so it would seem that local northern tradition underlies them. It may, therefore, be significant that in the seventh-century vassal treaty imposed by Esarhaddon on King Baal of Tyre, among the deities invoked to punish disloyalty to the terms of the treaty are the god Beth-el, ᵈ*Ba-a-a-ti-ili,* and the goddess Anat-bethel, ᵈ*A-na*[?]-*ti-Ba-a-*[*a-ti-il*]*i),* who are asked "to give you over to the claws of a devouring lion." (See Borger, *Asarhaddon,* p. 109, lines 6–7; cf. also B. Mazar quoted by Weinfeld, *Deuteronomy,* 123, n. 4.) Note that in v. 28, the repatriated priest returns to Beth-el, where he instructs the settlers in the proper cult.

they were killing some of them. The periphrastic construction, employing a form of the verb "to be" (Heb. *hāyâ*) plus a participle, is a feature of Late Hebrew and is widely used throughout the unit vv. 24–33. See Joüon, *Grammaire,* 121g.

26. *rites of the god of the land.* Heb. *mišpāṭ* is used in BH in the sense of both "law, ordinance," as well as "customary behavior." In these connotations, it is like its semantic counterpart in Akk. *parṣu,* as already observed by E. A. Speiser, *WHJP,* 1.282. *Mišpāt* in v. 26 refers to the ritual practices incumbent upon the worshippers of YHWH of which the new settlers were ignorant. For *parṣu* in this sense, see B. Landsberger, *AfO* 2 (1924/25), 64–68.

27. *Let him go and settle there and teach them.* The verbal forms in MT alternate between singular and plural, so that it is not clear how many priests were ordered returned. Since the narrator tells of a single priest at the Beth-el shrine (v. 28) and the appointment of additional priests from among the people themselves (v. 32), the singular has been preferred in the translation. Cf. the remarks of Stade.

28. *he taught them how to revere YHWH.* The inscriptions of Sargon report that "tax and tribute were imposed" upon the residents of the province organized in Samaria "just as if they were Assyrian" (*ANET*³, 284). He also had them trained in proper conduct, which in Assyrian terms meant "revering god and king" (*palāḫ ili u šarri*) (*ARAB* 2.122). It is tempting to think that the similar wording of the biblical and cuneiform texts is evidence that v. 28 is "a verbatim reproduction . . . of a characteristic expression of Sargon's policy . . . effecting a religious homogenization of the disparate elements of the population" (S. Paul, "Sargon's Administrative Diction in II Kings 17:27," *JBL* 88 [1969], 73–74).

29. *But each nation made its own gods.* The making of idols in the service of the sundry foreign deities is mocked by the use of *ʿāśô, "to do, make," followed by the

personal names of various deities, as in v. 30. This usage is unattested elsewhere; cf. Judg 18:24, 31. The sense conveyed is as follows: The new settlers manufactured gods!

In addition, *ʿāśô* is found twice in v. 32, with two other distinct meanings, "to appoint, to officiate." Such undiscriminating usage seems to suggest the influence upon the writer of a linguistic substratum in which the verb "to do" had a wider range of meaning than attested in standard BH. Thus, for example, in Akk., *epēšu,* "to do," in conjunction with *dullu,* "task, service," means "to worship." This idiom could have influenced the choice of the verb *ʿāśô,* for by the late seventh century, scribes in Judah were multilingual, acquainted with both Aramaic and Akkadian terminology. If this is the case, then the present section polemicizes by means of a word play against the cult of the foreign settlers in Samaria: they do not "perform service" (*dullu epēšu*) to their gods; they merely "make" (*ʿāśô*) gods.

the shrines of the high places. This expression is peculiar to north Israelite cultic worship, cf. 1 Kgs 13:32; 2 Kgs 23:19; in both of these verses, the shrines are located in the "cities of Samaria" (see above to v. 24).

the Samarians. The gentilic *šōmĕrōnîm* is unique in the Bible, though it is known from extrabiblical sources as early as the beginning of the eighth century (see above, v. 24). Therefore, it is inadvisable to speak of it as an anachronistic coinage (as do Benzinger, Stade, Šanda, Gray) based upon the name of the Assyrian province *Samerīna.* The present translation is meant to distinguish between the former Israelite population, referred to here as *šōmĕrōnîm* and the Samarians of the Second Temple period.

30. *The people of Babylon made Succoth-benoth.* Babylon was destroyed by Sennacherib in 689 and its population dispersed (cf. *ARAB* 2.339–41). The identification of Succoth-benoth remains elusive; no Mesopotamian divinity by this name is known. It is hard to recover from MT the names *Marduk* and *Ṣarpanitu,* Babylon's chief deity and his consort (as suggested by Haupt). Gray accepts Ṣarpanitu, and eliminates the first element as an accretion. Some would connect Succoth with the god ^{d}SAG.KUD, identified with Saturn (cf. Šanda; G. R. Driver, *EI* 5 [1958], 18*), but the specific worship of him in Babylon is not known. (For the reading of the name as Sakkud and the relation to Sakkut—*sikkût* in MT—in Amos 5:26, see W. W. Hallo, *HUCA* 48 [1977], 15.)

The second element *-bĕnôt* is explicable as a form of the divine name ^{d}*Bānītu,* "the creatress," sometimes an epithet of Ishtar. (For personal names constructed with *Bānītu,* see J. J. Stamm, *Die akkadische Namengebung* [Leipzig: Hinrichs, 1939], 28, 224, 310.) It is known that the goddess was worshipped at her own temple among the Aramaean colonists at Syene in upper Egypt; see J. T. Milik, *Bib* 48 (1967), 557–59. E. Lipiński suggests translating MT *skwt bnwt* as "image of Banit(u)" (*UF* 5 [1973], 202–4).

the people of Cutha made Nergal. Cutha in central Babylonia was holy to Nergal, god of the plague and "lord of the underworld" (see WM 109); it joined Merodach-baladan, king of Babylon, in rebellion and was punished by Sennacherib (cf. *ARAB* 2.257–59).

the people of Hamath made Ashima. Two suggestions to identify the city of Hamath have been made: (1.) the well-known center on the river Orontes in north Syria conquered by Sargon in 720 (cf. *ARAB* 2.55 and below 19:13); (2.) Amate on the Uqnu river in Elam, taken in the battles of 711 (cf. *ARAB* 2.32).

Ashima is an unknown divinity, thought by some to be behind the obscure *ʾšmt* of

Samaria in Amos 8:14 (e.g. Gray). But the numerous discussions have only led to inconclusive results. Graphically the closest divine name is Eshmun, a Phoenician god of healing whose name appears as [d]*Ia-su-mu-nu* in the treaty of Esarhaddon with Baal of Tyre (*ANET*[3], 534a). The relation of Eshmun to the divine element Eshem attested at Elephantine and Seimios/Simia/Semea in Greek inscriptions remains uncertain. See the discussions of E. M. Kraeling, *The Brooklyn Aramaic Papyri* (New Haven: Yale University Press, 1953), 90; W. F. Albright, *Yahweh and the Gods of Canaan*, 149–50, 187, 227. Eshmun leads toward a north-Syrian identification for Hamath and to Aramaeans as exiles in Samaria.

31. *the Avvites made Nibhaz and Tartak.* Apparently, Avva is the Elamite city Ama (cf. *ARAB* 2.32) and the gods are the Elamite divinities Ibnahaza and Dirtaq (as identified by F. Hommel, *OLZ* 15 [1912], 118; idem, *Paul Haupt Anniversary Volume* [Baltimore and Leipzig: Johns Hopkins University, 1926], 159–68).

Adrammelech and Anammelech, gods of Sepharvaim. It is unlikely that Sepharvaim is to be identified with Sibrain (cf. Ezek 47:16) or *Sabara'in* (incorrect reading of *Šamara'in;* see Comment to 17:1–6). Nor does the attempt to explain the dual ending in Heb. *-ayim* by identification with the two quarters of the Babylonian city Sippar have much to commend it (so G. R. Driver, *EI* 5 [1958], 18*). R. Zadok pointed to the city Sipra'ani, a Chaldean toponym mentioned in the Murashu archive from Nippur (*JANES* 8 [1976], 115–16). The question of the identification is further complicated because of the gods worshipped by the Sepharvaites, and the custom of burning children to them.

The god names as preserved in MT do not represent known divinities in the Aramaean and/or Assyro-Babylonian pantheons. The emendation of the element *ʾdr* to *ʾdd* in the first name, suggested by A. Ungnad (*AfO* Beiheft 6 [1940], 58) and accepted by many (e.g. W. F. Albright, *Archaeology and the Religion of Israel*[5], 157–58; Montgomery-Gehman), would recover a deity *Adad-milki*, known from personal names in the cuneiform archive of Tell Halaf from the region of Harran and Gozan (cf. K. Deller, *Or* 34 [1965], 382–83). Recent doubts about this identification have not ruled out this reading (see S. Kaufmann, *JNES* 37 [1978], 101–9). The name Anammelech may be tentatively identified with An(u), the god of heaven, revered from earliest times throughout Mesopotamia; on this deity see T. Jacobsen, *The Treasures of Darkness* (New Haven and London: Yale University Press, 1976) s.v. (The eccentric rendition of *NAB*, "King Hadad and his consort Anath," cannot be commended.)

32. *They appointed some of their own number.* Clearly the model for this description is Jeroboam I, concerning whom similar cultic appointments are reported (cf. 1 Kgs 12:31; 13:33). Not just persons "from every class of the people" (1 Kgs 12:31, *NEB*) were made priests; in any cult, trained personnel are required, and Hebrew *miqṣôtām* does express selection (cf. Ehrlich, *Randglossen* ad 1 Kgs 12:31 and E. A. Speiser, *Genesis*, AB, ad 47:2). But whatever their qualifications, these officiants were not of the tribe of Levi and so were condemned by Dtr.

33. *they revered* YHWH *and (at the same time) they served their own gods.* A Deuteronomic word pair "revere" (*yrʾ*) and "serve" (*ʿbd*)—cf. Deut 6:13; 10:12, 20—has been broken up to express, by contrast, the impropriety of this mixed religion. On the use of this stylistic device, see E. Z. Melamed, *SH* 8 (1961), 115–53.

from among whom. Heb. *miššām;* lit. "from there." The point of view is that of a writer resident in the land of Israel, not that of an exile.

34–40. The language of the unit is Deuteronomistic throughout. The reference to the Sinai covenant in vv. 34–35, imposed upon "the sons of Jacob," shows that the writer refers back to the Israelites who were the object of the previous indictment in vv. 7–23.

34. *Until this day.* The phrase "until this day" picks up the story broken off by the lengthy digression in vv. 24–33 by means of *Wiederaufnahme,* the literary technique whereby an interrupted story is taken up and continued by repeating a key word or phrase. The functioning of this technique was set out by C. Kuhl, "Die 'Wiederaufnahme'—ein literar-kritisches Prinzip?" *ZAW* 64 (1952), 1–11, cf. I. L. Seeligmann, *Theologische Zeitschrift* 18 (1962), 314–25, and see the bibliography of early treatments in M. Fishbane and S. Talmon, *ASTI* 10 (1975/76), 144, n. 64.

the(ir) earlier practices. The repetition of this phrase in v. 40 marks off vv. 34–40 as a distinct literary unit. The reading in v. 40 and Luc. in v. 34 suggests that *kmšpṭm hrʾšwn* should be read in both verses. For *mišpāṭ* in the sense of "customary behavior," see above on v. 26.

sons of Jacob, whose name he changed to Israel. An unusual expression. This use of *śîm*—"put, place," in the sense of "change"—occurs only once more in Neh 9:7. Name changes (under royal command) are expressed by *hēsēb* in 2 Kgs 23:34; 24:17. For a close parallel to the present verse, cf. 1 Kgs 18:31.

41. *these nations.* As in vv. 26, 29, the foreign settlers in Samaria are once more referred to.

Comment

This section, like the previous one, divides structurally and thematically into two units: (1.) Verses 24–33 tell of the foreign settlers brought to Samaria over a period of decades and the circumstances under which they adopted Israelite religious practices. In addition to the renewed YHWH cult at Beth-el, they continue to worship the gods of their homelands. (2.) Verses 34–40 condemn the "sons of Jacob" for their abandonment of YHWH's Teaching. Verse 41 rounds off both units, by resuming unit 1. (Note the same procedure above in v. 23, which resumes v. 6.)

Unit 2 is independent of unit 1 and should be seen within the larger context of 2 Kgs 17, particularly the homily in vv. 7–23. There one reads that the abandonment of the Teaching led to Israel's removal from the land "until this day." The phrase "until this day" is taken up again in v. 34 by means of *Wiederaufnahme*—"resumptive repetition"—and marks unit 2 as the continuation of v. 23, its subject being the Israelites after the fall of Samaria. The view expressed in unit 2 states: Even after punishment—i.e., exile—Israel persisted in following "their earlier practices" and sought no return to YHWH.

Therefore suggestions to see unit 2 as a late, postexilic addendum further condemning the mixed ritual of the settlers in Samaria already excoriated in unit 1, cannot be accepted.[1] It is highly unlikely that any postexilic writer would speak of the foreigners as "sons of Jacob," bound by the covenant obligations of the *torah* (vv. 34, 35, 37). Furthermore idolatry among the residents of Samaria is never an issue in the literature of the Persian period. Even when the Samarians represent themselves as worshippers of YHWH for many generations (Ezra 4:2), reference is not made to the mixed cult depicted in 2 Kgs 17:24–33. Their rejection by the returnees from Babylonian exile is based rather on their ethnic foreignness.[2] Therefore unit 1, as well, should not be regarded as a postexilic polemic.[3]

Both units should be seen against the background of Josiah's cultic reforms and his expansion into the former territory of the northern kingdom. Josiah moved into Samaria to destroy the altar in Bethel and purge the other cities of their *bāmôt*-shrines (2 Kgs 23:15–19). The priests who served at these sites were slaughtered (v. 20), as one would slaughter pagan priests under the law of *ḥerem.* Who else but the priests "appointed" to serve at the shrines of the new settlers (cf. 17:32) would be so treated? To further legitimize Josiah's claim as the heir to northern Israel, the author of unit 2 discredits the Israelite exiles, who by their continued idolatry forfeit any rights to their former inheritance.[4]

[1] So, Burney, Šanda, Montgomery-Gehman, Gray, and Noth, *Überlieferungsgeschichtliche Studien* 85, n. 5.

[2] Kaufmann reasons that with respect to their national-historical identity, the Samarians remained non-Israelites, although they had abandoned their pagan ways after centuries of settlement in Israel among Israelites (who were not deported). See Kaufmann, *Toledot* 4.197–207; and the discussion in Cogan, *Imperialism and Religion,* 107–10.

[3] S. Talmon recently reiterated the view that 2 Kgs 17 "represent(s) one of the latest stages in the editorial processes which affected the Book of Kings . . . (and) arose from the post-Exilic author's intent to prevent integration (with) . . . the disreputable Ephraimite version of the Yahwistic religion." See S. Talmon, "Polemics and Apology in Biblical Historiography—2 Kings 17:24–41," in *The Creation of Sacred Literature,* ed. R. E. Friedman (Berkeley, Calif.: University of California Press, 1981), 57–75.

[4] A full explication of the present view was set out by M. Cogan, *JBL* 97 (1978), 40–44.

THE KINGDOM OF JUDAH UNTIL THE EXILE

XXXI. THE REIGN OF HEZEKIAH: REFORM AND REBELLION

(18:1–12)

18 1 It was in the third year of Hoshea son of Elah, king of Israel,
that Hezekiah son of Ahaz, king of Judah, became king. 2 He was
twenty-five years old when he became king, and he reigned twenty-
nine years in Jerusalem. His mother's name was Abi,[a] daughter of
Zechariah. 3 He did what was pleasing to YHWH, just as David, his
ancestor, had done. 4 It was he who abolished the high places, and
broke the sacred pillars, and cut down the pole of Asherah[b] and
smashed the bronze serpent that Moses had made; for until those very
days the Israelites were offering sacrifices to it. It was called
Nehushtan.[c] 5 In YHWH God of Israel he put his trust; there was no
one like him among all the kings of Judah following him, or among
those before him. 6 He was loyal to YHWH; he did not turn away from
him, but kept the commands which YHWH had given to Moses. 7 And
so YHWH was with him; in all that he undertook, he was successful.
He rebelled against the king of Assyria and was his vassal no longer.
8 He defeated the Philistines as far as Gaza and its border areas, from
watchtower to fortified city.

9 It was in the fourth year of King Hezekiah—that is, the seventh
year of Hoshea, son of Elah, king of Israel—that Shalmaneser, king of
Assyria, marched against Samaria and laid siege to it; 10 he captured
it[d] at the end of three years. In the sixth year of Hezekiah, that is the
ninth year of Hoshea, king of Israel, Samaria was captured. 11 The

[a] In 2 Chr 29:1, the name appears as Abiah.

[b] MT sing.; versions and 2 Chr 31:1 read pl.

[c] Lit. "he called it."

[d] MT "they"; read *wayyilkĕdāh,* with some mss.; cf. 17:6.

king of Assyria exiled Israel to Assyria and he settled them[e] in Halah and on the Habor, the river of Gozan, and in the cities of Media; 12 for they had not obeyed YHWH, their God; they violated his covenant—all that Moses, YHWH's servant, commanded. They would not obey and would not behave.

[e] Read *wayyanniḥēm,* with versions.

Notes

18 1. *It was in the third year of Hoshea.* The usual formula for recording regnal synchronisms between Judah and Israel, *bšnt . . . l . . . mlk yśr'l . . . ,* is here preceded by the anomalous *wyhy,* "it was." *Wyhy* appears regularly in date formulae, which introduce specific accounts (e.g. v. 9 and throughout Kings), and though it is attested in all the versions of the verse, except the Syriac, it can hardly be original.

The three synchronisms between Hezekiah and Hoshea in vv. 1, 9, 10 are contradicted by fixed extrabiblical evidence. Hoshea came to the throne in 732/31; his last and ninth year was 724/23, the year in which the siege of Samaria began. Hezekiah's first year was in reality Hoshea's sixth year. The three-year difference derives from the calculation made by the Judahite chronographer of Kings, who did not know that Hoshea's reign ended before the siege began, and that during these three years, Samaria had no king (see above, Comment on 2 Kgs 17). Hence the difference between the actual date and the artificial reckoning (H. Tadmor, *EncMiqr,* 4.286–89).

Hezekiah son of Ahaz. The king's name appears on a seal of one of his officers—*lyhwzrḥ bn ḥlqyhw ʿbd ḥzqyhw* "(belonging) to Yehozarah son of Hilkiah servant of Hezekiah" (R. Hestrin and M. Dayagi, *IEJ* 24 [1974], 27–29, and cf. Diringer, *Iscrizioni,* pp. 74–78, 241, 302). The Akk. transcription *Ḫa-za-qi-ya-ú* (OIP 2, p. 31, line 76) shows that the name should be understood as being composed of a verb in the perfect (*ḥāzaq*) plus the theophoric element (*yāhû*), and means "YHWH was strong, prevailed." The vocalization of MT is a subsequent development, after the second short *a* was dropped. The form of the name with the prefixed *yod* (*yḥzkyhw*) used in Chronicles (e.g. 2 Chr 29:1) is based on a noun pattern popular in the postexilic period and is not original. On the name and its vocalization, see at length Kutscher, *Isaiah Scroll,* 104–6.

3. *David, his ancestor.* The comparison with David appears only here and with reference to Josiah in 22:2, as part of Dtr.'s positive evaluation of these kings of Judah. Note the use in Isaiah's address to Hezekiah, "David, your father," in 20:5.

4. *and cut down the pole of Asherah.* In formulaic listings of cultic transgressions, the term appears in the plural (1 Kgs 14:23; 2 Kgs 17:10, 23:14). The objects referred to are probably sacred poles set up beside altars; cf. Deut 16:21. The use of *'ăšērâ,* in the singular, is restricted to the worship of the Canaanite goddess Asherah of the same name, whose cult is attested both in northern Israel (Judg 6:24, 30; 1 Kgs 16:33; 2 Kgs 13:6) and in Judah by the Asherah cults of Maacah the queen-mother (1 Kgs 15:13) and of King Manasseh (2 Kgs 21:3, 7). See the note to 21:3. Consequently the plural reading of the versions in the present verse and 2 Chr 31:1 may be preferable.

and smashed the bronze serpent . . . Nehushtan. The word **kattēt,* "to smash, crush," is the same root used in Deuteronomy to describe the disposal of the molten calf (*kātat,* Deut 9:21), in contrast to **ṭāḥōn,* "grind," used in Exod 32:20. Like Moses before him, Hezekiah is depicted as ridding Israel of an idolatrous relic. On the motivation behind the removal of this venerated cult object, as well as the other reforms, see the Comment.

Nehushtan. The name suggests both the material, *nĕḥōšet,* "bronze," and the shape, *nāḥāš,* "serpent," of this image, which Judahite tradition identified with the standard fashioned by Moses in healing those attacked by the fiery serpents (cf. Num 21:9). The association of serpents with fertility rites and the popular nature of this cult in Judah was correctly stressed by M. Haran, *EncMiqr* 5.826–27. Rowley's suggestion (*JBL* 58 [1939], 113–41) that Nehushtan was adopted after the capture of Jerusalem by David from a pre-Israelite Jebusite cult, remains highly speculative.

5. *there was no one like him among all the kings of Judah following him, or among those before him.* It is generally agreed that the last clause is a "clumsy" addition (so Montgomery-Gehman; cf. Stade, Šanda). Moreover the entire sentence contradicts the unlimited praise heaped by the Dtr. upon Josiah; cf. 23:25 (and 22:2, 19; 23:22). Burney's recasting, therefore, is attractive, though it lacks textual justification (*wlʾ hyh kmhw bkl mlky yhwdh ʾšr hyw lpnyw,* "there was no one like him among all the kings of Judah who were before him").

7. *And so* YHWH *was with him.* There is no need to emend the Hebrew *wĕhāyâ* (perfect tense with conjunction) to *wayyĕhî* (imperfect with *waw* consecutive) as do Stade, Gray. The breakdown of classical Hebrew style under the influence of late usage is to be felt in several passages in 2 Kings (cf. Driver, *Tenses,* 133). R. Meyer has argued, as did Jepsen before him, that this usage, so marked in 23:4–15 and the present verse, was peculiar to annalistic writing; see R. Meyer, "Auffallender Erzählungsstil in einem angeblichen Auszug aus der 'Chronik der Könige von Juda' " in *Festschrift F. Baumgärtel* (Erlangen, 1959), 114–23.

in all that he undertook. Lit. "to wherever he went forth." For this idiom, used to affirm the reward of those who are loyal to YHWH, cf. Josh 1:7, 8; 1 Sam 18:5; 1 Kgs 2:3; Prov 17:8.

He rebelled against the king of Assyria. The rebellion against Assyria is perceived as a positive act, singling out Hezekiah as a righteous king who trusted YHWH; this is in contrast to the slavish attitude of his father, Ahaz. Cf. above 16:7 and Tadmor and Cogan, *Bib* 60 (1979), 505–6.

8. *Gaza and its border areas.* The plural noun Heb. *gĕbûlêhā,* "its borders," is used in a similar phrase in 2 Kgs 15:16. The LXX reading in the singular (preferred by Gray) is probably owing to the translator. The southern coastal plain and the Philistine seaports had been an Assyrian sphere of influence since the days of Tiglath-pileser III. Hezekiah's attacks, besides being an open act of war, were probably coordinated with local anti-Assyrian elements, who rebelled with him after Sargon's death. These actions took place between 705 and 702. See further in the Comment.

from watchtower to fortified city. Cf. 17:9. Recent archaeological surveys and excavations in the Negev have uncovered a rather dense network of fortified sites, some with projecting towers. (Their date and provenance is still debated.) See R. Cohen, "The Iron Age Fortresses in the Central Negev," *BASOR* 236 (1979), 61–79; and earlier, B. Mazar, *EncMiqr* 4.633–35.

9–12. This résumé of 17:1–23 not only coordinated the dates of the fall of Samaria with those of the reign of Hezekiah, but served to contrast the Judahite king's pious acts, which brought him success, with the impious ways of his northern neighbors which led to their destruction (cf. v. 12).

9–10. For the synchronisms with the reign of Hoshea, see the note to v. 1. All modern translations have noted the wrong verse division; v. 10a concludes the sentence begun in v. 9. Cf. above 17:5.

11. *The king of Assyria exiled Israel.* For *Israel* LXX reads *Samaria,* which is preferred by Stade; but MT is retained, as it follows the text of 17:6.

he settled them. The translation follows the reading of the versions and 17:6 in which the verb *wyšb* stands in place of *wynḥm.* M. Held (*JANES* 11 [1979], 57) defended the vocalization of MT, "he led them," noting the Akkadian usage of the verb sequence *nasāḫu-warû/wabālu,* "to deport, to lead, bring."

Comment

In contrast to his father Ahaz, Hezekiah is portrayed as a just and righteous king, unlike other kings before or after him. In these qualities, he is likened to David, the founder of the dynasty. Hezekiah's loyalty to YHWH is evidenced by the cultic reform he undertook, the first of such scale in Judah's history, and by his rebellion against Assyria. Throwing off the yoke of Assyria represented a major departure from the policies of Ahaz, who had willingly yielded to Tiglath-pileser III and proclaimed himself "servant and son" (16:7) of the Assyrian king.

The cultic reform of Hezekiah began with the closing of the high places, those popular sanctuaries which had endured since the days of Israel's settlement in the land, and was accompanied by the purging of pagan accoutrements associated with these sites.[1] As a result, worship was concentrated at the single altar in the Temple of Jerusalem (cf. 18:22), from which the venerated Nehushtan image was removed.

What motivated so far-reaching a reform? The explanations offered by biblical commentators and historians have grossly misrepresented the nature of Hezekiah's actions. They have proceeded from the assumption that "so long as Judah was a tributary Assyrian vassal, that is to say, far into the reign of Hezekiah, the official Assyrian religion had a place alongside the traditional worship of Yahweh in the state sanctuary in Jerusalem."[2] Therefore, when Hezekiah rebelled against Assyria and proclaimed his independence, he

[1] The large horned altar of ashlar blocks found at Beer-sheba, and the altar of earth and unhewn stones from Arad, with which it has been compared, were both dismantled and abolished during the reforms of Hezekiah, according to the interpretation of Y. Aharoni (*Archaeology of the Land of Israel* [Philadelphia: Westminster, 1982], 229–34). But a consensus has not been reached on the date of the archaeological stratum of these finds. See below note to 23:8.

[2] Noth, *History,* 266.

quite naturally repudiated the Assyrian gods.[3] However, an examination of the pertinent Assyro-Babylonian evidence, essentially the royal inscriptions of the Sargonid kings, does not support this assumption. Vassals of Assyria were not required to follow Assyrian religious practices; nor did the Assyrians interfere with the local cults. Moreover, the high places were centers of Israelite worship, long established in Israel. The sacred pillars and sacred poles characterized the native cults, and Nehushtan was certainly not an Assyrian cult object.[4]

One should search, rather, for inner Judahite motivations for the Hezekian reform. And indeed M. Weinfeld put forward a suggestion that "Hezekiah destroyed the high places and outlying sanctuaries so as to bind the people closer to the Jerusalem sanctuary" at the time of his rebellion against Assyria. Weinfeld found an analogy in the act of Nabonidus, the last king of Babylonia, who, on the eve of the Persian attack in 539 B.C.E., gathered the divine statues from provincial cities into Babylon.[5] But the example of Nabonidus is not analogous to Hezekiah. The gathering of statues into Babylon was, as it seems, incidental, a hurried act of frenzy and despair in the face of great danger, and was not part of Nabonidus's policy of elevation of the moon god, Sin, above other Babylonian gods.[6]

As presented by the Deuteronomist, Hezekiah's cultic reform was the central religious act of his reign and should most likely be dissociated from his policy toward Assyria. An assured outcome of cult reform would have been the disruption of social and religious stability within Judah. At a time when efforts were being directed toward the physical fortification and provisioning for war, wise counsel would not have recommended cult reforms.

Hence the reform should be dated prior to 705 B.C.E., the date of Hezekiah's rebellion; but just how much earlier? In 2 Chr 29:3, the date of the reform is given as "the first year of his reign, in the first month." Several scholars have regarded this date as authentic and even coordinated it with extrabiblical evidence.[7] It appears now, however, that this date is a literary

[3] So, e.g., Robinson, *History,* 392–93; Bright, *History²,* 280; and repeated most recently by Herrmann, *History,* 257.

[4] For a thorough presentation of the evidence, see Cogan, *Imperialism,* 9–61; and independently, though from a different vantage point, McKay, *Religion in Judah under the Assyrians,* 13–19, 60–66.

[5] M. Weinfeld, "Cult Centralization in Israel in the Light of a Neo-Babylonian Analogy," *JNES* 23 (1964), 202–12.

[6] For the text of Nabonidus, see *ANET³,* 306b and Grayson, *Chronicles,* 109–10. Cf., too, the early discussion of S. Smith, *Babylonian Historical Texts* (London: Methuen, 1924), 103, and H. Tadmor, "The Inscriptions of Nabunaid: Historical Arrangement," *AS* 16 (1965), 351–63. Note that Smith's dates for the events are one year too low.

[7] E.g. Thiele, *MNHK²,* 150–52; J. M. Myers, *II Chronicles,* AB, 170; H. Tadmor, *EncMiqr* 3.97.

convention, indicating Hezekiah's early piety, and cannot be used for chronological purposes.[8] Thus while the date of the reform remains uncertain, it is reasonable to place it in the first decade of Hezekiah's reign, after 722, the year Samaria fell.

Essentially religious in character, Hezekiah's reform may be viewed against the background of the disaster that befell the northern kingdom of Israel between the years 732–720. Exhortations and prophecies, like those of Hosea, which called for penitence and a return to YHWH, were hardly exclusive to the North. The Assyrian invasions, the destruction of the land, and the successive deportations must have had repercussions in neighboring Judah. The political and religious leadership in Jerusalem saw in the downfall of Israel a forboding lesson: Was it not Israel's apostasy that brought about its demise? Could not similar deviations from the prescribed cult be pointed to within Judah? Micah's denunciation of the idolatrous practices in Judah (e.g. Mic 5:9–14) clearly had Samaria in mind (cf. 1:6, 9). Hezekiah's reform, then, can be viewed as directed against such practices, in the hope that Judah would be spared the divine wrath. (Over a century later, some of Jerusalem's elders remembered Hezekiah's piety and its saving effect; cf. Jer 26:17–19.)

Unlike the later reform of Josiah, Hezekiah's acts are not said to have stemmed from a written book of *Torah* (cf. 22:8, 11). But this lack is not a reason to deny a connection between Hezekiah and the Deuteronomic school. The reform program of Hezekiah finds its clearest echo in the laws of Deuteronomy, and the positive evaluation of the king by the Deuteronomist points in the same direction. It is here that the Deuteronomic cultic ideal was first put to the test, though its full development and publication was to come only much later under Josiah (on which, see the Comment on 2 Kgs 22).[9]

In the year 705, the Assyrian Empire extended from the Brook of Egypt in the West to the Persian Gulf in the East. Under Sargon, the neo-Hittite states in southern and eastern Anatolia had been annexed to the empire; the nomadic Indoeuropean Cimmerians, who endangered the northern borders of Assyria, were defeated; and Urartu and Media were pillaged. In the South-

[8] See M. Cogan, "Tendentious Chronology in the Book of Chronicles," *Zion* 45 (1980), 165–72.

[9] Scholars have noted the affinity between the prophecies of Hosea and the book of Deuteronomy, and have thus traced certain trends in Deuteronomy to northern Israel. See, in particular, Alt, *Kleine Schriften,* 2.250–75; and cf. von Rad, *Studies in Deuteronomy,* 68; and H. L. Ginsberg, s.v. *Hosea,* in *Encyclopedia Judaica* 8.1023–24. If this is so, then the course by which northern ideas reached Judah can be suggested: the refugees from Ephraim after 722 who resettled in Judah brought the proto-Deuteronomy to its new home.

Most recently M. Haran offered a novel suggestion, in which the Priestly Code served as the impetus for Hezekiah's reforms. See, in detail, *Zion* 45 (1980), 1–12; idem, *Temples and Temple Service in Ancient Israel* (Oxford: Oxford University Press, 1978), 141–44.

east, Sargon reconquered Babylonia (in 710) and crowned himself king of Babylon, under the new title "governor of Babylon" (*šakkanak Babili*). But in 705 he fell in battle, his body captured by the enemy, not recovered and not buried.[10] It was only natural that the ignominious death of this mighty ruler on the battlefield in Asia Minor should shake the lands subservient to Assyria.

Vassal states on the periphery of the empire assumed that Assyrian hegemony had come to an end. In no time Merodach-baladan II the Chaldean (721–710), who had been ousted by Sargon, recaptured Babylon and his lost throne.[11] Also in the West, on the Phoenician coast, and in Egypt, political circumstances took a new turn. In Egypt a militant king of the Nubian dynasty, Shebitku, came to the throne[12]; the peaceful relations on the Egyptian-Assyrian border in southern Philistia came to an end. The Nubian pharaoh found partners in Tyre, Philistia, and Judah, who banded together to oust the Assyrian presence from the area.

In this alliance, Hezekiah played a dominant role. He attacked cities in Philistia loyal to Assyria, as far as Gaza (18:8), in order to consolidate the resistance to Assyria. In the case of Ekron, he removed its pro-Assyrian king, Padi, and imprisoned him in Jerusalem (*ANET*^{3}, 287b). Judah's involvement with Egypt and its dependence upon Egyptian military support was criticized by Isaiah, but was no doubt a major factor in Hezekiah's designs (cf. e.g. Isa 31:1–3).

In his preparations for war, Hezekiah concentrated upon the fortification of Jerusalem. The city wall was strengthened,[13] and its water supply was guaranteed against the anticipated siege by cutting a tunnel under the walls, to carry the waters of the Gihon spring to the Siloam Pool within the city.[14] At the entrance to this tunnel, an official inscription commemorating this feat of ancient engineering was placed; it is the only monumental inscription in Biblical Hebrew from the First Temple Period.[15] The provisioning of stores

[10] For the sources and a discussion of the obscure historical circumstances of Sargon's death, see H. Tadmor, *JCS* 12 (1958), 97–98. An Assyrian literary composition from a later date shows Sennacherib searching by means of liver omens for an explanation of "Sargon's sin" which led to his death (Tadmor, *EI* 5 [1958], 150–63).

A biblical echo of these events can be found in Isa 14:4b–21, where the Assyrian(!), not Babylonian, conqueror, depicted as "left lying unburied like loathsome carrion," is no doubt Sargon (H. L. Ginsberg, *JAOS* 88 [1968], 49–53).

[11] See J. A. Brinkman, "Merodoch-baladan II," in *Studies Presented to A. Leo Oppenheim,* 6–53.

[12] Kitchen dates his accession to 702 (*Third Intermediate Period,* 383).

[13] Cf. 2 Chr 32:5; Isa 22:9–10; and the massive city wall discovered by N. Avigad, *IEJ* 20 (1970), 129–134 and Plate 29 therein; see in the present volume, Plate 2.

[14] Cf. 2 Kgs 20:20; 2 Chr 32:3–4, 30; Isa 22:11.

[15] For the text, see Appendix I, No. 7; cf. *ANET*^{3}, 321; and a photograph of the slab, now in Istanbul, see Plate 4; cf. *ANEP*^{2}, 275.

throughout Judah reported in 2 Chr 32:28 completes this picture of military preparedness.[16] All these activities can reasonably be dated to 705–701, the years during which Sennacherib was engaged in reestablishing Assyrian rule in the East, leaving the West temporarily unattended.

[16] As a result of the latest excavations at Lachish, it has been proved that both the four-winged and two-winged *lmlk* impressions belong to level 3, i.e. the end of the eighth century (D. Ussishkin, *BASOR* 223 [1976], 1–13). Y. Aharoni, *The Land of the Bible*[2], 394–400, views all the royal *lmlk* seal impressions found at numerous sites throughout Judah as evidence for Hezekiah's reorganization of the kingdom, in the period immediately prior to the Assyrian invasion. Cf., too, the discussion of N. Na'aman, "Sennacherib's Campaign to Judah and the Date of the *lmlk* Stamps," *VT* 29 (1979), 61–86.

XXXII. SENNACHERIB'S CAMPAIGN TO JUDAH

(18:13–19:37)

18 13 In the fourteenth year of King Hezekiah, Sennacherib, king of
Assyria, attacked all of Judah's fortified cities and seized them.
14 Whereupon Hezekiah, king of Judah, sent a message to the king of
Assyria at Lachish: "I admit my guilt. Withdraw from me and[a] whatever you will impose upon me, I shall bear." The king of Assyria then
imposed (a payment of) three hundred talents of silver and thirty
talents of gold upon Hezekiah, king of Judah. 15 And so Hezekiah
turned over all the silver stored in the House of YHWH and in the
palace treasury. 16 At that time Hezekiah stripped the doors of the
Temple Hall[b] and the posts which he himself[c] had plated and delivered them to the king of Assyria.

17 The king of Assyria dispatched the Tartan, the Rab-saris, and the
Rab-shakeh from Lachish to King Hezekiah in Jerusalem, together
with a large force. They marched up to Jerusalem[d] and took up positions by the conduit of the Upper Pool on the Fuller's Field Road;
18 and they called for the king. Eliakim son of Hilkiah, the royal steward Shebna the scribe, and Joah son of Asaph the recorder came out to
them.

19 The Rab-shakeh spoke to them, "Tell Hezekiah, thus said the
Great King, the king of Assyria, 'What is this confidence of yours?
20 Do you think that plans and arming for war can emerge from empty
talk? Now,[e] in whom have you put your trust that you rebelled against
me? 21 Here now,[f] you put your trust in this splintered reed staff, in
Egypt; that if someone leans upon it, it pierces his palm and punctures
it. That's Pharaoh, king of Egypt, to all who put their trust in him!

[a] Read *weʾēt,* with mss., Luc., Syr., Targ.
[b] Lit. "Hall of YHWH."
[c] Lit. "Hezekiah, king of Judah."
[d] MT adds: *wyʿlw wybʾw,* a dittography; omitted by some mss., LXX, Syr. Vulg.
[e] Read: *wĕʿattâ* with several mss., Luc., LXX^{A}.
[f] Isa. 36:6; Luc., Syr. omit *ʿattâ.*

22 And if you tell me, It is in YHWH our God that we put our trust! Is
he not the one whose high places and altars Hezekiah removed, and
then ordered throughout Judah and Jerusalem, You must worship before this altar in Jerusalem? 23 Now, come make a wager with my
master, the king of Assyria: I will give you two thousand horses, if you
will be able to supply riders for them. 24 And so, how could you turn
down « »[g] one of my master's minor servants and trust in Egypt
for chariots and horsemen? 25 Now[h] was it without YHWH that I
marched against this place to destroy it? YHWH said to me, 'Attack
this country and destroy it!' "

26 Eliakim son of Hilkiah, Shebna, and Joah then said to the Rab-
shakeh, "Please speak Aramaic with your servants; we understand it.
Do not speak Judean with us within earshot of the people on the
wall." 27 But the Rab-shakeh answered them, "Was it to your master
and to you that my master has sent me to speak these words? Was it
not rather to the men sitting on the wall, who, together with you, will
have to eat their own excrement and drink their own urine?[i]" 28 Then
the Rab-shakeh stepped forward and called out loudly in Judean,
« »[j] "Hear the message of the Great King, the king of Assyria.
29 Thus said the king, 'Do not let Hezekiah deceive you, for he cannot
save you from me.'[k] 30 And do not let Hezekiah have you put your
trust in YHWH, by saying, 'YHWH will surely save us; and this city will
not be handed over to the king of Assyria.' 31 Do not listen to
Hezekiah; for thus said the king of Assyria, 'Send me a gift and surrender to me! Then each one of you will eat of his own vine and of his
own fig tree and will drink the water of his own cistern; 32 until I come
to transfer you to a land like your own land, a land of grain and new
wine, a land of bread and vineyards, a land of olive oil and honey. Stay
alive and don't die.' Do not listen to Hezekiah, when he incites you by
saying, 'YHWH will save us!' 33 Did any of the gods of the(se) nations
ever save his land from the king of Assyria? 34 Where are the gods of
Hamath and Arpad? Where are the gods of Sepharvaim?« »[l]
<Where are the gods of Samaria?>[m] Did they save Samaria from
me? 35 Who of all the gods of the countries was able to save his land

[g] MT has the additional word *pḥt.* See note.
[h] Read *wĕʿattâ* with mss., LXX[b], Syr. (cf. n. *e*).
[i] Qere substitutes euphemisms and points ketib accordingly. See note.
[j] MT adds *wydbr,* omitted by some versions.
[k] Read *mydy* with some mss. and versions, MT *mydw.*
[l] Omit *hnʿ wʿwh,* with LXX, Luc., Isa 36:19; see note.
[m] Add with Luc. and Vulg. See note.

from me, that YHWH should be able to save Jerusalem from me?"
36 They remained silent « »[n] and did not answer a word, for it
was the king's order, "Do not answer him!"

37 Thereupon Eliakim son of Hilkiah, the royal steward, Shebna the
scribe, Joah son of Asaph the recorder came to Hezekiah, with their
garments rent, and reported the Rab-shakeh's message to him.
19 1 When King Hezekiah heard this, he rent his garments and put
on sackcloth and entered the House of YHWH. 2 He sent Eliakim, the
royal steward, Shebna the scribe and the elder priests, dressed in sackcloth, to Isaiah son of Amoz, the prophet.[o] 3 They told him, "Thus
said Hezekiah, 'This day is a day of distress, of rebuke, and of contempt. Children have come to the breach, but there is no strength for
the birth. 4 Perhaps YHWH your God will listen to all the words of the
Rab-shakeh, whom his master the king of Assyria sent to taunt the
living God and will punish him for the words which YHWH your God
has heard. So do offer a prayer for this last remnant!' "

5 Now when the servants of King Hezekiah came to Isaiah, 6 Isaiah
said to them, "Speak thus to your master: Thus said YHWH, 'Do not
be frightened by the words you have heard by which these attendants
of the king of Assyria reviled me. 7 Behold, I will put a spirit in him, so
that he will hear a report and return to his own country, and I will
strike him down by the sword in his own country.' "

8 Now the Rab-shakeh withdrew, and since he heard that the camp
had moved from Lachish, he found the king of Assyria engaged in
battle at Libnah. 9 He (the king of Assyria) received a report about
Tirhakah, king of Ethiopia: He has set out to do battle with you. So
again he sent messengers to Hezekiah: 10 "Speak thus to Hezekiah,
king of Judah, 'Do not let your God deceive, the one in whom you put
your trust, by thinking that Jerusalem will not be given over to the
king of Assyria. 11 Now surely you have heard what the kings of Assyria did to all the lands—destroying them! And you—will you be
saved? 12 Did the gods of the nations save them whom my ancestors
destroyed,[p] Gozan and Haran and Reseph and the Edenites of Telassar? 13 Where is the king of Hamath and the king of Arpad and the
king of Lair, Sepharvaim, Hena, and Iwwah?' "

14 Hezekiah received the letter[q] from the messengers and read it. He

[n] Read *wyḥryšw* with LXX and Isa 36:21 for MT *whḥryšw*. MT adds *hʿm* "the people."
[o] *nābîʾ* is better placed at the end of the verse as in Luc. and Isa 37:2.
[p] Some mss. and Isa 37:12 read *hšḥytw*. Cf. note.
[q] Read sg. with Luc. Targ.; MT pl. (dittography of following *m*).

then went up to the House of YHWH; Hezekiah spread it out before
YHWH, 15 and Hezekiah prayed before YHWH, "O YHWH, God of
Israel, enthroned upon the cherubim, You, alone, are God of all the
kingdoms of the earth. It was You who made heaven and earth.
16 Turn your ear, O YHWH, and listen; open your eyes, O YHWH, and
look. Listen to the message that Sennacherib has sent[r] to taunt the
living God. 17 It is true, O YHWH, that the kings of Assyria have laid
waste the nations and their lands, 18 and put[s] their gods to fire—for
they are not gods, but only man's handicraft, mere wood and stone;
thus they were able to destroy them. 19 But now, O YHWH, our God,
save us from his hand, so that all the kingdoms of the earth may know
that You, YHWH, alone, are God."

20 Then Isaiah son of Amoz sent a message to Hezekiah: "Thus said
YHWH, God of Israel, 'I have heard your prayer to me concerning
Sennacherib, king of Assyria. This is what YHWH has spoken concern-
ing him:

21 "Maiden Daughter Zion
despises you, scorns you.
Daughter Jerusalem
shakes her head[t] after you.
22 Whom have you taunted and reviled?
Against whom have you raised your voice?
And raised your eyes heavenward?
Against the Holy One of Israel!
23 Through your messengers you taunted YHWH[u], by saying,
With my many chariots[v], it was I . . . .[w]
I ascended mountain peaks, the far reaches of the Lebanon.
I felled its tallest cedars, its choicest[x] firs.
I entered its remotest lodge, its rich woodlands.
24 It was I who dug and drank strange waters,
And with the soles of my feet I dried up the Niles of Egypt.
25 Have you not heard? From of old, I did it.
In ancient days, I fashioned it[y]. Now I have brought it about—

[r] Read *šlḥ* with some mss., LXX, Syr., Vulg., Isa.
[s] Read with Isa 37:19 *wntn.* 1Q Isa[a] has *wytnw.*
[t] LXX[B], Syr. and 1Q Isa[a] read *r'šh.*
[u] Mss. read tetragram; MT: "the Lord."
[v] Mss., qere and versions: *brb rkby;* MT: *brkb rkby.*
[w] Luc. adds: *ʿšyty ḥyl.* See note.
[x] Read *mbḥr* with some mss. and Isa 37:24.
[y] Omit *waw* with Isa 37:26, 1Q Isa[a] and versions.

and it is: Fortified cities crashing into ruined heaps,
26 Their inhabitants powerless, dismayed, and confounded.
They were like grass in the field, and fresh pasture;
Like straw on rooftops, blasted by the east wind.[z]
27 <Your every action>[a'] and your every pursuit, I
know.« »[b']
28 Because you have raged against me, and your uproar rings in
my ears,
I will put my hook in your nose and my bridle through your
lips,
and turn you back on the very road by which you came.
29 This shall be the sign for you:
This year you shall eat from the aftergrowth,
next year from the self-sown;
but in the third year, sow and reap,
plant vineyards and enjoy their fruit.
30 The remaining survivors of the house of Judah shall add on
roots below and produce fruit above.
31 For a remnant shall emerge out of Jerusalem,
And a survivor from Mount Zion. The zeal of YHWH[c'] shall
effect this.
32 Therefore, thus said YHWH concerning the king of Assyria:
He shall not enter this city, nor shall he shoot an arrow there.
He shall not move up defenses before it,
nor throw up a siege mound against it.
33 He shall go back[d'] by the same road he came; but into this
city,
he shall not enter. The word of YHWH.
34 For I will defend this city and save it, for my own sake
and for the sake of David, my servant.'"'

35 That night, YHWH's angel went out and struck the Assyrian camp
—185,000 men! At daybreak there were dead bodies all about.
36 So Sennacherib, king of Assyria, broke camp and left. He returned to Nineveh, where he resided. 37 Once, as he was worshipping
in the House of Nisroch, his god, Adrammelech and Sharezer, <his

[z] Read with 1Q Isa[a] *hnšdp lpny qdym.*
[a'] Restore with 1Q Isa[a] *qmk.* Omitted by haplography.
[b'] Omit *wʾt htrgzk ʾly.* Dittography of v. 28.
[c'] Qere, mss. and versions (Isa 37:32) add *ṣbʾwt.*
[d'] Read *bʾ* with mss., versions, Isa 37:34.

sons >,e′ struck him down with the sword and then fled to the land of Ararat. Esarhaddon, his son, became king.

[e′] Read *bnyw* with qere, ms. versions, and Isa 37:38. Omitted in MT.

Notes

18 13. *In the fourteenth year of King Hezekiah.* This date has been a crux to modern commentators, ever since the recovery of Assyrian documents from the reign of Sennacherib, which pinpoint the year of the Assyrian campaign against Judah as 701 B.C.E. The textual evidence seems to be self-contradictory. From vv. 9, 10, it is inferred that Hezekiah began his reign in 727 and was on the throne when Samaria fell in 722. His fourteenth year, therefore, would be 713, a date which cannot be coordinated with the Assyrian evidence. For this reason, a number of scholars (e.g. W. F. Albright, *BASOR* 100 [1945], 22; E. R. Thiele, *MNHK*[2], 118–40) have rejected the synchronisms in vv. 9, 10 and preferred the date in v. 13, thus dating Hezekiah's accession to 715/14. Moreover, the date in v. 13 cannot be integrated with the chronological data on Hezekiah's successors, and those who consider this date pivotal in their chronological system, emend the fifty-five years of Manasseh (2 Kgs 21:1) to forty-five years (so Albright) or assume a ten-year coregency between Hezekiah and Manasseh (so Thiele).

Other scholars, however, as well as the chronological scheme adopted in this commentary, prefer to date the accession of Hezekiah to 727/26 (e.g. Lewy, Begrich, Tadmor). To avoid manipulation of the chronological data, "the fourteenth year" is taken as the date which originally introduced the prophetic story of Hezekiah's illness and his miraculous recovery, 2 Kgs 20, at which time he was granted an additional fifteen years (20:6). These two figures, fourteen years and fifteen years, add up to the total sum of Hezekiah's reign, i.e. twenty-nine years (18:2) (so, with J. Lewy, *OLZ* [1928], 158–59). The present position of the date in v. 13a is secondary, probably from the hand of Dtr. or a still later chronographer.

(Hezekiah's accession in 727/26 is borne out by the dateline in Isa 14:28, "in the year of the death of Ahaz," the same year in which "the staff that beat Philistia was broken"—i.e. Tiglath-pileser died—both in 727; cf. J. Begrich, *Zeitschrift der deutschen morgenländischen Gesellschaft* 86 [1933], 66–79.)

Verses 13b (beginning with Heb *ʿālâ,* "attacked") through 16 consist of excerpts from a Judahite chronicle (vv. 13b–15) and a Temple chronicle (v. 16). Their original date or heading might be recovered from 20:1, "in those days"; cf. other examples of this style in 2 Kgs 16:5, 6. In these two chronistic excerpts, Hezekiah is referred to as *Ḥizkîyâ melek yĕhûdâ,* "Hezekiah, king of Judah," while in the prophetic narratives that follow he is *hammelek Ḥizkîyāhû,* "King Hezekiah." This is corroborative evidence for the separation of the date and the sources presented here, for in v. 13a, he is also styled "King Hezekiah."

Sennacherib, king of Assyria. In Akk. *Sin-aḫḫē-erība,* which means "(the god) Sin compensated for (dead) brothers." The LXX *sennachereim* is closer to the original pronunciation. On the transcription of the name of the moon god Sin with *s* rather

10. Residents of Lachish leaving for exile. *Drawing by Judith Dekel. Reproduced from D. Ussishkin,* The Conquest of Lachish by Sennacherib, *Tel Aviv, 1982.*

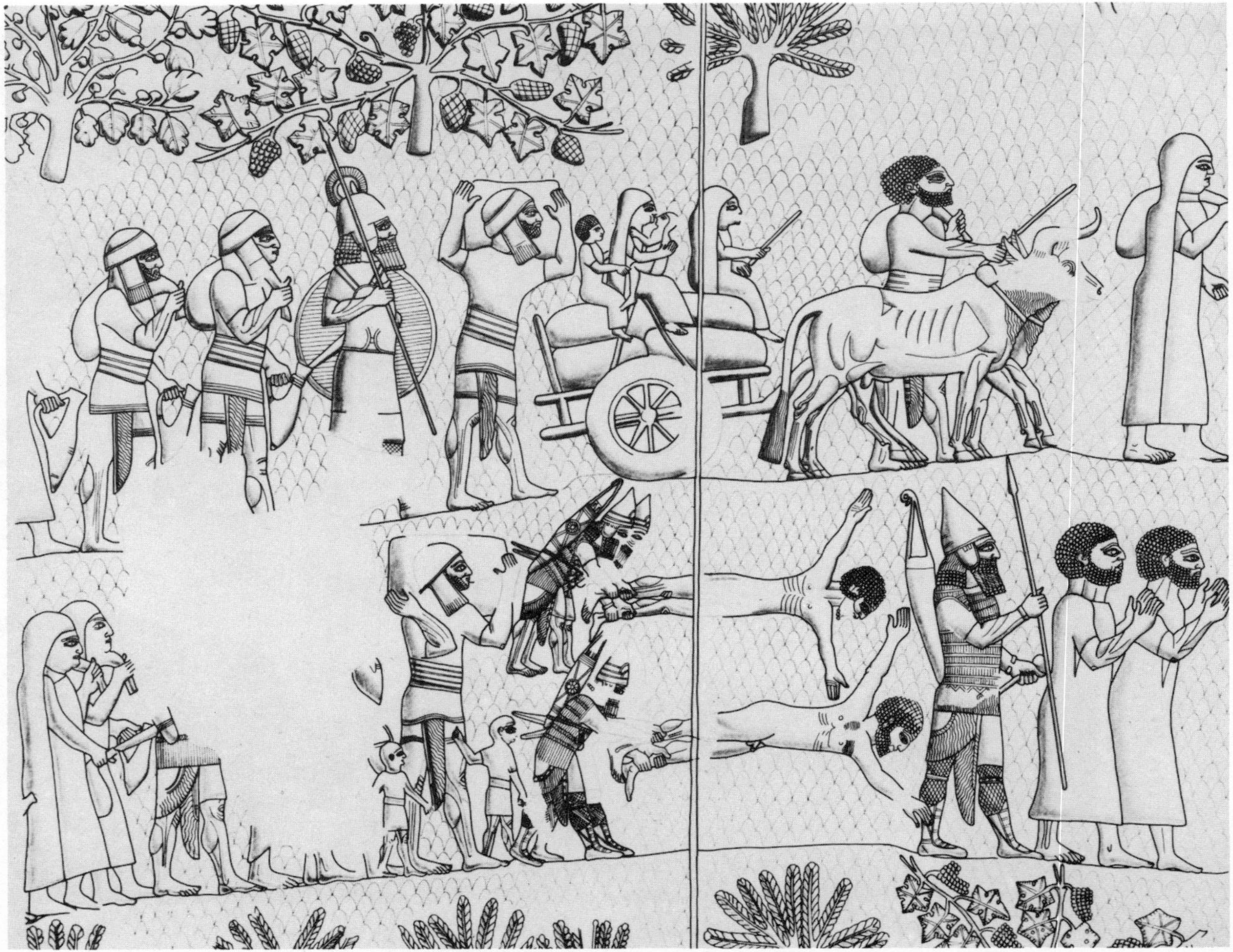

(a.)

11. Fragments of Assyrian stela of Sargon II found in excavation at (a.) Samaria and (b.) (opposite page) Ashdod. *Collection of Israel Dept. of Antiquities.*

(b.)

12. Seals and seal impressions of royal officials:

(a.) "Shema, servant of Jeroboam," *Collection of Israel Dept. of Antiquities.*

(b.) "Amos, the scribe," *Israel Museum, Jerusalem.*

(c.) "Jaazaniah, servant of the King" (cf. 2 Kings 25:23). *Collection of Israel Dept. of Antiquities.*

(d.) "The Governor of the City." (cf. 2 Kings 23:8). *Israel Exploration Society.*

13. Assyrian vessels, 8th–7th cent. B.C.E. Limestone bowl, Tell el-Qitaf; pottery bottle, Ramat Rahel. *Collection of Israel Dept. of Antiquities.*

14. "Pillar Astarte"—female pottery figurine. *Hecht Collection, Haifa.*

15. Crescent-shaped bronze standard and bell, Assyrian citadel at Tel Sera^{c}, seventh century B.C.E. *Ben-Gurion University of the Negev.*

16. Clay brick construction—Assyrian type, 7th cent. B.C.E., Tel-Jemme. *Israel Exploration Society.*

than the expected *š*, reflecting Babylonian usage, see A. R. Millard, *JSS* 21 (1976), 8–9, 13.

14. *to the king of Assyria at Lachish.* A monumental wall relief from the palace of Sennacherib in Nineveh commemorates the battle over the city and the deportation of its inhabitants, all of which took place under the personal direction of the king (see *ANEP*², 371–73). This is the only battle scene in the campaign of 701 B.C.E. to be thus depicted and points out the strategic importance of Lachish, in whose environs the main Assyrian camp was apparently pitched during the hostilities in Judah.

Recent archaeological excavation at Lachish has conclusively identified Level 3 as the one which fell to Sennacherib. See D. Ussishkin, *Tel Aviv* 4 (1977), 28–60.

three hundred talents of silver and thirty talents of gold. Sennacherib recorded that the amount paid by Hezekiah was 30 talents of gold and 800 talents of silver (*ANET*³, 288). The exact correspondence between the amounts of gold rendered is indeed striking. Therefore, the discrepancy between the 300 and 800 talents of silver might be explained by the assumption that the Assyrian record included the precious metals stripped from the Temple doors (v. 16). In addition the Assyrian text, recorded on the receiving end in Nineveh, is much more detailed; it contains a long list of booty taken from Judah not even hinted at in 2 Kgs 18. The biblical data may be incomplete at this point.

16. *At that time Hezekiah stripped the doors of the Temple Hall and the posts.* This appended note from Temple records (introduced by the formulaic "at that time") relates that Hezekiah was constrained, as was Ahaz his father under similar circumstances (cf. 2 Kgs 16:17–18), to remove the rich overlay from the entrance to the main Temple Hall, in order to meet the heavy indemnity forced upon him by his suzerain.

Citing the value placed upon wood and wooden objects in the tribute lists of Assyrian kings, M. Elat makes the novel suggestion that the doors themselves, not merely their metal facing, were shipped to Nineveh (*Economic Relations,* 63). Note, however, that **qṣṣ* is used of "cutting off, stripping" metals in 16:17 and 24:13.

The Heb. *ʾōmĕnôt,* translated as "posts," is a *hapax legomenon,* and may be related to the root meaning "support" (cf. *BDB* 52). But the construction details of the Temple entrances contained in 1 Kgs 6 do not include these items. The versions differ in their renderings: Targum has *ʾaskopiāʾ,* "thresholds"; LXX *esterigmena,* "braces."

The doubt cast upon Hezekiah as the benefactor of the Temple (so e.g. Klostermann, Stade, Šanda) has no textual or historical support. The repetition of the king's name and title a second time in v. 16b, while a bit awkward, may indicate the original wording of this datum as recorded in its source. Considering Hezekiah's interest in promoting the Israelite cult and his acknowledged wealth (see below 20:13), it would certainly have been in character for this king to have renovated the Jerusalem sanctuary.

17. *the Tartan, the Rab-saris, and the Rab-shakeh.* Tartan, lit. "viceroy" (Akk. *turtānu),* also in Isa 20:1, was the highest official after the king and occasionally replaced him when the latter did not campaign. Cf. RLA 2.460; and E. Klauber, *Assyrisches Beamtentum,* Leipziger Semitistische Studien, Vol. 3 (1910), 60–63.

Rab-saris is a loan word from Akk. *rab ša rēši* (LÚ.GAL SAG), lit. "chief eunuch"; the *rab-saris* was often dispatched on military duties at the head of Assyrian forces, e.g. by Tiglath-pileser III to Tyre (*ARAB* 1.803). (Most translations of the title in Assyrian royal inscriptions are incorrect, as they are based on an obsolete reading of the ideogram SAG as *šaqê,* considered by Klauber, op. cit., 89; e.g. *ARAB,* passim;

ANET³, 282b; Wiseman, *DOTT*, 56–57; in detail, H. Tadmor, in *Essays in honor of David Noel Freedman*, 279–85).

Rab-shakeh, Akk. "the chief butler," occasionally written *rab šaqê*, but mostly in ideogram GAL BI.LUL, was a high official whose duties were usually restricted to the court and the king's person. He never took part in military campaigns.

Doubts concerning the authenticity of the three-member Assyrian delegation, originally raised by H. Winckler and followed by almost all modern commentators in which the delegation is reduced to only the Rab-shakeh as in Isa 36:2 are not valid. Since Sennacherib himself participated in the campaign to the West in 701 B.C.E., it was only natural that he be accompanied by his personal attendants. The reason why the Rab-shakeh, and not one of the officers higher in rank, addressed the Judeans should be sought in the Rab-shakeh's fluency in the language of Judah. He might even have been of Israelite extraction, from a noble family exiled to Assyria (as suggested by H. Tadmor, *EncMiqr* 7.323–25).

the conduit of the Upper Pool on the Fuller's Field Road. The site is mentioned once again in Isa 7:3, but in neither case is there sufficient geographical detail to locate the pool or its water source. M. Burrows reviewed the major suggestions (*ZAW* 70 [1958], 221–27; cf. idem, *IDB* 2.850–51) and opted for the lower end of the eastern hill of Jerusalem as it reaches the Kidron Valley. B. Mazar (*EncMiqr* 3.824, 827–28) favors a location in the north at the upper end of the Tyropoeon Valley, outside the city walls, in an area both wide and flat enough to accommodate the force which accompanied the Assyrian delegation. For a suggestion to identify the "camp of the Assyrians" mentioned in Josephus, *Wars* v. 303, 504 on the ridge of the northwest hill of Jerusalem with the site of Sennacherib's expeditionary force, see D. Ussishkin, *IEJ* 29 (1979), 137–42.

18. *they called for the king.* Sennacherib's message was to be delivered to Hezekiah directly, and indeed it is written with second masculine sing. verbs.

the royal steward . . . the scribe . . . the recorder. The delegation of Judahite courtiers sent to receive the Assyrian conditions was composed of the ranking ministers in Judah. The title *ʾăšer ʿal habbayit*, lit. "who is in charge of the house"—i.e., the "royal steward," is known from the reign of Solomon onward (1 Kgs 4:6) in both Judah and Israel (16:9; 18:3; 2 Kgs 15:5). A Hebrew seal of the seventh century B.C.E. bears the inscription *[l]ydw ʾšr* [ʿ]*l hbyt*, "Belonging to Iddo, the Royal Steward." See N. Avigad, *Festschrift Rëuben R. Hecht* (Jerusalem: Koren, 1979), 119–20.

The appearance of the royal steward at the head of the listing may be due to the personal influence of Eliakim at the court of Hezekiah, as much as to the supposed growth in the power this office achieved over the years (cf. the remarks of Mettinger, *Solomonic State Officials*, 88, who notes the relatively low placement of the steward in the list at 1 Kgs 4:6). Eliakim and Shebna (whose title there is *sōkēn;* on which see the note to 1 Kgs 1:2) both appear in a prophecy of Isaiah (Isa 22:15–25) in which Shebna is forewarned of his impending replacement by Eliakim as steward because of his haughty bearing. Apparently, by the year 701, Shebna had been demoted, but not yet ousted completely from government service as the prophet had predicted. N. Avigad has argued that the sepulcher of a royal steward in the Kidron Valley east of Jerusalem belonged to Shebna and is the very one spoken of by Isaiah (22:16). See Avigad, "The Epitaph of a Royal Steward from Siloam Village," *IEJ* 3 (1953), 137–52.

Nothing is known about Joah son of Asaph, other than his service as state recorder.

19. *Tell Hezekiah, thus said the Great King.* In the Rab-shakeh's speech, Hezekiah

is always referred to by his personal name, without royal title, while the Assyrian king is always designated as the *Great King,* a translation of the Akk. *šarru rabû,* the foremost title of every Assyrian king from the days of Shamshi-Adad I on. See M.-J. Seux, *Épithètes royales akkadiennes et sumériennes* (Paris: Letouzey et Aré, 1968), 248 ff. It originated in a north-Syrian title and was typical of the Hittite kings. In Hebrew, it appears on an ivory discovered at Nimrud (*Iraq* 24 [1962], 45–49). For the alteration with *mlk rb* in LBH and Aramaic, see J. Greenfield, Proceedings of Fourth *WCJS,* 118–19.

What is this confidence of yours? Heb. **bṭḥ,* "trust, confide," occurs in various forms seven times in seven verses (as Childs, *Isaiah and the Assyrian Crisis,* 85, remarked). The theme of trust is common in Assyrian historical inscriptions when describing Assyria's enemies: they trust in their own strength, put their trust in their gods, etc. (cf. e.g. *ARAB* 1.445, 472; 2.153, 252, 785). For the Akk. verb *takālu,* "to trust," cf. *AHw* 1304, and C. Cohen, *IOS* 9 (1979), 39–41.

20. The verse is difficult; our translation follows Ehrlich. The opening of the message rings of proverbial origin. In Prov 14:23, *dĕbar śĕpātayim,* "empty talk," mere talk, as contrasted with toil and work, leads only to poverty; *ʿēṣâ* ("plans") and *gĕbûrâ* ("arming") are paired in proverbs; cf. Prov 8:14, Job 12:13. The dispatch continues with a parable in v. 21 and a sarcastic wager, all indicative of propagandistic modes of speech. A similar use of parables is known in Assyrian royal correspondence—e.g. Esarhaddon's letter to the Babylonians, *ABL* 403. Cf. note to 14:9 above.

21. *this splintered reed staff.* Egypt is dubbed a reed staff, probably because of the richness of cane in its marshy waters; cf. Ezek 29:6. In order to wound the person leaning upon such a staff, the reed would have to be split at its end (Heb. *rāṣûṣ*)—i.e. not having a clean break at a node. On the image, see Haupt, ad loc.; Ehrlich, *Randglossen* ad Isa 36:6; and in general O. Kaiser in *Wort und Geschichte,* Festschrift K. Elliger, AOAT 18 (1973), 106. Egypt's inability to come to the aid of its Philistine allies is mocked by Sargon, who described Pharaoh as *šarru lā mušēzibu,* "a king who cannot save," (H. Winckler, *Die Keilschrifttexte Sargons* [Leipzig: E. Pfeiffer, 1889], 18). His general Re'e was likened to "a shepherd (*rēʾû*) whose flock was plundered." See R. Borger, *JNES* 19 (1960), 49–53, and the note on 2 Kgs 17:4.

22. That the Rab-shakeh should have known of Hezekiah's reform of Judahite cultic practice is not in itself strange. Affairs of state in vassal kingdoms were certainly reported in Nineveh by Assyrian agents, and the cult centralization spoken of in this verse and in v. 4 would certainly have been noted. It may even be supposed that the reform was introduced within Judah without much popular support and so could have served the polemical purposes of the Assyrian speaker. See further in Comment.

23. *Come make a wager with my master.* Heb. *hitʿāreb,* lit. "pledge yourself," only here and understood from the use of *ʿārôb* in other contexts, e.g. Gen 43:9, Prov 17:18. The *hithpael* form conveys the sense of reciprocal action and competition. See the discussion of Z. Ben-Hayim, *Leš* 44 (1980), 85–99, on the root *ʿrb* and its derivatives.

two thousand horses. A very large number! The size of cavalry in the Assyrian army and the provisioning of horses is discussed by M. Elat, *Economic Relations,* 69–82, and Yadin, *Art of Warfare in Bible Lands,* 297–302.

24. *how could you turn down one of my master's minor servants.* The idiom *hēšîb pānîm,* "reject, refuse," with reference to a request (cf. 1 Kgs 2:16, 17, 20), seems to connote the wager proposed by the Rab-shakeh, who refers to himself as his master's minor servant. The meaning of "repulse" with military overtones, noted in *BDB* 999b

(cf. Gray, *NAB*) is unattested. Only Ehrlich noted the irony of this sentence; cf. too Luzzatto.

MT has the additional word *peḥâ* "governor," a loanword in Hebrew and Aramaic from Akkadian *pīḫātu* (*AHw*, 862; cf. E. Y. Kutscher, "*Pḥwʾ* and Its Cognates," *Tarbiz* 39 [1961], 112–19). But this substantive creates a lengthy construct chain, a syntactic aberration hardly permissible in BH. *Pḥt* may be omitted, taking it either as a gloss on the words "master's servant," (so Stade, Montgomery-Gehman) or dittography (Ehrlich, *BH*[3]). It is witnessed, however, in all ancient versions and is retained in many modern translations.

25. *YHWH said to me, 'Attack this country.'* That YHWH had called upon Sennacherib to attack Judah is not an idea necessarily drawn from the prophecies of Isaiah (e.g. Isa 10:5–6; cf. Childs, *Isaiah and the Assyrian Crisis*, 84), but was an idea current in Assyrian political thought. Royal inscriptions often describe local deities abandoning their faithful to join the Assyrian side. The use of direct speech here is so far unique, but is understandable as a rhetorical device. It is not unlike Sargon's claim that his conquest of Babylon came about as a call of Marduk to rescue the Babylonians from the illegal rule of Merodach-baladan (*ARAB* 2.31). Similarly, in his Babylonian inscription, Cyrus tells that he was called by Marduk "to march against his city" (cf. *ANET*[3], 315). On this theme, see E. Bickerman, *JBL* 65 (1946), 262–68, and Cogan, *Imperialism*, 9–21, 111. The notion that YHWH sent Sennacherib against Judah because of Hezekiah's breach of loyalty to Assyria, sworn allegedly in YHWH's name, has been rightly criticized by Childs, *loc. cit.* Moreover the Assyrian evidence, reexamined, shows that Hezekiah was not under a loyalty oath when he rebelled. See H. Tadmor, "Treaty and Oath," 150–51.

26. *Please speak Aramaic.* The request to speak Aramaic is not surprising, as Aramaic and not Akkadian was the language of the Assyrian Empire west of the Euphrates. See R. A. Bowman, "Arameans, Aramaic, and the Bible," *JNES* 7 (1948), 65–90; H. Tadmor, "The Aramaization of Assyria," in *Mesopotamien und seine Nachbaren*, H. J. Nissen and J. Renger, eds., Berliner Beiträge zum Vorderen Orient 1 (1983), 449–70. Official scribes who wrote Aramaic, alongside those who wrote cuneiform, are depicted on palace reliefs from the days of Tiglath-pileser III on. Cf. e.g. *ANEP*[2], 367.

Do not speak Judean with us. This is the only reference to the language of Judah in contemporary sources. The Hebrew spoken is referred to as Judean, in contrast to the dialect spoken at the same time in the northern kingdom. For the evidence of extrabiblical documents on these two dialects, see Cross-Freedman, *Early Hebrew Orthography*, 57. As a whole, Hebrew was called "the language of Canaan" (cf. Isa 19:18).

27. *to eat their own excrement and drink their own urine.* Qere substitutes *ṣōʾātām*, "filth," and *mê raglêhem*, "water of the legs." The ketib *šênêhem*, "their urine," is apparently plural, like Akk. *šīnāti*; *ḥarêhem*, "their excrement," may be related to the forms *ḥry ywnym* (2 Kgs 6:25) and *mḥrʾt* (10:27). See ad loc.

28. The superfluous *wydbr* in MT may have arisen from a mistaken copying of the following *dbr hmlk*.

31. *Send me a gift and surrender!* Heb. *ʿăśû ittî bĕrākâ.* Only occurs here. The uncommon use of *ʿāśâ* as an auxiliary verb indicates an Aramaic or Akkadian calque; and cf. note to 17:29. In some Akkadian dialects, *šulmānam epēšu* is used in the sense of "to exchange or send gifts"—cf. *CAD* E 221. (On *šulmānu*, "gift," see above to 16:8.) Hebrew *bĕrākâ*, "greeting," (2 Sam 8:10) also has the extended meaning of "gift" (Josh 15:19; 1 Sam 30:26; 2 Kgs 5:15).

For *yāṣāʾ ʾel* "coming out" from a besieged place, in the meaning "surrender"; cf. 1 Sam 11:3, Jer 38:17, 18.

Then each of you will eat. On the syntactic construction, using the imperative (*ʾiklû*) rather than the jussive to express greater intention, see Driver, *Tenses,* 65.

32. The promise made here that conditions in exile would be comparable to those found in the homeland was not mere rhetoric. It was in Assyria's interest to care for the deportees both during the journey to the lands of resettlement, as well as in their new homes, an interest motivated by a desire to make maximum use of the manpower and resources these exiles represented. (See the remarks of Obed, *Mass Deportations,* 41–74.) Deportees from the West were resettled within Assyria proper, and in Sennacherib's days many were brought to Nineveh to populate the newly rebuilt capital.

34. *Where are the gods of Hamath and Arpad?* Sennacherib is depicted here as boasting of victories over cities which, in fact, were conquered by earlier Assyrian kings. Hamath and Samaria were taken by Sargon in 720; Arpad by Tiglath-pileser III in 740.

The second half of the verse is a crux, variously interpreted already in antiquity. MT has the unfathomable *hnʿ wʿwh* (omitted in Isa 36:19). The Targum rendered this verbally as "Were they (the gods) not transported and carried off captive?" As proper nouns, the words appear in the textually sound passage 2 Kgs 19:13 with *ʿwh* resembling the town Avva mentioned in 17:24; *hnʿ* remains an enigma. The end of the verse, however, requires a preceding question, like the one found in Luc. and Vulg.; certainly the foreign gods could not be thought of as having failed to defend Samaria.

36. *They remained silent.* MT adds *hāʿām,* "the people." But how could the king have given an order to the people to remain silent before the confrontation with the Rab-shakeh, when only during the negotiations did it become known to Jerusalem's defenders that they were the object of the Assyrian's speech? See v. 27. Therefore the words "the people" looks like an explanatory, but incorrect gloss, missing in LXX and in Isa 36:21.

19 **1.** *He rent his garments and put on sackcloth.* The rending of garments and the donning of sackcloth as rites of mourning are well attested, especially in times of crisis. Cf. e.g. Isa 22:12, Jonah 3:5–6, and above 2 Kgs 6:30.

3. *This day is a day of distress, of rebuke, and of contempt.* Hezekiah's message to the prophet is twofold. It conveys the sense of humbling which Sennacherib's victories have induced, here termed "rebuke"; and at the same time, it calls attention to the blasphemies against YHWH hurled by the Rab-shakeh.

Children have come to the breach. A proverbial saying which appears here and in similar fashion in Hos 13:13. Heb. *mašbēr* has been translated both as "breach, mouth of womb" (*BDB* 991a and *KB* 572a), as well as by "birthstool" (Targ., followed by *NJPS*). Luzzatto astutely noted that the image depicts the "breaking forth" of the fetus into the world, the noun form *mašbēr* being a gerund. Cf. the semantically similar use of **pārôṣ,* "break through, out," in Gen 38:29.

5. *Now when the servants of King Hezekiah came to Isaiah.* The present placement of this verse in the story seems, at first blush, strange, especially after v. 3, in which the king's message was already delivered to the prophet. (Note the verb *wayyōʾmĕrû,* imperfect with *waw*-consecutive, "they told.") Verse 3 anticipates the meeting of the messengers and the prophet, and so, in v. 5, this moment is passed over and center stage is given over to Isaiah's response. Additional instances of this syntactic usage in

which strict chronological sequence is sometimes abandoned are discussed by Driver, *Tenses,* 75, 76 Obs.

6. *attendants of the king of Assyria.* Heb. *naʿar* is usually "attendant" (cf. 5:20 and the note there) and is used here sarcastically in a reference to the highest Assyrian officers. *NEB* renders "lackeys."

6. *Do not be frightened by the words you have heard.* This short oracle of support and encouragement, which opens with the phrase *ʾal tîrāʾ,* "do not be frightened," is similar in style and content to extrabiblical oracles in the West Semitic tradition. Ba'al-shamayn, the god of Zakur of Hamath, promises him through seers: *ʿl tzḥl ky ʾnh hml [ktk . . .] . . . wʾnh ʾhṣlk mn kl[. . .,* "Fear not, for I have made you king . . . and I shall deliver you from all[. . ." (Cf. *ANET³,* 501; see Comment to 13:1–9.) In Assyrian texts from the reign of Esarhaddon and Ashurbanipal, the goddess Ishtar encourages these frightened and anxious kings with oracles, which open with the formulaic "Fear not!" (*lā tapallaḫ*). Cf. *ANET³,* 605–6. For a full discussion of the biblical and comparative material, see J. C. Greenfield, Proceedings of Fifth *WCJS,* Jerusalem, 1969, 174–91; cf. also, Tadmor, in *Unity and Diversity,* 43.

7. *I will put a spirit in him.* I.e. "I will delude him" (*NJPS*). The content of the report is not stated, but whatever it might have been, Sennacherib is pictured as behaving differently than expected, and it is this divinely contrived rumor which will be his undoing. In 1 Kgs 22:20–23, a "lying spirit" in the mouths of 400 prophets leads Ahab to his death at Ramoth-gilead.

so that he will hear a report and return to his own country. Because of the complicated editorial history behind the present text, the fulfillment of this prophecy takes place in two stages. The rumor to be heard (v. 7, *šāmaʿ*) is the report (v. 9, *wayyišmaʿ*) of Tirhakah's approach. But the continuation of this story line is in v. 37, where it is told that Sennacherib actually returns home and is subsequently assassinated. For a critical discussion of the editing and historical circumstances reflected in the sources, see in detail the Comment below.

7–9. The repetition of the verbs *šāmaʿ,* "heard," and *šāb,* "returned," several times in three verses has caused some confusion in the textual transmission, as evidenced by the differences in the ancient versions and in Isa. In such a case, the Hebrew text of Kings is best retained.

8. *Libnah.* For the location of this site in the Judean Shephelah in the vicinity of Lachish, see the note to 2 Kgs 8:22.

9. *Tirhakah, king of Ethiopia.* During the time of Sennacherib's campaign, Tirhakah was not yet king; and according to certain chronological reckonings, he was still a child in 701. Note particularly, W. F. Albright, *BASOR* 130 (1953), 8–11, who follows the findings of M. F. L. Macadam, *The Temples of Kawa* (London: Oxford University Press, 1949). Most recently it has been argued that Tirhakah was indeed of age and could well have been at the head of the Ethiopian army force which engaged Sennacherib at Eltekeh. Full details are given by Kitchen, *Third Intermediate Period,* 383–87 and idem, *JANES* 5 (1973), 225–31. The title "king of Ethiopia" in the present context is admittedly anachronistic, for only in 690 did Tirhakah ascend the throne.

So again he sent messengers to Hezekiah. The composition of the second Assyrian delegation is not specified; nor is a face-to-face encounter with Jerusalemites described. Rather, this time anonymous messengers deliver a letter (v. 14) to Hezekiah directly.

11. *destroying them.* Heb. *lĕhaḥărîmām.* Šanda's suggestion to emend the text to

lĕhaḥărîbām, because of the improbability that the Assyrians practiced the Israelite form of *ḥerem*—ban—is unnecessary. In late BH, the verb *heḥĕrîm* is used in the general sense of "to destroy"; cf. Jer 50:21, 26; 51:3; 2 Chr 20:23; Dan 11:44.

12. *my ancestors.* The reference is to Sennacherib's predecessors, the kings of the Assyrian empire of the ninth century.

destroyed. Heb. *šiḥătû* in *piel;* in some mss. and Isa 37:12 *hišḥîtû* in *hiphil.* But this interchange of verbal constructions is attested elsewhere, without any change in meaning; e.g. 2 Sam 24:16 and 1 Chr 21:15.

Gozan. See above on 2 Kgs 17:6.

Haran. An important site on the upper Balikh, on the trade routes running East–West, Haran (Akk. *Ḫarrānu*) was annexed by Assyria in the ninth century. It continued as a major religious center for the cult of the moon god, revered by both the local Aramaean population and by their Assyrian overlords. See J. N. Postgate, RLA 4.122–25.

Reseph. The city of Raṣappa is located in the Sindjar plain of upper Mesopotamia (cf. Forrer, *Provinzeinteilung,* 12), and was the capital of one of the largest Assyrian provinces in the ninth and eighth centuries.

Edenites of Telassar. The people of Bit Adini (cf. Amos 1:5), conquered by Shalmaneser III, were deported from their homes on the Euphrates south of Haran and were resettled in Telassar. On wars in the territory of Bit-Adini, see cf. *CAH*[3] 3/1.260–64. Telassar corresponds to *Til-Aššuri,* "Mound of the Assyrians," possibly to be sought in the Zagros region along the lower Diyala River (so R. Zadok, *JANES* 8 [1976], 123–24). (The name Telassar is not a corruption of Tel-Bashir as suggested by Winckler, *KAT*[3], 39, n. 3, and followed by Dhorme, *Recueil É. Dhorme,* 265, [Paris: Imprimerie nationale 1951], and *JB* and Gray.)

12–13. Sennacherib's call to Hezekiah to surrender recounts past victories as proof that no one was ever able to stand up to the might of Assyria. Verse 12 speaks of the gods who could not save their nations; v. 13 speaks of defeated kings. The toponyms in v. 12 are likely places where Israelite deportees were settled (e.g. Gozan and Haran; cf. above 17:6), while those in v. 13 represent the homelands of the new settlers in Samaria transplanted there by the Sargonids (e.g. Hamath and Sepharvaim; cf. above 17:24). These references were intended to impress upon Hezekiah that continued rebellion would only lead to disaster, as it had in Israel.

Hamath. See above 17:24.

Arpad. A north Syrian city taken by Tiglath-pileser in 740 B.C.E., after a three-year siege, and turned into an Assyrian province. It is mentioned alongside Hamath in Isa 10:9. See RLA 1.153.

Lair. Lair is the city Laḫiru in northeastern Babylonia, as was recognized by A. Sarsowsky, *ZAW* 32 (1912), 146, and G. R. Driver, *Aramaic Documents of the Fifth Century B.C.* (Oxford: Clarendon Press, 1957), 6:1 and p. 57. (Montgomery-Gehman and *NAB* still translate erroneously: "the city/cities.").

Sepharvaim. See above 17:24.

Hena and Iwwah. See above 18:34.

15–19. Even though presented as extemporaneous, Hezekiah's prayer conforms to the known form of petition; the call for God's intervention is motivated by the divine self-interest, inasmuch as he had been reviled in Sennacherib's message. For an introduction to this prayer type, see M. Greenberg, *Biblical Prose Prayer* (Berkeley: University of California Press, 1983).

The Deuteronomic echoes in Hezekiah's prayer are manifest, a clear sign of its compositional origin: *"man's handicraft"* or *"mere wood and stone,"* cf. Deut 4:28; *"YHWH alone is God,"* cf. Deut 4:35; *"to destroy them,"* cf. Deut 12:2; *"kingdoms of the earth,"* cf. Deut 28:25, Jer 15:4 and 24:9. The theme of creation, uncommon in the Deuteronomistic writers, becomes an important element in postexilic liturgy. See the remarks of Weinfeld, *Deuteronomy,* 39.

15. *and Hezekiah prayed before YHWH.* The appearance of the king within the Holy of Holies, facing the Ark of the Covenant and the outstretched wings of the protecting cherub figures, may point to the privileged position granted Hezekiah, in that he was permitted entry into the sanctum restricted to priests. It was not the king's "sacral status" (so Gray), but rather the dire crisis facing Israel, combined with Hezekiah's acknowledged cultic good name, which allowed this interruption of ritual injunction.

O YHWH, God of Israel. Luc., Syr., and Isa 37:16 read, "O YHWH of hosts" (*ṣĕbāʾôt*), which is the regular formula associated with the image of the Lord who sits upon a cherub throne (cf. 1 Sam 4:4, 2 Sam 6:2). T. D. N. Mettinger discusses the derivation of the formula and its concrete background in the art of the ancient Near East in *Studies in the Period of David and Solomon,* 109–38.

18. *and put their gods to fire.* Read *wĕnātôn,* infinitive absolute, with Isa 37:19. The gods of the nations are portrayed as helpless blocks, whose nondivinity is proved by their inability to save themselves from destruction by fire. Yet it should be noted that Assyrian practice was in fact more tolerant than allowed by this polemic. Usually the gods of the conquered nations were treated with respect, for the Assyrians held that the gods abandoned their followers, thus handing them over to the conqueror. Often the divine statues were brought to Assyria, where they were installed in chapels until sent home. Seldom were the statues actually destroyed, as was done, for example, by Sargon's troops, who in the heat of battle smashed the gods of Urartu (Cogan, *Imperialism,* 22–41). Luzzatto (*Commentary on Isaiah,* ad Isa 37:19) recognized this point even before the discovery of Assyrian monuments, basing his comments upon Roman analogues.

21–28. The answer to Hezekiah's prayer is delivered by the prophet as a taunt or mocking song. The meter with three beats to two has often led scholars to class this as a *qînâ* dirge. Early studies on the metrical problems involved are those of K. Budde, *ZAW* 12 (1892), 31–37; idem, *JThS* 35 (1934), 307–13; T. J. Meek, *Crozer Quarterly* 18 (1941), 126–31. Numerous modifications have been made to Budde's theory (cf. e.g. the introduction of D. R. Hillers to *Lamentations,* AB, xxx–xxxvii), on which D.N.F. remarks, "My earlier views ["Acrostics and Metrics in Hebrew Poetry," *HTR* 65 (1972), 367–92] must now be qualified as follows: The so-called *qînâ* rhythm (3:2) is generally supported by the evidence, especially in Lamentations 1–4, although there are numerous exceptions. Overall a detailed analysis of the pattern in those chapters of Lamentations support Budde's hypothesis. To achieve line-by-line regularity or conformity to a pattern would require extensive rewriting of poems. There is a falling rhythm, but it is closer to 7:6 than 8:5, although there are examples of both, and the general 3:2 stress count holds up quite well, especially in Lamentations 2–3."

While there are clear echoes of Isa 10:13–14 in this oracle, other elements are later than Isaiah's time; therefore most commentators see these verses as a late interpolation. Cf. e.g. Skinner, *Isaiah,* Cam B, 288; Šanda; Childs, *Isaiah and the Assyrian Crisis,* 103.

21. *despises you.* Heb. *bāzâ* should be taken here as a perfect, in line with the rest of

the verbs in the verse, against the massoretic accents (so, already, Qimḥi, Luzzatto), which imply the participle.

shakes her head after you. Heb. *rōʾš hēnîʿâ.* This idiom is commonly taken to be a gesture of mockery (e.g. *BDB* 631; Gray), and appears in parallel construction with the verbs *bôz* and *lāʿôg* as in our verse. Cf. too Ps 22:8 and 109:25. But more than scorn is involved in this shaking of the head. As seen in Lam 2:15 and the equivalent idiom *hēnîd bĕrōʾš,* "shake, toss head," (e.g. Jer 18:16; Job 2:11; Ps 69:21), the gesture is one of sorrow and commiseration. No small amount of irony is involved here, as the prophet depicts the attacked consoling the attacker, and this by saying, "Poor Assyria, how you do suffer!"

23. *it was I . . .* Meter would seem to favor the addition present in Luc: *ʿśyty ḥyl,* "I was triumphant, valiant." See the remarks of K. Budde, *JThS* 35 (1934), 310–11. The verbs in the imperfect should all be pointed with the *waw*-consecutive, in order that all action be in the past tense; thus *wāʾekrôt,* "I felled"; *wāʾābōʾâ,* "I entered"; *wāʾaḥărib,* "I dried up" (v. 24). The use of the cohortative form in *wāʾābōʾâ* is extended in 1Q Isa[a] 37:24–25 to all verbs: *wʾkrwth, wʾḥrybh.* In LBH, the form no longer conveys modal sense and is freely added. Cf. the remarks of Bergstresser, *Grammatik,* 2.50.

24. *Niles of Egypt.* Heb. *yĕʾôr* is the Egyptian name of the Nile, the plural *yĕʾōrê* refers to the numerous branches of the Nile in the Delta, cf. Isa 7:18. The poetic form of the name Egypt, *māṣôr,* rather than the more common *miṣrayîm,* is used here and in Isa 19:6 and need not be emended (as does Gray). Note the same image of "drying up" the Nile waters in both texts. The first Assyrian king to reach Egypt was Esarhaddon in 671; it was he who also boasted of providing his troops with water drawn from wells in the arid desert south of Rapiah. Cf. *ANET*[3] 292b. An entirely different, though problematic, solution is now offered by H. Tawil (*JNES* 41 [1982], 195–206), who identifies *māṣôr* with Mt. Muṣri, north of Assyria, whose waters Sennacherib diverted to irrigate Nineveh and its environs (some time between 700 and 694 B.C.E.)

25. *and it is.* Heb. *wthy.* The pointing of MT translates as "and you shall be." This has been construed with the following phrase to mean I have appointed you to carry out the destruction of cities and their inhabitants. But the preceding verb *hēbîʾ,* "bring about," finds its complement in *wthy,* and the latter should be pointed *wattĕhî* (so LXX). Cf. similar usage in Deut 18:22; Ezek 39:8.

crashing into ruined heaps. The reading in Isa 37:26 *lhšʾwt,* with the *aleph,* for the Kgs *lhšwt,* is the standard form. On this orthographic variance, cf. *GKC* 23f.; and for the punctuation, cf. ibid., 53q.

26. *blasted by the east wind.* MT *šdph lpny qmh* was rendered by medieval exegetes, with some difficulty: "blasted before it (i.e., corn) is grown." *Qmh* belongs with the following verse (see below) and the missing word *qdym,* which completes the image, is now restored by 1Q Isa[a] 37:27. Cf. Gen 41:6, 23.

27. < *Your every action.* > Heb. *qmk wšbtk;* restored with 1Q Isa[a], and so already in LXX. Massoretic *qmh* at the end of v. 26 derives ultimately from *qmk.* (Stade and Šanda review the early discussion of this crux.) On the idiom "your rising up and your sitting down," cf. Deut 6:7, 11:19; Ps 139:2.

28. *your uproar.* Heb. *šaʾănankâ,* "your complacency." But LXX and Targum, as well as early commentators (e.g. Qimḥi, Ibn-Janah) understood the word as if it was read: *šĕʾônĕkā,* "your uproar, tumult." This recalls a well-known Mesopotamian literary topos of the punishment of mankind by the god Enlil, who was distressed by the uproar (*ḫubūru*) on earth; *ANET*[3], 104b, 106 and W. G. Lambert and A. R. Millard,

Atra-Ḫasīs (Oxford: Oxford University Press, 1969), 73, 107. (On *ḫubūru,* "din, noise," see *CAD* Ḫ 220 and J. J. Finkelstein, *JBL* 75 [1956], 329–30, for its biblical cognate *ḥōbēr ḥeber,* Deut 18:11; Ps 58:6).

I will put my hook in your nose. Here, too, the image finds its parallel in the treatment of Assyria's enemies—e.g. on the Zinjirli stele, Esarhaddon is depicted as leading two prisoners, apparently Baal of Tyre and Tirhakah of Egypt, by a rope tied to a ring which pierces their lips; cf. *ANEP*², 447. Captive kings were often displayed together with wild animals in the main square of Nineveh to their public disgrace; cf. *ARAB* 2.529, 829. In Ezek 19:4, 9, the princes of Judah, referred to as "young lions," are captured by the enemy (i.e. Babylonia) by means of hooks, an apt simile in light of the Assyrian practice; cf. too 2 Chr 33:11 on Manasseh's incarceration.

29. *aftergrowth.* Heb. *sāpîaḥ.* Cf. Lev 25:5. The word appears as a loan in the late Babylonian dialect of Akkadian as *sippīḫu,* "wild growth"; see W. von Soden, *UF* 13 (1981), 163, and *AHw* 1049a.

self-sown. MT *sāḥîš;* Isa 37:30 *šaḥîs;* 1Q Isaᵃ *šʿys.* A *hapax legomenon,* whose meaning is derived from the context. The sign to Hezekiah is that the aftergrowth would suffice for two years and that only in the third year would normal fieldwork be resumed. The deprivations of war would continue, not out of any lingering fear of the Assyrians (so, Ehrlich), but as a result of the destruction they had wrought in the land. This miraculous provisioning is a sign of YHWH's zeal at work in Israel. (This interpretation was earlier suggested by Luzzatto, but went unnoticed in subsequent research.)

The intentional devastation of enemy countryside is amply attested in Assyrian records; e.g. Tiglath-pileser III ravaged the environs of Damascus by cutting its orchards (*ARAB* 1.776), and did the same in Chaldea (*ARAB* 1.792). Cf. the relief in R. D. Barnett and M. Falkner, *The Sculptures of Tiglath-pileser III* (London: British Museum, 1962), plate xxxiii. The biblical injunction in Deut 20:19–20 against the wanton destruction of trees seems to be a reaction against the Assyrian practice. See above at 2 Kgs 3:19.

For a sign of encouragement tied to an event in the distant future, cf. Exod 3:12.

32–34. This second oracle is considered by many commentators to be the original reply of Isaiah to Hezekiah's prayer, which followed directly after v. 20. Note that both replies end with the same prediction: Sennacherib will return (Heb. *yāšûb;* cf. v. 28: *wahăšîbōtîkā)* by the same way which he came.

From Sennacherib's account of his investment of Jerusalem (see the Excursus), it is clear that no actual assault upon the city employing siege works was made. These are specifically mentioned with regard to the forty-six cities and towns taken in the Shephelah and are vividly depicted on the Lachish relief.

34. *For I will defend this city.* Cf. Isa 31:5 for another promise of YHWH's defending Jerusalem, apparently from the same period. Cf. Childs, *Isaiah and the Assyrian Crisis,* 58.

for my own sake and for the sake of David, my servant. This phrase is a unique coining, but the idea that YHWH acts for "his own sake" can be traced back to the plague traditions in Exod 10:1 and 11:7, while in Ps 23:3, 25:11, 106:8, and in late prophecy (Jer 14:7, 21), concern for God's reputation is well attested. "For the sake of David" is a Dtr. phrase; cf. above on 1 Kgs 11:32. In the present passage, then, these two components have been combined to express regard for the Temple City and the Davidic dynasty.

35. *YHWH's angel.* The appearance of the angel (Heb. *malʾāk,* lit. "messenger") rather than YHWH himself looks like a purposeful device of the storyteller; YHWH's *messenger* seeks redress from Sennacherib's *messengers,* who came to "taunt the living God." The traditions in Sir 48:20–21 and Josephus *Antiquities* x.19–21 which speak of a plague or pestilence visited upon the Assyrians represent later theological rationalizations of the miraculous deliverance. See further in Excursus.

185,000 men. A similar use of exaggerated numbers in divine punishment can be found in 2 Sam 24:15, where 70,000 die in a three-day plague. The destruction of the Assyrian army in this miraculous fashion mirrors Isaiah's predictions concerning the punishment of the tool who rose up against its wielder (cf. Isa 10:15). In particular, note, "To break Assyria in My land, to crush him on My mountain," 14:25; "At eventide, lo, terror! By morning, it is no more," 17:14.

Several rationalistic attempts have been made to render this story plausible. S. Feigen thought that the number slain was only 185 men; this figure was arrived at by assuming that originally the text read 185, followed by an *aleph*—i.e., *ʾîš,* which was misinterpreted by the Massoretes as *ʾelep,* "thousand" (Feigen, *Missitrei Heavar* [New York, 1943], 88–117). However, on the rhetorical use of numbers, see M. H. Pope, *IDB* 3.563–66. More recently, W. von Soden, noting that plagues are reported in Assyrian sources as sometimes upsetting military campaigns, considered the possibility that a plague in Sennacherib's camp cut down the besieging forces, though he would not accept so large a number (*Festschrift H. E. Stier* [Munster: Aschendorff, 1972], 43–51). It would appear that the caution expressed by A. Kuenen (*Prophets and Prophecy,* 296–97) over a century ago against literal interpretation of this miracle story is still valid.

At daybreak there were dead bodies all about. The dangers of night which pass with morning light was a popular image associated with divine salvation—e.g. in prayers: Ps 46:6, 90:14, 143:8; Lam 3:22f.; and in historical accounts: Exod 11:4, 2 Kgs 3:20, 2 Chr 20:20; cf. Isa 17:14; cf. the discussion of J. Ziegler, "Die Hilfe Gottes 'am Morgen' " in *Studien Nötscher, Bonner Biblische Studien* 1 (1950), 281–88.

36. *So Sennacherib, king of Assyria, broke camp and left.* J. Lewy, *OLZ* (1928), 156–58, took this to be the concluding verse of the chronistic account in 18:13b–15. Other accounts in 2 Kgs, in which tribute is exacted, end with the withdrawal of the attacking force after payment is rendered. Cf. e.g. 12:18–19; 15:19–20.

Accordingly Stade's suggestion to emend the text by omitting "where he resided" (Heb. *wyšb*), which repeats the previous action with a similarly written verb (Heb. *wyšb,* "he returned"), is attractive. Cf. too Šanda's observation that the verse is "overloaded" with verbs.

37. *Once, as he was worshipping.* On the use of the participial clause, see Driver, *Tenses,* 165.

House of Nisroch, his god. The name of the god Nisroch (Heb. *nsrk*) is obviously a corruption, as no divinity with that name is known. That it may be an intentional alteration of the name of some Mesopotamian god (e.g. Marduk or Nusku) is a reasonable suggestion; likewise the location of the Nisroch Temple remains, for the present, enigmatic. Cf. B. Landsberger-Th. Bauer, *ZA* 37 (1927), 70; J. P. Lettinga, *VT* 7 (1956), 105–6. E. G. Kraeling (*JAOS* 53 [1933], 335–46) correctly rejects the idea that the murder took place in Babylon.

Adrammelech and Sharezer his sons struck him down with the sword. As confirmed by the Babylonian Chronicle, "Sennacherib, king of Assyria, was killed by his son in a rebellion" (Grayson, *Chronicles,* 81:34–35). This is further corroborated by a tradition recorded by Nabonidus (cf. *ANET³,* 309a) and still later in Berossos (cf. S. M. Burstein, *The "Babyloniaca" of Berossus* [Malibu, Calif.: Undena, 1978], 24:3; Luckenbill, *Annals of Sennacherib,* 162).

In these ancient sources, a single son and not two, as in v. 37, is mentioned. Most recently, S. Parpola adduced new evidence to show that Sennacherib's murderer was Arad-Ninlil (pronounced "Arda-milissu"), who was bypassed in the line of succession in favor of Esarhaddon, a younger son. The form in Berossos (in an excerpt by Abydenos) is Adramelos, virtually identical with the Assyrian name. Accordingly the biblical Adrammelech would be a slight corruption of the original name. (*r* and *d* have interchanged by metathesis, and *k* may have entered the text as a late scribal error for *s.*) See in detail S. Parpola, in *Death in Mesopotamia,* 171–82.

A son named Sharezer is not attested in any other source, but there is no reason to doubt that he was Adrammelech's accomplice. The theophoric element of the name is missing; Winckler, *KAT³,* 84, n. 3, reconstructed the name as [Nabu]-shar-uṣur, who was governor of Markasi and eponym in 682 B.C.E.

The notion that Sennacherib was "perhaps crushed alive under a winged-bull colossus guarding the temple where he had been praying at the time of the murder" (Parpola, op. cit., 175) is based upon an outdated translation of a passage in Streck, *Assurbanipal,* 38, iv: 70–71; cf. *CAD* S 160.

the land of Ararat. I.e., Urartu, modern Armenia. Esarhaddon mentions "brothers" who contested his accession, but not the place of their refuge (*ANET³,* 289). Yet his insistence that the king of Shupria, in southern Urartu, extradite runaway Assyrians might be linked to the present story. See *ARAB* 2.593–96. On the source of the information in this verse, see Comment.

Esarhaddon, his son became king. Akk. *Aššur-aḫ-iddin(a),* "(the god) Ashur has given a brother". The place name Ashur appears in Hebrew as *ʾšwr;* in the present personal name, Akk. *š* shifted to *s* as in the name Sargon (cf. above to 15:29).

Though appointed by Sennacherib as his legitimate successor, Esarhaddon faced a revolt led by the two patricidal brothers, both of whose names are preserved only in biblical tradition; upon their flight to Urartu, Esarhaddon entered Nineveh and assumed the throne (cf. *ANET³,* 289–90).

Comment

The extensive account of Sennacherib's campaign to Judah divides into two discrete sources—A: 18:13b–16, a chronistic record; and B: 18:17–19:37, prophetic narratives. This division, first suggested by B. Stade,[1] and confirmed by most critics ever since, is based upon perceptible differences in style and

[1] B. Stade, *ZAW* 6 (1886), 214–21. A full survey of critical opinion was given by L. L. Honor, *Sennacherib's Invasion of Palestine* (New York: Columbia University Press, 1926), 45–48, and was more recently reviewed and confirmed by Childs, *Isaiah and the Assyrian Crisis,* 73–103.

scope. Source A is a terse, factual account "without moral judgement,"[2] derived from an archival document; while source B is a lengthy, discursive narrative, revolving around the Rab-shakeh's speech and the role of the prophet Isaiah in the miraculous salvation of Jerusalem. A and B are further distinguished by the form of Hezekiah's name and title. In A, he is *ḥizqîyâ melek yĕhûdâ,* "Hezekiah, king of Judah"; in B, *hammelek ḥizqîyāhū:* "King Hezekiah."[3]

Source A records Sennacherib's attack upon Judah and the fall of the Judaean walled cities, which prompted Hezekiah's resubmission to Assyrian overlordship. It reports the exact amount of gold and silver paid as indemnity from the royal and temple treasuries. Verse 16, introduced by the phrase *bāʿēt hahîʾ,* "at that time," is an appended note on the stripping of the Temple to meet the heavy Assyrian payment. The date in v. 13a belongs to the prophetic story in 2 Kgs 20 and is not integral to A (see above, note to 18:13). J. Lewy thought that the conclusion of this account is now to be found in 19:36, and as in other cases (e.g. 13:18–19) ends with the withdrawal of the enemy after tribute was rendered.[4] According to Lewy, A was to be reconstructed as:

> [In his days (?)] Sennacherib, king of Assyria attacked all of Judah's fortified cities and took them. Hezekiah, king of Judah sent a message to the king of Assyria at Lachish: "I admit my guilt. Withdraw from me and whatever you will impose upon me, I shall bear." The king of Assyria then imposed (a payment of) three hundred talents of silver and thirty talents of gold upon Hezekiah, king of Judah. And so Hezekiah turned over all the silver stored in the Temple and in the palace treasury. Sennacherib, king of Assyria then broke camp and left, and he returned to Nineveh.

(However, 19:36 has more often been taken as the conclusion of source B on which see further below.)

It has been noted that source A agrees in great measure with Sennacherib's own account of his Judaean campaign. Were these two sources the only evidence for the events of the year 701, little further discussion would be necessary. But it is the essential incongruity of source B with both A and the Assyrian record which has constituted the core of the intensive debate on Sennacherib's campaign.

Source B contains the story of two Assyrian missions to Hezekiah demanding the surrender of Jerusalem and the two pronouncements by Isaiah pre-

[2] So Montgomery-Gehman, 482.

[3] Note the same distinction in terminology in the stories of Joash in 2 Kgs 12. In vv. 5–17, a narrative concerning Temple renovations, he is *hammelek Yĕhōʾāš,* "King Joash"; in vv. 18–19, a chronistic piece, perhaps from Temple archives, he is *Yĕhōʾāš melek yĕhūdâ,* "Joash, king of Judah."

[4] J. Lewy, "Sanherib und Hizkia," *OLZ* 31 (1928), 156–57.

dicting the salvation of the city. Modern critics usually take it to be a literary blend of two parallel prophetic narratives and divide the text into two parallel strands, B_1 and B_2, both relating substantially the same event.[5]

B_1 (18:17–19:9a, 36) opens with the appearance of a high-level Assyrian embassy at the gates of Jerusalem, met by the representatives of King Hezekiah. The Rab-shakeh, the chief cupbearer—third in rank in the Assyrian hierarchy—delivers an official message (in first person singular, as if Sennacherib were addressing Hezekiah directly) on the hopelessness of further resistance to Assyria. Provoked by the lack of response and the request to speak Aramaic, the Rab-shakeh turns to the defenders of the city with a mixture of threat and ridicule. Overcome with grief at these demands, Hezekiah turns to the prophet, who in a brief "salvation oracle" foretells the sudden withdrawal of the Assyrian king due to an unspecified rumor. B_1 ends with Sennacherib "breaking camp" and returning to Nineveh (19:36).

An appearance by an Assyrian dignitary before the walls of a besieged city such as portrayed in B_1 is paralleled by a similar situation recorded in Nimrud letter ND 2632.[6] There two Assyrian officials take their stand before the Marduk Gate of Babylon and plead with the citizenry to abandon their support of Ukin (or Mukin)-zeri, the Chaldean king of Babylon (ca. 730). In this case, too, the besieged refuse to be intimidated by the Assyrian threats. Other Assyrian documents also refer to diplomatic persuasion used as a stratagem,[7] and on a relief from Sargon's palace in Khorsabad, a pictorial representation of an appeal in the midst of battle can be found.[8] Furthermore, Sennacherib's message (18:19–25), while delivered in the language of Judah, bears close affinities to the style and the ideas expressed in Assyrian royal inscriptions: e.g. YHWH is depicted as cooperating with Sennacherib, having dispatched

[5] The recent attempt to interpret B as a single unit by H. M. Gevaryahu, in *Oz LeDavid, Studies Presented to D. Ben-Gurion,* 351–75 (Hebrew), was amply criticized by Childs. Stade's reasoning remains basically intact; the parallel elements in the text are explainable only by positing two separate tradition strands.

[6] The letter was published by H. W. F. Saggs, *Iraq* 17 (1955), 23–24; and cf. the discussion by Childs, op. cit., 80–82.

[7] In the oracular queries addressed by Esarhaddon and Ashurbanipal to the sun god Shamash, the plans of attack upon enemy cities include: "Making a direct attack, breaking through (and) undermining (walls) . . . starvation . . . and persuasion (lit. *pî ṭābi,* "good words"); see J. A. Knudtzon, *Assyrische Gebete an den Sonnengott* (Leipzig: E. Pfeiffer, 1893), Text No. 1. Obverse 9; 12. Obverse 10; 150. Obverse 5, Reverse 10. Note, too, the letter addressed by Ashurbanipal directly to the inhabitants of Babylonia during his efforts to put down the rebellion led by his brother Shamshshum-ukin (*ABL* 301; translated: A. L. Oppenheim, *Letters from Mesopotamia* [Chicago: University of Chicago Press, 1967], 169–70).

[8] See Yadin, *Art of Warfare,* 425; and *EncMiqr* 7.324.

him against Judah.[9] It can hardly be denied that the Hebrew text preserves the original argumentation of the Rab-shakeh, whose Hebrew rhetoric so impressed his hearers that it became the focus of the B_1 tradition. And yet, like similar speeches in the writings of Thucydides, the biblical text does not contain the *ipsissima verba* of the speaker.

In source B_2 (19:9b–35), the Rab-shakeh does not figure any longer; Sennacherib's demands are transmitted through unnamed messengers in letter form. The central motif in B_2 is the scorning of YHWH by the Assyrian monarch; consequently, in Hezekiah's prayer the defense of YHWH's fame stands in bold relief. The role of Hezekiah in the crisis is particularly underscored in B_2. Without intermediary (as in B_1), the scion of David appears in person before YHWH (19:14–19), and in his prayer Hezekiah calls for divine action to prove the blasphemies of Sennacherib wrong. Isaiah's answer to Hezekiah, a short oracle, secondarily expanded by vv. 22–32, promises the divine protection of Jerusalem. The story concludes with the miraculous salvation of the city; the Assyrian camp is decimated by YHWH's angel.

Affinities to Assyrian royal inscriptions can be found in B_2 as well. The self-boasting of Sennacherib in the mouth of the prophet (19:23–24) closely resembles *topoi* employed in the annals of the ninth and eighth centuries, especially the motifs of traversing difficult passes, cutting mighty trees, and supplying the army with water.[10]

Having delineated the individual accounts B_1 and B_2, can their *Sitz im Leben* be suggested? To what period can the composite B account as it now stands be dated? B_1 bears the markings of authentic events, close to the time of Sennacherib's invasion; inasmuch as persons, places, situations are all vividly recalled, it would seem that B_1 was composed under the impress of the events themselves. That Sennacherib's retreat is explained as caused by a rumor may mean that the true nature of the "report" (19:7) was either unknown or immaterial by the time of the storytelling. B_1 may have originated then, perhaps orally at first, within the first generation of Isaiah's disciples. B_2 arose considerably later; it bears the imprint of the Deuteronomic school. Hezekiah's prayer is suffused with language typical of the Deuteronomists. The role of the just king, for whose dynasty's sake Jerusalem is rescued, accords well with Dtr.'s evaluation of Hezekiah (cf. 18:5–6). Yet the hero is clearly the prophet Isaiah, who derides Sennacherib's hubris, paraphrasing the boasting of the Assyrian king. His speech echoes the Egyptian campaigns of Esarhaddon or Ashurbanipal (671 or 669 B.C.E.). This would suggest that

[9] For a full exposition, see C. Cohen, "Neo-Assyrian Elements in the First Speech of the Biblical Rab-šaqê," *IOS* 9 (1979), 32–48; and most recently P. Machinist, "Assyria and Its Image in the First Isaiah," *JAOS* 103 (1983), 719–37.

[10] Cf. e.g. Grayson, ARI 2.544, 546, 557, 561, 565; and Luckenbill, *ARAB* 2.54, 118, 142, 244–45, 557.

B_2, as well, originated within the circles of Isaiah's disciples, but two or three generations later than the prophet.

At what stage of transmission, then, were B_1 and B_2 amalgamated? In spite of the acute observations of Childs, this question cannot be satisfactorily answered. B_1 and B_2 could have been blended into a single account within prophetic circles, prior to its inclusion by the Deuteronomist in his history.[11] The story of Jerusalem's salvation in the composite B account, a prophetic prediction which had come true, easily found its place within a work, one of whose main schema was the "system of prophetic predictions and exactly noted fulfillments."[12]

Yet a third and final stage in the editorial process of the Sennacherib pericope can be distinguished. The factual notation on Sennacherib's assassination and the identity of his murderers and their place of refuge (in v. 37) could only have been derived from a Babylonian chronicle. Such chronicles, which recount the history of relations between Babylonia and Assyria, are Babylonian in origin and were extensively copied in the Neo-Babylonian period. It stands to reason that the late editor of Kings, who was responsible for the reworking of the Merodach-baladan tale (cf. esp. 20:16–19), excerpted this notation from a Babylonian chronicle.[13] Thus the Sennacherib pericope ends with yet another *topos,* the punishment of the Assyrian king for his hubris—the affronting of YHWH and his sacred city. In exactly the same manner as the biblical writer, the last Babylonian king, Nabonidus, justifies Sennacherib's murder: Sennacherib, who desecrated Babylon in 689 B.C.E. and carried off the Marduk statue to Assyria, is punished by Marduk, who "made his own son murder the king of Assyria."[14]

[11] There is nothing in 19:9, which bridges B_1 and B_2, to help identify the redactor of the two stories, unless the mention of Lachish at the end of v. 9 is assumed to derive from 18:14, source A. If so, Dtr. would be responsible for this cross-reference.

[12] G. von Rad, *Studies in Deuteronomy,* 78–83. Clements, in his recent work *Isaiah and the Deliverance of Jerusalem, JSOT* Sup Series 13 (1980), followed the analysis of Childs as to the separation of the "Isaiah narratives" into two accounts, B_1 and B_2. However, Clements attributes the miraculous salvation of Jerusalem in 19:35 to the final redactors who blended the two sometime during the Josianic Age. These redactors were also responsible for the emphasis placed upon the belief in the inviolability of Jerusalem and the divine protection of the Davidic dynasty, ideas which were "essentially an interpretation, made in the perspective of Josiah's reign, of events which had taken place more than half a century earlier in the reign of Hezekiah" (Clements, 85). However, the position adopted in this commentary is that the so-called "Zion traditions" were already embedded in the original Isaiah tradition (so also Childs, 50–63) and are not a retrospective religious interpretation of Deuteronomistic circles at the end of the seventh century (as Clements admits, 63).

[13] This editor also added "and in his own country, I will strike him down by the sword," in 19:7, so as to close the circle. Thus, as predicted by the prophet, the Assyrian was personally punished for his blasphemies.

[14] *ANET*[3], 309.

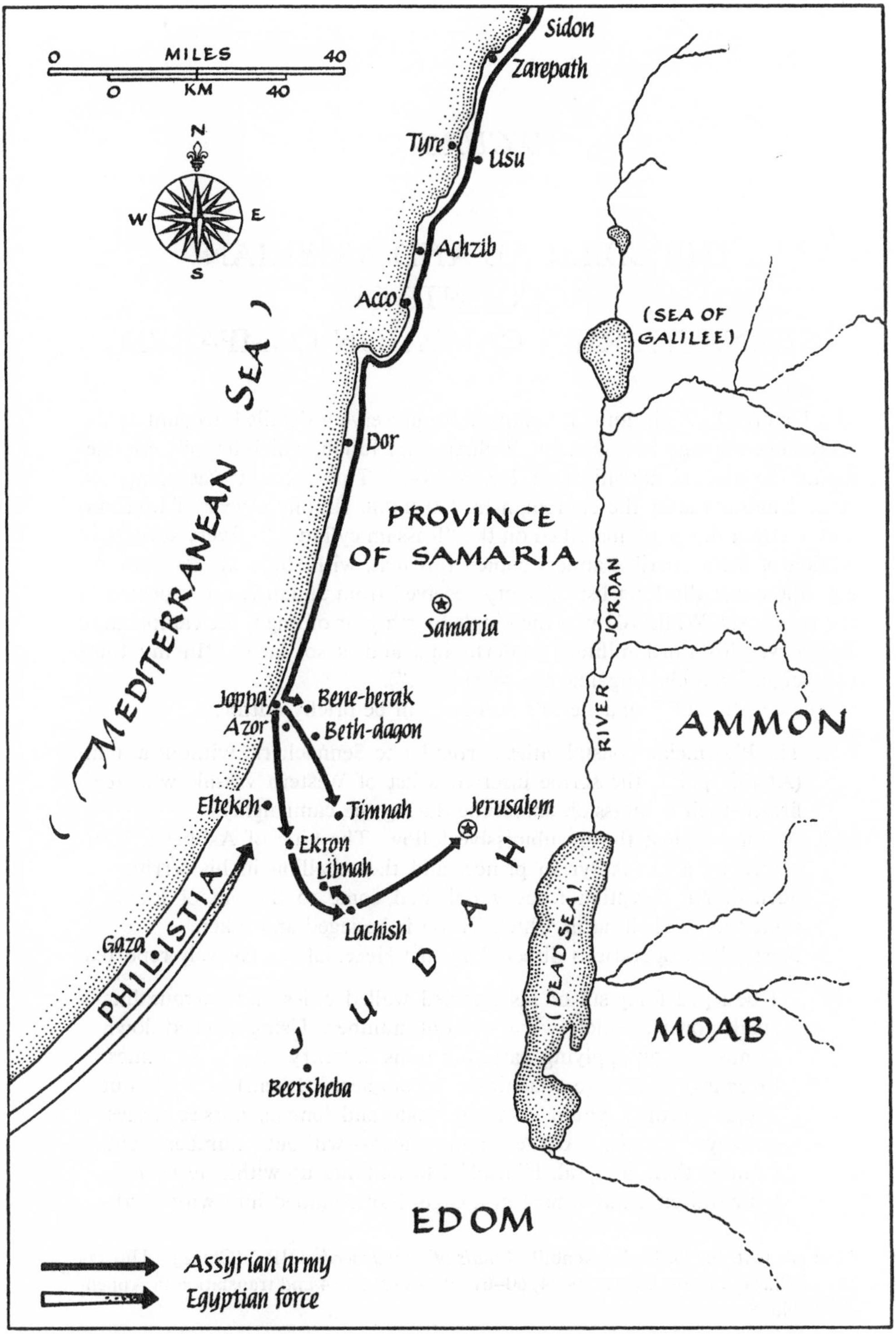

SENNACHERIB'S CAMPAIGN TO THE WEST
701 B.C.E.
2 KINGS 18:13–19:37

EXCURSUS

THE BIBLICAL AND ASSYRIAN ACCOUNTS OF SENNACHERIB'S CAMPAIGN COMPARED

The historical inscriptions of Sennacherib preserve a detailed account of the Assyrian campaign to Phoenicia, Philistia, and Judah, which happily complements the biblical narratives in 2 Kgs 18–19. This account was composed several months after the campaign in 700 B.C.E. (Eponym year of Metunu) and is extant in a copy inscribed on the "Rassam cylinder."[1] Every successive edition of Sennacherib's annals copied this text, with slight abbreviations—e.g., the unusually long list of booty received from Judah is not repeated in the later texts. While 701 was the king's fourth year of reign, the campaign to Judah was his third military undertaking, and is so dated ("In my third campaign, I marched against the West . . .").

The contents of Sennacherib's account can be briefly outlined:

1. The Phoenician coastal cities surrender to Sennacherib without a fight. (At this point, the scribe inserted a list of Western vassals who reaffirmed their submission sometime during the campaign.)
2. Actions against the unsubmissive follow. The king of Ashkelon is replaced by a pro-Assyrian prince, and the rebellion in his territory is quelled. An Egyptian force which had come to the aid of Ekron is routed at Eltekeh, after which Ekron is besieged and taken.
3. Next follow operations directed against Hezekiah, extensively reported:

> I besieged forty-six of his fortified walled cities and surrounding small towns, which were without number. Using packed-down ramps and by applying battering rams, infantry attacks by mines, breeches, and siege machines, I conquered (them). I took out 200,150 people, young and old, male and female, horses, mules, donkeys, camels, cattle, and sheep—without number—and counted them as spoil. Himself, I locked him up within Jerusalem, his royal city, like a bird in a cage. I surrounded him with earth-

[1] For the text, see D. D. Luckenbill, *Annals of Sennacherib,* OIP 2 (Chicago: University of Chicago Press, 1924), 29–34, 60–61; cf. *ARAB* 2.284 and translation in Appendix I, No. 8.

> works, and made it unthinkable (lit. "taboo") for him to exit the city gate.

These intense measures broke the back of Judaean resistance, and Hezekiah yielded. He paid a heavy tribute, which was not carried off immediately as booty, but delivered at a later time in Nineveh. (The late editions of Sennacherib's annals—the Taylor Prism and the Oriental Institute Prism—are the ones usually translated in collections of extrabiblical sources, e.g., *ANET*³, 288. But the list of tribute in these editions is much shorter than in the Rassam cylinder, translated here.)

> He sent me after my departure to Nineveh, my royal city, his elite troops (*urbi*) and his best soldiers—which he had brought into Jerusalem as reinforcements[2]—with 30 talents of gold, 800 talents of silver, choice antimony, large blocks of carnelian, beds (inlaid) with ivory, armchairs (inlaid) with ivory, elephant hides, ivory, ebony wood, boxwood, garments with multicolored trim, garments of linen, wool (dyed) red-purple and blue-purple, vessels of copper, iron, bronze and tin, chariots, siege shields, lances, armor, daggers for the belt, bows and arrows, countless trappings and implements of war, together with his daughters, his palace women, his male

[2] This translation is based on the reading *iršû tillāte* (OIP 2, 34:41). As pointed out by A. Ungnad, *ZA* 38 (1929), 196, this reading is to be preferred to *iršû baṭlāte,* "were left without work." *Baṭlāte* is a plural form of *baṭiltu* (cf. *CAD* B 176) and a *hapax legomenon* in Akkadian; whereas the Old Babylonian term *tillātu,* "help, auxiliary troops" (*AHw* 1358), though obsolete in the royal inscriptions of the first millennium, was still in use in the Omen literature of the period. So e.g. "the king will have auxiliary troops" (*tillāti iraššī*); E. Leichty, *The Omen Series Šumma Izbu* (Locust Valley, N.Y.: J. J. Augustin, 1970), 117:33; cf. similar omens 116:21, 118:43, 127:67. Thus the whole passage should be taken as a relative sentence—i.e. the elite troops were sent by Hezekiah with the heavy tribute to Nineveh. This translation was correctly recognized by W. F. Albright in his critique of *ANET*¹, in *JAOS* 71 (1951), 263; and so too E. Ebeling in H. Gressman, ed. *Altorientalische Texte zum Alten Testament* (2nd ed., Berlin and Leipzig: de Gruyter, 1926); D. J. Wiseman in *DOTT* 67 and R. Borger in K. Galling's *Textbuch zur Geschichte Israels* (2nd ed., Tübingen: J. C. B. Mohr, 1968), 69. Luckenbill's renderings in OIP 2 and *ARAB* 2.240 should be corrected accordingly.

As for *urbi,* "elite troops," the translation follows Theo Bauer *Inschriftenwerk Assurbanipals* (Leipzig: J. C. Hinrich 1933), 1, where the term is found parallel to LÚ *tebû,* "attack troops." Under no circumstances can *urbi* refer to Arabs, who are always rendered *Aribi* in cuneiform texts. See in detail I. Ephʿal, *JAOS* 94 (1974), 110. Tadmor, ("The Aramaization of Assyria," 454), suggests that *urbi* is a West Semitic loanword in Akkadian; cf. Hebrew *ʾōrēb,* Josh 8:12, 19:21; Judg 20:36–38; and Aramaic Ahiqar 99.

> and female singers. He (also) dispatched his personal messenger to deliver the tribute and to do obeisance.

> This list of tribute is the longest and the most detailed enumeration recorded in any of the Sennacherib inscriptions, and its inclusion suggests that the author of this account sought to underscore that even without taking Jerusalem, Hezekiah had been totally subdued and that Judah was once more an Assyrian vassal.

Shortly after the decipherment of the cuneiform inscription, the agreements and disagreements between the Assyrian and the biblical accounts became the subject of a scholarly debate which has continued up to the present without a consensus having been reached. As an example of agreement between the two accounts, one may compare the tribute rendered by Hezekiah (see the note to 18:14). The disagreements, on the other hand, are blatant and seemingly irreconcilable. Sennacherib's account claims that Hezekiah capitulated and was reduced to vassal status once again. The prophetic narratives in 2 Kgs 18–19 report that Sennacherib's army suffered a massive blow at the hand of YHWH and retreated from Judah.[3]

To resolve this most basic disagreement, the two-campaign theory has been proffered and upheld by such noted adherents as H. Winckler, R. W. Rogers, W. F. Albright and more recently J. Bright.[4] This theory suggests that the biblical account embraces data relating to two separate campaigns of Sennacherib to Judah. The campaign of 701 reported in Sennacherib's account and in 2 Kgs 18:13–16 ended in an Assyrian victory and a reassertion of hegemony over Judah. A second campaign to Judah, in the later years of Sennacherib (after the capture of Babylon in 689), for which no Assyrian records survive, ended in an Assyrian setback; Sennacherib suffered a defeat, retreated to Nineveh, and was assassinated shortly thereafter. This undated campaign is the one reported in the prophetic narratives in 18:17–19:37.

[3] Much stress has been placed on the reference to the Ethiopian king Tirhakah in 2 Kgs 19:9 as the army commander who engaged Sennacherib, for inasmuch as Tirhakah came to the throne in 690, he obviously could not have been king in 701. The publication of the Kawa texts and their interpretation as offered by Macadam suggested that Tirhakah was born in 710 and that at age twenty he was summoned to his brother Shebitku's side to serve as coregent for six years. W. F. Albright concluded that it was "impossible for him to take part in any military activity directed against the Assyrians until 688 or later" (*BASOR* 130 [1953], 9).

But a thorough reinvestigation by K. A. Kitchen of the chronology of the Nubian dynasty has led to new results. Tirhakah was crowned sole king in 690 and had already been of age in 701; thus he could have been at the head of the Egyptian forces which engaged Sennacherib at Eltekeh (Kitchen, *Third Intermediate Period,* 161–72). No disagreement exists, therefore, between 2 Kgs 19, which mentions Tirhakah, and the Rassam cylinder. (On his title "king of Ethiopia," see note to 19:9.)

[4] See Bright, *History*[3], 298–309, and the bibliography cited 298, n. 4.

The two-campaign theory has been criticized by the majority of commentators, and the present authors, as well, do not find it an acceptable solution to the problem of disagreeing sources. Its weaknesses are both historical and methodological.

1. A historical analysis of the reign of Sennacherib shows that the Assyrian monarch was not obliged to undertake a second campaign to the West after the impressive victory of 701. Hezekiah's rebellion stemmed from the special circumstances of the year 705; Sargon's death and the regaining of the throne of Babylon by Merodach-baladan had led to the high expectation that Assyrian might was collapsing. After Judah had been laid waste in the first campaign, what motivation can be suggested for a second rebellion by Hezekiah, especially if the supposed rebellion took place in the years immediately following the destruction of Babylon in 689? Babylon's fate surely served as a warning of what awaited the unsubmissive. It is hardly any wonder that Sennacherib did not have to campaign for close to a decade until his death. The world lay at Assyria's feet.

Furthermore, if Sennacherib had been forced to retreat shamefully from Judah—an embarrassing fact that the proponents of the two-campaign theory claim has been purged from Assyrian records—then Esarhaddon would have had to reconquer the West. But from Esarhaddon's inscriptions it is learned that Manasseh, king of Judah, was among the twelve Western kings who submitted to Esarhaddon early in his reign. Not even when Sennacherib was assassinated and inner strife flared up within Assyria did the vassal states rebel. The only conclusion is that there was but one Assyrian campaign to Judah and this in 701.[5]

2. Methodologically, the two-campaign theory misrepresents the evidence at hand. The sources—Sennacherib's annal account (the "Rassam cylinder"), the excerpt from the Judaean royal annals (18:13–16), the two prophetic narratives (B_1 and B_2)—are treated as if they were all of the same literary genre and of equal value in historical reconstruction. Thus the B_2 narrative which contains the story of a miraculous divine intervention on Hezekiah's behalf and which clearly evidences late reworking (e.g. 19:24) is treated as having the same degree of reliability as a chronicle or royal inscription.

3. The two-campaign theory also creates new problems while seeking answers to the old ones. The reader is asked to assume that events separated by at least twelve years have been telescoped into a single story; i.e. the report of Hezekiah's heavy tribute paid during the first campaign has been coordinated

[5] Winckler's suggestion (*Untersuchngen,* 36–38; cf. Bright, *History*[3], 309, n. 25) to take Sennacherib's raid upon the Arabs in 690 as evidence for further campaigning in the West cannot be sustained. The events took place prior to the fall of Babylon and apparently involved nomadic tribes west of Babylon who had supported the Chaldean rebels. The correct sequence of events is now presented byEphʿal, *The Ancient Arabs,* 112–25.

with prophetic stories which derive from Hezekiah's second rebellion. Is one also to assume that the Deuteronomistic historian thought to cover up Hezekiah's initial failure with the story of Sennacherib's retreat from Judah many years later? And if this is so, why did he mention the tribute payment at all?

The richness of literary evidence for the events of 701, as conflicting as it is, is no different from the sometimes contradictory reports that issue forth from modern-day battlefields and official government sources. Each report represents a partisan view and is grist for the historian's mill. These sources may be utilized in historical reconstructions only after having been analyzed critically, using tools appropriate to their literary categories.

Another ancient story, that related by Herodotus concerning Sennacherib's retreat from Egypt, has often been brought into discussions concerning the campaign of 701. Opinions range from seeing in it "without doubt" an account parallel to 2 Kgs 18–19,[6] to others who hold it to be "somewhat dubious."[7] The story tells of "Sennacherib, king of the Arabs and Assyrians," who came against Egypt with a large army. While encamped at Pelusium,

> one night, a multitude of field mice swarmed over the Assyrian camp and devoured their quivers and their bows and the handles of their shields likewise, insomuch that they fled the next day unarmed and many fell. And at this day a statue of the Egyptian king stands in Hephaestus' temple, with a mouse in his hand, and an inscription to this effect: "Look on me, and fear the gods."[8]

Josephus, while relating this story, notes that Herodotus "is in error, calling him king of the Arabs, instead of king of the Assyrians."[9] This criticism can now be extended. Not only was Sennacherib not king of the Arabs, but he never conducted a campaign as far as the border of Egypt, certainly not in 701. It was Sennacherib's son, Esarhaddon, who first attacked Egypt in 674/73, and as related in the Babylonian Chronicle:

> On the fifth day of Adar, the Assyrian army was defeated in Egypt.[10]

It was this defeat at the entrance of Egypt, as S. Smith astutely observed, which lived on in Egyptian memory.[11] In addition, as Esarhaddon himself records, the Arabs of northern Sinai had led the Assyrian army to watering holes and thus made possible a second, this time successful campaign against

[6] So Montgomery-Gehman, 497–98; cf. Gray, 694.
[7] Bright, *History*³, 288.
[8] Herodotus, Book II, 141.
[9] Josephus, *Antiquities* x.19.
[10] Cf. Grayson, *Chronicles*, 84:16.
[11] S. Smith, *CAH*¹ 3.74, 85.

Egypt in 671.[12] This cooperation would explain the strange combination of "Arabs and Assyrians" in the title of the king given by Herodotus.

Moreover, the focal point of the story, the destruction of the Assyrian arms by mice, is far from being a trustworthy historical datum. Those who would coordinate the biblical account and Herodotus, interpret both in rationalistic terms. Mice are traditional carriers of plagues; thus it was the outbreak of a plague within the Assyrian camp which caused the death of 185,000 men—this despite the distance which separates Jerusalem and Pelusium. As has been pointed out by classical scholars, mice were a symbol of the plague in Greek folklore and the god Apollo Smintheus (lit. "mouse") was depicted with a mouse in his hand. All of which suggests that Herodotus recast his "Egyptian" material in Greek terms.[13]

Methodologically, however, the question to be posed is not so much the connection between the two accounts, but rather: What was the source of the Herodotus story? Was his source indeed "Egyptian" or were his informants Greeks settled in Egypt who "transferred to an Egyptian statue an interpretation familiar (to them) from their homeland"[14]? Recently, A. Rofé has raised the possibility that the Herodotus story is an echo of the Jerusalem story. Considering that in the literature of the Second Temple period, the motif of Sennacherib's defeat at the hand of YHWH's angel continued to develop, perhaps Jewish immigrants brought the story to Egypt, where its focal point was transferred to Egypt.[15]

From all this, it is clear that Herodotus's account has nothing to do with Sennacherib's invasion of Judah, but is a later reflection either of Esarhaddon's campaign against Egypt, or Sennacherib's failure recorded in the legendary account in 2 Kings.

Finally, considering the nature of the sources, a reconstruction of the route of Sennacherib's advance on Judah, viz., the sequence of attacks upon Judaean settlements, and the timing of the encounter with the Egyptian forces at Eltekeh, is presently unachievable. Too many particulars remain unknown —e.g., the size of the armies and their outfitting, the defense preparations undertaken in anticipation of the Assyrian attack—all of which determined the logistics on the battlefield.[16]

[12] Cf. *ANET³*, 292b.

[13] See the discussion by W. Baumgartner, "Herodots babylonische und assyrische Nachrichten," in *Zum Alten Testament und seiner Umwelt* (Leiden: Brill, 1959), 306.

[14] Baumgartner, op cit., 308.

[15] Rofé, *Israelite Belief in Angels*, 217; and see the note to 19:35 above.

[16] The arrows presented on the map on page 245 are meant to suggest only the general direction of the Assyrian advance. Among the recent attempts to sketch this advance, see N. Na'aman, *VT* 29 (1979), 61–86; K. A. Kitchen, "Egypt, the Levant and Assyria in 701 B.C." in *Fontes Atque Pontes*, Festschrift for H. Brunner, Ägypten und Altes Testament 5 (Wiesbaden, 1983), 243–53.

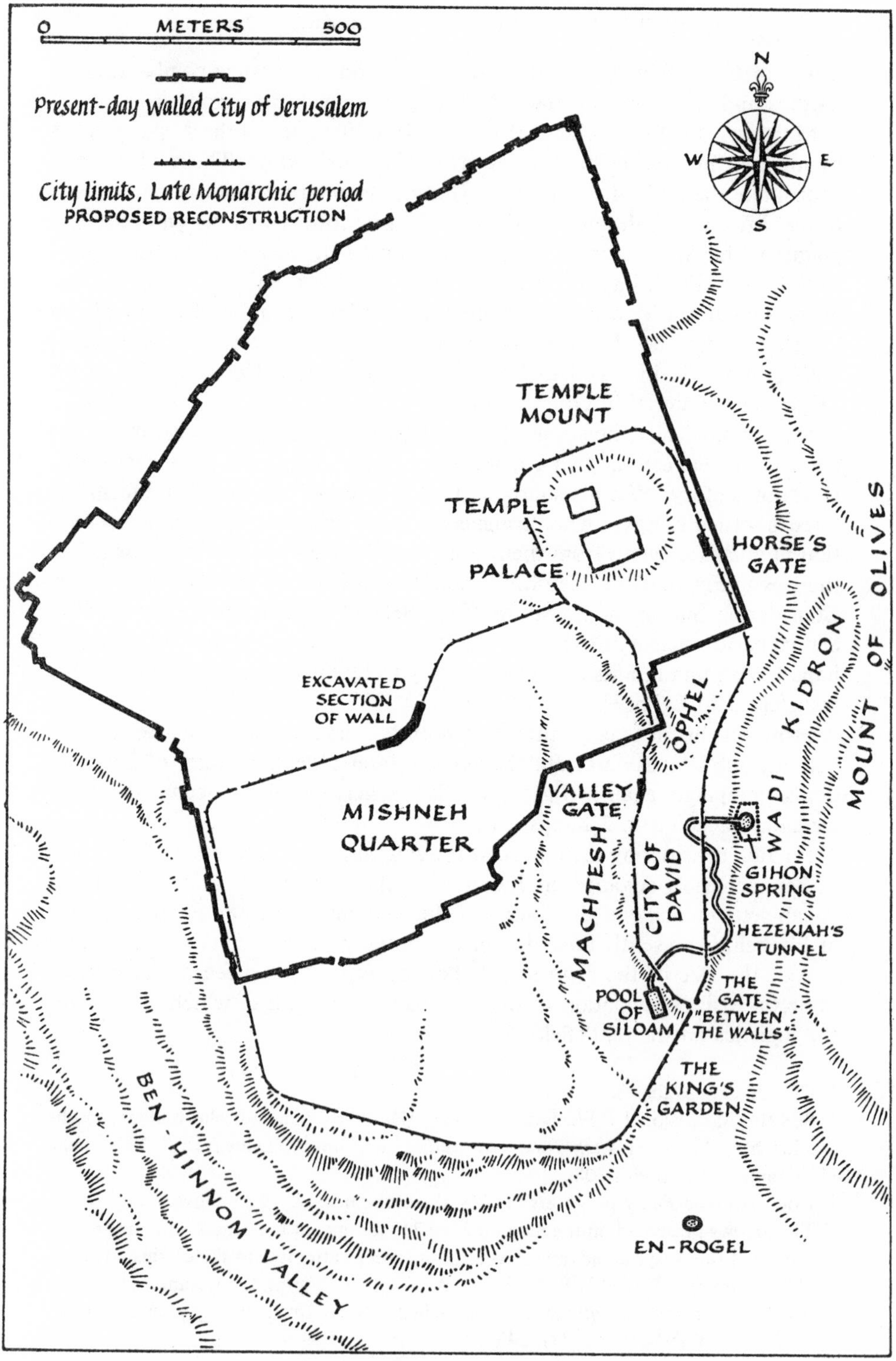

JERUSALEM IN THE
8TH AND 7TH CENTURIES B.C.E.

XXXIII. HEZEKIAH'S ILLNESS AND RECOVERY

(20:1–11)

20 1 In those days, Hezekiah became mortally ill. The prophet Isaiah
son of Amoz came to him and said to him, "Thus said YHWH, 'Prepare your testament, for you are about to die; you shall not recover.' "
2 Whereupon he turned toward the wall and prayed to YHWH,
3 "Please, O YHWH, remember how I served you faithfully and loyally,
and did what was pleasing to you." And Hezekiah wept bitterly.
4 Isaiah had not left the middle courtyard,[a] when the word of YHWH
came to him: 5 "Return and say to Hezekiah, ruler of my people, 'Thus
said YHWH, God of David your ancestor: I have heard your prayer; I
have seen your tears. Now, then, I will heal you. Within three days
you shall go up to the House of YHWH. 6 I will add fifteen years to
your life. I will save you and this city from the hand of the king of
Assyria, and I will protect this city, for my own sake and for the sake
of David my servant.' " 7 Then Isaiah said, "Fetch a fig cake." They
brought one and placed it upon the boil and he recovered. 8 Hezekiah
said to Isaiah, "What is the sign[b] that YHWH will heal me and that
within three days I shall go up to the House of YHWH?" 9 Isaiah
replied, "This will be the sign for you from YHWH, that YHWH will
perform what he promised: The shadow has moved ahead ten steps;
can it return ten steps?" 10 Hezekiah said, "It is easy for the shadow to
lengthen ten steps; not so for it to go back ten steps." 11 So the prophet
Isaiah called to YHWH, and He moved the shadow back the ten steps
which <the sun>[c] had gone down on the Ahaz dial.

[a] Read *hâṣēr* with qere, mss. versions; MT *hāʿîr,* "the city."
[b] Read *hāʾôt.* Cf. LXX; *hē* lost through haplography.
[c] Add *haššemmeš;* cf. Isa 38:8 and see note.

Notes

20 1. *In those days.* Heb. *bayyāmîm hāhēm,* an editorial phrase, like "then," "at that time," "in his days," which links narrative units originally independent. It was suggested above, 18:13, that "in the fourteenth year" formerly stood at the head of the present pericope. See discussion, ad loc.

2. *Prepare your testament.* Heb. *ṣaw lĕbêtekā,* lit. "give instructions concerning your household"; cf. 2 Sam 17:23 and 1 Kgs 2:1 (with *ʾet* rather than *ʾel*). In Mishnaic Hebrew, the noun *ṣāwāʾâ* is used regularly for dispositions and verbal wills (Jastrow, *Dictionary,* 1265).

you shall not recover. Heb. *wĕloʾ tiḥyeh,* lit. "you shall not live." **ḥāyâ* indicates restoration to health after critical illness, e.g. 1 Kgs 17:22.

toward the wall. Hezekiah turned away from whoever was present in the room in order to obtain solitude. Cf. 1 Kgs 21:4.

3. *I served you faithfully and loyally.* Hezekiah's very short prayer is composed entirely of Dtr. phraseology. See Weinfeld, *Deuteronomy,* 333–35. The usual idiom *hālak bĕderek* PN, "followed the ways of PN." is replaced here by *hithallēk lipnê,* lit. "walked before." Speiser recognized that the *hithpael* form has a durative sense, indicating iterative and habitual behavior (Speiser, *Genesis,* AB, ad 5:22 and idem, *Oriental and Biblical Studies,* 505–14).

The Hebrew idiom can be fully appreciated through comparison with its Akkadian counterpart. As Muffs penetratingly observed, *ina maḫar* PN *ittanallaku šalmeš,* lit. "to walk constantly before PN loyally," said of royal and temple servants, expresses the quality of their service. Such service, loyally performed, is rewarded by kings through grants of land and by the gods through grants of blessing and long life (Y. Muffs, *Studies in Aramaic Legal Papyri from Elephantine* [Leiden: Brill, 1969], 203–4). In Biblical Hebrew, *hithallēk lipnê* describes man's constant and faithful service of YHWH (cf. Gen 24:40, 48:15) and is usually followed by a request for reward.

In this verse, Hezekiah prays for recovery from his illness, but the request is unspoken. It is implicit, however, in the idiom chosen on this occasion. For other expressions of service, *ʿāmad lipnê,* "stood before," cf. 1 Kgs 1:2; *rāṣ lipnê,* "ran before," cf. 1 Kgs 1:5. Cf. also M. Weinfeld *JAOS* 90 (1970), 186.

4. *the middle courtyard.* The graphic corruption of *hāṣēr* to *hāʿîr* was shown by H. Orlinsky to be post-LXX (*JQR* 30 [1939–40], 34–39). The MT reading is not supported by the known topography of Jerusalem, as there was no quarter called "middle city." On the structure of the temple courts, cf. 1 Kgs 6:36.

5. *ruler of my people.* The term *nāgîd,* "ruler," is an archaism. It is common in the historical literature of the early monarchic period (1 Sam 9:16, 10:1; 2 Sam 5:2, 6:21, 7:8; 1 Kgs 1:35). Dtr. employs *nāgîd* with reference to Hezekiah because of its association with David. See Comment to 1 Kgs 1:35.

Within three days. This formulaic expression designates the completion of a short span of time, and is especially common in prose tales. The prophet Hosea promised quick and full recovery of battered Israel using the same expression; cf. Hos 6:1–2. Y. Zakovitch analyzed the formula in *The Pattern of the Numerical Sequence Three-Four in the Bible,* Ph.D. dissertation, Hebrew University, 1977, 1–37 (Hebrew).

6. *I will save you and this city.* The promise of rescue does not make sense in the present context, for both Hezekiah and Jerusalem had been rescued in the preceding chapter. Neither does the suggestion of many commentators (e.g. Šanda, Montgomery-Gehman) that v. 6 contains partial glosses based upon 19:34 answer the problem. Even a glossator would have seen that his words were superfluous after the reported destruction of the Assyrian army and Sennacherib's retreat. It should be noted that the phraseology of the verse relates well with v. 5, both echoing the favored status of the Davidic dynasty, and thus seems to be integral to the unit. It is probable, therefore, that the story of Hezekiah's illness originally preceded the narrative of Sennacherib's campaign and that it contained a prophecy of personal as well as national salvation. Later the story was removed to its present position in chapter 20. (See Comment for further discussion of editorial revisions and suggested date of the events.)

7. *Fetch a fig cake.* The evidence from Jewish and classical sources on the widely held belief that dried figs had medicinal qualities is collected in J. Feliks, *Plant World of the Bible,* 38 (Hebrew). For Ug. *dblt,* "fig cakes," used both as condiments and as a therapeutic, see now C. Cohen and D. Sivan, AOS 9, 40–41.

They . . . placed it upon the boil. Heb. *šĕḥîn* embraces a wide category of skin diseases. Because of the reported seriousness of Hezekiah's illness, the *šĕḥîn* from which he suffered has been diagnosed as Pemphigus, a disease characterized by severe blistering. See J. Leibovich, *EncMiqr* 7.421–22.

and he recovered. The prophet's therapeutic act was indeed effective, judging from the use of *wayyeḥî,* with *waw*-consecutive (cf. note to v. 1). But this fact does not coordinate well with the following request by Hezekiah for a "sign that YHWH will heal me." Medieval exegetes suggested distinguishing between Isaiah's act, performed out of sympathy for the ailing king and which only alleviated the suffering and the real cure, which was in God's hands (cf. Qimḥi, Abarbanel, ad loc.).

Modern translators resort to setting off v. 7 from the rest of the narrative (so e.g. *NJPS*) or translate the verb as anticipatory "that he may recover" (so e.g. *NAB*). But the most natural way to take the verse is as translated—"and he recovered"—and to understand it as a second tradition, one in which Isaiah appears as a healer and wonder-worker, in the style of Elijah and Elisha. That this is the plain sense of the text can be seen from the position of the verse in the parallel text in Isa 38. There the healing act was removed to the end of the story, after the miracle of the sundial, and set as the last act in the drama; cf. v. 21.

9. *The shadow has moved ahead ten steps; can it return ten steps?* As in other instances involving a prophetic sign, the attention of the audience is directed to the miraculous by posing a question (cf. Num 20:10; Ezek 37:3). Thus Isaiah asks, "The shadow has already moved ten degrees, just as your life has passed and you are near death. Let me ask you and tell me: Is it natural for the shadow to turn back ten degrees, which you should compare to your returning to life and health and moving about, unlike the death you are approaching, for another fifteen years?" (so Abarbanel; cf. earlier Josephus, *Antiquities* x.28). Many other commentators take MT *hlk* as if it were *hylk,* interpreting the entire sentence as a question.

10. *It is easy for the shadow to lengthen.* Heb. **nāṭâ* is used to describe the increasing length of the shadows as the afternoon approaches; cf. Judg 19:8; Jer 6:4.

11. *which the sun had gone down.* The verb *yārĕdâ,* "went down," third feminine sing., requires a feminine noun. The parallel text in Isa 38:8, although a bit garbled, twice refers to the feminine noun *šemeš,* "sun," as moving back and forth, thus caus-

ing a change in the length of the shadow. *Šemeš* is supplied in the present verse from Isaiah.

the Ahaz dial. All commentators agree that *maʿălôt ʾāḥāz,* "steps/degrees of Ahaz," is to be understood as a device by which the hours of the day were read as the sun moved across the sky. Targ. Vulg., LXX to Isa 38:8 and the Qumran scroll IQ Isa[a] read *bmʿlt ʿlyt ʾḥz* "on the dial of the Ahaz roof chamber," which has been taken as a reference to a sundial associated with the structure erected by Ahaz for worship of the astral deities. Cf. 2 Kgs 23:12 and the view of S. Iwry, "The Qumran Isaiah and the End of the Dial of Ahaz," *BASOR* 147 (1957), 27–33. That the dial was in fact incorporated within the structural features of the roof chamber was suggested by Yadin, who compared it to a model of a house excavated in Egypt which contained two flights of stairs used for telling time (Y. Yadin, "The Dial of Ahaz," *EI* 5 [1958], 91–96).

Comment

The exposition of the story of Hezekiah's illness is rendered difficult because of several inconsistencies within the narrative; their clarification sheds light on the editing of Kings as a whole. After announcing impending death to Hezekiah, Isaiah returns to correct his prophecy: Hezekiah will recover and will be granted fifteen additional years of life. The prophet proceeds to treat the king's disease with a fig cake, and "he recovered" (v. 7). Hezekiah then asks, "What is the sign that YHWH will heal me?"—to which Isaiah responds with a sign associated with the movements of the shadow on the sundial atop the roof structure erected by Hezekiah's father Ahaz. The inner logic of the story is disturbed by v. 7, for if the king had indeed recovered, there is little warrant to ask for a sign of future healing. The parallel text in Isa 38 offers help.

2 Kgs 20:1–6	‖	Isa 38:1–6
20:7–8	‖	38:21–22
20:9–11	‖	38:7–8
———		38:9–20

Two significant variants appear in Isa 38:

1. A psalm of thanksgiving, vv. 9–20, ascribed to Hezekiah, is recited by him upon recovery. These verses are lacking in 2 Kgs 20. Moreover, this is one of the rare instances outside the Psalter where a personality other than David is the author of a psalm; cf. the prayer of Hannah in 1 Sam 2:1–10.

2. 2 Kgs 20:7–8 (in a shortened form) stand as the last verses in Isa 38:21–22. Verse 22 is a fragment of a verse, as compared with 2 Kgs 20:8, and no longer makes sense in the rearranged story of Isa 38. Is it possible to suggest which text, Kings or Isaiah, was committed to writing first? Isa 38:22 proves that the *Vorlage* with which the Isaiah editor worked must have been similar

to the text of Kings. The rearrangement in Isaiah sought to smooth out the difficulty of 2 Kgs 20:7 noted above, by removing it to the end of the chapter; therefore the text of Kings is earlier. The editor of Isaiah was apparently not prepared to forego the fig-cake tradition altogether.

Returning now to 2 Kgs 20, if v. 7 were to be deleted, a consistent story would be obtained, with the language of v. 5 picked up again in v. 8 ("heal," "third day," "go up to the House of YHWH."). Consequently, the tradition in v. 7 concerning Hezekiah's illness, in which Isaiah is represented as active in healing the sick king, using the marvelous means of a fig cake (not unlike similar marvels told of Elijah and Elisha) may be taken as independent of the remainder of the narrative.

But even after recognizing the literary autonomy of the fig-cake tradition, its position within 2 Kgs 20 still remains problematic. Did Dtr. simply set the two stories at his disposal back to back, without attempting to join them editorially? Such simple collocation is not unparalleled in other biblical texts; cf. the two "first" meetings of Saul with David and the two introductions of David, 1 Sam 16:18–23 and 17:55–58. Or did Dtr. understand the stories as two stages in Hezekiah's recovery (stage 1, in which Isaiah performs a symbolic act, followed by stage 2, a God-sent healing marked by the sundial sign)? Whatever the case, the editor of Isaiah did not find Dtr.'s solution for the placement of the two traditions acceptable and so reworked his text accordingly.[1]

[1] The problem of comprehending the sequence of events may be behind the curious omission of Isa 38:21 (2 Kgs 20:7) from the Qumran scroll IQ Isa[a]. A later scribe, in another hand, added the missing verse in the margin. Was the omission due to homoioteleuton (cf. S. Talmon, *Qumran and the History of the Biblical Text* [Cambridge, Mass.: Harvard University Press, 1975], 330) or can it be inferred that the *Vorlage* of the Qumran scroll of Isaiah lacked the fig-cake tradition (cf. Y. Zakovitch, *Beth Mikra* 17 [1972], 302–5)? The Isaiah text, shown above to be secondary, may have circulated in both a shorter and a longer version, but this does not prove that a text of Kings without the fig-cake tradition was also in circulation. All ancient versions of Kings, especially LXX, resemble MT; and there is no evidence at Qumran to support the suggestion that the text of Kings was still fluid at so late a date as the Qumran Isaiah.

XXXIV. THE EMBASSY OF MERODACH-BALADAN

(20:12–21)

20 12 At that time, Merodach-baladan[a] son of Baladan, king of Babylon, sent letters and a gift to Hezekiah, for he had heard that Hezekiah
had taken ill. 13 Hezekiah was pleased[b] with them and he showed the
envoys[c] his entire storehouse—the silver, the gold, the spices and the
fine oil, his armory, and everything in his treasuries. There was not a
thing in his residence or in his realm that Hezekiah did not show
them.

14 Then Isaiah the prophet came to King Hezekiah and asked him,
"What did these men say? And from where did they come to you?"
Hezekiah replied, "They came from a distant land, from Babylon."
15 And he said, "What did they see in your residence?" Hezekiah said,
"They saw everything in my residence. There was not a thing in my
treasuries that I did not show them." 16 Thereupon Isaiah said to
Hezekiah, "Hear the word of YHWH, 17 'Now, in days to come, everything in your residence and that which your ancestors have amassed
up until today shall be carried off to Babylon. Nothing shall be left
behind,' said YHWH. 18 And some of your very own offspring, whom
you will have fathered, will be taken captive[d] to serve as eunuchs in
the palace of the king of Babylon." 19 Hezekiah said to Isaiah, "The
word of YHWH which you announced is just." For he thought: At least
there will be peace and security in my lifetime.

20 The rest of the history of Hezekiah and all his exploits, and how
he constructed the pool and the conduit to bring water into the city,
are indeed recorded in the annals of the kings of Judah. 21 So Hezekiah
slept with his ancestors and Manasseh his son succeeded him.

[a] So with mss. and Isa 39:1; MT *Berodach.*
[b] Read *wyśmḥ* for *wyšmʿ,* with Isa 39:2; some mss., Luc., LXX, Vulg., Syr.
[c] Lit. "them."
[d] Ketib: *yqḥ;* qere: *yiqqāḥû,* so in Isa 39:7. Final *waw* lost in ketib through haplography.

Notes

20 12. *Merodach-baladan, son of Baladan, king of Babylon.* A Chaldean prince of the Bit-Yakin tribe of southern Babylonia, Marduk-apla-iddina was king in Babylonia from 722–710 (during the days of Sargon II of Assyria) and for nine months in 704–703. The history of his rule is the subject of the comprehensive study by J. A. Brinkman, "Merodach-Baladan II," *Studies Presented to A. Leo Oppenheim,* 6–53.

The name of his father is unattested in cuneiform sources. The Hebrew "son of Baladan" may be an abbreviated form of a name whose theophoric element has been lost through haplography, thus *bn<nb>bldn,* "son of <Nabu>baladan." A. R. Millard reads the name as Bēl-iddin(a), a name attested in a late Aramaic endorsement as *blʾdn* (*Tyndale Bulletin* 21 [1971], 125–26).

13. *Hezekiah was pleased with them.* The reading of Isa 39:2 is not only attested in all the versions and some mss. to the present verse, but it suits the context better (Ehrlich); *wyšmʿ* looks like "a scribe's mistake . . . who erred in hearing *ʿayin* in the very next word *ʿlyhm*" (Luzzatto).

his entire storehouse. Heb. *bêt nĕkōtô.* A hapax legomenon, apparently an Akk. loan word, *bīt nakkamti,* "store, treasure house" (see *AHw* 721b–722a; and for references and discussion, Cohen, *Biblical Hapax Legomena* 40, 67, nn. 110, 112). Considering that BH attests to the native term *ʾôṣār,* "treasury," the borrowing of a foreign word would seem to be redundant and therefore puzzling. In the context of Assyrian royal inscriptions, *bīt nakkamti* was a depository for the booty of foreign campaigns. Perhaps the term signifies a particular Assyrian architectural style, which was borrowed by Hezekiah in constructing the depository for his vast treasures (cf. 2 Chr 32:27).

the fine oil. Rabbinic commentators thought that the reference here was to the balsam, for the production of which the Jordan Valley was renowned (cf. Rashi, Qimḥi, NEB, NJPS: "fragrant oil.").

his armory. Heb. *bêt kēlāyw,* another unique term, associated only with Hezekiah's Jerusalem. The Sargonid kings of Assyria built special armories (*ēkal māšarti*) which enclosed vast complexes for storing and training purposes. (On these buildings, their construction and use, see G. Turner, *Iraq* 32 [1970], 68–85.) Was this building another borrowing by Hezekiah under the strong impact of Assyrian imperial style?

17–19. The language of the prophecy and the king's reaction is that of Jeremiah, not Isaiah. Note, in particular, "in days to come" (Jer 7:32, 9:24, 16:14, 19:6, et al.; not once in Isaiah); "which your ancestors amassed" (cf. Jer 20:5; cf. 15:13, 17:3); "peace and security" (Jer 14:13, 33:6). For other indications of the late, post-Dtr. nature of this scene, see Comment below.

18. *some of your very own offspring, whom you will have fathered.* The verse contains a doublet, thus producing a poetic line. For MT *ʾšr yṣʾw mmk,* IQ Isa^{a} reads: *ʾšr yṣʾw mmʿk,* lit. "who will issue from your loins." This reading was already anticipated by Stade and preferred by Burney, Šanda, and Gray. But the Hebrew text echoes the promise to Abraham that "from you shall go forth" (*mmk yṣʾw*) kingly descendants (cf. Gen 17:6).

19. *"The word of* YHWH *which you announced is just."* Hezekiah appears at first to be piously resigned to the fate determined for him by YHWH. Cf. the reaction of Eli in

1 Sam 3:18. But the explication of his statement (note the second *wayyʾōmer*) is far from complimentary.

At least there will be peace and security in my lifetime. Heb. *hălôʾ ʾim,* lit. "Is it not so that." In Isa 39:8, the word *kî* substitutes for the somewhat awkward construction of 2 Kgs, clearly bringing out the asseverative force of the statement. The resignation to divine will is here interpreted as based, not upon humility, but upon Hezekiah's self-concern: "At least I will be spared the stern consequences of my act."

20. *the pool and the conduit to bring water into the city.* The Siloam tunnel, part of Hezekiah's fortification of Jerusalem in preparation for his war against Assyria, is discussed in the Comment to 18:1–12. The course of the tunnel and the task involved in its drilling are studied by Ruth Amiran, in *Jerusalem Revealed* (Jerusalem: Israel Exploration Society, 1975), 75–78.

21. The concluding statement on Hezekiah's death is filled out in Luc: "and he was buried with his fathers in the City of David," while Chronicles reports his burial "in the upper part of the graves of David's sons" (2 Chr 32:33). Cf. similar statements in 2 Kgs 8:24; 15:38; 16:20.

Comment

1. The nature of the embassy from distant Babylonia has intrigued ancient and modern commentators alike; all agree that more than meets the eye is behind the statement that the Babylonians came to visit the ailing Hezekiah. The Chronicler reasoned that whereas the Babylonians were famed for their interest in astronomy and astrology, they naturally came to inquire about the wondrous retreat of the shadow (cf. 2 Chr 32:31). Josephus, perhaps basing himself upon Berossus, speculated that the King of Babylon sent envoys . . . "to Hezekiah and invited him to become his ally and friend."[1] This approach, which has adherents down to this day, looks for corroborative evidence in the history of Merodach-baladan. Since he was Assyria's constant foe, the visit to Judah is to be viewed within the wider political context of his anti-Assyrian activity.

What is the record of Merodach-baladan vis-à-vis Assyria? Merodach-baladan came to the throne after the death of Shalmaneser V in 722 and remained the unchallenged king of Babylonia, backed by the Elamites, until 710. In that year Sargon invaded Babylonia and after several months routed both the Chaldean army and their Elamite supporters. Merodach-baladan fled, and Sargon assumed the throne. Sargon's death on the battlefield in 705 was seized upon by Assyria's antagonists. After a month's reign by the virtually unknown Marduk-zakir-šumi, Merodach-baladan regained the throne of Babylonia. According to Babylonian King List A, he reigned nine months.[2]

[1] Josephus, *Antiquities* x.30.

[2] See A. K. Grayson, RLA 6.93, line 14.

Sennacherib's first campaign, 704–703,[3] put an end to this short reign and to Merodach-baladan's hold on the south.

If indeed the Merodach-baladan embassy to Hezekiah had political aims, during which of his two terms as king of Babylon did it occur? It is unlikely that Merodach-baladan would have had the occasion to instigate rebellions, or for that matter to initiate a state visit of the sort described, while fighting for his life in 704–703 against the massive Assyrian attack. It is more reasonable to place the embassy during the period of his first reign, when he "enjoyed a ten-year respite from interference from the north."[4]

At this point, the biblical tradition of Hezekiah's "fourteenth year" should be considered once again. It has already been argued above that the date "in the fourteenth year" (18:13) is integral to the illness tradition in 20:1–11, rather than to the stories of Sennacherib's campaign to Judah. The embassy of the Babylonian king, whatever its background might have been, is intrinsically linked to this tradition. Thus the date of Hezekiah's fourteenth year, 713, emerges as the date of Merodach-baladan's embassy.[5] The year 713 was the year during which plans for rebellion were being fomented by Ashdod, and there are indications in Assyrian sources and in the prophecies of Isaiah that Judah was involved in these plans.[6] That Babylonia was a coconspirator

[3] It is commonly held that Sennacherib was recognized as king of Babylon for two years, 704–703. However, the passage in the Babylonian Chronicle is broken and all that can be read is: "Year 2 . . . [ ]" (cf. Grayson, *Chronicles,* 76:12). This passage may be restored (in accord with formulaic usage): "For two years, there was no king [in Babylon]." Cf. Grayson, *Chronicles,* 81:28. If so, the Chronicle would reflect the same tradition of chaos in the land of Babylon, without recognizing the Assyrian Sennacherib as king as that recorded in the Ptolemaic Canon, which reads here: *abasileuta*—"kingless period, two years."

In accord with this suggestion is L. D. Levine's study of Sennacherib's first campaign, which raises the possibility that Sennacherib began his thrust against Babylonia in 704 and which lasted thirteen months (*JCS* 34 [1982], 28–58).

[4] Brinkman, in *Studies Presented to Oppenheim,* 13. Sennacherib engaged Merodach-baladan once more in 700, when the Chaldean prince fled to the swamps in the direction of the Persian Gulf and "was never heard of again" (OIP 2.85:7–10). For the idiom *šadāšu ēmid,* "disappear forever," see *CAD* E 140a.

[5] For details, see the discussion in the note to 18:13, above. A recent study by A. K. Jenkins (*VT* 26 [1979], 284–98) of the "fourteenth year" date concludes that the tradition of the deliverance of Jerusalem belongs to the reign of Sargon and the period of the revolt of Ashdod. This requires the assumption that the actual circumstances of the year 712 were forgotten in one or two generations, to be transferred to Sennacherib, of whom it was known that he defeated Hezekiah. But such misinterpretation would indeed be odd.

[6] After deposing the Assyrian appointee Aḫimetu, the rebel Iamani of Ashdod sent to "the rulers of Philistia, Judah, Edom and Moab . . ." as well as to Egypt to join him in resisting Sargon (see *ANET*[3], 287a; *ARAB* 2.195). That Judah and its king Hezekiah did become involved is reflected in the oracle from the year of the Assyrian

cannot be said for sure; at the very least Merodach-baladan would have given his blessing to the enterprise.

Returning to the question raised at the outset as to the nature of the embassy, there is no hint in the story that its purpose was to instigate rebellion. Its mission was the maintenance of diplomatic good will with the strongest of Assyria's western vassals. Judah apparently was still free to conduct relations with its neighbors, and the Babylonians—who probably travelled to the West by the Arabian desert route rather than the north-Syrian–Damascus route—may have been interested in promoting trade in the West through the brokerage of their Arab allies.[7] Comparable to the Babylonian embassy would be the visit of the queen of Sheba, probably economic in purpose, but certainly not lacking political implications (see Comment on 1 Kgs 10:1–10).

2. The story of Hezekiah's illness appeared, in all likelihood, as the first of two blocks of prophetic traditions, and it carried the date "in the fourteenth year." In that critical year, as conceived by the Deuteronomist of Josiah's age, Hezekiah faced two crises: illness and war. Regarding the illness, Isaiah worked wonders and the king recovered, with fifteen years being added to his life. Faced with the threat of war with Assyria, the prophet advised Hezekiah of YHWH's determination to rescue Jerusalem and its Davidic ruler. At a later stage in the growth of the book of Kings, the illness story was removed to its present position in 2 Kgs 20, giving precedence to Sennacherib's campaign (18:13b–19:37). The date "in the fourteenth year" was left in place and the editorial phrases "in those days," and "at that time" tied the rearranged narratives together. When could such a transposition have taken place and for what purpose? The conclusion of 2 Kgs 20 holds the editorial key. Verses 17–19, in particular, are critical of Hezekiah and clearly lay the blame for the spoliation of Jerusalem and the exile of the royal family at his feet. This criticism must derive from the hand of the late Deuteronomist (Dtr_2), inasmuch as it contradicts the image developed by Dtr_1 of the faithful King Hezekiah, ever loyal to YHWH. The punishment for unseemly pride as announced by Isaiah is directed toward the king and his family, and does not hint either at the destruction of Jerusalem or exile for Judah. Such critical reinterpretation of Hezekiah may, therefore, reasonably be dated to the initial

Ashdod campaign in Isa 20, which was to serve as a warning against foreign entanglements. And it is still possible that the "Azekah Inscription" (BM 82-2-23, 131) joined to K.6205 by N. Na'aman (*BASOR* 214 [1974], 25–39) belongs to the reign of Sargon and to the events on the border of Judah in 712. For the earlier discussion, see H. Tadmor, *JCS* 12 (1958), 79–84 and A. Spalinger, "The Year 712 B.C. and Its Implications for Egyptian History," *Journal of the American Research Center in Egypt* 10 (1973), 95–101.

[7] Merodach-baladan's close relations with the Arabs are mentioned by Sennacherib in OIP 2.51:28.

period of Babylonian hegemony over Judah in 598–586.[8] The language of this criticism is strikingly akin to that of Jeremiah (see the notes to vv. 17–19).

In transferring the illness story with its new ending to its present position, the late editor did not smooth out the inconsistencies which he himself had created—e.g., 20:6. His interest was focused solely upon his new message: YHWH had saved Jerusalem, his sacred city in the past and would do so again. At the same time, caution was urged upon those who supported a pro-Babylonian political line, considering that the earlier association with Babylon had brought about the present sorry state of affairs.[9] And indeed an oblique reference to this fictionalized Isaianic prophecy appears in 24:13, proving that YHWH's word is reliable.

[8] The argument for the pre-exilic date of 20:12–21 is presented by the present authors in *EI* 16 (1982), 198–201. About the same time, Clements put forward a similar analysis in *Isaiah and the Deliverance of Jerusalem,* 64–67. Montgomery-Gehman had dated these verses to the years immediately following Jehoiachin's exile; the post-586 date suggested by other scholars (e.g. Burney, Šanda, Gray) is unsuitable.

[9] R. E. Clements recently discussed the question of the redaction of Isaiah's prophecies close to the fall of Jerusalem, in *VT* 30 (1980), 421–36. Cf., too, P. Ackroyd, "An Interpretation of the Babylonian Exile: A Study of 2 Kings 20, Isaiah 38–39," *SJTh* 27 (1974), 329–52.

XXXV. THE REIGN OF MANASSEH

(21:1–18)

21 1 Manasseh was twelve years old when he became king and he
reigned fifty-five years in Jerusalem. His mother's name was
Hephzibah. 2 He did what was displeasing to YHWH, imitating the
abominations of the nations whom YHWH dispossessed before the Israelites. 3 He rebuilt the high places which Hezekiah his father had destroyed; he erected altars to Baal; he made a pole of Asherah, just as
Ahab king of Israel had done; he bowed down to all the heavenly host
and worshipped them. 4 He built altars in the House of YHWH, of
which YHWH had said, "In Jerusalem, I will establish My name." 5 He
built altars to all the heavenly host in the two courtyards of the House
of YHWH. 6 He passed his son through fire; he practiced soothsaying
and sorcery, and dealt with persons who consult ghosts and spirits,
greatly displeasing YHWH to his anger.[a] 7 He set the idol of Asherah,
which he made, in the House, of which YHWH had said to David and
to Solomon his son, "In this House and in Jerusalem which I have
chosen out of all the tribes of Israel, I will estabish My name forever.
8 And I will not cause Israel to wander again from the land which I
gave to their ancestors, provided that they will carefully observe all
that I commanded them—all the Teaching which my servant Moses
commanded them." 9 But they did not listen, and Manasseh misled
them to do evil, more than the nations whom YHWH destroyed before
the Israelites.

10 Then YHWH spoke through his servants, the prophets, 11 "Since
Manasseh, king of Judah has done these abominable things, worse
than anything the Amorites before him did, and has caused Judah to
sin with his idols; 12 therefore, thus said YHWH, God of Israel, 'I am
about to bring disaster on Jerusalem and Judah,[b] so that it will resound in both ears of all who hear it.[c] 13 I will stretch the measuring

[a] Read *lhkʿysw,* with versions and mss. Final *waw* lost through haplography.
[b] A few mss. and LXX read: "and on Judah."
[c] Read with qere: *šmʿh;* Ketib: *šmʿyw*

line[d] of Samaria and the plummet of the House of Ahab over Jerusalem; and I will wipe out Jerusalem, as a plate is wiped clean and turned over on its face.[e] 14 I will abandon the remnant of My inheritance and hand them over to their enemies, so that they become spoil and plunder for all their enemies, 15 because they did what was displeasing to Me. They have been angering me ever since the day that their ancestors left Egypt, until this day!' "

16 And what is more, Manasseh shed innocent blood, so much so that he filled Jerusalem from end to end, apart from causing Judah to sin by displeasing YHWH.

17 The rest of the history of Manasseh and all that he did and his sinful acts are indeed recorded in the annals of the kings of Judah. 18 So Manasseh slept with his ancestors and he was buried in the garden of his residence, in the garden of Uzza; and Amon his son succeeded him.

[d] Read *qaw* (construct state) with many mss. for MT *qāw*.
[e] Read *māḥô wĕhāpôk*.

Notes

21 1. *Manasseh was twelve years old when he became king.* Manasseh's name appears in the contemporary records of the Assyrian kings, Esarhaddon and Ashurbanipal. He is first mentioned among the twenty-two Assyrian vassal kings of the West who were ordered by Esarhaddon to perform task work, transporting timber and stone colossi from the Lebanon to Nineveh for the royal storehouse (*Menasī/Minsī šar māt Iaudi,* "Manasseh, king of Judah"; *ANET³,* 291; cf. Appendix I, No. 9). On another occasion, these same kings of "Hatti and the sea coast" were required to help build *Kār-Aššur-aḫ-iddina,* "Port Esarhaddon," on the site of the destroyed city of Sidon in 676 (*ANET³,* 290b). About ten years later, during the reign of Ashurbanipal, Manasseh provided troops for the Assyrian campaign to Egypt. Here, too, he is listed second after Ba'al of Tyre (note the variant reading *Me-na-se-e* in Streck, *Assurbanipal,* 138:25; cf. *ANET³,* 294).

A stamp seal of the early seventh century B.C.E. bears the inscription *lmnšh bn hmlk,* "(Belonging) to Manasseh, son of the king" (N. Avigad, *IEJ* 13 [1963], 133–36). But this seal is not likely to be that of the biblical Manasseh, as once thought, for the script is now identified as Moabite (J. Naveh, *BASOR* 183 [1966], 29, n. 24; idem, *Early History of the Alphabet* [Jerusalem: Magnes, 1982], 101).

Manasseh's young age upon coming to the throne gave rise to a number of computations in Jewish sources, which showed that he was born after Hezekiah recovered from his illness, and that until the fourteenth year of his reign, Hezekiah had not concerned himself with the question of an heir. Cf. Josephus, *Antiquities* x.25; *b. Ber.* 10a.

Indeed, the difficulty felt by the rabbis concerning the ages of the kings of Judah (between Ahaz and Josiah) on ascending the throne is a real one. If Hezekiah was twenty-five years old when he took the throne and reigned twenty-nine years (cf. 18:2), Manasseh must have been born in Hezekiah's forty-second year. It is therefore highly unlikely that Manasseh was his firstborn. Perhaps all the previous heirs had died, leaving the throne to Manasseh, or perhaps Manasseh's older brothers were bypassed for reasons unknown.

Suggestions to emend the text or to posit a ten-year coregency between Hezekiah and Manasseh are made by W. F. Albright, *BASOR* 100 (1945), 22, n. 30; Thiele, *MNHK*², 157–59; and Tadmor, *EncMiqr* 4.304, nn. 7, 8.

3. *he erected altars to Baal; he made a pole of Asherah, just as Ahab king of Israel.* Ahab's cultic deviations are described in 1 Kgs 16:31–33. LXX reads *altar,* in the sing. here and in vv. 4, 5; where the plural is certainly to be preferred for the worship of the host of heaven.

He bowed down to all the heavenly host and worshipped them. The heavenly host, *ṣĕbāʾ haššāmayim*—i.e., the sun, moon, stars, and the planets (cf. 23:5; Deut 4:19)—was worshipped at the altars in the two temple courts (21:5) and on the roof of the palace (23:12), by bowing, censing, and libations. Jeremiah witnessed the private, family worship of the "Queen of Heaven" (Jer 7:18), which was popular in Jerusalem and Judah (cf. 23:5). Reverence for celestial bodies can be traced back to the second millennium B.C.E. in Syria-Palestine, as part of common Semitic tradition; in Deuteronomy itself it is noted that the Canaanites worshipped the "host" prior to Israel's entry into the land (Deut 4:19). A convenient summary of the literary evidence for this phenomenon is given by M. Dahood, in *Le antiche divinità semitiche,* ed. S. Moscati (Rome: Università di Roma, 1958), 65–94.

There is nothing particularly Mesopotamian about the astral cults. Biblical texts are too general in their descriptions to allow definite identifications with particular astral deities, though commentators admit that the listings are "typically Syrian" (cf. Šanda, Montgomery-Gehman). For further discussion on the source of this worship, see Comment and the note to 23:11 on "sun chariots."

5. *He built altars . . . in the two courtyards of the House of* YHWH. The location of these two courtyards has puzzled most commentators, inasmuch as the floor plan of the Temple in 1 Kgs 6 gives details only for the construction of the "inner court," cf. 6:36. From the present verse and from its counterpart in 23:12, one cannot specify the exact placement of these altars in the very large enclosed area of the "outer court." Cf. the terms in Jer 36:10; Ezek 44:19, 21.

6. *He passed his son through fire.* Deuteronomic terminology distinguishes between the practice of the nations who "burn" (**śārôp*) their children in service of their gods (Deut 12:31; 2 Kgs 17:31) and the practice of apostate Israelites who "pass their sons and daughters through fire" (**heʿĕbîr bāʾēš*) (16:3; 21:6). If this distinction is not merely euphemistic, then something other than actual sacrifice is meant by "passing through fire." In Deut. 18:9, "passing through fire" appears together with sundry Canaanite divinatory acts which are outlawed in Israel; this verse is the *Vorlage* for the present accusation against Manasseh.

At the same time, it must be admitted that in prophetic denunciations of the cultic mispractice of Israel, there are no distinctions between burning, sacrificing, slaughtering, and passing children through fire (cf. Jer 7:31, 19:5, 32:35; Ezek 16:20–21, 23:29). And it may be more than fortuitous that just at the time that Judah's kings, Ahaz and

Manasseh, are reported to have passed their sons through fire, a hint of burning children appears in documents from the Assyro-Aramean cultural realm.

In Neo-Assyrian economic documents, the penalty clauses against future litigation sometimes include the statement: *māršu ana* ^{d}*Sin išarrap marassu rabīte itti 2 sūtu dam erēni ana* ^{d}*Bēlet-ṣēri išarrap,* "He will burn his son to Sin. He will burn his eldest daughter with twenty silas of cedar balsam to Belet-ṣeri." (The texts were collected and discussed by K. Deller, *Or* 34 [1965], 382–86; M. Weinfeld, *UF* 4 [1972], 144–49; Cogan, *Imperialism,* 81–83.) Deller suggested that the harsh penalty could be circumvented by dedicating the children to the Temple; in this he was followed by Weinfeld, who interpreted the biblical evidence as "signifying dedication or transference to the sacred authority." But M. Smith (*JAOS* 95 [1975], 477–79) insists that "the texts mean what they say" and are not to be taken figuratively; infant sacrifices were stipulated in Assyria and actually performed in Israel.

Thus while child sacrifice cannot be totally excluded—it is attested on the part of Mesha, 2 Kgs 3:27, and is behind the image in Mic 6:7: "Shall I give my firstborn for my transgression, the fruit of my body for my sins?"—a less extreme act, with magical-divinatory significance may define Manasseh's sinful deed. (A. R. W. Green thoroughly investigated the cultural background of this practice in *The Role of Human Sacrifice in the Ancient Near East,* ASOR Dissertation Series 1 [1976].) On Molech worship, see below the note to 23:10.

he . . . dealt with persons who consult ghosts and spirits. The listing is based on Deut 18:10–11, somewhat abbreviated. **ʿāśâ,* "make, construct," is understood here, with Ehrlich, as meaning "have recourse to" (cf. 1 Sam 8:15) and not "appoint" as in 2 Kgs 17:32. The verse refers to Manasseh's active participation in illicit cults, not to royal appointment of practitioners (as in most translations). On the wide range of meaning of *ʿāśâ* in late BH, see the note to 17:29.

The term for "soothsaying," *ʿônēn,* often appears parallel to *kĕšāpîm* as a general term for sorcery, whose original technique is unrecoverable. Cf. Isa 2:6; Jer 27:9; Mic 5:11.

The terms "ghosts" (*ʾôb*) and "spirits" (*yiddĕʿōnî*) refer to the practice of necromancy, and from Lev 20:27, it is clear that they are distinct from the mediums who conjure them. It has been shown by Hoffner that *ʾôb* is an ancient term, attested in most Near Eastern languages, for a "ritual pit" through which mortals communicated with the chthonic deities of the underworld. (In Sumerian: ab [.lal]; in Hittite: *a-a-bi;* in Ugaritic: *ʾeb;* in Neo-Assyrian: *apu.*) In Hebrew, the semantic development seems to be from "pit" to "spirit of the pit." Isa 29:4 preserves reference to the "whispering sounds" in the act of calling the spirits earthward. The woman who calls Samuel up from the grave in 1 Sam 28:7 is a *baʿălat ʾôb,* one having access to a sacred spot from which the deities (cf. esp. v. 13) arose. For a full discussion of the relevant texts, see H. Hoffner, "Second Millennium Antecedents to the Hebrew *ʾôb,*" *JBL* 86 (1967), 385–401; and earlier M. Vieyra, *Revue hittite et asianique* 69 (1961), 47–55; cf. *CAD* A 2.201a. I. L. Finkel discusses necromancy in ancient Mesopotamia in *AfO* 29–30 (1983–84), 1–17, as a technique to exorcise restless ghosts as well as to learn the future.

7. *He set the idol of Asherah, which he made, in the Temple.* To judge by the evidence, Manasseh's introduction of an idol into the Temple building itself was the first such desecration of the Temple. (It is not stated that the "abomination made for Asherah" by Maacah was placed in the Temple, 1 Kgs 15:13.) The image referred to

by Ezekiel (8:3, 5) stood in the courtyard, so it may not be the same one erected by Manasseh. Manasseh's act is alluded to only once more in Jer 7:30.

The goddess Asherah appears frequently in the Ugaritic epics of the mid-second millennium B.C.E., where she is the consort of El, and bears the titles *ʾaṯrt ym*, "Asherah of the sea," and *ʾaṯrt ṣrm*, "Asherah of the Tyrians." Hence, the prominent place of Baal and Asherah in the cult of Samaria during the days of Ahab is understandable, considering Jezebel's Phoenician background and assuming the continuity of the Asherah cult in the Phoenician cities over the centuries (cf. 1 Kgs 16:32–33; 18–19).

Reed contends that the wooden object or pole associated with the goddess was not a sacred tree or grove but the image of the goddess herself (W. L. Reed, *The Asherah in the Old Testament* [Fort Worth: Texas Christian University Press, 1949]; idem, *IDB* 1.250–52). Cf. above the note to 18:4.

New epigraphic finds have recently reopened the scholarly discussion on the nature of the goddess Asherah and her relation to the official Israelite cult. In excavations of a ninth- eighth-century B.C.E. caravanserai at Kuntillet ʿAjrud (fifty-five miles northwest of Eilat), two large pithoi inscribed with blessing formulas were recovered: *brkt ʾtkm lyhwh šmrn wlʾšrth*, "I bless you by YHWH of Samaria and his Asherah"; *brktk lyhwh tmn wlʾšrth*, "I bless you by YHWH of Teiman and his Asherah." An inscription on a wall of an eighth-century burial chamber at Kh. el-Kom (eight miles west of Hebron) reads: *brk. ʾryhw. lyhwh . . . lʾšrth*, "Blessed be Uriyah by YHWH . . . (and) by his Asherah." (Z. Meshel, *Kuntillet ʿAjrud, A Religious Centre from the Time of the Judaean Monarchy on the Border of Sinai*, Israel Museum Catalog 175 [Jerusalem, 1978]; A. Lemaire, *RB* 84 [1978], 595–608). In addition, drawings on the fragments of the same storage jars at ʿAjrud show two representations of the Egyptian god Bes and a seated female playing a lyre. The iconographic motif of a single musician (see P. Beck, *Tel Aviv* 9 [1982], 31–36) has been reinterpreted by W. G. Dever (*BASOR* 255 [1984], 21–37) as representing the goddess Asherah; taken together with the texts, Dever thinks that at ʿAjrud "she was revered as the consort of Yahweh." But this radical suggestion is far from conclusive, as the relationship between the drawings and texts is still to be proven, and full publication of the texts has yet to appear.

Whatever the case, the new evidence on the association of YHWH and Asherah throws light on the "nonorthodox" popular religion against which the reforms of Hezekiah and Josiah were directed.

8. *I will not cause Israel to wander again from the land.* Heb. *hēnîd regel*, "to wander," appears only here. The Chronicler replaced this unusual idiom with the more common *hēsîr*, "remove"; cf. 2 Chr 33:8. After the construction of the Temple, the period of Israel's wandering and insecurity came to an end; and, as stated in Nathan's prophecy to David, the nation would dwell in safety (cf. 2 Sam 7:10). But exile need not necessarily be inferred from this verse; see further in Comment.

my servant Moses. A Deuteronomistic expression, cf. 1 Kgs 8:53, 56.

9. *Manasseh misled them.* Luc. expanded here, apparently reading *wayyatʿēb*, "he acted abominably," for MT *wayyatʿēm*, "he misled." Ehrlich preferred this reading, comparing 1 Kgs 21:26, where Ahab is described as acting most abominably, and this may well be the source of the Luc. expansion.

12. *it will resound in both ears of all who hear of it.* For the alternate punctuations *tiṣṣalnâ/ tĕṣillênâ* (1 Sam 3:11), "will ring," cf. *GKC* 67g. The expression appears again in 1 Sam 3:11, Jer 19:3. The figure is that of a resounding echo in the person's

ears created by the terrible news of impending disaster. The qere *šōmʿāh,* "he who hears it," agrees with the preceding feminine noun *rāʿâ,* "disaster."

13. *wiped clean and turned over.* The verbs are read as infinitive absolutes, rather than as perfects, as pointed out in MT. Two proverbial images are used here ironically:

a. The measuring line and plummet are ordinarily tools of construction, but when employed by YHWH, as in the present case, they aid in destruction. Cf. Isa 34:11, Lam 2:8. The standard for judging Judah is that by which Samaria was measured, and the hint of upcoming disaster rings clear (cf. Amos 7:7–9).

b. The turning over of a dish at the completion of a meal indicates satiation—i.e. no further consumption of the table's spread. Vividly conveyed by this image are two statements: not only are a city and its people wiped out, but YHWH as well, has had his fill of Judah's sinning and can take no more.

Most recently, K. Deller and K. Watanabe (*ZA* 70 [1980], 211–13) have pointed to a similar Akkadian expression for wiping a dish clean (*šukkulāt diqārī*) to get at the last crumbs of food.

14. *the remnant of My inheritance.* I.e., Judah. Cf. 17:18b. The people of Israel as YHWH's inheritance (*naḥălâ*) appears in prayer contexts in Deut 9:26, 29 and 1 Kgs 8:51, 53, where attention is called to the special relationship between YHWH and his people. In the present instance, even this status cannot deflect the decision to punish Judah. The use of *naḥălâ* to refer to people and not to land appears earlier in the Song of Moses, Deut 32:9: "For YHWH's share is His people, Jacob his own inheritance."

16. *And what is more.* After the lengthy list of cultic aberrations (vv. 2–7), an accusation from the social realm is introduced by *wĕgam,* a particle primarily denoting addition, but in this case a climax; cf. 24:4. C. J. Labushagne treated "The Emphasizing Particle *Gam* and Its Connotations," in *Studia . . . T. C. Vriezen* (Wageningen: H. Veenman, 1967), 193–203.

Manasseh shed innocent blood. Legend has it that the prophet Isaiah, among other YHWH loyalists, met his end during a campaign of terror which sought to eliminate the opposition to Manasseh's policies (Josephus, *Antiquities* x.38; *b. Sanh.* 103b). Such stories are based on the comparison between Manasseh and Ahab of Israel, who was remembered for his persecution of the prophets in Samaria. Cf. e.g. 2 Kgs 9:7. At the same time, it should be noted that in the prophetic literature of the late monarchic period, the expression "to shed innocent blood" referred to oppression of the poor and the underprivileged—cf. e.g. Jer 7:6; 22:3, 17; Ezek 22:6ff, 25ff. Thus Manasseh's reign was regarded by the Deuteronomist as the period during which social inequities originated with the king.

17. *all that he did and his sinful acts.* This is the only instance in the book of Kings in which cultic misconduct appears in the concluding formula to the reign of a king. Even Jeroboam I is spared this reprobation—cf. 1 Kgs 14:19. But although this evaluation is certainly that of the Deuteronomist, it is not unreasonable to think that cultic matters as affairs of state were recorded in the royal annals, but without critical judgment. For Mesopotamian analogues, cf. e.g. Grayson, *Chronicles,* 129:4, 5.

18. *he was buried in the garden of his residence.* After Hezekiah, no additional burials took place within the City of David, indicating perhaps a lack of space in the royal sepulchers there (so S. Yeivin, *JNES* 7 [1948], 30–45). As a result of a recent

archaeological survey, the suggestion to locate the royal sepulchers in the City of David, at the site of the tomb chambers discovered by R. Weill some seventy years ago, must be reconsidered (D. Ussishkin, *BA* 33 [1970], 33–46).

in the garden of Uzza. It has often been thought that Uzza is a variant of the name of king Uzziah, and that this leper king's private garden was pressed into service at this time. Cf. Yeivin, op. cit., 34–35. B. Mazar, on the other hand, would identify Uzza with the person of the same name in 2 Sam 6:8 and suggests locating the Garden of Uzza (and Perez-uzzah) at the cemetery discovered in the village of Siloam, east of the City of David (*EncMiqr* 6.624 and idem, *The Mountain of the Lord* [Garden City, N.Y.: Doubleday, 1975], 187).

Comment

1. King Manasseh as described by the Deuteronomist was an enthusiastic idolator, wholly bent on abandoning the Mosaic Law in his private worship, as well as in the public cult. An inveterate sinner, Manasseh is compared to another infamous sinner, Ahab king of Israel, whose cultic offenses had led to the downfall of the dynasty of Omri. To support his charge against Manasseh, the worst of all the kings of Judah, Dtr. compiled the longest list of misdeeds of any he assembled. Above and beyond this, Manasseh is accused of "shedding innocent blood," filling Jerusalem to the brim (cf. v. 16). Later tradition interpreted this in light of Ahab's judicial murder of Naboth, and so told of the persecution of YHWH's prophets, unto death, by Manasseh.[1] But unlike Ahab, who was personally held responsible for his sin (see 1 Kgs 21:20–22, 22:38), Manasseh enjoyed a long reign of fifty-five years, the longest in the history of the Davidic dynasty.

A specific problem in the first part of this chapter concerns vv. 7–9. S. R. Driver, following Kuenen and Wellhausen, regarded these verses as part of the body of the unit and not linked to the intrusive passage vv. 10–15.[2] Other scholars take vv. 7–9 as a redactional addition, together with vv. 10–15.[3] The

[1] Josephus explicates 21:16: "He killed all the righteous among the Hebrews, nor did he spare even the prophets, some of whom he slaughtered daily" (*Antiquities* x.38). Isaiah is counted among those that perished, in *b. Sanh.* 103b; *b. Yebam.* 49b; L. Ginzberg, *Legends of the Jews,* 4.278–79; 6.372–75; C. C. Torrey, *Lives of the Prophets, JBL* (Monograph Series) 1 (1946), 34.

[2] See S. R. Driver, *Introduction to the Literature of the Old Testament* (9th ed., Edinburgh: T & T Clark, 1913), 197–98; cf. also Burney.

[3] So e.g. Skinner; Šanda; Cross, *Canaanite Myth and Hebrew Epic,* 285–87. The syntactic difficulty of v. 8a and the conditional perspective of v. 8b led R. E. Friedman to include vv. 8–9 in the redactional addition ("From Egypt to Egypt: Dtr_1 to Dtr_2," in *Traditions in Transformation* [Winona Lake, Ind.: Eisenbrauns, 1981], 176–78); cf. earlier Gray. In Nelson's reappraisal of this unit, even vv. 4b, 5, 6b and 7b are from Dtr_2 (*Double Redaction,* 65–69).

point of debate is the question whether the verses imply the threat of exile, and if so, would they come from the hand of an exilic redactor. But it should be emphasized that the motif of exile extensively employed in treaty curses and prophecies can in no way be evidence *ipso facto* for an exilic date. Exile was a main tool of the Assyrian Empire and was effectively applied to the peoples west of the Euphrates after the mid-eighth century. It can be recognized as an authentic motif in the speech of the Rab-shakeh in 2 Kgs 18:31–32. Unlike vv. 10–15, in which the fate of Judah has been irrevocably sealed, vv. 7–9 touch on the possibility of averting punishment: "provided that they will carefully observe all that I commanded them." Such statements which held out hope no doubt encouraged Josiah to make a new covenant, in a national act of repentance. Verses 7–9 are, therefore, part of the original Deuteronomistic critique of Manasseh, and are not necessarily secondary or intrusive.

On the other hand, the intrusive nature of the unit vv. 10–15 has been recognized by most modern commentators. The verses "interfere with the connexion and wear the appearance of being insertions made after the original narrative was completed."[4] The unit represents a somewhat later stage in the presentation of Manasseh and is closely related to the prophecies of doom and exile so common to the book of Jeremiah. In vv. 10–15, anonymous prophets are said to have warned that Jerusalem would be arraigned as Samaria had been in its days; the awful verdict was in; it just had to be executed. This is not unlike Jeremiah's sermon at the Temple gates, in which he compared Jerusalem to Shiloh (cf. Jer 7:1–15). With F. M. Cross, the author of these verses, is then likely to be a later Deuteronomistic writer of the Exile (identified by the siglum Dtr_2).[5]

2. The decidedly one-sided portrayal of Manasseh is drawn in order to prepare the reader for the next stage in Judah's history, the reign of Josiah, the great reformer. Manasseh is the complete antithesis of Josiah; not a single positive act is recorded for his evil reign. Yet the Chronicler's account of Manasseh (2 Chr 33:1–20) records two items which seem historically credible:

a. Manasseh was arrested and confined by the king of Assyria, and subsequently returned to the throne (vv. 11–13). This imprisonment and reinstatement agrees well with Assyrian activities in the West, and especially with Ashurbanipal's often lenient policy of pardoning rebellious vassal kings. Cf. e.g. Necho's return to Egypt, *ANET*[3], 296–97.[6]

[4] Driver, *Introduction,* 198–99.

[5] Cross, *Canaanite Myth and Hebrew Epic,* loc. cit.

[6] The historical background of Manasseh's imprisonment in Babylon still avoids detection. See the note to 21:1 above and the discussions of Bright, *History*[3], 311–12; Cogan, *Imperialism,* 67–69.

b. The outer defense walls of Jerusalem were strengthened and troops stationed in various Judaean fortresses (v. 14).[7]

These passages from Chronicles make it all the more evident that the Deuteronomistic historian focused solely upon one element, that of Manasseh's cultic offenses, which in his view determined Judah's future and which were expressly the object of Josiah's reform.

3. What was the nature of Manasseh's cultic innovations, so negative as to be regarded as the cause of Judah's downfall? Until just recently, historians viewed these acts as a reflection of Assyrian imperialism—i.e., as a loyal vassal of Assyria, Manasseh was required to revere Assyrian gods, by introducing their cult into Judah's national shrine.[8] A question remained as to whether this requirement was part of the treaty obligations imposed upon Manasseh[9] or whether Manasseh willingly adopted Assyrian practices so as to court favor with his overlord.[10] In either case, Manasseh's idolatry was seen to be of foreign imperial origin.

Recent inquiry, however, into the nature of Manasseh's "apostasy" has shown that this view does not accord with what is known of Assyrian imperial policy.[11] As observed in discussing the altar erected by Ahaz (see the Comment on 16:10–16), there is no evidence that Assyria demanded adherence to Assyrian religious practices or interfered in any way in the native cults of their vassals. No Assyrian "vassal treaty" (the *adê* documents) contains clauses referring to cult matters. Indeed it may even be questioned whether a "vassal treaty"—i.e. a loyalty oath, similar to the one imposed by Esarhaddon on his eastern vassals, was ever imposed upon Manasseh.[12]

Manasseh's idolatry, rather than being a foreign import, should be interpreted as the revival of certain autochthonous, Canaanite, and/or Israelite practices, against which prophets spoke out regularly. The renewal of worship at the high places, the Baal altars, the Asherah image, and worship of the heavenly host "are all known to have been found in the land at a much earlier date, well before the advent of the Assyrians."[13] Assyrian cults are nowhere mentioned in our text.

Though Dtr. depicted Manasseh as solely responsible for Judah's apostasy,

[7] D. Bahat suggests that the "wall of substantial appearance" from the eighth to seventh centuries uncovered on the eastern slope of the City of David by K. Kenyon is the wall of Manasseh (*IEJ* 31 [1981], 235–36).

[8] Cf. e.g. Noth, *History,* 266, 272; Bright, *History³,* 312, n. 5; Herrmann, *History,* 259–60.

[9] So M. Tsevat, *JBL* 78 (1959), 199.

[10] E.g. R. Kittel, *Geschichte des Volkes Israel,* (Gotha: F. A. Perthes, 1922), 2.483–84.

[11] See Cogan, *Imperialism,* 42–61.

[12] See most recently Tadmor, "Treaty and Oath," 151.

[13] From the extensive discussion by J. W. McKay, *Religion in Judah Under the Assyrians 732–609 B.C.,* 20–44 (esp. 43); cf. too Cogan, *Imperialism,* 72–88.

it is unlikely that acts such as those listed to his discredit could have succeeded for so long without support in court circles and among the people. It may be submitted that the idolatry of Manasseh's age was a popular reaction to the religious policies of Hezekiah, which set in after that king's death. Hezekiah's cult reform did not prevent the disastrous rout of Judah at the hands of Assyria. Rather than meeting defeat and disaster on the hills of Judah, as prophesied by Isaiah (cf. e.g. Isa 10:12–19), Assyria reached the apogee of its power. During the reign of Esarhaddon, Assyria reasserted its presence in the West and after several campaigns against the Nubian kings, went on to conquer Egypt (671 B.C.E). The promised salvation did not come; the time was ripe for reaction. Groups directly hurt by the Hezekian reforms, the rural priesthood and perhaps even prophets outside the Isaianic circle, might well have supported the retrograde policies of Manasseh. Clearly these would hardly have been the innovations of a teenage king. Yet one should not exclude the personal element in this. Manasseh rejected his father's zealous pietistic ways, perhaps not unlike Sennacherib's total reversal of the political and religious policies of Sargon, his father (whom he never mentions in any of his inscriptions).

In analogous fashion, disillusionment can be observed in the age following the cult reform of Josiah. The abandonment of idolatrous cults during the Josianic reform, accompanied as it was with promises of renewed national well-being, was followed by the enslavement of Judah to Babylon. And here, as evidenced by the statement of the exiles in Egypt in Jer 44:15–19: "Ever since we stopped making offerings to the Queen of Heaven and pouring libations to her, we have lacked everything, and we have been consumed by the sword and by famine,"—the lesson to be learned was that the pagan gods had been angered, and in order to reverse the course of events, they were to be embraced once again.

XXXVI. THE REIGN OF AMON

(21:19–26)

21 19 Amon was twenty-two years old when he became king, and he
reigned two years in Jerusalem. His mother's name was Meshullemeth, daughter of Haruz, from Jotbah. 20 He did what was displeasing to YHWH, just as Manasseh his father had done. 21 He followed all
his father's ways; he worshipped the idols which his father worshipped
and he bowed down to them. 22 He abandoned YHWH, the God of his
fathers, and did not follow YHWH's way.
23 Amon's courtiers plotted against him, and they killed the king in
his residence. 24 But the People of the Land killed all those who had
plotted against King Amon, and the People of the Land set Josiah, his
son, on the throne as his successor. 25 The rest of the history of Amon
(and)[a] what he did are indeed recorded in the annals of the kings of
Judah. 26 They buried[b] him in his own tomb in the garden of Uzza,
and Josiah his son succeeded him.

[a] Many mss., Luc., Targ., and Syr. read: "and all that" (cf. 1:18, 14:15, 16:19).
[b] Read *wykbrw*, with many mss.

Notes

21 19. *Amon was twenty-two years old when he became king.* According to this entry, Amon was born in Manasseh's forty-fifth year, which would make him one of his youngest sons. Another case of a young son succeeding his father, who had reigned for an unusually long period is that of Ramesses II (ca. 1290–1224 B.C.E.), whose twelve eldest sons had died before he was succeeded by his thirteenth son Merneptah (cf. *CAH*^{3} 2/II.232).

The assassination of Amon after just two years on the throne (v. 23) might have been connected with the question of succession to the throne. See further in the Comment.

Meshullemeth, daughter of Haruz, from Jotbah. Opinions differ widely as to the identification of this town:

a. Jotbah is taken as identical with Talmudic Yoṭbath (in Josephus *Iotapata*), and *[Ia-]aṭ-bi-te* in the annals of Tiglath-pileser III, in the lower Galilee. This northern town, together with Rumah (cf. 23:36), also in the Galilee, would point to the policy of Judah's kings marrying women from northern Israel, thus strengthening their ties with the former Israelite state (Forrer, *Provinzeinteilung*, 61; B. Maisler, *Yediot* 1 [1933], 2–3, n. 11).

b. Jotbah may be the desert site Jotbath (Num 33:33f.) in the vicinity of the Gulf of Aqaba. Together with the Arab name Haruz, the Arab or Edomite origin of the family is thus indicated (so Montgomery-Gehman, Gray).

c. The text is emended by H. L. Ginsberg to read: Juttah (cf. Josh 15:55, 21:16 —for the "nonexistent Jotbah") in the Hebron hills, and is taken to be evidence for the recovery of this area by Judah during the reign of Manasseh (*A. Marx Jubilee Volume* [New York: Jewish Theological Seminary, 1950], 349–50, n. 12).

The first identification (a) seems preferable because of its complementary historical deduction.

24. *But the People of the Land killed all . . .* On the term *ʿam hāʾāreṣ* as a social force in late monarchic times in Judah, see the note to 2 Kgs 11:14, and the Comment there.

Comment

The short, two-year reign of Amon is depicted as simply the continuation of the age of idolatry fostered by Manasseh. Amon did not stray far from his father's ways. His reign was brought to an abrupt end by a palace coup. He was assassinated by a group of courtiers ("Amon's servants," v. 23), and his young son Josiah was placed on the throne by the "People of the Land."

This laconic report of a major crisis in the history of Judah has given rise to several scholarly conjectures as to the background of the murder of the king. A. Malamat has offered an explanation in international terms.[1] He postulated that Amon was killed by an anti-Assyrian party, which would have Judah join an area-wide uprising against Ashurbanipal in 640. With the approach of the Assyrian army to Syria, and especially with the capture of Akko (related in the latest edition of Ashurbanipal's annals; cf. *ANET*^{3}, 300b), the moderates gained the upper hand, placated Assyria, and elevated young Josiah to the throne. This reconstruction rested upon synchronizing the death of Amon, usually dated to the years 641/640 and the Assyrian campaign to the West, presumed to have taken place in 639 (following the accepted ordering of Ashurbanipal's campaigns). However, a revised chronology of the histori-

[1] A. Malamat, "The Historical Background of the Assassination of Amon King of Judah," *IEJ* 3 (1953), 26–29.

cal inscriptions of Ashurbanipal has shown that the Akko episode cannot be dated later than 644/643.[2] Moreover, the capture of Akko was not part of a campaign to the West, but was a local, small-scale punitive action, the date of which might have been earlier than 644.[3] No connection between that Assyrian action and the assassination of Amon in 640 can, therefore, be established.

Another suggestion was advanced by E. Nielsen; he explains the assassination in terms of inner Judahite politics, the struggle between the followers of Manasseh's religious policies and the opposition of the Jerusalem priesthood, the circle whose interests were hurt most by those policies.[4]

But as matters stand now, the reasons for Amon's murder remain elusive, and the question should be left open. Court histories of the Ancient Near East are replete with examples of kings murdered, sometimes by their offspring who were bypassed in the line of succession. (See above, on the discussion of the murder of Sennacherib in the Comment to 2 Kgs 18–19). In Judah, too, such fraternal rivalries cannot be ruled out. During his long reign, Manasseh ruthlessly silenced his opponents, supported, as seems likely, by the presence of the Assyrian army in the land. Only after Manasseh's death, and coincidentally with the retreat of Assyria from the West, did countercurrents begin to surface, in so violent a form as regicide.

Throughout this period, the stabilizing factor in Judah was the *ʿam hāʾāreṣ,* "the People of the Land," who remained loyal to the Davidides. As in the case of Jehoash (2 Kgs 11), so here too they appear at a moment of dynastic crisis to insure the continuation of the House of David, by placing Josiah on the throne. If the analogy to Joash be extended, it can also be argued that even though the *ʿam hāʾāreṣ* avenged the violent death of Amon, they were not supporters of the religiopolitical policies of Manasseh and his successor. This is seen from the thrust of Josiah's actions, after a decade of rule by the *ʿam hāʾāreṣ* during Josiah's minority; the influence upon the king of these circles, loyal to Israelite tradition was striking. From the death of Amon until the fall of Judah in 586, the "People of the Land" repeatedly came forward whenever the dynasty was endangered. They were also among the first to be punished by Judah's conquerors (cf. e.g. 23:35).

[2] H. Tadmor, XXVth International Congress of Orientalists (Moscow, 1960), 240; cf. too M. Cogan and H. Tadmor, *Or* 46 (1977), 81–85.

[3] Ephʿal, *The Ancient Arabs,* 158, n. 547.

[4] E. Nielsen, "Political Conditions and Cultural Developments in Israel and Judah During the Reign of Manasseh," Proceedings of Fourth *WCJS,* Papers (Jerusalem, 1967) 1.103–6.

XXXVII. THE REIGN OF JOSIAH: THE GREAT REFORM

(22:1–23:30)

22 1 Josiah was eight years old when he became king, and he reigned
thirty-one years in Jerusalem. His mother's name was Jedidah, daughter of Adaiah from Bozkath. 2 He did what was pleasing to YHWH; he
followed all the ways of David, his ancestor, straying neither to the
right nor to the left.

3 In the eighteenth year of King Josiah, the king sent Shaphan, the
scribe, son of Azaliah, son of Meshullam, to the House of YHWH:
4 "Go to Hilkiah the high priest and have him sum up the silver that
has been brought to the House of YHWH, which the keepers of the
threshold have collected from the people. 5 Let them deliver[a] it to the
workmen in charge of the House of YHWH, and they will pay it to the
workmen of the House of YHWH, who are to repair the House, 6 to
the carpenters, builders, masons, and to buy timber and quarry stone
for repairing the House. 7 Note that the silver delivered to them is not
to be audited, for they deal honestly."

8 Hilkiah the high priest said to[b] Shaphan the scribe, "I have found
the book of the Teaching in the House of YHWH." Hilkiah gave the
book to Shaphan and he read it. 9 Shaphan the scribe came to the king
and reported back to the king, "Your servants have melted down the
silver found in the House, and they delivered it to the workmen in
charge of the House of YHWH." 10 Then Shaphan the scribe told the
king, "Hilkiah the priest gave me a book," and Shaphan read it before
the king. 11 When the king heard the words of the book of the Teaching, he rent his garments. 12 The king then ordered Hilkiah the priest,
Ahikam son of Shaphan, Achbor son of Micaiah, Shaphan the scribe,
and Asaiah the king's servant, 13 "Go, inquire of YHWH on my behalf,
on behalf of the people, and on behalf of all Judah concerning the
words of this book that has been found. For great indeed is YHWH's

[a] So with qere *wĕyittĕnūhû.*
[b] Read *ʾel* with mss. and versions.

wrath that has been kindled against us, because our ancestors did not
obey the words of this book, to do all that is prescribed for us."
14 So Hilkiah the priest, Ahikam, Achbor, Shaphan, and Asaiah
went to Huldah the prophetess, wife of Shallum, son of Tikvah, son of
Harhas, the keeper of the wardrobe—she lived in Jerusalem in the
Mishneh quarter—and they spoke with her. 15 She said to them,
"Thus said YHWH, God of Israel, 'Say to the man that sent you to me,
16 "Thus said YHWH: I am about to bring disaster on[c] this place and on
its inhabitants, all the words in the book which the king of Judah has
read. 17 Because they have abandoned Me and they made offerings to
other gods, so as to anger Me by all their practices, My wrath is
burning against this place and it will not be extinguished." 18 But as
for the king of Judah, who sent you to inquire of YHWH, thus you shall
say to him, "Thus said YHWH, God of Israel: As for the things which
you heard, 19 since you took fright and you humbled yourself before
Me,[d] when you heard that I promised to turn this place and its inhabitants into a horror and a curse, and you rent your garments and wept
before Me, I, too, have heard—the word of YHWH." 20 Therefore I will
gather you to your ancestors, and you will be gathered to your grave
in peace. You will not behold all the disasters which I am bringing on
this place.' " So they reported back to the king.
23 1 Then the king sent for all the elders of Judah and Jerusalem to
assemble before him. 2 The king went up to the House of YHWH, and
with him all the men of Judah, all the residents of Jerusalem, the
priests, and the prophets, all the people, young and old. He read out to
them all the words of the book of the covenant which was found in the
House of YHWH. 3 The king stood by the pillar and he concluded the
covenant before YHWH, to follow YHWH, to keep his commandments,
his injunctions, and his laws with all their heart and soul, to uphold
the terms of this covenant written in this book. And all the people
committed themselves to the covenant.

4 The king then ordered Hilkiah the high priest, the deputy priests,
and the keepers of the threshold to remove from the Temple Hall[e] all
the objects made for Baal, Asherah, and all the heavenly host. He
burned them outside of Jerusalem on the terraces of the Kidron and
had their ashes carried to Bethel. 5 He put an end to the idolatrous

[c] Read *ʿal* for *ʾel,* corresponding to the following preposition; cf. 2 Chr 34:24.
[d] Read *lĕpānay* with Luc.
[e] Lit. YHWH's Hall.

priests who had been installed by the kings of Judah to offer sacrifices[f] at the high places in the cities of Judah and the environs of Jerusalem —those who sacrificed to Baal, to the sun and moon and planets, all the heavenly host. 6 He removed the (idol of) Asherah from the House of YHWH to the Kidron Valley outside Jerusalem; he burnt it in the Kidron Valley and beat it to dust, and then scattered the dust over the common burial ground. 7 He tore down the houses of the sacred males within the House of YHWH, where women weave coverings for Asherah.

8 He brought in all the priests from the cities of Judah, and defiled the high places where the priests had offered sacrifices, from Geba to Beer-Sheba. And he tore down the high places of the gates, by the entrance of the gate of Joshua, governor of the city, on a person's left at the city gate. 9 But the priests of the high places did not ascend the altar of YHWH in Jerusalem, though they ate unleavened bread together with their fellow (priests). 10 He defiled the Topheth in the Ben-hinnom[g] Valley, so that no one could pass his son or daughter through fire to Molech. 11 He did away with the horses which the kings of Judah had dedicated to the sun, at the entrance[h] to the House of YHWH, near the chamber of Nathan-melech, the officer of the precincts; and he burnt the chariots of the sun. 12 The king tore down the altars on the roof of the upper chamber of Ahaz that the kings of Judah had made, and the altars that Manasseh had made in the two courtyards of the House of YHWH. He hastily removed them from there,[i] and he threw their rubble into the Kidron Valley. 13 The king defiled the high places east of Jerusalem, south of the Mount of the Destroyer, which Solomon king of Israel had built for Ashtoreth, the detestation of Sidon, for Chemosh, the detestation of Moab, and for Milcom, the abomination of the Ammonites. 14 He broke the sacred pillars; he cut down the sacred poles, and filled their places with human bones.

15 Moreover the altar in Bethel, the high place which Jeroboam, son of Nebat, had made, causing Israel to sin, even that altar and the high place, he tore down. He burned the high place, making dust of it, and burned the pole of Asherah. 16 When Josiah looked about and saw the graves which were there on the mountainside, he sent and took the

[f] Read *wyqṭrw* (pl.) with LXX, Targ., for MT *wyqṭr* (sing.).
[g] So with qere; ketib *bĕnê.*
[h] Lit. "from entering."
[i] Read: *wayyĕriṣṣēm miššām*. See note.

bones out of the graves. He burned (them) on the altar, and thus defiled it, in accordance with the word of YHWH foretold by the man of God, who had foretold these things.[j] 17 He asked, "What is this marker I see?" The men of the city replied, "The grave of the man of God who came from Judah. He foretold all these things which you did to the altar at Bethel." 18 He then ordered, "Leave it alone! Let no one disturb his bones." So they spared his bones and the bones of the prophet, who came from Samaria. 19 Josiah also removed the shrines of the high places in the cities of Samaria which the kings of Israel had made to provoke <YHWH's anger>.[k] He did to them just as he had done in Bethel. 20 He slaughtered all the priests of the high places who were there on the altars, and burned human bones on them. Then he returned to Jerusalem.

21 The king issued an order to all his people: "Celebrate the Passover of YHWH your God, as prescribed in this Book of the Covenant." 22 Indeed, a Passover such as this had not been celebrated since the days of the Judges who judged Israel and all the days of the kings of Israel and the kings of Judah; 23 only in the eighteenth year of King Josiah was such a Passover of YHWH celebrated in Jerusalem. 24 Moreover, Josiah stamped out those who consult ghosts and spirits, the household images and the idols, all the detestations which had appeared in the land of Judah and in Jerusalem, in order to fulfill the words of the Teaching written in the book which Hilkiah the priest found in the House of YHWH. 25 There was no king like him before, who turned back to YHWH with all his heart, with all his soul, and with all his might, in accord with the entire Teaching of Moses; and after him, no one arose like him.

26 Yet YHWH did not turn away from his great wrath which had flamed up against Judah, for all the things by which Manasseh angered him. 27 YHWH said, "I will also remove Judah from my sight as I removed Israel; for I will spurn this city which I have chosen, Jerusalem, and this Temple of which I said, 'My name shall be there.' "

28 The rest of the history of Josiah and all that he did are indeed recorded in the annals of the kings of Judah. 29 In his days, Pharaoh Necho, king of Egypt, set out for the river Euphrates to the king of Assyria. When King Josiah confronted him, (Necho) put him to death at Megiddo as soon as he had seen him. 30 His attendants drove his body from Megiddo and brought him to Jerusalem; and they buried

[j] On the long addition in LXX, see note.
[k] Read with versions: *lhkʿys <ʾt yhwh>*; see note.

him in his own tomb. Then the People of the Land took Jehoahaz son of Josiah and anointed him; they made him king to succeed his father.

Notes

22 **1.** *Josiah was eight years old when he became king.* The name *Yō'šīyāhû* apparently appears in an abbreviated form as the name *Yā'ōš* in the Lachish letters (*ANET*[3], 322) and perhaps in the Arad astracon C (cf. the remark of W. F. Albright, *ANET*[3], 569, n. 17).

Because of Josiah's young age upon ascending the throne, it is more than likely that Judah's policies were set by regents, who reared the king during his minority. The identity of these regents is unknown; but they probably belonged to the *'am ha'āreṣ*, who placed Josiah on the throne (see above, 21:24).

Jedidah . . . from Bozkath. A city in the Judaean Shephelah, listed in Josh 15:39 as situated between Lachish and Eglon.

2. *He did what was pleasing to* YHWH *. . . straying neither to the right nor to the left.* A stock phrase in Deuteronomy and in Deuteronomistic writing, in which **sûr*, "to turn" (e.g. Deut 2:27, 5:29, 17:20, 28:14), replaces **nāṭô* of the earlier narrative literature (e.g. Num 20:17, 22:26). This verse is the first part of the Dtr. formula of evaluation, completed in 23:25, which frames the history of Josiah and describes him in terms unparalleled for any other king of Judah. The climax of Deuteronomistic presentations of righteous and sinful kings has unmistakably been reached.

3. *In the eighteenth year.* LXX adds "in the eighth month." Taken together with the celebration of the Passover in the same year (cf. 23:22–23), the timetable for 2 Kgs 22–23 was conceived as covering four months, with the year beginning in Tishri. See further in Comment.

4. *sum up the silver.* MT *wĕyattēm;* the *hiphil* of **tmm* appears only here in this sense. Ancient translations exhibit a variety of readings, as do the modern ones. Some follow LXX and read *waḥătōm*, "seal up" (*BH*[3]); most prefer Luc. (which here and in v. 9 has the same verb) *wĕyattēk*, "melt down" (Šanda, Montgomery-Gehman, Gray, and *NAB, NEB* and cf. R. Weiss, *JBL* 82 [1963], 189, n. 6).); Klosterman emends to *witakkēn*, "measure out," (cf. 12:12). Considering such divergencies, MT is preferred (so Stade).

Hilkiah the high priest. Heb. *hakkōhen haggādôl.* In 25:18, the title appears as *kōhēn hārō'š.* On the question whether the title is authentic in pre-exilic contexts, see the note on 12:11.

According to the genealogical lists of the high priesthood, Hilkiah was the son of Shallum of the family of Zadok (cf. 1 Chr 5:38–39, 9:10–11; Ezra 7:1; Neh 11:11). The gap in these lists reaching back from the reign of Josiah to the days of Solomon suggested to B. Mazar that the Zadokite priests were rehabilitated by Josiah (after their ouster from the high priesthood following the death of Solomon for unknown reasons); they played an influential role in furthering the present cultic reforms (*EncMiqr* 1.133; 3.161). H. J. Katzenstein (*JBL* 81 [1961], 377–84) suggested that the Zadokites returned to serve as early as Hezekiah's reform.

Hilkiah is also the name of the father of the prophet Jeremiah, one of the priests at Anathoth, but there is no hard evidence that this priestly family ever served in the

Jerusalem sanctuary. (Qimḥi at Jer 1:1 identified the two; and cf. a recent revival of this idea by Wilson, *Prophecy and Society in Ancient Israel,* 222–23.)

5. *They will pay it to the workmen.* Verse 5b is not a doublet of 5a (contra. Benzinger). In 5a the workmen are the regular maintenance crew in the Temple, not equipped to undertake the major repairs envisioned. They were to hire (Heb. *wĕyittĕnû;* cf. 12:12 *wayyôṣîʾūhû*), the professional artisans enumerated in v. 6. The corresponding description in 12:12, 16 also speaks of two groups of workmen.

to repair the House. Heb. *lĕḥazzēq bedeq habbāyit,* lit. "to strengthen the breaches." See the note on 12:6.

6. *carpenters, builders, masons.* Several types of skilled workers were employed: builders (*bōnîm*) and masons (*gōdĕrîm*). There is no reason to emend *gōdĕrîm* (lit. "wall-builders") to *gōzĕrîm* ("hewers") (so Ehrlich, Montgomery-Gehman, Gray). Cf. above 12:12–13.

7. The verse is part of the royal order; in 12:16, the auditing/accounting (**ḥiššēb*) refers to the work performed.

8. *the book of the Teaching.* Heb. *sēper,* lit. "a writing, record," may be reasonably understood as a written scroll (cf. Ezek 2:9). Papyrus sheets were in common use in Israel as in Egypt; in special cases, parchment was the rule. (M. Haran, "Book-Scrolls in Israel in Pre-Exilic Times," *JSS* 33 [1982], 161–73). For *sēper* as letter, cf. 2 Kgs 5:5, 10:6; Esth 1:22, 3:13, 8:10, 9:20 and 30. See too the note to 23:2.

he read it (i.e. the book). From the language of this verse and v. 10, one cannot determine the compass of the book of Teaching found by Hilkiah and read by Shaphan. For **qārôʾ,* "read," with pronominal suffix, cf. Jer 36:21; with the particle *bĕ-,* "from, out of," 36:6, 8. Only the explicit description in vv. 22–23 establishes that the whole scroll was read before Jehoiakim in a single audience, but such a description is lacking in the present verse.

9. *Your servants have melted down the silver.* Heb. *hittîkû.* **Nātôk* in *qal,* "to pour out," is said of water, Job 3:24; cf. of rain (in *niphal*) Exod 9:33; 2 Sam 21:10; and of divine wrath in prophetic literature, e.g. Jer 42:18; Nah 1:6. In *hiphil,* it is used in metallurgical contexts, cf. Ezek 22:20, 22. For a discussion of melting down metals, a procedure well attested in the ancient Near East, see note to 12:11.

11. *he rent his garments.* Josiah's reaction to hearing the words of the book was deep remorse. Rending garments and weeping aloud are well-known signs of grief—cf. e.g. Gen 37:29; and above 2:12, 19:1.

12. *Hilkiah . . . Ahikam . . . Achbor . . . Shaphan . . . Asaiah.* The identity of the persons who made up the delegation to obtain divine guidance presents a problem. In addition to the two central actors known so far, Hilkiah and Shaphan, three new individuals are introduced. Two of them, Ahikam and Achbor, are listed before Shaphan. If Ahikam was the son of Shaphan, the royal scribe, how can his mention in the list before that of his father be explained? Hence it has been inferred that Shaphan, Ahikam's father, is not identical with Shaphan, the scribe (cf. e.g. Šanda). Ahikam would then be a very influential person at court; and indeed, some years later, he intervened to save Jeremiah's life (cf. Jer 26:24). (S. Yeivin, on the other hand, sees Shaphan in both cases as the same person; cf. *Tarbiz* 12 [1941], 255.) Ahikam's son, Gedaliah, was appointed by Nebuchadnezzar to be governor of Judah after the destruction of the Temple—cf. 25:22.

Achbor, son of Micaiah, is mentioned in Jer 26:22 and 36:12 as the father of Elnathan, one of the most prominent officials at Jehoiakim's court. In 2 Kgs 22:12, a generation earlier, the father himself appears as a key official of Josiah. On Achbor's granddaughter Nehushta, see the note to 24:8. (A certain Coniah, son of Elnathan, the army commander, or *śár haṣṣābāʾ*, is mentioned in Lachish Letter No. 3 [*ANET*³, 322]. Is he a grandson of Achbor in the present verse?)

As for Asaiah at the end of the list, nothing is known of him or his post outside of the present context, but his participation in the delegation indicates that he was a ranking official. The title *ʿbd hmlk* appears on several stamp seals—e.g. "Jaazaniah, the king's servant" (cf. 25:23).

13. *YHWH's wrath that has been kindled against us.* God's wrath (*ḥēmâ*) is depicted in terms of fire (cf. Deut 32:22), here with the verb **yṣt* "kindle, burn" (cf. v. 17); in related literature with **bʿr,* "burn," (cf. Jer 4:4, 21:12, 44:6); **ntk,* "pour out," (cf. Jer 7:20, 42:18); and **špk,* "pour," (cf. Jer 10:25).

The old derivation of *ḥēmâ* from **yḥm,* "be hot," is now abandoned by *KB*³, 313, in favor of its relationship to the Akk. cognate *imtu,* "poison, foam," (*CAD* I–J, 139–41). M. Gruber (*Nonverbal Communication,* 513–50) would translate "venom" in this passage, as well as those which refer to "venomous creepers" (Deut 32:24), "poisoned" arrows (Job 6:4), and "poison of wine" (Hos 7:5).

all that is prescribed for us. Heb. *kātûb ʿālênû.* The only other instance of this construction is in Ps 40:8, *kātûb ʿālay,* usually rendered as "prescribed for me" (e.g. *NEB, NAB*). Luc. reads *kātûb ʿālāyw,* "written on it" (i.e. "the book"), cf. 2 Chr 34:21; this is preferred by Stade, Burney, Montgomery-Gehman.

14. *Shallum . . . keeper of the wardrobe.* A similar title was held by one of the staff of the Baal Temple in Samaria: "in charge of the vestments"; cf. 10:22. A like functionary is known from near contemporary Babylonian texts: *ša ina muḫḫi ṣubāti;* cf. *CAD* Ṣ 225b. Yeivin (*Tarbiz* 12 [1941], 261) took Maaseiah, a guard in the Temple, to be the son of the same Shallum, in the present verse; cf. Jer 35:4.

she lived in Jerusalem in the Mishneh quarter. A city quarter by this name (lit. "the second" [-city?]) is referred to by Zephaniah (1:10) in association with the hills of the city and the Maktesh-quarter. B. Mazar identifies the Mishneh as the suburbs of the City of David which developed on the Western Hill of Jerusalem during the late monarchic period (*EAEHL* 2.591). Excavation in this area has now uncovered an extensive settlement on the Western Hill enclosed by a city wall during the days of Hezekiah (N. Avigad, *The Upper City of Jerusalem* [Jerusalem: Shikmona, 1980], 54–60 [Hebrew]).

Huldah is the only woman prophet noted in the history of both kingdoms. The inquiry through Huldah, rather than through one of the better-known prophets—e.g. Jeremiah or Zephaniah—has been explained in various ways. Rabbinic savants considered "women to be merciful," so that Huldah could be expected to deliver a lenient oracle, more so than the doom-speaking men of her age (cf. *b. Meg.* 14b; Qimḥi; and for a modern echo, Šanda). Klostermann fancifully reconstructed a genealogy whereby Huldah was the grandam of the prophets, who at ninety-three years of age, had lived through the days of both Hezekiah's reform and Manasseh's apostasy. Jeremiah at this stage was still an inexperienced youth. Most recently, R. R. Wilson (*Prophecy and Society in Ancient Israel,* 219–23) traced Huldah (through her husband Shallum, taken by him to be the uncle of Jeremiah, cf. Jer 32:7) to north Israelite/Ephraimite priestly circles who were instrumental in fostering Josiah's reforms. Huldah was a court prophet, consulted on state matters, as required by the code in Deut 18:1–8.

For all this, it should be noted that in the seventh century B.C.E., in particular, at the court of the Assyrian kings, women prophets (*raggintu,* lit. "caller") often delivered messages concerning the safety of the king and the granting of divine protection against his enemies. These prophetesses are quoted in the Neo-Assyrian letters *ABL* 439 and 149; for which cf. S. Parpola, *Letters from Assyrian Scholars,* AOAT 5/1 (Neukirchen-Vluyn, 1970), 228–30, 270–71. A collection of such prophecies addressed to Esarhaddon is translated by R. D. Biggs in *ANET*³, 605. Cf. too, H. B. Huffmon, *IDB* Sup, 699–700.

15–20. On the double address of Huldah to Josiah (vv. 15 and 18) and the structure of her prophecy in general, see the Comment.

18. *As for the things which you heard.* The Hebrew has a hanging clause, which Montgomery-Gehman consider an anacoluthon. Most other commentators rewrite the text and join it to v. 19, as did the ancient translations. E. W. Nicholson (*Hermathena* 97 [1963], 96–98) restored *ʿal* at the beginning of the problematic words, translating: "Thus said YHWH . . . concerning the things which you heard."

The intent of the message is clear: Josiah could look forward to personal pardon; since he had heard and taken YHWH's word to heart, the Lord would respond in kind. "I heard" at the end of v. 19 echoes "I heard" in v. 18.

19. *since you took fright.* Heb. *rak lĕbābĕkâ,* lit. "your heart was soft." This idiom is used in parallel to verbs of fear and timidity; cf. Deut 20:3, Isa 7:4, Jer 51:46, 2 Chr 13:7. Here it describes Josiah, overcome by the warnings in the book of the Law read to him. Other translations suggest "penitent" (Moffat), "willing heart" (*NEB*).

to turn this place . . . into a horror and a curse. This threat is based upon Deut 28:37, in which Israel's wretched condition in exile becomes a byword among the nations. Cf. Jer 19:8; 24:9, et al.

20. *I will gather you to your ancestors.* This expression is used primarily in early literature—e.g. Gen 25:8, 17, 35:29; Num 20:24; and with reference to Moses in Deut 32:50. (In these instances, the noun used is always *ʿam,* "kin"; in the present verse, *ʾābôt,* "fathers.") Josiah is the only king of whom this apparently archaic expression is used.

you will be gathered to your grave in peace. Heb. *qibrōtêkā,* "your graves"; Šanda, Montgomery-Gehman, *BH*³ read *qĕbūrātĕkā* (cf. 23:30). The reference to ancestors at the beginning of the verse may have suggested the pl. noun "graves"—i.e., family sepulchers.

The promise of an untroubled death is contradicted by the violent end met by Josiah at Megiddo reported in 23:29. This verse, then, must be part of the original prophecy by Huldah. See the discussion of this matter in the Comment.

23 1. *all the elders of Judah and Jerusalem.* The *zĕqēnîm* are mentioned here for the first time in 2 Kings; for other assemblies of elders, see above on 1 Kgs 8:1 and 20:7. The term harks back to the early tribal and pre-monarchic organization of Israel, where authority was vested in the elders of the local communities, who apparently had not completely disappeared even at this late date. For discussions of their role, see J. L. McKenzie. "The Elders in the Old Testament," *Bib* 40 (1959), 522–40; J. Liver, *WHJP* 3. 190–91; H. Reviv, *Beer-sheva* 1 (1973), 204–15 (Hebrew). It may even be argued that "the elders" were part of the political leadership of Judah throughout the Monarchy; their "disappearance" from the sources reflects historiographic considerations, rather than historical reality. See H. Reviv, *The Elders in Ancient Israel, A Study of A Biblical Institution* (Jerusalem: Magnes, 1983), 95–111 (Hebrew).

The expression *Judah and Jerusalem,* common in late pre-exilic literature, distinguishes between the capital city and the rest of the kingdom of Judah. For the greater part of the seventh century, especially after the retreat of Sennacherib, Jerusalem was the most significant component of Judah.

2. *the men of Judah.* Heb. *ʾîš yĕhūdâ.* An old term, which in Davidic times meant "Judah-at-arms" (so H. Tadmor *JWH* 11 [1968], 49–57); it is used here anachronistically. The distinction between the citizenry of the capital and that of the countryside was made previously in v. 1. Cf. Jer 4:4, 17:25, and earlier Isa 5:3.

young and old. Lit. "small and great." A merismus describing the totality of the population. Cf. 1 Sam 5:9; 30:2; Jer 6:13; 8:10; 31:34. In Akkadian, the semantic parallel is *ṣeḫer u rabi;* cf. *CAD* Ṣ 184.

the words of the book of the covenant. In light of the Aramaic usage of *spr* in the Sefire treaty (I Cb 3–4): *mly sprʾ zy bnṣbʾ znh,* "the words of the inscription (which is) on this stele," Fitzmyer would interpret the present passage as "the words of the covenant inscription" (*CBQ* 22 [1960], 456).

3. *The king stood by the pillar.* Heb. *ʿal hā ʿammûd.* Targum renders "platform" (cf. Josephus, *Antiquities* x.63: *epi tou bematos*). Qimḥi noted that the parallel account in 2 Chr 34:31 reports the king standing "at his place" (*ʿomdô*), the place reserved for royalty. For this construction, see the note to 2 Kgs 11:14, where the same term appears.

the people committed themselves to the covenant. Heb. *wayyaʿămōd babbĕrît,* is a difficult expression, which appears only here. Klostermann emended to *wayyaʿăbēr* comparing Deut. 29:11 and the "passing" (**ʿbr*) through the pieces of the covenant spoken of in Jer 34:18. However, in 2 Chr 34:31, the verb is read in *hiphil* as: *wayyʿămēd,* "He—Josiah—enforced the covenant upon . . ." This usage in Chronicles is consistent with LBH, in which **ʿmd* replaces **qwm,* especially in expressions for establishing or confirming a covenant, oath, or promise (A. Hurvitz, *A Linguistic Study of the Relationship Between the Priestly Source and the Book of Ezekiel,* Cahiers *RB* 20 [1982], 94–97 discusses this replacement.) The *qal* reading of the present verse, then, might be the semantic equivalent of the early expression **kārôt bĕrît.*

4. *the terraces of the Kidron.* Heb. *sĕdēmâ* is of unknown etymology; the variety of translations point up the difficulty, e.g. "field" (*BDB,* NJPS); "open country" (*NEB*), "slopes" (*NAB*), "terraces" (*KB*); LXX^{B} transliterates the word. Within the context of Deut 32:32; Isa 16:8; Hab 3:17, in which *sĕdēmâ* appears in parallel to "vine," it should mean "creeping plant" (so Ibn-Janah) or "trellis." Hence the present translation, "terrace," the common location for viniculture in Israel. L. E. Stager (*JNES* 41 [1982], 111–21) has studied the excavated areas of the City of David to seek the exact place of these terraces. (Gray's "limekilns" is based upon a back formation from Luc. and an emended text.)

5. *idolatrous priests.* Heb. *kōmēr/kĕmārîm. kumru* priests appear in Old Assyrian documents from Cappadocia and once in a Mari document from the days of Shamshi-Adad I, king of Assyria (*CAD* K 534–35). The term does not appear in Babylonian or Assyrian of the first millennium, except for the reference to a *kumirtu* priestess as the title of an Arabian queen in an inscription of Ashurbanipal (*CAD* K 532, cf. *ANET*^{3}, 301, n. 1). In Aramaic, *kumrāʾ* is the common term for priest (cf. *DISO* 122). The idolatrous priests spoken of in this verse were, therefore, officiants of West Semitic cults (Baal, Asherah et al.) typical of the religious amalgam in the Assyrian empire of the West. They can hardly have been Assyrian cult officiants, since the term was not

used in any dialect of Akkadian in the first millennium. Nor is there direct textual support for the suggestion that the *kumru* priests were "presumably the prototype of Greek *kybebos* 'gallus' " (so W. F. Albright, *From Stone Age to Christianity*[2] [Garden City, N.Y.: Doubleday, 1957], 234, n. 46).

planets. Heb. *mazzālôt* has long been recognized as a loanword from Akk. *manzaltu,* the fixed locations of the stars in heaven. (The same term is used for positions of rank at court and in the army; cf. *CAD* M 1.228–29; and the early discussions in *KAT*[3], 628, and Šanda). LXX transliterates both here and in Job 38:32, *mazzārôt.* But in Job, the word might refer to a specific constellation; cf. M. H. Pope, *Job,* AB, ad loc.

6. *He removed the idol of Asherah from the House of* YHWH. This Asherah image had been installed by Manasseh (cf. 21:7 and see the note there). The repeated acts of destruction carried out against it—burning, grinding, scattering the dust—recall the description of the extirpation of the golden calf. In both Exod 32:20 and Deut 9:21, Moses is said to have burnt, ground to fine dust and scattered its remains "in the wadi that comes down the mountain." In similar fashion, the writer relates that Josiah rid himself of the odious idol of Asherah. For a Ugaritic parallel of multiple demolition and its relation to the Biblical passages, see the discussion of S. E. Loewenstamm, "The Making and Destruction of the Golden Calf," *Bib* 48 (1967), 481–90; idem, *Bib* 56 (1975), 330–43.

7. *sacred males.* Heb. *qĕdēšim.* It is an open question whether these persons were or were not male "cult prostitutes" (cf. *NEB, NAB, NJPS*). See the note to 1 Kgs 14:24.

where women weave coverings for Asherah. Heb. *bāttîm,* translation *ad sensum.* Early translations reflect the difficulty in understanding this word, which is normally "houses"; LXX has *chetiein,* likely a corrupt transliteration of MT (cf. Montgomery-Gehman); Targum *mĕkôlîn,* "curtains." Qimḥi, apparently combining several suggestions, offered "curtain enclosures," thus retaining the primary meaning of *bayit.* Šanda and G. R. Driver (*JBL* 55 [1936], 107) connect the word with Arab. *batt* and translate it as "vestments." H. Gressmann (*ZAW* 24 [1924], 325–26) compared the bedecking of cult images referred to in Ezek 16:16 and Jer 10:9. (The fashioning of woven and embroidered garments used to adorn the statues of the gods in Mesopotamia is discussed by A. L. Oppenheim, *JNES* 8 [1949], 172–93.)

8. *the priests from the cities of Judah.* These are priests (*kōhănîm*) of YHWH, in contradistinction to the idolatrous priests (*kĕmārîm*) of v. 5.

from Geba to Beer-sheba. As shown by B. Mazar (*Yediot* 8 [1939], 105–7), this Geba is best identified with a Geba recorded by Eusebius, as "five miles from Gophna on the road to Neapolis," and not with Geba of Benjamin. The phrase *from Geba to Beer-sheba* sets off the territorial limits of Josiah's New Judah, on the analogy of the phrase *from Dan to Beer-sheba* from the days of the United Monarchy; cf. 1 Kgs 5:5; as such it reflects the penetration of the reform deep into what had been the Assyrian province of Samaria (see vv. 15–20). (Still, A. Demsky considers it "preferable to identify the cultic center at Geba with the well-known *bāmâh* of Gibeon," *BASOR* 212 [1973], 31.)

he tore down the high places of the gates. A difficult passage because of the plural construction. Most critics have accepted the emendation of G. Hoffmann (*ZAW* 2 [1882], 175) and read *bāmat haśśĕʿîrîm,* "high place of the goat demons." (For this cult, cf. Lev 17:7 and 2 Chr 11:15.) Without emendation, the text might be construed in one of two ways: (1.) the high places (pl.) refer to cultic installations at city gates across the country and to a particular *bāmâ* of the sort referred to at the end of 8b; (2.)

bāmôt is singular in meaning, referring to one structure in one location; cf. the comments of P. H. Vaughn, *The Meaning of 'Bama' in the Old Testament* (Cambridge, U.K.: Cambridge University Press, 1974), 13–14, and N. H. Snaith, *VT* 25 (1975), 115–18.

the gate of Joshua, governor of the city. Heb. *śár hāʿîr,* apparently the highest official in the city administration (cf. 1 Kgs 22:26). The unique seal from seventh-century Judah with the text inscribed in a cartouche *śr hʿr,* "governor of the city," and a scene of royal symbolism of Assyrian derivation, might refer to one of the governors of Jerusalem (cf. N. Avigad, *IEJ* 26 [1976], 178–82; G. Barkai, *Qadmoniot* 10 [1977], 69–71). See Plate 12(d). In contemporary Assyria, two similar titles are known: *rab āli* and *ša muḫḫi āli,* "city governor, mayor"; the distinction between these two functions, however, is yet to be elucidated.

If Jerusalem is the city spoken of, no further evidence for a gate by this name is available. It would also be rather unusual for a gate in the capital city to be named after a contemporary city governor. Of special interest, therefore, is the ingenious suggestion of Y. Yadin (*BASOR* 222 [1976], 5–17) that v. 8b speaks of the city gate at Beer-sheba and that the structure on the left side of the city gate, excavated by Y. Aharoni at Beer-sheba, was the *bāmâ* where the monumental altar originally stood. (The excavators of Tel Beer-sheba, contrariwise, maintain that the altar and the cult structure are associated with King Hezekiah and his reforms at the site; see Z. Herzog, A. F. Rainey and Sh. Moshkovitz, *BASOR* 225 [1977], 49–58.)

The details concerning the location of the high place, on the left as one enters the city gate, points to the writer's personal acquaintance with this installation and is a sign of contemporaneity. (Technically these words are a footnote to the preceding description.)

9. *But the priests of the high places.* This verse can also be considered a "footnote," which interrupts the description of the reform acts. It refers to the fate of those rural priests brought into Jerusalem (v. 8a) and their status at the Temple. If the reading *maṣṣôt,* "unleavened cakes," is correct, and it is supported by all versions, it may be either a generic term for grain offerings (cf. e.g. Lev 2:4, 5, and the remarks of Rashi for the rabbinic view) or a reference to *maṣṣôt,* "unleavened cakes," consumed at the Passover celebration called for by Josiah; cf. below vv. 21–23.

The restriction reported here contravenes the injunction of Deut 18:6–8, in which Levitical clergy are granted full rights when they choose to come to the sanctuary city (see further in the Comment). It is, however, not unlike the limitations placed upon physically blemished priests by Lev 21:22–23 (pointed out by R. E. Friedman, *Exile and the Biblical Narrative,* Harvard Semitic Monograph 22 [1981], 65–66).

10. *He defiled the Topheth in the Ben-hinnom Valley.* Topheth was the cultic installation at which children were offered to the god Molech. Probably the word refers either to the stand over the fire upon which the child was placed or to the hearth as a whole; etymologically, it may be cognate to Ugaritic *ṯpd* and to Aramaic *špt,* "to set (on the fire)"; and cf. Hebrew, *šĕpōt hassîr,* "set the pot (on the fire)," in 2 Kgs 4:38. Discussions of the term are to be found in W. R. Smith, *The Religion of the Semites* (repr. New York: Meridian, 1956), 377 n. 2; N. H. Tur-Sinai, *Language and Book*[2] (Jerusalem: Mosad Bialik, 1954), 499–500 (Hebrew); W. F. Albright, *Yahweh and the Gods of Canaan* (Garden City, N.Y.: Doubleday, 1969), 234–44, 275.

The Ben-hinnom Valley is commonly identified with Wadi er-Rababi southwest of the City of David, and the location of Topheth in the last open area before the valley meets the Kidron Valley at En-rogel (J. Simons, *Jerusalem in the Old Testament* [Leiden: Brill, 1952], 10–12, 52, n. 2). Cf. Josh 15:8, 18:16, and Jer 19:2.

The excavations at the precinct of the goddess Tanit at Carthage, often referred to as "topheth," unearthed in reality a large cemetery containing urn burials of the charred remains of humans and animals, mostly dating from the fourth-century B.C.E. These deposits have been interpreted in line with the written reports of late antiquity that the Carthaginians practiced human sacrifice, especially in times of great crisis. But the excavated burial grounds in the Phoenician colonies, as well as those known from the homeland, are wrongly termed "topheth," which is known only from biblical sources. (The most recent work at the site is summarized by the excavator, L. E. Stager, in *New Light on Ancient Carthage,* [Ann Arbor, Mich.: University of Michigan, 1980] 1–11, 131–33.)

pass his son or daughter through fire to Molech. For "pass through fire," see the note to 21:6.

The identity of the deity to whom children were dedicated in this fashion is much debated. On the basis of 1 Kgs 11:7, a singular reference to Milcom, god of the Ammonites, as Molech, has led to the identification of the two (so Gray, *ad loc.;* cf. earlier Ibn-Ezra and Nachmanides ad Lev 18:21); but in 2 Kgs 23:10 and 13, the two gods are distinct. The name Molech derives from **mlk,* "to rule" and *melek,* "king"—and appears as an element in the names Adrammelek and Anammelek, gods to whom children were burned (2 Kgs 17:31). Because of the association of "burning children" to Adad and that god's epithet "king," M. Weinfeld considered Molech identical with Adad (*UF* 4 [1972], 135–54). But if Jeremiah can be trusted, sacrifices to Molech were offered at the installation of Baal (Jer 32:35), which suggests that Molech might be a general epithet associated with a number of deities. Eissfeldt's study of Punic inscriptions (*Molk als Opferbegriff im Punischen und Hebräischen und das Ende des Gottes Moloch* [Halle: M. Neimeyer, 1935]) led him to take the term *mlk* as a sacrificial term, a "votive offering"; but this interpretation is unacceptable in biblical texts (though adopted by M. Noth, *Leviticus,* 148 at 20:5) in which Molech is exclusively the name or an epithet of a god.

The polemics of Jeremiah (7:31, 9:5, 32:35) and Ezekiel (16:20–21, 23:29) raise the further possibility that in certain circles, Molech sacrifices were offered to YHWH and were considered by these worshippers to be a sign of ultimate devotion to God (cf. Mic 6:7). See the notes to 2 Kgs 3:27, 16:3, 21:6.

11. *the horses which the kings of Judah dedicated to the sun.* White horses served important ritual functions in Assyria and were associated with the gods Ashur and Sin. They are mentioned in penalty clauses for violations of contracts; e.g. "He shall tie/dedicate (*irakkas/iddan*) four white horses (*sisê piṣûte*) at the feet of Sin of Harran." (The documentation was collected by E. Weidner, *BiOr* 9 [1952], 157–59.) Shamash, the sun god (i.e. his emblem) rode a horse-drawn chariot on festal days, as did other Mesopotamian deities. Therefore, the mention of horses in the present verse suggests that rites similar to those known in Assyria had gained popularity in Judah. (The spread of this Mesopotamian cult into Judah under Manasseh and Amon is discussed in Cogan, *Imperialism,* 86–88.)

For **nātôn* in the sense of "to dedicate," cf. Num 3:9, 8:19, I Chr 6:33, as elucidated by E. A. Speiser, "Unrecognized Dedication," *IEJ* 13 (1963), 69–73.

the officer of the precincts. Heb. *parwārîm* is an old crux, still unresolved. A similar word, *parbār,* in a description of the Temple layout, 1 Chr 26:18, is usually connected with this term, and both are taken as a loanword from Persian *frabar,* "court, vestibule" (so e.g. E. Lipiński, *Studies,* 156–57).

Though the use of a Persian word in Chronicles can be expected in a work composed in the Persian period, it is unlikely to have been known to the Deuteronomistic historian(s) even in the latest strata of Kings. If it is indeed Persian, then *parwārîm* would be a late gloss. But its derivation from Old Persian is open to doubt (oral observation by Prof. S. Shaked) and perhaps best left as a hapax.

Oestreicher's suggestion (*Das deuteronomische Grundgesetz,* 54) to derive it from Sumerian *é.babbarra,* "house of the shining sun," the name of the Shamash temple at Sippar, is arresting, but seems farfetched.

12–13. The long periodic sentences ending with a verb need not be late insertions (as suggested by Gray); the break in the narrative sequence with the *waw*-consecutive may be intentional, calling notice to the removal of cultic structures of long standing.

12. *The upper chamber of Ahaz.* For a connection between the upper chamber (*ʿălîyâ*) constructed by Ahaz and the Ahaz sundial (*maʿălôt*), see the note to 20:11 and the discussion of S. Iwry cited there.

He hastily removed them from there. MT *wayyāraṣ miššām,* "he ran from there," is better read as *hiphil, wayyĕrîṣēm,* lit. "he hastened them, kept them distant," (*BDB* 930b). (The second *mem* was lost through haplography.) This is preferable to taking the verb as **rāṣôṣ,* "crush" (so Burney, *NEB, NAB* and already Qimḥi), which is used mostly to describe oppression (e.g. 1 Sam 12:3, 4; Amos 4:1), and is not part of Dtr.'s vocabulary for destruction.

13. *Mount of the Destroyer.* MT *har hammašḥit* is a word play on *har hammišḥâ,* "Mount of Ointment," i.e., the Mount of Olives (cf. Mishna *Mid.* 2.4 for the name). This pun makes use of the verb **hašḥît,* "to destroy, ruin, act wickedly," employed in Deuteronomic writing in reference to abandoning YHWH's way. Cf. e.g. Deut 4:16, 25; 31:29; Judg 2:19.

For the construction of these altars by Solomon to the gods of Israel's neighbors, cf. 1 Kgs 11:5–7. The editorial hand responsible for the description of Solomon's sins is also to be recognized at work here.

15. *He burned the high place.* If MT is retained, the burning would refer to those items of the cultic installation which were combustible, especially the pole of Asherah noted at the end of the verse. But burning a high place is unexampled elsewhere. In light of Deuteronomic language describing the eradication of idolatrous objects, where altars are smashed (**ntṣ*), sacred pillars are broken (**šbr*) and sacred poles chopped down (**gdʿ*) and burned (**śrp*) (cf. esp. Deut 12:3 and 7:5), one expects here a reference to a sacred pole. LXX reads "and broke its stones," which might reflect an original *wyšbr ʾt mṣbth.* To emend MT to read *wyšbr ʾt ʾbnyw* (so Stade, Burney, Šanda et al.) is unacceptable, as such an expression is unattested. Here, as in v. 6, the objects are repeatedly destroyed, though the scattering of their ashes is not noted.

16. *in accordance with the word of YHWH foretold by the man of God.* This editorial explication refers to the prophecy in 1 Kgs 13:2, which foretold the destruction of the Bethel altar by Josiah. The syntax of the MT seems garbled because of the repetition of *ʾăšer qārāʾ,* and perhaps this is a dittography. Either *ʾăšer qārāʾ* or even the entire phrase at the end of the verse, which appears again in v. 17, should be excised. After the words "the man of god" (*ʾyš hʾlhym*), LXX versions add: *en to estanai Ieroboam en te eorte epi to thusiasterion. kai epistrephas* (Luc. *Iosias*) *eren tous ophthalmous autou*

epi taphon tou anthropou tou theou. Retroverted into Hebrew: *bʿmd yrbʿm bḥg ʿl hmzbḥ wypn wyśʾ ʾt ʿynyw ʿl qbr ʾyš hʾlhym,* "When Jeroboam stood by the altar on the festival day, he (Josiah) turned and saw the grave of the man of God . . ." This additional clause has been accepted as genuine by most commentators and translations. If so, the shorter text in MT resulted from homeoteleuton. Or perhaps in some earlier stage of the tradition, the words of the prophecy which mentioned Josiah by name (1 Kgs 13:2) were quoted *in toto* after v. 16b to point up the fulfillment of ancient prophecy; they were later excised when the story was brought down to its present compass. See further in the Comment.

17. *"What is this marker I see?"* Heb. *ṣîyûn;* cf. Jer 31:21. In Ezek 39:15 the marker locates the still unburied dead in the war with Gog.

the grave of the man of God. The irregularity of the construct form with the definite article here and at the end of the verse, "the altar at Bethel," have been considered elliptical forms of expression; cf. *GKC* 127f.; and earlier Qimḥi, ad loc.

which you did to the altar. Heb. *ʿāśîtā ʿal. ʿAl* in a hostile sense, rather than "upon," is noted in *BDB* 757b, but this verse in 2 Kgs is not cited. In the original prophecy in 1 Kgs 13:4, *qārāʾ ʿal* means "proclaim against."

18. *So they spared his bones.* So with *NEB,* rather than "left undisturbed" as in *NAB, NJPS.*

The old prophet, whose bones were buried alongside those of the man of God from Judah, came from Bethel, not Samaria (1 Kgs 13:11). Moreover, Samaria had not yet been built in the days of Jeroboam I. Its mention here is anachronistic and betrays the usage of the seventh century when Samaria was a regional territory, juxtaposed to Judah.

19. *removed the shrines of the high places in the cities of Samaria.* Josiah proceeds according to the prophecy in 1 Kgs 13:32, into which the current language of Dtr. has crept. See the note to v. 18 on the use of the term "Samaria."

to provoke <YHWH's anger>. The verb *lhkʿys,* "to anger, provoke to anger" always appears with an object; cf. 1 Kgs 16:13, 26, 33; 22:54; 2 Kgs 17:11; 21:6.—which Luc., LXX, Vulg., Syr. supply.

20. *He slaughtered all the priests of the high places.* In contrast to his behavior in Judah (vv. 8–9), Josiah massacred the priests who served at the high places in the North, treating them as if they were idolatrous, though they are called *kōhănîm.* This was in the spirit of the law requiring the punishment of Israelite cities that strayed from YHWH, cf. Deut 13:13–19. Atrocities of this type were part of the norm of warfare of the Assyrian kings in the days of the Empire—cf. e.g. the descriptions of the wars of Ashurnasirpal II in *ARI* 2.546, 547, 549, 571, 585, 587 and Shalmaneser III in *ANET³,* 277–78.

21–23. The narrative resumes vv. 1–3, which had been interrupted by the lengthy insertion of the acts of reform (vv. 4–14, 15–20). This was the first centralized celebration of Passover, since the days of Israel's entry into the land; the last reported Passover is in Josh 5:10–11. With the eradication of the rural shrines, the Jerusalem sanctuary remained the sole site available to hold the sacrifice, as directed by Deut 16:5–6. (M. Haran has strongly argued for the antiquity of the requirement to offer up the paschal sacrifice in one of the temples outside the chosen place, as opposed to most critics who view the Passover as originally a family rite; cf. *Temples and Temple Service,* 343–48.)

24. *those who consult ghosts and spirits.* For these practitioners, see the note to 21:6.

household images. Heb. *tĕrāpîm.* Attested in early literature (Gen 31:19; Jud 17:5; 1 Sam 19:13) and only here in the Dtr. history, these images have been the subject of much conjecture. The most reasonable etymology is to connect *tĕrāpîm* with Hittite *tarpi(š),* a spirit both protective and malevolent, which appears in lexical texts parallel to Akk. *šēdu,* "a daemon" (H. Hoffner, *JNES* 27 [1968], 61–68). Their mention alongside the ephod and necromancers suggests that *tĕrāpîm* were used as a mantic device.

25. *with all his soul, and with all his might.* The unqualified commendation of Josiah is based on Deut 6:5 and is unique in the entire Deuteronomistic history; its terms echo the praise of Moses in Deut 34:10: Moses was the unsurpassed prophet; Josiah, the unsurpassed king. Such a perspective must have originated in a post-Josianic period.

29. *In his days.* An archival quotation; see the note to 2 Kgs 8:20.

Pharaoh Necho. Necho II, king of Egypt (610–595 B.C.E.). The historical background of his reign is reviewed by A. Spalinger, "Egypt and Babylonia: A Survey (c. 620 B.C.–550 B.C.)," *Studien zur Ägyptischen Kultur* 5 (1977), 221–244; and see the Comment below.

set out . . . to the king of Assyria. Heb. *ʿālâ ʿal,* not "marched against" as in most translations. The writer of this passage could not have been ignorant of Egypt's role as Assyria's ally at this crucial time in history. Note that *ʿal* often interchanges with *ʾel* in late texts; see *BDB* 757a. (*NEB*'s rendering, "set out to help," is influenced by modern historical knowledge.)

(Necho) put him to death . . . as soon as he had seen him. The Chronicler renders this encounter differently: The king, mortally wounded, was transferred to Jerusalem and died there; cf. 2 Chr 35:23–24.

30. *anointed him.* Anointing of kings is mentioned only in three instances in Kings—of Solomon (1 Kgs 1:45), Jehoash (2 Kgs 11:12) and Jehoahaz, all cases of irregular succession (as observed by Qimḥi). See the note to 9:6. In the present instance, a younger son was preferred to his older brother, the reasons for which are discussed in the Comment.

Comment

1. *The International Setting.* In contradistinction to the age of Manasseh, when Assyrian pressure was actively felt in the West, in particular during the campaigns of Esarhaddon and Ashurbanipal to Egypt, Josiah's reign occurred during the days of Assyria's decline and fall. By the middle of the seventh century, Assyria had lost control of Egypt; and for over a decade was involved in wars in Babylonia and Elam. Babylon was reconquered in 648 B.C.E. after a long siege; Elam was ravaged and its capital Susa finally pillaged and destroyed by 645. On its northern borders, the Empire was troubled by the activity of nomadic hordes, the Cimmerians (or in the opinion of some scholars, the Scythians).[1] Evidence for Assyrian operations in the lands

[1] For a comprehensive summary of the problem, with a survey of current views, see H. Cazelles, "Sophonie, Jérémie et les Scythes en Palestine," *RB* 74 (1967), 24–44. As to

neighboring Judah can be gleaned from the latest of Ashurbanipal's historical inscriptions. These tell of campaigns against the Arabs in the area of Damascus and the Transjordan, and of a punitive expedition against Ushu, the coastal section of Tyre—all before 643 B.C.E.[2] To this same period belong the two economic documents written in Neo-Assyrian found at Gezer,[3] which attest to imperial jurisdiction at a major Israelite city.

Shortly after 640, the written sources cease and very little is known of Assyrian history during the last decade of Ashurbanipal's reign. After the king's death in 627 B.C.E., there is reason to believe that Assyria was much weakened by internal strife stemming from the struggle between claimants to the throne. In 626 Babylonia rebelled and achieved independence, under Nabopolassar, a prince of Chaldean descent. A bitter struggle between the rival successors in Assyria, Sin-shar-ishkun and Ashur-etil-ilani, and Nabopolassar ensued.[4]

Our main source of information is the Babylonian Chronicle Series, which covers most of the years 627–594 B.C.E., from the revolt of Nabopolassar through the early years of Nebuchadnezzar.[5] It is from these Chronicles that one learns that Egypt came to the aid of the faltering Assyrians and sent forces to Mesopotamia in 616 to fight against the Babylonians. Meanwhile Nabopolassar had joined with the Median king, Cyaxares, also a major military power at this time. In 614 the city of Ashur fell, and two years later the capital Nineveh was captured and sacked. For a few years the western part of the Assyrian Empire, with the city of Haran as its center, resisted under the last Assyrian king, Ashur-uballit II. In 610 Haran, too, fell to the Babylonians.[6]

---

the Scythian eruption into Syria-Palestine, often inferred from Herodotus (*History* 1.103–6), cf. Bright, *History³*, 315; and A. R. Millard, "The Scythian Problem," in *Glimpses of Ancient Egypt*, Studies in Honour of H. W. Fairman, eds. J. Ruffle, G. A. Gaballa, and K. A. Kitchen (Warminster: Aris and Phillips, 1979), 119–22.

[2] For the texts see *ANET³*, 297–301; and for their analysis, see I. Ephʿal, *The Ancient Arabs*, 142–69.

[3] The documents are dated 652 and 649 and are published in R. A. S. Macalister, *The Excavation at Gezer* (London: Palestine Exploration Fund, 1912), 1.23–29.

[4] The chronological problems regarding the last three decades of Assyria have not been fully resolved. Basic studies are those of R. Borger, *WZKM* 55 (1959), 63–76, and idem, *JCS* 19 (1965), 59–78; J. Oates, *Iraq* 27 (1965), 135–59; W. von Soden, *ZA* 68 (1967), 241–55; J. Reade, *JCS* 23 (1970), 1–9.

[5] The Babylonian Chronicles were published by C. J. Gadd, *The Fall of Nineveh* (London: Luzac, 1923) and D. J. Wiseman, *Chronicles of Chaldaean Kings* (London: British Museum, 1956), and now appear, re-edited, in A. K. Grayson, *Chronicles*, 87–104. Cf. Appendix I, No. 10.

[6] The Babylonian Chronicle (Wiseman, *Chronicles*, 58:38) mentions the *Umman-manda* as allies of the Babylonians. This is the customary term by which northern barbarians are referred to and in the Chronicles must mean the Medes; the identification is assured by the letter published by F. Thureau-Dangin, *RA* 22 (1925), 27–29.

To what extent are events during the reign of Josiah linked to these international affairs? Viewed from the standpoint of the Deuteronomistic historian, Josiah's actions are a reaction to the decadent age of Manasseh. Viewed on the political level, Judah's resurgence under Josiah, including his activity in Samaria (cf. 23:15–18), must have coincided with and resulted from the retreat of Assyria from Judah's borders and the termination of the former's century-long sovereignty over that region.

It is very hard to establish the date when Assyria lost both its hold over the province of Samaria and its hegemony over Judah. The earliest possible date is in the 630s; another possibility would be 627 B.C.E., the year of Ashurbanipal's death. Josiah's thirty-one years of reign come, then, during a critical stage in the history of the ancient Near East.

2. *The Great Reform.* Dtr. proceeds directly to a description of the events in Josiah's eighteenth year, which are for him the crowning point of Judah's history. In this free composition, Josiah is depicted as concerning himself with the physical restoration of the Temple. In highlighting this act, Josiah's piety is underscored, for it was a primary duty of ancient Near Eastern monarchs to care for and to maintain the temples of the gods.[7]

The story of the Temple repairs is modeled on the older account in 2 Kgs 12, which relates in much detail how in the days of Jehoash, the king ordered repair work on YHWH's house. The verbal similarities between these two stories (e.g. 22:5–6 and 12:12–13; 22:7 and 12:16), which have often been pointed out, are not sufficient cause to postulate that both derive from Temple archives.[8] The description of the repairs in 2 Kgs 22 is abbreviated, with only the preparatory stages of the work reported. The conclusion of the narrative, which would have told of the repair work itself, is nowhere given (cf. 12:15—"they repaired . . . the Temple"). Moreover, unlike 2 Kgs 12, in which the high priest Jehoiada is a main actor, in 2 Kgs 22, it is the king who is shown to be versed in Temple matters. In a royal decree, Josiah orders the disbursement of money to the skilled workmen. The historian has set Josiah in center stage, but since the main subject of the present account was to be the Book of Teaching and the king's reaction to its discovery, the repair story is given in very brief form.

The account opens abruptly with a statement by Hilkiah, the high priest, that he has found the Book of Teaching. Shaphan receives the book and reads it, and is so deeply impressed by its contents, that he reports its discovery to the king. After hearing the words of the Book, Josiah is thrown into a state of

The role of the Scythians in the destruction of Assyria has been grossly overstated (cf. the remarks of I. M. Diakonoff, *VDI* 1981, No. 2, 40 and 63).

[7] See the remarks of H. Frankfort, *Kingship and the Gods* (Chicago: University of Chicago Press, 1948), 265–69.

[8] So e.g. Burney.

shock. Can this book that had such a profound effect upon all its hearers be identified?

It has become an accepted maxim in biblical scholarship ever since De Wette's *Dissertatio Critica* in 1805 that the book is Deuteronomy or its early nucleus.[9] Josiah's act of cultic reform (cf. 23:4–14, 21–24), which culminated in the centralization of all worship in Jerusalem, are presented in terms and style almost identical to that of Deuteronomy. Moreover no other book of the Pentateuch besides Deuteronomy requires cultic centralization in YHWH's chosen city. Josiah's mournful reaction to the book also points to Deuteronomy, in which the legal code concludes with lengthy maledictions, a dire warning to all violators of YHWH's covenant. Deuteronomy presents itself as a covenant, and from a literary point of view the book has the structure of a political treaty.[10] It is, therefore, cardinal for the understanding of the Josianic reform that it is described as having emerged from "the book of the covenant which was found in the Temple" (23:2), i.e. the book of Deuteronomy or a significant part of it. But can the report of this find be taken at face value?

The discovery of old documents during repairs of temples is an attested phenomenon in the ancient Near East. From Egypt come reports of scrolls discovered in the masonry of buildings, and in Mesopotamia ancient foundation deposits and stelae were eagerly sought and their recovery faithfully recorded.[11] But whether the Book of Teaching brought forward by Hilkiah was a bona fide find at the time of repairs to the Temple in Jerusalem or was purposefully presented as such, cannot be ascertained.[12] At issue is the date of

[9] A succinct presentation of the critical position can be found in S. R. Driver, *Deuteronomy,* ICC, xliv–xlv. For surveys of recent opinion on this issue, see E. W. Nicholson, *Deuteronomy and Tradition* (Philadelphia: Fortress, 1967), 1–7; N. Lohfink, *IDB* Sup, 229–32. M. Noth, *Überlieferungsgeschichtliche Studien*, 92, n. 1, thought it unnecessary to prove this point once again and accepted the identification as a given.

[10] See the detailed studies of Weinfeld, *Deuteronomy,* 39–157; D. J. McCarthy, *Treaty and Covenant,* AnBib 21A (1978), 157–87.

[11] See the early discussion of E. Naville, "Egyptian Writings in Foundation Walls and the Age of the Book of Deuteronomy," *PSBA* 29 (1907), 232–42. Mesopotamian evidence was collected by S. Euringer, "Die ägyptischen und keilschriftlichen Analogien zum Funde des Codex Helciae," *BZ* 10 (1912), 13–23; W. Speyer, *Bücherfunde in der Glaubenswerbung der Antike,* Hypomnemata 24 (1970), 125–28. The last Babylonian king Nabonidus is especially known for his search for older documents and in several instances it can be shown that their style influenced his own inscriptions. On this interest of Nabonidus in historical antecedents, see G. Goossens, *RA* 42 (1948), 149–59, and the texts in S. Langdon, *Neubabylonische Königsinschriften* (Leipzig: J. C. Hinrich, 1912), 218–29, 234–43; idem, *AJSL* 32 (1915), 102–17.

[12] M. Smith discusses ancient "misattributions" and "forgeries" in "Pseudepigraphy in the Israelite Literary Tradition," *Pseudepigrapha I,* Entretiens sur l'antiquite classique XVIII (1972), 191–227.

the book of Deuteronomy, which if one accepts the position adopted for over a century in biblical scholarship, was composed in the seventh century, though it may well include older material from northern Israel.[13]

Although the "discovery" of the book is credited to Hilkiah, himself either a reinstated Zadokite or from the priestly circle living at Anathoth (see the note to 22:4), others, a new elite, comprising priests, scribes, and prophets (cf. 23:2), supported Josiah and may be seen behind the promotion of the new reforms.

Most prominent among the king's supporters is the prophetess Huldah, whose response to Josiah's inquiry is given in somber tones: the fate of Judah is sealed, just as written in the book; but as a reward for his personal contrition, Josiah will die "in peace" before the doom overtakes his kingdom (22:15–20). Many recognize here the hand of the later Deuteronomistic historian, who has worked over the original prophecy of Huldah. The prediction of unrelenting doom "against this place," which does not consider the possibility of repentance, would not have encouraged Josiah to proceed with his reform.[14] A positive divine word, now transformed into a prophecy of woe by vv. 16, 17, 20b, originally strengthened him in his task. At the same time, the incongruity between the promise to Josiah that he would die "in peace" and his untimely death at Megiddo (23:29) identifies vv. 19–20a as part of the original kernel of the prophecy.[15] The late rewriting surprisingly did not eliminate this incongruity, which runs contrary to the historiographic viewpoint of the Deuteronomistic circle, for whom the fulfillment of prophecy played a key role. These words of Huldah remain a striking example of unfulfilled prophecy.[16]

Encouraged by Huldah's prophecy, Josiah convenes a grand assembly of

[13] See the works cited in note 9 of the Comment to 18:1–12, and R. E. Clements, *VT* 15 (1965), 300–12.

[14] "Huldah did not speak in this way, at any rate if her advice was followed by Josiah" (A. Kuenen, *Prophets and Prophecy in Israel,* 440).

[15] This is the opinion of most commentators, e.g. Benzinger, Montgomery-Gehman, Gray, whose arguments are summarized by Nelson, *Double Redaction,* 76–79. R. E. Friedman, *Exile and Biblical Narrative,* 25, considered these verses, with arguable signs of both Deuteronomistic editors, to be "too complex to unravel." The attempt to smooth over the obvious contradiction by taking "in peace" as referring to national well-being, rather than to Josiah's personal fortune (e.g. Thenius) cannot be sustained. Note the usage of "in peace" in 1 Kgs 2:6 and Jer 34:5. Šanda took "in peace" as an unexplained marginal gloss.

Y. Kaufmann (*Toledot,* 1.98–100) maintained the integrity of vv. 15–20 as authentic, prereform prophecy, by interpreting the "disasters" about to befall Jerusalem (22:20) as a general indictment of idolatry in the mode of ancient prophetic rebuke and not as prediction of destruction and exile.

[16] The pattern of prophecy and fulfillment pointed out by G. von Rad as a structural element in Dtr.'s work is here broken (von Rad, *Studies in Deuteronomy,* 78–82).

all Judah, from the capital and the countryside, priests and prophets, the entire population—young and old. They undertake the obligations of the "newly recovered" book of the covenant and pledge their loyalty to YHWH. To demonstrate compliance with the Teaching, Josiah proclaims the celebration of the Passover, whose observance was unlike any other in past history,[17] indeed, a finishing touch inspired by the Deuteronomic ideal (cf. Deut 16:1–7).

The historicity of the description given here may, however, be limited, for it comes from the hand of a partisan of the Deuteronomic school of thought and is constructed from the start to propagate the ideology of that school. Thus it is made to appear as if all events flow from the finding of the Book of Teaching. The Chronicler, in 2 Chr 34–35, presented a different order of events, one in which the Book does not play as central a role as in 2 Kgs 22. Yet in whatever way the divergent account in Chronicles is to be understood (see below), 2 Kgs 23:1–3 states that for the first time in the history of the monarchy, the entire community undertook a covenantal obligation to observe the divine ordinances based upon a Book of Teaching. In this respect, the Josianic covenant can rightly be seen as a new departure in the history of Judah.[18] This departure involves more than just oath taking. For the first time, a Book of Teaching is set as the constitutive base of the community of Judah, and with this act the first steps were taken to collect and codify Israel's legal and literary heritage. The emergence of Deuteronomy into the public realm marked the beginnings of the Pentateuch.[19]

Now, the description of the entire community undertaking an oath of loyalty to YHWH is literarily similar to the descriptions of oath ceremonies in Assyria during the days of Sennacherib, Esarhaddon, and Ashurbanipal. So, for example, in order to insure the undisturbed transfer of rule from father to son, Ashurbanipal reports that his father "gathered the people of Assyria, young and old, from the upper and the lower seas, and had them take an oath by the gods and enforced the(ir) obligations."[20] In addition, as has been shown in several studies, there is a distinct affinity between some of the curses which conclude the covenant in the book of Deuteronomy and those in the "vassal treaties" of Esarhaddon.[21] But questions relating to the literary ori-

[17] The literary connection between the act of covenant making and the Passover was pointed out by Thenius and Kostermann.

[18] This has been the opinion of all historians from J. Wellhausen, *Israelitische und jüdische Geschichte*[4] (Berlin: G. Reimer, 1901), 134–35, through M. Noth, *History*, 275–77.

[19] For apt remarks on the formation of the "Torah book," cf. Y. Kaufmann, *The Religion of Israel* (Chicago: University of Chicago Press, 1960), 172–75.

[20] Cf. *ANET*[3], 289 and Streck, *Assurbanipal*, 4, lines 18–22.

[21] The material was treated most recently by Weinfeld, *Deuteronomy*, 116–46; see the earlier studies of D. R. Hillers, *Treaty Curses and the Old Testament Prophets*, BibOr 16 (1964) (with reservations on the extent of Mesopotamian influence noted on 86–87); and R. Frankena, *OTS* 14 (1965), 122–54.

gins of Deuteronomy should not be combined with issues concerning Josiah's act of covenant making. The loyalty oath in Sargonid Assyria concerned itself with the newly appointed successor and in this respect can be compared to the covenant undertaken by the people to protect the succession of Johoash (2 Kgs 11:17). But there is no parallel anywhere in the ancient Near East to an entire community swearing allegiance to its God as depicted in 2 Kgs 23:1–3. Josiah's act and the biblical concept of a covenant made between God and people remain unique.[22]

Inserted into the narrative of the covenant ceremony is a detailed description of the eradication of all illicit cults in the Jerusalem Temple and throughout Judah, undertaken by royal decree and carried out with zeal and thoroughness (23:4–14). Eradicated were practices mentioned in Kings for the first time—e.g. the dedication of horses to the Sun god (23:11), alongside others which had been introduced into the capital a long time before by King Solomon—e.g. the high places dedicated to Chemosh and Milcom (23:14). In addition, the high places at which YHWH was worshiped were desecrated, and their priests were gathered into Jerusalem, where their service in the Temple was restricted (23:9).

Two major issues have been the focus of scholarly debate concerning Josiah's reform: (1.) the nature of the measures and their relationship to the Book of Teaching found in the Temple, and (2.) the chronology of the enactments. The influential study of T. Oestreicher called attention to the fact that the reform as described sought to purge Judah of foreign cults—i.e., they aimed for *Kultusreinheit,* "cult purity," not *Kultuseinheit,* "cult centrality."[23] The cults eradicated were taken by him to be Assyrian cults, signs of Judah's vassaldom, and their elimination was tantamount to rebellion. Josiah thus declared his political independence from the Assyrian empire. At the same time the closing of the high places was merely a temporary measure meant to prevent Assyria from appeasing the local god YHWH during the expected campaign to punish Josiah. It was not an act of centralization.

Several weak points in this position prevent adopting the proposed interpretation of events. While Josiah's reforms did give expression to Judah's newly acquired political independence, it should be noted that open rebellion against Assyria is not reported of Josiah as it is in the case of Hezekiah (cf. 18:7). Assyria had retreated from the area by the time Josiah acted. Furthermore, as has been previously shown, the Assyrian royal cult was never imposed upon Judah, not even in the dark days of Ahaz or Manasseh. As for the

[22] In this usage, the loyalty oath was adopted to insure the accession of Esarhaddon and of later Assyrian kings down to the days of Ashurbanipal's successors, Sin-sharishkun and Ashur-etil-ilani, about the time of Josiah's convocation. On the Assyrian oaths and their antecedents in the second millennium B.C., see now, H. Tadmor, "Treaty and Oath."

[23] T. Oestreicher, *Das deuteronomische Grundgesetz,* BFCT 27/4 (1923), 37–58.

foreign cults which were practiced in the Jerusalem Temple and in the Judaean countryside, they were typical of the cultic amalgam which had developed in the western regions of the Assyrian empire as a result of the massive population shifts enforced by the conqueror. The worship at the high places, according to the Deuteronomistic view, was a long-standing aberration of the cult of YHWH. That their closing was more than just a temporary measure is proved by the thoroughgoing defilement of both the high places and the Topheth (23:8 and 10). Certainly the intent was not to reinstitute Topheth once the Assyrian threat passed!

In addition, a clear-cut separation between cult purity and cult centrality does not exist in the book of Deuteronomy. The law of centralization in Deut 12 is introduced by a statement requiring the eradication of the manifold Canaanite cult sites throughout the land (Deut 12:2–4), and a single chosen site is enjoined upon Israel. Josiah acts in accordance with this law. By desecrating the rural shrines, he perforce centralizes worship at a single site; Jerusalem and its Temple are the direct beneficiaries of the Reform.

As to the question of the chronology of the enactments, it has been suggested that the presentation in 2 Chr 34–35 is historically more reliable than 2 Kgs 22–23. Accordingly, Josiah's first moves were in 632, his eighth year (2 Chr 34:3), the year of Ashurbanipal's death.[24] The increased confusion in Assyria and Babylonia allowed Josiah to proceed more vigorously, and by 628, his twelfth year, an open break with his overlord took place. But a functional connection between the death of the Assyrian monarch and events in Judah can no longer be claimed. It is now apparent that Ashurbanipal died in 627, though the battle of succession may well have begun earlier.[25] On the other hand, it has recently been argued that the report in Chronicles, which places the beginning of the reform in 628, may be but an artificial scheme based on the notion that a pious king acts early in his reign to attend to cultic matters, without any prompting by prophets or books of Law.[26]

Whatever the case concerning that report in Chronicles may be, Josiah's reforms may reasonably have begun sometime before the finding of the Book. The date "the eighteenth year" in 2 Kgs 22–23 should not be taken at face value, for the narration of events there by the Deuteronomistic historian makes Josiah's every act flow from this discovery. Not only is the reader under the impression that events have been telescoped into just a few months, but one might expect that the physical refurbishing of the Temple would have

[24] S. Smirin, *Josiah and His Age* (Jerusalem: Mosad Bialik, 1952), 53–58 (Hebrew); F. M. Cross and D. N. Freedman, *JNES* 12 (1953), 56–58; cf. Bright, *History*^{3}, 317–18.

[25] W. von Soden, *ZA* 68 (1967), 241–55. The date "year 8" in 2 Chr 34:3 would then correlate with the battles on the eve of Ashurbanipal's death.

[26] M. Cogan, "Tendentious Chronology in the Book of Chronicles," *Zion* 45 (1980), 165–72.

included its cultic rehabilitation as well. On historical grounds, by about 625 B.C.E., Josiah was already free of any vassalage to Assyria. This would have permitted his expansion into the northern territories prior to his eighteenth year (22:3). But lacking firmer evidence, free of historiographic considerations, exact dates for the various stages of Josiah's reform cannot be fixed.

3. *Josiah in North Israel.* Josiah carried his reform measures into the territory of the former kingdom of Israel, here called Samaria/Samerina, the name it bore under Assyrian rule. The sanctuary ("high place") of Bethel, founded by Jeroboam son of Nebat, of all the cultic sites desecrated and devastated by Josiah, is singled out for special notice. The king further defiles these sites by burning human bones upon them, at the same time sparing the bones of the two prophets buried at Bethel.

Nowhere in this account does the writer tell of the fate of the mixed cults and their worshippers in the repopulated city of Samaria and the cities of that province, cf. 17:24–33. Yet the polemic against these cults in 17:24ff. is terminologically tied up with the narrative in 23:15–20 (cf. the similar usages: "cities of Samaria," 17:24, 23:19; "shrines of the high places," 17:29 and 32, 23:19; "priests of the high places," 17:32, 23:20). The narrative further states that "until this day" one could observe these syncretistic practices—that is, until Josiah purged the north of its idolatry. Though not specifically mentioned in 23:19–20, the new YHWH cult in the Assyrian province of Samaria was exterminated along with the old Israelite cult. The manner in which the priests are slaughtered (v. 20) is in line with the punishment specified in Deut 13:13–19 for the man who has gone astray after foreign gods. (It is of significance that the officiants are called *kōhănîm,* "priests," and not *kĕmārîm,* "idolatrous priests.") In sum, the polemic in 17:24–33 is part of the Josianic propaganda written in support of Josiah's reform in the north.[27]

By all these acts, Josiah fulfilled an ancient prophecy, which an unnamed man of God had pronounced against Jeroboam's altar (1 Kgs 13:1–3, 32). That prophecy, in its present rendition, can only be considered a *vaticinium ex eventu:* "While Jeroboam was standing on the altar to offer sacrifice, he (the man of God) cried out against the altar: 'O altar, altar! Thus said YHWH, "A son shall be born to the House of David, Josiah by name, and he shall slaughter upon you the priests of the high places who offer sacrifices upon you, and human bones shall be burned upon you" ' " (1 Kgs 13:1b–2). It serves the historian as another example of the theme "Prophecy and Its Fulfillment," so central to the historiographic perspective in Kings.[28] The prophecy serves, as well, as the ideological basis for Judah's triumph over the

[27] See above the Comment to 17:24–33 and M. Cogan, *JBL* 97 (1978), 40–44.

[28] In this case, the protagonist, Josiah, is the unwitting executor of the word of God. Josiah proceeds, unaware of the ancient prediction—cf. v. 17. The message of the tale is clear: "The word of God did come about in due time, even without the factor of a conscious decision on the part of the king who fulfilled it" (U. Simon, "I Kings 13: A

rival northern kingdom. By eradicating the ancient cult center at Bethel, a symbol of Jeroboam's rebellion, Josiah squared the account once and for all and reestablished Jerusalem's centrality.

Finally, one may surmise that the Deuteronomistic historian concluded his account of Josiah with a statement of appraisal, v. 25 or its like. But as vv. 25b, 26, 27 contain clear intimations of the final punishment of Judah, it appears that the later editor reworked the end of that account.

4. *Death at Megiddo.* The history of Josiah and the reform acts of his eighteenth year was the final and culminating chapter in the first edition of the Book of Kings. A later editor added the brief statement on his death at Megiddo (23:29–30).

In order to understand the circumstances which led to the tragic encounter between Necho and Josiah at Megiddo in 609, the relations between Egypt and Judah during the preceding decades must be considered, particularly after the withdrawal of Assyria from the West. An enigmatic statement in Herodotus relates that Psammetichus besieged Ashdod for twenty-nine years. Such a long siege is incredible: but if this statement is based upon a reliable historical tradition, one might suggest that the city fell to the Egyptians in the king's twenty-ninth year, i.e. 635.[29] In addition, an Egyptian stele dated to 612 includes a claim by Psammetichus to suzerainty over the Phoenician coast.[30] Furthermore, Babylonian Chronicles record that an Egyptian force fought at the side of Sin-shar-ishkun, king of Assyria, as early as 616.[31] While the route taken by the Egyptians northward is unknown, it has been suggested that it was by the Megiddo pass, and that Megiddo had been transferred by Assyria to Psammetichus to serve as "a logistic base, or at least a vital way station, for the Egyptian army in campaigns to Syria."[32] Though this picture is sketchy at best, there is no evidence for direct hostilities between Egypt and Judah, despite the revived expansionist policy of the Saitic dynasty, until 609.

The year 609 is a watershed in the history of Judah. The Babylonian Chronicle for that year reports that in July (Tammuz) a large Egyptian army crossed the Euphrates, marched toward Haran, and laid siege to the city. Haran was in the hands of the Babylonians, who had ousted the last Assyrian king, Ashur-uballit II; though the continuation of the passage in the Chroni-

---

Prophetic Sign—Denial and Persistence," *HUCA* 47 [1976], 81–117, and esp., 110–11).

[29] For this interpretation of Herodotus ii, 157, see H. Tadmor, *BA* 29 (1966), 101–2. The destruction of stratum 3a (VII) at Ashdod was identified by the excavators with this Egyptian action (M. Dothan, *Atiqot* 9–10 [1971], 71, 115).

[30] K. S. Freedy and D. B. Redford, *JAOS* 90 (1970), 477.

[31] Grayson, *Chronicles,* 91, line 10.

[32] A. Malamat, "Josiah's Bid for Armageddon," *JANES* 5 (1973), 267–78. Malamat correctly rejects any relation between the defeat of the Syrians at Magdolus (Herodotus ii.159) and the Megiddo episode in 2 Kgs 23; see below the Comment to 24:7.

cle is broken, it appears that even with Egyptian aid, the Assyrians could not dislodge the Babylonians from the city.[33] The king of Egypt at this time was no longer Psammetichus I, but Necho II, who had come to the throne at the end of the preceding summer.[34] Necho continued the policies of his father, assisting Assyria during her final death throes.

Modern historians are of the opinion that Josiah's appearance at Megiddo sought to stop the Egyptian advance; if so, this signaled the end of the *modus vivendi* which had prevailed in the territory of Israel after Assyria's withdrawal. Was Josiah prompted by the capture of the Assyrian stronghold at Haran by the Medes and the Babylonians in 610, or by the accession of Necho II, a new, yet untried king to the throne in Egypt? Some have even surmised that the king of Judah aligned himself at this crucial stage with Babylonia, fearing an Assyro-Egyptian revival.[35]

Each of these attempts at understanding what happened at Megiddo proceeds on the assumption that Josiah met Necho in a military engagement, based on the explicit account to that effect in 2 Chr 35:20–24. This, however, is not borne out by 2 Kgs 23:29, in which the description borders on the cryptic. If one follows the laconic passage in 2 Kgs 23:29, which is the only contemporary evidence, there was no battle or military move. (Hebrew *wayyēlēk . . . liqrā'tô* does not necessarily imply warlike action.) Josiah came to meet Necho at Megiddo,[36] and as M. Noth observed, "Necho succeeded in some way or other in seizing the person of Josiah" and killing him.[37]

There can be little doubt that the sudden and tragic death of Josiah was considered a calamity by his contemporaries. Later tradition recorded that "the prophet Jeremiah composed a song of lament for his funeral, which

33 Grayson, *Chronicles,* 96, lines 66–68. I. M. Diakonoff, *VDI* 1981, No. 2, 38, n. 37 restores the line: *ana kašādi illik* [*ul iṣ*]*ṣabtū,* "(The army) set out to capture (Haran); they [did not] take it."

34 For the chronology, see E. Hornung, *Zeitschrift für ägyptische Sprache* 92 (1966), 38f.; Freedy and Redford, *JAOS* 90 (1970), 474.

35 For these suggestions, see among others, R. Kittel, *Geschichte⁵,* 2.532–34; Robinson, *History,* 424; Bright, *History³,* 324–25.

It has also been conjectured that a Scythian attack on Ashkelon preceded the Megiddo affair; cf. e.g. A. Spalinger, *Journal of the American Research Center in Egypt* 15 (1978), 49ff. But the whole notion of a Scythian invasion of ancient Palestine at that time is problematic, as it is based solely on a late tradition found in Herodotus; see further the criticism of R. P. Vaggione, " 'Over All Asia': The Extent of the Scythian Domination in Herodotus," *JBL* 92 (1973), 523–30; cf. also M. Avi-Yonah, "Scythopolis," *IEJ* 12 (1962), 123–34.

36 A. C. Welch (*ZAW* 43 [1925], 255–60) thought that Necho summoned Josiah to explain his suspicious conduct. What took place at Megiddo was "not so much a battle as a court-martial."

37 M. Noth, *History,* 279.

remains to this day."[38] The Deuteronomistic historian must have been hard put to account for the death of the hero of his narration, a righteous king, the greatest since David. The astonishing fact is that 2 Kgs 23 offers no explanation for the events at Megiddo. The historian could not reconcile Josiah's death with his world view of just retribution; nor could his death be accommodated to Huldah's promise that "you will be gathered to your grave in peace" (22:20).[39] Two centuries later Josiah's death is attributed to his refusal "to listen to Necho's words according to God's order" (2 Chr 35:22)[40]; in a subsequent rationalization, it was inattention to the warning of Jeremiah the prophet which led Josiah to his end (1 Esdr 1:28–29).

Into the breach created by the loss of the king stepped the People of the Land, who, as in similar circumstances in the past when the regular succession to the Davidic throne was upset (cf. 11:14, 15:5, 21:24), appointed the new king, Jehoahaz/Shallum, one of Josiah's younger sons (see the note to 23:31). The reasons for his preference over the older brothers are not stated. Some have suggested that it was his hostile attitude toward Egypt which recommended him and made Jehoahaz the leader of the anti-Egyptian faction in Judah,[41] a view which might be supported by Ezekiel's description of the king as a "young lion" tearing prey and devouring men (Ezek 19:3–4).

[38] 2 Chr 35:25; Josephus, *Antiquities* x.78; cf. also 1 Esdr 1:30. Rabbinic exegesis found further reference to this tragedy in "the mourning of Hadad-rimmon in the plain of Megiddon" (Zech 12:11). Cf. Targum, ad loc.; *b. Meg.* 3a; *b. Moʿed Qatan* 28b.

[39] Josephus seems to have altered his *Vorlage,* the text of Chronicles, to suit his Greek-speaking audience. He interprets Josiah's action thus: "It was Destiny (*variant:* fated boastfulness), I believe, that urged him on to this course, in order to have a pretext for destroying him." And then Josephus adds other details: "As he was marshalling his force and riding in his chariot from one wing to another, an Egyptian archer shot him . . ." This heroic description has at its base 2 Chr 35:23–24, which in turn is strikingly similar to the one in 1 Kgs 22, of Ahab at the battle of Ramoth Gilead. Both accounts speak of "dressing up for war" and the wounding of a king by a bowman; cf. above 1 Kgs 22:29–34.

[40] S. B. Frost thoughtfully discusses "the deuteronomic historians' rather halfhearted attempt to deal theologically with Josiah's death," in "A Conspiracy of Silence," *JBL* 87 (1968), 369–82. H. G. M. Williamson (*VT* 32 [1982], 242–48) critically evaluates the development of the Chronicler's account.

[41] E.g. W. F. Albright, *JBL* 51 (1932), 92; S. Yeivin, *Tarbiz* 14 (1941), 264–65; and Qimḥi's early comment on plans by Jehoahaz to avenge his father's death.

XXXVIII. THE REIGN OF JEHOAHAZ

(23:31–35)

23 31 Jehoahaz was twenty-three years old when he became king, and
he reigned three months in Jerusalem. His mother's name was
Hamutal, daughter of Jeremiah of Libnah. 32 He did what was displeasing to YHWH, just as his ancestors had done. 33 Pharaoh Necho
imprisoned him at Riblah in the land of Hamath, ending his reign in
Jerusalem,[a] and he imposed an indemnity on the land of one hundred
talents of silver and a talent of gold. 34 Then Pharaoh Necho made
Eliakim son of Josiah king to succeed Josiah his father, changing his
name to Jehoiakim. He took Jehoahaz and brought him[b] to Egypt,
where he died. 35 Jehoiakim paid Pharaoh the silver and the gold, but
assessed the land so as to pay the amount set by Pharaoh. He exacted
the silver and the gold from the People of the Land, each according to
his assessment, so as to pay Pharaoh Necho.

[a] Read with qere: *mmlk;* ketib *bmlk.*
[b] MT: "He came"—i.e. Jehoahaz; LXX and 2 Chr 36:4 read *wayyĕbîʾēhû.*

Notes

23 31. *Jehoahaz.* His original name was evidently Shallum, as shown by the dirge over the king's misfortune in Jer 22:10–12 and by the Davidide genealogy in 1 Chr 3:15: "The sons of Josiah: the firstborn, Johanan; the second, Jehoiakim; the third, Zedekiah; the fourth, Shallum." It is generally agreed that the name Jehoahaz was taken as a "throne name" upon his accession (A. M. Honeyman, *JBL* 67 [1948], 13–26, and R. de Vaux, *Ancient Israel,* 107–8). But the new name, with the theophoric element *yhw,* may have been taken in order to have the name conform with those of Josiah's other three sons. Characteristic of the spirit of the age after Josiah's reform was the popularity of names composed with the divine name (H. Torczyner, *Lachish I* [London, 1938], 28–29), though W. E. Albright (*JBL* 51 [1932], 85, n. 25) suggested that Shallum was a hypocoristicon for *šlmyhw.* The name is now attested on a late seventh-century stamp seal: *lyhwʾḥz bn hmlk;* "(Belonging) to Jehoahaz, son of the king" (N. Avigad, "A Group of Hebrew Seals," *EI* 9 [1969], 9).

33. *ending his reign in Jerusalem.* The exchange of *m* (qere) for *b* (ketib) may not be

altogether necessary, if the *beth* is taken as an ablative; see the note to 14:13 and cf. Josh 3:16 for a similar exchange.

Riblah in the land of Hamath. At administrative and military center in the north Lebanon Valley, at Tel Zerrʿa on the Orontes River thirty-four km south of Homs. During the period of Assyrian administration in north Syria, a fortress/checkpost was located at Riblah (see *Iraq* 25 [1963], 79–80: Nimrud letter ND 2766); the site later served as headquarters for Nebuchadnezzar during his campaigns in the West (cf. 25:6, 20).

a talent of gold. The number of talents of gold has fallen out in MT. Luc. has "ten talents"; LXX has "one hundred," which is too high and can hardly be correct. In tribute lists, the amount of silver in relation to gold is much greater—cf. e.g. the payment of Hezekiah in 18:14. See also the discussion of M. Elat, *Economic Relations,* 29–42 (Hebrew).

34. *changing his name to Jehoiakim.* In the case of Eliakim, the suzerain changed his name in minimal fashion, the theophoric element *yhw* replacing *ʾēl.* The change of name may have been connected with an oath of loyalty sworn to the new overlord, not unlike the practice attested for the kings of Assyria. Necho's father, Psammetichus I was renamed Nabushezibanni by Ashurbanipal when installed as a district ruler under Assyrian aegis (*ANET*³, 295).

35. *He exacted the silver and the gold.* Heb. *nāgaś ʾet,* with double accusative is not attested elsewhere. The words "the silver and the gold" might better follow "to pay Pharaoh Necho." Cf. 15:20, also a statement concerning taxation imposed to pay an indemnity.

Comment

A short three months after ascending the throne, Jehoahaz faced Necho, who upon his return from the unsuccessful siege of Haran, brought Judah under direct Egyptian hegemony. Because Jehoahaz apparently represented a policy inimical to Egypt, Necho removed him from the throne; he was exiled to Egypt, where he died (cf. Jer 22:10–12). A heavy indemnity was imposed upon the country, and another son of Josiah, Eliakim/Jehoiakim was elevated as king. He remained an Egyptian vassal until Nebuchadnezzar II advanced upon the region.

XXXIX. THE REIGN OF JEHOIAKIM

(23:36–24:7)

23 36 Jehoiakim was twenty-five years old when he became king, and
he reigned eleven years in Jerusalem. His mother's name was Zebidah[a]
daughter of Pedaiah of Rumah. He did what was displeasing to
YHWH, just as his ancestors had done.
24 1 In his days, Nebuchadnezzar, king of Babylon marched forth;
and Jehoiakim became his vassal for three years. Then he turned and
rebelled against him. 2 YHWH let loose bands of Chaldeans, Aramaeans, Moabites, and Ammonites against him. He let them loose against
Judah to destroy it, in accordance with the word of YHWH spoken
through his servants the prophets. 3 This was entirely YHWH's intent,
directed against Judah, to remove them[b] from his sight, because of all
the sins that Manasseh committed; 4 and also because of the innocent
blood which he shed. He filled Jerusalem with innocent blood so that
YHWH would not forgive. 5 The rest of the history of Jehoiakim and all
that he did are indeed recorded in the annals of the kings of Judah.
6 So Jehoiakim slept with his ancestors and Jehoiachin his son succeeded him. 7 The king of Egypt did not leave his country any more,
for the king of Babylon seized all that had belonged to the king of
Egypt, from the Wadi of Egypt to the River Euphrates.

[a] Qere: *Zebudah.*
[b] Read *lhsyrm,* with LXX; *mem* lost in MT through haplography.

Notes

23 36. *Jehoiakim was twenty-five years old.* If this was his age on coming to the throne, then Josiah was fourteen years old when Jehoiakim was born, possibly too young. Two suggestions on how to resolve this problem have been put forward: either make Jehoahaz an older brother (cf. W. F. Albright, *JBL* 51 [1932] 85) or emend Jehoiakim's age (cf. Tadmor, *EncMiqr* 4.304, n. 10).

Pedaiah of Rumah. Identified as Aruma near Merom in the Upper Galilee or Ruma in the Netophah Valley (Aharoni, *Land of the Bible*[2], 403). In either case, this is another example of the ties established by Josiah with northern Israel; see note to 21:19.

24 **1.** *Nebuchadnezzar king of Babylon.* Nebuchadnezzar II, son of Nabopolassar, the founder of the Neo-Babylonian Empire, took the throne upon is father's death in August 605 (Wiseman, *Chronicles,* 69 = Grayson, *Chronicles,* 99, line 10). The Heb. form of the name *nbkdrʾṣr* in Jer 21:2, 7; 22:25; Ezek 26:7; 29:18–19, while less common than the form *nbkdnʾṣr* in the present verse, is a historically more accurate representation of Akk. *Nabu-kudurrī-uṣur,* "O Nabu, protect my offspring." (Older explanations of the name took *kudurru* as meaning "boundary, boundary stone"; but lexical evidence makes this less likely; see J. A. Brinkman, *Post-Kassite Babylonia,* 104, n. 565; CAD K 497.) On an Aramaic tablet from the king's thirty-fourth year, the name is spelled *[n]bwkdrṣr mlk [bb]l* (J. Starky, *Syria* 37 [1960], 100, B, lines 5–6).

marched forth. Heb. *ʿālâ* is generally followed by an object introduced by *ʿal* or *ʾel*—e.g. 17:3, 18:9, 23:29, which is missing in the present verse. The simplest solution is to suggest that *ʿālāyw,* "against him," was lost through haplography. (Some Luc. mss read here: *epi tēn gēn,* "against the country.") For the historical background of Jehoiakim's submission, see the Comment.

he turned. I.e. he recanted, reneged on his oath of allegiance. For **šûb* in this sense, cf. Jer 34:11, 16.

2. *YHWH let loose . . .* LXX^{B} omits YHWH, thus allowing the subject to be construed as Nebuchadnezzar. This reading, however, is difficult, since the direct antecedent of the verb "he let loose" would then be Jehoiakim. Hebrew would require the specific mention of Nebuchadnezzar as subject. Though LXX is favored by many critics, YHWH as subject may be retained as original, from the pen of the historian (Dtr_2) and not a later gloss.

bands of Chaldeans, Aramaeans, Moabites, and Ammonites. Though Nebuchadnezzar's official title is "king of Babylon," his people are referred to as Chaldeans by Judaean and later Greek sources. Cf. e.g. Jer 37:5, 8, 9; Hab 1:6. The Neo-Babylonian records refer to the Chaldeans as Babylonians (*Akkadû,* i.e. Akkadians). In the somewhat earlier Assyrian records, the Chaldeans appear alongside eastern Aramaeans as *Kaldu Aramu* (Streck, *Assurbanipal,* 30.97–98). It is this usage that is present in 2 Kgs 24:2 and Jer 35:11. (R. C. Steiner explains the interchange of the biblical form *kaśdîm* and the cuneiform *kaldû* as the substitution of fricative *s* by lateral *l* [AOS 59, 137–43]; cf. too D. O. Edzard, RLA 5.296.) The early history of the Chaldeans is reviewed by Brinkman, *Post-Kassite Babylonia,* 260–67; and *idem, Or* 46 (1977), 304–9. Therefore the emendation of "Edomites" (*ʾdm*) for "Aramaeans" (*ʾrm*) which is sometimes suggested (Stade, Klostermann, Benzinger, Burney, cf. Gray) is both textually and historically unwarranted. Edom itself may have been in a state of rebellion (cf. Jer 27).

It is sometimes claimed that the animosity between Judah and Edom, evidenced in prophetic invective (e.g., Ezek 35; Obadiah) and national laments (Lam 4:21–22; Ps 137:7), had its origin in the Edomite attacks upon Judah during this decade. But without the emended verse 24:2, specific references to clashes between the two are not available. This is not to deny that Edom was a hostile force on Judah's southern border at this juncture; note the warning against an Edomite advance in the eastern Negev voiced in Arad ostracon no. 24, line 20 (Y. Aharoni, *Arad Inscriptions,* [Jerusalem: Israel Exploration Society, 1981], 46). Cf. the cautious statement of J. R. Bartlett, "Edom and the Fall of Jerusalem," *PEQ* 114 (1982), 13–24.

The addition in Luc., "and the Samaritans," is probably a late polemic and cannot be trusted.

to destroy it. Heb. *lĕhaʾăbîdô.* Only here in Kings. The verb appears again in this sense in the maledictions in Deut 28:51, 63, in conjunction with the threat of exile.

4. *because of the innocent blood which he shed.* Šanda noted that a similar accusation was directed against Jehoiakim by Jeremiah (Jer 22:17). But while Šanda's observation is correct, syntax requires relating v. 4 to the preceding verse, whose subject is Manasseh. Dtr_2 repeats the charge already brought against Manesseh in 21:16.

5. *annals of the kings of Judah.* This is the last time that these annals are referred to. Can this be taken to mean that with the end of Jehoiakim's reign the annals ended? The writing of royal annals most likely continued even during the turbulent decade which followed the exile of Jehoiachin, though additions to a summary work, such as the annals of the kings of Judah may not have been made. Noth (*Überlieferungsgeschichtliche Studien,* 78, 86f.) credits all the information on Judah's last years to the Baruch narrative (Jer 39–41). See further in the Comment to 2 Kgs 25.

6. *Jehoiakim slept with his ancestors.* Luc. and LXX to 2 Chr 36:8 add that Jehoiakim "was buried in the Garden of Uzza with his ancestors." Jeremiah's invective that the king would "be buried like an ass" (Jer 22:19) finds its echo in a tradition mentioned by Josephus (*Antiquities* x. 97), while rabbinic midrash sought to harmonize the varying reports (*Lev.Rab.* 19.6). Bright speculates that Jehoiakim was assassinated during the siege (*History*[3], 327).

7. *Wadi of Egypt.* Usually identified with Wadi el-Arish; cf. 1 Kgs 8:65. The proposal of N. Na'aman ("The Brook of Egypt and Assyrian Policy on the Border of Egypt," *Tel Aviv* 6 [1979], 68–90) to identify it with Wadi Besor, which reaches the Mediterranean farther to the north, near Gaza, was criticized by A. Rainey (*Tel Aviv* 9 [1982], 131–32).

Comment

The story of Jehoiakim's eleven-year reign (608–598 B.C.E.) is devoted entirely to his relations with his Babylonian overlord, with only the briefest of Deuteronomistic evaluations (v. 37). There was no need for further comment, for the fate of Judah had been sealed (24:3–4).

In 605 a decisive victory was won over the Egyptian army at Carchemish by the Chaldean forces led by Nebuchadnezzar, the crown prince.[1] This victory was followed up with a campaign throughout all of Syro-Palestine (*māt Ḫatti*) by King Nebuchadnezzar who ascended the throne upon the death of his father. In Kislev (= December), 604, the city of Ashkelon was captured and plundered and its king taken prisoner.[2] These events can be coordinated with the solemn fast proclaimed "in the ninth month of the fifth year of Jehoiakim" (Jer 36:9) and explain quite well the agitation in Jerusalem. Necho was unable to meet the Babylonian challenge and thus the Egyptian designs on Philistia and the Phoenician coast were put to rest. It is this state of affairs which is behind the summary statement in 2 Kgs 24:7: "The king of

[1] See Wiseman, *Chronicles,* 68 = Grayson, *Chronicles,* 99, lines 1–7. The rout of the Egyptians at Carchemish is recalled in the date of Jer 46:2.

[2] Wiseman, *Chronicles,* 68 = Grayson, *Chronicles,* 100, lines 18–19.

Egypt did not leave his country anymore, for the king of Babylon seized all that had belonged to the king of Egypt, from the Wadi of Egypt to the River Euphrates." Somewhat later, Jehoiakim submitted to Nebuchadnezzar and became his vassal for three years (604–602).[3]

Despite his initial successes, Nebuchadnezzar suffered a major setback in the winter of 601/600, when he set out to attack Egypt proper. The site of the battle is not recorded in any source,[4] but its outcome is certain. Nebuchadnezzar was forced to withdraw all the way to Babylonia. In the following year, he did not campaign; he stayed at home refitting "his numerous horses and chariots."[5] Under these circumstances, Jehoiakim saw a chance to free himself from Babylonian vassalage and so rebelled. Nebuchadnezzar's response was to attack with garrison troops stationed in the West. Apparently during these attacks, Jehoiakim died.[6]

[3] The Aramaic letter of King Adon requesting aid from his lord, the pharaoh of Egypt, against "the forces of the king of Babylon who have reached Aphek" belongs to this period. Note the phrase *wṭbth ʿbdk nṣr,* "and your servant has remained loyal," indicating the vassal status of Adon (*KAI,* No. 266; H. L. Ginsberg, *BASOR* 111 [1948], 24–27). Recently B. Porten, on the basis of the newly discovered hieratic notation on the reverse side of the letter, identified Adon as king of Ekron, rather than of some other Philistine city (*BA* 44 [1981], 36–52, with full bibliography).

[4] It has been suggested that behind the tradition of Necho's defeat of "Syrians" at Magdolus (Herodotus ii, 159) lie the events of 601 B.C.E. See K. S. Freedy and D. B. Redford, *JAOS* 90 (1970), 475, n. 57; E. Lipiński, *AION* 32 (1972), 235–41. A. Malamat discusses the identification of Magdolus with Migdol in the eastern delta and the possible relevance of the date in Jer 46:13, *JANES* 5 (1973), 275–76.

[5] Wiseman, *Chronicles,* 70 = Grayson, *Chronicles,* 101, lines 5–8.

[6] There is no hint in contemporary records, either biblical or cuneiform, that Jehoiakim was exiled to Babylonia. The tradition of his arrest "in chains to be brought to Babylon" in 2 Chr 36:6 cannot be corroborated by any other source (otherwise J. M. Myers, *II Chronicles,* AB, 218).

The item in Dan 1:1–2, that in Jehoiakim's third year Nebuchadnezzar despoiled the Temple and exiled some Judaeans, often cited in this connection, cannot be used for historical purposes; the book of Daniel is not on a par with 2 Kings and the Babylonian Chronicle. "The third year" is a literary topos, like the "the third day" (e.g. Gen 22:4), "the third month" (e.g. Exod 19:1), "the third year" (e.g. 1 Kgs 22:2); see the discussion of S. Loewenstamm, *Tarbiz* 31 (1961), 227–35, and H. Tadmor, *AS* 16, 354, n.19. One should consider the possibility that the tradition in Dan 1:1–2 derives ultimately from the text of 2 Chr 36:6. See also the remarks of L. F. Hartman and A. A. DiLella, *Daniel,* AB, 128f.

The year 605, the third year of Jehoiakim, was the year of the battle of Carchemish. Nebuchadnezzar reached the land of Hamath, but not Jerusalem. He reached Judah, at the earliest, in 604, Jehoiakim's fourth year. (A. Malamat, *VT* Sup 28 [1975], 131, would postpone his arrival to 603, and emends the text in Daniel from "third" (*šlš*) to "sixth" (*šš*); cf. idem, *IEJ* 18 [1968], 142, n. 10.)

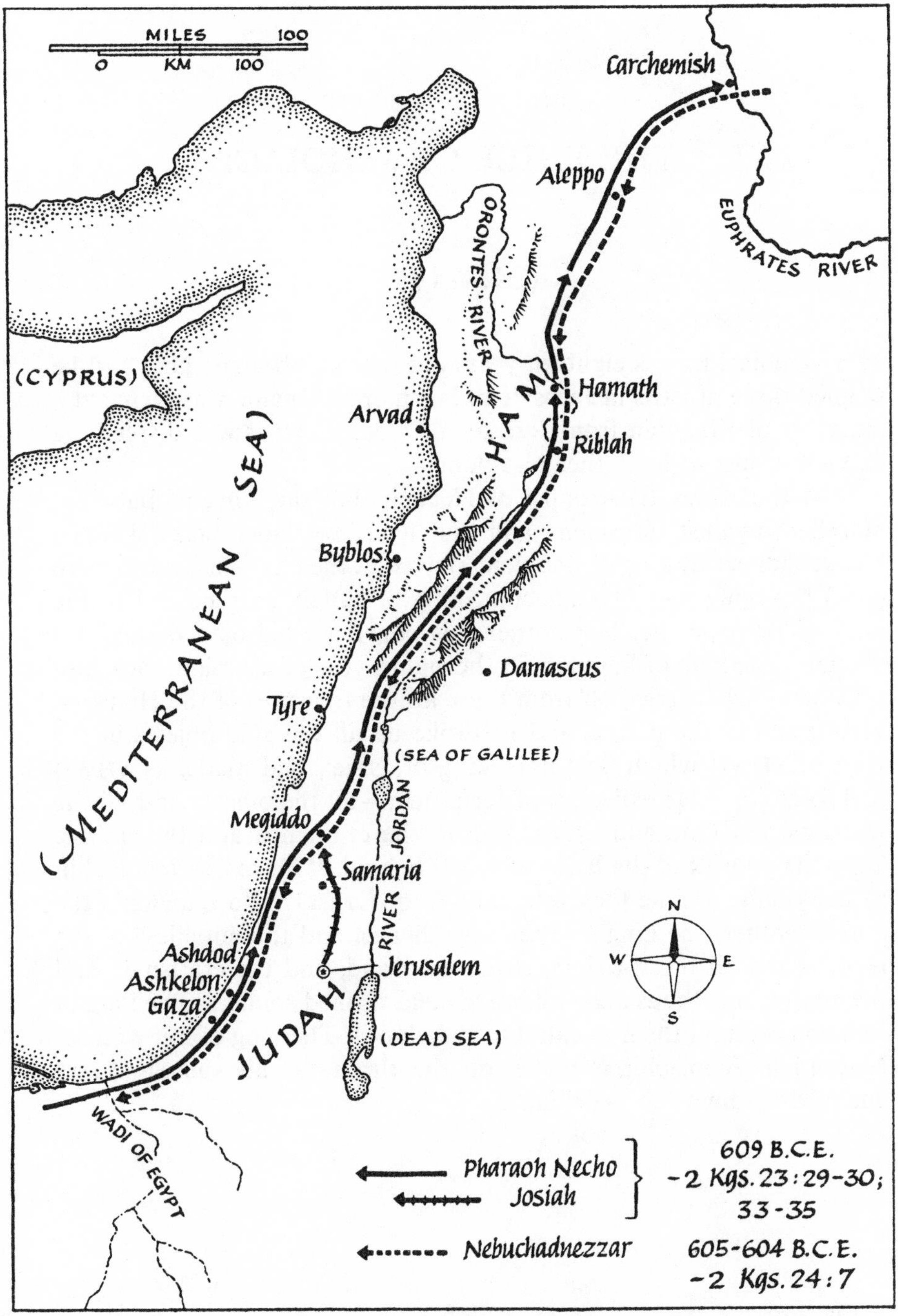

EGYPTIAN AND BABYLONIAN CAMPAIGNS
END OF 7TH CENTURY B.C.E.

XL. THE EXILE OF JEHOIACHIN

(24:8–17)

24 8 Jehoiachin was eighteen years old when he became king and he
reigned three months in Jerusalem. His mother's name was Nehushta,
daughter of Elnathan from Jerusalem. 9 He did what was displeasing
to YHWH, just as his father had done.
10 At that time, the troops[a] of Nebuchadnezzar, king of Babylon,
marched[b] against Jerusalem, and the city came under siege. 11 When
Nebuchadnezzar, king of Babylon, arrived at the city—his troops were
(still) besieging it— 12 Jehoiachin, king of Judah, surrendered to the
king of Babylon: he, his mother, his courtiers, his officers, and his
officials. The king of Babylon, in the eighth year of his reign, took him
prisoner. 13 He carried off from there all the treasures of the House of
YHWH and of the palace, and he broke up all the gold objects in the
Hall of YHWH which Solomon, king of Israel, had made, as YHWH
had foretold. 14 He exiled all of Jerusalem—all the officers and all the
warriors, ten thousand exiles, and all the craftsmen and the smiths.
Only the poorest of the land[c] were left behind. 15 He exiled Jehoiachin
to Babylonia; and he took into exile from Jerusalem to Babylonia the
king's mother, the king's wives, his officials, and the notables[d] of the
land, 16 and all the warriors, seven thousand, and the craftsmen and
the smiths, one thousand—all brave men, trained soldiers. The king of
Babylon brought them as exiles to Babylon. 17 The king of Babylon set
Mattaniah, Jehoiachin's[e] uncle, on the throne as his successor and
changed his name to Zedekiah.

[a] Lit. "servants of."
[b] Read with qere plural, for ketib sing.
[c] Read *dallat hāʾāreṣ* for MT *dallat ʿam hāʾāreṣ*. See note.
[d] Read with qere *ʾyly*, for ketib *ʾwly*.
[e] Lit. "his uncle."

Notes

24 8. *Nehushta, daughter of Elnathan.* For Elnathan, a high court official, cf. Jer 26:22; 36:12, 25; and the note to 2 Kgs 22:12 above.

Jehoiachin. The king's name appears in several variant forms: *yhwykyn* (2 Kgs 24 passim); *yknyhw* (Jer 24:1); *yknyh* (Jer 28:4); *knyhw* (Jer 22:24). (Note that in Jeremiah, the verbal element precedes the theophoric.) The name on the stamp seal, *ʾlʾlykm nʿr ywkn,* "Belonging to Elyakim, steward of Yawkin," was taken by W. F. Albright to be that of Jehoiachin (*JBL* 51 [1932], 77–106); but it seems that this identification can no longer be maintained. The seal belongs to a class of private stamp seals (as shown by N. Avigad, *Magnalia Dei,* 294–300) and, on paleographic as well as archaeological grounds, is to be dated to the late eighth century, cf. D. Ussishkin, *BASOR* 223 (1976), 1–14, and F. M. Cross, "The Seal of Miqnêyaw, Servant of Yahweh," in *Ancient Seals and the Bible,* eds. L. Gorelick and E. William-Forte (Malibu: Undena, 1983), 57–58.

In cuneiform documents dated to 592, Nebuchadnezzar's thirteenth year, Jehoiachin and his five sons are mentioned as recipients of food rations, distributed to them and others resident in Babylon, to the sons of Aga, the king of Ashkelon, and various foreign artisans (Tyrians, Elamites, Egyptians, Persians, Lydians). There his name is transcribed: *[Ia]-ʾ-ú-kīnu* and *Ia-ku-ú-ki-nu.* Zadok holds that these forms represent **Yahū-kīn,* "an Aramaic form meaning *'Yhw* is righteous, reliable,' which was used as the royal name by the Aramaic-speaking Babylonians" (Zadok, *The Jews in Babylonia,* 19). (Note that *ku* interchanged with *ḫu* in Neo-Babylonian, as in the transcription of the name Judah, *Ia-a-ḫu-du/Ia-ku-du.*) Besides the king, other Judaeans received grants as well—e.g. Ur(i)milki, Gadi-ilu, Qanayama, Shalamyama, Samakuyama (*yama* stands for the theophoric element *yaw*). The texts were published by E. Weidner, *Mélanges Dussaud* (Paris: P. Geuthner, 1939), 2.923–35 (cf. *ANET*^{3}, 308) and were discussed by Zadok, op. cit., 39–40.

10. *the city came under siege.* The length of the siege is unknown. The entry in the Babylonian Chronicle reads: "Year seven (of Nebuchadnezzar). In the month of Kislev (= December) 598, the king of Babylonia mobilized his troops and marched to Hatti (i.e. the West). He encamped against the city of Judah. On the second of Adar (= March 16) 597, he captured the city and seized its king" (Appendix I, No. 10; Wiseman, *Chronicles,* 72–73 = Grayson, *Chronicles,* 102, lines 11–12). It is possible that Jerusalem came under siege by army units stationed in the region prior to the mustering of troops reported in the Chronicle.

12. *in the eighth year of his reign.* It is unusual to date an event by the regnal year of a foreign ruler—cf. too 25:8, Jer 52:28–30. The notation indicates that the writer was familiar with the official practice of the Babylonian conqueror or perhaps was even in his employ.

The Babylonian Chronicle Series records the fall of the city at the end of Nebuchadnezzar's seventh regnal year. It was some time later, as much as several months later, that the exiles actually left Jerusalem for Babylon, hence the "eighth year" in the present verse. (Nebuchadnezzar himself probably left soon after the surrender in order to be in the capital for the celebration of the New Year on the first of Nisan, a formal requirement for all Babylonian kings; cf. the remarks of D. N. Freedman, *BA* 19 [1956], 56.)

13. *he broke up all the gold objects.* Heb. *wayĕqaṣṣēṣ;* lit. "he cut into pieces." In 16:17, 18:16, the verb denotes the stripping of metals; here the cast objects are turned into bullion.

While there is evidence for the delivery of Temple vessels to the Babylonians already in 597 (Jer 27:16–18, 28:3), the sweeping statement of v. 13—*all* the treasures of the Temple—which conflicts with 25:13–15, can only be judged to be editorial exaggeration. On its source, in a prophetic word, see the Comment.

14. *He exiled all of Jerusalem—all the officers and all the warriors, ten thousand exiles.* The sum total of exiles from Jerusalem reported in this verse is 10,000, while in the duplicate accounting in vv. 15–16, the total is 8,000—i.e. 7,000 warriors, 1,000 craftsmen and smiths. Both traditions give only approximations in round numbers; more exact numbers would have been recorded in Babylonian documents. Though no such documentation has survived from the Neo-Babylonian empire, using Assyrian administrative practices as a model, it may be assumed that Babylonian practice was similar.

Another tally of exiles in year 7 of Nebuchadnezzar is preserved in Jer 52:28: 3,023 Judaeans. This appears to be the sum of deportees from the countryside, not from Jerusalem, which was conquered only in year 8 (cf. A. Malamat, *IEJ* 18 [1968], 154). The other tallies in Jer 52:29, 30, from years 18 and 23 of Nebuchadnezzar, also refer to minor deportations of Judaeans.

the craftsmen and the smiths. Heb. *ḥārāš,* "skilled worker," whether in wood or metal, cf. 22:6.

Heb. *masgēr,* only here and in v. 16, is of unknown etymology. The obvious connection with **sgr,* "to close, shut," leads to "gate keepers" (Targum), "siege builders" (Thenius, who compares Jer 13:19; *KB* 541). Montgomery-Gehman derives from Arabic *sajara,* "to roast in an oven," and translates "metal-smith," comparing *zāhāb sāgûr* (1 Kgs 6:20), "refined gold" (cf. *BDB* 689).

the poorest of the land. MT has *dallat ʿam-hāʾāreṣ* which, as Talmon pointed out, is a conflate reading of *dallat hāʾāreṣ* (2 Kgs 25:12) and *dallôt hāʿām* (Jer 52:15). The present verse is similar to the double reading in Isa 24:4, *mĕrôm/ʿam-hāʾāreṣ* (S. Talmon, *Textus* 4 [1964], 119). In neither case is the social class *ʿam hāʾāreṣ,* "People of the Land," referred to.

15. *the notables of the land.* Heb. *ʾêlê hāʾāreṣ,* cf. Ezek 17:13. Jer 27:20 substitutes the class term *ḥōrîm,* "nobles," known mostly from LBH of the Persian period (Neh 2:16; 4:8, 13; cf. above 1 Kgs 21:8, 11).

17. *Mattaniah, Jehoiachin's uncle.* He was the last son of Josiah, by the same mother as Jehoahaz; see 23:31, cf. Jer 25:1. In 2 Chr 36:10, he is "his brother"; but this was subsequently corrected by LXX to read "his father's brother," to bring the verse into line with the genealogy in 1 Chr 3:15.

changed his name to Zedekiah. Here, too, the hegemon changes the name of his vassal, as was the case with Eliakim/Jehoiakim (23:34), as though creating a new personality. But Mattaniah's new name, *Ṣidqîyāhû,* "YHWH is my vindication," had wider implications. It has been suggested that the name was chosen to fit Jeremiah's prophecy concerning *ṣemaḥ ṣaddiq,* "the true shoot," of the house of David (Jer 23:5–6). But as J. Liver pointed out (*The House of David* [Jerusalem: Magnes, 1959], 56–59

[Hebrew]), the prophecy dates from the reign of Zedekiah and in fact expresses disappointment with the new king, whose name evokes unfulfilled hopes. The future Davidide, not the reigning king, will be the true shoot; his name will be *YHWH ṣidqēnû.* See J. Bright, *Jeremiah,* AB, 144, 146. (D.N.F. suggests a different parsing of Jer 23:5–6: "Behold! Days are coming. And I will establish for David a branch (*ṣemaḥ*); a righteous one (*ṣaddîq*) who will reign; a king who will prosper, and he will do justice . . ." and compares these verses to Zech 6:2, in which *ṣemaḥ* stands by itself.)

The Babylonian Chronicle also records that Nebuchadnezzar "appointed there a king of his choice" (Appendix I, No. 10, Wiseman, *Chronicles,* 72 = Grayson, *Chronicles,* 102, line 13).

Comment

Jerusalem was taken on the second of Adar in the seventh regnal year of Nebuchadnezzar (= March 16, 597; see above the note to v. 10). Jehoiachin, the royal family, and his court were deported, together with the elite of the country, the choice troops, and the artisans. Because the king had surrendered, the city itself was spared wrack and ruin, though it was heavily penalized. The royal and temple treasuries were looted and carried off to Babylon. Mattaniah, the king's uncle, was set on the throne; but he began to count his regnal years only after Jehoiachin and his entourage departed for Babylonia—i.e., after Nisan 597 (see the note to 25:2).

The duplication of sources describing Jehoiachin's exile was noted long ago. Verses 13–14 have been seen a "later insertion," "secondary," and "extravagant."[1] But upon close examination, v. 13 exhibits certain peculiarities which set it apart from the rest of the account. It alone refers to all the treasures of the Temple and royal house being taken to Babylon. The verse ends with an allusion to an earlier prophecy, "as YHWH had foretold," which had predicted these events. Stade suggested that v. 13, and v. 14 as well, were misplaced and referred to the second exile eleven years later, when the Temple was destroyed.[2] However, Jer 27:18 and 28:3 show that during Zedekiah's reign, Temple vessels were already in Babylon, taken there by Nebuchadnezzar at the time of Jehoiachin's exile. If v. 13 is deleted, then there would be no record in Kings of this spoliation of 597 attested to in Jeremiah. Hence the kernel of v. 13 is authentic. The reference to the prophetic word should, moreover, be associated with the prophecy in 20:16–18, there attributed to Isaiah, with which v. 13 is linked, both semantically and thematically. In that prophecy, the prospect is that of total exile: "Everything in your residence

[1] So Burney, Gray, Montgomery-Gehman, ad loc.

[2] B. Stade, *ZAW* 4 (1884), 271–77.

and that which your ancestors have amassed up until today shall be carried off to Babylon." The prophecy is posterior to the events of the reign of Hezekiah and expresses the outlook of the late Deuteronomistic historian of Kings, Dtr_2 (see Comment to 20:12–21).

XLI. THE REIGN OF ZEDEKIAH: THE FALL OF JERUSALEM

(24:18–25:21)

24 18 Zedekiah was twenty-one years old when he became king, and
he reigned eleven years in Jerusalem. His mother's name was
Hamutal, daughter of Jeremiah from Libnah. 19 He did what was displeasing to YHWH, just as Jehoiakim had done. 20 Because of YHWH's
wrath did these things happen to Jerusalem and Judah, until he rid
himself of them. Thus Zedekiah rebelled against the king of Babylon.
25 1 In the ninth year of Zedekiah's[a] reign, in the tenth month, on
the tenth day of the month, Nebuchadnezzar king of Babylon
marched against Jerusalem, he and all his forces, and he encamped
against it. They built a siege wall all about, 2 so that the city was under
siege until the eleventh year of King Zedekiah. 3 <In the fourth
month,>[b] on the ninth day of the month, the hunger became severe in
the city; even the People of the Land had no bread. 4 Thus the city was
breached. <Zedekiah> and all the soldiers <fled>[c] by night,[d] leaving through the gate between the two walls which was near the king's
garden; and though the Chaldeans were all around the city, he made
off by the Arabah road. 5 But the Chaldean forces pursued the king
and overtook him in the steppes of Jericho, as all his troops dispersed.

6 They captured the king and brought him to the king of Babylon at
Riblah. He passed sentence[e] upon him. 7 They slaughtered Zedekiah's
sons before his own eyes and (then) blinded Zedekiah. He put him in
fetters and had him brought to Babylon.

8 In the fifth month, on the seventh day of the month—it was the
nineteenth year of King Nebuchadnezzar, king of Babylon—
Nebuzaradan the chief cook, an officer of the king of Babylon, came to
Jerusalem. 9 He burned the House of YHWH and the Palace and all the

[a] Lit. "his."
[b] Add with Jer 52:6; cf. 39:2.
[c] So, partially restored, with Jer 39:4. See note.
[d] Read *laylâ; hē* dittography; cf. Jer 52:7.
[e] MT: "they"; read *wayĕdabbēr . . . mišpāṭîm* with Jer 52:9.

houses of Jerusalem—every large house[f] he burned down. 10 All the
Chaldean forces that were with[g] the chief cook tore down the walls of
Jerusalem all about. 11 Then Nebuzaradan the chief cook exiled the
rest of the people left in the city and those who had deserted to the
king of Babylon—the rest of the masses. 12 But from the poor of the
land, the chief cook left some to be vine dressers and field workers.

13 The Chaldeans broke up the bronze columns in the House of
YHWH, and the stands and the bronze Sea in the House of YHWH; and
they carried the bronze away to Babylon. 14 They took the pots, the
shovels, the snuffers, the spoons, all the bronze vessels used in the
service. 15 The chief cook took the fire pans and the sprinkling bowls,
those of gold and of silver. 16 The weight of all these vessels was incal-
culable: two columns, one Sea, and the stands, which Solomon had
made for the Temple. 17 The height of one column was eighteen cubits
and its capital was bronze. The height of the capital was five[h] cubits,
and on the capital all around was a meshwork with pomegranates, all
of bronze. The other column was exactly like it, with its meshwork.

18 The chief cook took Seraiah the high priest, Zephanaiah the deputy priest, and three keepers of the threshold. 19 And from the city, he
took an official who was in charge of the fighting men and five of the
king's personal attendants who were found in the city, and the scribe[i]
of the army commander who mustered the People of the Land, as well
as sixty of the People of the Land who were in the city.
20 Nebuzaradan the chief cook took them and brought them to the
king of Babylon at Riblah. 21 The king of Babylon had them struck
down and put to death in Riblah in the land of Hamath. Thus Judah
was exiled from its land.

[f] Read *bayit* for MT *bêt;* and see note.
[g] Insert *ʾet* with some mss. and Jer 52:14.
[h] So with Jer 52:24 and 1 Kgs 7:16; MT has "three."
[i] Read *sōpēr* with Jer 52:25.

Notes

24 20. *rid himself of them.* Heb. *hišlīkô.* For the anomalous pointing of the infinitive with *ḥireq,* rather than *pataḥ,* see *GKC,* 53 l.

25 1. *In the ninth year.* Heb. *bišnat hattĕšîʿît.* For the construct form, cf. 2 Kgs 17:6. Lachish ostracon no. 20 opens with the same date: *btšʿt byw*[*m* . . ."] "on the ninth (year of Zedekiah?) *da*[*y* . . .]"

They built a siege wall all about. Heb. *dāyēq,* a word of unknown etymology. It appears again in Ezek 4:2; 17:17; 21:27, as distinct from the *sōlĕlâ,* "ramp," heaped up in the siege of Jerusalem. Its cognate is attested, only once, in a text of Esarhaddon, describing his conquest of Shubria, southwest of Lake Van, in 672 (Th. Bauer, *ZA* 40 [1931], 253, n. 31; cf. *CAD* D 27):

[. . .] *epiš qabli u tāḫazi dāyiku ibbalkitūni,* "[my troops?] climbed over the siege wall to do battle" (Borger, *Asarhaddon,* 104., col, ii, line 8).

2. *until the eleventh year of King Zedekiah.* The chronological scheme which accommodates most of the biblical and extrabiblical data is based upon the assumption that Zedekiah started counting his regnal years in Nisan (= Spring), 596. His eleventh year is, then, 586/85 B.C.E. (H. Tadmor, *JNES* 15 [1956], 226–30; idem, *EncMiqr* 4.274–76; cf. D. J. A. Clines, *Australian Journal of Biblical Archaeology* 2 [1972], 9–34). The intricate problems involved in dating events during Judah's last two decades are worked out in different fashion by E. R. Thiele, *MNHK*², 161–73; and by A. Malamat, *IEJ* 18 (1968), 137–56; idem, *VT* Sup 28 (1975), 123–45.

4. *The city was breached.* The siege machines and battering rams (*kārîm*) which finally broke through the defenses of the beleaguered city are not described here, but do appear in Ezekiel's description of Jerusalem's fall; cf. Ezek 4:2.

<Zedekiah> and all the soldiers <fled> by night, leaving through the gate. The text of Kings, which lacks a verb and does not mention the king who is the object of the ensuing chase (see v. 5), is restored on the basis of Jer 39:4 and 52:7: *wybrḥw ṣdqyhw wkl ʾnšy hmlḥmh lylh wyṣʾw drk šʿr* . . . The inclusion of the information on the arrival of the Babylonian officers in Jer 39:3, necessitated the recasting of the verse in Jeremiah. But as this detail is not included in 2 Kgs 25:4, the verb *wayyibrĕḥû,* "they fled," is placed at the head of the sentence as required by Hebrew syntax.

the gate between the two walls. This gate is located in the southeast wall of the City of David and may be identical with the Gate of the Spring (i.e. Rogel spring) in Neh 3:15. The double-wall construction seems to refer to the additional wall built by Hezekiah to protect the Siloam pool; cf. Isa 22:11, 2 Chr 32:5.

the Arabah Road. For this steppe land in the Jordan Valley rift, from south of the Sea of Galilee to Eilat, cf. Josh 11:2, 2 Sam 2:29, Deut 1:1; cf. the "sea of the Arabah," i.e., the Dead Sea, 2 Kgs 14:25. The escape route to the Arabah probably led through Wadi Kelt, which exits in the vicinity of Jericho, where Zedekiah was overtaken (v. 5).

6. *Riblah.* See the note to 2 Kgs 23:33.

He passed sentence upon him. Heb. *wayĕdabbēr ʾittô mišpāṭîm* occurs in similar contexts in Jer 1:16 and 4:12. The notion of *dabbēr mišpāṭîm* is not that of a trial in which the accused is charged and then pleads his case before a verdict is rendered, but an arraignment before a superior, during which the violater is rebuked and punished forthwith. Therefore, although the Akk. *dinam dabābu,* "to plead a case," (see *CAD* D 10) appears to be akin to Heb. *dabbēr mišpāṭ* as in Isa 32:7 ("and the needy when they plead their case"), this is not so in the present instance (otherwise Montgomery-Gehman). A fair trial before a judge is not applicable here. (Hence *NEB*'s "he [i.e. Zedekiah] pleaded his case before him" misconstrues the scene.) Zedekiah was charged with breaking an oath of loyalty to his overlord, and under the circumstances, he could only plead for mercy. His case was not unlike that of the king of Shubria, whose eloquent plea after admitting his guilt was nevertheless turned down by Esarhaddon (*ARAB* 2.593). Cf. Ezek 5:8 *ʿāśîtî mišpāṭîm,* not "trial," but judgment, i.e. "punishment," like Akk. *šipṭam šakānu,* "to punish," (cf. e.g. "I punished all the unsubmissive," Streck, *Assurbanipal,* 80, line 120).

The interchange of singular and plural in 2 Kgs 25 creates a confused picture. The verb in MT vv. 6 and 7a are in the plural, and would seem to refer to the Chaldean forces (v. 5); whereas MT v. 7b is cast in the singular and refers to the king of Babylon. The versions and Jer 52:9–10 read the verbs in vv. 6b and 7 in the singular, so that it was Nebuchadnezzar who accused and himself dealt punishment to Zedekiah; Jer 52:10 adds "the king of Babylon" twice so as to make this more explicit. Jer 39:6 adds *wĕʾet kōl ḥōrê yĕhūdâ šāḥaṭ melek bābel,* "and the king of Babylon slaughtered all the nobles of Judah." This datum is a summary of 2 Kgs 25:18–20a, recording the additional slaughter at Riblah. The writer of Jer 39 did not continue the story beyond the capture of Zedekiah, but focused upon the personal fate of the prophet Jeremiah. Jer 52:10b is based upon 39:6. (The variation *ḥōrîm/śārîm* is in accordance with LBH usage—cf. e.g. Jer 27:20, Neh 6:17, 13:17.)

7. *and (then) blinded Zedekiah.* Blinding was a common punishment of the rebellious slaves in the ancient Near East. It is mentioned in the vassal treaty between Ashur-nirari V, king of Assyria, and Matti-ilu, king of Arpad, among the curses pronounced against a future violator: *ēnâšu lunappil,* "May he (i.e. the enemy) tear out his eyes" (*AfO* 8 [1932–33], 22, Reverse VI, 2; *ANET*[3], 533b). On the other hand, references to blinding of large numbers of captives probably relate to gouging out only one eye; this method left the mutilated as a usable slave force. Cf. the remarks of P. Machinist, *Assur* 3/2 (1982), 18, n. 41 for the Mesopotamian practice. This is the background of the demand of Nahash the Ammonite to the men of Jabesh-gilead: "I will make a pact with you on the condition that everyone's right eye be gouged out" (1 Sam 11:2), as interpreted by F. M. Cross, "The Ammonite Oppression of the Tribes of Gad and Reuben: Missing Verses from 1 Samuel 11 Found in 4Q Samuel[a]," in *History, Historiography and Interpretation, Studies in Biblical and Cuneiform Literatures,* ed. H. Tadmor and M. Weinfeld (Jerusalem: Magnes, 1983), 148–58.

fetters. Heb. *nĕḥuštayim,* lit. "fetters of bronze." The usage is archaic, for in the late Iron Age, fetters were commonly made of iron, as shown by the Akkadian term *birīti parzilli,* "iron fetters" (*CAD* B 254–5); cf. *kablê barzel,* "chains of iron" (Ps 105:18; 149:8).

Jer 52:11 adds: *wayyitĕnēhû bĕbêt happĕquddōt ʿad-yôm môtô,* "and he put him in the guard house until the day of his death." This item, absent as it is in both 2 Kgs 25 and Jer 39, was apparently not recorded in the original sources describing Zedekiah's fate. Had it been so, one would expect to find it in 2 Kgs 25. It probably derived ultimately from an additional source or some personal knowledge of the author(s) of Jer 52.

Bêt happĕquddōt is a hapax. If connected with *pĕquddōt* in Ezek 9:1, it means "house of punishment"; cf. M. Greenberg, *Ezekiel,* AB, ad loc. (The corresponding Akk. term is *bīt maṣṣarti,* "prison," lit. "place of confinement." See *CAD* M.1 340–41.)

8. *In the fifth month, on the seventh day of the month.* Luc. reads: "ninth day"; Jer 52:12: "tenth day." Rabbinic tradition explained away the discrepancies by viewing the varying dates as the beginning and end points of the destruction; *b. Ta ʿan* 29a; Tosepta 4.10. The day of national mourning was set on the ninth of Ab; cf. Josephus, *Antiquities* x.135.

Nebuzaradan, the chief cook. Nebuzaradan (Akk. *Nabû-zēr-iddina,* "Nabu has given me offspring") the *rab nuḫatimmu,* "chief cook," is mentioned second in a list of courtiers of King Nebuchadnezzar, followed by the chief of the royal guard, the *ša rēši* (cf. *ANET*[3], 307; note that the *mašennu,* "officials," come first in the list). His Hebrew title *rab ṭabbaḥîm* is then a loan translation; cf. the use of **ṭbḥ,* "to slaughter, cook," in 1 Sam 8:13, 9:23, 24. The title has often been interpreted quite literally, but incorrectly, as "chief executioner" (e.g. *BDB* 371; Montgomery, *Daniel* ICC, 155); the same holds true for Potiphar, who was also *śar haṭṭabbāḥîm* (Gen 37:36, contra. E. A. Speiser, *Genesis,* AB, 291–92). Titles of this kind ("chief cook", "chief cupbearer") originated in the circumstances of court service; under special conditions, these trusted individuals were dispatched on missions, e.g. the Rab shakeh of Sennacherib (cf. 2 Kgs 18:17) or Nehemiah in the days of Artaxerxes (cf. Neh 2:1). Toward the close of the Neo-Assyrian empire, the chief cook served as an eponym (M. Falkner, *AfO* 17 [1954–56], 105, s.v. Sailu).

Nebuzaradan is missing from the list in Jer 39:3. But the name Nergalsarezer, there repeated twice, must be an error and should be corrected in its first occurrence to Nebuzaradan. The enigmatic *smgr* is to be taken as a transcription of the title, Sin-magir, a Babylonian minister (W. von Soden, *ZA* 62 [1972], 84–90; cf. *AHw* 1045). (Note that in the present verse, the title has been translated; unlike the titles *Rab shakeh* and *Rab saris,* which retain the original Assyrian, *rab ṭabbāḥîm* is itself a Hebrew translation.)

an officer. Heb. *ʿebed,* lit. "servant." The alternate reading in Jer 52:12 should be noted: *ʿōmēd lipnê* (with LXX), "a servant, attendant," lit. "one who stands by." This appears to be a translation of the Akkadian title *manzaz pani,* "a personal attendant" (*CAD* M.2 233–34); cf. too the verbal form in Jer 40:10.

9. *every large house.* Heb. *kōl bêt gādōl.* The construct form *bêt,* "house of," led Targum to translate *bāttê rabrĕbayā',* "houses of the nobles." But *gādôl* is always used adjectively when expressing "importance" as in 2 Kgs 4:8 or 5:1. The transposition *bêt kōl gādôl* suggested by Ehrlich and Šanda does not help in this regard. Hence it is better to read *bayit. NEB*'s "including the mansion of Gedaliah" is apparently based on the emendation of J. Zuckerbram, "Variants in Editing," *Melilah* 3–4 (1950), 21, who thought that the present reading developed from an abbreviated writing *byt gdl* for *byt gdlyhw.*

11. *those who had deserted.* For the idiom *nāpôl ʾel,* see the note at 7:4.

the rest of the masses. Heb. *yeter hehāmôn.* Jer 52:15 reads *hāʾāmôn* "artisans," preferred by Benzinger, Burney, Gray, *NEB, NAB.* But as Thenius earlier observed, such a corrected text would serve as a poor contrast to 2 Kgs 24:14. Moreover, *hāmôn,* "crowd," appears in battle contexts indicating a massive array of troops; cf. Judg 4:7; Ezek 39:11; Dan 11:11–13. Akk. *illatu,* "host, troops, pack," carries the same semantic range as the Hebrew (*CAD* I–J 82–85).

12. *vine dressers and field workers.* Heb. *lĕkōrĕmîm ûlĕyōgĕbîm* (with qere and Jer 52:16). The second element of this pair is as yet unexplained. LXX offers only a transcription of the Hebrew word (*gabin*); the Targum translates (and note inversion): *maplĕḥîn bĕḥaqlin ûbĕkarmîn,* "workers in the fields and the vineyards." Some have noted that the ketib in 2 Kgs 25:12 and the vocalization of Jer 39:10 *gēbîm* seems to reflect the Hebrew word *gēb,* "pit, trench, cistern" (cf. 2 Kgs 3:16; Jer 14:3), and adopt this reading here (e.g. Klostermann). The usual word pair *sādeh* and *kerem,* "field and vineyard" (e.g. Exod 22:4; Num 16:14, 20:17) points to the general sense of the phrase (Zuckerbram [above, note 9]).

13–15. The fashioning of these Temple vessels is described in the Solomonic account of the Temple construction; for the pillars, cf. 1 Kgs 7:15–22; the bronze Sea, 7:23–26; the stands, 7:27–37; the pots, 7:45; the shovels, 7:40; the snuffers, 7:50 (there made of gold! cf. also the notice from the days of Joash in 2 Kgs 12:14); the spoons, 1 Kgs 7:50; the fire pans, 7:50; the sprinkling bowls, 7:50.

16. *The weight of all these vessels . . .* The list of large bronze objects, repeating items mentioned in the previous verses, might be a booty count, perhaps of Babylonian origin. But a similar counting and repetition is to be found in 1 Kgs 7:40–47; cf. esp. vv. 44 and 47, which very likely inspired the present epitome. The editor, here, quoted the Solomonic list with modifications; e.g. the twelve bronze bulls which held the Sea were not enumerated, for they had been sent by Ahaz in payment to Tiglath-pileser; cf. 2 Kgs 16:17. (Jer 52:20 incorrectly includes the twelve bulls in its listing.)

17. The pillars and their design are treated in a single verse; Jer 52:23 gives additional details, though somewhat garbled. Both passages are derived from 1 Kgs 7:15–20.

18. *Seraiah the high priest.* In 1 Chr 5:40, it is specifically recorded that his son Jehozadak was led off to Babylon, with the rest of the exiles.

Zephaniah the deputy priest. Some years earlier Zephaniah was the chief officer responsible for maintaining order in the Temple (Jer 21:1 and 29:25ff.). His father Maaseiah was a "keeper of the threshold," with an office in the Temple (Jer 35:4).

The specific functions of these highest-ranking priests is nowhere described in the Bible; and though a similar administrative structure is known to have existed in the main temple of the god Ashur in the city of Ashur, even there the specific tasks of the *šangû rabû*, "chief priest," and the *šangû šaniu*, "deputy priest," cannot be defined (B. Menzel, *Assyrische Temple* [Rome: Pontifical Biblical Institute, 1981], 1.194–97).

The priestly titles in this verse appear again in 2 Kgs 12:10–11 and 22:4, and see the notes there.

19. *the king's personal attendants.* Heb. *rōʾê pĕnê hammelek;* cf. Esth 1:14. In both verses, the term is a calque formation of the Akk. *dāgil pāni,* "subject, servant," lit. "one who beholds the face" (A. L. Oppenheim, *JAOS* 61 [1941], 258, and *CAD* D, 23). The cognate Hebrew expression is *ʿōmēd ʿal/lipnê,* "to stand/wait upon." Normally, Hebrew *rāʾô pĕnê* carried the nuance "to have an audience with a superior," as in Exod 10:28–29, 2 Sam 14:24, 28. Jer 52:25 reads: "seven personal attendants," as in Esth 1:14.

Comment

1. A unique situation exists with regard to the text of the present unit; an almost verbatim copy of it is preserved in Jer 52, which serves as an appendix to the book of Jeremiah's prophecies.[1] In actuality, Jer 52:1–27 parallels 2 Kgs 24:18–25:21, except for a few textual variants (in vv. 10–11). The Deuteronomistic evaluation of Jehoiakim (Jer 52:2) and the manner in which the punishment by exile is presented (Jer 52:3, 27) are the hallmarks of the book of Kings and not Jeremiah. Thus the composition of the unit is certainly attributable to the late Deuteronomistic editor, Dtr_2.

[1] Jer 51:64 concludes with: "Thus far, the words of Jeremiah." Rudolph (*Jeremiah,* HAT, ad loc.) notes the possible displacement of this concluding phrase from 51:58.

A second recital of the fall of Jerusalem and Zedekiah's tragic end is found in Jer 39:1–14. This unit is also related to 2 Kgs 25:1–21, though it is considerably shorter. In addition, woven into Jer 39:1–14 is another story, that of the fate of Jeremiah and his treatment at the hands of his Babylonian captors.[2] The signs of Deuteronomistic editing are lacking entirely in Jer 39.

The suggested relationship between these three texts may be set out schematically as follows:

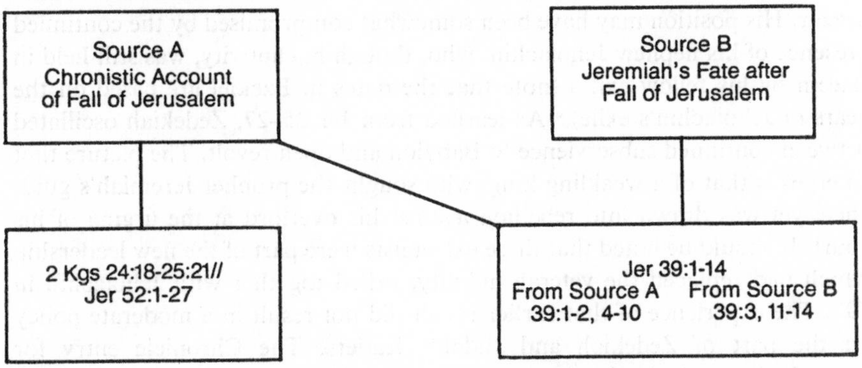

Textually, the manuscript which served as the model for MT 2 Kgs 25 seems to have been poorly preserved, for it exhibits more than a few instances of haplography (see the notes to vv. 4, 7) and erroneous readings. With the help of the copy in MT Jer 52, the faulty text in 2 Kgs 25 can be restored in several instances.

At the same time, the most recent work on the LXX of Jeremiah by E. Tov suggests that the Hebrew *Vorlage* of the LXX was a shortened edition of Jeremiah "and the expanded text of MT (is) a later form of the book."[3] Applying this principle to Jer 39, one arrives at the following stemma.

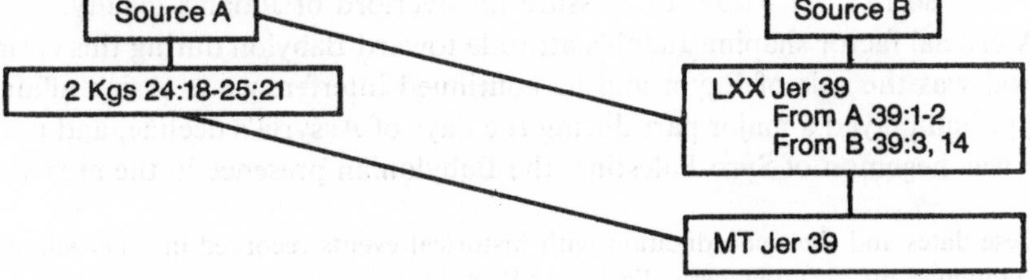

[2] The shortness of the account in Jer 39 may have prompted a late hand to append the fuller version now in Jer 52. Note that Jer 39 did not specifically mention the burning of the Temple (see v. 8) or give the list of Temple booty (cf. 2 Kgs 25:13–17).

[3] See E. Tov in *Le Livre de Jérémie*, ed. P.-M. Bogaert (Leuven: Leuven University Press, 1981), 145–67.

2. The Babylonian Chronicle Series continues to relate the major events of Nebuchadnezzar's reign down to the king's eleventh year (594/593 B.C.E.). In his eighth, tenth, and eleventh years, Nebuchadnezzar again campaigned in Hatti, i.e. Syro-Palestine. For the following years, the chronicle series is not extant; for events in Judah, therefore, historical reconstruction depends entirely upon the biblical data, supplemented here and there by indirect references in Egyptian sources.

Zedekiah (596–586 B.C.E.) took the throne as a sworn vassal of Nebuchadnezzar. His position may have been somewhat compromised by the continued presence of his nephew Jehoiachin, who, though in captivity, was still held in esteem by his fellow exiles (note that the dates in Ezekiel are based on the years of Jehoiachin's exile).[4] As learned from Jer 25–27, Zedekiah oscillated between continued subservience to Babylon and open revolt. The picture that emerges is that of a weakling king, who sought the prophet Jeremiah's guidance, yet was drawn into rebellion against his overlord at the urging of his court. It should be noted that these extremists were part of the new leadership which had replaced the veteran nobility, exiled together with Jehoiachin in 597. The experience of that earlier revolt did not result in a moderate policy on the part of Zedekiah and Judah's leaders. The Chronicle entry for Nebuchadnezzar's tenth year reports strife inside Babylonia:

> From the month of Kislev until
> the month of Tebet, there [was] a rebellion
> in Babylonia . . . he executed many of [his army?]
> He personally [captured] his enemy.[5]

This is the background against which the meeting in Jerusalem of representatives of Edom, Moab, Ammon, Tyre, and Sidon, was convened the following summer to plan revolt (Jer 27:3).[6] But this rebellion died at birth. Three months later, in Kislev of his eleventh year, Nebuchadnezzar came west,[7] and in the course of the year, Zedekiah sent a mission (which he himself may have headed—so MT Jer 51:59) to reassure his overlord of Judah's loyalty.

A crucial factor shaping Judah's attitude toward Babylon during this entire period was the role of Egypt and its continued interference in Asian affairs. Egypt had played a major part during the days of Assyria's decline, and until 605 was hegemon of Syro-Palestine; the Babylonian presence in the area was

[4] These dates and their coordination with historical events recorded in other sources are tabulated by M. Greenberg, *Ezekiel,* AB, 8–11.

[5] Grayson, *Chronicles,* 102, line 22.

[6] This meeting could not have taken place during Zedekiah's accession year as argued by N. Sarna (*EI* 14 [1979], 89*–96*). The date in Jer 27:1 is doubtful on textual grounds and historically improbable. The event is to be coordinated with the heading in 28:1, referring to the king's "fourth year."

[7] Grayson, *Chronicles,* 102, lines 25–26.

after all a new factor, Nebuchadnezzar's failure to invade Egypt in 601 only underscored the feeling that the supremacy of Babylon under the Chaldeans was a passing phenomenon. From the point of view of the Syro-Palestinian states, Egypt's power seems not to have been discredited by Nebuchadnezzar's yearly campaigns in Hatti. Consequently, the "triumphal progress" of Psammetichus II to Palestine in 592, though basically a peaceful journey, was intended "to broadcast his military success in the Sudan, and to galvanize his allies and subjects in hither Asia by his presence against the Babylonian menace."[8]

Whether this manifestation of power had an immediate effect is unclear, for the exact date of the outbreak of Zedekiah's rebellion (2 Kgs 24:20) is not given. Malamat places it early in 589, after the accession of Apries,[9] but the possibility of rebellion as early as 591 should not be excluded.[10]

Nebuchadnezzar's retaliation seems to have been slow in coming. Not until January 587 (= 10 Tebeth, in Zedekiah's ninth year, 25:1) did a Babylonian force lay siege to Jerusalem. For the next eighteen months, with the exception of the short respite occasioned by the arrival of Egyptian units (Jer 37:5, 11),[11] the city's defenders held off the superior Chaldeans. Nebuchadnezzar himself may not have been present during the lengthy siege of the city. A Neo-Babylonian royal inscription (from Wadi Brisa in the Lebanon) tells of his engagement against a "foreign enemy" who had stirred up the local population in Lebanon against his rule;[12] Egypt was behind these disturbances as well.[13]

Jerusalem was finally subdued by hunger, perhaps the most effective factor in siege operations employed by the great empires (25:3). In July 586 (= 9 Tammuz, in Zedekiah's eleventh year, 25:3), the city was broken into. Zedekiah escaped under the cover of night, but was captured and brought to trial before Nebuchadnezzar at Riblah. He was subjected to cruel punishment for breaking his oath of loyalty and then sent off to Babylon to die.

Nebuchadnezzar then ordered Jerusalem and its Temple razed, and the order was carried out on August 16, 586 (= 7 Ab; cf. 25:8). Conquest and looting were insufficient punishment for the capital city that had proven itself

[8] K. S. Freedy and D. B. Redford, *JAOS* 90 (1970), 478–80; and earlier M. Greenberg, *JBL* 76 (1957), 304–9. For corrected dates of this Egyptian move, see A. Malamat, *VT* Sup 28 (1975), 141, n. 40; and cf. H. Cazelles, in *Le Livre de Jérémie* (above, n. 3), 36–38.

[9] So, A. Malamat, *VT* Sup 28 (1975), 142.

[10] Cf. M. Greenberg, op. cit. (above, n. 8).

[11] On the relevance of passages in Ezek 29, 30 to these events, see Freedy and Redford, op. cit. (above, n. 8), 47–74.

[12] *ANET*^{3}, 307.

[13] Cf. the remarks of M. Noth, *History*, 286; and H. J. Katzenstein, *History of Tyre*, 320.

recalcitrant so many times;[14] the city's destruction establishes that there were no plans to reconstitute Judah around a Babylonian provincial center in Jerusalem.

As to the extent of the exile, no total number of the deported is given in Kings (unlike the first deportation under Jehoiachin in 24:16). According to Jer 52:29, 832 Jerusalemites were exiled in Nebuchadnezzar's eighteenth year, a year before the city's fall, but this may represent the first phase of the principal deportations still to come.[15] The only record in Kings is the summary, untallied, in 25:11 and the list of high officials who held out in the city until the end, 25:18–19. Does it mean that the late editor had no detailed information on the exiles? Or did he prefer a general statement that would parallel the one on the fall of Samaria and the exile of Israel in 2 Kgs 17:6? Whatever the reason for this deficiency in Kings, it is known that no new settlers were brought to replace the exiled, or the thousands who no doubt were killed or escaped to neighboring lands.

3. Significantly, unlike the earlier historian, Dtr_1, who expounded upon the righteousness of YHWH's judgment against the northern kingdom in the lengthy homily in 2 Kgs 17:7–23, the later Deuteronomistic historian, Dtr_2, did not expatiate upon the fall of Jerusalem. He satisfied himself with a chronistic, matter-of-fact report on Zedekiah's last rebellion (24:20b–25:21a). At the same time, he enclosed this final chapter of the history of Judah within a frame, and in so doing gave expression to his historiographic viewpoint:

> 24:20a: "Because of YHWH's wrath did these things happen to Jerusalem and Judah, so as to rid himself of them . . ."
>
> 25:21b: "Thus Judah was exiled from his land."

Further comment at this juncture may have been difficult for this historian, who had lived through the destruction and exile. He, unlike Ezekiel (Ezek 24:27), was struck dumb by the terrible fate which had overcome his people.

Finally, it should be noted that the historian concluded his narrative in pedantic fashion, with a detailed list of Temple treasures carried off to Babylon (25:13–17). But these details, when set over against the lengthy description at the outset of the monarchic history of the building's construction and outfitting (1 Kgs 6–8), point once again to one of the major Deuteronomic concerns—the centrality of the Solomonic Temple. The return of these Temple treasures marked the beginning of the new era of restoration for a later historian (Ezra 1:7–11).

[14] See E. J. Bickerman, "Nebuchadnezzar and Jerusalem," *PAAJR* 46–47 (1979–80), 69–85.

[15] See A. Malamat, *IEJ* 18 (1968), 154; idem, *VT* Sup 28 (1975), 134; idem, *WHJP* 4/I.219.

XLII. GEDALIAH, A BABYLONIAN GOVERNOR IN JUDAH

(25:22–26)

25 22 Now as for the people left in the land of Judah, those whom
Nebuchadnezzar king of Babylon left behind, he appointed Gedaliah
son of Ahikam son of Shaphan over them. 23 When all the officers of
the army, they and their men,[a] heard that the king of Babylon had
appointed Gedaliah, they came to Gedaliah at Mizpah: Ishmael son of
Nethaniah, Johanan son of Kareah, Seraiah son of Tanhumeth the
Netophathite and Jaazaniah son of the Maacathite, they and their
men. 24 Gedaliah gave his oath to them and their men: "Do not be
afraid to serve[b] the Chaldeans. Stay in the land; serve the king of
Babylon and it will go well with you." 25 But in the seventh month,
Ishmael son of Nethaniah son of Elishama, one of the royal line, came
with ten men and they struck down Gedaliah and he died, as well as
the Judaeans and the Chaldeans who were at Mizpah with him.
26 Then all the people, young and old and the army officers set out and
went to Egypt, for they were afraid of the Chaldeans.

[a] Read: *wʾnšyhm* with versions and Jer 40:7, cf below vv 23b and 24.
[b] Read: *mēʿăbôd* with Jer 40:9

Notes

25 22. *Gedaliah son of Ahikam son of Shaphan.* Gedaliah was of a prominent Jerusalem family His grandfather was the scribe during the reign of Josiah (2 Kgs 22.3), and his father was a member of the mission sent to Huldah (22:12 and see note there) and later intervened to save Jeremiah from the mob threatening the prophet's life (Jer 26:24). Gedaliah, too, was likely in the king's service, if he is identified with the person of the same name on the seal impression of the late seventh century found at Lachish *lgdlyhw ʾšr ʿl hbyt* "Belonging to Gedaliah, the Royal Steward" (*Lachish III* [London Oxford University Press, 1953], 348). While serving as the Babylonian appointee in Mizpah, Gedaliah enjoyed the support of Jeremiah, the prophet being one of the few who remained loyal to him (Jer 39·14; 40·1–6; cf S. Spiegel, in *ALEI AYIN The Salman Shocken Jubilee Volume* [Jerusalem Shocken, 1948–52], 9–16 [Hebrew])

23. *Mizpah.* Cf. 1 Kgs 15:22. Excavations at Tell-en-Naṣbeh (eight miles north of Jerusalem), identified with Mizpah, did not uncover a destruction level of the early sixth century. Cf. E. Stern *BA* 38 (1975), 32–37. On this basis, M. Noth (*History,* 288) suggested that Mizpah had been spared the fate of the capital, which was razed and left uninhabited. If the territory of Benjamin in its entirety had indeed surrendered to Nebuchadnezzar, it could well have served as a refuge for the Judaeans left in the land (so A. Malamat, *JNES* 9 [1950], 226–27).

Johanan son of Kareah. MT Jer 40:8 reads, "Johanan and Jonathan, sons of Kareah"; LXX for this verse has the short reading of 2 Kgs 25:23.

Seraiah son of Tanhumeth the Netophathite. Jer 40:8 reads, "and the sons of Ephai the Netophathite." Netopha is a city in northern Judah in the vicinity of Bethlehem; cf. 1 Chr 2:54 and Neh 7:26. Two of David's heroes hailed from Netopha (2 Sam 23:28–29).

Jaazaniah son of the Maacathite. A seal found at Tell-en-Naṣbeh bears the inscription: *ly'znyhw ʿbd hmlk,* "belonging to Jaazaniah, servant of the king," and may have belonged to the army officer in v. 23 (W. F. Badè, *ZAW* 51 [1933], 150–56). Maacah is more likely the Calebite clan Maacah (1 Chr 2:48) than the Aramaean kingdom of Beth-Maacah (so e.g. *NEB, NAB*). Maacah clearly appears in Judaean contexts in 2 Sam 23:34 and 1 Chr 4:19.

24. *Gedaliah gave his oath to them.* Though the subject matter of the oath is not stated, it no doubt contained a solemn promise that the army officers, who just recently had fought against Nebuchadnezzar, would not be punished. Hence Gedaliah's call: "Do not be afraid to serve the Chaldeans." The fuller account in Jer 40 reports that Gedaliah also promised to represent the officers before the Babylonian authorities. The same passage legitimizes the seizure of lands abandoned by the exiles to Babylon.

to serve the Chaldeans. Read *mēʿăbôd* as in Jer 40:9 for MT *mēʿabdê,* "servants," which is meaningless.

25. *they struck down Gedaliah and he died.* The bloody attack by Ishmael and his band was solely upon the government; other Judaeans, who were part of the official entourage, were forcibly taken to Ammon (Jer 41:10).

Comment

1. These five verses are a précis of a fuller account of Gedaliah's term of office now found in Jer 40:7–41:18. Since no awareness of Jeremiah or his activity is evidenced, it may have been composed of data drawn from a common source at an early stage of transmission, prior to its incorporation into the book of Jeremiah.[1] The following relationships are to be noted:

2 Kgs 25:23–24	<	Jer 40:7–9
2 Kgs 25:25	<	Jer 41:1a,2,3
2 Kgs 25:26	<	Jer 41:16–18

[1] A common source for 2 Kgs 25:22–26 and parts of Jer 40 is posited by G. Wanke, *Untersuchungen zur sogenannten Baruchschrift, BZAW* 122 (1971), 115–16.

2. Unlike the Assyrian imperial policy, the Neo-Babylonian monarchs did not transfer masses of new settlers to newly conquered Judah. So whereas in Samaria a new ethnic group developed out of the fusion of native Israelites and foreign settlers, Judah remained sparsely settled during the period of Babylonian rule. Judah's center shifted northward to Mizpah in Benjamin, an area which had not suffered heavy destruction during the siege of Jerusalem. Jerusalem itself and the ruined site of the Temple still maintained their sacred status (cf. Jer 41:5). A Judaean nobleman, Gedaliah son of Ahikam, was appointed as administrator of local affairs. His official title is unknown, which does not help to determine the exact status of Judah at this juncture. Was Judah a province of which Gedaliah was governor? Or had some sort of interim status with minimal Babylonian supervision been imposed? As it happens, no Neo-Babylonian administrative records which could shed light on the administration of the provinces survive. Nor do the royal inscriptions relate to matters of military and political significance. In view of standard Assyrian practice, the appointment of a local noble is unprecedented. Yet it might be compared to the position of the local Delta princes in Egypt under Esarhaddon and Ashurbanipal (*ANET*^{3}, 294–95) or to that of Zerubbabel and Nehemiah under the Achameneans.

The report of the flight to Egypt which abruptly closes this account is markedly passed over without editorial comment; the statement given here affirms that YHWH's judgment was carried out *in full:* "Thus Judah was exiled from its land" (cf. v. 21). The exiles in Babylon viewed Gedaliah's murder as the death blow to national existence, and instituted fast days to mourn this loss, as well as the destruction of Jerusalem and the Temple (cf. Zech 7:5; 8:19).

The duration of the political arrangements under Gedaliah is unknown, but the impression is that it lasted only a few months, or at most a year. His assassination by a member of the royal family was hardly an act of rebellion against Nebuchadnezzar; it was rather a case of vendetta against a collaborator with the Chaldean enemy carried out by extremists. Such a small band of men could not have hoped to rid themselves of the yoke of Nebuchadnezzar. [2]

Is this capsule history of Gedaliah from the same hand as the rest of 2 Kgs 25? As it is devoid of value judgment and explicit message, the author of this addition—his time and place—cannot be determined. At the very least, the verses point out that after 586, no framework, political or religious, around which national existence could rally, survived in Judah.

[2] Though Ishmael did have the backing of Baalis, king of the Ammonites (Jer 40·14; 41 10), a full scale uprising against Nebuchadnezzar so soon after the fall of Jerusalem was impractical.

XLIII. EPILOGUE: RELEASE OF JEHOIACHIN

(25:27–30)

25 27 In the thirty-seventh year of the exile of Jehoiachin king of Judah, in the twelfth month, on the twenty-seventh day of the month, Evil-merodach, king of Babylon, in his accession year, pardoned Jehoiachin king of Judah < and released him >[a] from prison. 28 He spoke kindly to him and set his throne above those[b] of the kings who were with him in Babylon. 29 He changed his prison garb and he received permanent provisions[c] by his favor for life. 30 His allowance was a permanent allowance from the king, daily for life.

[a] Add *wayyôṣēʾ ʾōtô,* with Luc., LXX, and Jer 52:31.
[b] Read *lĕkissēʾ* with Jer 52:32.
[c] Lit. "He ate (his) food regularly."

Notes

25 27. *in his accession year.* Heb. *bišnat molkô,* which corresponds to Akk. *rēš šarrūti,* is that portion of the year from the king's accession until the first of Nisan, after which the first official regnal year begins. This period is not counted in the total years of the king. In Aramaic, the term is *rʾš mlkwt* (A. Cowley, *Aramaic Papyri of the Fifth Century B.C.* [Oxford: Clarendon Press, 1923], 6.1–2; and Daliyeh papyrus No. 1.1 (F. M. Cross, in *New Directions in Biblical Archaeology* [eds. D. N. Freedman and J. C. Greenfield, Garden City, N.Y.: Doubleday, 1971], 48); in Phoenician *št mlk* (G. A. Cooke, *A Text-book of North-Semitic Inscriptions* [Oxford: Clarendon Press, 1903], No. 6, line 1). Cf. also H. Tadmor, *EncMiqr* 7.312–14.

Evil-merodach. Amel-marduk was the son and successor of Nebuchadnezzar, 562–560 B.C.E. For a discussion of his reign, see R. H. Sack, *Amel-Marduk 562-560 B.C.E.* AOATS 4 (1972).

pardoned. Heb. *nāśāʾ rōʾš,* lit. "lifted the head." The expression is used several times in Gen 40:13, 19, 20; there, too, in the sense, "to take note of, to pay special attention to" (Speiser, *Genesis,* AB, 308; idem, *BASOR* 149 [1958], 17–25 [= *Oriental and Biblical Studies,* 171–86]; and now M. Gruber, *Nonverbal Communication,* 598–613.)

28. *He spoke kindly to him.* Heb. *waydabbēr ʾittô ṭōbôt.* Recent studies have suggested that *dabbēr ṭōbôt* can be understood in a covenantal sense, "a type of legal arrangement" (so e.g. A. Malamat, *BAR* 3.197; M. Fox, *BASOR* 209 (1973), 41–42; M. Weinfeld, *Maarav* 3 [1982], 27–53). But while Heb. *ṭōbâ* as well as Aram. *ṭābtāʾ*

and Akk *ṭābtu* can refer to treaty relations (W L. Moran, *JNES* 22 [1963], 173–76), not every benevolent act points to a formal covenantal setting. *Ṭōbâ* still maintains its more general meaning of "grace" and in the present instance should be taken to mean that Jehoiachin was released through an act of amnesty on the occasion of Evil-merodach's accession to the throne. See further on *dĕbārîm ṭôbîm* in 1 Kgs 12 7

the kings who were with him in Babylon. Perhaps some of the kings who are mentioned on the "Unger Prism" of Nebuchadnezzar, e.g. the king of Tyre, the king of Gaza, the king of Sidon, the king of Arvad, the king of Ashdod (*ANET*[3] 308a) were still alive in 562

29 *by his favor* Heb *lĕpānāyw* For this idiom, cf Gen 6·11, 17 18, 43 33, and the comment by Speiser, *Genesis*, AB, 51

30 *allowance.* Heb *ʾărūḥâ*, here and in Jer 40·5 and Prov 15 17, is of unknown etymology LXX has *hestiatoria*, "food allotment", Targ., *šĕrûtāʾ*, "meal " The Akk origin suggested in the lexicons (Gesenius, K-B) is problematic **Arhītu*, "monthly duty," is a very rare word, appearing only in Old Babylonian (*CAD* A, 2 258); *iarahhu*, "a fine quality barley" (*CAD* I–J, 325), appears only in lexical texts.

Verse 30 may be an explicatory comment on v 29 concerning his daily provisions; or it may refer to an additional allowance of personal items, e g. oil used for cosmetic purposes, as understood by the Targum

Comment

The release of Jehoiachin from prison is the last historical notation recorded in Kings and is an addition by an exilic writer acquainted with the event Sometime during the reign of Nebuchadnezzar, Jehoiachin had fallen into disfavor for an unspecified reason, accusations of treason, for which such a punishment would have been appropriate, were common at the courts of the ancient Near East. He was thrown into prison and languished there until the act of amnesty upon the accession of Evil-merodach The daily rations issued to Jehoiachin after his release (v 30) are not those issued to him in Nebuchadnezzar's thirteenth year (see above, note to 24 8), but were a new issue some thirty years later [1]

What might have been the purpose of this final *postscriptum?* This passage appears nonintegral to the book of Kings, it contains none of the phraseology typical of Deuteronomistic editing, nor does it articulate any of the historiographic tenets of the Deuteronomic school Consequently it cannot be invested with the theological significance ascribed to it by von Rad

> But the Deuteronomist saw yet another word as active in the history, namely, the promise of salvation in the Nathan prophecy, and it, as well as the threat of judgment, was effectual as it ran through the course of history Had it too creatively reached its goal in a fulfillment? The Deuteronomist's history leaves this question open Yet, closing as it does with

[1] Gray's statement concerning these documents is misleading.

the noted about the favor shown to Jehoiachin (2 Kgs 25:27ff.), it points to a possibility with which Jahweh can resume.[2]

Rather than holding out the promise of salvation through the renewal of the Davidic dynasty,[3] these verses are merely an epilogue by an exilic writer who brought the narration of Jehoiachin's life up to date.[4] Exilic readers might have found some measure of consolation in the preferred treatment of their aged king; from this point of view the book of Kings does end on a positive note.[5] But the restoration of Israel, in Deuteronomic terms, required a return to YHWH:

> When they sin against You . . . and You are angry with them and deliver them to the enemy, and their captors carry them off to an enemy land, near or far; and then they take it to heart in the land to which they have been carried off, and they repent and make supplication to You in the land of their captors, saying: "We have sinned, we have acted perversely, we have acted wickedly," and they turn back to You with all their heart and soul . . . give heed in Your heavenly abode to their prayer and supplication, uphold their cause, and pardon your people (1 Kgs 8:46–53; cf. Deut 4:25–31, 30:1–20).

The Deuteronomistic historian(s) responsible for the final edition of Kings did not speak in these terms; the harsh realities of the destruction and the rigors of the exile were apparently too close at hand to entertain such high hopes.[6] It was for others to guide the community of Israel in their search for return.

[2] G. von Rad, *Old Testament Theology* (New York: Harper & Row, 1962) 1.343.

[3] The "good" shown to Jehoiachin is a rather thin thread upon which to hang the "firm affirmation of the theologian that the promise . . . [of Yahweh to] the Davidic house still endures and therefore the word can be trusted" (so W. Brueggemann, "The Kerygma of the Deuteronomistic Historian," *Interpretation* 22 [1968], 387–402).

[4] Cf. Noth, *Überlieferungsgeschichtliche Studien,* 87 (E.T., 74).

[5] The motif of the elevation of a Judaean to a position of influence at a foreign court was a popular one in exilic literature, e.g., the story of Daniel at the court of Nebuchadnezzar, and that of Mordecai at the court of Ahasuerus.

[6] Cross agrees that vv. 27–30 are too meager to find in them a Deuteronomic message, and explains the "strange shape of the Exilic edition" as due to the "fidelity (of the exilic editor) in preserving intact the work of the Josianic Deuteronomist" (*Canaanite Myth and Hebrew Epic,* 277–89). Cross finds the theme of hope and restoration in other Dtr. passages, as had H. W. Wolff, "Das Kerygma das deuteronomistischen Geschichtswerkes," *ZAW* 73 (1961), 171–86 (E.T. in *The Vitality of Old Testament Traditions,* eds. H. W. Wolff and W. Brueggemann [Atlanta: J. Knox, 1975], 82–100). Cf. too Nelson, *Double Redaction,* 123.

Appendixes

APPENDIX I: A SELECTION OF EXTRABIBLICAL TEXTS RELATING TO 2 KINGS

1 MESHA, king of Moab
The Moabite Stone (Latest edition *KAI*, No. 181 Translations. *ANET*[3], 320; *DOTT*, 196–97)

I am Mesha, son of Chemosh[yat], king of Moab, the Dibonite. My father reigned over Moab thirty years and I reigned after my father I built this high place for Chemosh in Qarho (or "the citadel") because he saved me from all the kings and let me gaze (triumphantly) upon all my enemies. Omri, king of Israel, oppressed Moab many years for Chemosh was angry with his land. His son succeeded him and he, too, said, "I will oppress Moab." [Thus] he said in my days, but I gazed (triumphantly) over him and his house, while Israel has utterly perished forever Omri had taken possession of a[ll of the la]nd of Medeba and dwelt there during his lifetime and half the lifetime of his son(s), forty years, but Chemosh restored it in my days. I built Baal-meon and I made the reservoir in it, I built Kiriathaim Now the men of Gad had dwelt in the land of Ataroth from of old and the king of Israel had built Ataroth for himself But I fought against the city, I took it and slaughtered all the people of the city *to satisfy* Chemosh and Moab. I captured the Ariel of *David* and dragged it before Chemosh in Kerioth I settled there the men of Sharon and Maharith Then Chemosh said to me, "Go, take Nebo from Israel!" I marched at night and fought against it from the break of dawn until noon, I took it and slaughtered everyone—7,000 men, *boys*, women, *girls*, and maidens, for I had devoted it to Ashtar-Chemosh I took from there [vessels] of YHWH and dragged them before Chemosh The king of Israel had built Jahaz and settled it while fighting me; but Chemosh drove him out before me. I took two hundred men from Moab, all *leaders*, and led them against Jahaz and took it to add it to (the territory of) Dibon

I built Qarho (or "the citadel"), the walls of the parks, and the walls of the Ophel, and I built its gates and I built its towers and I built the king's house and I constructed the *retaining walls* of the reser[voirs for wa]ter within the city Now there was no cistern inside the city, within Qarho (or "the citadel"), and I said to all the people, "Make yourselves each one a cistern in his house" I cut the ditches at Qarho (or "the citadel") (employing) the captives of Israel. I built Aroer; I made the road by (Wadi) Arnon. I built Beth-bamoth for it had been destroyed. I built Bezer for it was in ruins, [ ] fifty (?) [me]n of Dibon, because all Dibon was subject (to me). I was king over [ ] hundreds of towns which I added to the land. I built [Me]deba and Beth-diblathen and Beth-meon and I set there . . . and as for Hauronen, there dwelt there . . . and Chemosh said to me, "Go down and fight against Hauronen." So I went down . . . [ ] and Chemosh [dwelt] there in my days . . . from there . . . and I . . .

2. SHALMANESER III, king of Assyria (859–824 B.C.E.)

A. Basalt statue (Latest edition: E. Michel, *WO* 1/2 [1947], 57–58, col. I:14–II:1. Translations: *ARAB* 1.681; *ANET*³, 280)

I defeated Adad-idri of Damascus together with twelve kings, his helpers. Twenty-nine thousand of his brave fighters, I laid down like (slaughtered) sheep; the remainder of his troops I pushed into the Orontes River (and) they fled to save their lives. Adad-idri disappeared forever; Hazael, son of a nobody, seized the throne. He called up a large army and set out to engage me in battle. I fought against him, defeated him, and captured his camp. He fled to save his life. I marched as far as Damascus, his royal city [and cut down his] orchards.

B. Marble slab (Edition: F. Safar, *Iraq* 7 [1951], 11–12, col. III:45–IV:15)

In the eighteenth year of my rule, I crossed the Euphrates River for the sixteenth time. Hazael of Damascus put his trust in his vast army and called up his troops in great number. He made Mt. Senir, a mountain peak facing the Lebanon, his fortress; 16,020 of his combat troops I killed; 1,121 chariots, 470 riding horses, as well as his camp, I seized. He fled to save his life. I followed (and) besieged him (lit. "locked him up") in Damascus, his royal city. I cut down his orchards and burned his stocks of grain. I marched as far as the mountain(s) of Hauran. Countless cities I destroyed, tore down, and burned, and carried off their spoil. I marched to Mt. Ba'ali-rasi, at the head of the sea facing Tyre and set up my royal stele there. I received tribute of Ba'ali-manzeri of Tyre (and) Jehu, "son of Omri." On my return, I ascended Mt. Lebanon and set up my royal stele alongside the stele of Tiglath-pileser, the great king, my ancestor.

C Black Obelisk (Latest edition E. Michel, *WO* 2 [1955], 140, Band 2. Translations. *ARAB* 1 590; *ANET*³, 281, *DOTT*, 48)

I received the tribute of Jehu, "son of Omri", silver, gold, a golden bowl, a golden vase(?), golden goblets, golden buckets, tin, a royal scepter, and javelins.

3 ADAD-NIRARI III, king of Assyria (811–783 B.C E.)
Tell al-Rimah stele (S. Page, *Iraq* 30 [1968], 141–42, lines 6–12)

He received 2,000 talents of silver, 1,000 talents of copper, 2,000 talents of iron, 3,000 multicolored garments, and linen garments as tribute from Mari' of Damascus. He received the tribute of Joash of Samaria, of the Tyrians, and of the Sidonians. He received tribute from all the kings of Na'iri land

4 TIGLATH-PILESER III, king of Assyria (745-727 B.C E.)

A Iran stele (L. D Levine, *Two Neo-Assyrian Stelae from Iran*, Royal Ontario Museum, Art and Archaeology Occasional Paper 23 [1972] col II 1 23, cf H Tadmor, *ITP*, St. IIIA, 1–23)

The kings of Hatti, the Aramaeans of the western seashore, the Qedarites and Arabs Kushtashpi of Kummuh, Rezin of Damascus, Menahem of Samaria, Tubail of Tyre, Sibatbail of Byblos, Urik of Que, Sulumal of Melid, Uassurme of Tabal, Ushhiti of Atuna, Urballa of Tuhana, Tuhame of Ishtundi, Uirimi of Hubishna, Dadi-il of Kaska, Pisiris of Carchemish, Panammu of Sam'al, Tarhulara of Gurgum, Zabibe queen of the Arabs, tribute of silver, gold, tin, iron, elephant hide(s), ivory, blue-purple and red-purple garments, multicolored linen garments, dromedaries, she-camels, I imposed upon them

B From the Annals (Latest edition H Tadmor, *ITP*, Ann 18, lines 4' 7' Translations *ARAB* 1 779; *ANET*³, 283)

x captives from the city of -bara, 625 captives from the city of [ ] [captives from the city of] Hannathon, 650 captives from Ku[x captives from the city of Jo]tbah, 656 captives from the city of Sa[ ] the cities of Rumah and Merom [ ]

C Summary inscription (Latest edition H Tadmor, *ITP*, Summ 4, lines 15 19' Translations *ARAB* 1 817, *ANET*³, 284, *DOTT*, 55)

The land of Israel [ ] its hosts [ ] all of its people, [ ] I carried off [to] Assyria Pekah, their king [ ] and I installed Hoshea [as king] over them, 10 talents of gold, x talents [of silver], their [ ] I received from them, and [to Assyria, I carr]ied them off

D. Clay-tablet inscription (Latest edition: H. Tadmor, *ITP,* Summ 7, Reverse, lines 7′–13′; Translations: *ARAB* 1.801; *ANET³,* 282; *DOTT,* 55–56)

[The tribute] of Kushtashpi of Kummuh, Urikki of Que, Sibittibi'il of [Byblos, Hiram of Tyre, Pisiris of Carchemish,] [Eni-]ilu of Hamath, Panammu of Sam'al, Tarhulara of Gurgum, Sulu[mal of Melid, Dadi-il of Kashka,] [U]assurme of Tabal, Ushhitti of Tuna, Urballa of Tuhana, Tuham[mi of Ishtunda, Urimme of Hubishna,] [Ma]tanbi'il of Arvad, Sanipu of Ammon, Salamanu of Moab, [ ] [Me]tinti of Ashkelon, Jehoahaz of Judah, Qaushmalaka of Edom, Mus[ ], Hanunu of Gaza, gold, silver, lead, iron, tin, multicolored garments, linen garments, the garments of the lands, wool (dyed) red-purple, [all kinds of] costly articles, produce of the sea (and) dry land, the yield of their country, royal treasures, horses, mules, broken to the yo[ke . . . I received].

5. SHALMANESER V, king of Assyria (727–722 B.C.E.)

Excerpt from the Babylonian Chronicle Series (Latest edition: A. K. Grayson, *Assyrian and Babylonian Chronicles,* 73:27–31)

In the month of Tebeth, day 25, Shalmaneser ascended the throne in Assyria and Babylonia. He demolished Samaria.
The fifth year. Shalmaneser died in the month of Tebeth. Five years Shalmaneser ruled Babylonia and Assyria. In the month of Tebeth, day 12, Sargon ascended the throne in Assyria.

6. SARGON II, king of Assyria (722–705 B.C.E.)

A. Prism Inscription (C. J. Gadd, *Iraq* 16 [1954], 179, col. 4:25–41; cf. H. Tadmor, *JCS* 12 [1958], 34)

[The Sa]marians who had come to an agreement with a [hostile] king not to do service or to render tribute to me, did battle. In the strength of the great gods, my lords, I fought with them; 27,280 people together with their chariots and the gods in whom they trust, I counted as spoil. 200 chariots I organized as a royal unit from among them and the rest of them I settled in Assyria. I restored the city of Samaria and settled it more densely than before (and) brought there people from the lands of my conquest. I placed my eunuch over them as governor and counted them as Assyrians.

B. From the Annals (A. G. Lie, *The Inscriptions of Sargon II* [Paris: P. Geuthner, 1929], 20, 22, lines 120–25; Translations: *ARAB* 2.17–18; *ANET³*, 286)

(In the seventh year of my rule . . .), the Tamud, Ibadidi, Marsimani, Haiapa, the far-off Arabs, desert dwellers who know neither overseer nor commander, who had not brought any king their tribute, I defeated them with the aid of Ashur, my lord, and exiled their remnant; I settled them in Samaria. I received tribute from the pharaoh of Egypt, Samsi queen of the Arabs, It'amra the Sabaean, and from kings of the seashore and desert: gold, ore of the mountains, precious stones, ivory, ebony seeds, all kinds of aromatics, horses, (and) camels.

7. HEZEKIAH, king of Judah (727–698 B.C.E.)
Siloam Tunnel Inscription (Latest edition: *KAI*, No. 189. Translations: *ANET³*, 321; *DOTT*, 210.)

[ ] the tunnel. This is the matter of the tunnel: While [ ] (were) still [ ] the axe(s) toward one another, and while there were still three cubits to be [tunneled, there was heard] a voice calling to his fellow, for there was a fissure (?) in the rock on the right [and on the left]. And on the day when the tunnel was cut through, the stone cutters struck toward one another, ax against ax. Then the water flowed from the source to the pool for 1,200 cubits, and the height of the rock was 100 cubits above the heads of the stone cutters.

8. SENNACHERIB, king of Assyria (705–681 B.C.E.)
From Rassam Prism Inscription (D. D. Luckenbill, *Annals of Sennacherib*, 29–34, col. II:37–III:49; 60, lines 56–58. Translations: *ARAB* 2.239–40, 284; *ANET³*, 287–88; *DOTT*, 66–67).

In my third campaign, I marched against Hatti. The awesome splendor of my lordship overwhelmed Lulli, king of Sidon, and he fled overseas and disappeared forever. The terrifying nature of the weapon of (the god) Ashur overwhelmed his strong cities, Greater Sidon, Lesser Sidon, Bit-zitti, Ṣariptu, Mahaliba, Ushu, Akzib, Akko, walled cities (provided) with food and water for his garrisons, and they bowed in submission at my feet. I installed Taba'lu on the throne as king over them and imposed upon him tribute and dues for my lordship (payable) annually without interruption.

The kings of Amurru (i.e. the West), all of them—Minihimmu of Samsimuruna, Tuba'lu of Sidon, Abdiliti of Arvad, Urumilki of Byblos, Mitinti of Ashdod, Puduilu of Beth-Ammon, Chemosh-nadbi of Moab,

Ayarammu of Edom—brought me sumptuous gifts, rich presents, fourfold, and kissed my feet

(As for) Ṣidqa, king of Ashkelon, who had not submitted to my yoke, I deported and sent him to Assyria, (together with) his family gods, he, himself, his wife, his sons, his daughters, his brothers, and all his descendants. I set Sharruludari, son of Rukibti, their former king, over the people of Ashkelon and imposed upon him the payment of tribute (and) presents to my lordship; he (now) bears my yoke.

In the course of my campaign, I surrounded and conquered Beth-Dagon, Joppa, Banai-Barqa, Azuri, cities belonging to Ṣidqa, who did not submit quickly, and I carried off their spoil. The officials, the nobles, and the people of Ekron who had thrown Padi, their king, (who was) under oath and obligation to Assyria, into iron fetters and handed him over in a hostile manner to Hezekiah, the Judaean; because of the offense they committed, they were afraid The kings of Egypt, (and) the bowmen and chariot corps and cavalry of the kings of Ethiopia assembled a countless force and came to their (i.e. Ekronites') aid. In the plain of Eltekeh, they drew up their ranks against me and sharpened their weapons. Trusting in (the god) Ashur, my lord, I fought with them and inflicted a defeat upon them The Egyptian charioteers and princes, together with the charioteers of the Ethiopians, I personally took alive in the midst of the battle I besieged and conquered Eltekeh and Timnah and carried off their spoil I assaulted Ekron and slew its officials and nobles who had stirred up rebellion and hung their bodies on watchtowers all about the city The citizens who had committed sinful acts, I counted as spoil and the rest of them, who had not sinned, I ordered their release I freed Padi, their king, from Jerusalem and set him on the throne as king over them and imposed tribute for my lordship over him

As for Hezekiah, the Judaean, who had not submitted to my yoke, I besieged forty-six of his fortified walled cities and surrounding small towns, which were without number Using packed-down ramps and by applying battering rams, infantry attacks by mines, breeches, and siege machines, I conquered (them). I took out 200,150 people, young and old, male and female, horses, mules, donkeys, camels, cattle, and sheep, without number, and counted them as spoil Himself, I locked him up within Jerusalem, his royal city, like a bird in a cage I surrounded him with earthworks, and made it unthinkable (lit "taboo") for him to exit by the city gate. His cities which I had despoiled, I cut off from his land and gave them to Mitinti, king of Ashdod, Padi, king of Ekron and Ṣilli-bel, king of Gaza, and thus diminished his land I imposed upon him in addition to the former tribute, yearly payment of dues and gifts for my lordship

He, Hezekiah, was overwhelmed by the awesome splendor of my lordship, and he sent me after my departure to Nineveh, my royal city, his elite troops and his best soldiers, which he had brought into Jerusalem as reinforcements, with 30 talents of gold, 800 talents of silver, choice antimony, large blocks of carnelian, beds (inlaid) with ivory, armchairs (inlaid) with ivory, elephant hides, ivory, ebony-wood, boxwood, garments with multicolored trim, garments of linen, wood (dyed) red-purple and blue-purple, vessels of copper, iron, bronze and tin, chariots, siege shields, lances, armor, daggers for the belt, bows and arrows, countless trappings and implements of war, together with his daughters, his palace women, his male and female singers. He (also) dispatched his personal messenger to deliver the tribute and to do obeisance.

9. ESARHADDON, king of Assyria (681–669 B.C.E.)
From Prism A (Latest edition: R. Borger, *Asarhaddon,* 60–61, col. V:54–VI:1; Translations: *ARAB* 2.690; *ANET³,* 291)

I mobilized the kings of Hatti and the Trans-Euphrates (lit. "on the other side of the river"): Ba'lu king of Tyre, Manasseh king of Judah, Qaushgabri king of Edom, Musuri king of Moab, Ṣilbel king of Gaza, Mitinti king of Ashkelon, Ikausu king of Ekron, Milkiashapa king of Byblos, Matanba'al king of Arvad, Abiba'al king of Samsimuruna, Puduilu king of Beth-Ammon, Ahimilki king of Ashdod, twelve kings of the seacoast . . . ten kings of Iadnana (Cyprus), in the midst of the sea, together twenty-two kings of Hatti, the seacoast, and the (islands) in the midst of the sea, and I gave them orders and had them transport . . . under great difficulties, whatever was necessary for my palace at Nineveh, the city of my lordship.

NOTE: The same list of kings, with two minor changes, appears in the Prism C inscriptions of Ashurbanipal: Iakinlu, king of Arvad, and Amminadbi, king of Beth-Ammon (Streck, *Assurbanipal,* 2.138–40, col. I: 23–47. Translations: *ARAB* 2.876; *ANET³,* 294).

10. Excerpts from the Babylonian Chronicle Series (Latest edition: A. K. Grayson, *Chronicles,* 95, 100, 101; Translations: *ANET³,* 563–64; *DOTT,* 77, 78, 80)

(610/609 B.C.E.) Year 16. In the month of Iyyar, the king of Babylonia mobilized his troops and marched to Assyria. From [the month of . . .] Marchesvan, they marched about victoriously in Assyria. In the month of Marchesvan, the Umman-manda [who] had come [to the ai]d of the king of Babylonia, joined their armies and marched to Haran [against

Ashur-uball]ıt who had taken the throne of Assyrıa. Ashur-uballıt and the army of Eg[ypt] whıch had come to [hıs aıd] were overcome by fear of the enemy and aban[doned] the cıty [   ] they crossed The kıng of Babylonıa reached Haran [   ] captured the cıty, he carrıed off much spoıl from the cıty and the temple. In the month of Adar, the kıng of Babylonıa left theır [   ] He returned home and the Umman-manda (ı e the Medes), who had come to the aıd of the kıng of Babylonıa, pulled back

(609/608 B.C E.)   Year 17   In the month of Tammuz, Ashur-uballıt, kıng of Assyrıa, a large Egyptıan army [   ] crossed the rıver (Euphrates) and marched agaınst Haran to conquer (ıt)   They defeated the garrıson statıoned ınsıde by the kıng of Babylonıa   they encamped agaınst Haran Untıl the month of Elul, he assaulted the cıty, though he could not take ıt [   ], he dıd not pull back The kıng of Babylonıa marched to the aıd of hıs army

(604/603 B.C E) Year 1 of Nebuchadnezzar In the month of Sıvan, he mobılızed hıs troops and marched to Hattı Untıl the month of Kıslev, he marched about vıctorıously ın Hattı All the kıngs of Hattı came before hım and he receıved theır rıch trıbute He marched to [Ashk]elon ın the month of Kıslev and captured ıt, he seızed ıts kıng, plundered ıt, and carrıed off ıts spoıl He turned the cıty ınto a heap of ruıns. In the month of Shebat, he marched and [returned] to Babylon

(601/600 B C E) Year 4 The kıng of Babylonıa mobılızed hıs troops and marched to Hattı [They marched about vıctor]ıously ın Hattı In the month of Kıslev, he took charge of hıs army and marched to Egypt The kıng of Egypt receıved the news and mob[ılızed?] hıs army In open battle, they ınflıcted casualtıes on one another and each suffered great losses The kıng of Babylonıa and hıs troops turned and [went back] to Babylon

(598 597 B C E) Year 7 In the month of Kıslev, the kıng of Babylonıa mobılızed hıs troops and marched to Hattı He encamped agaınst the cıty of Judah, and on the second of Adar, he captured the cıty and he seızed (ıts) kıng A kıng of hıs choıce, he appoınted there; he to[ok] ıts heavy trıbute and carrıed ıt off to Babylon

APPENDIX II: THE CHRONOLOGY OF THE DIVIDED MONARCHY

JUDAH		*ISRAEL*	
Rehoboam	928–911	Jeroboam I	928–907
Abijah	911–908	Nadab	907–906
Asa	908–867	Baasha	906–883
Jehoshaphat	870–846	Elah	883–882
Jehoram	851–843	Zimri	882
Ahaziah	843–842	Tibni	882–878
Athaliah	842–836	Omri	882–871
Joash	836–798	Ahab	873–852
Amaziah	798–769	Ahaziah	852–851
Azariah	785–733	Jehoram	851–842
Jotham	758–743	Jehu	842–814
Ahaz	743–727	Jehoahaz	817–800
Hezekiah	727–698	Jehoash	800–784
Manasseh	698–642	Jeroboam II	789–748
Amon	641–640	Zechariah	748–747
Josiah	639–609	Shallum	747
Jehoahaz	609	Menahem	747–737
Jehoiakim	608–598	Pekahiah	737–735
Jehoiachin	597	Pekah	735–732
Zedekiah	596–586	Hoshea	732–724

* The dates follow the chronological reconstruction in H. Tadmor, *Chronology, EncMiqr* 4.245–310; see further, idem, *WHJP* 4/1, 44–60.

APPENDIX III: CHRONOLOGIES OF THE ANCIENT NEAR EAST

1. Kings of Assyria

Shalmaneser III	859–824
Shamshi-Adad V	824–811
Adad-nirari III	811–783
Shalmaneser IV	783–773
Ashur-dan III	773–755
Ashur-nirari V	755–745
Tiglath-pileser III	745–727
Shalmaneser V	727–722
Sargon II	722–705
Sennacherib	705–681
Esarhaddon	681–669
Ashurbanipal	669–627
Ashur-etil-ilani Sin-shum-lishir Sin-shar-ishkun	627–612
Ashur-uballit II	612–609

2. Kings of Babylonia: The Chaldean Dynasty

Nabopolassar	625–605
Nebuchadnezzar II	605–562
Amel-Marduk	562–560
Neriglissar	560–556
Labashi-Marduk	556
Nabonidus	556–539

* The dates of the kings of Assyria and Babylonia given here are reckoned from their accession year; the native Mesopotamian practice was to count from the first full year following the accession, which began in Nisan (= March/April). J A. Brinkman in A. L. Oppenheim, *Ancient Mesopotamia* (Revised ed., Chicago: University of Chicago, 1977), Appendix. Mesopotamian Chronology of the Historical Period, 335–48, follows the Mesopotamian practice.

3. *Kings of Egypt: 25th (Nubian) Dynasty*

Pi(ankhy)	747–716
Shabako	716–702
Shebitku	702–690
Tarharqa	690–664
Tantamani	664–656

26th Dynasty

Psammetichus I	664–610
Necho II	610–595
Psammetichus II	595–589
Apries	589–570
Amasis II	570–526
Psammetichus III	526–525

2 KINGS

INDEX OF BIBLICAL AND OTHER REFERENCES

I. BIBLE

II. APOCRYPHA

III. QUMRAN SCROLLS

IV. JOSEPHUS

V. RABBINIC LITERATURE

NON-HEBREW WORDS AND PHRASES DISCUSSED

I. Akkadian

abat šarri qabû / zakāru 80
abu 32
adê mēšu 205
amāru 156
amšali 111
ana balaṭ 8, 57
ana māt Aššur utīr 192
apu 267
aradka u marūka anāku 187
arānu 138
arḫītu 329
āšipu 8, 64
bābu / bāb maḫīri 81
badqu 137
baṭlāte 247
bēru / bēr qaqqari 8, 65
birīti 318
bīt maṣṣarti 318
bīt nakkamti 259
dāgil pān šarri 8, 320
dāyiqu 317
dīnam dabābu 317
dullu 211
ēkal māššarti 259
ēnāšu lunappil 318
epēšu 211
epqu 63
garābu 63
gugudānu lūṣûma 63
guḫlu 111
ḫalla / zê summāti 79
ḫapû 205
ḫarūbu 79
ḫaṭû 22
ḫawû 8, 205
ḫubūru 237, 238
iaraḫḫu 329
igisû 188
illatu 319
imtu 283
ina pāni / ina īni aqāru 27
ina tarṣi PN 186
ina ūmīšuma 186
itti nišē māt Aššur amnūšunuti 177n.
karašu 82
kēnu 189
kibru / kibrātu 65
kilili 111
kilīlu 128
kî līṭūtu 157
kīma dayašti adīš 144
kudurru 306
kulūlu 128
kumirtu 285
kumru 285
lāsimu 116
lā tapallaḥ 74, 234
maltaktu 115
manzaltu 286
manzaz pāni 319
maqātu 82
mār bārî 32
mār ḫabbatu 80
māršu ana DN *išarrap* 267
māru 32, 80
mašennu 318
maštaku 115
mēsu / mēšu 205
mūdē šarri 114
nanmurru 156
nāqidu 43
nasāḫu 218
nīd aḫi 161
nīru 95
palāḫ ili u šarri 210
pānu 63
parṣu 210
pīḫātu 232
pî ṭābi 242n.
qaštu malîtu 110
qerītu 74
quppu 138
rab āli 287
rab ḫanšē 26
rab nuḫatimmu 8, 318
rab ša rēši 229
rab šaqê 230
raggintu 284
rēʾû 231
rēš šarrūti 328

II Aramaic

III Greek

IV Hittite

V Persian

VI Sumerian

VII Ugaritic

KEY TO THE TEXT

Chapter	*Verse*	*Text Section*
1 Kgs 22	52–54	I
2 Kgs 1	1	I
2 Kgs 1	2–18	II
2 Kgs 2	1–18	III
2 Kgs 2	19–22	IV
2 Kgs 2	23–25	V
2 Kgs 3	1–27	VI
2 Kgs 4	1–44	VII
2 Kgs 5	1–27	VIII
2 Kgs 6	1–7	IX
2 Kgs 6	8–23	X
2 Kgs 6	24–33	XI
2 Kgs 7	1–20	XI
2 Kgs 8	1–6	XII
2 Kgs 8	7–15	XIII
2 Kgs 8	16–24	XIV
2 Kgs 8	25–29	XV
2 Kgs 9	1–37	XVI
2 Kgs 10	1–36	XVI
2 Kgs 11	1–20	XVII
2 Kgs 12	1–22	XVIII
2 Kgs 13	1–9	XIX
2 Kgs 13	10–13	XX
2 Kgs 13	14–25	XXI
2 Kgs 14	1–22	XXII
2 Kgs 14	23–29	XXIII
2 Kgs 15	1–7	XXIV
2 Kgs 15	8–31	XXV
2 Kgs 15	32–38	XXVI
2 Kgs 16	1–20	XXVII
2 Kgs 17	1–6	XXVIII
2 Kgs 17	7–23	XXIX
2 Kgs 17	24–41	XXX
2 Kgs 18	1–12	XXXI
2 Kgs 18	13–37	XXXII
2 Kgs 19	1–37	XXXII
2 Kgs 20	1–11	XXXIII
2 Kgs 20	12–21	XXXIV
2 Kgs 21	1–18	XXXV
2 Kgs 21	19–26	XXXVI
2 Kgs 22	1–20	XXXVII
2 Kgs 23	1–30	XXXVII
2 Kgs 23	31–35	XXXVIII
2 Kgs 23	36	XXXIX
2 Kgs 24	1–7	XXXIX
2 Kgs 24	8–17	XL

Chapter	*Verse*	*Text Section*
2 Kgs 24	18–20	XLI
2 Kgs 25	1–21	XLI
2 Kgs 25	22–26	XLII
2 Kgs 25	27–30	XLIII